Ireland the Best

JOHN MCKENNA AND SALLY MCKENNA

Published by Collins
An imprint of HarperCollins Publishers
Westerhill Road
Bishopbriggs
Glasgow G64 2QT
www.harpercollins.co.uk

Collins® is a registered trademark of HarperCollins Publishers Ltd

1st edition 2018

Text © John McKenna and Sally McKenna
Maps © Collins Bartholomew 2018

John McKenna and Sally McKenna assert their moral right to be
identified as the authors of this work.

A catalogue record for this book is available from the British Library.

ISBN 978-0-00-824881-9   10 9 8 7 6 5 4 3 2 1

Printed and bound in China by RR Donnelley APS Co Ltd

If you would like to comment on any aspect of this book,
please contact us at the above address or online.
e-mail: **the.best@harpercollins.co.uk**

Contents

Section 5 *Galway*

Section 6 *Regional Hotels & Restaurants*
The Best Places to Eat & Stay in Ireland's East

Section 8 *Good Food & Drink*

Section 9 *Historical Places*

Section 10 *Outdoor Places*

Section 11 *Strolls, Walks & Hikes*

Introduction

Ireland the Best is the distillation of the 30 years we have spent travelling, traversing, researching, walking, hiking, shopping, eating and drinking in every corner of our little island.

The book is a companion to series originator Peter Irvine's bestselling *Scotland the Best*, and utilises the same design template, with one single objective in mind: we want you to discover the finest things that Ireland has to offer, whether you are seeking out an exemplary country pub, a beautiful place to spend the weekend on an island off the coast, an original piece of Irish woodcraft, or the hottest restaurant in Belfast city.

We spend a lot of our life on the road, travelling the highways and byways of Ireland, North and South. And, yes! It is a wonderful job. Irish food, for example, has relentlessly improved over the last three decades as the country develops more confidence in its culinary history, and its exemplary ingredients. Ireland has a fascinating past, sculpted by the great characters – knights, saints, writers, architects, freedom fighters, clerics, politicians, artists – who have shaped the nation, whether for good or for ill. We have loved discovering the castles and keeps, the graveyards and follies, the beaches and gardens that illuminate a picture of Irish culture going right back to pre-history.

The places in this book represent a personal choice, and we're always seeking and learning more. We love to hear of new places to visit, destinations in which to eat, discoveries to enjoy. Writing about Irish crafts has become a new passion, as we seek out the best Irish craftsmen and women, whether they be jewellers, leatherworkers, potters, woodworkers, knife-makers or weavers.

Ireland the Best uses a series of codes – look out for ATMOS, which are the places we think have a unique atmosphere which singles them out. Also location is measured in one to three Ls depending on the exquisiteness of the setting. The walks have their own codes, alerting you to how much of a challenge they present. We also look at features such as hotels that are dog friendly, restaurants that are ideal for families, places that are proud to be gay, whether an attraction is free, and explain the price you can expect to pay for a restaurant meal.

Please email us at **the.best@harpercollins.co.uk** with your feedback, good or bad. We will also welcome suggestions for future editions at the same email address, with brief reasons why you think they should be included.

John and Sally McKenna

How To Use This Book

There are three ways to find what you are looking for in this book:

1. There is a comprehensive index at the back.
2. The book can be used by category, e.g. you can look up the best restaurants in the South West, or the best scenic routes in the whole of Ireland. Most entries have an item number in the outside margin. These are in numerical order and allow easy cross-referencing.
3. Start with the maps and see how individual items are located, how they are grouped together and how much there is to see and do in any particular area. Then just look up the item numbers. If you are travelling around Ireland, we would urge you to use the maps, and this method to find the best of what an area or town has to offer.

Top tip: as a general guide and when searching by using the maps, items numbered below 1530 generally refer to places to eat and stay.

Most items have a code which gives (1) the specific item number; (2) the map on which it can be found; and (3) the map co-ordinates. For space reasons, items in Dublin, Belfast, Cork and Galway are not individually marked on the map although they do have co-ordinates in the margin to give you a rough idea of location. A typical entry is shown below, identifying the various elements that constitute the entry:

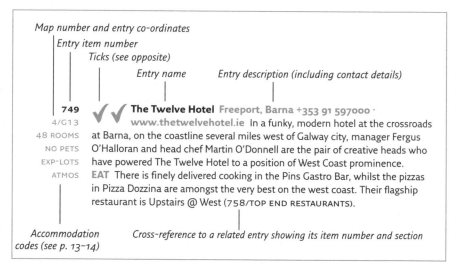

Map number and entry co-ordinates

Entry item number

Ticks (see opposite)

Entry name   *Entry description (including contact details)*

749   ✓✓   **The Twelve Hotel** Freeport, Barna +353 91 597000 ·
4/G13   www.thetwelvehotel.ie In a funky, modern hotel at the crossroads
48 ROOMS   at Barna, on the coastline several miles west of Galway city, manager Fergus
NO PETS   O'Halloran and head chef Martin O'Donnell are the pair of creative heads who
EXP-LOTS   have powered The Twelve Hotel to a position of West Coast prominence.
ATMOS   **EAT** There is finely delivered cooking in the Pins Gastro Bar, whilst the pizzas
             in Pizza Dozzina are amongst the very best on the west coast. Their flagship
             restaurant is Upstairs @ West (758/TOP END RESTAURANTS).

Accommodation   *Cross-reference to a related entry showing its item number and section*
codes (see p. 13–14)

A Note On Categories

Dublin, Belfast, Cork and Galway, the largest cities, are covered in the sections 2, 3, 4 and 5. We recommend that you use a city map, or a smartphone/satnav, in tandem with the book.

When consulting the maps, we have divided the country into East, South East, South West, West, North West and Northern Ireland.

From Sections 9 to 13, the categories are based on activities, interests and geography and are Ireland-wide.

Section 14 covers the islands, beginning at the islands near to Dublin, and circling the entire country.

Ticks For The Best There Is

Although everything listed in the book is notable and remarkable in some way, there are places that are outstanding even in this superlative company. Instead of marking them with a rosette or a star, they have been 'awarded' a tick.

✓ Specially Recommended

✓ ✓ Among the Very Best in Ireland

✓ ✓ ✓ The Best in the World or Simply Unique

Listings generally are not in an order of merit, although if there is one outstanding item it will always be at the top of the page, and this obviously includes anything which has been given ticks. Ticks also indicate exceptional value for money.

The Codes

1. The Item Code
At the left-hand margin of every item is a code which will enable you to find it on a map. Thus **1260** 3/J21 should be read as follows: **1260** is the item number, listed in simple consecutive order; 3 identifies the particular map at the back of the book; J21 is the map co-ordinates, to help pinpoint the item's location on the map grid.

2. The Accommodation & Property Code
Beside each recommended accommodation or property is a series of codes, as follows:

16 ROOMS	LL
MAR–DEC	MED.INX
NO TV	NO KIDS
NO C/CARDS	NO PETS
DF	ATMOS
FF	☕

ROOMS indicates the current number of bedrooms in total (ie to give an idea of size). No differentiation is made as to the type of room.

MAR–DEC shows when the accommodation is open. No dates means it is open all year. It is always advisable to check an establishment is open before travelling.

NO TV means there are no TVs in the bedrooms.

NO C/CARDS means the establishment does not accept credit cards.

DF denotes a place that welcomes dogs, although often with conditions. Check in advance.

L, LL, LLL indicate places in outstanding locations. L is set in a great location; LL denotes a very special setting; and LLL indicates a world-class spot.

CHP, MED.INX, MED.EX, EXP, LOTS indicates the general cost of the accommodation based on an average twin or double room rate. Many hotels change rates daily depending on occupancy, but the broad prices associated with each band are: CHP = under €80; MED.INX = €80–120; MED.EX = €120–150; EXP = €150–200; LOTS = €200+.

NO KIDS does not necessarily mean children are unwelcome, only that special provisions are not usually made; ask in advance. In other cases, children are welcome, often with special rates.

NO PETS indicates that the hotel does not generally accept pets.

ATMOS indicates a place whose special atmosphere is an attraction in itself.

☕ indicates a property with an exceptional tearoom.

3. The Dining Codes

The price codes refer to the cost of an average dinner per person with a starter, main course and dessert. It excludes wine, coffee and extras. Prices are based on 2017 rates. Where a hotel is notable also for its restaurant, this is identified by **EAT** on a separate line below the main accommodation description, with details following.

Within the text of an entry, LO means last orders at the kitchen. Some restaurants close earlier if they are quiet and go later on request.

10pm/10.30pm means usually 10pm Mon-Fri, 10.30pm at weekends. It's common for restaurants to open later at weekends.

CHP, MED.INX, MED.EX, EXP, LOTS indicates the general cost of the meal per person, and the broad prices associated with each band are: CHP = under €20; MED.INX = €20-35; MED.EX = €35-70; EXP €70-90; LOTS = €90+

4. The Walk Codes

Beside each of the many walks in the book is a series of codes as follows:

3-10KM

CIRC/XCIRC

1-A-1

Most walks are a set length and the distance will be shown, but a range such as 3-10KM means the walk(s) described may vary in length between the range shown (3 to 10km in this case). CIRC means the walk can be circular, while XCIRK shows the walk is not circular and you must return more or less the way you came.

The 1-A-1 Code:

First the number (1, 2 or 3) indicates how easy the walk is.

1 the walk is easy

2 medium difficulty, e.g. standard hillwalking, not dangerous nor requiring special knowledge or equipment.

3 difficult; care and preparation and a map are needed.

The letters (A, B or C) indicate how easy it is to find the path.

A the route is easy to find. The way is either marked or otherwise obvious.

B the route is not very obvious, but you'll get there.

C you will need a map and preparation or a guide.

The last number (1, 2 or 3) indicates what to wear on your feet.

1 ordinary outdoor shoes, including trainers, are probably okay unless the ground is very wet.

2 you will need walking books

3 you will need serious walking or hiking boots.

Apart from designated walks, the 1-A-1 code is employed whenever there is more than a short stroll required to get somewhere, eg a waterfall or a monument.

Abbreviations

As well as the codes in the left-hand margin, we use abbreviations within the main entries. The most common ones are:

N, S, E, W - north, south, east, west

TGP - time of going to press

AYR - all year round

BYOB - bring your own bottle

Céad Míle Fáilte

Famously Big Attractions

Among the locations that regularly feature in the top free and paid visiting attractions, these are really worth seeing. Find them under their item numbers.

The Book of Kells Dublin Report: 401/DUBLIN ATTRACTIONS.
Guinness Storehouse Dublin Report: 403/DUBLIN ATTRACTIONS.
Newgrange Stone Age Passage Tomb Co Meath Report: 1582/PREHISTORIC.
Giant's Causeway Co Antrim, NI Report: 1652/LANDSCAPE.
The Titanic Experience Belfast, NI Report: 561/BELFAST ATTRACTIONS.
Cliffs of Moher Co Clare Report: 1654/LANDSCAPE.
National Gallery of Ireland Dublin Report: 405/DUBLIN ATTRACTIONS.
Irish Museum of Modern Art Dublin Report: 406/DUBLIN ATTRACTIONS.
National Botanic Gardens Dublin Report: 409/DUBLIN ATTRACTIONS.

OTHER UNMISSABLES ARE:

1
3/B21
1A
3/B21
FOR VISITOR
CENTRE

✓✓✓ **Skellig Islands** Co Kerry Visiting the UNESCO World Heritage Skelligs is an unpredictable journey given its westerly island location. But, if you do make it across in the boat with your dozen or so fellow *Star Wars* fans, hoping to see it for themselves, then you witness the fruits of the extraordinary determination of the monastic mind: just how did the monks build the Monastery, the Oratory, St Michael's Church, and the incredible beehive-shaped, corbelled dwelling cells, and how on earth did they manage to survive here for centuries. Before you go, call in to the **Skellig Experience Visitor Centre** The Skellig Experience, Valentia Island, Co Kerry +353 66 99476306 · www.skelligexperience.com to help understand the magic or simply enjoy the Skelligs from dry land. 10am-7pm 7 days, July and Aug, closing earlier during the rest of the year.

2
4/D14

✓✓ **Poll na bPéist** Inis Mor, Aran Islands, Co Galway *Poll na bPéist* – or The Worm-Hole – is an extraordinary straight-sided rectangle, measuring some 20ft by 50ft, which has been cratered in the limestone on the southern edge of Inis Mór, close to the fort at Dun Aonghasa. It is the largest of the 'puffing holes' on the island, subterranean passages that connect the sea to the land. It is somewhat strange that the island's most striking natural curiosity doesn't have an attendant myth, though modern writers tend to extrapolate the word *bpéist* to mean 'serpent', rather than 'worm.' Get close to it on a stormy day and the sound of the roaring water will terrify you. Divers use it for competitive competitions, bless 'em.

3
1/R15

✓✓ **Glendalough** Bray, Co Wicklow · www.heritageireland.ie The Glendalough Valley is known as the Valley of the Two Lakes, and within it there is a 6thC monastic settlement founded by St Kevin. The surrounding area is now the Wicklow Mountains National Park. Today there is a visitor centre and a series of trails and walkways around the site. Open all year, and extremely busy. There is a cute craft shop, no destination restaurants within the immediate zone, but Glendalough Green in nearby Laragh is recommended (846/THE EAST). See also Report: 1819/PILGRIM PATHS.

4
3/R2

✓ **Carrick-a-Rede Rope Bridge** 119a Whitepark Rd, Ballintoy, Co Antrim, NI +4428 20769839 · www.nationaltrust.org.uk/carrick-a-rede This is another of those sites where it pays to go early, or late, as only a few people are allowed on the bridge at any one time and, even in quiet periods, you'll probably have to queue. Best to avoid high season altogether, and be aware that they sometimes close the bridge if it's blowing a westerly. How different it all is now to

1755 when the brave salmon fishermen threw a rope between the mainland and the nearby island rocky island, and used it as a bridge, and then launched their boats from the island into the sheer rocky bay below. In early spring or late autumn, when there aren't too many people, it is a magical place to see guillemots, and traverse the bridge without taking a breath. The walk down to the bridge takes about 15-20 minutes. 9.30am-7pm, closing earlier outside the months of July & Aug.

5
3/Q2
✓**Bushmills Distillery** 2 Distillery Rd, Bushmills, Co Antrim, NI +4428 20733218 · www.bushmills.com 'One of the world's most interesting distilleries' is how the drinks writer Michael Jackson described the elegant Bushmills Distillery. The association with distilling dates back to 1276, and the first licence to any distillery was granted to Bushmills in 1608, allowing them to claim to be the world's oldest distillery. Distillery tours are excellent: fun; enlightening; humorous, and not to be missed. All day, 7 days, starting at noon on Sun. Slightly shorter hours off season.

6
3/K21
✓**The Jameson Experience** Midleton, Co Cork +353 21 4613594 · www.jamesonwhiskey.com Distilling has been taking place in Midleton since 1825, when the three Murphy brothers – David, James and Jeremiah – bought the site. Today, the Jameson Experience takes place in the beautiful Victorian heritage centre, and it's a splendid way to get your head around the world of whiskey in 75 minutes. The sister site, on Bow Street in Dublin, reopened in early 2017 after a massive and expensive refurbishment, which allowed them to create three different interactive tours. All day, 7 days, last tour 4pm. Shorter hours in winter.

7
5/G10
AYR
📷
FREE
ADMISSION
✓**Museum of Country Life** National Museum of Ireland, Turlough Park, Castlebar, Co Mayo +353 94 9031755 · www.museum.ie/Country-Life The collection is curated by the National Museum of Ireland and includes artefacts from Irish history collected through craft, farming, hunting and domestic life looking at growing, harvesting and using materials such as straw and rushes, looking at how people lived, and how they hunted, grew food and ate. The curation is artful, and extremely moving. Tue-Sat 10am-5pm, Sun 2pm-5pm.

8
5/E10
✓**Croagh Patrick - The Holy Mountain** Meermihil, Murrisk, Co Mayo +353 98 64114 · www.croagh-patrick.com The holy mountain of St Patrick, Croagh Patrick, is just outside the village of Murrisk in Co Mayo. The mountain is 746m high, and easily walkable, though at the summit it becomes very steep with free-falling rocks that move disconcertingly under your feet as you edge forward, sometimes on all fours. There is an annual Pilgrimage up the mountain on what is known as Reek Sunday, the last Sunday in July. At the summit there is a chapel. The National Famine monument, an eerie and beautiful statue of a coffin ship, is at the base of the mountain. There is a Visitor Centre, *Teach na Niasa*, at the entrance to the hill walk, opposite the National Famine Monument. Views from the mountain top are spectacular. Reports: 1132–1144/IF YOU'RE IN WESTPORT.

9
5/H6
✓**Sliabh Liag Cliffs** Teelin, Carrick, Co Donegal +353 9700000 · www.sliabhliag.com The 600m-tall Sliabh Liag cliffs are amongst the highest in Europe, considerably higher than the more popular Cliffs of Moher, though not as tall as Croaghaun on Achill Island. But because you can drive almost to the summit, though the road is narrow and has many lay-bys to allow cars to pass, the cliffs are unusually accessible. Walking the summit is challenging, and requires you to traverse the One Man's Path, which is about a metre wide. Close to the summit there is a Napoleonic tower. Fuel up at the Ti Linn coffee shop at the visitor centre before you head for the heights. Sliabh Liag Boat Trips depart from Teelin Pier on the N side of Donegal Bay.

Great Ways to Get Around

10 **By Barge or Narrowboat** Shannon Princess, Glasson, Athlone, Co Westmeath +353 87 2514809 · www.shannonprincess.com; Riversdale Barge Holidays, Ballinamore, Co Leitrim +353 71 9644122 · www. riversdaleholidays.com With five en suite cabins, the Shannon Princess cruises the River Shannon, the longest river in Ireland. This is a floating boutique hotel, with a deck side spa pool and a restaurant. Cruises are generally 6-7 days duration and can be booked either by the cabin, or with an exclusive Charter. The Riversdale barges are actually modified narrowboats that have been widened. You can navigate the Shannon-Erne waterway in these Widebeam barges, with space for up to seven berths. Hire by the week. This company are boat builders in addition to hiring the vessels.

11 **By Luxury Train** Belmond Grand Hibernian, Reservations +4420 31171300 · www.belmond.com Ireland's first luxury rail experience offering 2-, 4-, and 6-night journeys, departing from Dublin and exploring both the N and S. The train is relatively modern, with an observation car, dining car and private en suite cabins.

12 **With Horse or Donkey** Clissmann Horse Caravans, Cronybyrne, Rathdrum, Co Wicklow +353 404 46920 · www.clissmannhorsecaravans.com Try a leisurely holiday with an Irish Cob horse, who will pull your home through the Wicklow landscape. Or go for a 7-day walk with a friendly donkey, who will walk beside you and carry your load.

13 **By Vintage VW Van** Retro Camper Ltd, The Barn, Puddenhill Activity Centre, Moorepark, Garristown, Co Meath +353 1 8355679 · www. retrocamper.ie For your inner hippie, self-drive a Classic VW. Retro Camper hires out 1970s campers with wide windows and a lift-up roof to give you a bit more space. And everybody smiles at you when you drive a VW bus. Tours recommended include Wild Atlantic Way, N. Ireland, and Ireland East.

14 **By Jaunting Car (pony and trap)** Killarney, Co Kerry +353 64 6631068 · www.killarneydaytour.com There are two recommended pony and trap jaunts in Killarney: First, opposite the Muckross Park Hotel (1041/THE SOUTH WEST) is a lay-by where you can hail a driver, to take you leisurely through Muckross Park down to the Torc Waterfall. Another spectacular bus/jaunting car and boat tour is organised through Killarney Day Tour, who pick up at your hotel, drive to nearby Kate Kearney's Cottage, take the pony and trap through the Gap of Dunloe (1656/LANDSCAPE), take a boat across Loch Léin and then a bus back to your hotel.

15 **By Currach** Boyne Boats Adventure, Oldbridge, Drogheda, Co Meath +353 86 361 6420 · www.boyneboats.ie The traditional Currach boat originates from Kerry in the SW, but you can find them here in the NE as part of Boyne Boats' Battle of the Boyne tour where eight paddlers can employ the same paddling techniques used to train the Iron Islanders in *Game of Thrones*.

16 **By Plane** Aer Arann, An Caislean, Inverin, Co Galway +353 91 593238 · www.aerarannislands.ie Aer Arann has been flying to the Aran Islands since 1970, bringing visitors and islanders and cargo to the three western islands daily. Take the plane from Connemara Airport to any of the three islands, alternatively charter a plane, or join one of their scenic tours.

17 **By Helicopter** Executive Helicopters, Galway, Co Galway +353 90 9749764 · www.executive-helicopters.com Private helicopter charter company, specialising in trips over Dublin city, and the Cliffs of Moher where a 15-minute tour includes a free glass of Prosecco. On a fine day you'll see the Aran Islands, Hag's Head, Spanish Point Bay and Green Island – one of the few places in the world where sharks can be caught on rod and line.

18 **Under Sail** Charter Ireland, Galway · www.charterireland.ie; Sovereign Sailing, Kinsale · www.sovereignsailing.com; Baltimore Yacht Charters · www.baltimoreyachtcharters.com Sailing in Ireland is underdeveloped due to unpredictable weather and limited marina facilities. Visitor facilities are good in the Royal Cork Yacht Club, Crosshaven, the world's oldest yacht club, dating back to 1720. Kinsale is close by, with two marina facilities. Further west there are good anchorages and visitor moorings in Glandore, Castletownsend, Schull and Crookhaven. There are marinas in Baltimore and Sherkin Island. Further west there is a fishing port at Castletownberehaven, with a marina at nearby Bere Island. Heading N, there is a charming marina at Dingle (Daingean Uí Chúis). Further N up the W Coast towards Galway there is a visitor marina in the heart of Galway City. As marinas are few and far between, it's important that sailors are comfortable with anchoring operations and have access to a dinghy.

19 **On Foot** The Ulster Way, N. Ire · www.walkni.com Ireland has a network of walking routes, and one of the very best of them is the Ulster Way which links a series of quiet walkways with interlocking road routes, designed to take you the fastest route to the next walk. The whole walk circles the entire province. Don't miss the Mourne Wall which passes over 15 mountains. Report: 1767/WAYS.

20

FEB-MAR

The Six Nations Tournament · www.rbs6nations.com In a good year, when Ireland are winning the rugby, the Six Nations brings the country to a halt. In Dublin city, where the home fixtures take place, there is an invasion of fans, who drive the cost of hotel rooms skywards.

21

17 MAR

St Patrick's Day · www.stpatricksfestival.ie The festival of Ireland's national saint is observed less at home than with the greening of buildings and cities worldwide, especially in big ex-pat cities like New York. Parades take place throughout Ireland, the grandest of which is in Dublin.

22

EASTER
WEEKEND

Galway Food Festival · www.galwayfoodfestival.com Down at the pier and throughout the town over the Easter Holiday with a massive tent of great food producers, plus a host of cooking demos. If the weather is good, it's a case of al fresco picnics overlooking the River Corrib for the hungry hordes.

23

APR

West Waterford Festival Of Food · www.westwaterfordfestivaloffood.com Featuring the best market of any Food Festival in Ireland, around the square in pretty Dungarvan. This one attracts Ireland's foodies like no other and great guest chef dinners sell out in seconds.

24

MAY BANK
HOL
WEEKEND

Connemara Mussel Festival · www.connemaramusselfestival.com A wonderful celebration of seafood, and more importantly, the community in N Connemara. Most of it takes place in the charismatic Paddy Coyne's Pub, which has a headstone in the beer garden. All great craic, as they say.

25

MAY BANK
HOL
WEEKEND

Lit Fest · www.litfest.ie Ballymaloe House in E Cork hosts a festival of all things literary in food. Set in the lovely surroundings of Ballymaloe House and cookery school, it has attracted a wealth of international food people such as Claudia Roden, Alice Waters, and Rene Redzepi.

26

MAY

Baltimore Wooden Boat Festival · www.baltimorewoodenboatfestival.com An impressive line up of traditional Irish wooden craft in W Cork, and those who take part in the races take it very seriously indeed. A food fair on the pier accompanies.

27

MAY

Fastnet Short Film Festival · www.fastnetfilmfestival.com Schull village, in deepest West Cork, has no cinema yet still manages to host an international film festival. Everywhere from the town hall to the local pubs get converted to screens as the town absorbs itself in short movies and an international film maker's prize.

28

MAY-JUN

Listowel Writer's Week · www.writersweek.ie Characterful Festival of Words, running since 1970, in the Kerry birthplace of some of Ireland's most famous writers – John B Keane, Brendan Kennelly, Bryan MacMahon and others.

29

MAY-JUN

Derry Fleadh · www.fleadhcheoil.ie Part of the International Fleadh (pron. flaa) – see below, **Fleadh Cheoil**, this festival attracts enormous crowds in Londonderry (Derry) celebrating city life and traditional music.

30

JUN

Ocean To City · www.oceantocity.com Ocean to City, An Rás Mór is a longdistance rowing race where participants, both amateur and professional, journey from Cork harbour to Cork city centre via the River Lee using all sorts of craft, including kayak, currach, skiff, longboats or canoes. You need your own boat and have to complete the race in the time allowed, but the experience is open to all. Register via the website.

31 **Vantastival** · www.vantastival.com Musical Festival in Co Louth's Beaulieu
JUN House and Gardens. You don't need a VW, but it helps.

32 **Cat Laughs** Kilkenny · www.thecatlaughs.com Kilkenny's comedy festival
JUN attracts all the big names in Stand Up from all over the world to Ireland's most
beautiful city.

33 **Corpus Christi** · www.dublindiocese.ie Takes place in June, in towns and
JUN villages around Ireland. White lilies in shop windows line the route, known
colloquially as The Procession.

34 **Bloom** · www.bloominthepark.com Ireland's largest garden festival takes
JUN BANK HOL place on the June Bank Holiday weekend in Dublin's Phoenix Park and, whilst
WEEKEND it's not quite the Chelsea Flower Show, there are many creative and delightful
gardens.

35 **SÓ Sligo** · www.sligofoodtrail.ie Sligo has put a lot of work into its many
JUN attributes. There's great surfing here, good pubs, and great food. The Festival
presents a trail of foodie treats that has put Sligo on the culinary map.

36 **The Irish Maritime Festival** · www.maritimefestival.ie Annual celebration of
JUN the sea in Drogheda, Co Louth. On shore actions include food fairs and music, off
shore includes ships and the Boyne Swim.

37 **Bloomsday** · www.bloomsdayfestival.ie Celebrating the work of James Joyce,
16 JUN this festival runs for a week in June around the 16th, the date on which Joyce set
his masterpiece, *Ulysses*. Lots of people dress in period costume, and if you get the
chance to hear anyone reading *Finnegan's Wake*, jump at it.

38 **Body & Soul** · www.bodyandsoul.ie Ireland's summertime music and arts
JUN SOLSTICE festival – something akin to Burning Man, but with green fields and rain instead of
WEEKEND desert and pyromaniacal fires.

39 **Picnic In The Park** · www.corkmidsummer.com Ten days of music, theatre,
JUN SOLSTICE dance, food and visual arts taking place throughout Cork over midsummer June.

40 **Dublin Kite Festival** · www.dublinkitefestival.ie A great family event in North
JUN Bull Island repainting Dublin's skies in a rainbow of colour. Their website tells you
how to build a kite.

41 **B.A.R.E. In The Woods** · www.barefestival.com Fast becoming one of
JUN Ireland's premier music festivals, it takes place in Garryhinch Woods, Portarlington,
Co Laois.

42 **Mourne International Walking Festival** · www.visitmournemountains.co.uk
JUN One of many walking festivals around Ireland, dotting the great trails that all parts
of the country have to offer. We love the Mourne walks for the long stone wall that
stretches over fifteen mountains and into the distance.

43 **Hinterland Festival** · www.hinterland.ie Formerly Hay Festival, in Kells, Co
JUN Meath, this is a celebration of literature and writing in Ireland.

44 **West Cork Chamber Music Festival** · www.westcorkmusic.ie/
JUN–JUL   chambermusicfestival Bantry fills with people carrying piano stools and cello
cases. The concerts are world-class, the musicianship is spell-binding, and the
various town venues turn into places to hear music of great beauty. 'One of the
world's finest festivals of chamber music' said *The Observer*.

45 **SeaFest** · www.seafest.ie Ireland's national maritime festival in Galway.
JUN–JUL   A celebration of everything to do with the sea in one of the great seaside cities.

46 **The Curragh Irish Derby** · www.curragh.ie Like many other derbies, race day
JUN–JUL   is as much about the dressing up and the corporate hospitality as it is about the
betting and the ponies.

47 **West Cork Literary Festival** · www.westcorkmusic.ie/literaryfestival
JUL   The Literary Festival in Bantry gets bigger and more dynamic every year, with
authors arriving from all over the world to talk about their work and give writing
workshops.

48 **The Twelfth Orangefest** · www.culturenorthernireland.org The twelfth
12 JUL   of July is the culmination of the marching season, when members of the Orange
Order and Black Preceptory take to the streets to commemorate the Battle of the
Boyne and other battles from the island's history. Many city centre businesses,
including some restaurants and shops, close for around two weeks at this time.

49 **Willie Clancy Summer School** · www.scoilsamhraidhwillieclancy.com An
JUL   important date in the Irish traditional music calendar is the Willie Clancy Summer
School in Miltown Malbay in Co Clare. The festival commemorates the town's best-
known uilleann piper, and the festival has been running since 1973.

50 **Earagail Arts Festival** · www.eaf.ie All the stuff you would expect from an arts
JUL   festival: theatre, music, visual arts.... then throw in a bit of carnival and circus, and
you've got the Earagail Arts Festival. It all takes place in the NW, in Donegal.

51 **Reek Sunday** · www.croagh-patrick.com Reek Sunday Pilgrimage takes place
JUL   on the last Sunday in July, on the Mountain of Croagh Patrick in Co Mayo, when
over 25,000 pilgrims visit the Reek, some walking barefoot. The Chapel at the Reek
is 764m high at the top of the mountain. Views of Clew Bay and the surrounding
hills are spectacular.

52 **Galway International Arts Festival** · www.giaf.ie Galway is a city with a rich
JUL–AUG   arts heritage, and some terrific venues, including the atmospheric Druid Theatre.
The GIAF celebrates theatre, opera, music, visual art, and above all, spectacle! Look
out for the fantastic parades organised by the Macnas collective. Galway has been
designated as the European Capital of Culture 2020.

53 **Galway Race Week** · www.galwayraces.com Celebrated more for the craic
AUG   than the horse racing, race week is still a big event in Galway's social calendar,
even though Irish politicians have grown wary of using it for deal-making, as they
did in the past.

54 **The Big Grill** · www.biggrillfestival.com Pit-masters and grill maestros from
AUG   Ireland and the rest of the world bring their flames to what is one of Dublin's most
dynamic food festivals. Fantastically imaginative use of flames and flesh.

55 **Outburst Queer Arts Festival** · www.outburstarts.com Northern Ireland isn't
AUG generally known for its tolerance, understanding, or its lack of phobias, so all the
more reason to celebrate this splendid LGBTQ+ festival in the Northern capital.

56 **Dublin Horse Show** · www.dublinhorseshow.com A Dublin institution, and as
AUG much about dressing up and sitting in the stands and drinking champagne as it is
about show jumping.

57 **Taste of Cavan** · www.tasteofcavan.ie Cavan's annual food festival attracts
AUG huge audiences – massive audiences – for the food demos and tastings by local
and visiting chefs.

58 **Fleadh Cheoil na hÉireann** · www.fleadhcheoil.ie A major event in Ireland's
AUG traditional music calendar, as Ireland's young musicians, singers and dancers
throughout the country compete to be able to call themselves All-Ireland Champion.

59 **Kilkenny Arts Festival** · www.kilkennyarts.ie One of the premier arts
AUG events, with music, dance, theatre, talks, exhibitions and family events in Ireland's
craft capital.

60 **Schull Calves Week** · www.shsc.ie A mini Cowes, hence the name, this sailing
AUG festival at the start of August is based in Schull harbour and Roaring Water Bay. The
final race is the Fastnet Race, famous as the destination for the biennial offshore
yacht race organised by the Royal Ocean Racing Club in the UK.

61 **Masters of Tradition** · www.westcorkmusic.ie/mastersoftradition A
AUG five-day festival in August with some of the best Irish music you could hear
anywhere. Organised by West Cork Music and curated by violinist Martin Hayes.
Expect magic from the musicians as they play to respectful, appreciative and
dedicated audiences.

62 **Cruínniu na mBád** · @KinvaraCruinniu Traditional sailing festival in Kinvara,
AUG Co Clare, celebrating the traditional commercial fleet of Turf Boats. Mass is held on
the Sunday for the Blessing of the Boats, and there is fancy dress, sea swimming
and a village fete.

63 **Puck Fair** · www.theringofkerry.com/puck-fair If we told you that this
10-12 AUG festival involves a goat, would you believe us? You just have to be there to
understand. It's a Kerry thing, and it's to do with celebrations of a fruitful harvest as
well as getting our own back on Oliver Cromwell.

64 **Rose of Tralee** · www.roseoftralee.ie A beauty pageant, but one with a
AUG difference, the organisers argue. What can we say. It's the Rose of Tralee. It's been
going since forever.

65 **Electric Picnic** · www.electricpicnic.ie Ireland's leading music and arts
SEPT festival, held in Co Laois at the 1st weekend of September, attracts the biggest
bands and best names in comedy and the arts. *McKennas' Guides* organise the food
tent, known as Theatre of Food, so come and find us and say "Hello".

66 **ABV Beer Festival** · www.abvfest.com Craft beer festival in Belfast in
SEPT September, celebrating everything there is to celebrate about the art of brewing
beer. Northern Ireland has some ace brewers, and the selection of local and
international brews you can discover is magnificent.

67
SEPT **Lisdoonvarna Matchmaking Festival** · www.matchmakerireland.com
Yes, in the days of Tinder, there still is a matchmaking Festival in Lisdoonvarna, Co Clare.

68
SEPT **Liffey Descent** · www.canoe.ie/liffey-descent Marathon canoe and kayak race on the River Liffey. Paddlers from all over the world take part in the 28km race, with 10 weirs and 1 portage. It starts at Straffan Weir, Co Kildare, and watching from the bridges, as paddlers fall into the water, is as much a sport as the race itself.

69
SEPT **The All Ireland** · www.gaa.ie Hurling and Gaelic Football are two of the most balletic and beautiful sports to watch, hurling in particular. Teams are organised according to counties, and rivalries are particularly intense. The 'Clash of the Ash' is when Ireland's county GAA champions battle with *hurl* and *sliotar* to win the All Ireland Hurling Final.

70
SEPT **National Ploughing Championships** · www.npa.ie 'The Ploughing' is a ginormous roving agricultural exhibition that has captured the imagination of the country and is now one of the biggest festivals in the world. Interestingly, the organisation, despite its scale, is still handled by the family who initially created the event. Wellies needed.

71
SEPT **Waterford Harvest Festival** · www.waterfordharvestfestival.ie Having come through the doldrums, Waterford's festival of food in the autumn is shaping up to be a great East Coast celebration of local culinary creativity.

72
SEPT **Galway Oyster Festival** · www.galwayoysterfestival.com The Galway Oyster Festival is making an effort to get back to its roots and to take its place as one of the premier festivals in the city.

73
SEPT **Dingle Food Festival** · www.dinglefood.com Dingle Food Festival is a huge beanfeast where all the town's shops, restaurants, art galleries and pubs host tastings of local food. Getting a room in the town during the festival season is the only problem when coming down to the peninsula.

74
OCT **Dublin Marathon** · www.sseairtricitydublinmarathon.ie Dublin is well suited to hosting a Marathon, which explains why this event is so successful. The weather is clement for running, and the route follows a single lap, including a section in the Phoenix Park.

75
SEPT-OCT **Dublin Theatre Festival** · www.dublintheatrefestival.com With its many famous playwrights, Ireland is a hub of good theatre, and Dublin's Festival celebrates it with more than two weeks of new and classic theatre productions.

76
OCT **Savour Kilkenny** · www.savourkilkenny.com Popular food festival, with a large market that stretches around atmospheric Kilkenny Castle on the weekend and lots of extremely well-organised tastings, events and demos.

77
OCT **Guinness Cork Jazz Festival** · www.guinnessjazzfestival.com Long running jazzers' fest that attracts many of the big names in jazz to Cork city, though these days the jazzers are interspersed with more accessible and popular musos.

78 **Food On The Edge** · www.foodontheedge.ie Recently founded in Galway
OCT city, but already making enormous impact globally, Food on the Edge is a two-
day symposium of internationally famous chefs and food enthusiasts with
lofty aims and genuine ambitions to make the world better through food and
cooking.

79 **Burren Winterage** · www.burrenwinterage.com A celebration of
OCT transhumance, when cattle are traditionally herded up to over-winter in the Burren
hills of Co Clare. The tradition is key to maintaining the biodiversity of the unique
Burren landscape.

80 **Galway Jazz Festival** · www.jazzfest.com Galway does great food, great
OCT theatre, great festivals, and it goes without saying they understand how to
promote and celebrate jazz. Cool cats, don't you know.

81 **Belfast International Arts Festival** · www.belfastinternationalartsfestival
OCT .com It used to be known as the Festival at Queens, which gives a sense of the
academic nature of this very serious and significant arts festival. Expect world
premieres, plenty of spectacle and a fantastic international line up of music,
theatre and the arts.

82 **Other Voices** · www.othervoices.ie Getting to Dingle (Daingean Uí Chúis)
DEC always feels like a pilgrimage and that, along with its winter scheduling, gives this
festival a unique vibe. Musicians from all over the world join Irish musicians in
what was once a chance to record for Irish TV, but now is a full-blown festival with
gigs all over town.

83 **The Late Late Toy Show** · www.rte.ie Curl up on the sofa with the kids and
DEC the cocoa every year, and watch RTÉ television's slightly cringe-making Christmas
bonanza when toys and children collide on screen.

84 **The Bacon Rasher** Invented in Waterford in 1820 by butcher Henry Denny who found that sandwiching long flat pieces of pork between two layers of dry salt helped the meat to last much longer. He later successfully exported the idea to other countries such as Denmark.

85 **The First Guided Missile** Invented by Louis Brennan, born in Castlebar, Co Mayo. Mr Brennan was also said to have invented the first tilting monorail train, and an early type of helicopter. The first guided missile was a defensive weapon and it was never fired in anger.

86 **The First Commercial Submarine** Invented by John Philip Holland from Co Clare, the son of a lighthouse keeper who became a Christian Brother and taught mathematics and music in Drogheda, Co Louth, in what is now Scholars Townhouse Hotel. Report: 861/THE EAST.

87 **The Cream Cracker** Invented by WR Jacobs at his bakery in Bridge Street, Waterford. He also invented the **Fig Roll**.

88 **Confession** When Irish monks started spreading their faith throughout Europe in 7thC, they brought with them their tariff books. These were the first penitentials, and became the basis of the Christian Church's system of penance, whereby you could confess your sins to a priest, who would consult the book, award the penance, and the sins would be forgiven.

89 **Splitting the Atom** Ernest Walton, who first split the atom, was born in Dungarvan, Co Waterford. He is one of nine Irish men and women to receive the Nobel Prize.

90 **The First Maternity Hospital** The Rotunda in Dublin was the world's first Maternity Hospital, built in 1745.

91 **The DeLorean Sports Car** The real hero of the *Back to the Future* movies, a gullwing sports car, built in a factory near Lisburn. Only 9,000 cars were built. DeLorean was later charged with drug dealing and fraud, and acquitted. Enthusiasts continue to hold DeLorean conventions.

92 **Quiz** In 1780 James Daly, a Theatre Manager, invented the word Quiz. His intention was to introduce a meaningless word into the English language, within 24 hours. He succeeded.

93 **Rubber Soles** Humphrey O'Sullivan was a printer, an Irish immigrant from Skibbereen, who got fed up walking the stone floor while working on the press. So he began to use a rubber mat, and then cut two pieces from the mat the size of his heels. They worked so well, he patented them.

94 **The Titanic** The name Titanic comes from the Ancient Greek word meaning gigantic. The boat was built in Belfast, by Harland & Wolff shipbuilders, who actually built three liners for the White Star Line, *RMS Olympic* and *HMHS Britannic* being the other two. The building was overseen by chairman William James Pirrie, who also served as Lord Mayor of Belfast (561/BELFAST ATTRACTIONS).

95   The Publican Undertaker It was commonplace in Ireland for the local publican to also act as the local undertaker. This happened because the Coroners Act of 1846 allowed a dead body to be brought to the cool cellar of the pub before further arrangements were made. The legislation was removed in 1962, but the publican undertaker was still a feature of Ireland until recent times.

96   The Irish Pub There are Irish pubs all over the world, styled and fashioned to look like the pubs you find in Ireland. These are faux Irish pubs. To find a true Irish pub, you have to come to Ireland, where we have plenty of them. Their USP is the craic, a virtually untranslatable term that suggests spontaneity, a shared conviviality, conversation, and a welcome for all.

97   Guinness The global success of Arthur Guinness's stout means that the drink is indelibly associated with Ireland. Arthur used an inheritance of £100 to buy a brewery in Leixlip and, on selling this, moved to Dublin where he took over a disused brewery in 1759. By 1799 he had decided to brew only porter, and Guinness steadily took over the globe (403/DUBLIN ATTRACTIONS).

98   Irish Music Traditional Irish music is oral in character, which is to say it is transmitted in performance, and preserved in memory. Traditional Irish musicians do not perform with scores, and the repertory changes with each performer and performance. The principal instruments are fiddle, accordion, bodhran, whistle and uilleann pipes, whilst the guitar has become increasingly popular. Sean-nós (old-style) singing – where a singer performs unaccompanied, perhaps holding the hand of the person sitting next to them – is thought to be linked to French trouvères, and Irish music, in pitch, rhythm, and thematic content, resembles traditional music of Western Europe.

99   The Irish Coffee Irish coffee is indelibly associated with the chef, Joe Sheridan, who was working at the airport in Foynes, Co Limerick, when he created the drink, in 1943. Dubliners, however, suggest he had learnt the drink whilst working in the city. Mr Sheridan later worked at the airport in Shannon, before emigrating to the USA in 1952 where he worked at Buena Vista bar in San Francisco, the bar that is particularly associated with the drink and which still serves 2,000 Irish coffees per day.

100   The Coffey Whiskey Still Aeneas Coffey was from Dublin, and is to distilling what Henry Ford was to the motor car. His invention of a new way to distill whiskey, via his invention of the patent still, allowed whiskey to be made more quickly and cheaply than the slow pot still method. Under-appreciated in Ireland, Coffey moved to England and his patent still changed everything in the world of distilling.

101   The Miner's Safety Lamp Dr William Clanny is credited for saving the lives of many miners, by inventing an oil lamp that was much safer than the naked candle flames that were extremely dangerous in the presence of flammable and explosive gases in the mines.

102 **The Rechargeable Nickel-Zinc Battery** Dr James Drum was a brilliant student of chemistry from Dundrum, in Co Down. His inventions include a fine soap, and a way to keep peas green after they were canned. He then turned his attention to an alkaline battery that could be rapidly charged. The battery was used successfully for electric trains.

103 **Riverdance** Designed as a 7-minute interval act during the 1994 Eurovision Song Contest, the music for *Riverdance* was written by Bill Whelan, and the two principal dancers were Jean Butler and Michael Flatley. By its 20th anniversary, the show had been seen by more than 23 million people, and annual revenues are in excess of $20m.

104 **A Cure for Leprosy** Irishman Vincent Barry, from Cork, led the medical research team that discovered a compound that ultimately led to a treatment for leprosy.

105 **The Beaufort Scale** Sir Francis Beaufort, inventor of the wind force scale that still bears his name, was a naval commander who was born in Navan in 1805.

106 **Modernist Architecture** The designer Eileen Gray's famous house in the South of France – e1027 – built between 1926 and 1928 is arguably the first piece of modernist architecture ever realised. Ms Gray, who was born in Enniscorthy in 1878, also created the most expensive piece of 20thC furniture when her 'dragon chair' was sold at Christie's for £19.4m in 2009.

107 **A Cure For Cancer, Ageing Rocks and the first Colour Photography** Inventor John Joly from Offaly first developed a method for using radiotherapy to treat cancer. He also developed the techniques to accurately estimate the age of a geological period, based on radioactive elements present in minerals. He also invented the Joly Colour Process, which was the first successful method of producing colour photographs from a single plate.

108 **The Royal Ballet** The Royal Ballet was founded by Dame Ninette de Valois, born in Co Wicklow in 1898. She was born Edris Stannus, and spent much of her childhood in Co Laois. Dame Ninette lived to be 103 years old.

109 **The Modern Tractor** Harry Ferguson, famously nicknamed the 'Mad Mechanic', designed a tractor and plough that coupled together to form a single unit. The new system would revolutionise farming. Ferguson was also the first Irishman to fly, in 1909, when he ascended to a height of 12 feet and flew almost 400 feet in a monoplane he built himself.

110 **The Ejector Seat** Invented by Sir James Martin, an engineer from Co Down. The first seat was tested using a dummy, and the second was bravely tested by an Irish fitter, Bernard Lynch. The ejector seat was adopted by the RAF, and every British military plane fitted with one.

111 **Shorthand** John Robert Gregg, from Monaghan, invented a system of speed writing in 1888, that became what is now called shorthand, and was adapted to several languages.

112 **The Hypodermic Syringe** Francis Rynd was a doctor based in Dublin. He invented the hypodermic syringe, and administered the world's first subcutaneous injection at the Meath Hospital in 1844.

113 **The Induction Coil** Rev Nicholas Callan invented the electric induction coil in 1836 in Maynooth, and the self-enacting dynamo, both of which are still used. His inventions and instruments can be seen in the Science Museum in Maynooth College, Co Kildare.

114 **Flavoured Potato Crisps** Potato crisps were originally sold in a greaseproof paper bag, with a twist of salt, until Tayto magnate, Joseph 'Spud' Murphy developed a technique which allowed seasoning to be added during manufacturing. Murphy, and his colleague Seamus Burke, produced the world's first Cheese & Onion, and Salt & Vinegar flavours, and then sold the rights to the technology.

115 **Seismology** Robert Mallet, a Dublin man, was instrumental in the construction of the Fastnet Rock lighthouse. He then developed a process which could measure the speed of waves in surface rocks after dynamite explosions, after an experiment carried out on Killiney beach. This was the beginning of seismological research. Indeed, he coined both the words 'seismology' and 'epicentre'.

116 **Perforated Stamps** The facility to tear apart individual stamps exists thanks to the invention of the first postage stamp perforating machine, which was invented by Irishman Henry Archer in 1848. He sold the patent to the Postmaster General in the UK for £4,000.

117 **The Kelvin Scale & The First Atlantic Telegraph Cable** The creation of an absolute scale of temperature (the Kelvin scale) was invented by William Thomson, Lord Kelvin, who was born in Belfast in 1824. Thomson was also knighted for his work on the laying of the undersea Atlantic Telegraph Cable which stretched from eastern Newfoundland to Valentia, Co Cork, in 1865.

Ireland's Film Locations

DUBLIN
Educating Rita Trinity College.
The Commitments Temple Bar.
My Left Foot Mulligan's Bar, Poolbeg Street.
Once Walton's World of Music shop in Dublin, and Killiney Hill Park

THE NORTH
Game of Thrones The Dark Hedges and other locations in Co Antrim, NI.

THE SOUTH EAST
Saving Private Ryan Curracloe, Co Wexford
Redwater Dunmore East and the sea stacks at Ballydowane Bay, Co Waterford.
Brooklyn Enniscorthy, Co Wexford.

THE EAST
Braveheart Dunsoghly Castle Finglas Co Dublin and Trim Castle, Bective Abbey and The Curragh all in Co Meath.
Laurence Olivier's Henry V and Stanley Kubrick's Barry Lyndon; Ella Enchanted and **The Tudors** all filmed in Powerscourt, Co Wicklow
P.S. I Love You filmed in the Sally Gap, Co Wicklow

THE WEST
Man of Aran Inis Mor, Aran Islands.
The Ballroom Of Romance Ballycroy, Co Mayo
Dancing At Lughnasa Glenties, Co Donegal
Harry Potter & The Half Blood Prince and **The Princess Bride** Cliffs of Moher, Co Clare
Ryan's Daughter Dingle Peninsula, Co Kerry and the Cliffs of Moher, Co Clare. Dingle was also the location for Far And Away
The Quiet Man Maam Valley, Connemara and Cong, Co Galway
The Field and **The Guard** Leenane and Killary Harbour, Co Galway

THE SOUTH WEST
Angela's Ashes Limerick City, Co Limerick
Excalibur Derrynane, Co Kerry
The Irish RM Castletownshend, Co Cork
War of the Buttons Union Hall, Co Cork
Michael Collins Beál na mBláth, Co Cork
Moby Dick Youghal, Co Cork
Star Wars Episode VII: The Force Awakens Skellig Michael, Slea Head, Co Kerry
Star Wars Episode VIII: The Last Jedi Three Castle Head, Co Cork
The Lobster Park Hotel, Kenmare, Co Kerry

the Best

of Dublin

The Best of the Major Hotels

118
1/R13
192 ROOMS
NO PETS
EXP-LOTS

✓ **The Conrad** Earlsfort Terr, D2 +353 1 6028900 · www.conradhotels3. hilton.com Peachy location, directly across from the National Concert Hall, the Conrad mixes an ideal setting with a subdued, classy design style that has a timeless and comforting feel. General Manager Martin Mangan heads up a superb team, and sometimes the only problem is yet another member of staff asking if they can do something for you.
EAT The Gulliver's Travels-themed cocktails in Lemuel's bar are a blast. Excellent cooking from chef Dmitry Stroykov means that at every junction the team are out to impress. For pub grub and craft beer, Alfie Byrne's Pub.

119
1/R13
265 ROOMS
LOTS

✓ **The Shelbourne** 27 St Stephen's Grn, D2 +353 1 6634500 · www.theshelbourne.ie The grand dame of Dublin hotels is back to its best after a period of ownership changes. It's not just an hotel: it's a place to be, and you can simply sit by the fire in the foyer and watch the life of Dublin happen. There is a gym, a pool and a salon – best accessed from the street – along with a good basement barber shop. Staff manage to cope with the extraordinary jamboree of Dublin life with great patience.
EAT A drink in the Horseshoe Bar is a rite of passage, and meeting up for tea in the Mayor's Lounge is akin to sharing a salon with friends, so long as you can get a table. The cooking in the Saddle Room restaurant is good rather than stellar.

120
1/R13
142 ROOMS
NO PETS

✓ **The Merrion Hotel** Upr Merrion St, D2 +353 1 6030600 · www.merrionhotel.com Twenty years ago they skillfully fused four Georgian townhouses to create the Merrion Hotel, probably the most high-profile 5-star destination in Ireland. Since then the hotel has been shorthand for a level of luxury service that aims to read the customer's mind before the customer even knows what they would like.
EAT The afternoon tea service is exemplary, there is a gorgeous garden – the only hotel garden in the city – and eating choices range from the expensive, starry Restaurant Patrick Guilbaud (140/TOP END RESTAURANTS) to the handsome Garden Restaurant. Chef Ed Cooney has been one of the most creative and consistent talents in Dublin for the last two decades, and his culinary work is as meticulous as it gets. His menus have a lightness, a delicacy, that is utterly winning: this is great modern cooking. Cocktails are in No 23 Cocktail Bar.

121
1/R13
205 ROOMS
NO PETS
LOTS

✓ **The Westbury** Balfe St, D2 +353 1 6791122 · www.doylecollection.com The Doyle family is synonymous with Irish hotels and hospitality going back over the decades and the Doyle Collection hotels are top-notch. The large lounge and meeting area of the Westbury – just directly up the stairs from the main entrance – has been home to a million informal meetings and gatherings.
EAT The group have made major strides to establish distinct culinary identities for their restaurants – Wilde, and Balfes Bar & Brasserie. Only problem is getting a table, especially at weekends. Cocktails in The Sidecar. The company also own the well-run Croke Park Hotel.

122
1/R13
187 ROOMS
NO PETS
LOTS

The Marker Hotel Grand Canal Sq, Docklands, D2, +353 1 6875100 · www.themarkethoteldublin.com Grand Canal Square is the first Dublin square to have been created since the great Georgian Squares were laid in the 18thC, and the Marker Hotel set out to give the city a defining destination. The open lobby area boasts the most complex cantilevered structure ever built in Ireland, in order to create uninterrupted sightlines from bar to lobby. The rooftop terrace and bar offer 360° views of the city. There is a 23m infinity-edge pool and a spa, and some fine artworks.

EAT Head chef Gareth Mullins oversees an ambitious team in The Brasserie, and it's worth noting that even the hotel's buffet breakfast is well achieved. Simple cooking in the Marker Bar is a good choice if you're attending a show in the nearby Grand Canal Theatre.

123 **Radisson Blu** Golden Lane, D8 +353 1 8982900 · www.radissonblu.com/
1/R13 royalhotel-dublin The ten-year-old Radisson Blu sits just behind the narrow,
150 ROOMS medieval streets surrounding Dublin Castle, a couple of blocks down from
MEX.EX St Patrick's. Some of the landmark buildings nearby may be in disrepair but, like all the streets in this part of D8, this mix of ceremonial, ecclesiastical, residential, corporation, and student living is a place where anyone can feel connected. Lots of natural light in the rooms and public rooms, a calming, earth colour scheme; helpful staff close the deal.

124 **The Gibson Hotel** Point Sq, D1 +353 1 6815000 · www.thegibsonhotel.ie
1/R13 Funky modern hotel at the end of the Luas red line, very close to the 3Arena but
252 ROOMS also in a strategically clever part of town that offers good access to the Bord Gáis
MED.EX Energy Theatre, the Convention Centre and Croke Park. Given its location with 21stC Dublin building up around it, the hotel could sit back. It tries a little bit harder than that though. Don't miss the Gibson Clock.

125 **The Clarence Hotel** 6 Wellington Quay, D2 +353 1 4070800 ·
1/R13 www.theclarence.ie Stops and starts with planning applications and
50 ROOMS development plans have hindered the development of the Clarence Hotel –
EXP famously part-owned by Bono and The Edge from U2 – over the last dozen years. The original hotel is an architectural gem, the rooms are restrained and have aged well, and both The Octagon Bar and the Study are islands of calm and charm amidst the mad tide of a Temple Bar weekend.

EAT Chef Oliver Dunne runs the restaurant – Cleaver East – and there is Texan bbq and whiskeys in their Bison Bar.

126 **The Morrison** 15 Ormond Quay Lwr, D1 +353 1 8744039 ·
1/R13 www.morrisonhotel.ie Owned by Russia's wealthiest woman, Elena Baturina,
145 ROOMS and operated under Hilton Hotel's DoubleTree brand, The Morrison has a superb,
NO PETS River Liffey location, close to the pedestrian Millennium Bridge. Manager Patrick Joyce and his team focus their restaurant cooking on the Josper grill, and the bar is a lively place for cocktails.

The Best Individual & Boutique Hotels

127
1/R13
98 ROOMS
NO PETS
MED.EXP–LOTS

Brooks Hotel 62 Drury St, D2 +353 1 6704000 · www.brookshotel.ie
Many visitors to the city argue that Brooks Hotel is the best destination in the city. Manager Anne McKiernan has a formidable team under her charge, many of whom have been here for aeons. Their experience and professionalism shine through and they are, above all, a team.
EAT Chef Pat McLarnon is one of the great intellects of the Irish kitchen, a thinker and forager who produces beautiful, elegant cooking in Francesca's Restaurant. Breakfast is first rate, and the style of the rooms is restrained and intimate. Good whiskeys in Jasmine Bar and Cafe Lounge.

128
1/R13
16 ROOMS
NO PETS
MED.INX
ATMOS

Kelly's Hotel Dublin 35 Sth Gt George's St, D2 +353 1 648 0010
Kelly's is a smart choice for those who want good accommodation at decent prices, something increasingly hard to find in Dublin. The rooms are small, but the style is big and imaginative and the housekeeping is excellent.
EAT Breakfast is served in the excellent L'Gueuleton Restaurant, next door, and in addition to their own Candle Bar, there are two cult Dublin pubs – Hogan's and The Secret Bar – just down the stairs.

129
1/R13
72 ROOMS
DF
LOTS

Dylan Dublin 4 Eastmoreland Pl, D4 +353 1 6603000 · www.dylan.ie
Pop stars tend to favour the Dylan – Kylie stayed here! – and the hotel has added 28 new rooms to try to catch up with the shortfall of space in the Dublin hotel market. Everything, right down to the cooking in the Tavern Restaurant, is an exercise in style, all of it trying very hard to be hip and knowing.

130
1/R13
ROOMS
DETAILS
PRICE

The Dean Hotel 33 Harcourt St, D2 +353 1 6078110 · www.deandublin.ie
The Dean Hotel is part of the McKillen family's Press Up group, which has been developing properties and opening restaurants in the city at breakneck speed over the last several years. The Dean exhibits the group's strengths – hip design, smart young millennial crowd, a terrific nous for what is fashionable, whether it's pizza, or bourbon, or Netflix on your Samsung television – and its popularity has meant they are already developing another boutique hotel just down the street. Stylish colourful rooms, but do note that Harcourt St at night is the noisiest place in the city.
EAT The top-floor Sophie's Restaurant has great views of the city, and good pizzas.

Superior Lodgings

131
1/R13
21 ROOMS
MED.EXP
ATMOS

✓✓ **Number 31** 31 Lower Leeson St, D4 +353 1 6765011 ·
www.number31.ie The wooden mews door opens, you take several steps across the walled courtyard, then step in the door of No 31, a glimpse of the Picasso print on the wall signals that you are in that rarest of Dublin destinations: a modernist masterpiece. If you have always wanted to have your own villain's lair, straight from a James Bond movie, then here it is, a step away from Dublin's Leeson Street. Actually, No 31 is two houses: a 60's-era modernist mews, and a fine Georgian house that opens onto Fitzwilliam St. Noel Comer is a great host, and breakfasts are sublime.

132
1/R13
48 ROOMS
NO PETS
MED.INX-MED.
EXP

✓ **Pembroke Townhouse** 90 Pembroke Rd, Ballsbridge,
D4 +353 1 6600277 · www.pembroketownhouse.ie Manageress Fiona Teehan has fashioned a distinctive breakfast offer in Pembroke Townhouse, one that is as fine as any in the city. In particular, it is the handmade treats for guests that make Pembroke stand out, and which show the sort of bespoke care at which this high, handsome Georgian destination excels: a little glass of homemade cordial when you arrive; delicious biscuits with tea. Excellent sitting rooms with coffee also allow for meetings. 24-hour larder available. Many staff members have worked here for many years: always a good sign.

133
1/R13
37 ROOMS
NO PETS
MED.EXP

Ariel House 50 Lansdowne Rd, D4 + 353 1 6685512 · www.ariel-house.net
Is there a better breakfast than the one prepared by Jenny McKeown and her team in Dublin's Ariel House, a sturdy, red-brick Victorian terrace of houses just adjacent to the Aviva stadium in Ballsbridge? When you talk about benchmark standards of sourcing, cooking and serving an Irish breakfast, Ariel House is going to be at the very top of the list. Chef Rose Murphy also takes endless painstaking care over their signature afternoon teas, and the fact that you don't have to be a resident is a special bonus. Good rooms, great housekeeping, always filled with regular guests.

134
1/R13
9 ROOMS
NO PETS
EXP

Cliff Townhouse 22 St Stephen's Gn, D2 +353 1 6383939 ·
www.theclifftownhouse.com This classic St Stephen's Green Georgian house is sister to the acclaimed Cliff House Hotel (1270/COUNTRY HOUSE HOTELS), in Co Waterford. It has two fine restaurants, but of note are the nine rooms for guests at the top of the house. They are stylish and compact, and four of the rooms have views of the park. The group have recently taken over the running of Cliff at Lyons, at the big Lyons estate in Co Kildare, just south of Dublin.
EAT Sean Smith's seafood cookery is smart and how wonderful to have a decent selection of edulis and gigas oysters as well as cooked oyster dishes. Seafood is the smart choice, though there are good beef dishes. Urchin Bar (225/SEAFOOD).

135
1/R13
LOTS
ATMOS

✓ ✓ ✓ **Chapter One** 18 Parnell Sq, D1 +353 1 873 2266 · www.chapteronerestaurant.com Stop a random sample of Dubliners on the street to ask them which is the city's finest restaurant, and a sizeable majority will tell you that it is Chapter One. That's not just because chef-patron Ross Lewis and his team offer superb modern Irish cooking, in an intimate and luxe basement space, beside the Hugh Lane Gallery. It's also because this is a restaurant that people have enormous affection for, and will return to at any and every opportunity – so many birthdays are celebrated here that their theme tune should be 'Happy Birthday'. Head chef Eric Matthews and his team send out food for the gods in one of the best cultural experiences you can enjoy in Ireland, and value for money is exceptional. Lunch Tue-Fri, dinner Tue-Sat.

136
1/R13
LOTS

✓ ✓ **L'Ecrivain** 109 Lwr Baggot St, D2 +353 1 6611919 · www.lecrivain.com We have eaten in L'Ecrivain since Derry and Sallyanne Clarke first opened, in 1989, when the restaurant was in a tiny basement just off Baggot Street, and the consistency of the cooking throughout that long history has been not just impressive, but also imperious. Today, the L'Ecrivain crew, under head chef Tom Doyle, forge Mr Clarke's muscular and elegant style of food as assuredly as ever. Food and wine service is top-notch, the dining room and the private dining rooms are happy, buzzy places, and the restaurant's Dublinesque lack of pretension is just darling. Lunch Thur-Fri, dinner Mon-Sat.

137
1/R13
LOTS

✓ ✓ **The Greenhouse** Dawson St, D2 +353 1 676 7015 · www.thegreenhouserestaurant.ie Mickael Viljanen's cooking is an event. Every dish the chef sends out from the kitchen in The Greenhouse is a spectacular answer to the question: will this blow your mind, and your tastebuds? No other chef in the city works as hard to win your love, so abandon yourself to the embrace of the tasting menu, and choose the accompanying wine selections from the awe-inspiring list. The tasting menus also allow you to see how Mr Viljanen orchestrates a tapestry of connecting flavours, right through the courses, from first bite to last. It's not the greatest room, at the St Stephen's end of Dawson St, but from the first taste you will only have eyes for what's on the plate. Lunch & dinner Tue-Sat.

138
1/R13
EXP

✓ **Dax** 23 Pembroke St Upr, D2 +353 1 6761494 · www.dax.ie Olivier Meisonnave has reunited with an old partner, the chef Graham Neville, and together this pair has propelled Dax to the top of the Dublin dining apex. Mr Neville is one of the best cooks, M. Meisonnave is one of the best sommeliers, and together they are squeezing out sparks in this plush basement restaurant space. Neville has an almost Federer-like command of his ingredients, which makes the high prices well worth the money. There are many fine wines on the list if you have the wherewithal, but also a good selection by the glass. Service is sublime. Lunch & dinner Tue-Sat.

139
1/R13
MED.EXP

✓ **Amuse Restaurant** 22 Dawson St, D2 +353 1 6394889 · www.amuse.ie It's commonplace to have people tell you that Conor Dempsey's cooking is their favourite food in Dublin, and that Amuse also offers some of the best value in the capital. In his ability to marry Japanese flavours with French-style technique, Mr Dempsey has carved out something unique: it's not fusion cooking, but something altogether more elemental, and altogether more elegant. A great list of wines and a polished, calm dining room further explain why Amuse is so many people's favourite. Lunch & dinner Tue-Sat.

140   ✓ **Restaurant Patrick Guilbaud**   21 Upr Merrion St, D2 +353 1 6764192 ·
1/R13   **www.restaurantpatrickguilbaud.ie** The inspectors from the Guide Michelin
LOTS   love RPG, and garland it with two stars year after year, the only restaurant in the
city and country to be so favoured. It's a grand, gilded palace of a place, right
beside the 5-star Merrion Hotel, facing Government buildings, and the cooking is
ultra-professional. It has many admirers amongst Dublin's professional and
business classes who can afford its sky-high prices. Personally, we aren't amongst
that cohort. Lunch & dinner Tue-Sat.

The Best Modern Irish Cooking

141   ✓✓ **Forest Avenue**   8 Sussex Terr, D4 +353 1 6678337 ·
1/R13   **www.forestavenuerestaurant.ie** You cross over the canal onto Upr
MED.EX   Leeson St to get to John & Sandy Wyer's benchmark restaurant, but this tactile
room burns with city centre energy, thanks to John Wyer's unique take on modern
Irish cooking. Mr Wyer is one of the best chefs, his kitchen gets steadily better with
each year. Vegetables take equal prominence alongside meats and fish, and
flavours and textures are defined with rare precision. All wines by the glass, service
sharp but informal; excellent value. Lunch Thur-Sat, dinner Wed-Sat.

142   ✓✓ **Bastible**   111 Sth Circular Rd, D8 +353 1 4737409 ·
1/R13   **www.bastible.com** Barry FitzGerald's first venture as chef-patron, in a
MED.EX   stripped-back, dark-coloured room at the Leonard's Corner end of the Sth Circular
Rd, opened at full speed, and won a devoted audience in a matter of weeks. The
reason why is simple: Bastible cooking is polished, direct and delicious, and the
3x3x3 menu keeps the kitchen fully focused on delivering one successful plate after
another. Wines are well chosen, and value for money is excellent for such
ambitious cooking. Lunch Fri-Sun, dinner Wed-Sat.

143   ✓✓ **Heron and Grey**   Blackrock Market, 19a Main St, Blackrock,
1/R13   Co Dublin +353 1 2123676 · www.heronandgrey.com Andrew Heron
MED.EX   and Damien Grey won a star from the Guide Michelin in their first year of business,
which means it's all-but-impossible to get a table in their tiny room in the centre
of the jumble of the Blackrock Market. But, if you have the patience, persist:
Damien Grey's 6-course menus can really deliver with flavours and textures that
will knock you out and his cheese course dish, in particular, is a modern
masterpiece. Great wines from Andrew Heron underscore the food. Two menus
are offered – Omnivore and Herbivore. Dinner Thur-Sat. They do not cater for
Vegan or Lactose Intolerant.

144   ✓✓ **The Fumbally Café**   Fumbally Lane, D8 +353 1 5298732 ·
1/R13   **www.thefumbally.ie** Everything about The Fumbally is unorthodox.
CHP   The room looks like an auction house, staffed by avant-garde Situationists.
There is no head chef, and the food is cooked by a rotating bunch of cooks, so
you never know exactly what will be on the menu. And yet, somehow, Aisling
Rogerson and Luca d'Alfonso make it all work, right down to the shots of
fermented cabbage and ginger juice, and the pig's head terrine with black garlic
potatoes, probably because they attract serious creative talents to work in the
kitchen. Daytime Tue-Sat.

145 ✓✓ **The Winding Stair** 40 Lwr Ormond Quay, D1 +353 1 8727320 ·
1/R13 www.winding-stair.com Elaine Murphy took over what was once
MED.EX Dublin's most iconic bookshop and promptly turned it into one of Dublin's
TERRACE most iconic dining rooms. Views over the Ha'penny Bridge and the River Liffey,
and gutsy modern cooking with superb Irish ingredients, means that eating
here is one of the city's defining experiences. Elaine also operates four other
truly exceptional restaurants in the city: The Woollen Mills (167/CASUAL
RESTAURANTS), The Yarn (213/PIZZA), The Washerwoman (347/BARS WITH GOOD
FOOD) and The Legal Eagle (339/BARS WITH GOOD FOOD). Lunch & dinner 7 days.

146 ✓ **Forest & Marcy** 126 Leeson St Upr, D4 + 353 1 6602480 ·
1/R13 www.forestandmarcy.ie Ciaran Sweeney is the head chef at F&M, the
MED.EX little sister restaurant to John & Sandy Wyer's Forest Avenue, just around the
corner. The room isn't much more than a long bar with a few high tables and
chairs, and you can't book a seat, so be prepared to wait. But this is cooking
worth waiting for – unusual pairings on small plates such as goat's curd with
guanciale, or mussels with pickled sea spaghetti, seem perfectly logical; the
signature dish of fermented potato bread is not to be missed. Excellent wines.
Lunch Fri-Sat, dinner Wed-Sun

147 ✓ **Assassination Custard** 19 Kevin St Upr, D8 + 353 87 9971513 The name
1/R13 comes from a pudding that James Joyce's wife, Nora, made for Samuel
CHP Beckett when he was recuperating in Paris after being stabbed by a pimp. Ken
NO C/CARDS Doherty and Gwen McGrath's tiny café, opposite the Garda Station is as strange
as its name – it has only two tables, and the decor is chicest bedsit – but this
pair are mighty cooks, so join the queue for tripe sandwiches, lamb heart curry,
nduja rolls with ricotta, kohlrabi tonnato. AC is a true Dublin original – surreal;
inspiring; an utter maverick. Lunch Mon-Fri. Bookings taken for parties in the
evening, BYOB, 6-12 people.

148 ✓ **Delahunt** 39 Camden St, Lower, D2 +353 1 5984880 · www.delahunt.ie
1/R13 Owner Darren Free spent 18 months bringing the historic building of
MED.EX Delahunt – it's name-checked in James Joyce's Ulysses – back to its full Victorian
splendour. It's a gorgeous room with a smart cocktail bar on the first floor, and
concise menus – 4 choices each course – mean that chef Dermot Staunton
delivers with authoritative consistency. Excellent wine list offers many choices
by the glass, and the cocktail bar is one of the most stylish in the city. Dinner
Tue-Sat, lunch Thur-Fri.

149 **Clanbrassil House** 4 Clanbrassil St Upr, D8 · www.clanbrassilhouse.com
1/R13 Head chef Grainne O'Keeffe is one of the city's hottest talents, and heading up the
MED.INX kitchen in Clanbrassil House, the second venture from the wildly successful team
at Bastible, will really let her show her mettle. Short, skilled menus are beautifully
sourced, and value for money is exceptional. As with Bastible, it will be necessary
to book well in advance. Excellent wines.

150 **Craft** 208 Harold's Cross, D6W +353 1 4978632 · www.craftrestaurant.ie
1/R13 Phil Yeung's intimate restaurant, up the hill in quiet, suburban Harold's Cross, is
MED.EX worth the punt out of town, for cooking that shows craft – and hard work – with
every plate. His food is harmonious, even when the pairings are unlikely. The mix

of graft and culinary craft delivers cooking with more verve and ambition than one would expect from the restaurant's setting. Lunch Fri & Sat, dinner Wed-Sat, brunch Sun.

151 **Mr Fox** 38 Parnell Sq West, D1 +353 1 8747778 · www.mrfox.ie

1/R13 Anthony Smith's basement restaurant is around the corner from the Rotunda
MED.EX Hospital, on Dublin's Parnell Sq. Whilst opinion is divided on the room itself, it is unanimous on the finely tuned cooking the kitchen turns out. All the en vogue tastes and techniques are here but Mr Smith's cooking is sincere and professional, and he gets the flavours down on the plate. Save space for their jokey puddings, which include a much-Instagrammed walnut whip homage. Lunch & dinner Tue-Sat.

152 **The Pig's Ear** 4 Nassau Street, D2 +353 1 6703865 · www.thepigsear.ie

1/R13 If your idea of a visit to Dublin includes dinner whilst staring over the cricket
MED.EX pitches on the campus of Trinity College, then Stephen McAllister's restaurant is for you: the views from the three floors of The Pig's Ear are enrapturing. Mind you, when the food arrives, you won't be looking out the windows. Lunch & dinner Tue-Sat.

153 **Hatch & Sons** The Little Museum of Dublin, 15 St Stephen's Gn, D2 ·

1/R13 www.hatchandsons.co In the basement underneath the Little Museum of Dublin,
CHP Hatch & Sons achieves a rare feat: it makes traditional Irish dishes seem utterly
ATMOS contemporary. It does this through sympathy and understanding, not through pyrotechnics. Sourcing is superb, right down to offering Barry's tea from Cork, probably the finest blend of tea in the world. Supper served on Wed and Thurs: spiced beef with soda bread; beef and Guinness stew; fruit crumble. Daytime 7 days.

154 **One Pico** 5 Molesworth Pl, D2 +353 1 6760300 · www.onepico.com

1/R13 Owner Eamonn O'Reilly has been doing the good thing here in a luxe series of
MED.EX rooms just off Kildare St and Molesworth St, and an excellent crew means he also has time to run the starred The Greenhouse, just around the corner on Dawson St. Chef Ciaran McGill's cooking has lots of imagination and is as lavish as the clubbable rooms; this is a great place for a big celebration or an expense account treat. Lunch & dinner 7 days. No buggies, prams or child seats.

155 **Locks** 1 Windsor Terr, Portobello, D8 +353 1 4163655 ·

1/R13 www.locksrestaurant.ie One of the longest established restaurants in the
MED.EX south city, Locks has been gazing out on the canal since the 1980's, in a tree-lined location between the bridges at Portobello and Harold's Cross. It's a pretty room in a pretty part of town, and chef Conor O'Dowd produces cooking to match. Excellent wine list with many good choices by the glass makes it easy to linger and enjoy the view. Lunch Fri-Sun, dinner Tue-Sat.

156 **Suesey Street** 26 Fitzwilliam Pl, D2 +353 1 6694600 · www.sueseystreet.ie

1/R13 A delightful terrace is one of the attractions of Suesey Street, at the Leeson St end
MED.EX of Fitzwilliam Place. An equal attraction is the general manager, John Healy, a witty and charming man who is an Irish TV celebrity. And, finally, the smart bistro-style cooking seals the deal, being unpretentious and inviting. Nice simple lunch dishes also makes Suesey Street a good choice for daytime eating.

157   **Taste at Rustic**   17 Sth Gt George's St, D2 +353 1 5267701 ·

1/R13   www.tasteatrustic.com Celebrity chef Dylan McGrath has a cluster of

EXP   restaurants adjacent to one another in this zone on George's St and Exchequer St, with Taste at Rustic the flagship. Here he offers his personal take on sushi, sashimi, omakase and nabemono, with meat and fish cooked on the Robata grill. Mr McGrath also runs Rustic Stone which offers a mash up of steak-cooked-on-volcanic-stone, and raw and health foods, all of which show his freewheeling culinary imagination.

158   **Old Street Restaurant**   Old St, Malahide, Co Dublin +353 1 8455614 ·

1/R13   www.oldstreet.ie There is a top-notch team of talents at work in the no-

EXP   expense-spared (Eames chairs!) Old Street Restaurant – chefs Fergus Caffrey and Chris Fulham are both fast-emerging talents, whilst front-of-house supremo Denise O'Brien is one of the best in the business. The food comes at city-centre prices, but the ingredients are blue chip, and the Sunday menus are more keenly priced. TGP early days for a hugely ambitious project. Lunch & dinner Wed-Sat, 1pm-7pm Sun.

159   **Restaurant Forty One**   41 St Stephen's Gn, D2 +353 1 6620000 ·

1/R13   www.residence.ie Many people believe that because Restaurant Forty One

LOTS   is housed in a posh St Stephen's Green Georgian townhouse that it's a stuffy place to eat. In fact, even though it is stylish and expensive, the place is nicely unpretentious, and chef Peter Byrne's cooking is spot on. If you have something special to celebrate, then lunch or dinner in the light-filled first floor Front Room, looking out over the Green is hard to beat. Lunch & dinner Tue-Sat.

Brasseries & Bistros

160
1/R13
MED.EXP
ATMOS

✓ **Hugo's** 6 Merrion Row, D2 +353 1 6765955 · www.hugos.ie Gina Murphy, the owner of Hugo's, is one of the great figures in Dublin hospitality, and for a decade she has steered Hugo's through bad times and good, and always made it seem as if she was relishing every minute. With a young head chef, Margaret Roche, in the kitchen, the menus move seamlessly through time. This is friendly, punchy bistro food, with good wines and beers and the room's energised atmosphere makes Hugo's a gem. Lunch & dinner Tue-Sun (no lunch Sat).

161
1/R13
MED.INX
FF

✓ **O'Connell's** 135 Morehampton Rd, D4 +353 1 2696116 · www.oconnellsrestaurant.com Tom O'Connell is one of the great hospitality veterans of Dublin, but he's also a restaurateur who doesn't stand still, so every visit to the comfortable and welcoming O'Connell's – formerly a pub in the centre of Donnybrook village – brings some new discovery that the boss has brought home with him. Mind you, it's the old-school touches, like the roast chicken carved tableside, served with stuffing and gravy that bring us back to Donnybrook. The room, and the cuisine, are ageless and charming. Lunch Tue-Sun, dinner 7 days.

162
1/R13
MED.INX

✓ **Richmond** 43 Richmond St Sth, D2 +353 1 4788783 · www.richmondrestaurant.ie Owner David O'Byrne and chef Russell Wilde offer a Greatest Hits selection of modern cooking in this atmospheric and comfortable room, just a stone's throw from the canal at the top of Richmond St. Everything is powerfully savoury, and perfect for a hearty appetite. Early bird menus offer excellent value. Dinner Tue-Sun, brunch Sat & Sun. No kids under 12 after 7pm.

163
1/R13
MED.EXP
ATMOS

✓ **Pichet** 15 Trinity St, D2 +353 1 6771060 · www.pichet.ie Pichet is one of the city's busiest restaurant rooms, thanks to chef Stephen Gibson's punchy, brasserie-savoury cooking, and thanks to the classic styling of the room with its banquettes and bentwood chairs. The cooking is extra-tasty, and it's done with a light touch. A newly added cocktail bar, and a tapas menu, are just the ticket for making a late night of it with some classy tunes. Lunch & dinner Mon-Sun.

164
1/R13
MED.EXP

Bang Restaurant 11 Merrion Row, D2 +353 1 4004229 · www.bangrestaurant.com On the narrow strip of Merrion Row, to the east of St Stephen's Green, Bang has been a solid sender of good, soulful cooking for many years. Its longevity means it tends to get overlooked by the media, but its many regulars value not just the comfortable rooms, but also the consistent and flavour-filled food. Pre-theatre menus are excellent value for money. Lunch Thur-Sat, dinner 7 days.

165
1/R13
MED.EXP

Coppinger Row Off Sth William St, D2 +353 1 6729884 · www.coppingerrow.com The Bereen brothers, Marc and Conor, made the reputation of Coppinger Row on the back of good, finely detailed Mediterranean cooking, excellent cocktails, and a room that was always suffused with energy. The dishes rock all around the Med and they make for zestful, happy eating, whilst the cocktails and gins are great. The brothers also have Charlotte Quay restaurant, down on Dublin's Grand Canal Dock, with menus that veer more towards North African flavours. Lunch & dinner 7 days.

The Best Cafés & Casual Restaurants

166
1/R13
CHP
DF

Fia 155b Rathgar Rd, Rathgar, D6 +353 1 4413344 · www.fia.ie
Keith Coleman and his team run one of the smartest destinations in Rathgar,
directly across the road from the Church of the Three Patrons. They aren't doing
anything new: they are simply doing everything better. Their sourcing is impeccable,
which allows them to concentrate on getting those all-important details right, and
it's no surprise that you need to get here early at weekends to get a seat. Charming
staff, water bowls outside for the doggies, great vibe. Daytime Tue-Sun.

167
1/R13
MED.EX
TERRACE

The Woollen Mills 42 Lower Ormond Quay, D1 + 353 1 8280835 www.
thewoollenmills.com
There is nothing quite like a Dublin eating house which has one menu section
headed: Gruel. But there is nothing gruel-like about the Woollen Mills version of
Dublin coddle, or indeed the excellent stout sausage served with wild garlic champ.
And not only do you get good grub here, you also get one of the best roof terraces
in the city, and some of the best views over the Ha'penny Bridge and the River
Liffey. Open Lunch & dinner 7 days.

168
1/R13
MED.INX

Brother Hubbard North 153 Capel St, D1 +353 1 4411112 ·
www.brotherhubbard.ie Garrett Fitzgerald and James Boland's two cafés,
here and **Brother Hubbard South** on Harrington St, are distinguished by
superlative staff members, young folk whose energy gives super-hero status to the
food they cook. The daytime offering is excellent, but the evening Middle Eastern
menus are special indeed. At this stage, the Brother is part of the fabric of the city.
TGP they are developing a large new space on the corner of Capel St which will
have a multi-function use. North: open lunch 7 days, dinner Wed-Sat; South: open
daytime 7 days.

169
1/R13
CHP

The Pepperpot Cafe Unit 22A, Powerscourt Townhouse Centre,
59 William St S, D2 +353 1 7071610 · www.thepepperpot.ie
The Pepperpot is a legendary address in Dublin. Up on the first mezzanine level in
the Powerscourt Centre, their secret is the scrambled eggs, widely regarded as the
best in the city, and available all day. But, here's the thing: everything else is as
good as the scrambled eggs. For many food lovers, the Pepperpot is the best café in
the city. Breakfast & lunch 7 days.

170
1/R13
CHP

3fe 7 Sussex Mews, Sussex Terrace, D4 · www.3fe.com Colin Harmon
created the coffee revolution in Dublin, and he and his team are amongst the
most important players in the city. The barista standards they set right from their
beginnings drive the company today, and whilst the coffee is benchmark good, the
cooking is also nifty and delicious. Minimalist room, maximalist staff and
customers. No reservations. Breakfast, coffee & lunch 7 days. There is another 3FE
on Grand Canal St Lower, selling coffee paraphernalia.

171
1/R13
CHP

Five Points 288a Harold's Cross Rd, D6 · www.fivepointshx.com Five
Points took off like a rocket upon opening, thanks to some inspiring cooking
from Adam Sheridan and Hilary O'Hagan-Brennan, both former 3fe crew. Whilst
the coffee heritage is sound, it's been the quality of the cooking that has fired
everyone up. A busy, buzzy room in Harold's Cross is just the space to enjoy it.
Breakfast & lunch 7 days.

172
1/R13
CHP

Camerino Bakery, Cakery & Coffee Shop 158 Capel St,
D1 +353 1 5377755 · www.camerino.ie Caryna Camerino intended to
backpack through Ireland for a few days but, fifteen years later, this Canadian expat

is still here. For that, the citizens of Dublin are grateful indeed, for Ms Camerino is a most wonderful baker, and her Capel St shop and café has become a fixture in one of Dublin's most dynamic food zones. 'Lovin' from the Oven' is Ms Camerino's tag line, and you taste it in every bite. Breakfast & lunch Mon-Sat.

173 ✓ **Olive Skerries** 86a Strand St, Skerries, Co Dublin +353 1 8490310 ·
1/R13 www.olive.ie Peter and Deirdre Dorrity are great restaurateurs, for a simple
CHP reason. They know they have to let their staff 'exercise their heart', to borrow a quote from Danny Meyer, New York's greatest restaurateur. Putting their staff at the top of their list of priorities means those happy staff put the customer's happiness at their top of their To-Do list. And that is why Olive Café and Olive Deli are a cornerstone of the culture and community of Skerries. Daytime 7 days.

174 **The Cake Café** The Daintree Building, Pleasants Pl, D8 +353 1 4789394 ·
1/R13 www.thecakecafe.ie The mismatched, bricolage style of the Cake Café may look
CHP ramshackle, but don't be fooled: everything the team do in this small but charming room is considered down to the last detail. There is a bamboo bedecked courtyard for days when the sun breaks through, which creates a great urban escape, even though you are just adjacent to Camden St. And it's not just cake: this is one of the best brunch destinations, and the savoury lunches are excellent also. Daytime Mon-Sat.

175 **Gallagher's Boxty House** 20 Temple Bar, D2 +353 1 6772762 ·
1/R13 www.boxtyhouse.ie Padraic Og Gallagher is the most successful restaurateur in
MED.INX Temple Bar, and his Boxty House is perennially packed. The boxty concept is simple – it's a delicious potato pancake – served here with a wide variety of different accompaniments. The Boxty House is also a place to enjoy Irish stew, Dublin coddle, and beef and stout stew. Mr Gallagher is a widely-published authority on the Irish potato, and he's also an excellent craft brewer: don't miss those superb Jack Smyth stouts and ales. Lunch & dinner 7 days.

176 **Two Pups** 74 Francis St, D8 · @twopupscoffee Kevin Douglas and Zoe Ewing-
1/R13 Evans have a little room, resurrected from dereliction with up-styled hipster chic, in
CHP the Liberties area, close to St Patrick's Cathedral. Along with excellent coffee there is great food, mostly vegetarian. Two Pups is part of The Francis St Collective, so you can splurge on vintage clothing, limited-edition frocks, and even get your hair done. Super cool. Lunch Mon-Sat.

177 **Oxmantown** 16 Mary's Abbey, City Markets, D7 +353 1 8047030 ·
1/R13 www.oxmantown.com The star of the City Markets area, between Capel
CHP St and the Four Courts just north of the river, Oxmantown has long been celebrated for the sheer class of its offer, from sandwiches – amongst the best in town – to soups, salads and cakes. Conor Higgins and Amie Costello have an appetite for hard work and an appetite for what is good. Everyone has an opinion on which of their signature sandwiches is the best, so make your mind up by trying them all. Daytime Mon-Fri, till 4pm.

178 **Juniors Deli & Cafe** 2 Bath Avenue, D4 +353 1 6643648 · www.juniors.ie
1/R13 At the very busy intersection that separates Ballsbridge from Ringsend in D4,
MED.INX Juniors is tiny, which means the rush to get a table at weekends is intense. Brothers Paul and Barry have won a great reputation for rock-steady cooking over the last decade, producing NYC-style sandwiches at lunch, and Italian-accented food in the evenings. Confident, friendly team; always a smart choice. Lunch, brunch & dinner 7 days. This company also operates Paulie's Pizza, (215/PIZZA).

179 · **101 Talbot** 101 Talbot St, D1 +353 1 8745011 · www.101talbot.ie Thirty years
1/R13 young, and ever-youthful, the upstairs 101 Talbot was the pioneer restaurant in
MED.INX this zone of Dublin 1, when the St was a culinary wasteland. Today, under the
gentle care of Neil and Jenny, it's one of the best northside choices for punky, fun
cooking with real style. The split-level room is always welcoming, and the energy at
weekends is mesmerising. Lunch & dinner Tue-Sat.

180 · **Meet me in the Morning** 50 Pleasants St, D8 · @meetmeinthemorningcafe
1/R13 You don't need to be a Dylanologist to fall in love with MMITM. Owner Brian
CHP O'Keeffe is an award-winning coffee champion, and the brews are just one reason
to head to Pleasants St, a short stroll from busy Camden St. The brunch cooking is
especially imaginative and invigorating, anchored by their home-made flatbreads.
Grain bowls expertly composed, and don't miss their doughnuts. Breakfast & lunch
Tue-Sun.

181 · **Press Café** The National Print Museum, Beggar's Bush, Haddington Rd,
1/R13 D4 +353 87 6546458 · www.presscafe.ie Elaine Toohill has a sweet conservatory
space for her café, in the National Print Museum, at Beggars Bush on Haddington
Rd. Ms Toohill's cooking has some verve. It's a real sweet spot for brunch, and you
can even browse the cookbooks that have inspired the boss's dishes. Breakfast &
lunch 7 days.

182 · **Cloud Café** 43 North Strand Rd, D3 +353 89 2204588 · www.cloudcafe.ie
1/R13 Between the Irish Financial Services Centre and Fairview Park, and painted with
CHP a winning baby blue exterior, Cloud Café sources well, and disposes well, so you
eat ingredients grown in the community gardens behind the shop, and any waste
returns there to make healthy compost. Soups, salads, sandwiches on good
sourdough, nice brunch dishes and great coffee. Breakfast, coffee & lunch 7 days,
till 4pm.

183 · **Mayfield Eatery** 7 Terenure Rd Nth, D6W +353 1 4926830 ·
1/R13 www.mayfield.ie Mayfield is an unusual enterprise, a fusion of restaurant,
MED.INX bric-a-brac shop, and performance space, where they stage small theatre and
TERRACE opera productions. Energetically run by two guys who are both named Kevin Byrne,
they offer an all-day menu, which runs right through until late between Thurs and
Sat, adding special dinner dishes to the mix. Lots of atmosphere, and a nice al
fresco terrace. They also operate the next door deli and café, Fragments, with good
foods to buy and Italian-inspired dishes to enjoy with prosecco on tap. Daytime 7
days, dinner Thu-Sat.

184 · **KC Peaches** 27 Nassau St, D2 +353 1 6336872 · www.kcpeaches.com
1/R13 Katie Cantwell's quartet of Dublin destinations offer a taste of West Coast
CHP cooking – that's West Coast USA, not Galway, as Ms Cantwell is a Seattle native.
You can fashion your own salad bowl or sandwich from the kaleidoscope of fresh
ingredients, and with a health-filled focus on wholefoods – 'Slow food fast' is how
they describe it – KC delivers good eating. Nice rooms make for good zones for
hanging out. Daytime and early dinner, LO 7pm-8pm. Other branches on Dame St,
Stephen's Green and Pearse St.

185 · **Soup Dragon** 168 Capel St, D1 +353 1 8723277 · www.soupdragon.com
1/R13 Niamh and Fiona opened Soup Dragon back in 2000, and their stalwart cooking
CHP has been a backbone to Capel St ever since. Great imaginative soups underpin the
offering and there is good savoury and sweet baking and zesty juices. Breakfast &
lunch Mon-Fri.

186   **Simon's Place Café**   22 Sth Gt George's St, D2 +353 1 6797821

1/R13   @SimonsPlaceCafe More than 20 years ago, Simon McWilliams found a little

CHP   space in the George's St Arcade, spent a few quid doing it up, let everyone pin up posters about the gigs they were playing, made some nice sandwiches and soups and brewed good tea, and everyone agreed that it was a good thing. More than 20 years later, everyone still agrees. Breakfast & lunch Mon-Sat.

187   **Camden Kitchen**   3 Camden Market, Grantham St, D8 +353 1 4760125 ·

1/R13   www.camdenkitchen.ie A few paces off the main strip at the top end of Camden

MED.INX   St, Padraic Hayden's bistro is understated, intimate and unpretentious, and has built a formidable reputation for excellent cooking. CK is the sort of place, and has the sort of prices, that Dublin should boast of having in every nook and cranny. But, as it doesn't, the trip to Grantham St to enjoy pork neck terrine, or mackerel with ponzu vinaigrette, or apple and blackberry crumble, is a trip well made. Lunch Wed-Fri, dinner Tue-Sat.

188   **Green 19**   19 Camden St Lwr, D2 +353 1 4789626 · www.green19.ie Part of the

1/R13   dizzying array of restaurants on Camden St, Stephen Murray's Green 19 has built

MED.INX   its name on fine cocktails and great value cooking – the value here is amongst the best in town. Get things going with a Jesus, Rosemary and Joseph cocktail – who could resist? – then get stuck into a Wicklow game pot pie, or the cauliflower steak. They have extended their weekend brunch offer to both Saturday and Sunday, and some blue corn tacos and a house Bloody Mary seems like a good start to the weekend. Lunch & dinner 7 days.

189   **Urbun Cafe**   Unit 2 Watermint Old, Bray Rd, Cabinteely, D18 +353 1 2848872

1/R13   · www.urbunn.ie Katie Gilroy sold her baked goods at farmers' markets before

CHP   she opened up Urbun, and a lack of money meant that she had no choice about fashioning a minimalist interior for this cracking café, in Cabinteely Village. Breakfast, lunch and brunch are simple, and deftly executed. Ms Gilroy is also the dynamo behind Buckle Up, an Aussie-influenced café at the green in Sandymount, D4. Breakfast & Lunch 7 days.

190   **Corner Bakery**   17 Terenure Rd N, D6 +353 1 4906210 · www.cornerbakery.ie

1/R13   This colourful shop is – appropriately – one of the cornerstones of the buzzy food

CHP   culture of Terenure. For a dozen years, the team have baked real breads, cakes, biscuits, made real sandwiches, created scrummy wraps, and baked cakes that make your days special – who's for a slice of Schwarzwaelder kirschtorte? Daytime 7 days.

191   **Queen of Tarts**   Cork Hill, Dame St, D2 +353 1 6707499 ·

1/R13   www.queenoftarts.ie Is there anything nicer on a warm Dublin afternoon than

CHP   a madeleine and a cup of tea in Queen of Tarts, on Cork Hill opposite the City Hall in Dublin? Well, maybe a cup of coffee and a breakfast of potato cake and bacon in Queen of Tarts on Cow's Lane, down in Temple Bar. The Fallon sisters, Regina and Yvonne, have built a devoted following for their superb cooking, which means it is virtually impossible to get a table in the little room on Cork Hill. It's worth waiting. Breakfast, lunch & tea, till 8pm. Also at Cow's Lane, Dame St.

192   **Kennedy's Food Store**   5 Fairview Strand, D3 +353 1 8331400 ·

1/R13   www.kennedysfoodstore.com People feel comfortable in Sarah Kennedy's trio

CHP   of food destinations, and everyone who walks in behaves as if they are a regular. Ms Kennedy's food is simple, clean and clever, and you could eat it several times a week, which is how the team not only sailed through the recession, but also opened the newest branches of the business. It's a bomb-proof model for a modern Dublin food business. Daytime 7 days. Branches in Raheny, Clontarf and Phibsboro.

193 **The House** 4 Main St, Howth, Co Dublin +353 1 8396388 ·
1/R13   www.thehouse-howth.ie Karl Dillon's restaurant is a home from home for many
MED.EXP   Howth residents, not least because it offers one of the smartest kids' menus you
FF   will find anywhere: grilled ham and cheddar on sourdough; Sloppy Joe; homemade
spag bol with Desmond cheese; pork and leek sausages with mash. Aside from the
youngsters, locals love the fact that there is music, purchasable art on the walls,
and a real feeling that The House is a centre not just for eating, but for sharing
time and conviviality. All day & dinner 7 days.

194 **Eathos** 15 Baggot St Upr, D4 +353 1 6298090 · www.eathosdublin.com
1/R13   The aesthetic may have been borrowed from the original and ground-breaking
Ottolenghi style of presentation, but Lisa and Peter Murrin's pretty café, Eathos,
has its own modus operandi. They do refer to beef and chicken and fish as
'protein' but more important is the fact that they source carefully, so the drinks
are excellent, the sweet baking is pretty irresistible, and the healthfulness of the
cooking is confidently delivered. Walk-ins only. Daytime Mon-Sat.

195 **Green Beards** 23 Dunville Ave, Ranelagh, D6 +353 1 5588401 ·
1/R13   www.greenbeards.ie Ray and Kevin use a Norwalk cold-pressing juicer and a
CHP   Good Nature juicer in their search to make their cold-pressed juices as nutrient
rich as possible, and to minimise oxidation. It's worked with the public, as they
now have a second branch in Donnybrook, and supply several of the best food
stores and cafés in the city. Good coffee from local roasters Two Fifty Squared, nice
healthful foods on the funky shelves. Daytime 7 days. Also at Morehampton Rd,
Donnybrook.

196 **Cocu Kitchen** 9 Baggot St Upr, D4 +353 86 1303319 · www.cocu.ie
1/R13   Emilia Rowan has opened three branches of Cocu in double-quick time, as
Dubliners hunger for the zappy, healthy food that Cocu produces. The shops get
very busy at lunchtimes, especially on Baggot St and Hatch St, as office workers
seek an alternative to the desk sandwich. Excellent coffees and juices complement
the foods, and the name is a riff on counter-culture. Daytime Mon-Sat. Other
branches at Hatch St, and Chatham St, D2.

197 **Honey Truffle Kitchen** 45 Pearse Street, D2 +353 87 9864964 · www.
1/R13   honeytruffle.ie Owner Eimear Rainsford was one of the team who made the
CHP   food offer at the Avoca cafes a by-word for excellence, and here on the sunny side
of Pearse Street she shows that same culinary sharpness in a range of bounteous
salads, savoury dishes and sandwiches and excellent coffee. A coronation chicken
sandwich and a cup of Baobab coffee, and you are definitely on the sunny side of
the street alright. Daytime Mon-Fri.

198 **Metro Cafe** 43 William St S, D2 +353 1 6794515 · www.metrocafe.ie
1/R13   With 21 years service to the city, Metro has seen the changes come and go, but
CHP   has mostly seen its customers return time and again. The food and drink offer is
TERRACE   rock-steady: Metro meatball sandwich; bangers and mash with onion gravy; Irish
beef stew served with a Waterford blaa. Sitting under the verandah on the street,
enjoying the sunshine along with your flat white, is part of what Dublin is. All day
7 days.

Where to Eat Brunch

199 ✓ **Two Boys Brew** 375 North Circular Rd, D7 · www.twoboysbrew.ie
1/R13   Kevin Roche and Taurean Coughlan are local heroes and critical darlings, who
CHP   brought their experience of living and working in Oz, and a lean, light, modern
Antipodean design ethic, home to northside Dublin and made it work from day
one. Daytime 7 days. Closed 4pm. Walk-ins only, no bookings.

200 ✓ **Overends Restaurant, Airfield** Overend Way, Dundrum, D14 +353 1
1/R13   9696666 · www.airfield.ie Airfield is a 38-acre working farm which has been
CHP   run as a charity since 1974. Enjoying a weekend family brunch, in conjunction with
FF   exploring the farm and garden – and seeing their Jersey cows being milked – is a
treat, and the fact that much of what you eat is grown in the gardens outside is an
added delight. Late summer is the optimum time to visit, when garden is in full
production. Daytime Mon-Fri, brunch Sat-Sun. All day coffee menu.

201 **The Cookbook Cafe** 57a Glasthule Rd, Sandycove, Co Dublin +353 1 5997999
1/R13   · www.cookbookcafe.ie Chef Audrey McDonald's husband is the well-known disc
MED.EX   jockey Tom Dunne, so this modern, colourful destination on the main strip of little
ATMOS   Glasthule village provides brilliant vinyl music selections at weekends as you enjoy
dishes curated from McDonald's favourite cookery books: Bobby Flay's quesadilla;
Ottolenghi plate. Nice drinks too. Daytime Tue-Sun, dinner Thur-Sat.

202 **Ember** Milltown Shopping Centre, Milltown Rd, D6 · www.ember.ie
1/R13   +353 1 4443783 In the middle of a shopping strip, chef Greg O'Mahoney corrals
MED.EX   the Med and the Middle East into smart brunch dishes – huevos benedictos; roast
squash with feta and lentils – and uses his Basque-style grill to create smoked
Ember burger. Manager Paddy Scully and his team are fleet and professional and,
with little serious cooking in this part of S Dublin, Ember is valuable. Lunch Tue-Fri,
brunch Sat & Sun, dinner Tue-Sun.

203 **The Pigeon House Cafe** 11B Vernon Avenue, Clontarf, D3 ·
1/R13   www.pigeonhouse.ie +353 1 8057567 Paul Foley and Brian Walsh work hard
MED.INX   to look after every customer, which means they even have a brunch menu for
FF   children. The smallies can decide on scrambled egg on toast, or pancakes with
banana and Nutella, whilst the adults can ease into the day with a Bellini. It's a
busy popular spot, so make sure to have reservation. Enjoy a long walk on Bull
Island afterwards. Daytime & dinner 7 days. Second Pigeon House Cafe at The
Delgany Inn, Co Wicklow.

204 **Farmhill Cafe & Restaurant** 9 Farmhill Rd, Goatstown, D14 ·
1/R13   www.farmhill.ie +353 1 4413871 With the talented Anita Thoma in charge of
MED.INX   the kitchen, it's worth the trek out to Goatstown at the weekend to enjoy brunch
dishes that are anchored around some of the best Irish artisan ingredients. If
you are making the journey, make sure to have a reservation. Value for money
excellent. Daytime Tue-Fri, brunch Sat & Sun, dinner Thur-Sat.

205 **Charlotte Quay** Millennium Tower, Ground Floor, Charlotte Quay Dock,
1/R13   Ringsend Rd, D4 · www.charlottequay.ie +353 1 9089490 · With a two-for-
CHP   one brunch cocktail offer at weekends, Conor and Mark Bereen's Charlotte Quay
restaurant is a smart choice for weekend eating. The menu is concise and focused
– Billionaire's BLT; forager's breakfast; pastrami and eggs; the Full Charlotte with
smoked beans and poached eggs – the room is welcoming and atmospheric and, of
course, the waterside location at Grand Canal Dock, just off the Ringsend Road, is
pure darling. Lunch & dinner 7 days. Brunch at weekends.

206 **Bibi's** 14b Emorville Avenue, D8 · www.bibis.ie +353 1 4547421 Many
1/R13 Dubliners regard the Bibi's brunch as the best in the city, which explains why
MED.INX you may have to wait for a table in either of their two rooms on any given day.
TERRACE Maisha and Geoff Lenehan's concise menus steer clear of the fry-up options
found elsewhere, and signature dishes such as Turkish eggs, or roast squash with
poached eggs and chilli butter, are clean and satisfying. Tables outside the café, on
Ovoca Rd, are a treat when the sun shines. Daytime 7 days, Dinner Thur.

207 **Slice** 56 Manor Pl, Stoneybatter, D7 +353 1 4456100 · www.asliceofcake.ie
1/R13 Brunch starts early and ends late at the weekend in Slice, a sister restaurant to
CHP the acclaimed Cake Café, and one of the places that has put Stoneybatter on the
food lover's radar. The choices are enigmatic and creative and a stroll in the nearby
Phoenix Park beforehand will stoke the appetite nicely. Daytime Mon-Fri, all day
brunch Sat & Sun.

208 **San Lorenzo's** Castle House, 73-83 Sth Gt Georges St, D2 +353 1 4789383 ·
1/R13 www.sanlorenzos.ie They only allow you 75 minutes to have brunch in San
MED.EXP Lorenzo's, such is the pressure on seats at the weekend, and such is the regard
for their immodestly entitled 'Brunch of Champions'. The music is turned up to 11,
the room is packed, the energy is crazy, and if you would like to quietly peruse the
Sunday newspapers, then go someplace else, because they start the party early in
San Lorenzo's. Daytime & dinner 7 days.

209 **Hey Donna** 137 Rathmines Rd Lwr +353 1 491 3731 · www.joburger.ie Serial
1/R13 restaurateur Joe Macken turns his sights on the Middle East with Hey Donna,
MED.INX offering sharing plates of baba ghanoush, ember-baked beets; slow-roasted carrots
with carrot-top pesto, and a series of grill dishes: beef kofta; sumac chicken;
Berber-spiced lamb chops. The canteen seating and the canteen vibe is as well-
judged as the Ottolenghi meets April Bloomfield grub. Very smart; terrific fun.
All day 7 days.

210 **Whitefriar Grill** 16 Aungier St, D2 +353 1 4759003 · www.whitefriargrill.ie
1/R13 Halfway up Aungier St, the Whitefriar was one of the first destinations to offer
MED.EXP a dedicated brunch menu, and whilst it is known primarily as a steakhouse, the
brunch dishes offer some nice riffs on the weekend classics. If you have the
appetite, you can order their signature ribs 'n' rump, a combination of rump steak
and barbecue ribs. Dinner 7 days, brunch Sat-San. The same team run Bow Lane, a
funky bar, right next door: www.bowlane.ie.

211 **Storyboard** Clancy Quay, Islandbridge, D8 · www.storyboardcoffee.com
1/R13 Chef Laura Caulwell is ex-Fumbally and ex-Ballymaloe, which is pretty much the
MED.EXP best cv you can get in Irish cooking. Owner Jamie Griffin got the right talent for his
Islandbridge cafe, on Clancy Quay, and Ms Caulwell relishes turning every foodie
norm upside-down on her hand-written menus: black rice porridge for the rice
bowl; miso greens for egg on toast; caraway mayo with sausage sandwich. Lean
room, vivid food, excellent coffee. Daytime 7 days.

The Best Pizza

212 ✓ **Gaillot et Gray** 59 Clanbrassil St Lwr, D8 +353 1 4547781
1/R13   **@GaillotGrayP** Emma Gray and Gilles Gaillot made their name selling
CHP   pizzas out of an old, rigged-up Citroen van, before setting up shop at the top of
DF   Clanbrassil Street, just down from the canal. Their Gallic signature is the use of
Emmental cheese, rather than Parmesan, so these are pizzas with a French
accent, from a Grand-Mere oven, and they are rockin'. BYOB. Daytime & dinner
Tue-Sat, till 10pm.

213 **The Yarn** 37 Liffey St Lwr, D1 · www.theyarnpizza.com Between The
1/R13   Woollen Mills and The Grand Social – look for the neon sign saying Pizza +
MED.INX   Booze – The Yarn is home to some very hip pizzas and cocktails. The pizza style is
TERRACE   somewhere in between the thin-crust Neapolitan style and a crisper Roman style
and, with an Aperol and Prosecco spritz in the other hand, sitting at a table on the
terrace with the roof rolled back and the sun shining, the Yarn delivers in spades.
Dinner 7 days.

214 **Dublin Pizza Company** 23 Aungier St, D2 +353 1 5611714 ·
1/R13   www.dublinpizzacompany.ie Michael Ryan's pizza shack hit Dublin with a
CHP   bang when he opened on Aungier St in mid-2016, and the combination of superb
ATMOS   ingredients – many from their own garden and polytunnels in Stoneybatter, just
across the river – and the original approach of Mr Ryan has proven to be a bombproof
formula. The pizzas are an homage to Irish artisan cheeses and ingredients such
as whiskey-cured Irish salamis, and the addition of a daily steak sandwich means
everyone is happy. Join the queue. Dinner 7 days. Open till midnight.

215 **Paulie's Pizza** 58 Upr Grand Canal St, D4 +353 1 6643658 · www.juniors.ie
1/R13   Barry and Paul McInerney focus on Neapolitan-style pizza here at Grand Canal
MED.INX   St, whilst allowing themselves a detour to New York style pie, and some house
ATMOS   specials like the Roxy and Zoe's, where they get to throw on the chillies and the
nduja. A small selection of antipasti and pasta dishes keeps everything tightly
under control, and the only problem is getting a seat. Dinner 7 days. Also from this
company, **Junior's Deli & Cafe** and the **Old Spot** gastropub.

216 **Manifesto Restaurant** 208 Lwr Rathmines Rd, D6 +353 1 4968096 ·
1/R13   www.manifestorestaurant.ie In addition to serving some of the most highly
MED.INX   regarded Italian cooking in Dublin over the last 20 years, Lucio Paduano's
ATMOS   restaurant also produces ace pizzas, including the award-winning Don Corleone
and the Mamy. The wine list covers the entire vinous landscape of Italy and offers
an embarrassment of riches, with many wines available by the glass. Lunch Sat &
Sun, dinner 7 days.

217 **Dave's Wood Fired Pizza Co.** George's St Arcade, D2 +353 86 7724744 ·
1/R13   www.davespizzas.ie Dave's pizza has been one of the staples of Dublin market
CHP   life, but even with a smart new home in the George's St Arcade, you can still find
them working the markets at the weekend. There are seven pizzas on offer in the
Arcade, along with flat breads and a nifty breakfast calzone. Marlay Park Market
Saturdays and Sundays, People's Park Market Sundays.

218   **C O T T O**   46 Manor St, Stoneybatter, D7 + 353 1 5522918 · www.cotto.ie
1/R13   Cotto is a sister restaurant to the excellent Oxmantown, but the speciality here is
MED.INX   pizza, cooked at dinnertime during the week, with a more conventional brunch
menu at weekends. Conor Higgins is a super-smart cook who knows how to keep
things simple and how to deliver balance and trueness. The room is lean and
simple, the drinks are good. Brunch Sat & Sun, dinner Wed-Sun.

219   **Cirillo's**   140 Baggot St, D2 +353 1 6766848 · www.cirillos.ie James Cirillo
1/R13   was practically reared in Dublin's original Italian restaurant – Nico's, on Dame St,
MED.INX   where his dad was a chef – so bringing home the true tastes of Neapolitan pizza
was written on his DNA. There are nine Neapolitan pizzas, and five pizza bianche,
as well as a small selection of pastas and starters, and the pizzas use fine Irish
ingredients, rather than simply importing everything. With plain tables, bentwood
chairs, dark wood shelves, nice wines and an intimate style, the interior hits the
right notes. Lunch & dinner Mon-Sat.

220   **Base Wood Fired Pizza**   18 Merrion Rd, Ballsbridge, D4 +353 1 4405100 ·
1/R13   www.basewfp.com Shane Crilly has grown his Base WFP chain from the original
MED.INX   pair of locations – in Terenure and Ballsbridge – to a collection of five restaurants.
For many pizza lovers who have followed Mr Crilly since 2008, it's hard to steer
away from the Base Classics. Daytime & dinner 7 days. Branches in Ballsbridge,
Stillorgan, Terenure, Lucan & Glenageary.

221   **Skinflint**   60 Dame Street, D2 · www.joburger.ie Joe Macken is a maverick
1/R13   Dublin restaurateur with a small assortment of restaurants that specialise in one
MED.INX   thing, whether that be burgers, chicken, beef or, in the case of Skinflint, pizza. It's
a quintessential hipster locale, with great sounds and cool drinks, and the pizzas,
with grilled crust, are quite different to everyone else's. Pretty much to the taste
of everyone under 25, but others might just find it too left-field. Lunch & dinner
Mon-Sun.

222   **Honest Pizza**   12 Dame Ct, D1 +353 1 6337727 · www.honestpizza.ie
1/R13   One element of the fine Honest To Goodness Café, run by Darragh and Martin, HP
CHP   is upstairs and amongst the range of lovely pizzas there is a good selection with
bianco bases. Dinner Tue-Tur, Lunch & dinner Fri-Sat.

Sophie's @ The Dean Report: 130/BOUTIQUE HOTELS.
Da Mimmo Report: 256/ITALIAN.

The Best Seafood Restaurants

223
1/R13
MED.INX

✓ **Fish Shop** 6 Queen St, Smithfield, D7 +353 1 4308594 ·
www.fish-shop.ie It started with a shack in a market and now, after just a few short years, Peter and Jumoke's little empire includes two of the best places to eat seafood in Dublin. Fish Shop, on Queen St, a stone's thrown from Mellows Bridge over the River Liffey, is a tiny, ascetic room, and a textbook demonstration of how to showcase fish and shellfish at its best. Their tiny space on Benburb St, just around the corner, is where they offer fish and chips (1447/FISH & CHIPS). Both rooms also offer superlative and surprising wines, all available by the glass. They serve only wild Irish fish, sourced and cooked on the day and the only problem is getting a seat. Dinner Wed-Sat.

224
1/R13
MED.INX
ATMOS

Klaw 5A Crown Alley, D2 · www.klaw.ie Klaw is a narrow little crab shack of a place, with a counter along one wall and a pair of high tables, but owner Niall Sabongi and his crew know their way around seafood. In 2017 they opened another new destination, **Klaw Poké**, where Niall Sabongi's take on Hawaiian poké happens in a hip room with a gorgeous zinc bar, behind which the man himself shucks oysters, blowtorches fish, and cracks jokes. You can fashion your own poké bowl, or choose one of their signature bowls and the lobster rolls are already legendary. Daytime and dinner 7 days.

225
1/R13
MED.EXP

Urchin The Cliff Townhouse, 22 Stephen's Gn, D2 +353 1 6383939 · www.theclifftownhouse.com The colourful, beach hut style of Urchin, in the basement of the elegant Georgian of The Cliff Townhouse (134/SUPERIOR LODGINGS), brings a touch of sun and sand to St Stephen's Green. Chef Sean Smith has fashioned a menu of seafood tapas to pair with an excellent cocktail selection. You can keep the price low by concentrating on the less-expensive tapas, but with good sounds and good drinks it's hard to slow the adrenaline in Urchin. Lunch Mon-Sat, dinner 7 days.

226
1/R13
MED.EXP

Lobstar 101 Monkstown Road, Monkstown, Co Dublin +353 1 5373323 · www.lobstar.ie Lobster does of course have the starring role in Veronika and Zsolt Zakar's Monkstown restaurant, one of many places to eat in this affluent Dublin suburb. The shellfish is served as lobster roll, lobster burger, lobster ravioli, lobster pot and split and grilled, and you can add half a lobster to your choice of steak. But there are also fish choices, a burger and chicken wings. Veronika oversees the small, bright room with quiet charm and, in spite of all the competition, Lobstar has found its audience quickly. Lunch Sat-Sun, dinner Tue-Sun.

227
1/R13
MED.EXP
ATMOS

Rosa Madre 7 Crow St, Temple Bar, D2 +353 1 5511206 · www.rosamadre.ie Luca de Marzio's little Temple Bar restaurant has a wet fish counter, so you get to see your dinner in its pristine, raw state before the kitchen works its magic. You can choose to have the day's catch grilled, oven-baked or salt-crusted, and these classic techniques allow the quality of the fish to shine. There are also classic pasta dishes – spaghetti alla vongole; tagliatelle with lobster – and very fine wines, some imported directly by Mr de Marzio himself. Lunch & dinner 7 days.

228 **Cavistons Seafood Restaurant** 58 Glasthule Rd, Sandycove, Co Dublin
1/R13 +353 1 2809245 · www.cavistons.com The Caviston family's food emporium
EXP is a legendary shop in pretty little Glasthule, and for the last 20 years they have
cooked the seafood that is one of their major specialities and served it in their
small, always packed restaurant. Don't miss a visit to the shop, a clamorous and
delightful temple of delicious things. Lunch Tue-Sat, dinner Thur-Sat.

229 **Aqua** 1 West Pier, Howth, D13 +353 1 8320690 · www.aqua.ie Housed in
1/R13 a handsome building right at the end of Howth's West Pier, Aqua offers achingly
MED.EXP glorious views out across the sea to Ireland's Eye but when the Aqua signature
dishes begin to arrive at the table, you will only have eyes for the food. Elegant
dining, with assured cooking and lovely wines, in a gorgeous room. Lunch &
dinner Tue-Sun.

230 **The Oar House** West Pier, Howth, D13 +353 1 8394568 · www.oarhouse.ie
1/R13 A fine old stone cottage on the pier, with flags fluttering and tables outside to catch
MED.INX the sun, is the perfect setting for chef John Aungier and fishmonger Sean Doran
TERRACE to strut their stuff. Check the blackboard and the wet fish display before making
up your mind. The laid-back nautical theme of the room puts everyone in a good
mood. The same team operate the Octopussy tapas bar on the pier. Lunch &
dinner 7 days.

231 **King Sitric Fish Restaurant & Accommodation** East Pier, Howth, D13 +353
1/R13 1 8325235 · www.kingsitric.ie Aidan and Joan McManus's restaurant has been in
MED.EXP operation for more than 40 years. The upstairs restaurant on the pier at Howth is a
TERRACE formal, comfortable room, with beautiful sea views, in which to enjoy good wines
and Mr McManus's classic seafood cookery. There are eight guest rooms, each
named after Irish lighthouses, whilst the informal East Café Bar on the ground floor
has good seafood dishes, boards and platters, and nice food for children. Dinner
Wed-Sat, lunch Sun.

232 **Crabby Jo's** 14 West Pier, Howth, D13 +353 1 8323999 · www.crabbyjos.com
1/R13 On the West Pier at Howth, so an important place to know if you've enjoyed a
MED.INX blustery family day out, and need to get the bairns filled up on the Little Nippers
FF menu: mini fish and chips; steak strips with mash; baby bowl of mash. And then a
chocolate brownie, of course, while they finish colouring in the fishes. Daytime &
dinner 7 days.

The Best Burgers & Steaks

233 **Bujo** 6a Sandymount Green · www.BuJo.ie Owner Michael Sheary has stepped
1/R13 the bespoke burger business up another notch with Bujo, situated right beside the
MED.INX wooded green in pretty Sandymount. Every detail of the delivery of the burger –
from bread to beef to bacon, right down to the skin-on fries – has been thought-
through, and then delivered anew. Hip room, beers from Wicklow Wolf, and a crew
who relish their work complete a dynamic new attraction in D4. A walk along the
Sandymount Strand (461/DUBLIN WALKS), followed by a beer and a Bujo burger, is
just the ticket.

234 **Dillinger's** 47 Ranelagh, D6 +353 1 4978010 · www.dillingers.ie Dillinger's
1/R13 owner John Farrell is one of the city's busiest restaurateurs, but what is interesting
MED.EX about his portfolio is the fact that each destination is different. His Ranelagh
outpost, Dillinger's, is his tribute to American-style dining, so there is a particularly
fine burger – frequently rated amongst the best in Dublin – served with paprika
onions, also rib-eye and bavette steaks. The brunch menu majors in the American
classics, cocktails are cool, and locals tend to have more than one 777 margarita.
Brunch Sat & Sun, dinner 7 days

235 **Bunsen** 36 Wexford St, D2 +353 1 5525408 · www.bunsen.ie Bunsen gets
1/R13 the votes of many Dubliners for the city's best burger. Owner Tom Gleeson studied
CHP the discipline obsessively – when he wasn't working in Le Bernardin and The Fat
Duck – and everything is considered down to the last detail. You can get a burger,
or a cheeseburger; you can double up on either of those; you can get shoestring
fries, hand-cut fries, and sweet potato fries. The food arrives on trays, and it's tasty,
zappy, umami-rich fare. Expect to queue. Lunch & dinner 7 days. Also at Temple
Bar, 3 South Anne St, and 4 French Church St, Cork.

236 **The Chop House** 2 Shelbourne Rd, Ballsbridge, D4 +353 1 660 2390 ·
1/R13 www.thechophouse.ie Chef-proprietor Kevin Arundel uses 35-day dry-aged
MED.EX beef from Cairn's farm in Co Louth for his signature steaks, at this bustling bar and
restaurant close to the Aviva stadium. There is rib-eye, fillet, porterhouse, and cote
de boeuf for two, along with a Hereford beef burger. They also offer a quartet of
dishes using fish, chicken and lamb. A slick and impressive gastropub that's always
busy. Lunch Mon-Fri & Sun, dinner Mon-Sat.

237 **The Butcher Grill** 92 Ranelagh Village, D6 +353 1 4981805 ·
1/R13 www.thebutchergrill.ie A converted butcher's shop on the main strip of
MED.EX Ranelagh, the Butcher Grill is intimate and atmospheric, and the meaty dishes are
good. They do a good deal with a cote de boeuf special for two people early in the
week, and the restaurant has all the efficiency and slickness of the various places
run by serial restaurateur John Farrell. Kids welcome for brunch only, not during
dinner. Brunch Sat & Sun, dinner Wed-Sun.

238 **Jo'Burger** 4 Castle Market, D2 · www.joburger.ie Joe Macken cracked the
1/R13 formula of good food and good times, took the burger out of the fast food school,
MED.INX and the place was packed from day one. The formula is simple: select your burger –
TERRACE beef; lamb; chicken; veggie; fish fillet – then customise it one of 20 different ways,
and add a few extras. There is a bunch of side dishes, a raft of sauces, and that's it.
You can now also choose your location, with the extra branch in Smithfield
village, D7".

239 **Featherblade** 51b Dawson St, D2 +353 1 6798814 · www.featherblade.ie
1/R13 Chef Paul McVeigh marinates his signature featherblade steaks for 24 hours before
MED.EXP they are finished on the grill. Focusing on a single dish has proven to be a formula
for success, and Featherblade is usually rockin' with people getting their steak
knives out, especially late at night. The featherblade is usually supplemented by
another steak choice – hanger steak, usually – and there is a smoked burger
served at lunchtime which has become as much of a signature dish. Lunch &
dinner 7 days.

240 **Bobo's** 72 Middle Abbey St, D1 +353 1 5380800 · www.bobos.ie Bobo's
1/R13 signature Cashel burger, with the great Tipperary blue cheese and rocket, tomato
MED.INX and smoked bacon, is one of the city's best. The original Wexford St location is the
most atmospheric of their three destinations. They also offer burger riffs with lamb,
chicken and fish, and there are two vegetarian choices using mushrooms and
falafel. Other branches on Dame St and Wexford St. Lunch & dinner 7 days.
Open till 4am Sat.

241 **Wowburger** 11 Wellington Quay, D2 +353 86 0563144 · www.wowburger.ie
1/R13 Wowburger has been winning the critical kudos for burger excellence since it
MED.INX opened, and has speedily opened three branches in the city. The original hut is
sited in the Workman's Club, a bar and music venue on Wellington Quay, and the
offer is simplicity itself: burgers, burgers with bacon, burgers with cheese; fries
with garlic butter; shakes and sundaes, with free toppings. The second branch is
downstairs in the fantastically atmospheric Mary's Bar, on Wicklow St, and the
third is at the triangle in Ranelagh. Lunch & dinner 7 days.

The Best Vegetarian & Vegan Restaurants

242
1/R13
MED.INX
ATMOS

✓**Cornucopia** 19 Wicklow St, D2 +353 1 6777583 · www.cornucopia.ie
Deirdre McCafferty's restaurant is one of the longest established restaurants in the city – it opened in January 1986 – and it's cherished by Dubliners as an always reliable destination for good vegetarian and vegan cooking, all day, every day. People have lined up at the service counter with their trays for more than 30 years, deciding what they will choose from the dishes described on the blackboards, and knowing they will enjoy wholesome and deeply-considered food. There are three dining rooms, all looking out onto Wicklow St, but with an average of 500 customers per day, it can be tricky getting a seat. Breakfast, lunch & dinner 7 days

243
1/R13
MED.INX

✓**Veginity** Richmond Pl Sth, Rere 26 Richmond St Sth, D2 ·
www.veginity.com Aussie chef Mark Senn is the man who has made Veginity into one of the city's cult dining destinations. It's plant based cooking, sure. And it comes out of a food truck, yes, situated in a warehouse. But what makes Veginity special is the fact that it's superb cooking. Mr Senn's skills are truly universal, so his menus hop from continent to continent and country to country. Look out for the green neon 'V' sign. There is a second Veginity truck operating out of Eatyard, beside the Bernard Shaw pub, serving 'fish' and chips. Dinner Thur-Sat.

244
1/R13
MED.INX

Sova Food Vegan Butcher 51 Pleasants St, D8 +353 85 7277509 ·
@SovaVeganButcher After Mr Sova became vegan, he started doing pop-up restaurant evenings, and ran a market stall stocked with his foods. That has led to a pleasant, minimalist little room where he offers plant-based dishes that often have carnivorous names – king scallops with kelp caviar; seitan steak; lentil and aubergine meatballs; seitan doner kebab. Best of all, he makes it work, right down to the vegan Irish breakfast they have created for weekend brunch. Lunch Wed-Sun, dinner Wed-Sat.

245
1/R13
CHP

Umi Falafel 180 Rathmines Rd Lwr, D6 +353 1 4976028 ·
www.umifalafel.ie The Umi falafel story has proven to be quite a success, with two restaurants in Dublin and a third in Cork city, and we will be surprised if there aren't more to come. Their signature dishes are the Lebanese falafel (tahini sauce, Lebanese bread) and the Palestinian falafel (chilli sauce, pitta pocket). Most of their dishes are vegan. Nice juices too, and keen prices. Lunch & dinner 7 days. Umi Falafel also at 13 Dame St and 11 Academy St, Cork.

246
1/R13
CHP

Blazing Salads 42 Drury St, D2 +353 1 6719552 · www.blazingsalads.com
Lorraine and Pamela Fitzmaurice have been cooking good vegetarian food for Dubliners since 1982, and opened their wholefood deli on Drury St in 2000. You help yourself to the salads and hot dishes in the buffets, construct the lunch you want, then pay according to the weight of your chosen dishes. You can stand at the window ledge and eat, as there is no seating, but this doesn't deter their ardent customers, who come back again and again. Daytime, Mon-Sat.

247 **Happy Food** Yoga Hub, 27 Camden Pl, D2 +353 85 9630292 ·
1/R13 www.happyfood.ie Lenka Potysova's bright little room in the Yoga Hub, in
CHP Camden Place just off the Camden St, offers plant-based daytime food. It's a
quiet little haven, with a peaceful courtyard garden, and is a well-kept secret.
Daytime Mon-Sat, LO 3pm.

248 **Little Bird** Sth Circular Rd, Portobello, D8 · www.little-bird.ie This pretty
1/R13 pastel blue café and yoga studio, at the Leonard's Corner end of Sth Circular Rd,
TERRACE is not exclusively vegetarian, but plant-based dishes dominate. Badger & Dodo
DF coffees, Wall & Keogh teas, and dog bowls and doggy seating area outside. Daytime
7 days, till 8pm Mon-Fri.

▬▬▬ The Best of The Middle East

249 **Silk Road Cafe** Chester Beatty Library, Dublin Castle, D1 +353 1 4070770
1/R13 · www.silkroadcafe.ie A self-service cafe in the elegant space of the Chester
CHP Beatty Library in the elegant space of Dublin Castle is one of the best secrets
in the city. Ibrahim Phelan cooks authentic Middle Eastern food, and even old
warhorses such as moussaka, or chicken tagine, are fresh and elemental. They
also serve a very unusual afternoon tea, with a mixture of savoury and sweet
dishes. Might be a problem getting a table during lunchtime. Daytime 7 days,
'til 4.15pm.

250 **Moro Kitchen by Dada** 21 Camden St, D2 +353 1 4758816 ·
1/R13 www.morokitchen.ie With a pair of sweet and lovely dining rooms, colourfully
CHP fitted out with furniture and bricolage which owner Aziz Nouhi brought back from
Marrakech, Moro Kitchen has just the right feel, with just the right Moroccan
street food. Downstairs is the café and takeaway, and you can also order online
for home delivery. On Sth William St, Nouhi's **Dada Moroccan Restaurant** is
simpler, but equally classic and good value. Brunch Sat & Sun, lunch & dinner
7 days.

251 **El Bahia** 37 Wicklow St, D2 +353 1 6770213 · www.elbahia.com A staple
1/R13 of Wicklow St since 2000, El Bahia has all the Moroccan furnishing to set the
MED.INX mood, and all the Moroccan culinary classics: Marrakech tagine; braised cow's
tongue with harissa; merguez with tomato sauce; Berber couscous. Dinner
Tue-Sun, lunch Sat & Sun.

The Best Italian Tratts & Osterias

252
1/R13
MED.INX

✓ **Dunne & Crescenzi** Sth Frederick St, D2 +353 1 675 9892 ·
www.dunneandcrescenzi.com Dunne & Crescenzi personifies all the things
we want from a public place to eat – atmosphere, comfort, service, a sense of
community, a sense of well-being, delicious and well-understood cooking,
memorable wines. There's a special pleasure in suggesting to people that they
should eat in D&C when they visit or move to Dublin, and then hearing their
delighted reaction to the artful curation of Italian food, wine and service that Eileen
Dunne and Stefano Crescenzi have created. Daytime & dinner 7 days. Other
branches in Sandymount, Blackrock. They also operate L'Officina in Dundrum and
Kildare Village, Co Kildare.

253
1/R13

✓ **Osteria Lucio** The Malting Tower, Clanwilliam Ter, Grand Canal Quay,
D2 +353 1 6624198 · www.osterialucio.com Chefs Ross Lewis and Luciano
Tona got everything right from the off in Osteria Lucio, and created everyone's idea
of an archetypal Italian restaurant. Osteria food is comforting food, and that is what
you will find here, where standard ingredients are tweaked reverentially. The room
pulses with energy, and is already a favourite Dublin destination. Excellent pizzas
from the wood-fired oven. Lunch & dinner 7 days.

254
1/R13
MED.INX
ATMOS

Terra Madre Café 13 Bachelors Walk, D2 +353 8735300 ·
www.terramadre.ie With only 17 seats, all artfully mismatched, of course, this
cramped little basement on Bachelors Walk, on the northside of the River Liffey,
has more character than you could shake a stick at. Staff are straight from central
casting, especially Marco, and pretty much everyone loves it to bits. So, just ask
Marco to feed you. Nice wines, excellent value, but be careful on those stairs.
Lunch & dinner 7 days.

255
1/R13
MED.INX
TERRACE

Il Valentino 5 Gallery Quay, Grand Canal Harbour, D2 +353 1 6331100 ·
www.ilvalentino.ie Owen and Valentina Doorly's bright, busy bakery and café
has become one of the icons of Grand Canal Harbour, thanks to superb Italian
breads and savouries, and good coffee. It's the place for the best cannoli, and for
that perfect breakfast croissant, baked downstairs underneath the café, and for
a simple lunch, based on their formidable breads. A state-of-the-art filtration
system means the water for drinks and for baking is as pure as can be. Daytime
7 days.

256
1/R13
MED.EXP
ATMOS

Da Mimmo's 148 N Strand Rd, N Dock, D8 +353 1 8561714 ·
www.damimmo.ie Tino Fusciardi's northside restaurant offers expert pizzas and
some very fine pasta dishes, not least their fine take on spaghetti with clams. It's a
bustling, busy place, with robustly flavoured cooking that Dubliners just love, and
it's packed with both diners and folk turning up for takeaway. Good value wines
means dinner won't hurt the credit card. Lunch & dinner 7 days.

257
1/R13
CHP

Bottega Toffoli 34 Castle St, D2 · @Toffoli Elaine McArdle and Carlo Eremita
have a little, bare-bones room on Castle St, between Christchurch and City Hall
on Dame St, and they have built a mighty reputation for good pizzas – who can
resist a pizza named The Hangover – and fine piadina sandwiches. There might be
spaghetti on the menu and, then again, there might not be. It's as basic as it gets,
and that's the bit we like best. Lunch & dinner 7 days.

258 **Panem** 21 Lwr Ormond Quay, D1 +353 1 8728510 · www.panem.ie For 21
1/R13 years now, Ann Murphy has served baked focaccias, frittata, sandwiches and salads
CHP to the hungry people of Dublin, from the little riverside space that is Panem, and
in all that time Ms Murphy hasn't had to change a thing. There is a counter with
half-a-dozen stools inside the room, but there is nothing nicer than to take a
warm Siciliana focaccia out to the river and sit down on the boardwalk on a sunny
summer day. It's not actually compulsory to describe Panem as a 'hidden gem', but
that's what everyone calls it. Daytime 7 days.

259 **Pinocchio** Luas Kiosk, Ranelagh, D6 +353 1 4608800 ·
1/R13 www.flavourofitaly.net The original Ranelagh branch of Pinocchio, tucked
MED.INX in under the LUAS railway bridge, has been joined by a sister restaurant, on the
ATMOS splendidly named Pudding Row, in Temple Bar. The owners also operate a cookery
school, a catering company, and a specialist Italian travel company but, when
they aren't teaching and travelling, they have time to fire out the Italian trattoria
classics. Dinner from 4pm Mon-Wed, Lunch & dinner Thur-Sun.

Rosa Madre www.rosamadre.ie Report: 227/SEAFOOD.

The Best French Restaurants

260 **l'Gueuleton** 1 Fade St, D2 +353 1 6753708 · www.lgueuleton.com Dubliner
1/R13 Aoife Barker can cook French bistro dishes as well as the French themselves, and
MED.EXP her food makes the ultra-atmospheric l'Gueuleton a sure bet for a good night.
TERRACE Great room and whilst we find the dimmed light a little dark, others probably just
ATMOS find it romantic. Lunch & dinner 7 days.

261 **Chez Max** 133 Lw Baggot St, D2 +353 1 6618899 · www.chezmax.ie
1/R13 Max de Laloubie's French cafés may trade in every cliché about French eating that
MED.INX you could imagine, but Dubliners have taken these two cafés and the Epicerie to
TERRACE their hearts for more than a dozen years. The Baggot St café is considered to be
better, but if you need a fix of moules frites, or steak frites, or poulet a l'estragon,
then pull up a bentwood chair. Lunch & dinner 7 days.

262 **La Maison** 15 Castle Market, D2 +353 1 6727258 · www.lamaisondublin.com
1/R13 With bentwood chairs and small tables downstairs, behind the outdoor dining
MED.INX area, and a pretty red banquette running along the wall upstairs after you pass the
Doisneau photographs, La Maison conforms to every French bistro archetype you
can think of, even before you get to the menus. And when it comes to food, owner
Olivier Quenet brings home the classics from breakfast to dinner, all delivered with
professional calm. Daytime & dinner 7 days.

263 **Pearl Brasserie** 20 Merrion St Upr, D2 +353 1 6613572 · www.pearl-
1/R13 brasserie.com Classy, calm and comfortable, Pearl Brasserie has been one of the
EXP defining city centre restaurants. Sebastian and Kirsten are professionals from first
course to last, and have been since they opened in late 2000. The name brasserie
is misleading, because this is a quiet warren of rooms, with French classics crossed
with some Asian-influenced riffs. Set menus offer good value. Lunch & dinner
7 days.

✓ **Restaurant Patrick Guilbaud** Report: 140/TOP END RESTAURANTS.

The Best Tapas & Spanish Restaurants

264 **Port House** 64a Sth William St, D2 +353 1 6770298 · www.porthouse.ie
1/R13   A cave-like room, dimly lit with tiny spotlights and wall-to-wall candles makes
MED.INX   The Port House a great, romantic, date restaurant. The pintxos are good, the
classics such as lamb stew with paprika and peppers, and octopus a la gallega,
are good, and the wines and sherries are only excellent. With a no-reservations
policy, you may have to wait, but it's worth it. Sister restaurant Port House
Pintxo on Eustace St, is another moody, atmospheric basement, A third branch
is out at Dundrum shopping centre, and the latest addition is in London's Covent
Garden. Lunch & dinner 7 days.

265 **Las Tapas De Lola** 12 Wexford St, D2 +353 1 4244100
1/R13   · www.lastapasdelola.com The secret of Las Tapas de Lola is more than the
MED.INX   gutsy, flavourful little plates of tasty food that owners Anna and Vanessa create.
ATMOS   The secret, in fact, is the energetic abandon of everyone who gets swathed in
the room's hospitality, and the vibe. The small tables, bentwood chairs and red
cushions give the room the feel of a bar, which is more than appropriate for
tapas. Every classic Spanish dish you've ever heard of seems to be here, and
everyone is encouraged to enjoy themselves. Tapas is party food, which means
there's a gathering every night of the week. Dinner 7 days.

266 **La Bodega** 93 Ranelagh, D6 +353 1 4975577 · www.labodega.ie A narrow,
1/R13   somewhat cavernous room in Ranelagh Village is home to some of the best
MED.INX   Spanish cooking in town. Start with the classic pa amb tomaca – tasty toasted
bread with ripe, crushed tomatoes – then have the rich bacon croquetas. We
especially love the northern Spanish stews like the rich zarzuela with its intense
brew of mussels and prawns in shellfish stock, and their bacalao with pea purée
is the funkiest fish & chips you can get. Dinner 7 days, lunch Fri & Sat.

267 **Fade Street Social** Drury St, D2 +353 1 6040066 · www.fadestreetsocial.
1/R13   com Celebrity chef Dylan McGrath offers a tapas menu in the gastro bar of his
EXP   Fade Street empire. As one would expect from Mr McGrath, he bends the tapas
concept to his own will, so the dishes are nicely unconventional. Lunch & Dinner
Mon-Sun.

268 **Boqueria** 31 Church St, Howth, D13 +353 1 8322932 · www.boqueria.ie
1/R13   Chef Matt Fuller earned a good reputation for his tapas cookery in a little room in
MED.EX   Stoneybatter, before setting sail to head to Howth, in north Co Dublin, where the
restaurant occupies a pretty, cottage-style house on Church St, just up from the
harbour. This is de luxe cooking. Short list of Spanish wines are all well-chosen.
Lunch & dinner Tue-Sun.

269 **777** Unit 7 Castle House, Sth Great George's St, D2 +353 1 4254052 ·
1/R13 www.777.ie A beautiful jewel-box of a room, which from the outside on George's
MED.EX St looks like nothing whatsoever, is home to some of the best margaritas in the
ATMOS city. Everyone – but everyone – starts with a brace of these, then takes it from
there. It's all mad, raucous fun, and the only trouble is having a conversation as
the noise level rises to a margarita-fuelled crescendo. Dinner 7 days. Late opening
Thur-Sat, 'til 11pm/midnight.

270 **Taco Taco** 13 Dame Court, D2 · www.tacotacodublin.com Run by the team
1/R13 from nearby San Lorenzo's, Taco Taco shines brightest with its brunch dishes, and
MED.EX has brought something new to the city with dishes like duck hash, and Cajun-spiced
pork burrito, and chicken Parmesan with buttermilk waffles. They have brought the
signature baked Nutella cheesecake over from San Lorenzo's, and their margaritas
have a mighty reputation. Dinner 7 days, 'til 10pm/11pm, brunch Sat-Sun.

271 **K Chido Mexico** 18 Chancery St, Inns Quay, D7 +353 85 8230348 ·
1/R13 www.kchidomexico.com Well, this is the real dope: an old converted Citroen HY
CHP van serving Mexican street food, at the back of Fegan's fruit warehouse in D7, just
ATMOS around the corner from the Law Library. The tables and chairs are up-styled pallets,
the colour scheme is psychedelia-on-acid, the cooking is just lovely. Good coffee
from roasters Ariosa, and good Mexican sounds. Daytime 7 days.

272 **Cafe Azteca** 19-22 Lord Edward St, D2 + 3531 6709476 · www.azteca.ie
1/R13 Azteca is the real deal, serving Mexican food as it should taste, and not dumbed-
CHP down Tex Mex. Owner Hugo has created a menu specialising in burritos, taquitos,
enchiladas, quesadillas, with good Mexican wines to match the tacos al pastor.
Hugo also hosts cookery classes, so enquire if you want to learn more about the
subtlety of this ancient cuisine. Mon-Sat lunch & dinner, till 8pm/9pm.

273 **Pablo Picante** 4 Clarendon Market, D2 +353 1 6334245 ·
1/R13 www.pablopicante.com With four city locations, including a big new room on
MED.INX Aston Quay on the banks of the River Liffey, Colm McNamara's Pablo Picante is a
California-style burrito bar, which also offers tortas and paleo bowls. A tinga torta
and a bottle of beer is welcome anytime, and the sweet pepper vegetarian choice is
a good one. Fast turnover and lots of students queueing for the special price deals
sets the tone. Lunch & dinner 7 days. Branches of Pablo Picante can be found at
Baggot St, Fleet St, Temple Bar and Aston Quay.

274 **El Grito Taqueria** Merchants Hall, Merchant's Arch, Temple Bar,
1/R13 D2 +353 1 5584717 · @ElGritoMexicanTaqueria A hatch – just five seats, but
MED.INX you can take away – in the narrow walkway of Merchant's Arch as it traverses from
the River Liffey into Temple Bar, El Grito lets you choose your dish – tacos; burritos;
quesadillas – and then you decide which version of beef, chicken or pork filling you
want. Good, simple Mexican street food and, thanks to the pork broiler, the place to
get tacos al pastor. Lunch & dinner 7 days.

275 **Little Ass Burrito Bar** 32a Dawson St, D2 +353 1 6799694 · www.littleass.ie
1/R13 Having set up Little Ass in a tiny space on Dawson St, Philip Martin has since
CHP established Blanco Nino, a factory in Tipperary which produces authentic corn
tortillas, and it's those tortillas you will find in the best Mexican places to eat in
Ireland. There is now a much larger branch of Little Ass in Rathmines in D6, with
the same smart mix of tacos, boxes, quesadillas and burritos. A Sancho Panza and
a cold beer is alright by us. Lunch & dinner 7 days. Also at Rathgar & Rathmines.

The Best Asian Restaurants

BEST SUSHI AND JAPANESE

276 ✓ **Michie Sushi** 11 Chelmsford Ln, Ranelagh, D6 +353 1 4976438 ·
1/R13 www.michiesushi.com Michel and Anna of Michie Sushi have made sushi a
MED.INX part of Dublin life. They have done it by adhering to rigid standards – the freshest fish, chosen by Michel himself, painstakingly paired with select ingredients, balanced on perfectly cooked and seasoned sushi rice, and showing meticulous composition of the pieces. To this potent mixture Michel and Anna added friendly, urbane service, the sort of service that makes even sushi beginners feel at ease. We have watched Michie Sushi grow from a single, tiny room in Ranelagh to a chain of busy stores but, in reality, nothing has changed: Michie Sushi is always a pleasure. Lunch & dinner Tue-Sun. Branches also in Sandyford, Dun Laoghaire, IFSC and at Avoca Rathcoole and Kilmacanogue.

277 **The Ramen Bar** 51 William St S, D2 +353 1 5470658 ·
1/R13 www.kokorosushibento.com Behind the Kokoro Sushi Bento takeaway, you find
CHP The Ramen Bar, serving the best ramen in the city. In a dark, lacquered room, a place setting is prepared with a paper menu, a covetable wooden soup spoon and a pair of chopsticks. When you order from the paper sheet, they ring your order with biro, and shortly afterwards deliver bowls of steaming deliciousness. Owner Ian Conway imported a noodle-making machine from Japan, and it was worth it. Hungry folk should note that they will bring an extra portion of noodles if you still have broth remaining. Sushi and bento boxes sold from the shop at the front. Lunch & dinner 7 days. Second branch at 19 Liffey St.

BEST NEPALESE

278 ✓ **Monty's of Kathmandu** 28 Eustace St, D2 + 353 1 6704911 ·
1/R13 www.montys.ie In September 1997, Shiva and Lina Gautham got the doors
EXP open on their premises in Temple Bar, and brought a palette of new flavours and culinary ideas to the city. What distinguished Monty's is the quest for authenticity, so they offer domestic Nepalese cooking, but with a professional confidence, and with masterly tandoor skills ensuring that the smoky, barbecued trueness of the flavours is always present. Lunch Mon-Sat, dinner 7 days.

PAN-ASIAN

279 ✓ **Chameleon Restaurant** 1 Fownes St, Temple Bar, D2 +353 1 6710362
1/R13 www.chameleonrestaurant.com Ever since they won the first Taste of
MED.EX Temple Bar Award, back in 1995, Chameleon has stayed true to the ethos of what the competition sought to achieve: that the zone would be a funky, punky arrondissement of chef-patron places to eat. The rest of the zone has commercialised, but Kevin and Carol haven't, and eating in The Chameleon is an adventure. Still the star of Temple Bar. Takeaway menu available. Dinner Tue-Sun.

280 ✓ **Nightmarket** 120 Ranelagh, D6 +353 1 5385200 · www.nightmarket.ie
1/R13 Jutarat and Conor Sexton have rewritten the book on Thai cooking in the
MED.INX hugely popular Nightmarket. Jutarat's sharing-style dishes are alive with the thrill of lime and chilli, which animate the pork and prawn dumplings, the duck breast salad in baby gem leaves, the grilled mackerel with wok greens, the slow-cooked lamb with coconut milk and potatoes. This is thrilling cooking, and the restaurant has taken Ranelagh by storm. Superb wines, and very good value. Dinner Wed-Sun.

281
1/R13
MED.INX
ATMOS

Saba 2 Clarendon St, D2 +353 1 5631999 · www.sabadublin.com
One evening in Saba, no fewer than five staff members welcomed us with a warm 'Good evening!' before we had even reached our table. That's the sort of outfit Paul Cadden runs, both on Clarendon St in the centre of the city and in the slightly more informal Baggot St branch, just over the canal bridge. This is a first-class team, trained to the back teeth, and it means any evening is guaranteed good times and great Thai cooking. Start with one of their cocktails. Lunch & dinner 7 days. 2nd branch on Baggot St. Saba To Go takeaways in Rathmines, Windy Arbour, Dundrum & Deansgrange.

282
1/R13
MED.INX

Bread and Bones 7 Millennium Walkway, D1 +353 1 5346925 ·
www.breadandbones.ie B&B is a fun joint, and Jack Fox and Duncan McDonald and their team love to pile on those big flavours. The savoury baos are the star of the show, so settle into a booth made from an upcycled pallet, and don't forget to bring your inner Ninja warrior. Lunch & dinner 7 days.

283
1/R13
MED.INX

Pho Viet 162 Parnell St, D1 +353 1 8783165 · www.phoviet.ie Kim Nguyen and her family specialise in Vietnamese pho, a street food which offers a light broth and rice noodles to which you add chicken or beef, and vegetables. Nice clean rooms, and we love the fact that the Vietnamese curry is accompanied by baguette. There is a short wine list, but you can also BYOB, which incurs a small charge. Lunch & Dinner 7 days.

284
1/R13
MED.INX

Thai House 21 Railway Rd, Dalkey, Co Dublin + 353 1 2847304 ·
www.thaihouse.ie When Tony Ecock opened Thai House in 1997, Dublin had virtually no authentic Asian cooking. But Mr Ecock is one of those pioneering guys who sees an opportunity long before anyone else, and so he opened Thai House in a neat room in Dalkey, the posh village south of Dublin. He created a comfortable and welcoming series of rooms, offered superbly curated wines, and his team cooked delicious Thai food. The rest, of course, is history. Takeaway menu available. Dinner from 4pm Tue-Sun.

KOREAN

285
1/R13
CHP
ATMOS

✓ **Kimchi Hop House** 160 Parnell St, D1 +353 1 8728318 · www.hophouse.ie
Imagine a future where the Irish pub is gridded with a Korean eating house, and it will be this madcap, unique place. The pub is a Parnell St pub. The restaurant is a little eating house from a side street in Seoul. Owner Kyoung Hee Lee hasn't tried in any way to meld the two: she just lets them sit cheek-by-jowl, brother-by-sister, weirdness and incongruity, in stereo. Echt Korean cooking, and don't overlook the Japanese dishes which are highly regarded by Japanese residents of the city. Lunch & dinner Mon-Sun, till 11.30pm.

286
1/R13
CHP

Brothers Dosirak Super Asia Foods Supermarket, 27 Capel St, D1 ·
@dosirakbrothers The Brothers Dosirak is a little shebeen of an eating house, up a walkway beside the meat and fish counters at the side of the Super Asia Foods supermarket, near the River Liffey end of Capel St. The brothers are a cult team, thanks to cooking fine Korean food, and offering the sort of value for money that seems unbelievable in the overheated Dublin of today. Lunch & dinner 7 days.

287
1/R13
CHP

Han Sung 22 Gt Strand St, D1 +353 1 8874405 At the back of the Han Sung Asian Market, close to the Millennium Walk, is a little counter of Asian cooking, with the overhead menus offering rice dishes, stir-fries, jjigae, noodle dishes, all served buffet style. There are long tables and benches to share in front of the counter, under the skylight. All day till 9pm, 7 days.

The Best Chinese Restaurants

288
1/R13
MED.EXP
ATMOS

✓**Hang Dai** 20 Camden St, D2 +353 1 5458888 · www.hangdaichinese.com
Ireland has never seen anything like Hang Dai. The room is luridly coloured, loud, raucous, and chaotic, the Oriental restaurant from a sci-fi movie made real, on Camden St, in Dublin's new restaurant quarter. In the midst of the tumult, chef-patron Karl Whelan calmly wields his knife. Mr Whelan is the Zen antidote to the most original restaurant the capital has seen, and his calmness brings forth mighty foods. Meanwhile, partner Will Dempsey pulls it all together with superb staff and getting a table is the hard bit. Dinner Tue-Sat.

289
1/R13
MED.EXP

✓**China Sichuan** The Forum, Ballymoss Rd, Sandyford Ind Est, D18
+353 1 2935100 · www.china-sichuan.ie A ride on the DART out to the China Sichuan yields some of the finest ethnic cooking in Ireland. The newer menu dishes show a kitchen at the height of its powers, though you could happily stay with the Sichuanese classics they have cooked for decades. It's a good idea to ask owner Kevin Hui what the kitchen has been up to, and to trust them with your order. The room is luxurious, but it's a little disappointing to see Irish diners still opting to use knives and forks, ordering their own main course, and not embracing the sharing ethos that is at the heart of Sichuanese and Chinese eating. Lunch & dinner 7 days.

290
1/R13
MED.INX

✓**M&L** 13 Cathedral St, D1 +353 1 8748038 · www.mlchineserestaurant.com
Angie and Graeme's ethnic restaurant is the place to get the real deal. In a city where most Chinese restaurants maintain two menus – one for Westerners, one for Chinese – in M&L you can tell the waiters that you want sliced whelk with scallions, or the cold stomach of pork with raw vegetables, and they won't bat an eyelid. M&L is unusual, also, in that the greeting is warm and sincere and service is helpful, so tell them you want to get far out of your comfort zone. Lunch & dinner 7 days.

291
1/R13
MED.INX

Good World 18 Sth Gt George's St, D2 +353 1 6775373 The Good World is the best place in Dublin to order dim sum, from a large menu with all the classics: char siu bun; glutinous rice with lotus leaf; marinated chicken feet; turnip paste; spicy beef tripe; egg custard bun. They also do a pretty neat Peking duck. Dim sum until late, closes 2am, 7 days.

292
1/R13
MED.INX

Ka-Shing 12a Wicklow St, D2 +353 1 6772580 · www.kashing.ie Manager Marcus Hoo's Wicklow St institution is popular for dim sum, but let the team know that what you want is the strange stuff such as the chicken feet, the scallops on the shell with vermicelli and black beans, and you will eat very well here. Lunch & dinner 7 days.

293
1/R13
MED.INX

Duck 15 Fade St, D2 +353 1 6718484 · www.duck.ie Roast duck and crispy pork belly are the things to target in this Hong Kong BBQ meats deli, the duck being sourced from the highly successful Silver Hill Foods, in Co Monaghan, and cooked in a Bullet oven. The blackboard announces the daily special – lemon chicken; duck red curry – and they pair nicely with the starchy staples of rice and noodles. Lunch & dinner 7 days.

PARNELL STREET – DUBLIN'S CHINATOWN

294
1/R13
MED.INX

Lee Kee 100a Parnell St, D1 +353 83 4500922 Parnell St is Dublin's Chinatown, home to cheap and cheerful Chinese restaurants, which morph and metamorphose according to some lunar law we are unfamiliar with. Lee Kee, however, managed by Rikan Liu, has been a steady destination for true Chinese food, so come here for sea whelks, for jellyfish and cucumber salad; oyster and tofu soup, pig's ear salad; duck tongue. Decent service, too. Lunch & dinner 7 days.

295
1/R13
MED.INX

Sichuan Chilli King 100 Parnell St, D1 +353 1 8783400 · @SichuanChilliKing Manager Lee Xu oversees the spicy Sichuanese classics in Chilli King, so step out and go for the boiled beef slices in fiery sauce, the ma po tofu, the fish braised with beancurd. Lunch & dinner 7 days.

The Best Indian Restaurants

296
1/R13
EXP

✓**Pickle Restaurant** 42 Camden St, D2 +353 1 5557755 · www.picklerestaurant.com What chef-patron Sunil Ghai does in Pickle is simple: he takes basic things and through complex, finessed technique, he transforms them utterly. The dishes hide the effort needed to create them, and simply offer powerful tastes and textures. It's a masterly performance, and such red-hot cooking has made Pickle one of the biggest hits in Dublin. Lunch & dinner 7 days.

297
1/R13
MED.EXP

✓**Rasam** 18 Glasthule Rd, Dun Laoghaire, Co Dublin +353 1 2300600 · www.rasam.ie Owner Nisheeth Tak and head chef Dayal Negi squeeze out the culinary sparks in Rasam, one of the best-loved restaurants in Dublin. Rasam was ahead of the pack when it opened in 2003, upstairs above The Eagle Pub on the main strip of Glasthule, and offered Dubliners the true flavours of the Indian subcontinent. Whilst Rasam was an eye-opening experience then, its strength has been to maintain that level of enchantment, and many customers are regulars dating back to the early days. Dinner 7 days.

298
1/R13
EXP

Ananda Sandyford Rd, Dundrum Town Centre, D14 +353 1 296 0099 · www.anandarestaurant.ie The flagship of the small Jaipur chain of restaurants redefined ethnic eating, and our expectation of Asian dining, when Ananda first opened back in 2008. In the ensuing years, the restaurant has been characterised by an enviable consistency, along with a dynamic creativity that makes the marriage of Irish ingredients and ethnic techniques and seasonings seem utterly logical. Service is excellent, and pricing is very fair for cooking of such intricacy. Dinner 7 days & Sun lunch.

299
1/R13
MED.EXP

Kinara Kitchen 17 Ranelagh Village, D6 +353 1 4060066 · www.kinarakitchen.ie Sean Collender and Shoaib Yunus are creative restaurateurs, and they have made both Kinara and its Ranelagh sister, Kinara Kitchen, amongst the best-loved destinations for Pakistani cooking in Dublin. The Clontarf room has lovely sea views, and ace cooking, especially the tandoor specialities and the vegetarian dishes. In Ranelagh, the restaurant is unusual in offering an award-winning selection of cocktails in the upstairs bar, and the drinks are amongst the best-fashioned cocktails in town. Out in Malahide, Kajjal has notched up a decade of serving excellent food in this pretty seaside village. Other branches in Clontarf & Malahide. Dinner 7 days.

300
1/R13
MED.INX

Konkan 46 Upr Clanbrassil St, D8 +353 1 4738252 · www.konkan.ie Clanbrassil St is where you go to find the southern Indian specialities of Konkan. There is great value in the early-bird menus, and in the wine list. A second branch in Dundrum looks after the suburbs, and of course they do takeaway, and delivery. They've been doing the job well since 2004. Dinner 7 days. 2nd branch in Dundrum, opp the Garda Station.

Party Rooms & Late Night Restaurants

301
1/R13
EXP
ATMOS

✓**Luna** 2-3 Drury St, D2 +353 1 6799009 · www.supermisssue.com Serial restaurateur John Farrell's hippest destination is a basement room that manages to tick every box: a beautiful, glamorous space; great staff; smart food and, above all, the kind of atmosphere that feels like everyone is on the way to a party. Painstaking attention to detail helps people to suspend reality when they are in Luna: it looks and feels like a restaurant in a Martin Scorsese wiseguy movie, and that's before the dessert trolley arrives. Mr Farrell sells a beautiful dream. Dinner Wed-Sat, LO 11pm.

302
1/R13
MED.EXP
ATMOS

Trocadero 4 St Andrew's St, D2 +353 1 6775545 · www.trocadero.ie Everyone who has lived in Dublin has a story about the Troc, about the great times they had, about the laughter, the craic, about losing their keys, their credit cards, about how they don't recall getting home. The stories don't mention the food, which is fine, because the food is there to facilitate the good times. Dinner Mon-Sat, LO 11.30pm on theatre nights. Booking advisable.

303
1/R13
MED.EX

The Green Hen 33 Exchequer Street, D2 + 353 1 6707238 · www.thegreenhen.ie Looking like something between a prototypical Dublin bar and a quintessential French bistro, The Green Hen is a fun space just off the main shopping street in central Dublin. People come for the steaks, especially, which are well sourced and properly served. The two floors are kitted with classic bistro chairs and tables, and the room is popular with visitors as well as locals. A late-night menu is served until the early hours on Fri & Sat, along with wines and cocktails. Lunch & dinner Mon-Sun, LO 1am Fri & Sat.

304
1/R13
MED.EXP

Super Miss Sue 2 Drury St, D2 +353 1 6799099 · www.supermisssue.com Street-level sister to the basement Luna next door, this is a modish, neon-lit and narrow space with smart, diner food. Lunch & dinner 7 days, LO 11pm Thu & Sat. Their sister chipper, Cervi, is open till midnight. Report: 1450/FISH & CHIPS.

305
1/R13
MED.INX

Crackbird 34 S William St, D2 · www.joburger.ie Joe Macken's temple to the diversity and deliciousness of chicken has all the familiar tropes – upcycled furniture; remnants of the Chinese restaurant it used to be; zappy, spicy, finger-lickin' food that isn't afraid of the deep-fat fryer. Above all, it's mighty fun, and it doesn't take itself too seriously; just the vibe that you need for that late-night feed. Lunch & dinner 7 days, LO 10pm Mon-Wed, 11pm Thur-Sat, 9pm Sun.

The following restaurants serve food until late at the weekend. Booking is recommended.

✓**Hugos** 'Til 11pm Report: 160/BRASSERIES.

✓**Hang Dai** 'Til 11pm Report: 288/CHINESE.

✓**Kimchi Hop House** 'Til 11.30pm Report: 285/ASIAN.

777 'Til midnight Report: 269/MEXICAN.
Good World 'Til 2am Report: 291/CHINESE.
The Exchequer Wine Bar 'Til 11pm Report: 345/BARS WITH GOOD FOOD.
Dublin Pizza Co 'Til midnight Report: 214/PIZZA.

306 **Eat Yard** 9-18 Sth Richmond St, D2 · www.the-eatyard.com As you would
1/R13 hope from an eclectic meld of street food traders, the variety is dazzling, and
ATMOS quality levels are sky high. There is also a stage for demos and discussions, and a
flea market. Lunch & dinner Thur-Sun.

307 **147 Deli** 147 Parnell St, D1 +353 1 8728481 · @147deliparnell Barry
1/R13 Stephens' deli has some atypical food to go alongside the reuben and the
meatball sub, so head to Parnell St for mushroom and quinoa burger; chickpea
and roasted squash with tahini dressing; chipotle chicken with pineapple salsa.
All day Mon-Sat.

308 **Poulet Bonne Femme** Avoca, 13 Suffolk St, D2 +353 1 6674215 ·
1/R13 www.pouletbonnefemme.com Gavin McCarthy and Sarah Mitchell are the
masters of rotisserie chicken, and have steadily expanded the range of meats
beyond birds, so you can enjoy pork, beef, ham and lamb, and they will even cook,
bone and roll an Xmas turkey for your festive table. Four locations in Avoca stores,
and one in the vast Dundrum centre in south Dublin. All day, 'til 4.30pm, 7 days.
Look out for PBF in other Avoca stores and in markets.

309 **Temple Bar Food Market** Meeting House Sq, D2 +353 1 9059189 For the last
1/R13 25 years, the market in Temple Bar has given artisans their best showcase in the
ATMOS city. It's a wonderful location for shopping, but also for grazing as the quality of the
cooked food offerings is exceptionally high. Sat 10am-5pm.

310 **Grand Canal Market** Mespil Rd, D4 · www.irishvillagemarkets.ie
1/R13 This market is one of several run by Irish Village markets, both in the city and the
suburbs. The offer from the stallholders is diverse so join all the office workers who
cram the banks of the canal. Thurs 11.30am-2pm.

311 **People's Park Market** Dun Laoghaire The Sunday market in the lovely Dun
1/R13 Laoghaire park is more of an eating than a shopping market, as southsiders
ATMOS meander through the stalls having Sunday lunch on the hoof. Sunday 11am-4pm.

312 **The Birdcage Bakery** 21 Harcourt Rd, D2 +353 1 4783820 ·
1/R13 @BirdcageBakery This tiny little place, no more than a counter, a few seats and
a few shelves, is noteworthy for their fine Italian baking, good breakfasts and nice
coffee. Breakfast, lunch & coffee Mon-Fri, LO 3.30pm.

313 **Alchemy Juice Company** 5 Leeson St Lwr, D2 + 353 1 6706217 ·
1/R13 www.alchemyjuice.ie Interesting to know that Alchemy uses a process of
trituration and hydraulics to press their juices, but it's more interesting to know
that they are utterly delicious, and we would walk across town for a Turmeric Tonic.
Nice free-from food as well. Open daytime Mon-Sat, LO 2.30pm Sat.

314 **Sprout & Co** 63 Dawson St +353 1 7645908 · www.sproutfoodco.com
1/R13 The Kirwan brothers, Jack and Theo, have been colonising Dublin in double-quick
time, first with their wholesome drinks, then with their healthy food to go. Open
daytime Mon-Sat. Sprout Kitchens also at Lwr Mount St, Sir John Rogerson's Quay,
Ballsbridge.

The Best Original Pubs

315
1/R13
ATMOS

✓✓✓ **The Long Hall** 51 Sth Gt George's St, D2 +353 1 4751590 With an original interior dating from 1880, the Long Hall is one of the glories of Dublin drinking. If there is a bar in Heaven, then it will look exactly like The Long Hall, an exuberant temple of alcohol and affability.

316
1/R13
ATMOS

✓ **Doheny & Nesbitt** 5 Baggot St Lwr, D2 +353 1 6762945 · www.dohenyandnesbitts.ie Founded by William Burke in 1850, and one of the most glorious examples of pub Victoriana in the city. Well known as home-from-home for civil servants and barristers, unpublished poets and would-be intellectuals who together constitute 'The Doheny & Nesbitt's School of Economics'.

317
1/R13

✓ **John Kavanagh, The Gravediggers** 1 Prospect Sq, Botanic, D9 +353 1 8307978 Situated next to Glasnevin cemetery – hence the name The Gravediggers – this is one of the best pubs in Dublin, and the essence of its distinguished history and management under the Kavanagh family – it is now run by the 8th generation – is evident in every detail of the bar. The food offer, served in the lounge by Ciaran Kavanagh, is extremely good.

318
1/R13

The Brazen Head 20 Lwr Bridge St, Merchants Quay, D8 +353 1 6779549 The oldest drinking establishment in the city, and sources suggest travellers may have been taking refreshments here as far back as the 12thC. Evocative, atmospheric, and host at various times to Robert Emmet, Wolfe Tone, Daniel O'Connell, the leaders of the United Irishmen.

319
1/R13
ATMOS

Kehoe's 9 Sth Anne St, D2 +353 1 6778312 This quaint little pub, just off Grafton St, is often overlooked, but for us it's one of the most charming of the authentic Dublin pubs.

320
1/R13
ATMOS

Grogan's 15 Sth William St, D2 +353 1 6779320 · www.groganspub.ie At the rere of the Powerscourt Centre, many Dubliners have a special affection for the beautiful, unchanged Grogan's. 'No music, no television, no nonsense. It's a place to return to in search of yourself' said *The Irish Times*. Having a pint helps the search.

321
1/R13

Mulligan's 8 Poolbeg St, D2 +353 1 6775582 · www.mulligans.ie There has been a pub on the site of Mulligan's since 1782, and perhaps it's that lengthy history – and their reputation for pouring an excellent pint of stout – that seems to inspire a particular reverence for Mulligan's. John F. Kennedy used to drink here regularly, back in 1945, when he worked for the Hearst newspaper company.

322
1/R13

The Duke 9 Duke St, D2 +353 1 6799553 · www.thedukedublin.com On the corner of Duke St and Duke Lane, the bar occupies numbers 8 and 9, and the latter is named Gilligan's. Famous literary pub in the past, it is today the starting point for the much-loved Dublin Literary Pub Crawl.

323 **Davy Byrne's** 21 Duke St, D2 +353 1 6775217 · www.davybyrnes.com
1/R13 James Joyce wasn't the only Irish artist who put Davy Byrne's legendary pub to artistic use. Many other artists and writers, and politicians – Edna O'Brien; Harry Kernoff; William Orpen – have found the pub to be a conduit for their work. Davy Byrne himself retired from the bar as long ago as 1939 and, although legend records that he did not stand his customers a drink, he did offer Arthur Griffith a bottle of wine on the house in January 1922, when the treaty establishing Irish independence was signed.

324 **Neary's** 1 Chatham St, D2 +353 1 6778596 · www.nearys.ie A former owner
1/R13 of Neary's managed somehow to combine running this classic Victorian pub with carrying out the arduous duties of acting as Honorary Consul to the Republic of Guatemala. Famous home for actors, both working and resting, as the back door opens onto a laneway across from the Gaiety Theatre. Nice clubby feel, nice lounge upstairs.

325 **Toner's** 139 Baggot St Lwr, D2 +353 1 6763090 · www.tonerspub.ie The story
1/R13 is told that Toner's is the only Dublin pub that W.B. Yeats ever visited. When Oliver Gogarty chose Toner's as the place to bring Yeats, he chose well, for it's a classic bar, with a lovely snug just inside the door.

326 **The International** 23 Wicklow St, D2 +353 1 6779250 · www.international-
1/R13 bar.com Full disclosure: this was our favoured Dublin pub many years ago, when we joined up with everyone else from *Hot Press* magazine to welcome the weekend with pints of stout. It hasn't changed a bit since then, and it's still dear to our hearts.

327 **The Palace Bar** 21 Fleet St, Temple Bar, D2 +353 1 6717388 · www.
1/R13 thepalacebardublin.com The exterior of The Palace is always festooned with
ATMOS an extravagant display of flowers, and inside is one of the vital Dublin pubs, unchanged and charming.

328 **The Stag's Head** 1 Dame St, D2 +353 1 6793687 Yes, there is a stag's head
1/R13 in The Stag's Head, an architectural jewel of a pub whose style, rather curiously, evokes an almost ecclesiastical atmosphere. Its beauty means it has proven popular with film crews and, if you sit down in here in the afternoon as the light streams through the stained glass windows, you will feel you are in a temple. Beautiful snug, too.

329 **McCaffreys Hole In The Wall** Blackhorse Ave, D7 +353 1 8389491 · www.
1/R13 holeinthewall.pub This is the longest pub in Ireland, and has a fine restaurant and wine shop as well as the series of interlocking rooms that house the bars. Its origins date all the way back to 1610 and, thanks to the hard work of the McCaffrey family, it's in fine hands.

The Best Traditional Irish Music Pubs

330 ✓ **The Cobblestone** 77 King St N, Smithfield, D7 +353 1 8721799
1/R13 · www.cobblestonepub.ie *The* cult destination for authentic music sessions.
ATMOS The pub doesn't look like much from the outside, a reminder of the original
grimness of Smithfield before it began to be gentrified, but the Mulligan family who
own the bar have been involved in music for generations, and the music making is
serious. Sessions every night, also bluegrass, folk, uilleann pipers, all in the
Backroom.

331 ✓ **O'Donoghue's** 15 Merrion Row, D2 +353 1 6607194 · www.odonoghues.ie
1/R13 A legendary haunt for musicians who stage fine music sessions, O'Donoghue's
ATMOS is particularly famous as the bar where fabled group The Dubliners first came
together to play. On a busy night, which is every night, the bar at the front
redefines the term 'crowded'. Yeah, that little guy sitting over in the corner is Bruce
Springsteen.

332 **The Celt** 81 Talbot St, D1 · www.thecelt.ie Trad sessions every evening, starting
1/R13 around 9.30pm in an old-style city centre pub that is festooned with memorabilia,
and packed with tourists.

333 **O'Shea's Merchant** 12 Lwr Bridge St, Merchant's Quay, D8 +353 1 6793797
1/R13 Traditional sessions and ballads seven nights in a bar that has hosted many now-
famous Irish musicians long before they ever caught fame. Set dancing on Mon
night.

334 **Devitts** 78 Lwr Camden St, St Kevin's, D8 +353 1 4753414 · www.
1/R13 devittspub.ie Good music sessions include a traditional session on Thurs, held in
the bar, whilst the other sessions happen upstairs on Thurs, Fri & Sat.

335 **McNeills** Capel St, D1 +353 1 8747679 · @McNeillsPubSessions Lovely old
1/R13 Capel St pub, with good sessions on Thurs and Fri, and a nice open fire to warm
you on those dark and stormy nights.

336 **The Temple Bar** 47 Temple Bar, D2 +353 1 6725286 One of the busiest Temple
1/R13 Bar pubs has ballad sessions every evening. Good luck getting a seat amidst all the
tourists.

337 **Johnnie Fox's Pub** Glencullen, Co Dublin +353 1 2955647 · www.jfp.ie
1/R13 One of a number of pubs that claim to be the 'Highest pub in Ireland'. It's a big
ATMOS draw for tourists thanks to their hooley nights and musical sessions, and they
have buses leaving from the centre of Dublin to take you all the way up the hills
to Glencullen.

338 **Whelan's** 25 Wexford St, D2 +353 1 4780766 · www.whelanslive.com
1/R13 International acts as well as local up-and-coming musos flock to one of the city's
best venues. In a perfect world, you were in Whelan's the night that Jeff Buckley
played.

The Porterhouse www.theporterhouse.ie Dublin's first craft beer pub and
brewery has music sessions most nights and, of course, excellent ales: don't miss
the oyster stout. Report: 348/CRAFT BEER.

Bars with Very Good Food

339
1/R13
MED.EXP

✓✓ **The Legal Eagle** 1 Chancery Place, Inns Quay, D7 +353 1 5552971 · www.thelegaleagle.ie Elaine Murphy's gastro pub has been praised as offering 'joyous' cooking, and that's the truth: who wouldn't find delight in beef suet pudding with crushed swede, or wild rabbit, bacon and cider pie, or homemade jelly and ice cream. It's a city pub – just across the street from the Four Courts – but this is big, brassy country cooking, and the kitchen pulls it off with flying colours. Great beers, great sounds, great service, and the Eagle is someplace special. Lunch & dinner 7 days.

340
1/R13
ATMOS

✓ **L. Mulligan Grocers** 18 Stoneybatter, D7 +353 1 670 9889 · www.lmulligangrocer.com The L. Mulligan team are blessed with a Nostradamus-like prophetic vision. They were already into craft beer when they opened in 2011. They were into gin and whiskey, they were into irony, upcycling, using the pub as a shop, brewing collaborations and monthly quizzes, things that are now, of course, the staples of our lives. Above all, they were deep into making tasty, unpretentious grub. Dinner Mon-Fri, lunch & dinner Sat & Sun.

341
1/R13
ATMOS

✓ **The Bernard Shaw** 11 Richmond St Sth, D2 +353 1 9060218 · www.thebernardshaw.com The young folk love the wicked vibes of the Bernard Shaw, with its Big Blue Bus – an old Routemaster bus, parked in Eatyard beside the bar – and its ramshackle bar, which looks like a stage set from *Mad Max*. The pizzas are great, the coffee is too strong, but the vibe is irresistible. 4pm-late Mon-Fri, Lunch & dinner Sat & Sun.

342
1/R13

Ashton's Gastropub 11 Vergemount, Clonskeagh, D6 + 353 1 2830045 · www.ashtonsgastropub.ie Paul Lenehan and Ronan Kinsella run two of the best gastropubs in Ireland – Harte's, on the square in Kildare town, south of the city, and the Dew Drop Inn, in Kill, Co Kildare – and the same confident nous and experience is evident in the menus at Ashton's. Lunch & dinner, 7 days. BEST Irish craft beers, gins and whiskeys seal the deal. Lunch & dinner, 7 days.

343
1/R13

The Old Spot 14 Bath Ave, Sandymount, D4 +353 1 6605599 · www.theoldspot.ie Under the same ownership as the nearby Paulie's Pizza and Junior's, The Old Spot delivers zappy, savoury food downstairs in the bar. Upstairs in the restaurant there is more ambitious fare. Lunch & dinner 7 days.

344
1/R13

Workshop Gastropub George's Quay, D2 +353 1 67706 · www.theworkshopgastropub.com Before its makeover, the Workshop was a tatty, well-loved old boozer called Kennedy's. The refurb managed to retain a lot of the intimacy, whilst also giving it an upstairs restaurant – The Peppercorn Room. Popular place for lunch for nearby office workers who scarf down chicken BLTs and burgers on brioche. Lunch & dinner 7 days.

345   The Exchequer 3-5 Exchequer St, D2 +353 1 6706787 · www.
1/R13   theexchequer.ie Good cooking and hip cocktails in a trad pub is something
ATMOS   everyone now emulates, and while the cooking here doesn't reinvent the
wheel, it offers an array of good savoury assortments including a special
Sunday roast for 4 people at an all-in price. Lunch & dinner 7 days.

346   Merrion Inn 188 Merrion Rd, D4 +353 1 2693816 · www.themerrioninn.
1/R13   com Fearghus McCormack and his team work hard to get beyond the
traditional expectations of what people think Irish pub cooking can be, in
this big, stylish pub, across the road from St Vincent's Hospital. Lunch &
dinner 7 days.

347   The Washerwoman 60 Glasnevin Hill, D9 +353 1 8379441 · www.
1/R13   thewasherwoman.ie You could sum up Elaine Murphy's restaurant
MED.EXP   mantra as: "Simple things, done beautifully". The food in her restaurants
is unpretentious, well-rooted, and out here in Glasnevin, she practises the
mantra that has served her so well in Dublin city centre, where she runs
The Winding Stair, The Woollen Mills and The Yarn. The care in the cooking
reflects the care in the sourcing. Put these ingredients on a plate in
these lovely rooms, and you have a very happy destination. Lunch & dinner
7 days.

The Chop House Report: 236/BURGERS & STEAKS.

348
1/R13
ATMOS
The Porterhouse 16 Parliament St, D2 +353 1 6798847 ·
www.theporterhouse.ie The Porterhouse is something of a Holy Grail for
beer lovers, for it was here on Parliament St that the group's mighty march to bring
people something other than monolithic, macro beers got underway. What they
wanted to bring the world was Oyster Stout, and Wrasslers XXXX and Hop Head,
and a clatter of other drinks that challenged conformity. For their pains, they
succeeded beyond imagining. They also operate the huge Porterhouse Central, on
Nassau St, and the Dingle Distillery.

349
1/R13
ATMOS
57 The Headline 56 Clanbrassil St Lwr, D8 +353 1 5320279 ·
www.57theheadline.com Geoff Carty offers two house beers – Two Sides –
in addition to almost two dozen craft beers, and they have no macro beers. There
are 10 rotating taps, and tasting trays. Just as importantly, they have good food,
well-sourced and smartly delivered, and their bright and airy upstairs bar is a very
good spot for dinner.

350
1/R13
ATMOS
The Black Sheep 61 Capel St, D1 +353 1 8730013 · www.galwaybay
brewery.com This is our favourite of the Galway Bay Brewery pubs in the city, at
the Parnell St end of Capel St. Calm and efficient staff somehow manage to cope
with the crowds, and the guest selection of beers is always a thrill.

351
1/R13
Against the Grain 11 Wexford St, D2 +353 1 4705100 · www.galwaybay
brewery.com The first Dublin bar to be opened by the Galway Bay Brewery proved
to be a sure-fire success, and paved the way for the eight other GBB pubs that have
followed. Excellent beers are matched by some tasty food.

352
1/R13
J.W. Sweetman 1 Burgh Quay, D2 +353 1 6705777 · www.jwsweetman.ie
Sweetman brews five beers on site here in a bar which dates back to 1756, so this
is a real brewpub, and it was one of the pioneers in the craft beer revolution.
Head to Burgh Quay then for a taste of: red ale; weiss; pale ale; porter; and blonde,
and you can sample them all on a tasting tray, and even take them away in a
Growler.

353
1/R13
T. O'Brennan 15 Upr Dominick St, Phibsborough, Co Dublin +353 1 8307934
· www.tobrennans.com From the team behind 57 The Headline, here is the
Northside destination for craft beer heads, and for whiskey and gin fans. Geoff
Carty and his team did a superlative restoration job here on Upr Dominick St, close
to the N1 road northwards, and their beer list is formidable: a core selection on
draught is added to with a rotating series of taps, and the bottle and can selection
is great. Tasting trays of Irish whiskeys, and a beautiful interior, will make you order
up that second drink.

354
1/R13
The Taphouse 60 Ranelagh, D6 +353 1 4913436 · www.taphouse.ie
David Kelly's Taphouse, just across from The Triangle in Ranelagh, is notable not
just for great beers, but also for delicious food – burgers; sliders; tacos; flatbreads.
There is a short selection of cocktails, but their attitude towards craft beers is
shown by the fact that they recommend the Munique glass, and the list is only
brilliant, and includes a sampler tray of four beers. If you don't want the party to
stop, they sell Growlers of beer to take away up to 10pm.

355 **Blackbird** 82 Rathmines Rd Lwr, D6 +353 1 5591940 · @Blackbird
1/R13 Rathmines Blackbird is an enormous pub, just as you hit the commercial strip
Df of Rathmines. Their tap list is only mighty, and is abetted by a great selection of
rotating beers, and an excellent beer garden with retractable roofing. It's been
a big hit ever since they opened, and their success is another element of the
regeneration of Rathmines. Water bowls for the dogs, of course.

356 **The Hill** Old Mountpleasant, D6 +353 1 4978991 · www.thehillpub.ie
1/R13 Derek and Daragh have more than 20 taps operating in The Hill, a century-old
pub at the green in Old Mount Pleasant in Ranelagh, which they took over and
niftily refurbished in 2016. Along with the drinks they have food cooked by the
Lucky Tortoise pop-up, which revolves around dim sum style dishes – scallion
pancake; vegetable wontons; okonomiyaki. Good gins and cocktails.

357 **Underdog** Brogan's Bar, 75 Dame St, D2 Barry and Paddy combined their
1/R13 extensive craft bar experience to open Underdog, in the basement underneath
ATMOS Brogan's, on Dame St, close to the Olympia Theatre. Their tap list is spectacular,
with 18 beers on tap and 50 more craft beers in bottles and cans, aided by the
fact that the bar is not affiliated to any brewery. Fresh cask opened at a special
price at 5pm each Friday.

358 **The Bull & Castle** 5 Lord Edward St, D8 +353 1 4751122 ·
1/R13 www.fxbuckley.ie The B&C was one of the first Dublin pubs to mix a creative
food identity with a craft beer identity. It's owned by the butchering family of
F. X. Buckley, so it's a great place for a well-hung steak, as well as a craft beer,
and a well-made gin and tonic, from a huge list of gins. There is also a seafood
bar upstairs. It's enormously popular, especially with tourists who have been
checking out Christ Church (410/DUBLIN ATTRACTIONS).

Alfie Byrne's Report: 118/MAJOR HOTELS.

The Best Places to Drink Cocktails

359
1/R13
ATMOS

✓ **Vintage Cocktail Club** 15 Crown Alley, Temple Bar, D2 +353 1 6753547 · www.vintagecocktailclub.com A three-storey, hidden away location in Temple Bar – the VCC is behind a nondescript black door with only a crown-like logo to alert you that you have found the place. Mixologist Gareth Lambe is one of the foremost Dublin drinks masters, but good drinks aren't the only attraction, and the small plates and boards they offer in the downstairs dining room are good. The drinks survey the history of cocktails in masterly fashion, from absinthe to tiki, and the signature cocktails are wickedly good. 7 days.

360
1/R13
ATMOS

The Blind Pig Speakeasy 18 Suffolk St, D2 +353 1 5654700 · www.theblindpig.ie Paul Lambert is one of the city's legendary cocktail creators, and The Blind Pig is his first speakeasy venture. It started life as a pop-up before settling on this atmospheric cavern-like basement with its low ceiling and exposed brick walls and high tables. Mr Lambert is a master mixologist, and has no time for fripperies like dirty martinis, so come here for his own creations and for cocktail classics. 7 days.

361
1/R13

Bow Lane 17 Aungier St, D2 +353 1 4789489 · www.bowlane.ie TGP one of the city's best chefs, Gavin McDonagh, has taken charge of the kitchen at this groovy cocktail lounge, so expect creative and unusual riffs on gastropub classics, from one of the great Dublin talents. Excellent drinks, of course. 7 days.

362
1/R13

The Candlelight Bar Siam Thai Restaurant, Dundrum Town Centre, Co Dublin +353 1 2964500 · www.candlelightbar.ie With his extravagant whiskers, Darren Geraghty of Candlelight looks like a mixologist who has stepped out of a Neil Gaiman book. He works his magic in the plush surrounds of the Candlelight Bar of the Siam Thai restaurant, in Dundrum. Long way to go for a drink, for sure, but worth it to enjoy one of Mr Geraghty's smoking Bloody Marys. 5pm 'til late 7 days.

363
1/R13
ATMOS
DF

MVP 29 Upr Clanbrassil St, D8 +353 1 5582158 · www.mvpdublin.com MVP is one of five pubs and venues run by the super-cool Bodytonic collective. Unlike conventional publicans, these guys are left of left-field, and their joints are fun, from the crazy Bernard Shaw to the wild Wigwam. MVP does great cocktails – the Heléna; the Poitín colada – and baked potatoes, because, you know, no one else would put those two things together, and make it work. There are also yoga classes, and you can bring your dog to sit by your feet as you sip a pink drink. 7 days.

364
1/R13

Koh Bar 6 Jervis St, Millennium Walkway, D1 +353 1 8146777 · www.koh.ie This popular bar and restaurant, on the Millennium Walkway, specialises in Asian cuisine, but over the last decade their original cocktail creations have won acclaim, and the list is a masterclass in the art of mixology, overseen by top-flight barkeepers. 7 days.

365
1/R13

The Liquor Rooms 6-8 Wellington Quay, D2 +353 87 3393688 · www.theliquorrooms.com In the basement of the Clarence Hotel, the Liquor Rooms is a cocktail bar as imagined by Baz Luhrmann: surreal, gaudy, fun. Nice to see a range of cocktails created to honour famous Irish women, so we'll drink an E-1027 to honour Eileen Gray. 7 days.

366 **Thundercut Alley** 6a Market Sq, Smithfield, D7 +353 1 8783281
1/R13 Tucked behind a big fridge door in the Gutterball hoagies shop, just off the Smithfield plaza, TCA is a surreal, over-the-top space with good cocktails to match with their wood-fired oven flatbreads. It's pretty essential to bring a sense of irony and a disco ball. Lunch & dinner Tue-Sun.

367 **Peruke & Periwig** 31 Dawson St, D2 +353 1 6727190 · www.peruke.ie The
1/R13 staff know their stuff in the lavish, indeed decadent, P&P rooms. Music themed cocktails. 7 days.

The Sidecar, Westbury Hotel Report: 121/MAJOR HOTELS.
The Exchequer Report: 345/BARS WITH GOOD FOOD.
Lemuel's, The Conrad Report: 118/MAJOR HOTELS.
The Marker Report: 122/MAJOR HOTELS.
Delahunt Report: 148/MODERN IRISH COOKING.

The Best Wine Bars

368 ✓✓ **Ely Winebar** 22 Ely Place, D2 +353 1 6768986 · www.elywinebar.ie
1/R13 Home to one of the best wines lists in the world, and some of the best
ATMOS wine bar staff in the world, Ely is also home to serious cooking. The Ely wine list
FF took two Wine Spectator Awards in 2017 and drinking something special here is one of the great delights of Dublin city, much aided by the hipness, humour and knowledge of the team. Lunch & dinner Mon-Sat.

369 ✓ **Piglet Wine Bar** Cow's Ln, Temple Bar, D2 +353 1 7070786 ·
1/R13 www.pigletwinebar.ie The kitchen in Piglet has to be the tiniest kitchen in
ATMOS the capital and yet, somehow, this little room sends out plates of food that are big with bold tastes and textures, and wines to match. Start with little snacks – duck gizzards; lardo with anchovy; smoked eel with bean purée – then proceed to a plate of pasta and let the owners choose wines to match. The room is ramshackle, the charm irresistible. Lunch & dinner 7 days.

370 **Etto** 18 Merrion Row, D2 +353 1 6788872 · www.etto.ie Etto is a tiny room,
1/R13 where you have to move over to let your dining companions in, on a traffic-choked
ATMOS strip just off St Stephen's Green. But, they have two secret weapons: a terrific selection of wines, and their signature hashed potatoes and Lyonnaise onions. Smart Italian ideas dominate and there isn't a bad bottle on the list. Lunch & dinner Mon-Sat.

371 **64 Wine** 64 Glasthule Rd, Sandycove, Co Dublin +353 1 2805664 ·
1/R13 www.64wine.ie Gerard Maguire's handsome wine shop on the gastronomic strip of Glasthule, south of Dun Laoghaire, is much-acclaimed, with a dazzling array of great wines, and an excellent by-the-glass choice. They have now added evening and brunch menus, having extended the kitchen, so it's now someplace to drink and eat, from something simple like a cheese platter to a cote de boeuf for two. Daytime, till 9pm/10pm 7 days.

372 Il Vicoletto 5 Crow St, Temple Bar, D2 +353 1 6708633 ·
1/R13 www.ilvicolettorestaurants.ie You don't expect to find a wine bar with an
amazing wine selection in Temple Bar, but here it is in the shape of Il Vicoletto, a
noisy, lively room where the wine shelves wrap around the walls, and where the
cellar is a sommelier's dream. Knowledgeable staff will guide you through the
labyrinth of Italian choices, whilst wine buffs will thrill to the selection of boutique,
single vineyard choices. Dinner 7 days from 4pm, lunch Fri & Sat.

373 Cavern 17 Baggot St Upr, D4 +353 85 8088266 · www.cavernbaggotst.com
1/R13 Down below the much-loved Baggot Street Wines is Cavern, where Garret Connolly
and his team serve excellent wines and interesting food. The principle is to place
simple foods with complex wines, and you can buy any bottle from the shop as
BYOB and pay a corkage charge. Lunch & dinner Tue-Sat.

374 The French Paradox 53 Shelbourne Rd, D4 +353 1 6604068 ·
1/R13 www.thefrenchparadox.com Tanya and Pierre's atmospheric wine shop and
ATMOS wine bar has been a Ballsbridge fixture for more than 15 years, a cheering and
colourful white-walled space with superb bottles and some very nice food. There
is a metal-topped Surgery bar downstairs around the wine shelves, and a dining
room upstairs. The food has never attempted to be anything other than a snapshot
of French classics but matched with those excellent wines and Tanya's charm, it's
irresistible. Lunch & dinner Tue-Sat.

375 Whelehans Wines The Silver Tassie, Bray Rd, Loughlinstown, Co Dublin
1/R13 +353 1 9011144 · www.whelehanswines.ie David Whelehan has brought
together a great team in his eponymous piece of wine heaven. It's a great stop to
buy wines, but also a great stop to drink them. For €5 corkage, you can drink any
bottle in the shop, but we love the weekly wines they showcase in the wine bar.
The foods on the menu are as smartly sourced as the wines, and a great team
makes sure every visit is a treat. Lunch & dinner 7 days.

376 Exchequer Wine Bar 19 Ranelagh, D6 +353 1 4215780 ·
1/R13 www.theexchequerwinebar.ie Whilst their Exchequer St outlet focuses on food
and cocktails, and is one of the city's best gastropubs, the Ranelagh outpost of the
Exchequer lets them focus on wines. There are no fewer than 40 wines available
by the glass – more if you include the Coravin system they use for fine wines – in
125ml and 175ml glass sizes. Wine buffs will enjoy trying to identify the daily
mystery wine: get it right, and they give you a bottle. Dinner 7 days.

377 Green Man Wines 3 Terenure Rd Nth, D6W +353 1 5594234 ·
1/R13 www.greenmanwines.ie David and Claire Gallagher both have deep backgrounds
in the wine trade, so their chosen wines are exemplary. But what galvanises
punters to head to Green Man at the weekends and to choose something good
from the shelves are the small plates and sharing boards which they serve with the
wines in the wine bar at the back of the shop. Simple food, brilliant wines, great
fun. Lunch & dinner Tue-Sun.

378 Bagots Hutton 6 Ormond Quay Upr, D7 +353 1 8788118 ·
1/R13 www.bagotshutton.com Brian Deery & Giovanni Fusciardi made a great success
of the original Bagots Hutton wine bar before moving to this cavernous big space
just north of the river. There is a wine bar, a shop, restaurant space, and music
performance space, arranged over three floors, and it's all on a scale rarely seen in
Dublin. Daytime & dinner 7 days.

The Best Coffee

379
1/R13

✔✔ **3fe** 32 Grand Canal St Lwr, D2 · www.3fe.com Colin Harmon is the godfather of Dublin's extraordinary coffee culture, the man who first made waves in international barista competitions before creating one of the most respected brands with 3fe, and educating a generation of baristas whilst he was at it. Lovely stylish stores, cool staff, nice food, and we even covet the T-shirts and baseball caps, never mind the coffee beans. No reservations. Breakfast, coffee & lunch 7 days. There is another branch of 3fe on Sussex Mews.

380
1/R13

✔✔ **Coffee Angel** 3 Trinity St, D2 · www.coffeeangel.com Karl Purdy was an respected restaurateur before switching careers, getting a little cart, and launching Coffee Angel on its unstoppable path. The shops are characterised by great coffee but also by superlative staff: these guys and girls are the business, and what they don't know about roasting and cupping isn't worth knowing. There are branches of Coffee Angel in Leinster St, Pembroke St, Sth Anne St, Custom House Quay and a mobile cart near the bridge at Spencer Dock.

381
1/R13

laine, my love 38 Talbot St, D1 · www.lainemylove.com The room is little more than a corridor, under the railway bridge at the Connolly Station end of Talbot St, but what counts is the fact that owner Ferg Brown is one of the great coffee roasters, with his own roastery, Roasted Brown, out in Delgany in Co Wicklow. Nice breakfasts and snacks to go with the brew. Breakfast and lunch Mon-Fri till 3pm.

382
1/R13

Legit Coffee Co 1 Meath Mart, Meath St, D8 +353 1 2225180 · www.legitcoffeeco.com Daniel Vossion transformed an old butcher's shop on Dublin's splendidly scattershot Meath St into Legit, and made the tables himself. His real skill lies in his baking, however, so don't miss the madeleines and the terrific sausage rolls amongst lots of other good savoury and sweet treats. Coffee from Baobab roasters in Co Kildare, abetted by guest roasters, teas from Wall & Keogh. Breakfast & lunch Mon-Sat.

383
1/R13

Bear Market Coffee 19 Main St, Blackrock, Co Dublin · www.bearmarket.ie The weekend queue for coffee and pastries at Bear Market is something to behold, and the success – and the style – of the room has led to a second branch, in the IFSC in central Dublin. Stephen Deasy and Ruth Hussey demonstrate judgement and good taste in every detail of the two shops, from the coffee beans – from Coffee Culture – to the food to the items on the shelf. Join the queue. Breakfast & Lunch 7 days.

384
1/R13

Vice Coffee Inc. 54 Middle Abbey St, D1 · www.vicecoffeeinc.com Tom Stafford is one of the city's premier baristas, so in the Wigwam space on Middle Abbey St, which they share with three other businesses, you will find superbly curated coffees, great toasted cheese sandwiches, and some ace doughnuts. If you are in the mood, do try their Irish coffee, a crazy drink that they manage to make sense of. Daytime 7 days.

385
1/R13

Urbanity Coffee The Glass House, 11 Coke Lane, Smithfield, D7 +353 1 8747288 · www.urbanitycoffee.ie Jason Mac an Tsionnaigh roasts his own coffee beans here in Urbanity, using a 12-kilo machine, and his style is influenced by the lighter roasts favoured by Scandinavian roasters. A large, minimalist room in The Glass House, signalled by a red neon 'coffee' sign, shows you the way to Coke Lane, so plonk yourself down on the benches for soft-fried eggs and chickpea couscous, and a perfect flat white. Breakfast & lunch 7 days, closes 4pm.

386 **Proper Order** 7 Haymarket, Smithfield, D7 · www.properordercoffeeco.com
1/R13 Niall Wynn won the Irish barista championship in 2017, so Proper Order, at the River Liffey end of the enormous Smithfield Sq, is the place to discover coffee nirvana. The shop is also notable for serving the brilliant work of the Sceal Bakery, and nothing beats a flat white and a morning cronut. Breakfast & Lunch Mon-Sat.

387 **Kaph** 31 Drury St, D2 +353 1 6139030 · www.kaph.ie Kaph is delightful, and 1/R13 pretty much everyone loves Chris Keegan's coffee shop. Beans are from 3Fe, there is a rotating gallery of artworks on the first floor, the music is excellent, and their arty approach makes Kaph another of those places that is making the Drury St zone special. Breakfast & lunch 7 days till 7pm.

388 **Full Circle Roasters** 21-28 Talbot Place, D1 +353 1 87 9699884 ·
1/R13 www.fullcircleroasters.ie Brian Birdy's coffee roasting company operates a small outlet at the Jacob's Inn Hostel, just off Talbot St. It's an unassuming place in which to enjoy top-notch coffee, and particularly good toasted sandwiches, made with just as much care and finesse as the coffee. Daytime till 3pm 7 days.

389 **Clement & Pekoe** 50 Sth William St, D2 · www.clementandpekoe.com
1/R13 Clement & Pekoe is unusual in that owners Simon and Dairine devote as much care and attention to making a perfect cup of tea as they do to fashioning a perfect flat white. It's an elegant series of rooms, with an excellent porch for lounging in the Creative Quarter, on Sth William St, and there is a sister branch on Essex St in Temple Bar. Breakfast & lunch 7 days, till 7pm weekdays, 6/6.30pm weekends.

390 **Granthams** 8 Aungier St, D2 +353 1 4758553 · www.granthams.ie
1/R13 Dave Regan is another 3fe graduate who transformed himself into an award-winning barista and, working alongside his brother-in-law, Paul Church, he has created a powerful critical reputation for Granthams. The coffee is Dark Arts, roasted in London by Regan's brother, and their toasted sandwiches are ace. These guys are out-there coffee heads, so don't miss their Epic Latte, which they create every week. Breakfast & lunch Mon-Sat.

391 **Bang Bang** 59a Leinster St North, Phibsborough, D7 +353 86 8576054
1/R13 · @bangbangD7 Brother and sister team Daniel and Grace use Silverskin coffee, roasted just up the road in Glasnevin, for their brews. You will also find vintage clothing, and lots of smartly curated deli foods. Phibsborough is being rapidly gentrified, and Bang Bang, with its quirky, amiable eccentricity is another transformatory step for the northside zone. Breakfast & lunch Tue-Sun.

392 **Two Fifty Square** Williams Park, Rathmines Rd Lwr, D6 +353 1 4968336 ·
1/R13 www.twofiftysquare.ie Tucked away just off the main strip of Rathmines, Adam McMenamin's Two Fifty Square is both a wholesale coffee roastery and a café. It's a big room, filled with light that pours in through transparent ceiling panels, and they offer all-day brunch dishes from a single page menu. They utilise every manner of making a perfect cup of coffee, so whether you want a V-60 or a Vietnamese-style iced coffee, you are in the right place. Breakfast & lunch 7 days.

393 **The Bald Barista** 68 Aungier St, D2 +353 1 3129980 · @thebaldbaristacafe
1/R13 Buzz Fendall is a Kiwi who has been turning Dubliners on to proper coffee from the early days of the coffee revolution. Mr Fendall is a larger-than-life character, which means his Aungier St room is always a buzzing destination For many Dubliners, the BB would be their first choice for a cup of joe. Breakfast, lunch & dinner, 7 days, 'til 8.30pm Mon-Thur.

394 **Badger & Dodo** 59 Francis St, Merchants Quay, D8 +353 1 8755400 ·
1/R13 www.badgeranddodo.ie Broc Lewin roasts his beans in Fermoy in north Co Cork, and sends them to 200 coffee shops throughout the country. The B&D space in the Cross Art gallery on Francis St is one of two cafés they operate themselves – the other is in Galway – and their kelly-green La Marzocco PB produces beautiful brews. There are also sandwiches, and lots of geeky coffee kit. Breakfast & lunch Mon-Sat.

395 **First Draft** 3 Curved St, Temple Bar, D2 · www.firstdraftcoffee.com On the
1/R13 first floor, above Filmbase, on Curved St in Temple Bar. Ger O'Donohue is one of the foundational coffee figures in Dublin, importing speciality coffee and offering barista courses. Have some fun by trying their Coffee Flight, which offers you the same coffee beans served three different ways. Food offering is meticulously sourced. Coffee, cakes & lunch Mon-Sat.

396 **Ebb & Flow** 56 Clontarf Rd, D3 +353 1 8532536 Dave Smyth's coffee shop in
1/R13 the smart northside suburb of Clontarf uses Full Circle Roasters beans as their
DF house brew, and Mr Smyth is actually a partner in that business. Their sandwiches are well made and use top-class ingredients whilst sweet things come from the benchmark Camerino Bakery. Make sure to bring your dog, as there is always a cool bowl of Clontarf tap water waiting for your beloved. Breakfast & lunch 7 days.

397 **Sasha House Petite** Drury St, D2 +353 1 6729570 · www.shpetite.ie A micro-
1/R13 roaster and bakery tucked into the ground floor of a multi-storey car park sounds downright weird, but there is nothing strange about what Natatie and her team roast and bake in Sasha House Petite. Good coffee is joined by very unusual baking, and if you are looking for Russian Easter bread, you won't find it anywhere else. Breakfast & lunch 7 days.

398 **Love Supreme** 57 Manor St, D7 +353 1 5496489 · www.lovesupreme.ie
1/R13 You've got to love a coffee shop named after John Coltrane's ageless musical masterpiece, and here it is, at the junction in hipster Stoneybatter. What you've also got to love about Ken and Karie Flood's place is the fact that the beans are from Roasted Brown, the hot chocolate from the brilliant Shana Wilkie, and the bakes and pies and signature sausage rolls are made by their own fair hands. Everything is pretty much Instagram ready. Daytime 7 days.

399 **Nick's Coffee Company** 20 Ranelagh, D6 +353 86 3838203 Nick Seymour
1/R13 and his team have been looking after the good people of Ranelagh for more than a decade, serving great coffee, using a mix of beans that they roast themselves, from a tiny, pretty space just at the entrance to the Ranelagh market. 7 days till 9pm

400 **Brother Sister** Ground Floor, Powerscourt Townhouse Centre, 59 Sth
1/R13 William St, D2 @brothersisterdublin Shoehorned into a tiny space beside the stairwell in the Powerscourt Townhouse Centre, Toure and Yvonne Kizza's little coffee space 'sells smiles and coffee' says Toure. Sweet things are sourced from blue-chip companies like Firehouse Bakery and Aungier Danger, and Brother Sister is small, but perfectly formed. Daytime Mon-Sat, till 8pm.

401
1/R13

✓✓✓ **The Book Of Kells** Trinity College, College Grn, D2
+353 1 8961000 · www.tcd.ie/visitors/book-of-kells The 9thC Book of Kells is one of the greatest creations of Western art, and has been described as Ireland's Sistine Chapel. A richly decorated, intricately drawn, and enormously colourful rendition of the four Gospels of the New Testament, it is now believed that the book was created on the island of Iona, off the west coast of Scotland, before being taken to the the Abbey of Kells. Today, the book is exhibited, page by page, in the 18thC Library building on the beautiful campus of Trinity College; it is a simply remarkable distillation of art and culture. The tour is self-guided. 7 days: 8.30am-5pm Mon-Sat, from 9.30am Sun. Shorter hours Oct-Apr.

402
1/R13
AYR
☞
FREE
ADMISSION
ATMOS

✓✓✓ **Trinity College** College Green, D2 +353 1 8961000 · www.tcd.ie Many people visit Trinity to see the Book of Kells (Report above) but the college campus also hosts the Science Gallery and the Long Room Library, a 65m-high library filled with 200,000 of the Library's oldest books. Treasures from the Library include one of very few copies of the 1916 Proclamation of the Irish Republic. The Science Gallery is a place 'where science and art collide'. No permanent collection, instead an eclectic mix of science, technology and arts. Science Gallery Café is a bright room serving good food all day and early evening.

403
1/R13

✓ **Guinness Storehouse** St James's Gate, D8 +353 1 4084800 · www.guinness-storehouse.com Spread over seven floors of interactive exhibitions that tell the story of Ireland's most famous beverage, the Guinness Storehouse® has become Ireland's leading tourist attraction, with visitor numbers heading towards 2 million each year. Visitors to the centre usually spend about 1.5 hours on a self-guided tour. The story began in 1759 when Arthur Guinness signed a 9,000-year lease for the brewery site, at an annual rent of £45. By 1799, Guinness was only brewing porter, having phased out the brewing of ale. Several restaurants. Everyone taking the tour gets rewarded with a pint in the Gravity Bar, on the top floor. 9.30am-7pm 7 days. Late opening July & Aug 9am-8pm.

404
1/R13
AYR

✓ **Kilmainham Gaol Museum** Inchicore Rd, Kilmainham · www.kilmainhamgaolmuseum.ie 'The opening and closing of the Gaol more or less coincided with the making and breaking of the Union between Great Britain and Ireland. During the intervening years the Gaol functioned like a political seismograph, recording most of the significant tremors in the often turbulent relations between the two countries', wrote Pat Cooke in *A History of Kilmainham Gaol*. The building opened in 1796 and closed its doors in 1924. Members of the Irish Republican movement were detained here, as well as convicts waiting to be transported to Australia. The Gaol is now a museum. 9am-6.45pm Jun-Aug 7 days. Shorter hours off season.

405
1/R13
AYR
FREE
ADMISSION
☞

✓ **National Gallery of Ireland** Merrion Sq West & Clare St, D2
+353 1 6615133 · www.nationalgallery.ie A €30m revamp overseen by superstar architects Heneghan Peng has given the formerly congested National Gallery 'the architectural equivalent of a Vicks nasal spray', said *The Observer*, all of which increased 'the lucidity and delight of the galleries'. There are many great works to enjoy: Caravaggio; Goya; Vermeer; Rembrandt; Jack Yeats; Monet, and the brilliant use of natural daylight enhances these great works, and enormously adds to the pleasure of spending several hours in the Gallery. World-class travelling exhibitions for which booking required. 9.15am-5.30/8.30pm Mon-Sat, 11am-5.30pm Sun.

406
1/R13
AYR
FREE ADMISSION
🗗

✓**Irish Museum of Modern Art** Royal Hospital Kilmainham, Military Rd, D8 +353 1 6129900 · www.imma.ie Aside from the treasures inside, the Royal Hospital, near the Heuston railway station at Kilmainham, is probably the finest 17thC building in Ireland. Styled on Les Invalides in Paris, it was completed two years before the Royal Hospital in Chelsea. It became IMMA in 1991 and aside from the work of celebrated modernists such as Louise Bourgeois, Lichtenstein, le Brocquy and Joseph Cornell, it is continually complementing the collection with new works by Irish and Irish-based artists. 11.30am-5.30pm Tue-Sat, noon-5.30pm Sun, closed Mon. Last admission 5.15pm.

407
1/R13
AYR
FREE ADMISSION

✓**National Museum of Ireland** Natural History Museum, Merrion Sq, D2 · www.museum.ie Four locations to the NM of I, here in Merrion Sq, aka 'The Dead Zoo' displays a zoological collection where the ground floor is dedicated to animals native to Ireland, and the upper floor features mammals of the world. Collins Barracks, which houses Decorative Arts & History, carries exhibitions on contemporary craft and design, with permanent exhibitions that include a retrospective of the ground-breaking designer Eileen Gray, as well as Irish Silver and Irish Country Furniture. The Kildare St Archaeology features many well-preserved artefacts from Bronze Age, Viking and Medieval Ireland. The Museum of Country Life is in Co Mayo (7/BIG ATTRACTIONS).

408
1/R13
AYR
🗗 FREE
ADMISSION

✓**Chester Beatty Library** Dublin Castle, D2 +353 1 4070750 · www.cbl.ie This splendid building houses the collection of Sir Alfred Chester Beatty (1875-1968). On display are paintings, calligraphies, painted scrolls, prints, drawings, manuscripts, and rare books. It is an astonishing collection of over 6,000 items, particularly Islamic and Asian decorative art objects. There are also travelling exhibitions, and a superb restaurant, Silk Road Cafe, serving a Middle Eastern menu. All day, 7 days, from 1am Sun (249/MIDDLE EAST).

409
1/R13
FREE ADMISSION
AYR   NO DOGS
🗗 ATMOS

✓**National Botanic Gardens** Glasnevin, D9 +353 1 8040300 · www.botanicgardens.ie 3km from the centre of the city, there are over 300 endangered species grown, including six that are already extinct in the wild, and the garden sees itself as like a modern Noah's Ark for plants. All day, 7 days. Reduced hours winter season.

410
1/R13
AYR

✓**Christ Church Cathedral** Christchurch Pl, D8 +353 1 6778099 · www.christchurchcathedral.ie Built overlooking the Viking settlement at Wood Quay, the entire area was subject to scandalous and unsympathetic planning. A road now separates the Cathedral from its original medieval quarter. Rebuilt in the 1180s by the Anglo-Normans, it is the place of the tomb of Strongbow. Henry II received communion here, apparently the first time to receive it after the murder of Thomas Becket in Canterbury. In 1742 the world premiere of Handel's *Messiah* was performed by members of the Cathedral choir in nearby Fishamble St. Renovated in the 19thC, when the flying buttresses were added. Location for the filming of *The Tudors*. All day till 7pm, 7 days, closing earlier in winter.

411
1/R13
AYR

Dublin Zoo Phoenix Park, D8 +353 1 4748900 · www.dublinzoo.ie One of the world's oldest zoos, spread over 28ha in the Phoenix Park, and housing more than 400 animals. Daily activities include feeding times and the new Zoorassic World reptile house features a daily reptile talk. The zoo also works with other wildlife organisations to help conserve wildlife throughout the world. Mar-Sept 9.30am-6pm. Last admission 5pm. Shorter hours off season.

412
1/R13
AYR

✔ **Marsh's Library** St Patrick's Close, D8 · www.marshlibrary.ie Very few 18thC buildings in Dublin are still being used for the purpose for which they were built. One such is Archbishop Marsh's perfectly preserved three-centuries old library, where more than 25,000 books sit on their original dark-oak bookcases with carved gables. All day, 5 days, closed Tue & Sun.

413
1/R13
☕
TERRACE
AYR

✔ **National Library of Ireland** 2 Kildare St, D2 +353 1 6030200 · www.nli.ie Not a lending library, but a place where people go to carry out research, perhaps to explore a family history, or seek out an obscure and arcane reference. Take a break from the books and head to their Café Joly, where you can order up a bowl of soup, a terrine, a stew or tagine. Value is keen, and they use the very best ingredients. A precious Dublin secret. Daytime Mon-Sat.

414
1/R13
☕
AYR

✔ **Dublin City Gallery, The Hugh Lane** Charlemont House, Parnell Sq N, D1 +353 1 2226660 · www.hughlane.ie Home to the re-created studio of painter Francis Bacon and, once you have seen Bacon's mighty mess, you will never criticise your teenager's room again. The modernist works are in fruitful conflict with the magnificent Georgian architecture and the refined elegance of the exhibition rooms, whilst the great Impressionist works seem right at home. Don't miss the extraordinary stained glass work of Harry Clarke, for our money an Irish artist to rival Jack Yeats. 9.45am-5/6pm 7 days, opens later at w'end.

415
1/R13

St Patrick's Cathedral St Patrick's Close, D8 +353 1 4539472 · www.stpatrickscathedral.ie St Patrick's is the National Cathedral for the Church of Ireland. The Cathedral building as it stands today was built between 1220-1259, but there has been a church on this site since at least the 10thC. In 1901 six Celtic grave slabs were discovered underneath the park next to the Cathedral, one of which was covering the remains of an ancient well. Speculation goes that this might be the well used by St Patrick to baptise people into the early Christian church on this site in the 5thC. The grave slabs are displayed inside the Cathedral. Jonathan Swift, author of *Gulliver's Travels*, was Dean of the Cathedral for 35 years in the 17thC. He is interred in a tomb at the entrance to the Cathedral. St Patrick's Cathedral Choir School choristers attend daily Matins. All day, 7 days.

416
1/R13
AYR

Irish Whiskey Museum 119 Grafton St, D2 +353 1 5250970 · www.irishwhiskeymuseum.ie This is a young museum, riding the wave in interest and enthusiasm in whiskey; choose between three tours. The bar serves whiskey cocktails and a selection of brands to taste. Opposite Trinity College. All day, 7 days.

417
1/R13
AYR
ATMOS

Little Museum of Dublin 15 St Stephen's Gn, D2 +353 1 6611000 · www.littlemuseum.ie 'Our goal is not to sell an ideology, but simply remember the past', say the Little Museum, a private museum, situated in one of the Georgian houses in Dublin's central St Stephen's Green. Showcasing a collection of domestic artefacts that were all donated to the museum in response to an appeal when the museum was launched in 2011. All day, 7 days.

418 **Dublinia** Christ Church, D8 +353 1 6794611 · www.dublinia.ie A hands-on
1/R13 interactive romp through the history of Dublin and its four exhibitions are particularly
AYR suited to families. Learn history by reliving it - they encourage you to put on Viking
clothing, play medieval games, experience a Viking ship. Learn about Medieval
Dublin, how archaeology works, or climb St Michael's Tower. All day, 7 days.

419 **GPO Witness History** General Post Office, O'Connell St Lwr, D1 +353 1
1/R13 8721916 · www.gpowitnesshistory.ie Opened to celebrate the centenary year
AYR of the Easter Rising. For the first time, the public was given access to Ireland's
historic GPO, one of the oldest working post offices in the world. The interactive,
CGI, audiovisual presentation of the exhibition has been likened to being in a video
game. All day, 7 days.

420 **Grand Lodge of Ireland** 17 Molesworth St, D2 +353 1 6761337 · www.
1/R13 freemason.ie Oldest Lodge in continuous existence, this is the second most
AYR senior lodge in the world. Architecturally stunning, and completely surreal, it is
more than worth a tour, which takes place each day at 2.30pm. One of the best
kept secrets in the city.

421 **The Irish Rock N Roll Museum** Curved St, Temple Bar, D2 +353 1 6351993 ·
1/R13 www.irishrocknrollmuseum.com This Temple Bar venue and recording studio is
AYR now home to a museum of rock'n'roll, featuring memorabilia from Irish rocks stars,
particularly Phil Lynott, U2, Rory Gallagher and The Scripts. All day, 7 days.

422 **The James Joyce Centre** 35 N Gr George's St, D1 +353 1 8788547 · www.
1/R13 jamesjoyce.ie For more than 20 years, the Joyce Centre has celebrated the life
AYR and work of the man whose writing defined the city. The Centre also arranges a big
celebration of Bloomsday – June 16th – each year.

423 **Royal Hibernian Academy** 15 Ely Pl, D2 +353 1 6612558 · www.rhagallery.ie
1/R13 The strikingly designed RHA has no fewer than five separate galleries, and the
AYR Academy has held an annual exhibition for almost 200 years. The exhibition
☐ disburses a significant prize fund via almost 20 awards each year, including the
RHA Gold Medal. The gallery's café, Coppa, is at the front of the building, facing Ely
Place, and serves Italian-influenced food. Daytime 7 days.

424 **Powerscourt Townhouse Centre** Sth William St, D2 +353 1 6794144 ·
1/R13 www.powerscourtcentre.ie Centre for fashion, craft, design, antiques and
AYR good food in a collection of forty boutiques and restaurants just off Dublin's main
shopping street. Recommended restaurants include Brother Sister (400/COFFEE),
and the Pepper Pot (169/CASUAL RESTAURANTS). All day, till 6pm/8pm, 7 days.

The Best Independent Shops
(Vinyl Stores, Bookshops & Galleries)

VINYL STORES

425 **Freebird Records** 15a Wicklow St, D2 +353 1 7079955 · www.freebird.ie
1/R13 Look for the tiny entrance to the Secret Book and Record Store, on Wicklow St, and
ATMOS you will also discover Freebird Records, who have been keepin' on keepin' on since
1978, a mighty tenure for a fine record store. Be prepared to spend a lot of time
browsing. 11am-6.30/7.30pm, 7 days.

426 **The R.A.G.E.** 16b Fade St, D2 +353 1 6779594 · www.therage.ie For seekers
1/R13 in search of PS2 or maybe a great Audio Technica vinyl deck, here is Mecca. RAGE
ATMOS (Record Art Game Emporium) has all the classic vinyl on LP and 45's, new and
second-hand. Downstairs is The Record Spot, and they also sell 'trendy' cassettes,
as well as games and gaming machines, new and second-hand. Super Mario lives!
10.30am-7pm Mon-Sat, noon-6pm Sun.

427 **Tower Records** 7 Dawson St, D2 +353 1 6713250 · www.towerrecords.ie
1/R13 Vinyl forms the guard of honour these days when you walk in Tower Records, at the
Trinity end of Dawson St. Sited behind the black discs are shelves and rows of CDs
and DVDs, and the bargain section is always interesting. Good audio gear as well,
and the staff know their stuff. 9am-7/8/9pm Mon-Sat, 11.30am-6.30pm Sun. Also
at O'Connell St in the Eason building.

428 **Spindizzy Records** 32 Market Arcade, Sth Gt George's St, D2 +353 1 6711711
1/R13 · www.spindizzyrecords.com In the George's St Arcade, Spindizzy has a good
selection of 45's and well-stocked new and second-hand vinyl, along with a lot of
CDs and DVDs. They also sell on www.disccogs.com, and offer a buy and collect
service – this saves on p&p and gives a chance to have a good look at the item.
10am-6.30pm Mon-Sat, noon-6pm Sun.

429 **All City Records** 4 Crow St, Temple Bar, D2 +353 1 6772994 ·
1/R13 www.allcityrecordlabel.com Olan O'Brien and the guys in All City run the whole
ATMOS show: record label; concert promoters; vinyl record heads; vendors of splendid
T-shirts; spray paint specialists who will help you become the next Maser; Temple
Bar stalwarts. All City is the shop that defines the Temple Bar aesthetic, something
that's often hard to find.

430 **Dublin Flea** Newmarket Sq, D8 · www.dublinflea.ie The super-atmospheric Flea
1/R13 market, on Newmarket Sq is a good spot for picking up vinyl. It's also home to the
Sceal Bakery stall, who produce some of the city's finest baking, and get your lunch at
the White Mausu stall for rice bowls and peanut rayu. Last Sun of every month.

BOOK STORES

431 ✓**Ulysses Rare Books** 10 Duke St, D2 +353 1 6718676 · www.rarebooks.ie
1/R13 If you desperately crave that signed first edition of Harry Potter, then Aisling
ATMOS and David Cunningham's acclaimed rare book store on Duke St is the place you
need to know. Whilst they are specialists in what Aisling calls 'The Big Five' –
Beckett; Heaney; Joyce; Wilde; Yeats – there are treasures galore here, like a 1935
Ulysses illustrated by Henri Matisse, and first edition Hans Christian Andersen.
9.30am-5.45pm Mon-Sat.

432 ✓ **The Gutter Bookshop** Cow's Lane, Temple Bar, D2; 20 Railway Rd,
1/R13 Dalkey +353 1 2859633 · www.gutterbookshop.com The Gutter scooped
the prize as Best Independent Bookshop at the 2017 British Book Awards, a big
gong for Bob Johnston's pair of modest Dublin bookshops. As Mr Johnston says,
'there are still enough people who want to buy books in a shop'. Don't miss.
10am-6.30/7pm Mon-Sat, 11am-6pm Sun.

433 ✓ **Books Upstairs** 17 O'Olier St, D2 +353 1 6778566 · www.booksirish.com
1/R13 Home to a hoard of wonderful books, and also home to the *Dublin Literary*
🖵 *Review*, overseen by Maurice Earls and Enda O'Doherty for the last decade. These
ATMOS guys like to lift the intellectual hood high, so the Review's essays are complex,
erudite and discursive. The shop itself is quietly charming. A fine café on the first
floor is home-from-home for Dublin's literary types, and the window seats are
much prized. 10am-7pm Mon-Fri, 10am-6pm Sat, 2pm-6pm Sun.

434 **The Winding Stair** 40 Lwr Ormond Quay, D1 +353 1 8726576 ·
1/R13 www.winding-stair.com A restaurant, and also a bookshop, which occupies the
ground floor of the building, on the north side of the river just by the Ha'penny
Bridge. The shops shares the lovely, well-worn vibe of the restaurant, and offers
new books at the front, and an extensive range of second-hand books in the rere.
10am-6/7pm Mon-Sat, noon-6pm Sun.

435 **Hodges Figgis** 56-58 Dawson St, D2 +353 1 6774754 · www.waterstones.
1/R13 com/bookshops/hodges-figgis It's easy to lose an hour or several in the
cloistering embrace of Hodges Figgis, as this spacious, 4-storey store swallows you
up and you get lost in browsing. Their Irish section is reckoned to be the largest
selection of books relating to Ireland to be found anywhere in the world. 9am-
6/7/8pm Mon-Sun, from noon Sun.

436 **Marrowbone Books** 78 The Coombe, D8 +353 1 5510495 ·
1/R13 www.marrowbone.ie There is a sweet, old-fashioned vibe to this little second-
ATMOS hand book shop, who invite you to bring your own coffee when you come in to
browse the books. Marrowbone is a definition of cult, from its daffodil-yellow colour
scheme to the determination of owners Lily Power and Brain Flanagan to bring the
city something different, left-field, nicely wonky. Daytime 6 days, closed Tues.

437 **Dubray Books** 36 Grafton St, D2 +353 1 6775568 · www.dubraybooks.ie
1/R13 We love the calm, clear layout of the Grafton St Dubray shop, whose brilliant design
makes the most of a narrow space, and showcases the books beautifully. Excellent
staff know their books backwards, and you will find the same authoritative
assistance in all their stores. 9am-9pm Mon-Fri, 9am-7pm Sat, 11am-6pm Sun.
Branches also in Blackrock, Dun Laoghaire, Rathmines, Stillorgan, Galway, Kilkenny
and Bray. 7 days.

438 **Chapters Bookstore** Ivy Exchange, Parnell St, D1 +353 1 8723297 ·
1/R13 www.chapters.ie Before settling into its capacious big store on Parnell St,
Chapters occupied various locations around the city. Today it has all the books you
can imagine, along with CDs and DVDs and a large second-hand section. It's a big
shop, but the staff still treat everyone like they treated us when they first opened
up that little place on Wicklow St, back in the early 80's. 9.30am-6.30/8pm
Mon-Sat, noon-6.30pm Sun.

439 **The Company of Books** 96 Ranelagh Village, D6 +353 1 4975413 ·
1/R13 www.thecompanyofbooks.ie In the centre of Ranelagh village, Anne and Gwen's shop has a very personal ambience, helped by the fact that the owners are so keen to make recommendations and offer suggestions. It's a precious place, as local estate agents well know when pointing out its cultural value to the village. 10am-6pm Mon-Sat, noon-6pm Sun.

440 **Big Bang Comics** Dundrum Shopping Centre, Co Dublin +353 1 21165093 ·
1/R13 www.dundrum.ie It's worth the trip out to Dundrum to enjoy the lavish interior of this store, and maybe to get involved when they have their Batman days or host their comic expo. John Hendrick and his staff know their graphic novels and comics from Neil Gaiman to Charles Burns, from the Silver Surfer to Swamp Thing. 9/10/11am-7/8/9pm Mon-Sun.

441 **Stokes Books** George's St Arcade, D2 +353 1 673584 ·
1/R13 www.georgesstreetarcade.ie Stephen Stokes' shop is a true Dublin institution, and offers everything from rare editions of books on Irish history to bargain offers and second-hand books. 10.30am-6pm Mon-Sat.

INDEPENDENT GALLERIES

442 **Kerlin Gallery** Anne's Lane, Sth Anne St +353 1 6709093 ·
1/R13 www.kerlingallery.com The Kerlin was designed by John Pawson, who created a serene, minimalist exhibition space on two floors that has been a home for many Irish and international modernists for 30 years. The Kerlin has been involved with the Venice Biennale for many years, and is particularly associated with the work of Sean Scully and Dorothy Cross. All day from 10am/11am Mon-Sat.

443 **Taylor Galleries** 16 Kildare St, D2 +353 1 6766055 · www.taylorgalleries.ie
1/R13 At the St Stephen's Green end of Kildare St, John and Patrick Taylor's gallery is home to many of the leading contemporary Irish artists of today: Sean McSweeney; Charles Tyrrell; Melita Denaro; Brian Bourke; John Shinnors; Martin Gale. There are two large group shows each year, during Aug and Christmas, whilst solo exhibitions occupy the rest of the calendar. 10.30am-5.30pm Mon-Fri, 11am-3pm Sat.

444 **The Douglas Hyde Gallery** Trinity College, D2 +353 1 8961116 ·
1/R13 www.douglashydegallery.com A pair of contemporary galleries in the Arts Building on the campus of Trinity College, they host many exhibitions of textiles, crafts, outsider art, and film, and welcome shows by leading international artists. 11am-6pm Mon-Fri, 'til 7pm Thur, 'til 5.30pm Sat.

445 **Gallery of Photography** Meeting House Sq, D2 +353 1 6714654 ·
1/R13 www.galleryofphotography.ie Housed in a beautiful, purpose-built space in Temple Bar's Meeting House Square, the GofP hosts many exhibitions, but also has photography workshops and darkroom facilities. Exhibitions range from graduate shows to the work of superstars like Steve McCurry, Robert Capa, Eve Arnold. Free admission.

446 **Molesworth Gallery** 16 Molesworth St, D2 +353 1 6791548 ·
1/R13 www.molesworthgallery.com Occupying two floors of a fine Georgian townhouse, the Molesworth hosts eight solo and two group exhibitions each year, and celebrated names associated with the gallery include John Kindness, Jennifer Trouton and Francis Matthews. Mon-Fri.

447   **Olivier Cornet Gallery** 3 Gt Denmark St, D1 +353 1 87 2887261 ·
1/R13   www.olivercornetgallery.com M. Cornet's gallery opened first in Temple
Bar in 2012 before finding a home on Gt Denmark St, between Parnell Sq and
Mountjoy Sq, an area already being talked up as the Parnell Sq Cultural Quarter. He
represents a small school of established artists in addition to the AGA – Associate
Gallery Artists – who are recent graduates. Tue-Sun.

448   **Kevin Kavanagh Gallery** Chancery Ln, D8 +353 1 4759514 ·
1/R13   www.kevinkavanaghgallery.ie Discreet gallery, on Chancery Lane, has been
home to leading Irish artists for almost 25 years. Mr Kavanagh has said that he
likes to introduce the work of a new artist each year, and he decides 'by keeping an
eye on what's going on'. Artists include Dermot Seymour; Diana Copperwhite; Mick
O'Dea; Sinéad Ní Mhaonaigh. Tue-Sat.

449   **The Rubicon** 10 St Stephen's Gn, D2 +353 1 6708055 · www.rubicongallery.ie
1/R13   Since 1995, Josephine Kelliher's city centre gallery has hosted ten exhibitions
annually, as well as participating in the major international art fairs. Gallery
artists include Eithne Jordan; Anita Groener; Tom Molloy, whilst guest artists have
included Hughie O'Donoghue; Nick Miller; Amelia Stein. Tue-Sat.

450   **Green on Red Gallery** Park Lane, Spencer Dock, D1 +353 87 2454282 ·
1/R13   www.greenonredgallery.com At the rere of the Convention Centre, and 100m
from the Spencer Dock Luas stop, Jerome Ó Drisceoil's gallery occupied a number
of different spaces in Dublin before settling in Docklands. In addition to the
exhibitions, there are performances and lectures, and associated artists include
Nigel Rolfe, Damien Flood; Mark Joyce; Caroline McCarthy. Wed-Sat.

451   **Cross Gallery** 59 Francis St, D8 +353 1 4738978 · www.crossgallery.ie
1/R13   Amidst the antique shops of Francis St, on the Liberties zone, Cross exhibits the
work of well-known painters such as Felim Egan and Mary Rose Binchy, as well as
exhibitions of classic 20thC furniture. Mon-Sat.

452   **The Printmakers Gallery** 25 Drury St, D2 +353 1 671 4978 · www.
1/R13   theprintmakersgallery.com This handsome gallery in the Creative Quarter of
Drury Street specialises in etchings, lithography, woodcut and drypoint. In addition
to an impressive roster of established artists – Brian Maguire; Bernadette Madden;
Syd Bluett – the gallery is also welcoming towards the work of newly graduated
artists.

Easy Walks in the City

453
1/R13
☑ **The Phoenix Park** · www.phoenixpark.ie One of the largest enclosed parks in any European capital, the Phoenix Park is an ancient playground, first envisioned as a deer park on behalf of Charles II in 1662. Visitors' Centre to explain the Park's history, full facilities, and a very good cafe. The Phoenix Cafe offers wonderfully vivid flavours and uses the produce from the gardens outside, and sells their vegetables. It gets very busy.

454
1/R13
☑ **The E & W Piers** Dun Laoghaire, Co Dublin Both the E and W piers at the harbour afford bracing seaside walks overlooking the bay. The W pier was constructed in the early 19thC and is 1,584m long. The W Pier Lighthouse was constructed in 1852 and automated in 1930. The E Pier gets more crowded with people who enjoy the 2.6km return journey. If you want to walk a bit further, the nearby People's Park is open near the E pier. It has a Fallon & Byrne restaurant. Market every Sunday.

455
1/R13
☑ **The Promenade** Clontarf, D3 Built on reclaimed land, landscaped in the '50s, the walkway is about 3km long, stretching from Fairview Park to the Bull Wall. It's a roomy 30m wide. Wind and Sails sculpture by Derry Sculptor Éamonn O'Doherty. The Memorial Seat is a tribute to Alfie Byrne, ten times Lord Mayor of Dublin, known as the 'Shaking Hand of Dublin'. Easter Island Moai stone head replica. The walkway is adjacent to St Anne's Park, which is another great walking amenity, with 4 boules courts, a par-3 golf course, a playground and the Red Stables Market, Sat, which has its own excellent café, Olive's Room, www. olivesroom.ie.

456
1/R13
☑ **DART to DART** Dalkey to Killiney, Co Dublin Starts at one DART station, and ends at the other. Hop off at Dalkey follow the Sorrento Rd, along Vico Rd, and then up Dalkey Hill via stone steps known as the Cat's Ladder. Great views when you reach the top. The pathway dips down, and then back up again, this time Killiney Hill, where you might be greeted by the site of paragliders. The Obelisk at the top of Killiney Hill was built to commemorate a famine in 1740. Taking the path down hill, this leads you to Killiney DART station. About 2km in distance.

457
1/R13
☑ **Cliff Path** Howth Head, Co Dublin Starting at the DART station, 6km loop walk along the cliff path at Howth Head. Signposting isn't great, but when it exists, it's a green arrow. Great views of Lambay Island and Ireland's Eye. The highest point of the walk is Beann Éadair (the Ben of Howth) 171m above sea level. Another walk in Howth is the walk to the Baily Lighthouse.

458
1/R13
The Iveagh Gardens Clonmel St, D2 · www.iveaghgardens.ie Known as Dublin's Secret Garden – formally designed in 1865 by Ninian Niven but with a much longer history. Original landscape features include grottoes, cascade waterfall, sunken garden, wilderness, woodland, and a yew maze. Gates close at dusk.

459
1/R13
North Bull Island Clontarf, D3 Low-lying sandbank, stitched together by the roots of marram grass stretching 5km, parallel to the shore off Clontarf in Dublin Bay. The beach stretching the length of the island is known as Dollymount Strand (known locally as the 'Dollier'). Nature Reserve, a UNESCO biosphere reserve and an EU Special Protection Area. Don't walk on the salt marshes! OS N050

460 **Herbert Park** Ballsbridge, D4 A circuit of Herbert Park is almost exactly a
1/R13   mile used by joggers and walkers to accurately measure their fitness progress.
There is a Lolly & Cooks café in the park, where you can buy a healthy breakfast
after your walk – www.lollyandcooks.com, and a fine little farmers' market
on Sunday. A row of hornbeam trees replaced an earlier planting of elms. The
Edwardian-style park has been in existence, pretty well unchanged, for just over
100 years, on old maps it is known as the Forty Acres.

461 **Poolbeg Lighthouse** Sandymount, D4 There are a lot of different walking
1/R13   options in Sandymount, the place where James Joyce stayed on the day of
Ulysses – 16 June 1904. The village has its own walking trail or you can choose
to walk the Great South Wall to Poolbeg Lighthouse. When constructed, the
Wall was the world's longest sea wall, and from the car park near the ESB
chimneys, it is a 4km walk to the Lighthouse. Industrial landscape with the
new Poolbeg Incinerator impacting on the skyline as well as the ESB chimneys.
Be aware of the tides if walking far out on the beach; the water comes in very
quickly.

462 **The Dodder Walk** Clonskeagh, Dublin The River Dodder is one of three
1/R13   main rivers running into Dublin – the Liffey and the Tolka being the other two.
5KM   You can walk a 5km path known as the Dodder Trail, starting at Bushy Park and
XCIRC trailing over riverbank and parkland, going through Dartry Park. If you end the
1-A-1 walk at Clonskeagh, you are near Ashton's Gastro Pub. Just saying. Report: 342/
☕   PUBS WITH GOOD FOOD. The river itself then travels through Donnybrook and
Ballsbridge, and joins the Liffey, along with the Grand Canal, at Grand Canal
Dock. The river becomes tidal where the Lansdowne Road Bridge crosses it, as
it goes over a weir.

463 **The Hell Fire Club** Montpelier Hill, Co Dublin On top of Montpelier Hill, 383m
1/R13 high is a ruined hunting lodge (from 1725), known locally as The Brass Castle.
The building, with its associated tales of bad boy debauched aristocrats, gives the
mountain its present-day name. Car park near the summit closes at dusk. There
are several short walks through the spruce forests, including the Hell Fire forest
loop, 5.5km, a moderate walk marked with a red way marker. Views of Dublin Bay
are breathtaking, best just as the sun is setting. OS N050.

464 **Dublin's Bridges** River Liffey Close your eyes and think of Dublin, and you'll
1/R13 probably see a view of, or from, a bridge. Views of the many bridges perfectly
capture the spirit of the city, particularly the Calatrava-designed harp-shaped
Samuel Beckett Bridge with its backdrop of the Conference Centre, or the Ha'penny
Bridge at sunset. There are 24 bridges over the Liffey. The oldest is Mellows Bridge,
though bridging the river goes back over a thousand years to the Viking wooden
constructions. Ha'penny Bridge gets its name from the toll that was charged when
the bridge was privately owned – a toll that would make a mint nowadays, with an
estimated 30,000 people walking over each day.

465 **Etihad Skyline Rooftop Tour at Croke Park** The arena is 17 storeys high, and
1/R13 from the roof there is a tour that visitors can take to see panoramic views of the
city. During the tour you will learn about the various landmarks. Online booking
from www.crokepark.ie/etihad-skyline.

466 **The DART** Dublin's inner city railway stretches from Howth in N Dublin to
1/R13 Greystones and Bray in Co Wicklow. There are 31 stops and both N and S of the city
train views can be immense.

St Michael's Tower 96 steps to the top of this medieval tower, see Dublinia
Report: 418/DUBLIN ATTRACTIONS.

Guinness Storehouse Gravity Bar Uninterrupted 360° views of the whole of
Dublin, stretching to the Dublin mountains. Report: 403/DUBLIN ATTRACTIONS.

Sophie's @ The Dean Hotel Great 360° views from this glass-lined rooftop
restaurant. Report: 130/BOUTIQUE HOTELS.

The Marker Hotel Rooftop Bar & Terrace One of the best views of Dublin is to
see the city at night from the Terrace. Report: 122/MAJOR HOTELS.

the
Best
of Belfast

The Best Places to Stay in Belfast

467
6/S6
61 ROOMS
MED.EXP

Ten Square Hotel 10 Donegall Sq +44 28 90241001 ·
www.tensquare.co.uk Ten Square is very comfortable, and its location behind City Hall couldn't be more central. It's also relatively quiet. The rooms have dark, minimalist interiors, both in the original Yorkshire House building and in the newer signature room extension. Breakfasts are good, with only two cooked items alongside a buffet; attention to detail is precise. Friendly staff. A brand new space, the Loft wine bar and lounge, with amazing views across City Hall, is in development.

468
6/S6
62 ROOMS
LOTS
TERRACE

The Merchant 16 Skipper St +44 28 90234888 ·
www.themerchanthotel.com Easily the most glamorous hotel in the city, this magnificently restored former Ulster Bank building is lavish in detail. There are 21 rooms in the Victorian wing, and a further 36 rooms with an Art Deco theme, so choose your favourite era when booking. Capacious suites are named for celebrated Northern Irish writers, poets and playwrights. The Great Room restaurant is the centrepiece of the complex and the former banking hall; there are no fewer than four bars. The open-plan style of the Great Room robs it of any intimacy, and the cooking has always been consistent, if pricey. There is a spa and gym, and a rooftop garden for private events.

469
6/S6
43 ROOMS
NO PETS
EXP
TERRACE
ATMOS

Bullitt 40a Church Lane +44 28 95900600 · www.bullitthotel.com
Borrowing its name, and imagery, from the famous movie, starring Steve McQueen and Jacqueline Bisset, Bullitt is cool, funky, and fun, and it's the hottest destination in the city. It's minimalist, colourful, and the staff – as you expect in Belfast – are delightful.

EAT The public rooms are essentially one great big space combining bar, coffee dock, and the Taylor & Clay restaurant, which specialises in meats cooked on their Asador grill. They serve a simple breakfast – granola and yogurt, fruit – brought to your door, though you can also grab a brioche bun, or cooked breakfast, downstairs. It's a big, raucous space in the evenings, especially at weekends.

470
6/S6
119 ROOMS
EXP
ATMOS

The Titanic Hotel 6 Queens Rd, Belfast +44 28 95082000 ·
www.titanichotelbelfast.com Historic brick building, once home to Harland & Wolff shipyard headquarters, now a luxury hotel. The fascinating building has been elegantly and sympathetically refurbished, especially the vaulted Drawing Office – where the Titanic was conceived, now the Harland Bar. Helpful staff, dressed in traditional tweed and leather uniforms are happy to give you an impromptu tour. The food offer has yet to find its feet, but the rooms are smashing. The building is adjacent to The Titanic Experience (561/BELFAST ATTRACTIONS).

471
6/S6
130 ROOMS
EXP

Fitzwilliam Hotel Gt Victoria St +44 28 90442090 ·
www.fitzwilliamhotelbelfast.com We've always found the Fitzwilliam to be a beacon of professionalism. The staff are clued-up and helpful, the rooms are luxe, and the location is perfect. It doesn't have the centre-of-the-city feel of The Europa, but that's a bonus. The many splendid local restaurants means that their own hotel restaurant has never established its identity, whilst the bar is a more commodious and comfortable space, and has good cocktails. Park directly across the street.

472 **The Europa** Gt Victoria St +44 28 90271066 · www.hastingshotels.com
6/3G Famously the most-bombed hotel in the world, The Europa is part of the
272 ROOMS Hastings Group, and they have worked hard to establish an up-market identity
LOTS recently. The quality of ingredients at breakfast has improved dramatically and,
given its reputation and location, it's always a bustling, happening place: at any
given moment there are a dozen conferences happening here, with consequent
pressure on the staff. The rooms are standard and comfortable, but parking
is a hassle, not helped by the concierges. Also part of the Hastings Group is
the Stormont Hotel, Upr Newtownards Rd and the Culloden Hotel overlooking
Belfast Lough, 10km outside Belfast.

473 **Tara Lodge** 36 Cromwell Rd +44 28 90590900 · www.taralodge.com
6/S6 Pristine housekeeping, excellent staff, and a quiet, University Zone location
34 ROOMS with free parking has helped Tara Lodge establish a stellar reputation. It's
MED.INX an unassuming place, and under manager Pauline McCullough there is a
NO PETS team of terrific women who are focused on service. The annexe rooms are
smaller, so pay extra to stay in the main house. Good breakfasts, but it's the
excellent service that makes it. With Botanic Station nearby, you can sightsee
by train.

474 **Malmaison** 34-38 Victoria St +44 121 4568613 · www.malmaison.com
6/S6 The Mal really shook up the style factor in Belfast hotels when it arrived in
62 ROOMS town, and it's still a funky, fashionable destination, even as others have
MED.EXP rushed to adopt its cool attitude. The dark palette of the decor has aged well,
even if it feels somewhat discordant at breakfast time. Dinner time suits the
style of the brasserie much better, but the cooking has struggled to establish
consistency and identity, as many guests head instead to the plentiful nearby
restaurants.

Belfast International Youth Hostel Report: 1306/HOSTELS.

Best Modern Ulster Cooking

475
6/S6
MED.EXP

✔✔✔ **OX** 1 Oxford St +44 28 90314121 · www.oxbelfast.com In OX, next to the River Lagan, chef Stephen Toman and sommelier Alain Kerloc'h have raised Northern Irish cooking to new heights. You get the impression that the team feel they can do anything and, when they put a plate of hay-baked celeriac with black garlic and sorrel on the table, and pair it with a glass of Pouilly-Fuissé, you realise they can. Tasting menu with wine pairing is the way to go. Lunch & dinner Tue-Sat.

476
6/S6
MED.EXP

✔✔ **James Street South** 21 James Street Sth +44 28 90434310 · www.jamesstreetsouth.co.uk Dynamic chef Niall McKenna has built an empire of restaurants in Belfast, but this is where it all started. A minimalist, bright room, tucked away close to City Hall, is the venue for head chef David Gilmore to max the flavours of excellent NI artisan produce: Dundrum crab with roasted lemons; Antrim beef with sea greens; razor clams with cider and broad beans. Value for money is exceptional, service is pretty perfect. Lunch & dinner Mon-Sun.

477
6/S6
EXP

✔ **Deanes Eipic** 28 Howard St +44 28 90331134 · www.deaneseipic.com Having brought stars and the acclaim of being the first woman to be voted best chef in Ireland, Danni Barry has handed on the kitchen reins at Eipic to her understudy, Alex Green, in a smooth and seamless handover. Mr Green has an impressive c.v., but he is back on home ground, having begun his career in the original Deane's. His food is elegant, subtle and controlled, and the menus are notable for a very fine vegetarian menu. Owner Michael Deane, liberated from the kitchen, has become a relaxed and humorous host, and Eipic is, in every way, epic. TGP Danni is moving on to Clenaghans near Moira. Dinner Wed-Sat, lunch Fri.

478
6/S6
MED.INX
ATMOS

✔ **Ginger Bistro** 68 Gt Victoria St +44 28 90244421 · www.gingerbistro.com Simon McCance is a lovely cook, and he has been serving nuanced, tasty, friendly food for years, in a simple, boho-chic little room just off Great Victoria St. Despite the years, his youthful touch and enthusiasm never falter, and every meal is fun, a tonic of good tastes and good times, and excellent value. Vegetarian dishes are a particular good. Dinner Mon-Sat, lunch Thur-Sat.

479
6/S6
MED.EXP

✔ **The Barking Dog** 33-35 Malone Rd+44 28 90661885 · www.barkingdogbelfast.com Michael O'Connor is one of those chefs who can do perfect: crispy pork belly bites; steak tartare; beef shin burger; squid ink linguini with Portavogie prawns; espresso creme brûlée.This explains why, for many food lovers, this atmospheric warren of rooms in an old Victorian house, is their favourite restaurant in Belfast. Mr O'Connor and his partner, manager Michael Fletcher, are flying high. Lunch & dinner Mon-Sun

480
6/S6
MED.INX
ATMOS

✔ **The Muddler's Club** Warehouse Lane, Cathedral Quarter +44 28 90313199 · www.themuddlersclubbelfast.com Gareth McCaughey is one of the most knowing chefs, who seems to have no blind spots, which means The Muddler's Club is a complete concept, from soup to nuts, from style to uniforms. He worked in great kitchens before opening this place, and he nailed it right from the get-go. Staff are superb, the room buzzes, and value for money is the best. Lunch & dinner Tue-Sat.

481 ✓**SHU** 253 Lisburn Rd +44 28 90381655 · www.shu-restaurant.com
6/S6   At the city end of the Lisburn Rd, Shu has glided through the Belfast
MED.INX dining scene like a luxury ship. Smooth and smart, calm and sophisticated, it's a room that has stayed at the top, thanks to Brian McCann's questing cooking, and owner Alan Reid's adroit stewardship. The confidence in the kitchen is mirrored by the team out front, hard-working folk who wear their considerable learning lightly. Shu is not just a destination, it's a Belfast institution. Lunch & dinner Mon-Sat.

482 **Howard Street** 56 Howard St +44 28 90248362 ·
6/S6   www.howardstbelfast.com Mission: Impossible in Belfast is the simple
MED.INX act of getting a table to eat Marty Murphy's cooking, and to enjoy the energy
ATMOS of Howard Street. The reason is Mr Murphy's big flavoured cooking, for here is a chef who supercharges his ingredients, using every device in the culinary book, and his food is super good to eat. So, keep on trying to get that table in one of Belfast's hottest rooms, because it's worth it for those flavours, and that buzz. Lunch & dinner Tue-Sat.

483 **Deanes at Queens** 1 College Gardens +44 28 90382111 ·
6/S6   www.michaeldeane.ie Chef Chris Fearon has been the man stoking the
MED.INX Mibrasa charcoal oven for the last decade in Michael Deane's University
TERRACE Quarter bar-restaurant. The bar has a full licence, and outside is one of the best terraces for dining. Mr Fearon's food reads straight-ahead but the precision and sophistication of his cooking and plating is a joy to eat, and everything tastes clean, fresh and vivid. Value for money is exceptional, service is Belfast good. Lunch & dinner Mon-Sat.

484 **Saphyre** 135 Lisburn Rd +44 28 90688606 ·
6/S6   www.saphyrerestaurant.com Joery Castel took up the reins at Saphyre
MED.EXP in early 2017, after many years working in The Boat House, out east in Bangor. The restaurant is a lavish design extravaganza, complete with Hermes fabrics, at the rere of designer Kris Turnbull's showroom. It's sited in a Grade-B listed church, which also houses the café and lounge. Early menus are fine value for money, and keep an eye out for their wine dinners. Wed-Sun lunch & dinner.

The Best Burgers & Steaks

485 **Bar + Grill** 21 James St Sth +44 28 95600700 ·
6/S6   www.belfastbargrill.co.uk A Josper grill is the secret weapon of Niall
MED.EXP McKenna's bare brick brasserie, next door to his up-market James Street South
ATMOS   restaurant. It's not just beef, however, as they also grill brill on the bone, pork
T-bone, spatchcocked chicken, and sea bream. A superb wine list features many
by the glass as well as magnums. Sunday roast features two roasts and Yorkshire
puds. Lunch & dinner 7 days.

486 **Deanes Meat Locker** 28-40 Howard St +44 28 90331134 ·
6/S6   www.michaeldeane.ie Using meat from superstar butcher Peter Hannan,
MED.EXP matured in a Himalayan salt chamber, means Michael Deane has only to
rustle up some beef fat chips and maybe a blue cheese sauce to go with your
Delmonico rib-eye, and you have meat heaven on your plate. There are other
brasserie classics but those NI steaks are the thing. Lunch & dinner Mon-Sat.

487 **City Picnic** 6 Castle St +44 28 90246194 · www.citypicnicbelfast.com At
6/S6   the rere of the old Anderson & McAuley store, the big, bright, glass-fronted City
Picnic boasts the city's best burger. That's up for debate, but what is true is the
smart mix of elements that Arthur McAnerney and Gavin Gregg have assembled.
It feels like a diner meets deli meets convenience store. Beer and wine are sold,
but it's not a place to linger. Lunch & dinner 7 days.

The Barking Dog The beef shin burger which chef Michael O'Connor
creates in The Barking Dog is one of the best in the country, not just the city.
Report: 479/MODERN ULSTER COOKING.

Where to Eat Brunch

488
6/S6
MED.INX

✓**Hadskis** 33 Donegall St +44 28 90325444 · www.hadskis.co.uk Hadskis is one of the city's nicest rooms at brunch time, a narrow room alongside Commercial Ct, in the Cathedral Quarter. The menus are straight-ahead and the execution is second to none. Brunch, Lunch & dinner 7 days.

489
6/S6
MED.INX

Neill's Hill 229 Upr Newtownards Rd +44 28 90650079 · www.neillshill.com Jonathan Davis's attractive and characterful room is a perfect east Belfast destination for toasted crumpets with egg and bacon or grilled grapefruit with banana, cinnamon and honey. Mr Davis is one of the city's best restaurateurs, and was one of the first people to colonise the Newtownards Rd as a food destination. Daytime & dinner 7 days.

490
6/S6
MED.INX
ATMOS

Permit Room Unit 6, McAuley House, Fountain St +44 28 90231394 · www.permitroom.co.uk Permit Room is the younger café sibling of the wildly successful Howard Street restaurant, run by chef Marty Murphy and front of house Niall Davis. Root and Branch coffee underpins their offering, and these guys like big, big flavours. The facade is unassuming, but inside it's a stylish room with mahogany walls and floor, and the drinks are very good. Great sound system, too. Daytime 7 days, dinner Fri & Sat.

491
6/S6
MED.INX

Town Square 45 Botanic Ave +44 79 38244851 · www.townsquarebelfast.com In one of the city's most handsome rooms, on the corner of Botanic Ave and Lwr Crescent – Town Sq is part of the fast-developing Crescent Townhouse. The brunch menu runs until noon in Botanic Avenue's hippest room, and with coffee from Roasted Brown in Wicklow, it's ideal for avocado on sourdough, or eggs Benedict. TGP Town Sq 2 is already in development. Daytime & dinner 7 days, till 1am Fri & Sat.

492
6/S6
MED.INX
ATMOS

Kaffe O 411 Ormeau Rd +44 28 90642434 · www.kaffeo.coffee Orla Smyth's handsome store is Scandinavian coolness personified. The room is beautifully styled, lit and decorated, to add to the enjoyment of superb coffees, roasted by Ricco Sorensen and imported from Copenhagen. The Nordic accent of Kaffe O comes out in force in the morning, and has a refreshin take on brunch. A cup of Belfast Brew, and you're off to the perfect start. All day till 9pm Mon-Thur, till 6pm Fri-Sun. Second branch on Botanic Avenue.

Bert's Café in The Merchant Hotel, Report: 468/PLACES TO STAY.

The Best Pizza

493 ✓ **Belfast Wood-Fired Pizza Company** 699 Lisburn Rd +44 28 90914903 ·
6/S6   @woodfireBT9 Ross O'Neile is really shaking up the pizza cart here. His
ATMOS   sourcing is superb: fresh mozzarella from Smyth McCann's dairy farm; his own
smoked scamorza; locally cured coppa, chorizo and salami from Ispini meats in
Moira; Abernethy butters; pork slow-roasted with Jameson Black Barrel whiskey;
benchmark Young Buck blue cheese; prawns from Portavogie. The result is
something unique. Nice rustic style with reclaimed wooden furniture, cool sounds
and, if you can't make it here, look out for their pizza van at festivals. Dinner from
3pm Tue-Sun.

494 **Honest Pizza Company** 153 Stranmillis Rd +44 28 90666100 ·
6/S6   www.honestpizzacompany.com Honest Pizza uses a 48-hour matured
sourdough base, and owners Andrew Porter and Michael Burnside have a purist
approach to pizza, though they do allow for local tastes that demand pineapple,
except their pineapples are freshly cut. Recycled Italian tomato tins hold sweet-
smelling basil plants. Dinner Wed-Sun.

495 **Greens Pizza** 549 Lisburn Rd +44 28 90666033 · www.greenspizza.com
6/S6   William Clark opened almost 30 years ago – it was called Pizza The Action,
back then – which makes Greens the Grandpa of Belfast pizza. The Lisburn
Rd branch expanded into the next-door building, and there is a second one at
Ballyhackamore. The crew also runs the ever-popular Café Conor, just across from
Queens. Greens is noted for its vegan pizzas, and corkage is inexpensive if you
bring your own wine. Lunch & dinner 7 days.

496 **Villa Italia** 39 University Ave +44 28 90328356 ·
6/S6   www.villaitaliarestaurant.co.uk Old-style Italian food and classic pizzas in one
of the longest serving restaurants – opened 1988 – in Belfast. Pizzas run through all
the classics including, of course, the Hawaiian. Dinner 7 days. All Day Sun.

Trusty Tratts & Italian Osterias

497 **Coppi** St Anne's Sq, Cathedral Quarter +44 28 90311959 · www.coppi.co.uk
6/S6   Named for the great Italian cyclist Fausto Coppi, this stylish room is one of the
MED.INX   busiest in the city, and you will find the crowds packing the place out at the
ATMOS   weekends. Chef Tony O'Neill takes Italy's greatest dishes – "Jamie's Italian on
steroids" was one description –and whilst there are benchmark meats from
superstar butcher Peter Hannan, the food would improve with better ingredients.
Vegan menu. Good cocktails, and a rockin' room. Lunch & dinner Mon-Sun.

498 **Il Pirata** 279 Upr Newtownards Rd +44 28 90673421 ·
6/S6   www.ilpiratabelfast.com Sister restaurant to the city centre Coppi, Il Pirata is a
MED.INX   lean, modern room with lean, modern Italian food. With fresh pasta and sourdough
ATMOS   breads coming from their own Pasta Factory in the city, quality and consistency are
reliable, and the minimalist, tiled room is lively, and very noisy. Lunch & dinner
7 days.

499 **Deane & Decano** 537 Lisburn Rd +44 28 90663108 · www.michaeldeane.ie
6/S6   Michael Deane's Lisburn Rd venture sees the great chef indulge his Italian leanings
MED.INX   but the offer in this busy room extends far beyond Italian classics, so there is
dressed crab, rump steak, even an all-day breakfast during the week. Good value,
and a smart, New York-style room. Daytime & dinner 7 days. Saturday brunch.

The Best Seafood Restaurants

500
6/S6
MED.INX

✓ **Deanes Love Fish** 28-40 Howard St +44 28 90331134 ·
www.michaeldeane.ie Michael Deane's seafood restaurant is the fish lover's choice in his trio of city centre restaurants, tucked between Deane's Eipic and Meat Locker. It's a classy, consistent and always busy space, arranged around the neat bar. The day's fish dishes are chalked on the board, and the menu ranges from classic seafood platter to fish and chips with proper tartare sauce. Lunch & dinner Mon-Sat.

501
6/S6
MED.INX
ATMOS

✓ **Mourne Seafood Bar** 34-36 Bank St +44 28 90248544 ·
www.mourneseafood.com Andy Rea is a great cook, and a great seafood cook. You will find his perennially busy seafood and oyster bar at the rere of the big Primark on Royal Ave, and it's one of the city's liveliest rooms. Mr Rea's food is direct and punchy. Lovely wines, superb Belfast staff. Mr Rea also runs the Belfast Cookery School. Lunch & dinner 7 days. Second Seafood Bar in Dundrum.

502
6/S6
MED.EXP

Tedford's 5 Donegall Quay +44 28 90434000 · www.tedfordsrestaurant.com
Facing the River Lagan, in between the Queen's Bridge and the Queen Elizabeth Bridge, Alan Foster's chic upscale restaurant is a calm, svelte space on three floors. Seafood is the thing to go for, and do start with a drink in the basement bar if you are visiting at the weekend. Lunch Thur-Fri, dinner Tue-Sat. (See also Tedford's Kitchen, Report: 515/CASUAL RESTAURANTS).

The Best Ethnic Restaurants

MEXICAN

503
6/S6
MED.INX
ATMOS

✓ **La Taqueria** 53 Castle St +44 7748 786654 · www.lataqueriabelfast.co.uk
Adam Lynas and his wife, Eliza, from Monterrey, have brought the true tastes, colours and drinks of Mexico to Belfast. Forget Tex-Mex dross, and enjoy a classic mezcal with superlative Nino Blanco corn tortillas; quesos fundidos made – interestingly – with mozzarella; chorizo verde quesadillas; pork and chili tamales; and beef steak fundidos. The cut-price decor with Dia de los Muertos murals adds to the authenticity. Dinner Tue-Sun, lunch Sat & Sun.

ASIAN

504
6/S6
MED.INX

Zen 55 Adelaide St +44 28 90232244 · www.zenbelfast.co.uk Eddie Fung's uber-glam Zen is dark and luxurious, with one of the largest Buddha statues in the country. There are fusion dishes, but the best bet is to go for the sashimi, sushi, maki rolls and teppanyaki specials. Cocktail list includes their own Zen-style drinks. Lunch & dinner 7 days.

CHINESE

505
6/S6
MED.INX
NO C/CARDS
ATMOS

Macau 271 Ormeau Rd +44 28 90691800 · www.macaubelfast.com
Macau is a plain, compact, paper tablecloth, BYOB restaurant, and it's the best bet for Chinese food in the city. If you hanker for soft-shell crab with cumin, or char siu and monkfish hotpot, or their mesmeric aubergine stuffed with prawn paste with fermented black bean sauce, then it's here. Make sure you book. Dinner Tue-Sat. No credit cards.

506
6/S6
CHP
NO C/CARDS

Same Happy Donegall Pass +44 28 90310507 Soup-based noodle dishes and barbecued meats are the backbone of the Same Happy menu that draws in Belfast's local Chinese community. It's not much more than a diner, but the char siu, the belly pork and the roast duck dishes are worth the detour. Lunch & dinner 7 days.

The Best Cafés & Casual Restaurants

507
6/S6
MED.INX
✓ **Deanes Deli Bistro** 44 Bedford St +44 28 90248800 · www.michaeldeane.ie Near to the Ulster Hall on Bedford St, Michael Deane's deli-bistro-wine bar shows he is as adept with punchy savoury cooking as he is with starry cookery. Perennially busy, so make sure to book; music at weekends; fine cocktails. Lunch & dinner Mon-Sat.

508
6/S6
CHP
ATMOS
✓ **Cast & Crew** Titanic Quarter, Queens Rd +44 28 90451400 · www.castandcrewbelfast.co.uk Out in the Titanic Quarter, Niall McKenna's café offers gourmet grub for truckers and builders and urban professionals: fish finger sandwiches; all-day Ulster fry; chilli dog; buffalo wings; Titanic burger. The cooking is knowing, evocative, and beautifully delivered. Daytime 7 days.

509
6/S6
Cyprus Avenue 228 Upr Newtownards Rd +44 28 90656755 · www.cyprusavenue.co.uk Richard McCracken has opened the latest pared-back, bistro-style room in the area. Cyprus Avenue is eclectic from breakfast to dinner, allowing the chef to bring world food influences to modern Ulster food. McCracken's experience - working with Helene Darroze, Tom Kitchin, Andrew Fairlie and Danny Millar – shows in precise and smart cooking. 9am-9pm 7 days.

510
6/S6
General Merchants 361 Ormeau Rd +44 28 90291007 www.generalmerchants.co.uk Tim Fetherston's General Merchants has been spreading Antipodean and Asian influences across the city. As serious about coffee as they are about food, they source their beans from The Barn in Berlin. Always busy, so expect to queue for your Melbourne breakfast and a cortado on Sat morning. Daytime 7 days, dinner Wed-Sat. Second branch on Newtownards Rd.

511
6/S6
Home 22 Wellington Pl +44 28 90234946 · www.homebelfast.co.uk Richard Haller's Home began life as a pop-up, but quickly became a favoured fixture of Belfast dining, thanks to outstanding signature dishes. Those classics remain on the menu in this ever-busy room in Wellington Pl, but Mr Haller has steered the menu towards more vegetarian and vegan dishes. It's also a terrific place for children, with a clever menu for youngsters. You can also get food-to-go and coffees from their deli counter. Daytime & dinner 7 days.

512
6/S6
CHP
Cafe Conor 11a Stranmillis Rd +44 28 90663266 · www.cafeconor.com Right across from the Queen's University campus, Conor has been a landmark destination for many years. Their Big Breakfast is a legendary feast, but there is lots more here than just fry-ups. Gorgeous Neil Shawcross paintings dominate the tall room. Value for money is keen. The popular Greens Pizza is a sister business. Daytime & dinner 7 days.

513
6/S6
MED.INX
Graze 402 Upr Newtownards Rd +44 28 90658658 · www.grazebelfast.com In amongst the cluster of neighbourhood restaurants – the zone has been christened Ballysnackamore – Neil Johnston and chef John Moffat describe Graze as part neighbourhood eatery, part bistro, but Mr Moffat's cooking can scale the stellar heights. He has a rare sympathy for ingredients. Mr Moffat worked with the best chefs in Belfast and Sydney, and his style is both rooted and cosmopolitan. Great gin selection in the plush bar. Lunch & dinner 7 days.

514   **Bistro Este** 221 Upr Newtownards Rd +44 28 90656976 ·

6/S6   www.bistrueste.com The cookery books all around little Bistro Este signals
MED.INX the dedication of the team, and this cooking, from chef proprietor David Adams,
ATMOS is properly personal. The sureness of touch makes this one of our favourite East
Belfast destinations. Service is only brilliant, and value for money is exceptional.
Lunch & dinner Tue-Sun.

515   **Tedford's Kitchen Bar & Restaurant 1** Lanyon Quay +44 28 90278823 ·

6/S6   www.tedfordskitchen.com Alan Foster has let his hair down with his Kitchen
MED.INX Bar. The informality and funkyness of Tedford's Kitchen couldn't be more unlike
the formality of Tedford's, its sister restaurant just down the road. Here, there are
swirling banquettes, high ceilings, neon lights, and some out-there cooking. Good
value, good drinks, excellent staff. Lunch & dinner Tue-Sat.

516   **NATIVE™** The MAC St Anne's Square,Cathedral Quarter, +44 28 90235053 ·

6/S6   www.themaclive.com Run by the excellent Yellow Door food company, the
CHP MAC menus showcase good local foods – Ewing's smoked salmon and prawn roll;
Doran's beef burger; Rockvale farm chicken salad. The short Native Bites menu
is a real treat, especially with a glass of craft ale, and with menus for vegetarians,
children, and a concise pre-theatre menu, everyone is well looked after. All day
7 days.

517   **Cafe Smart** 56 Belmont Rd, Belfast +44 28 90471679 ·

6/S6   www.cafesmart.co.uk Simon Maccabe's café is a staple of the Belmont Road,
a calm, colourful and welcoming room that is notable for displays of paintings by
local artists, including Mr Maccabe's grandmother, Gladys Maccabe. Good tasty
cooking, especially their fine, award-winning wheaten bread, brings the punters
back time after time, and it's all charming and heartfelt. Daytime 7 days.

Original Belfast Pubs

518
6/S6
ATMOS

✓ ✓ ✓ **Crown Liquor Saloon** 46 Great Victoria St +44 28 90243187 ·
www.nicholsonspubs.co.uk The Crown features in every tourist's
list, but don't let this deter you from enjoying this pub's Victorian Gothic interiors.
Owned by the National Trust, it was established in 1826 and the major
embellishments took place – at the hands of Italian craftsmen – in 1885. A
facelift in 1981 revived the phantasmagoric level of detail etched into every corner:
frankly, you need a drink or two to sober up from the orgy of design. Beautiful
snugs are the place to be on an afternoon when sunlight casts a benediction on
the interior.

519
6/S6
ATMOS

✓ **Sunflower Public House** 65 Union St +44 28 90232474 ·
www.sunflowerbelfast.com Everyone loves The Sunflower, like, big time.
They love the wit – a sign outside says: "No topless sunbathing, Ulster has suffered
enough." They love the pizzas. They love the far-out memorabilia, and the music
sessions and the monthly flea market and the beer garden and the fact that owner,
Pedro Donald, has swapped big beer brands for a diverse range of craft beers.

520
6/S6

Kelly's Cellars 30 Bank St +44 28 90246058 · www.kellyscellars.com
"A sanctuary in the wilderness" is how the writer Hugh McCarten described
Kelly's Cellars. The low, well-washed counter and the vaulted ceilings make you
think you have stepped back in time to 1720 when it first opened, and this is one
of the most authentic rooms in the city. Good music sessions, open fires, and big
crowds.

521
6/S6

Robinson's Saloon 38 Great Victoria St +44 29 90247447 ·
www.robinsonsbar.co.uk There are five different bar areas in the legendary
Robinson's. The two most significant are the beautiful Front Bar, restored after
a terrorist bombing, and Fibber Magee's, known for its nightly music sessions.
There is a bistro on the first floor, and pool tables and sports televisions in the loft.
Ground floor saloon with Titanic memorabilia.

522
6/S6
ATMOS

Lavery's Public Bar 12 Bradbury Pl +44 28 90871106 · www.laverysbelfast.com
Lavery's has been a mainstay of Belfast's drinking and socialising culture for almost
a century. There is music and DJs and pool tables on the upper floors, so it's the
traditional Pavilion public bar and the back bar and beer garden downstairs that are
most interesting for local pub culture. It's always packed. The same organisation
owns The Pavilion on the Ormeau Rd.

523
6/S6

The Morning Star Pottinger Entry +44 28 90235986 ·
www.themorningstarbar.co.uk Walk down narrow Pottinger's Entry, to find this
venerable old pub dating back to 1818. Upstairs there is a well-regarded restaurant,
with Victorian decor, and the owners work hard at sourcing good ingredients, have
their own herb garden, and an in-house butcher. No surprise, then, that steaks –
and big steaks – are a menu mainstay, so bring an appetite before you climb the
stairs, after an aperitif in the bar. Excellent staff.

524
6/S6

Duke of York 7-11 Commercial Court +44 28 90241062 ·
www.dukeofyorkbelfast.com The Duke has one of the classic bar interiors, a
cornucopia of pristine memorabilia that recalls the heydays of the distilling and

brewing trades and the newspaper industry. Its sister bars, The Dark Horse, The Friend at Hand and The Harp Bar, on Hill Street, are no less impressive.

525   **The Spaniard**   3 Skipper St +44 28 90232448 · www.thespaniardbar.com
6/s6   Across from the Merchant Hotel, on Skipper St, The Spaniard is – allegedly – the
DF   place Bill Murray heads to when he is in Belfast. Myriad images of the Sacred
ATMOS   Heart and the Blessed Virgin adorn the walls of this tiny bar, along with other
paraphernalia that makes it feel as if you have stepped into one of Neil Gaiman's
dreams. A large selection of rums is their USP, and its amiable grungy ethos.

526   **Muriel's Café Bar**   12 Church Ln +44 28 90332445 · @muriels.cafebar
6/s6   Sister bar to The Spaniard, and famous for its gin selection, and the ladies'
underwear hanging from the ceiling – Muriel's used to be a milliner's, back in the
day. The gin list is enormous, and the cocktails are bracing and imaginative. There
is some decent food, but having a Jawbox Gin in here is a rite of passage.

Belfast Bars with Good Food

✓ **Molly's Yard**   Report: 528/CRAFT BEER.

The Morning Star   Report: 523/BELFAST PUBS.

The Black Box   Report: 530/CRAFT BEER.

The John Hewitt   Report: 533/CRAFT BEER.

Dirty Onion & Yardbird   Report: 532/CRAFT BEER.

527 ✔ **Boundary Brewing Taproom** Portview Trade Centre, Newtownards Rd
6/S6 · www.boundarybrewing.coop The dynamic Boundary Brewing co-
ATMOS operative opens its tap room monthly, and in addition to guest brewers who take
over the taps, they offer food from the likes of Belfast Wood Fired Pizza, and
charcuterie from the talented Ispini artisans. There can be as many as 17 beers on
offer, and it's mighty fun – if slightly chilly: bring your duffle-coat – to mingle in this
old, industrial linen mill. Owner Matthew Dick and his cohorts are serious beer
heads and business heads, so watch this brewery grow.

528 ✔ **Molly's Yard** 59 Botanic Ave +44 28 90322600 · www.mollysyard.co.uk
6/S6 Molly's is run by the Scullion family, whose Hilden Brewery is the oldest craft
brewery in the country. A dozen Hilden brews are on sale – you can buy an ale sack
to take them home – and the beers are the perfect match for the tasty food that
Siobhan Scullion and her team prepares.

529 **Brewbot/Belfast** 451 Ormeau Rd · www.brewbotbelfast.com A brewbot
6/S6 is a beer brewing robot which can be controlled by an app on your smartphone.
TERRACE More importantly, however, Brewbot is a bricks-and-mortar craft beer bar, in a
ATMOS glass-fronted building with hipster industrial chic style, and a wine bar upstairs. In
its first two years Brewbot managed to feature no fewer than 600 breweries on tap
and in bottle, and their celebration evenings can see more than 20 beers on tap.
The room, dominated by a large central table, is devoid of ornament, and crammed
with character. 3fe coffee, Suki teas, pretty covered verandah at the front, and
beers to take away. The dynamic Galway Brewing Company have recently taken
over, and they are a bunch who really know their stuff, with many successful brew
pubs in Dublin and Galway.

530 **The Black Box** 18 Hill St +44 28 90244400 · www.blackboxbelfast.com
6/S6 You will notice the gorgeous mural on the wall of The Black Box first, and whilst
this historic premises is principally an arts centre, there is a smashing selection
of local and international craft beers in The Green Room, and the staff know their
stuff. The cooking is similarly focused, offering pizzas and even vegan stews, at
knockdown prices. Elsewhere there are good gigs, movies, street art walking tours
and much more.

531 **The Woodworkers** 20 Bradbury Pl +44 28 90871106 · @thewood
6/S6 workersbelfast This is part of the Lavery's group, and sited right beside their
off-licence and bar on Bradbury Pl. In a large, double-height room they offer seven
rotating taps of craft beers. A flight of four taster glasses is a great way to try the
new wave of NI craft brewers, and they also offer a Growler service. DJs at the
weekend.

532 **The Dirty Onion** 3 Hill St +44 28 90243712 · www.thedirtyonion.com
6/S6 The Dirty Onion looks super-modern, thanks to its dramatic wooden cross-beam
ATMOS exterior, but the building dates back to the 1680's. Owned by the Wolsey family
who have the slick Merchant Hotel nearby, you will have to queue at the weekends,
so go at a quieter moment and enjoy the artworks curated by the Belfast Print
Workshop. Upstairs is their Yardbird rotisserie chicken restaurant, whilst the bar
specialises in Boilermaker pairings of beers and whiskeys – a Roundstone Red Ale
with a glass of Hibiki Harmony should get your weekend off to a good start. Look
out for their own cask beer, whilst the whiskey selection is Whiskey Heaven.

533　**The John Hewitt**　51 Donegall St +44 28 90233768 ·
6/S6　www.thejohnhewitt.com The John Hewitt – named after one of Belfast's
ATMOS　finest poets – isn't 20 years old, yet it feels like it has always been here. Run by a
non-profit co-operative from the Unemployed Resource Centre, it was one of the
first places to take craft beers seriously, and to offer good bar food. Good beers
and gins, nice daytime food and excellent music sessions make the JH a jewel of
the city.

534　**Bittles Bar**　70 Upr Church Lane +44 28 90311088 · @BittlesBar Bittles is a
6/S6　real spot for chasing down new NI brews, from craft brewers such as Farmageddon,
Hilden, Northbound, Yardsman, Pokertree, Fifth Quarter and Ards Brewing. They
host a beer festival each May bank holiday, in addition to regular whiskey tasting,
and the whiskey room is a tippler's paradise. Don't miss the portraits of NI
celebrities.

535　**The Errigle Inn**　312 Ormeau Rd +44 28 90641410 · www.errigle.com
6/S6　The Errigle is one of the best-known destinations on the Ormeau Rd, and in
addition to the sports and comedy performances it is notable for having its own
beer society. There are more than 20 beers on tap, including local superstars such
as Hercules and Clearsky.

The Best Music Pubs

536　**McHugh's**　29 Queen's Sq +44 28 90509999 · www.mchughsbar.com
6/S6　McHugh's is allegedly the oldest surviving building in Belfast – Established
ATMOS　1711 – but these days it buzzes with the energy of youth, offering music and
entertainment from Thurs through to Sun in its three bars, and lots of good local
craft beers to enjoy as you listen to the sessions. There is traditional music, jazz,
DJs and modern sounds in the basement, and lots of food.

537　**Fibber Magee's**　38 Great Victoria St +44 29 90247447 · www.robinsonsbar.
6/S6　co.uk The snug back bar of the big Robinsons' pub complex, Fibber's is home to
ATMOS　traditional sessions.

538　**The Garrick**　29 Chichester St +44 28 90321984 · www.thegarrickbar.com
6/S6　One hundred and fifty years young, the Garrick is one of the city's most handsome
ATMOS　Victorian bars. Restored to its original glory – as a bar without televisions and
jukeboxes – it's a tasteful enclave dedicated to drinking, music sessions, and
eating. The craft beer and whiskey selection are excellent, but it's that curving bar,
and the way it welcomes you in, that makes this a special pub.

Great Places to Drink Cocktails

539
6/S6
ATMOS
✓ ✓ **The Merchant Cocktail Bar** 16 Skipper St +44 28 90234888 · www.themerchanthotel.com The lavish Merchant Hotel has two popular spots for cocktails – The Cocktail bar itself, with its swaddling luxury – and Bert's Jazz Bar. But it's extensive book of drinks in the Bar, all 10 chapters, that holds the allure in the Merchant, and mixologist Andrew Dickie is an award-winning exponent. The mint julep is particularly sublime. It's worth noting that New York's highest-rated cocktail bar, The Dead Rabbit, was opened by Sean Muldoon and Jack McGarry who started their cocktail careers in The Merchant. 7 days.

540
6/S6
TERRACE
ATMOS
✓ **The Perch Rooftop Bar** 42 Franklin St +44 28 90248000 · www.theperchbelfast.com The high style of The Perch is a delightful contrast to the dull ugliness of Franklin St. High above the city, this is one of the hottest places in town, a clamour of colour, crowds and cocktails. The drinks menu changes with the seasons and is concise and choice, and there are pizzas, served casual-style in a pizza box. 7 days.

541
6/S6
ATMOS
Rita's 44 Franklin St +44 28 90248000 · www.ritasbelfast.com Rita's has nine House Rules – 'Gentlemen, Please Remain So' – which puts us in mind of the legendary New York mixologist Sasha Petraske, and his famous Milk & Honey bar, which had eight house rules for civilised drinking. The beer list is sub-par, but the alcoholic teas, gins and cocktails run the entire gauntlet, and there is a selection of vintage spirits at sky-high prices. Mixologist Jonathan Shaw is amongst the highest regarded bartenders in the city, and he's a real seeker, so just ask what he recommends. 7 days.

542
6/S6
Shubar 253 Lisburn Rd +44 28 90381655 · www.shu-restaurant.com In the basement of Shu restaurant, one of the city's leading restaurants, Shubar offers a concise list of cocktail classics, and food is also served downstairs on Fri and Sat nights. Lunch & dinner Mon-Sat.

543
6/S6
Filthy McNasty 45 Dublin Rd +44 28 90246823 · www.thefilthyquarter.com It's the Filthy Chic cocktail bar in this big compendium of venues on the Dublin Rd that is of most interest to cocktail lovers. Bar manager David Kelly and his team know their stuff, so the cocktails are largely unadorned and classic in style, and all the better for it. There is also a fine beer garden, and an excellent range of craft beers. 7 days.

544
6/S6
AM:PM 38 Upr Arthur St +44 28 90249009 · www.ampmbelfast.com The interior of this 'bohemian' restaurant is so over the top that it requires a good cocktail to calm your racing heart in the face of such floral and fin de siecle overload, not to mention the avalanches of champagne bottles. The cocktail list sticks to the classics, whilst food is served from breakfast right through the day. 7 days.

545
6/S6
The Albany 701 Lisburn Rd +44 28 90664442 · www.thealbanybelfast.com Liquor & Food is what they promise in The Albany, a big, glass-fronted room on the Lisburn Rd, beside the Wood Fired Pizza Co. The cocktails are good, and you can buy a bottle of Pol Roger Sir Winston Churchill if the wind is in your sails. There should be more local beers on the list, although the array of spirits is extremely good. 7 days.

546 **The Northern Whig** 2 Bridge St +44 28 90509888 · www.thenorthernwhig.com
6/S6 Cathedral Quarter Cocktails are the speciality, so order up a Skipper Street Punch or a Waring Street iced tea (made with a syrup from the locally blended Nambarrie tea). The Whig is a classy, clubby big space and has won awards as best pub in the North, and they serve popular dishes – vegetable lasagne; dry-aged sirloin; Korean chicken – all day long. 7 days.

547 **Sweet Afton** Brunswick St +44 28 90248000 · www.sweetaftonbelfast.com
6/S6 In the city's Linen Quarter, Sweet Afton is part of a cluster of jointly-owned bars including Chinawhite, The Perch and Rita's. There are 10 signature cocktails, including a drink made for Robert Burns with bourbon and prosecco, and a selection of craft gins and neat wines. It's a characterful bar, though we would prefer fewer televisions, with an all-day food menu that majors on classics, along with a selection of steaks. 7 days.

The Best Wine Bars

548 ✓ **Cru Club** 451 Ormeau Rd · www.thecruclub.com Juliette McCavana and
6/S6 Olivier Machado opened their wine bar in early 2017. It's upstairs, above the
ATMOS celebrated Brewbot craft beer pub, and wines are matched with Continental and Irish artisan cheeses and hams. There are local gins and beers on the list, but with all the wines available by the glass, and with many coming from their preferred magnums, you'll find superb wines at decent prices. The room is lean and modernist, dominated by a long central table, and Olivier and Juliette are helpful, knowledgeable and fun. 5pm-1am Wed Fri, 2pm-1am/midnight Sat & Sun.

549 ✓ **OX Cave** 1 Oxford St +44 28 90314121 · www.oxbelfast.com Part of the
6/S6 success of Ox has been the extraordinary wine service the restaurant offers. In
MED.EXP fact, to get the best from the cooking, opt for the wine pairings suggested by
ATMOS sommelier Alain Kerloc'h. In the Ox Cave, right next door to the restaurant, the gentleman's club feel is quite distinct from the restaurant, and the wines take centre stage, with small plates of Irish charcuterie, artisan cheeses and breads to complement. There are regular tastings and events, and music at weekends. 4pm-late Tue-Sat.

550 **Deanes Deli Vin Cafe** 44 Bedford St + 353 28 90248830 ·
6/S6 www.michaeldeane.ie Michael Deane's wine cafe can boast its own label
MED.INX prosecco, sauvignon blanc, cab sauv and malbec. It's always busy, with small plates
ATMOS of cured meats, crispy squid and smoked salmon on sourdough, to match the wines. Daytime & dinner Mon-Sat.

The Best Coffee

551 ✓✓ **Established Coffee** 54 Hill St +44 28 90319416 ·
6/s6 www.established.coffee Mark Ashbridge and Bridgeen Barbour's
ATMOS Established is the Big Bang of coffee in Belfast. In an ultra-minimalist room in the
Cathedral Quarter, Ashbridge and Barbour brought the skills – he's an AeroPress
champion – and the perfectionist attitude that Belfast needed to kick-start a coffee
revolution. There are two daily beans on offer and a barista surprise, which is
always a good choice. They could coast on the coffee alone, but the food is as
precise and carefully chosen as the brews. Heavens above, Established even serve a
nice cup of tea. Day time 7 days, till 3pm.

552 ✓ **Root & Branch** 1B Jameson St · www.rootandbranch.coffee Ben Craig
6/s6 and Simon Johnston have established a vital destination just off the Ormeau
ATMOS Rd, in a tiny upstairs-downstairs room. They roast on site, and there is always nice
cake to go with that cup of Colombian as you sit on a sheepskin-covered chair.
These guys are serious, enthusiastic, and knowledgeable – when they tell you that
there is a hint of passionfruit in that Kenyan, you can bet it's there. Their Instagram
feed is a work of art, of course. Daytime 7 days.

553 **Guilt Trip Coffee + Donuts** 4 Orangefield Ln +44 79 99071903 ·
6/s6 www.guilttripcoffee.com The Guilt Trip guys have a sense of humour: along
ATMOS with coffee and donuts they also offer Not Coffee, which used to be known as tea,
or hot chocolate. They have the whole Williamsburg vibe down to a T: the lean
room, the vivid lighting, the manifesto, the T-shirts, the branding, the Instagram
feed, the tattoos. Donuts are baked fresh each day, whilst the coffee offer rotates
amongst various roasters. There is usually a long queue out the door. Daytime
Tue-Sat.

554 **The Pocket** 69 University Rd · www.thepocket.coffee A friendly coffee shop
6/s6 in a 150-year-old Georgian building. With beans from Dublin's 3fe, sourdough from
Zac's Bakehouse and pastries from Man Made, the template is bomb-proof. The
bricolage style – decorated with pages from *Alice in Wonderland* and with upcycled
elements – is charming, and when the sun shines there are chairs out front where
you can idly watch students being idle. Great spot to pick up a picnic if you are
heading to Botanic Gardens (568/BELFAST ATTRACTIONS). Daytime Mon-Sat.

555 **Common Grounds** 12 University Ave +44 28 90326589 ·
6/s6 www.commongrounds.co.uk This admirable enterprise donates all its profits
to two charities – Foodbank, and Global Kitchen – and half of the staff members
are volunteers. The cooking can be hit and miss, but the coffee is excellent, and
their baristas have the silverware to show their mastery of the AeroPress and the
tamper. Daytime Mon-Fri.

556 **Co Couture** 7 Chichester St +44 7888 899647 · www.ccocouture.co.uk
6/s6 Co Couture is actually more of a chocolate experience, but the coffee is regarded
respectfully as well, and often accompanied by a little delight, such as a chocolate
caramelised hazelnut with your flat white. They're very serious about what they do
here, and their masterclass sessions in chocolate are popular. Good brews, and the
hot chocolate is just the best. Daytime Mon-Sat.

557 **5A Lockview Road** 5A Lockview Rd · @5ACoffee 5A was originally known as
6/S6 The Bicycle Café, as many cyclists stopped here as they navigated the towpath
DF along the River Lagan at Stranmillis. It's about a minute's walk from the Stranmillis
ATMOS campus, and it's always packed, so the atmosphere is always fizzing. Excellent
coffee from Bailies Roasters, good sandwiches and baked goods, and there are
cycle parking slots, and a water bowl for your best hound. Be prepared to wait for a
table at the weekend. Daytime 7 days.

558 **The National Grande Café** 62 High St +44 28 90311130 ·
6/S6 www.thenationalbelfast.com A handsome converted bank building in the
TERRACE Cathedral Quarter, National Grande arranges a series of bars and clubs over no
fewer than four floors, and has the city's biggest beer garden. But aside from
alcohol, they are into coffee and teas – they have the superb local Suki teas in a
dozen varieties. Coffee is also taken seriously, with a weekly roast, microlot beans,
and AeroPress filters. Good spot for weekend brunch, when the menu runs late
into the afternoon. 9am-1am 7 days, till midnight Sun.

559 **Quartisan** 23 Waring St +44 28 90311116 · @quartisan Beside the CQHQ office
6/S6 suite on Waring St – look for the very funny wall mural – Quartisan is both artisan
food store and casual restaurant. They have acquired an excellent reputation for
doing things well, and with a revamp and a focus towards simple eating, it's a key
address in the zone. Daytime 7 days.

560 **District** 300 Ormeau Rd +44 28 90643603 · www.districtcoffee.co.uk
6/S6 With two superbly styled rooms on the Ormeau Rd and in Stranmillis, District has
quickly come to personify the new Belfast coffee culture: minimal styling; great
drinks; a brunch menu; supper club evenings with cutting-edge guest chefs;
gentrifying neighbourhoods; cold brews; and classy Belfast service. The beans are
from Man Versus Machine in Munich, and local roasters Bailies, and front man
Richard Stitt is a true professional. Second branch on Stranmillis Rd.

Belfast's Main Attractions

561
6/S6

✓ **The Titanic Experience** 1 Olympic Way, Queens Rd, Belfast, N. Ire +4428 90766386 · www.titanicbelfast.com The ever-enigmatic SS Titanic was built in Belfast's Harland & Wolff shipyard in 1911, and as everybody well knows, the White Star Line cruise liner sank on her maiden voyage from Southampton to New York on 15 April 1912. The magnificent Titanic Experience building, with its 72º lean, suggests the ship's hull, and glitters with a facade that is clad in aluminium sheetings that have been folded into asymmetrical shapes, and reflect in the water of Belfast harbour. The exhibition space is enormous; believe them when they say a proper visit takes hours. The building is sited just 100m from where the Titanic was launched; the Belfast skyline is still dominated by the two enormous shipyard cranes, Samson and Goliath. 9am-7pm Jun-Aug, with slight shorter hours rest of year.

562
6/S6
AYR
ATMOS

✓ **Game of Thrones Filming Locations** Self-Drive App Tour · #gotterritory is the hashtag and the App is available for Apple or Android. Hire a car or a motorbike and download the App, and you are on your way to exploring the accessible filming locations from *Game of Thrones*. Just like New Zealand, with *The Lord of the Rings* phenomenon, Belfast has put itself in the centre of the stunning locations that people associate with the Series.

563
6/S6
AYR
ATMOS

✓ **St George's Market** 12 East Bridge St +44 28 90435704 · www.stgeorges.market There are three distinct markets held under the canopy of the beautiful George's Market space. On Fridays, there is a living echo of the old fish market which stretches back decades in the city's history, and it is enhanced by other stallholders selling all manner of bric-a-brac. Saturday brings out the modern food artisans: this is the best day for food shopping. On Sundays, there is cooked food, lots of music, as the zone chills out, and given that little – or nothing – happens in Belfast on a Sunday morning, the market has provided a vital destination. Fri, Sat & Sun -3pm.

564
6/S6
AYR
🖵
FREE
ADMISSION

✓ **Ulster Museum** Botanic Gardens +44 845 6080000 · www.nmni.com The museum is home to a collection of art, artefacts and natural history, and offers the visitor hands-on activities, galleries and shopping. The building itself offers a history of 20thC architecture, with the contrast between the 1914 neo-classical original, and the brutalist 1960's extension. The contemporary art is outstanding, with works by Sickert, Nash, Stanley Spencer, Francis Bacon, Bridget Riley, Ivon Hitchens, Basil Blackshaw, and Colin Midleton amongst many others. There is also a coffee bar, serving goodies from Yellow Door. Daytime Tue-Sun.

565
6/S6
AYR

W5 Science Centre 2 Queen's Quay +44 28 90467700 · www.w5online.co.uk With more than 250 hands-on exhibits, W5 is a science experience that aims to provoke the curiosity and imagination of children. For the under 8s, there is a special play and discover area as well as a Climbit zone. Under 16s can design and build robotics and play virtual sports, and for older children there are exhibits that look at subjects like genetics and flight. All can learn about recycling, optical illusions or space, or take a K'Nex challenge. Terrific, engaging fun. 7 days.

566
6/S6
AYR
FREE
ADMISSION

Belfast Castle Estate & Cave Hill Antrim Rd +44 28 90776925 The silhouette of the basalt rocks at Cave Hill dominating the Belfast skyline is said to have inspired Jonathan Swift to write *Gulliver's Travels*. On the lower slopes you will find Belfast Castle Estate, built in 1870, with panoramic views. Outstanding adventure playground, walks and visitor centre. Cave Hill is named after its five caves, possibly early iron mines carved out during the Neolithic period. Archaeological attractions include McArt's Fort on the summit, an ancient ring fort. During WWII a German bomb, dropped apparently by accident, created a large crater. Private tours on request. Daytime 7 days.

Other Belfast Attractions

567   **HMS Caroline**   Alexandra Dock, Queens Rd · www.hmscaroline.co.uk
6/S6   The *Caroline* is a WWI Battle of Jutland cruiser, and the only remaining ship of the
AYR   Grand and High Seas Fleet. Even before you step aboard, take note of the mooring
system – a feat of engineering that allows the ship to rise and fall with the tide,
without moving laterally. The ship is a 122m light cruiser, built in 1914, which has
been moored in Belfast since 1924 and underwent significant restoration before
reopening in the Titanic Quarter in 2016. 7 days.

568   **Botanic Gardens**   Botanic Avenue +44 28 90314762 Designed by Sir Charles
6/S6   Lanyon, the beautiful Palm House, commenced in 1839, is one of the earliest
AYR   glasshouses made from cast iron and curvilinear glass. The Tropical Ravine, built
FREE ADMISSION   in 1889 and home to some of the oldest seed plants, is currently undergoing
extensive renovation. The parkland is set amongst 28 acres, and is part of the
Queen's Quarter encircling the university. 7 days.

569   **Belfast City Hall**   Donegall Sq +44 28 90320202 Christened 'the stone Titanic'
6/S6   by a former Lord Mayor, the city of Belfast is dominated by the magnificent
AYR   Portland stone Baroque revival mansion that was once a Linen Hall, and is now
FREE ADMISSION   home to Belfast City Council. Few other buildings exude the air of mercantile
wealth and confidence that City Hall reveals about the Edwardian city of Belfast.
Three 45-min tours per day. 7 days.

570   **Belfast Zoo**   Antrim Rd +44 28 90776277 · www.belfastzoo.co.uk As with
6/S6   all zoos, it's the feeding times you're interested in, so if you want to see the
AYR   Sumatran tiger then go Mon-Wed, Fri & Sun. There is a visitor's learning centre and
a Zoovenir shop. Don't miss the crowned sifaka lemur, and do bring your camera
and enter their photo competition. Note, visitors on the autism spectrum and their
friends and families are allowed visit the zoo an hour earlier on special days. 7 days.

571   **Crumlin Road Gaol**   53 Crumlin Rd +44 28 90741500 ·
6/S6   www.crumlinroadgaol.com Locally known as The Crum, for 150 years it was a
AYR   Victorian prison, but now it's a bar and grill, a conference centre, a venue setting,
ATMOS   and a place where visitors can take a guided tour of the gaol and hear of its
detainees, including condemned prisoners, suffragettes, loyalists and republicans,
hunger strikers and law breakers. The tour takes just over an hour. 7 days.

572   **Stormont Parliament Buildings**   Newtownards Rd +44 28 90521802 ·
6/T6   www.parliamentbuildings.org Belfast's Greek/Classical-style Parliament
FREE ADMISSION   Buildings are located just beyond the city centre, overlooking beautiful, sweeping
grounds. Known as "Parliament Buildings" - even though it is only one structure -
because the original plan was to include a separate law courts and administrative
block (neither of which were built). The structure now houses the Northern Ireland
Assembly, which was established after the Good Friday Agreement in 1998. Both
public and private tours are available.

The Best Independent Shops
(Vinyl Stores, Bookshops & Galleries)

GALLERIES

573 **MAC** 10 Exchange St +44 28 90235053 · www.themaclive.com MAC is
6/S6 the Metropolitan Arts Centre, and it's a great big event space with six floors and three galleries in the Cathedral Quarter. Its focus on visual arts is abetted by live performances, dance, theatre, comedy and family workshops. They commendably open for 363 days a year, and the building, by Hackett Hall McKnight, has won many architectural awards. 7 days till 7pm.

574 **Charles Gilmore** 1 Lanyon Quay, Oxford St +44 28 90311666 ·
6/S6 www.charlesgilmore.com We love the fact that Charles Gilmore suggests that if you want to visit his Lanyon Quay gallery, opposite the Law Courts, that you 'bump up onto the pavement in front of the gallery for 10 minutes' Ha! Can't imagine Sotheby's suggesting that! Mr Gilmore has represented many major Irish artists for more than 25 years – Anthony Murphy; Ian Gordon; Neil Shawcross; Emma Connolly – so get the car up on the pavement and never mind the traffic wardens. Daytime Mon-Sat.

575 **James Wray & Co** 14 James St S +44 28 90313013 · www.jameswray.ie
6/S6 Across the lane from Niall McKenna's acclaimed JSS restaurant, the handsome gallery specialises in the work of major modern Irish painters, but there is also 18thC work alongside large modern abstract pieces. Daytime Tue-Sat.

576 **The Eakin Gallery** 27 Lisburn Rd +44 28 90668522 · www.eakingallery.co.uk
6/S6 Alongside a busy framing service, the Eakin specialises in 20thC and 21stC Irish art, showcasing the work of artists such as JB Vallely, Basil Blackshaw, Markey Robinson, William Scott and many others. Daytime Mon-Sat.

577 **The Naughton Gallery at Queen's** University Rd +44 28 90245133 ·
6/S6 www.naughtongallery.org Named for the philanthropists Martin and Carmel Naughton, this visual arts gallery above the main hall of the university presents up to eight exhibitions per year, and is regarded as one of the best university galleries. Daytime Tue-Sun.

578 **Belfast Exposed** 23 Donegall St +44 28 90230965 ·
6/S6 www.belfastexposed.org Gallery of contemporary photographic works, from both local and international photographers. In addition to the exhibitions, they also run photographic courses and workshops. The Belfast Exposed Futures gallery features the work of new Northern Irish practitioners, and presents a graduate award. Daytime Tue-Sat.

VINYL STORES

579 ✓ **Sick Records** 78 North St +44 28 90319358 · @sickrecordsbelfast
6/S6 'Stay sick, kids!' advise the cool school heads who run Sick Records. So if you
ATMOS want to be the sickest cat with that new copy of *Space, Energy & Light: Experimental Electronic and Acoustic Soundscapes 1961-1988*, or the triple blue vinyl edition of *OK Computer* then you need to get over to North St. Yes, they do have Kendrick and Bowie, but it's the queer gear in Sick Records that is the big attraction. Excellent. Daytime Mon-Sat.

580 **Dragon Records** 58 Wellington Pl +44 7542 285995 ·
6/S6   @DragonRecordsBelfast Jeff Doherty's, shop, up the stairs at the corner
of Wellington Pl and below the tattoo parlour, has been rejuvenated with the
increased interest in vinyl, so climb the stairs if you want some Russ Meyer
soundtracks or Thai Beat A Go Go. Daytime Mon-Sat.

581 **Head** Unit 28, Castlecourt +44 28 90237226 · www.wearehead.com Head
6/S6   is part of a small chain of record stores – they are in Galway, Dublin and
Leamington Spa also – and their Belfast store in Castlecourt is renowned for
excellent staff. New releases and choice second-hand vinyl, DVDs and audio kit
as well. Daytime 7 days.

582 **Belfast Underground Records** 33 Queen St +44 28 95439405 ·
6/S6   www.belfastunderground.co.uk Look for the bright orange sign on Queen
ATMOS   St, and you will find more than just a record store. Underground also operates a
radio station – the station room is in the corner of the store and has five webcams
for streaming – a recording studio and a record label. Allow plenty of time for
browsing. Daytime Mon-Sat.

BOOK SHOPS

583 ✓ **No Alibis** 83 Botanic Ave +44 28 90319601 · www.noallibis.com
6/S6   No Alibis is the most famous bookstore in the city, and an iconic part of
ATMOS   Belfast's intellectual life. 'Without a doubt Northern Ireland's coolest bookshop'
gushed *The Guardian*. Lots of crime books, but also lots of signings, gigs, book
launches and noirish pulp. Excellent. Daytime 7 days, from 1pm Sun.

584 **Keats & Chapman** 21 North St +44 28 90776838 ·
6/S6   www.keatsandchapman.com Bill Burlingham's shop, piled from floor to
ATMOS   ceiling with books, and benefitting hugely from the boss's acumen, is a legendary
North St address. It has been described as 'a labyrinth of literature' and every genre
of book is on the shelves, and if you find some Flann O'Brien, it will explain the
name.

585 **Belfast Books Limited** 112 York Rd +44 28 90751466 · www.belfastbooks.co.uk
6/S6   BBL is about a mile from the city centre, on York Rd. Strong emphasis on books
about NI, in addition to a wide array of mainstream titles, and the store is an
important community hub. Daytime Mon-Sat.

586 **War On Want** 24 Botanic Ave +44 28 90247773 Yes, it's a charity
6/S6   bookstore, but WOW is a highly-regarded charity bookstore. Lots of new stock
is always carefully arranged and displayed, and prices are extremely keen.
Daytime Mon-Sat.

the
Best
of Cork

The Best Places to Stay in Cork

587
3/J21
182 ROOMS
MED-EXP
ATMOS

✓ **The River Lee** Western Rd +353 21 4252700 ·
www.doylecollection.com Every detail of the River Lee operation is considered, from the speedy reply to your booking and the information offered about the city, the superb breakfasts, the excellent bars and public rooms, the comfortable dining room. The character of the hotel has come together over time, and this means that whilst there is a confidence about the team, there is none of that self-congratulation that mars so many boutique hotels. These guys are hungry to impress you, from the moment you walk in. Pool and health club.

588
3/J21
48 ROOMS
MED-INX

Lancaster Lodge Lancaster Quay, Western Rd +353 21 4251125 ·
www.lancasterlodge.com There is a pared-back quality to the rooms and the public spaces in Lancaster Lodge, hard by the River Lee on the Western Rd. It's an ascetic aesthetic: they understand that less is more when it comes to design and interiors, so the feng shui is just spot on. The design means that Lancaster Lodge doesn't feel like a standard hotel – the 'boutique hotel' moniker they use to describe themselves really does apply here, especially if you get one of the superior rooms. Great value.

589
3/J21
93 ROOMS
ATMOS
EXP

Maryborough Hotel Maryborough Hill, Douglas +353 21 4365555 ·
www.maryborough.com Hidden away in 18 acres of mature grounds S of the city, in Douglas, the Maryborough is one of the city's most handsome mansions, built in 1710 by one of the city's merchant princes, Richard Newenham. The modern wing of the house has almost 100 rooms plus a spa and a conference wing. Over the years we have found the staff to be uniformly excellent, and Maryborough is a great escape, a city hotel away from the city.
EAT in Bellini's Restaurant. Chef Gemma Murphy is an ambitious cook, and she is helped by having a vegetable and herb garden to supplement her favoured artisan ingredients. Her cooking is colourful and creative. Here is a talent to watch. Also specialise in Afternoon Tea.

590
3/J21
200 ROOMS
MED.EXP

Clayton Hotel Lapps Quay +353 21 4224900 ·
www.claytonhotelcorkcity.com The Clayton has a great location – overlooking the river on Lapp's Quay – and comfortable rooms, but it is their English Market dinner menu, in the Globe Restaurant, that shows the ambition of this re-branded destination. This is one of the best ways to get the artisan flavours of the city, and there are Cork city craft beers to pair with the dishes.

591
3/J21
48 ROOMS
ATMOS
LOTS

Hayfield Manor Perrott Ave, College Rd +353 21 4845900 ·
www.hayfieldmanor.ie We all need a bit of de luxe treatment now and then, and that's what they deliver in Hayfield Manor, the grand former home of retail titans the Musgrave family, tucked away at the rear of University College Cork. Liveried staff, deep pile carpets and sumptuous beds, and an aura of peace at the edge of the city, make for a blast of luxury.

592 **Cork International Hotel** Cork Airport Business Park +353 21 4549800 ·
3/J21   www.corkinternationalairporthotel.com Manager Aaron Mansworth has
145 ROOMS   a great crew working alongside him in the Cork International Hotel and, if you
MED.INX   presumed that an hotel sited at an airport couldn't be anything other than an
FF   indifferent destination for red-eye fliers, think again. The rooms far exceed
expectations, the public spaces are fleek, and the cooking is focused and delicious.
In the New Yorker bar the menus appear conventional but the food is full of flavour.
Breakfast is cooked at a teppanyaki-style grill, and is also carefully achieved.
Superfast broadband.

593 **The Montenotte Hotel** Montenotte +353 21 4530050 ·
3/J21   www.themontenottehotel.com You get some of the finest views of Cork city
107 ROOMS   from the elevated perch of the Montenotte Hotel, particularly from the Panorama
EXP   Bistro and Terrace, and the hotel has benefited hugely from a big spend on
rooms and facilities by the Whelehan family. There is a fine swimming pool, good
apartments for longer stays, there is the Cameo cinema, and above all there are
engaged staff who really look after you. The city centre is a brief walk down the hill,
and a steep walk back.

594 **Hotel Isaacs** 48 MacCurtain St +353 21 4500011 · www.isaacs.ie A major
3/J21   upgrade of the deluxe rooms brought the accommodation in Isaac's in line with its
47 ROOMS   smartly refurbished Greenes restaurant, one of the city's best places to eat. Their
MED.EX   apartments are extremely useful for sleeping families at a decent cost in the city
centre, whilst the classic rooms are boxy and need the upgrade. But, the location is
superb, there is parking just around the corner.
     EAT Greenes Restaurant (Report: 600/MODERN CORK COOKING) and Cask (Report:
667/COCKTAILS) are two happening destinations.

595 **The Metropole Hotel** MacCurtain St +353 21 4643700 ·
3/J21   www.themetropolehotel.ie Owned by the same people behind the fine
112 ROOMS   Cork International and Airport Hotels, this 120-year-old piece of Cork's history
MED.INX   is being developed, big time, in conjunction with a brand new footbridge across
the River Lee. When completed, a 400-room complex with retail is promised,
and the new bridge should bring the Victorian Quarter close to the heart of
the city.

596 **Cork Airport Hotel** Cork Airport +353 21 4947500 ·
3/J21   www.corkairporthotel.com The simpler sister hotel to the plush
81 ROOMS   Cork International, the hotel is as close to the terminal as you can get. Lots of
MED.INX   thoughtful features: free parking; superfast broadband; gym; kids' playroom, and
the rooms are well appointed. Olivo Restaurant has an Italian theme.

597 **The Imperial Hotel Cork** South Mall +353 21 4274040 ·
3/J21   www.flynnhotels.com One of a small chain of Irish hotels owned by the Flynn
125 ROOMS   family, the Imperial's location on South Mall is A1, which makes it the perfect
MED.EXP   place to arrange to meet up in the bar and the lobby, as well as an ideal city
centre location for staying over. The hotel has been a mainstay of Cork city for two
centuries, and Charles Dickens stayed here, as did Michael Collins, whilst Franz
Liszt gave a recital in the hotel in 1843.

Best Modern Cork Cooking

598
3/J21
MED.EXP

✓✓ **Cafe Paradiso** 16 Lancaster Quay · +353 21 4277939 · www.cafeparadiso.ie When it opened in Oct 1993, Cafe Paradiso was already offering the food of the future, and chef-proprietor Denis Cotter and his business partner, Ger O'Toole, haven't stopped pushing the envelope in this pretty room on the Western Rd, and they are still 20 years ahead of everyone. The cooking in Paradiso doesn't use meat, but it's facile to call it vegetarian cooking. Instead, it's a cuisine open to every influence and its artful assemblage of these strands produces stunning food. May be the finest vegetarian restaurant in Europe. Dinner Mon-Sat.

599
3/J21
MED.INX
ATMOS

✓ **Farmgate Cafe** English Market · +353 21 4278134 · www.farmgate.ie Most restaurants look forwards for inspiration, but Cork's Farmgate Café, upstairs in the middle of Cork's English Market, behaves like an Italian restaurant: respecting the tradition, acknowledging the past, learning from the ancestors. The Café's menus are directed by the foods sold in the market – the tripe, the fish and shellfish, the corned beef, the mutton, the spuds and cabbage. Today, Rebecca Harte, and Mirco Fondrini, who runs the room, continue that proud tradition of culinary curatorship, and for many, Farmgate Café is a national treasure. Daytime Mon-Sat.

600
3/J21
EXP

✓ **Greenes Restaurant** 48 MacCurtain St + 353 21 4500011 · www.greenesrestaurant.com Bryan McCarthy's cooking in Greenes utilises all the on-trend techniques yet there is no doubt that every plate he sends out is his alone, and has his signature style. He creates a weave of ingredients but his goal is always the harmonious interaction of every ingredient. The arrival of the excellent sister establishment, Cask cocktail bar, just across the alleyway from the restaurant, on the middle of MacCurtain St, N of the river, is the perfect place for pre-dinner cocktails before heading in for some of the city's best cooking. Lunch & dinner Tue-Sat.

601
3/J21
MED.INX
ATMOS

✓ **Crawford Gallery Cafe** Crawford Gallery, Emmet Pl · +353 21 4274415 · www.crawfordartgallery.ie/dining 'We like to cook simple food with local ingredients', says Sinead Doran, chef at Cork's city centre Crawford Art Gallery, and she puts that mantra on the plate. Her food has no truck with the whims of fashion, so expect roasted bone marrow with parsley salad and sourdough; lamb's kidneys; leek and mature Coolea cheese tart. Ms Doran can also nail Middle Eastern chicken with bulgur salad as if she hailed from the Levant. Terrific staff work in one of the city's sweetest rooms, at the rear of the Gallery itself, and whilst the Crawford may be a 30-year-veteran, the cooking eats like the new kid in town. Great also for coffee and proper cakes at any time. Lunch Mon-Sat.

602
3/J21
MED.INX
ATMOS

✓ **Elbow Lane** 4 Oliver Plunkett St +353 21 2390479 · www.elbowlane.ie A fire which gutted the tiny interior of Elbow lane in late-2016 scarcely dented the momentum of Conrad Howard's flagship brew and smokehouse. Elbow Lane is the room that everyone wants to be in, so you need to arrive early as they don't take bookings. And when you do get seated in this little L-shaped room, start with one of their quintet of nano-brews, and match them with some artful cooking. This is in-your-face food, wild and punchy with smoky, deep flavours, and the people of Cork have taken to it as to the manner born. Dinner 7 days.

603
3/J21
MED.INX

✓ **Nash 19** 19 Princes St +353 21 4270880 · www.nash19.com Nash 19 is a place of subtle, classy elegance, and the pleasure of eating here is heightened by the brilliance of the staff: where does owner Claire Nash find all these personable, helpful young women? Ms Nash never lets anything slip, and attention to detail is paramount in every aspect. Breakfast is one of the city's best, lunch sees the queue go out the door. There are also rotating artworks to enjoy, and nice foods to take away from their pantry. Daytime Mon-Sat.

The Best Casual Restaurants & Cafés

604
3/J21
MED.INX

✓Ali's Kitchen Rory Gallagher Pl +353 21 2390681 · www.aliskitchencork.com Ali Honour is one fine cook, and she has a lean, Californian-style room in Rory Gallagher Pl to showcase her great breads, and the wonderful things she does with them. Ali's Kitchen is a great boon to the city, a destination with a great vibe where everything from the apple and vanilla custard doughnut to the rye poolish is top-notch. Daytime 7 days.

605
3/J21
CHP

✓The Rocket Man Food Co 38 Princes St · www.therocketman.ie 'Not fast food,' says Rocket Man supremo Jack Crotty, so this particular Rocket Man is not burning out his fuse. Instead, Mr Crotty has created a trio of key Cork destinations for some of the city's most imaginative food. Princes St is where you go for vibrant plant-based cooking. EAST in Winthrop Arcade, across from the GPO, is home to Mr Crotty's excellent riff on falafels. He's also at Mahon Point Farmers' Market & Douglas Farmers' Market and TGP opening up on Evergreen St.

606
3/J21
CHP

✓Idaho Café 19 Caroline St · www.idahocafe.ie Idaho expresses what may be the highest ideal in hospitality: it does what it does as well as it can do it, every day. It delivers the magic moments, and even with all its limitations – the room is tiny, somewhat cramped, always packed – it's a room you return to for those lovely breakfasts, that quiet mid-afternoon moment with a good cup of tea and a slice of cake. Richard and Mairead run a Cork institution, and don't miss their teeny tiny Idaho Gelato. Daytime Tue-Sat.

607
3/J21
MED.INX

✓Jacques 23 Oliver Plunkett St +353 21 4277387 · www.jacquesrestaurant.ie Jacque and Eithne Barry have been doing the good thing in Cork for almost 40 years, successfully keeping their menus and wine offering up to date, whilst always refining and finessing their food to embrace new styles and flavours. You can graze on tapas plates, or go the whole hog with the a la carte which offers lots of the best Co Cork ingredients. There are two entrances, just few doors from the GPO, in the centre of town. Lunch & dinner Mon-Sat.

608
3/J21
MED.INX

✓Orso 8 Pembroke St +353 21 2438000 · www.orso.ie Orso has brought an Ottolenghi influence to leafy Pembroke St, in the centre of Cork, and their menu of flatbreads, spicy salads, Lebanese pies and brilliant sweet treats means it's frequently impossible to get a seat. Coffee is expertly served – these guys are serious baristas – Elbow Lane beers are available by the bottle, and the cocktail list is short and smart. Daytime Mon-Sat, Dinner Tue-Sat.

609
3/J21
MED.EXP

Market Lane 5-6 Oliver Plunkett St +353 21 4274710 · www.marketlane.ie Market Lane is the conventional sister to the dynamic Orso and Elbow Lane members of the family, with more straight-ahead cooking that suits a wider demographic. It's always, always busy, and the set menus offer very good value. Lunch & dinner 7 days.

610
3/J21
MED.EXP

Cornstore Cornmarket St +353 21 4274777 · www.cornstore.ie Cornstore has a sister branch in Limerick city, and both are well-respected for reliable and confident cooking in bustling, fun rooms. Their steaks – dry-aged in house with Himalayan salt — are particularly good. They don't reinvent the wheel, they just concentrate on getting the classics rights. Good cocktails, craft beers and ciders. Lunch & dinner 7 days. Cornstore Limerick is open on Thomas St. +353 61 609000.

611   **Electric** 41 South Mall +353 21 4222990 · www.electriccork.ie Housed in
3/J21   one of the city's most beautiful art deco buildings, which backs on to the River Lee,
MED.EXP   Electric manages the artful job of offering something for everyone. The upstairs
TERRACE   Fishbar has one of the best balconies in the country looking out on the river and
ATMOS   the weir, whilst downstairs is a busy bar that does a bustling lunchtime trade, and
  great staff hold the whole shebang together. Lunch & dinner 7 days. Fishbar open
  for dinner.

612   **Dockland** Lapps Quay +353 21 4273987 · @DocklandCork Harold and Beth's
3/J21   Dockland is a great room, one of those city spaces where the comfort encourages
MED.EXP   you to exhale deeply as you sink into a deep, comfortable banquette. Harold's
  richly savoury cooking drives home this comfort apex. Value for money is excellent
  and it's an excellent weekend haunt for brunch and Bloody Marys – there are no
  fewer than half-a-dozen BMs to choose from to go with your Breakfast in Bread.
  Open all Day.

613   **Quinlan's Seafood Bar** 14 Princes St +353 21 2418222 · www.seafoodbar.ie
3/J21   Best known for the popular restaurants in towns like Killarney and Tralee, Quinlan's
MED.INX   have recently refurbished their Cork flagship. With their own fleet of fishing boats
  guaranteeing pristine fish, there is really only one way to go here. Lovely staff bring
  it all home. Lunch & dinner 7 days.

614   **House Cafe** Cork Opera House, Emmet Place +353 21 4270022 ·
3/J21   www.corkoperahouse.ie House is funky. Victor and Stephen operate a little
MED.INX   kitchen and counter to the left of the lobby in the Opera House, with some stools
  and some seats. But there is imagination in the cooking, the foods are cleverly
  sourced from the Cork markets, and it's a choice coffee stop. Good breakfasts, nice
  vibe. Open daytime Mon-Sat and every occasion the Opera House stages an event.

615   **Cafe Gusto** City Quarter, Lapp's Quay +353 21 4224099 · www.cafegusto.com
3/J21   It's almost 20 years since Gusto first opened on Washington St, and during that time
CHP   it has been a key element of Cork's identity as a city for good food. The menus play
TERRACE   to the great standards of the Mediterranean diet and everything is done accurately,
  and with consistency and imagination. Daytime Mon-Sat. There is a second branch
  of Café Gusto at 3 Washington St +353 21 425446

616   **The Workshop** Lios Cross, Ballygarvan +353 21 2373033 ·
3/J21   www.theworkshopcork.com Tucked away amidst the winding, climbing roads
CHP   around Cork's airport, and surprisingly close to the main runway of the airport
  itself, The Workshop is quaint, but serious about serving good, true cooking. Soups,
  sandwiches and salads are on the menu, all based on local ingredients. It's all
  very charming, the room is cosy, and there just might be some antique or piece of
  vintage gear that takes your eye. Daytime Tue-Sun.

617   **The Natural Foods Bakery** 26 Paul St +353 21 4614555 ·
3/J21   www.thenaturalfoodsbakery.com The Natural is one of the great Cork city
CHP   pioneers, renowned for singular baking – don't miss the cherry buns – but it's also
  the place for good soups, homemade breads, nice pies, fresh salads. Daytime Mon-
  Sat. Two other branches at Fitzgerald's Park and Blackrock, both open 7 days.

Best Vegetarian & Vegan Restaurants

618 **Quay Co-Op** 24 Sullivan's Quay +353 21 4317026 · www.quaycoop.com
3/J21 Thirty five years of service to the good people of Cork is the proud record of the
CHP left-field collective that is the Quay Co-Op. Their stately building on Sullivan's Quay
houses an enormous wholefood shop, and upstairs in the restaurant is the home of
Cork city vegetarian cooking. Lunch & dinner 7 days. Deli counter and coffee dock
with food available to eat in or take away.

619 **Umi Falafel** 11 Academy St +353 21 4274466 · www.umifalafel.ie The Cork
3/J21 city centre branch of the Dublin falafel chain is just off Patrick St. Most of the
CHP choices in their sandwiches, salads and mezze are vegan, and value for money is
very keen. Lunch & dinner 7 days.

620 **143V** Lwr Glanmore Rd +353 85 7651584 · @143vcork The ethos here in
3/J21 this little vegan hairdresser-turned restaurant, has something of a millennial
CHP feel: simple; unadorned; efficient. Find it close to Kent railway station, in a part of
the city that has gotten neglected over the last decade. The food is light, simple
and straightforward. The blackboard menu is smart and concise, and the room is
charming. All day till 8pm 7 days.

✓✓ **Iyer's** Unique southern Indian brahmin vegetarian cooking from Gautham
Iyer, who makes every single thing from scratch with his own hands.
Report: 638/INDIAN.

✓✓ **Café Paradiso** Café P may be the best vegetarian restaurant in Europe,
and has been the standard for vegetarian food in Cork for 25 years.
Report: 598/BEST MODERN CORK COOKING.

The Best Burgers & Steaks

621 ✓ **Coqbull** 5 French Church St +353 21 4278444 · www.coqbull.com
3/J21   Coqbull has been a hit since day one, and the fizzing, fun atmosphere and
MED.INX good, savoury cooking explains why. Start with a Coqtail, then wade into their
ATMOS   rotisserie chicken and burger selection. Superb staff maintain the party atmosphere
FF   24/7, which is however absent in the upstairs room. Lunch & dinner 7 days. There
is a second branch in Limerick.

622 **White Rabbit Bar & BBQ** 56 MacCurtain St +353 21 4552222 ·
3/J21   @whiterabbitcork The barbecue arrives on aluminium trays covered with
MED.INX white paper at this busy bar and restaurant at the Montenotte end of MacCurtain
St. Southern barbecue is their thing – beef brisket with Mi Daza stout barbecue
sauce; pork ribs with hot and tangy sauce; chilli nachos, in an enormous portion.
Beers from Rising Sons Brewery hit the right Cork city note. Lunch & dinner 7 days.

623 **Holy Smoke** Little Hanover St +353 21 4273000 · @HolySmokeCork
3/J21   John Relihan came back from his tenure as Jamie Oliver's UK pitmaster in
MED.INX Barbecoa to open up Holy Smoke. It's a big, industrial-chic space, a former
bonded warehouse tucked away in Little Hanover St, so the feel is just right for
expert barbecue, and some good burgers and a char-grilled flat iron steak. Decent
selection of beers, but the wine choice is petite. Dinner Wed-Sun.

624 **The Spitjack** 34 Washington St +353 21 239 0613 · www.thespitjack.com
3/J21   Richard Gavin's Washington St venture, in the midst of Cork's newly minted
MED.INX gourmet ghetto, is a rotisserie brasserie, something new for the city. The modern,
smart looking room is complemented by friendly staff, frequently checking that all
is to your taste, as well as the sight of large tanks where the homemade probiotic
drinks are maturing. Richard and Laura's mission was to open a restaurant with
a focus on high-quality Irish meat, and they have done just that. Daytime and
dinner 7 days.

625 **Gourmet Burger Bistro** 8 Bridge St +353 21 4505404 ·
3/J21   www.gourmetburgerbistro.ie Michael Condon has always used organically-
MED.INX reared beef and lamb in his burgers in GBB, a little room a few metres north of the
river on Bridge St.The style is simpler than some of the kitchen sink offers you find
elsewhere, and all the better for it. Small selection of wines and craft beers. Lunch
& dinner 7 days.

626 **Son of a Bun** 29 MacCurtain St +353 21 4508738 · www.sonofabun.ie Niall
3/J21   and Amanda O'Regan's bright, open-plan, exposed-brick room has been part of
MED.INX the MacCurtain St, north-of-the-river renaissance. They create a special burger
ATMOS   each month with a funky title – The Edible Hulk; Moulin Rouge, Sgt. Pepper; Mac
FF   Attack – which they advertise on murals across the city. Great fun, and we would
love to see a tie-up with a limited-edition craft beef for each new burger. Lunch
& dinner 7 days.

627 **West Cork Burger Company** Washington Street +353 21 2410300 · www.
3/J21   westcorkburgercompany.com Henry Hegarty made his reputation running
CHP   the excellent Wokabout market stalls, so he's a veteran of the food business.
His first bricks and mortar base on Washington Street, run with Cian Handley
and butcher Michael Twomey, offers a signature West Cork wagyu beef burger
alongside an Aberdeen Angus burger, and the team have thought through every
element. Good drinks, nice up-cycled design style and terrific staff makes for a
really rockin' room. Lunch & Dinner 7 days.

628 **Liberty Grill** 32 Washington St +353 21 4271049 · www.libertygrill.ie
3/J21   The Liberty is as rock-steady as a diner gets, with super-tasty brunch dishes
MED.INX served between noon and 5pm each day. The menu is extensive – from crab open
sandwich to six choices of burger – and the room always has a great vibe. Liberty
may be a veteran address in Cork's food zone on Washington St, but it's ever
youthful. Lunch & dinner Mon-Sat.

629 **Cafe Fresco** Glucksman Gallery UCD, Cork · www.glucksman.org
3/J21   The gorgeous Glucksman, in the midst of University College Cork's idyllic campus,
CHP   is just the place for weekend brunch in Fresco, their basement café, followed by a
trip round the gallery, a visit to the bookshop, then a stroll around the leafy groves
of academia. Quite lovely. Daytime Tue-Sat.

✓ **The River Lee Hotel** Sitting on the covered terrace of The Weir Rooms, looking
out on the River Lee whilst enjoying a smoked Cork boi sausage with chimichurri
is pretty hard to beat. Great location for meeting up. Report: 587/PLACES TO STAY.

✓ **Arthur Mayne's** Sunday brunch in this wonderfully kooky 120-year-old
pharmacy on Pembroke St offers nice, left-field cooking: little mermaid;
Benedictine; florence & the machine. Report: 665/WINE BARS.

✓ **Castle Cafe** Out in Blackrock, at the 16thC castle which is home to the
Observatory, the Castle Café offers one of the nicest al fresco terraces outside
the Café to eat, as well as comfy dining rooms. Brunch is inventive – corn and
feta cakes; ricotta pancakes; kiddie breakfast – and is served 7 days a week.
Report: 680/CORK ATTRACTIONS.

✓ **Ali's Kitchen** Some of the city's best baking is here in Rory Gallagher Place,
along with black pudding hash, mushroom florentine, hot smoked salmon.
Report: 604/CASUAL RESTAURANTS.

✓ **Crawford Gallery Cafe** The ground floor café in the city-centre Crawford is
one of the city's best rooms, with bright vivid brunch dishes: eggy brioche with
Kanturk bacon; poached eggs and Hederman's smoked salmon. Brunch 9am-4pm
Sat. Report: 601/MODERN CORK COOKING.

✓ **Nash 19** Claire Nash's benchmark restaurant has been a Cork icon for
25 years, and they roll out the brunch specials on Sat on Princes St: Blooming
Benedict with Crowe's bacon; eggs Royale with Arbutus toast. Brunch Sat. Report:
603/MODERN CORK COOKING.

Sober Lane Ernest Cantillon's hugely popular bar and courtyard, on Sullivan's
Quay close to the river, has a whacky brunch menu at the weekends, with croque
madame; brunch pizza, chorizo burrito. Dinner Mon-Fri, brunch & dinner Sat & Sun.
Report: 648/CRACKING CORK PUBS.

Electric Brunch is served upstairs, so you get views of the River Lee, Trinity Church
and St Fin Barre's Cathedral along with oysters mignonette; black pudding salad; wild
mushroom ragu. Brunch Sat & Sun noon-3pm. Report: 611/CASUAL RESTAURANTS.

The Sextant This clamorously busy bar, on the corner of the bridge over the
River Lee at Albert St, has a good reputation for its Sun brunch, served between
11am and 3.30pm. Report: 651/CRACKING CORK PUBS.

The Best Pizza

630
3/J21
CHP

✓**Palmento Pizza** Ballinlough, S Douglas Rd +353 21 4365241 ·
www.palmento.ie The Tavolieri family has been making fine pizzas in
Cork since 1972, but with Palmento Pizza, a big 55-seater in Douglas, Elio
Tavolieri has raised the bar. His base is a two-year-old sourdough starter, given
a 20-hour prove. Well-sourced ingredients and fast cooking in wood-burning
oven delivers a signature Neapolitan pizza with perfect charring; perfect
chewiness. Seasonal beers and European wines bring on the good times.
Dinner 7 days. Delivery to Douglas, Rochestown, Maryborough, Blackrock,
Ballintemple, Ballinlough, South Douglas Rd.

631
3/J21
CHP

Fast Al's Paradise Place · www.fastals.ie Alan Goulding is the pizza hero
of Cork city. All the best restaurant chefs respect and admire this guy and his
perfectionist approach to good pizza. He set the benchmark in the city, and he
has maintained that benchmark for almost 20 years. Anytime you have a slice
of Al's Fasthamlet, or the Alfather, is a good time indeed, and the staff are as
witty as it gets. Lunch & dinner 7 days. Other branches opposite the GPO at
Pembroke St and College Rd (5 mins from UCC).

632
3/J21
CHP

Volcano Wood Fired Pizza Mahon Point Market +353 86 7930062 ·
www.volcano.ie Simon Mould makes great pizzas, and at the markets
around Cork city where he brings his portable, home-built pizza ovens and sets
up his canopies, you will always find a long queue. Mr Mould and his team are
feverishly imaginative, so whilst there are Neapolitan and Sicilian classics, the
funky inventions are often the ones to go for: Ballinrostig gouda with cumin;
aubergine and feta; chorizo with jalapeno. Thurs 10am-3pm. Also at Wilton,
Tues, Midleton Sat, and Douglas markets.

633
3/J21
CHP

Iago 9 Princes St +353 21 4277047 · @Iago This benchmark delicatessen
sells pizza dough, to go, and all the other things you need to make great pizza.
Daytime Mon-Sat.

Sober Lane Report: 641/CRACKING CORK PUBS.

SPANISH

634 **Feed Your Senses** 27 Washington St West +353 21 4274633 ·
3/J21 @feedyoursense Rosa and Vincente have one of the tiniest rooms on
MED.INX Washington St, but the cosiness of Alimenta tus Sentidos is part of the charm and, when everyone is packed in sardine-tight and their good Spanish wines are flowing, no one cares that it's cheek-by-jowl eating. The food is Tapas' Greatest Hits and it's executed precisely and respectfully. The Spanish wines which they import themselves are also available to take away. Dinner Tue-Sun.

FRENCH

635 **Les Gourmandises** 17 Cook St +353 21 4251959 · www.lesgourmandises.ie
3/J21 Chef-patron Pat Kiely continues to fly the flag for classic-era French cooking in his
MED.EXP intimate Cook St restaurant, situated just down from the central Oliver Plunkett St. Soizic Kiely looks after the wines with winning expertise. Dinner Mon-Sat. The team behind Les Gourmandises supply the food for The Woodford Bar in the city centre. Report: 647/CRACKING CORK PUBS.

MEDITERRANEAN

636 **Star Anise** 4 Bridge St +353 21 4551635 · www.staranise.ie Virginie Sarrazin's
3/J21 chic little restaurant, just north of the river in the Victorian Quarter, is ageless
MED.EXP and unpretentious. The kitchen knows its way around the flavours of the Med blindfolded, which means the cooking is both delicious, and reliable. The wine list offers value; service is charming and efficient. Dinner Tue-Sat.

The Best Ethnic Restaurants

JAPANESE

637   ✓✓ **Miyazaki** 1A Evergreen St +353 21 4312716 · @miyazakicork
3/J21   Takashi Miyazaki's cooking, served in a takeaway with five little stools and
CHP   a counter, has won extraordinary acclaim, and has revealed to Irish people the
ATMOS   majesty of true Japanese cooking. You will spot the mural of the geisha as you
trudge up the hill from the river, at much the same time as you spot the queue
snaking out the door but, if ever cooking was worth the wait, this is it. Every dish
looks like a work of art, and the flavours are extraordinary. Make sure to ask about
the daily specials, which is where Mr Miyazaki and his team wheel out the
fireworks. Unique. A second outpost, ichigo ichie, close to the courthouse, is
planned as we write, which will have 30 seats and kaiseki-style dishes. Tue-Sun
from 1pm.

INDIAN

638   ✓✓ **Iyer's** 38 Pope's Quay +353 87 6409079 Iyer's could not be simpler.
3/J21   There are about seven tables, in a little room with a counter, on Pope's
CHP   Quay, north of the River Lee. The food is southern Indian vegetarian cooking, the
food of Gautham Iyer's birth place, Tamil Nadu, cooked according to Ayurvedic
principles, laid down millennia ago in the Vedic texts. The simplicity is purposeful:
Mr Iyer wants your focus to be on his cooking, and his cooking is like nothing else
in Ireland. Everything is made by Gautham Iyer, by hand, and the patience and the
love shines from every bite. Lunch Tue-Sat.

ASIAN

639   **Ramen Asian Street Food** Anglesea St +353 21 4317116 · www.ramen.ie
3/J21   Ramen serves street-smart Asian dishes – noodles; curries; and wok specials – and
MED.INX   it's a bomb-proof operation that appeals to everyone: it's not unusual to see a
FF   bunch of tweenies eating in here without a parent in sight. Students from UCC tend
to pack out the Dennehy's Corner branch, and don't forget to fill your cone with
soft-serve before you leave. Lunch & dinner 7 days. You can find Ramen branches
in Dennehy's Cross, Ballincollig, Douglas, Midleton, Wexford and Limerick.

Cracking Cork Pubs

640
3/J21
ATMOS
✓ Franciscan Well Brew Pub 14B North Mall +353 21 4393434 · www.franciscanwellbrewery.com The Franny Well was the first of a new generation of micro-brewery pubs in Cork city, when it opened in 1998. Set back through an archway on the elegant North Mall, the site was originally a Franciscan monastery, with a well that was believed to have curative powers. In addition to their signature beers, they conduct brewery tours, and have trad and jazz sessions. There is also a very fine beer garden, and some rather good pizzas from their Pompeii Pizza oven. The beers are now widely available – Molson Coors bought over the brewery in 2013 – but there's still nothing like enjoying a pint of Rebel Red in the beer garden.

641
3/J21
✓ The Hi-B 108 Oliver Plunkett St +353 21 4272758 · @HIBCork Switch off your mobile phone before climbing the stairs up to the legendary Hi-B, beside the chemist's shop on the corner of Oliver Plunkett St. Failure to do so may incur the displeasure of the owner, and get you ejected, a proud fate that will forever make you a true citizen of Cork. The Hi-B is unchanging, ageless, a tabernacle for drinking and talking, and maybe reciting a bit of poetry.

642
3/J21
ATMOS
✓ The Bierhaus Pope's Quay +353 21 4551648 · www.thebierhauscork.com Dave O'Leary's bar on Pope's Quay is a craft beer lover's heaven, and it has been one of the significant destinations on the fast-awakening Pope's Quay. They offer cask ales; serve up to 18 guest taps in addition to their own regular taps, and great new discoveries are just waiting for you in this Cork classic.

643
3/J21
Abbot's Ale House 17 Devonshire St, Shandon +353 21 4507116 There is an incredible array of craft beers for sale in the off licence on the ground floor of Abbot's, and upstairs the choice is just as fine, served by friendly, easy-going staff who know their game backwards.

644
3/J21
The Oyster Tavern 4 Market Ln, St Patrick's St +353 21 7355677 'A famous and elegant tavern' is how the Bushmills Irish Pub Guide described Cork's legendary Oyster Tavern, way back in 1994. Newly rebirthed and refurbed, this great destination, down a laneway leading into the English Market, has a glam, 1920's feel to the interior with tiled floors, and high seating giving it something of the feel of an English pub. Good food is sourced from the market and they can make a cracking bowl of chowder, and the manner of the staff is pure Cork.

645
3/J21
ATMOS
Canty's Bar 6 Pembroke St +353 21 4270566 · @CantysBar Daniel Canty first put his name over the pub on Pembroke St, way back in 1892. Owner Ger Buttimer keeps the pub in the old style, organises lots of music sessions, and there is always a great atmosphere.

646
3/J21
The Long Valley Bar Winthrop St +353 21 4272144 · www.thelongvalleybar.com There was a time when stern-faced ladies wearing white coats used to man the bar at The Long Valley, serving everyone big door-step sandwiches stuffed with spiced beef, all in an almost monastic silence. Whilst we are nostalgic for those days, the bar has smartened up and moved on, and installed televisions, but it's still a lovely spot for a pint of Beamish.

647
3/J21
The Woodford Paul St +353 21 4253931 · www.thewoodford.ie The Woodford is notable for some fine gastropub cooking, executed in association with Pat Kiely, of Les Gourmandises Restaurant, just across the city. But aside from beef and Guinness stew, it's also a high, handsome pub in which to enjoy Guinness in a glass, or to take a morning cup of coffee. Music sessions from Wed through Sun.

648 **Sober Lane** 5 Sullivan's Quay +353 21 4317979 · www.soberlane.ie With quiz
3/J21 nights, pizza nights, coin flip challenges, live music and whatever you're having
yourself, Sober Lane touches all bases for those looking for a spot of raucous fun.
It's always mad busy, both in the bar and in their capacious Courtyard, which draws
enormous crowds to watch Irish sporting fixtures.

649 **Mutton Lane** 3 Mutton Lane +353 21 4273471 @mutton.lane Housed down
3/J21 one of the many alleyways that lead from Patrick St into the English Market,
Mutton Lane has been pulling pints for 225 years, and still enjoys a unique, almost
medieval pallor, and candlelight. In a respectful tribute to its origins, back in 1793,
there are no televisions.

650 **The Oval Bar** 25 South Main St +353 21 4278952 · @oval.bar.9 Named for
3/J21 its unique interior ceiling, The Oval is today as it was in 1915, a classic Arts &
Crafts building with mullioned windows that owes more than a little to the style of
Charles Rennie Mackintosh. We love the curving bar, the studded banquettes, and
James Horan's centurion statue.

651 **The Sextant** 1 Albert St +353 21 4840667 · www.thesextant.ie Just across
3/J21 the de Valera bridge on the city's southside, the Sextant is famous for its raucous
TERRACE atmosphere, its beer garden, and for its Free Food Fridays, when the food starts
flowing at 6pm. DJs spin the discs at the weekends.

652 **Rising Sons Brew Pub** Cornmarket St +353 21 2414764 ·
3/J21 www.risingsonsbrewery.com You can take a tour of the Rising Sons micro-
brewery, and then enjoy a tasting of the several beers which they brew, including
any limited edition special releases. The pub itself is a big, busy spot which
specialises in sports games, and pizzas. The beers are also available in many other
bars throughout Cork city and county.

653 **The Abbey Tavern** 54 Gillabbey St +353 87 6738307 · @theabbeytaverncork
3/J21 The Abbey is loved by the art students of the nearby Crawford School of Art, who
don't find it too arduous to walk up the Hill to Gillabbey Street, at the rere of St Fin
Barre's Cathedral. Renowned for good tunes, as well as a fine pint of stout.

654 **Dennehy's Bar** 11 Cornmarket St +353 21 4272343 · @dennehys11 Step in
3/J21 the door and step back 50 years in time, to the era when the Dennehy family first
ATMOS opened the doors of the bar. Almost everything around Dennehy's in Cornmarket St
has changed but, in here, nothing whatsoever has changed. Priceless atmosphere,
and check out all those old currency notes covering the walls.

655 **The Porterhouse** Sheares St +353 21 4273000 · www.theporterhouse.ie
3/J21 The Porterhouse is part of the Dublin craft brewing group who were amongst
the pioneers in Irish brewing back in the 1990's, and it's part of the Mardyke
Complex, on Sheares St. The Porterhouse beers are excellent, so this is the place
for a Brainblasta or their classic Oyster Stout. There is also a short menu of staple
gastropub dishes.

656 **The Friary** 62 Shandon St +353 87 6680941 · @thefriarycork Look for the
3/J21 blue building with the letters 62 Wine above the door as you cross Griffith Bridge,
heading towards Shandon St. This darling little pub is part of the Cork Ale Trail, a
quintet of destinations in the area that have a specialisation in craft beers. There
are also quiz nights, karaoke, and music sessions in the upstairs attic.

657 **The Bodega** St Peter's Market, Cornmarket St +353 21 4273756 ·
3/J21 www.bodegacork.ie The Bodega is a most handsome big bar, housed in the old
St Peter's Market premises, in the Coal Quay area, also known as the Irish Market.
A nightclub with a late bar is a major attraction, and there is a fine terrace for
people watching.

658 **Tom Barry's Bar** 113 Barrack St + 353 21 431 8498 One of the jewels of
3/J21 gentrifying Barrack St, Tom Barry's is a favourite pub for many Leesiders. What's
not to love about a pizza menu where the pizzas are all named after famous
painters: the Picasso; the Salvador Dali; the Monet. Cosy fires inside, nice beer
garden at the back with lots of tables. Look out for the Peadar Lamb lightbox.

659 **The Castle Inn** Sth Main St +353 21 4277485 The Castle Inn is reputedly Cork's
3/J21 oldest working pub, and has been family run since 1939. There is a blazing fire,
ATMOS a cosy snug, good hard benches to sit on whilst you sip your pint and Mary, the
kindly lady behind the bar, is a Cork legend.

The Best Music Pubs

660 ✓**Sin E** 8 Coburg St +353 21 4502266 · @sinecork Open since 1889,
3/J21 Sin E translates as 'That's It' and is one of the city's most famous pubs for
ATMOS music, with sessions every evening. It's just north of the St. Patrick's Bridge, as you
cross the river into the Victorian Quarter, and next to the funeral parlour. Music
begins as early as 6.30 pm.

661 **The Corner House** 7 Coburg St +353 21 4500655 · www.thecornerhouse.ie
3/J21 The Corner House is one of the city's favourite bars for authentic music sessions.
It's home to the Lee Delta Blues Club, and was the original home to the Murphy's
Folk Club. The Lee Valley String Band also preside over many sessions, and there
are bluegrass sessions, and darling pints.

662 **An Spailpin Fanach** 28 South Main St +353 21 4277949 · @anspailpinfanach
3/J21 They have sessions every night of the week in the Spailpin Fanach, both in the bar
and upstairs. Nothing quite like a session with The Thirsty Scholars!

663 **Coughlan's Bar & Beer Garden** 7 Douglas St +353 21 4961751 ·
3/J21 www.coughlans.ie This pristine, flower-bedecked bar is one of the city's major
ATMOS music venues, and has won prizes for its showcase gigs. There is always a brilliant
TERRACE atmosphere, and the beer garden is heated.

664 **John Henchy's & Sons** St Luke's Cross · @HenchysBar Up the hill at
3/J21 Montenotte, this handsome big pub has Sat sessions with rhythm & blues and
classic rock, and DJ sets on Sun.

The Best Wine Bars

665
3/J21
MED.INX
ATMOS

✓ **Arthur Mayne's Pharmacy** 7 Pembroke St +353 21 4279449 ·
@arthur.maynes Arthur Mayne's is strange, in a David Lynch is strange kind of way, which is to say that it's strangely wonderful. Benny McCabe's food and wine bar is an old pharmacy, with numerous relics of the 120-year-old pharmacy stock and bric-a-brac on the shelves and in the cabinets. Behind the bar there is the restaurant, and it's also got an extremely unusual antique bathroom. And it's brilliant, even if you are just having a glass of wine in the bar. But if you can get a seat to eat, then the food is cleverly delivered on sharing boards, the sort of food that makes you want to open another bottle. Lunch & Dinner 7 days. Late Night open till 2/3am.

666
3/J21
MED.INX
ATMOS

✓ **L'Atitude 51** 1 Union Quay +353 21 2390219 · www.latitude51.ie Planning a trip to France for the summer? Don't bother. Instead, park the car on Union Quay, push open the doors of L'Atitude 51, sit down at that old butcher's block that doubles as a bar and take a look at the blackboard. Petit salé aux lentilles, with morteau sausage? Bavette? Tartiflette? Maybe a glass of Chateau Ventenac? The cooking and the vibe in Beverley Matthews' wine bar delivers that Anton Ego moment where you are delivered back to your first trips to La France Profonde. It's pure France, and pure Cork, and it's superb.
Lunch & dinner Mon-Sat.

Great Places to Drink Cocktails

667
3/J21
ATMOS
TERRACE

✓ **Cask** 48 MacCurtain St +353 21 4500913 · www.caskcork.com Mixologist Andy Ferreira has been hauling in the silverware for his cocktail creations in the serious competitions, and Cask is shaping up as the destination for lavish drinks in the Victorian Quarter of Cork. Ordering a Cork First, Ireland Second; or a Basil's Baldy Barber, has quickly become part of the rite of passage to being a true Corkonian. Nice outdoor space by the waterfall, but it does get madly jam-packed at the weekends. No surprise: there are some great talents at work in Cask. Evenings Mon-Sun.

668
3/J21

Pigalle 111 Barrack St · @BarPigalleCork Barrack St is quietly gentrifying, thanks to the efforts of destinations like Pigalle, who take their cocktails seriously. Nice sounds, and good staff who really enjoy their mixology. From 5pm 7 days.

669
3/J21

Edison 11-12 Washington St +353 21 427 3252 Housed in a former cinema, Edison has a good reputation for its cocktails, and there are also local Cork craft beers. Lots of music and DJs to boogie to as you sip a Tom Collins.

670
3/J21
TERRACE

Suas 4 South Main St +353 21 4278972 · www.suasbar.com Suas is up above Captain America's, which is itself up above Wagamama, on South Main St in the city centre, so it's the real rooftop deal. The cocktails are classics – elderflower Collins; Margarita; Long Island iced tea – abetted by shooters and small selection of wines. Great covered terrace gives all the rooftop views. 7 days.

Sober Lane Report: 648/CRACKING CORK PUBS.
Cornstore Report: 610/CASUAL RESTAURANTS.
The Weir, River Lee Hotel Report: 587/PLACES TO STAY.
Electric Report: 611/CASUAL RESTAURANTS.
Coqbull Report: 621/BURGERS & STEAKS.

The Best Coffee

671
3/J21

FILTER 19 Georges Quay +353 21 4550050 · @FILTER Eoin's tiny espresso and brew bar has a stellar reputation, and for many coffee lovers a trip to George's Quay, beside the river, is how you get the day started. The baking, sourced from Diva Boutique Bakery, is just as carefully chosen as the beans, and the narrow room, with its coffee bric a brac, is always friendly, laid-back and welcoming, and the barista skills are second-to-none. Good teas, of course, but those brews are worth the walk down the river. Second branch now open on N Main St, in St. Peter's Church. Daytime 7 days.

672
3/J21
ATMOS

SOMA Coffee Company 23 Tuckey St · @somacoffeecompany SOMA is the cool school, minimalist counterpoint to Cork city's more typical bricolage style of coffee house. Tucked away at the side of Bishop Lucey Park, on Tuckey St, just off Grand Parade, it's particularly notable for featuring coffees from West Cork Coffee, and also for some truly scrummy toasted sandwiches: mushroom with cheddar and spinach; Durcan's ham with brie. Good sounds encourage everyone to linger and have a second shot, and the staff are just darling. Daytime 7 days.

673
3/J21
ATMOS

Alchemy Coffee and Books 123 Barrack St · @AlchemyCoffeeandBooks Up the hill from the river, on the corner of slowly-gentrifying Barrack St and Fort St, Alchemy does the magic. It's a ramshackle space, packed with shelves of books and with a couple of tables outside on the street. The coffee, the cakes and the cooking are all top-notch, especially their signature sausage rolls. Great staff, some of whom even do their work barefoot. Daytime 7 days. Another branch, Alchemy 2 on Langford Row, which features a music store.

674
3/J21

Cork Coffee Roasters 2 Bridge St +353 87 7766322 · www.corkcoffee.com John Gowan was a fisherman before he hopped ashore at Seattle to learn his coffee craft as that city was becoming the world's coffee capital. Mr Gowan is one of the pioneer Cork coffee heads, and he is a talented, expert roaster, with the beans roasted on an original 1930's small batch roaster. His shops are funky and hip, as you would expect in Cork. Daytime 7 days. A second branch is open at 2 French Church St.

675
3/J21

The Bookshelf Coffee House 78 South Mall +353 21 2392576 · www.bookshelfcoffee.com Paul O'Carroll's coffee shop is housed in the old Cork Library, on South Mall, and you enter through the elegant limestone entrances of the library, which date back to 1792. Coffee is sourced from the Barn Roastery in Berlin, the cooking riffs on classic egg dishes for breakfast and brunch, with sandwiches the core lunchtime offer, all concocted and served with charm. Daytime 7 days. Second branch in Tralee +353 66 7179743

676
3/J21

Dukes Coffee Company 4 Carey's Ln Centre +353 21 4905877 www.dukes.ie Aidan Dukes' shop on Carey's Ln in the city centre has expanded to open a swish vinyl lounge, in the upstairs of Golden Discs on Patrick St, and this is one cool space in which to spin the black circles. The coffees are very fine and use the best local Cork roasters, and we would love to see a little more focus on the food so that all the potentials of Dukes are realised. All day 7 days.

677   **Union Grind**   4 Union Quay, Cork +353 21 4965605 · @Uniongrindcork

3/J21   The UG guys had a viral moment in Easter 2017 when they served their mochas inside a hollowed out Easter egg, setting off an internet storm. Gimmicks aside, the coffee is first class and crafted by some of the city's best baristas, the breakfasts and sandwiches are top-notch, and a seat outside on a sunny day beside the river on Union Quay is delightful. All day from 7.30am Mon-Fri.

678   **Priory Coffee**   Co North Main St, Cork · www.priorycoffee.com

3/J21
CHP
TERRACE   This dynamic coffee company has moved beyond their original home in Youghal – where they also serve excellent fish and chips in addition to excellent coffee – and set up stall on the corner of North Main Street. It's a classy stylish room, with good Badger & Dodo brews and some smart toasties: the smoked chicken is particularly good, and the crispy vegetable crisps served alongside are just the business. Daytime 7 days.

Cork's Main Attractions

679
3/J21

✓✓ **Cork English Market** Princes St +353 21 4924258 ·
www.englishmarket.ie Pig's tails, and 70% tumbes Peruvian dark chocolate bars. Drisheen – a blood pudding made of sheep's blood – and bottles of 2008 Pommard. Think of Cork's legendary English Market as Cockaigne, the mythical land of plenty, but Cockaigne as designed by Guillermo del Toro, a trawl of riches from the labyrinths of Irish culinary history, slung together surreally and cheek-by-jowl in the centre of the city. Its uniqueness lies in the fact that it straddles the ancient and the contemporary, seemingly without any tension, which means there is no other food market quite like it. Daytime Mon-Sat.

680
3/J21
AYR
☞

✓✓ **Blackrock Castle Observatory** Blackrock, Cork +353 21 4357917 ·
www.bco.ie The iconic riverside castle was built as a coastal defence fortification in the 16thC to protect Cork Harbour and Port. It is now a working observatory that delivers the science of space to children. Schools and families use the castle's interactive astronomy centre, exploring the formation of the planet and the universe, and its planetarium and sundial. It also operates as a lab for astronomical researchers from Cork Institute of Technology, and the Cork Astronomy Club bring their telescopes for regular observing sessions that are open to the public. The building is also home to the Castle Café. Also an occasional wedding venue. All day, 7 days. Restaurant open all day, till 8pm/9pm/9.30pm Tue-Sun.

681
3/J21
MAR-OCT

✓ **Cork Butter Museum** The Tony O'Reilly Centre, O'Connell Sq, Cork +353 21 4300600 www.corkbutter.museum Butter has always been hugely important to Ireland, both as an export and as the basis, and crowning glory, of Irish cuisine. The Cork Butter Museum looks at every aspect of this Irish success story, from its role in Irish culture, to the 19thC Butter Exchange, right down to actually making butter in the museum at noon on Tue, Thurs and Sat. All day, 7 days.

682
3/J21
☞
FREE
ADMISSION

✓ **Crawford Art Gallery** Emmet Place, Cork · www.crawfordartgallery.ie
The plaster Greek and Roman sculptures on the ground floor of the Crawford were brought to Cork in 1818, from the Vatican. The purpose was to give the Irish public a sense of Neo Classicism and Greco Roman culture, as well as the concept of antiquity. The permanent Crawford collection has over 2,500 works, and is a visually stunning mix of contemporary and traditional art. Performance artists also host their work here, and talks take place on a regular basis.Tours available. Café at the rere of the Gallery is one of the city's best. Report: 601/MODERN CORK COOKING. All day Mon-Sat.

683
3/J21
☞

✓ **Lewis Glucksman Gallery** University College Cork +353 21 4901844 ·
www.glucksman.org Like some beautiful but benevolent spaceship that has settled onto the campus of University College Cork, The Glucksman is one of those striking buildings that seems to be not of this earth: seen from certain angles, the O'Donnell + Tuomey construction seems to levitate amidst the trees. The feeling of floating is accentuated as you traverse the three floors of galleries. It's an utterly singular and successful piece of work, and the architecture serves perfectly to enhance the many visual arts exhibitions held here. Report: 629/BRUNCH. All day Tue-Sun.

684
3/J21

✓ **Shandon Sweets** 37a John Redmond St, Shandon +353 21 4507791
The last surviving handmade sweet factory in Ireland, Shandon Sweets was established in 1928, and the Linehan family really haven't made any significant changes since then to their extraordinary sweetie-making enterprise. You will get

the smell of sugar as you walk up John Redmond St, for this sweetie factory is a living museum of candy. Their iconic confectionery is Clove Rock, made in copper pans and boiled till it would take the fingerprints off you, and then the sweet is rolled and cut into traditional pink tubes, a masterpiece composed of water, sugar and glucose. Danny and Tony Linehan also make pear drops, butter nuggets, bullseyes. Pure Cork. Daytime Mon-Sat.

685 St Anne's Church & Shandon Bells Tower Shandon, Cork ·
3/J21 www.shandonbells.ie A feature of the skyline of Cork city, the Shandon Bells & Tower was known as the 'Four Faced Liar' because of its unpredictable time keeping on the four clock faces of the tower. Nowadays, the technology has improved, and the clocks all tell the right time. Climb the 18thC tower and enjoy a 360° view of the whole of Cork city. They even let you have a go at ringing the bells, and show the mechanism of Cork's giant clock. St Anne's Church itself is one of the oldest churches in the city. Entry to the tower open all day till 3pm/4pm/5pm, AYR 7 days.

686 Cobh Heritage Centre Cobh +353 21 4813591 · www.cobhheritage.com
3/J21 The Cobh Heritage Centre tells the many stories of hope and heartbreak that are indelibly associated with this historical town, overlooking Cork harbour – one of the largest natural harbours in the world, and last port of call before New York. Formerly known as Queenstown, Cobh was the place where many embarked either voluntarily or involuntarily on steamers, liners, cruisers, convict ships or coffin ships. Two famous boats that have an association with the port are the *Titanic*, which stopped one last time here before its ill-fated voyage, and the *Lusitania*, the Cunard liner torpedoed by a German submarine in 1915, whose survivors and victims were brought to Cobh. Nowadays it is also a centre that serves as a source of genealogy, where visitors come to find out about their Irish roots. Daytime 7 days.

687 Cork City Gaol Convent Ave +353 21 4305022 · www.corkcitygaol.com
3/J21 One of Cork's more unusual attractions is the private evening tour in Cork City Gaol, a spooky gathering around these Victorian cells. The minimum number of people per tour is 8, and the tour needs to be booked one week in advance. The Gaol building itself is a Georgian Gothic architectural gem, with the appearance more of a castle than a gaol. Daytime 7 days with pre-arranged evening tours.

688 Lifetime Lab Lee Rd +353 21 4941500 · www.lifetimelab.ie The Lifetime
3/J21 Lab is a science centre aimed at potential young scientists, engineers and mathematicians, bringing to life and explaining STEM education subjects through a series of interactive exhibitions that look at water, energy and waste. At the heart of the venture there is a playground that is a veritable Heath Robinson drawing brought to life. The carefully restored Victorian building which houses the exhibitions was the old Cork City Waterworks and the history and science bundled up in the building help to explain how a city works. Popular with school groups, the centre opens to the public for tours and is a popular visitor attraction. Daytime 7 days.

Blarney Castle Report: 1590/MONUMENTS.
Fota Wildlife Park Report: 1903/FAMILY ACTIVITIES.
Harper's Island Report: 1756/BIRDS.
Spike Island Report: 1990/THE ISLANDS.

The Best Independent Shops (Vinyl Stores, Bookshops & Galleries)

VINYL SHOPS

689 **Records and Relics** 14 Lancaster Quay, Washington St, Cork
3/J21 +353 21 2291594 · @RecordsandRelics Vintage vinyl, vintage clothes and, as owners Eilis Dillon and Colin Biggs says, vintage is how to express your authentic self in the modern world. Daytime Mon-Sat, till 7pm.

690 **Golden Discs** 4 Carey's Ln Centre +353 21 4905877
3/J21 www.dukes.ie Upstairs looking out over Pana (Patrick St), this groovy venture from the Dukes coffee house has punky staff, vinyl, home baking, rock history books, and strikes a nice balance between record shop and coffee shop. Daytime 7 days.

691 **Bunker Vinyl** The Basement, Ozalid House, Camden Pl +353 87 4329477 ·
3/J21 @bunkervinyl John Dwyer and Aileen Wallace's basement is both vinyl store and in-house studio space. As they say themselves: record shopping is cheaper than seeing a psychiatrist, and where better than a room where Iron Maiden rub shoulders with Sonic Sum and Van Morrison's *Saint Dominic's Preview*, which makes it pure Cork, of course. Daytime Tue-Sun, till 7pm

BOOKSHOPS

692 **Liam Ruiséal Bookshop** 49 Oliver Plunkett St +353 21 4270981 ·
3/J21 www.lrbooks.net The oldest bookshop in the city first opened in 1916, when it was called the Fountain Bookshop. They have a superb stock of Irish history books and Irish language publications, and it's a darling store. Daytime Mon-Sat.

693 **Vibes & Scribes** 2 Lavitt's Quay, Cork +353 21 4279535 ·
3/J21 www.vibesandscribes.ie Everyone has that crisis moment when you suddenly discover you need a new pair of knitting needles, and a copy of *The Hidden Life of Trees*. And that's why Vibes & Scribes exists. Lovely bookstore on the river, and all the yarns you could ever need. Also a craft supplies shop Vibes & Scribes on Bridge St. Daytime 7 days.

694 **Uneeda Bookshop** 71 Oliver Plunkett St +353 21 4270899 At the Patrick St
3/J21 end of Grand Parade, Uneeda is a city classic, selling vinyl, cassettes, second-hand books and more. Daytime Mon-Sat.

695 **The Time Travellers Bookshop** Wandesford Quay +353 21 4311921 ·
3/J21 www.timetraveller.ie Sister store to the original TTB in Skibbereen, West Cork, this is a meticulous antiquarian bookstore, with a particular specialisation in historical maps and collectable vinyl. They have an excellent online service, but nothing beats a slow browse around the shelves, with the promise of finding something you don't really need but do really want. Daytime Mon-Sat.

696 **The Shelf Bookshop** Georges Quay +353 21 4312264 ·
3/J21 www.theshelf.ie 'Every visit saves you money' is what they say in The Shelf, something Jeff Bezos never thought to say. Specialists in second-hand school books, and a lovely Cork shop. Daytime Mon-Sat. Another branch in Midleton.

Alchemy Coffee and **Alchemy 2** Report: 673/COFFEE.

GALLERIES

697 **The Lavit Gallery** 5 Fr Matthew St +353 21 4277749 · www.lavitgallery.
3/J21 com Beside the Cork RTE studios the Lavit was established as a not-for-profit gallery back in 1963, aiming to promote the work of Cork artists. Today, they represent more than 200 artists, and have a Student of the Year Awards annually. Major Cork artists – Tim Goulding; Carin McCana; Wendy Dison – mix with younger painters and sculptors, and it's one of the city's most beautiful spaces. Exhibitions 10.30am-6pm Tue-Sat.

698 **The Wandesford Gallery** Wandesford Quay, Clarke's Bridge +353 21
3/J21 4335210 · @CITWandesfordQuayGallery Part of the Cork Institute of Technology campus, and a beautiful gallery space which hosts a variety of exhibitions, featuring contemporary art, craft and design. Daytime Tue-Sat.

699 **2020 Art Gallery** Griffith House, N Mall, Sunday's Well +353 21 4291458
3/J21 · www.2020artgallery.com Sheelah Moloney first opened her gallery in little Ballydehob, in deepest West Cork, before moving to the city and to North Mall. 2020's specialisation is contemporary Irish art, and Ms Moloney is knowledgeable and helpful, and blessed with a good eye. Daytime Tue-Sat.

700 **The James Barry Exhibition Centre** Cork Inst of Technology CIT,
3/J21 Bishopstown Campus, Cork +353 21 4335860 · www.arts.cit.ie The gallery space in the Cork Institute of Technology hosts group and solo exhibitions.

WHERE TO STAY

701
3/J21
11 ROOMS
MED.EXP

Blindgate House Blindgate + 353 21 4777858 · www.blindgatehouse. com The area known as Blind Gate is just up from St Multose Church, so it's a nice quiet refuge when Kinsale gets overheated at the height of the season. We have always admired the style of Maeve Coakley's Blindgate House, and the fact that its conventional exterior hides one of the most lushly designed and precisely executed interiors in West Cork. But style doesn't win out over comfort in Blindgate, so this is a cosy house, and not one of those design traps that involves you suffering for someone else's art.

702
3/J21
22 ROOMS
EXP

Perryville House Long Quay +353 21 4772731 · www.perryvillehouse.com Andrew and Laura Corcoran's pretty in pink Perryville House overlooks the pierside as you come into town on the R600. It's a majestic, 200-year-old house, sumptuously comfortable and lavishly appointed. The addition of a bar and garden room has given guests another space in which to relax and enjoy a drink before heading out to dinner. Look out for their many flags.

703
3/J21
73 ROOMS

Actons Hotel Pier Rd +353 21 4779900 · www.actonshotelkinsale.com Overlooking the Marina, Actons is the oldest hotel in town, and has developed through several incarnations since opening in 1946, and is today in common ownership with the Trident Hotel, further down Pier Road. A big refurb in 2013 means the rooms are up-to-the-minute in style, and the views across to Scilly from the rooms at the front are spectacular. Good friendly staff, and lots of involvement with the local community, means there is always a happy buzz about the public rooms. A pool and leisure centre is an added bonus.

704
3/J21
39 ROOMS
EXP

The Trident Hotel World's End House, Lwr O'Connell St, Old Fort +353 21 4779300 · www.tridenthotel.com At the end of town, at the World's End, the Trident's rooms and suites offer extraordinary views across the harbour. Manager Hal McElroy has been in charge ever since we first stayed here in the late 1980's, and he has a great team alongside him. Casual food in the bar, more lavish dining in the Pier One restaurant.

705
3/J21
17 ROOMS

The Blue Haven 3 Pearse St +353 21 4772209 · www.bluehavenkinsale.com The Blue Haven has always been at the centre of Kinsale's tourism and food agenda, and was one of the original members of the Kinsale Good Food Circle, which made the town a dining destination more than four decades ago. Smart rooms mean the hotel has a neat boutique feel, and downstairs they offer a bar and bistro – with music each night – a seafood café – a plate of oysters and a glass of their Fairbourne Estate sauvignon is hard to beat – and a tapas wine bar.

706
3/J21
8 ROOMS
EXP

Long Quay House Long Quay, Sleveen +353 21 4709833 · www.longquayhousekinsale.com Between Perryville House and the Old Bank House, overlooking the pier, Peter and Rasa Deasy's handsome home has eight rooms for guests. Generous breakfasts typify the owners' meticulous attention to detail, and the house has been winning consistent plaudits since Peter and Rasa took over in 2015.

707 **Old Bank House** 10 Pearse St +353 21 4774075 ·
3/J21
17 ROOMS
MED.EXP
www.oldbankhousekinsale.com This handsome Georgian house is part of the Blue Haven Collection, owned by local man Ciaran Fitzgerald. The location – across from the pier, and opposite the two large gift shops, Cronin's and Boland's, couldn't be bettered, and as well as rooms they have an all-day café – The Gourmet Café – for coffee and sandwiches and sweet things, with a neat verandah at the front of the house where you can watch the world pass by. There is also a Take Out menu if you want to picnic down by the water's edge.

WHERE TO EAT

708 ✓**Fishy Fishy Cafe** Crowley Quay +353 21 4700415 · www.fishyfishy.ie
3/J21
MED.EXP
Tucked away just behind the Town Park, within site of the inner harbour, Fishy Fishy has been Kinsale's benchmark restaurant for more than a decade. Chef-proprietor Martin Shanahan rewired the operation of Fishy Fishy to ensure he was buying the best seafood direct from boats returning to Kinsale harbour. The pristine quality of the fish allows him to keep the cooking simple, which it has to be as the restaurant is so phenomenally busy. Lunch & Dinner Mon-Sun.

709 ✓**The Black Pig** 66 Lwr O'Connell St +353 21 4774101 ·
3/J21
MED.INX
TERRACE
ATMOS
@theblackpigwinebar Just outside the main strip of Kinsale on the hill road behind Actons Hotel, The Black Pig is a marvellously atmospheric wine bar with great cooking, and a delightful courtyard. Gavin and Siobhan take the simplest things and make them seem newly minted, freshly imagined. The dishes play perfectly to the restaurant's strength, which is to cook foods that match well with the magnificent wines they offer. You need to get there early, mind you, especially to get a seat in the courtyard on balmy evenings. Dinner Wed-Sun.

710 **Bastion** Market St +353 21 4709696 · www.bastionkinsale.com
3/J21
MED.EXP
Paul McDonald and Heather Noonan have brought a vivid culinary template to Kinsale, so enjoy gin and tonic foam with mackerel; monkfish carpaccio; braised rabbit with Iberico ham; or oyster Eton Mess. You can eat simply at the bar, you can enjoy small plates, or push the boat out and enjoy the prosecco on tap. Dinner Wed-Sun.

711 **Bruno's** 36 Main St +353 21 4777138 · @brunosrestaurantkinsale Bruno's
3/J21
MED.INX
is wonderfully atmospheric – imagine an enoteca in the Roman catacombs, with an ancient well in the centre – the bric-a-brac is funky, the wines are judiciously chosen, and the pizzas are made with a fermented sourdough starter, so they have winning flavour even before they are topped with San Marzano tomatoes and Toonsbridge mozzarella, or Jack McCarthy's black pudding with leeks, apple and pine nuts. Don't miss their own Italian wines. Dinner Wed-Sun.

712 **Koko Kinsale** Pier Rd +353 87 6110209 · @kokokinsale Overlooking the
3/J21
CHP
pier, opposite the main town car park, you find a little shop where Frank Keane switched career from seller of ceramics to artisan chocolatier, and he has enjoyed great success since he opened Koko in 2013. There are lovely original ideas here, such as the signature ginger-honey-seaweed combination, and look out for Balkan cherries soaked in kirsch, and the classic rum truffle. They also sell coffee to take away. Daytime.

713 **The Lemon Leaf Café** 70 Main St +353 21 4709792 ·
3/J21 @LemonLeafCafeKinsale The Lemon Leaf stands out as a special destination,
even in a town with the standards of Kinsale. The excellent food and drinks, the
elegant vibrancy of the room and the carefully chosen foods on the dresser, add to
the totality of Tracy Keoghan's smart café. That mid-morning cup of Ariosa coffee
will hit the spot, but so will the croque madame, or the sweet potato fishcakes with
lime and coriander mayonnaise. Everything is done just right, just so. Daytime
7 days.

714 **Man Friday** Scilly +353 21 4772260 · www.manfridaykinsale.ie Scilly is
3/J21 just across the harbour from the main collection of Kinsale destinations, and is
MED.EXP named for the many Cornish sailors who decamped to Kinsale. Philip Horgan's
Man Friday restaurant is one of the longest-established restaurants in Ireland, with
40 years of service and 40 years of making people happy, in one of the great party
rooms. It's classic cooking, always welcome and fun, with great service. Dinner
7 days.

715 **Max's** 48 Main St +353 21 4772443 · www.maxs.ie Anne Marie and Olivier
3/J21 Queva describe their restaurant as being 'quaint' and 'professional', though we
MED.EXP could also add 'unpretentious' to the roll-call of adjectives. Everything marries
well in this delightful set of rooms – the food; the decor with its artful bricolage;
the service, which is confident, and charming. The Quevas make it look easy,
and that is part of the charm of this Kinsale institution. Dinner 7 days. Closed
Bank Hols.

716 **The Supper Club** 2 Cork St +353 21 4772847 · www.thesupperclub.ie Around
3/J21 the corner from St John the Baptist Church, Tom Kay and his team in The Supper
MED.EXP Club have been pushing all the right buttons since they got the doors open. A
ATMOS well-chosen menu of food, good drinks and friendly service offers the true Kinsale
zeitgeist, and the cooking strikes the right note. Comfortable rooms, and keen
prices also. Dinner Wed-Sun.

717 **Toddies @ The Bulman** Summercove + 353 21 4772131 · www.thebulman.ie
3/J21 Overlooking the sea, just beyond Scilly, and just before Charles Fort, Toddies is
MED.EXP one of Kinsale's classic bars, housed in the comforting space of The Bulman, in
ATMOS pretty Summercove. Pearse O'Sullivan's cooking shows the confidence and class
of a cook with years of experience cooking in Kinsale under his toque. Start with
oysters cooked with lobster bisque and smoked Gubbeen cheese, then indulge
in Mr O'Sullivan's classic hake with brilliant local asparagus, and it's pretty
impossible to have a better food experience. Lunch & Dinner Mon-Sun. Live Music
at weekends.

✓ **The Coffee Shop** Report: 995/THE SOUTH WEST.

WHERE TO EAT & STAY

718 **9 Market Street** 9 Market St + 353 21 4709221 · www.ninemarketstreet.ie
3/J21 Just down from the historic Courthouse building, which is now the Kinsale Regional
3 ROOMS Museum, Leona and Dee's cooking in 9 Market St appears simple but here's the
MED.INX secret of No.9: this cooking is technically flawless, and the perfection of everything
they send out will stop you in your tracks. Nice rooms upstairs.

719 **Jim Edwards** Market Quay +353 21 4772541 · www.jimedwardskinsale.com
3/J21 On a small laneway, running up from the pier, where the Tourist Office building
7 ROOMS now sits, Jim Edwards pub has been serving classic cordon bleu style cooking in
MED.EXP their bar and restaurant for more than 40 years. One of their specialities is Kidneys
Madeira, their vegetarian dish is served in a mille feuille, there is a lobster tank,
and you can order grilled sole on the bone. Upstairs there are seven recently
refurbished bedrooms.

720 **Jo's Cafe & Rooms** 55 Main St + 353 087 9481026 · www.joskinsale.com
3/J21 In the middle of Main Street, Jo's offers five small rooms, which are very good
5 ROOMS value, and it's the spot for a freshly baked doughnut, and a cup of coffee, and while
CHP we're at it don't forget the breakfast brioche.

THE BEST PUBS

721 **The Spaniard Inn** Scilly +353 21 4772436 · www.thespaniard.ie This thriving
3/J21 pub is just across from the town on Scilly, opposite Man Friday's restaurant, and it's
a great place to hear traditional music.

722 **Tap Tavern** 9 Guardwell, Sleveen +353 21 4773231 Run by the formidable and
3/J21 welcoming Kinsale character Mary O'Neill, The Tap is said to be Kinsale's oldest
pub. Mary's son Brian is the man behind the Kinsale Ghost Tours.

THE BEST WALKS

723 **James Fort Walk** Old Fort, Kinsale James Fort is situated on a small
3/J21 promontory that juts out into Kinsale harbour. The ruins of the fort can only be
DF accessed by foot. Walk past Castlepark Village and into the Castlepark Marina, and
L take a narrow lane, bordered by Alexanders, to some quite steep steps, and up the
2-A-1 hill, from where the fort is signposted. The way up and around the promontory is
1-2 KM a series of mowed paths through wild-flower meadows. Bird song fills the air, and
whichever path you take around the promontory will be interesting and attractive,
with harbour views to E and W. Best to explore any of the paths, and if you want to
make it a circular walk, then walk down to Sandy Cove and back through Castlepark
Village. You won't get lost because the promontory is small. We've coded the walk
a 2, because access involves steps.

724 **Scilly Walk to Charles Fort** Scilly, Kinsale The Scilly Walk is a well-signposted
3/J21 pedestrian path that runs just alongside the harbour from the little hamlet of Scilly
L to Charles Fort. The walk takes in Summercove, and the Bulman Bar, so you can opt
1-A-1 for lunch here, or maybe make your destination the tea rooms at Charles Fort. If you
want to make the walk a little longer, then start at the Post Office in Kinsale. Take the
low road out of Kinsale that loops around the water's edge and up the hill to Scilly.
The pedestrianised Scilly Walk path starts just beyond The Spaniard pub; look for the
sign. Charles Fort is 4km from Kinsale. The walk is easy, but does involve steep hills.

BEST BEACHES

725 **Garretstown and Garrylucas Beaches** Kilcolman Marsh, The Old Head
3/J21 of Kinsale Garretstown and Garrylucas beaches are two adjacent white strand
L beaches near the Old Head, off the R604, 15km from Kinsale. The nearest village
is Ballinspittle. These are blue flag beaches with car parking, toilet facilities and
lifebuoys. Lifeguards are on duty during the bathing season. Access via ramps and
steps. Garretstown is a centre for watersports activities.

726 **The Dock Beach** Castlepark Marina, Kinsale The Dock Beach is on the
3/J21 promontory that is famous for being the site of James Fort. Access to the beach is
by foot, through the Castlepark marina. Drive to the marina and park, and look for
the 'Beach' sign. It's a two-minute walk to the little cove, which is popular with
kayakers as well as locals.

HISTORICAL ATTRACTIONS

727 **Charles Fort** and **James Fort** Summer Cove, Kinsale Much of Kinsale's history
3/J21 is recorded in the names of its pubs and shops - hence The Spaniard, 1601, or
L The Lord Kingsale. 1601 was the date of the Battle of Kinsale, when an alliance
CAFE of Spanish and Irish fought with the better organised English, who defeated the
alliance and — recognising the importance of this port – built two star-shaped
forts, opposite one another, on either side of the narrow waterway that leads into
the harbour. James Fort was the first to be built, and then re-built after the Battle
of Kinsale. Charles Fort, the larger of the two, was commenced in 1678, and used
as an army garrison until 1922. Today it houses a pretty tea rooms, and is open to
the public for guided tours, which last 1 hour.

728 **St Multose Church** Church St, Sleveen, Kinsale St Multose is a beautiful
3/J21 cruciform-plan church that dates back to 1190, St Multose being the Patron Saint
of Kinsale. It is one of the oldest Protestant churches in Ireland, dominated by a
Norman bell tower and steeply pitched slate roofs. Historically, it was the place
where Charles II was declared King of England. Church services are held at 8.30 am,
10 am and 11.30 am Sundays.

729 **Desmond Castle** and the **Wine Museum** Cork St, Kinsale Kinsale was
3/J21 always a successful and significant port, trading in butter, tobacco, wood, salt
and wine. It was the first port of call for shipping from America to the Continent,
and was well placed, with both a safe harbour and a river to transport supplies
from the surrounding countryside. Desmond Castle was the customs house in the
16thC and also served as an arms store for the Spanish during the Battle of Kinsale.
Today, the building hosts the International Museum of Wine Exhibition that
documents the influence and history of the Irish on the world of wine.
Guided tours last 30 minutes. You find Desmond Castle just near the Garda (Police)
station.

730 **Lusitania Museum and Memorial Garden and the Old Head Signal Tower**
3/J21 Old Head, Kinsale The Old Head is a spectacular headland 15km from the town
L of Kinsale, where a lighted beacon has stood since pre-Christian times. Nowadays,
the Old Head promontory itself is closed to the public, as it is the location for a
privately run golf course, but there are still regular open days for the lighthouse.
Near to the Old Head, you can access the 19thC Signal Tower which has been
restored and now houses a visitors' centre. The tall Martello tower, with incredible
views of the coastline, is one of 81 signal towers built by the British, where each
tower can see the tower on either side, and receive signals coded with flags and
balls. One of the highlights of visiting the tower is being able to take the stairs to its
roof storey, and enjoy the views. The centre is also home to the Lusitania Memorial
Garden and Museum, featuring artefacts from the Cunard Liner, sunk by a German
U Boat in WW1.

THE BEST ACTIVITIES

731 **Kinsale Harbour Cruises** Kinsale Quay +353 86 2505456 ·
3/J21 www.kinsaleharbourcruises.com With cruises on the *Spirit of Kinsale*
departing every hour, this is a great opportunity for visitors to see this beautiful
part of the country from the water. Tours give a seaside view of the harbour and
its marinas, the village of Scilly, Charles and James Fort and, most dramatically,
the Old Head and its lighthouse and signal tower. Great for families, as well as
hens and stags. This is a family-operated boat, and tours are well informed and
anecdotal.

732 **Kinsale Pottery and Arts Centre** Olcote, Ballinacurra +353 21 4777758 ·
3/J21 www.kinsaleceramics.com Situated in a converted stables just outside Kinsale,
both children and adults are welcome to join their pottery, glass, jewellery and
mosaic courses that are run here throughout the year. Groups are small and suit
beginners as well as enthusiasts. They are well kitted out with different kilns and
all the paraphernalia you need to bring home a piece of your own creativity.

733 **Kinsale Farmers' Market** Market Quay +353 85 7220259 ·
3/J21 @kinsalefarmersmarket Each Wednesday morning brings a charismatic group
of local artisans to the Market Quay, and there are lots of nice foods to snack on
even if you aren't shopping. 10am-2pm.

INDEPENDENT SHOPS & GALLERIES

734 **The Gallery Kinsale** 57 Main St, Sleveen +353 86 8448589 This independent
3/J21 gallery takes pride in displaying paintings of local scenes, painted by local Irish
artists, and also displays international contemporary art.

735 **Annabel Langrish Gallery** Market Lane +343 86 8352294 ·
3/J21 www.herongallery.ie The popular West Cork artist Annabel Langrish runs a
gallery of her work in Kinsale, as well as in her base in Ahakista on the Sheep's
Head Peninsula, further west, where she maintains her studio. Annabel's range is
becoming increasingly better known, thanks to her offshoot prints, tablemats and
cushions. If you love her work, then do try and visit her Heron Gallery in West Cork,
where she runs a charming cafe. Report: 1009/THE SOUTH WEST.

736 **Kinsale Bookshop** 8 Main St · www.kinsalebookshop.com Wooden
3/J21 floorboards and wall to ceiling wooden shelves in this low-ceilinged little book
emporium make the Kinsale Bookshop one of Cork's classic bookshops.

737 **Giles Norman Photography** 45 Main St +353 21 4774373 ·
3/J21 www.gilesnorman.com Black and white large scale landscape photography is
Giles Norman's signature, and his work features elegant portraits of many iconic
Irish places, as well as cityscapes of Dublin, Venice, New York and London.

738 **Enibas Irish Jewellery** Main St, Sleveen +353 21 4777022 · www.enibas.com
3/J21 Sabine Lenz is both a designer and creator, and for 25 years her jewellery work
has been one of the most distinctive artistic signatures of West Cork. The original
Enibas Boutique is in Schull, West Cork, and the collection is also available online.

the
Best
of Galway

The Best of the Major Hotels

739 **The Connacht Hotel** Dublin Rd + 353 91 381200 · www.theconnacht.ie
4/G13 This is a great big hotel, but it is extremely well run and, if you are staying in
358 ROOMS one of their suites with your family and can use the well-equipped kitchens,
NO PETS then The Connacht works out at offering extremely good value for money, and
MED.INX parking is free. It's a little way outside the city, but if you don't object to a good
walk then you can steer clear of hiring taxis.

740 **The G Hotel & Spa** Wellpark + 353 91 865200 · www.theghotel.ie
4/G13 The G may be the most luxe hotel in Ireland. With interiors by the milliner
101 ROOMS Philip Treacy, it's garish, glam and girlish. Don't worry that the location is less
NO PETS than ideal: the G is actually an ocean liner, and when you step in the doors, you
EXP leave the everyday world far behind. The rooms have smart TVs with access to
Netflix, and the spa is excellent. The glam interiors mean that every visit here
feels very special.
EAT Jason O'Neill is the chef in the hotel's main restaurant, gigi's, and his food
is gracious and well-judged. One small gripe: we wish the tables and chairs in
the dining room weren't so low. Daytime dinner 7 days. Afternoon tea noon–
6pm daily.

741 **Ardilaun Hotel** Taylors Hill +353 91 521433 www.theardilaunhotel.ie
4/G13 A kilometre from the city centre on leafy, suburban Taylor's Hill, the Ardilaun
123 ROOMS is something of a Galway institution, the place where you stay when you go
NO PETS back year after year for the Galway races. With a pool and leisure club and a
MED.EXP kids club, it's very family oriented.
EAT One of Galway's leading chefs, Ultan Cooke, is at the reins of the hotel's
Camilaun Restaurant, so the cooking has a much more modern temperament
than one would expect of a suburban hotel. There is also food in their Ardilaun
Bistro. Food served all day 7 days.

742 **Park House** Forster St, Eyre Sq +353 91 569219 · www.parkhousehotel.ie
4/G13 The quiet professionalism of the Park House makes it the first choice for many
84 ROOMS visitors to Galway. The location, close to Eyre Square, is perfect, and their junior
NO PETS suites allow up to 4 people in a room. But it's the staff who make it, and the
lively bustle of Boss Doyle's bar is always fun.

743 **Radisson Blu** Lough Atalia Rd + 353 91 538300 ·
4/G13 www.radissonhotelgalway.com Centrally located, and just beside the
261 ROOMS bus station, the dedicated team of local staff members lifts the Radisson out
NO PETS of the ordinary. The rooms facing Lough Atalia and the railway have the best
views, and the rooms are thoughtfully equipped. But it's the staff who make
the difference here, and they erase any sense of a standard corporate hotel.
EAT In Raw – Sushi In The Sky, chef Hisahi Kumagai fashions an excellent
menu of sushi with nigiri, maki, oshi and temaki on offer. There are also
sashimi choices, along with ceviche and tuna tartare, and a single offering
of barbary duck for carnivores. Lovely selection of sake, and incredible views.
Tue-Sat.

The Best Individual & Boutique Hotels

744 ✓ **The House Hotel** Lower Merchant's Rd, Spanish Parade, Latin Quarter
4/G13   +353 91 538900 · www.thehouse.ie The House is a splendid boutique
40 ROOMS hotel, with comfortable rooms and staff who work hard and take their job seriously.
MED.INX The rooms are beautifully designed and maintained, and the public rooms are an
NO KIDS important part of Galway's cultural life: everyone meets everyone here for drinks.
ATMOS It's popular with hen parties, mind you, but we're okay with that. The location
couldn't be bettered, and nearby car parking is inexpensive. 'The service is
outstandingly friendly,' wrote *The New York Times*.

745 **The Huntsman** 164 College Rd +353 91 562849 · www.huntsmaninn.com
4/G13 Stephen Francis and his crew are amongst the best hospitality teams on the west
12 ROOMS coast. Nothing at this bar and restaurant with rooms, on the edge of Lough Atalia,
MED.INX seems out of the ordinary, but when you stay here, you quickly see just how good
these guys are. Every return visit brings evidence of slow, steady improvement and
we particularly like the rooms, which are spacious and understated.
EAT The menus in the Huntsman Restaurant are filled with clever modern food
that they deliver with accuracy. Breakfast, Lunch & dinner 7 days.

746 **The Residence Hotel** 39 Dominick St +353 91 569600 ·
4/G13 www.theresidencehotel.ie Residence is a new boutique hotel from the same
20 ROOMS people who run the big Connacht Hotel. As well as modish, musicianly design
MED.EXP features – this is where all those old Rolling Stone covers have ended up – it's
got Nextflix, Nespresso, high-speed wifi and Belaire champagne. The location is
smack-bang in the city centre, and there is traditional and jazz music sessions in
the bar. The hang-on-the-door breakfast bag could be better, but there are lots of
very good breakfast options nearby.

747 **7 Cross Street Boutique Hotel** 7 Cross St + 353 91 530100 ·
4/G13 www.7crossstreet.com If you like those tiny Parisian hotels where every
10 ROOMS element seems shoehorned into the tiniest space imaginable, then you will love
MED.INX 7 Cross Street. The rooms are tiny, the noise from the street is never-ending, and
it's just the best fun. If you do need more space, however, the owners also offer a
very stylish self catering house on Nun's Island, just across the river.

748 **Corrib House Tea Rooms & Guest Accommodation** 3 Waterside
4/G13 +353 91 446753 · www.corribhouse.com This pretty Georgian house,
5 ROOMS overlooking the salmon weir and hard by the banks of the River Corrib, has been
MED.EXP winning a terrific reputation, thanks to the dedicated hard work of Victoria and
David Bohan who took over the house in 2011. There are five elegant rooms, and a
pretty tea rooms and restaurant where they serve breakfast and lunch for guests
and visitors.

The Best Hotels Outside Town

749
4/G13
48 ROOMS
NO PETS
EXP-LOTS
ATMOS

✓✓ **The Twelve Hotel** Freeport, Barna +353 91 597000 ·
www.thetwelvehotel.ie In a funky, modern hotel at the crossroads at Barna, on the coastline several miles west of Galway city, manager Fergus O'Halloran and head chef Martin O'Donnell are the pair of creative heads who have powered The Twelve Hotel to a position of West Coast prominence.
EAT There is finely delivered cooking in the Pins Gastro Bar, whilst the pizzas in Pizza Dozzina are amongst the very best on the west coast. Their flagship restaurant is Upstairs @ West (758/TOP END RESTAURANTS).

750
4/G13
16 ROOMS
NO PETS
LLL
ATMOS
LOTS
FF

✓ **Ballynahinch Castle** Recess +353 95 31006 ·
www.ballynahinch-castle.com Ballynahinch manager Patrick O'Reilly controls things with great expertise and experience at the helm of this beautiful Castle, which has seen the creation of new rooms and a thorough upgrade of the hotel. The grounds are spectacular, and Ballynahinch has always been the most egalitarian of the big castles.
EAT In The Owenmore Restaurant there are beautiful views of the grounds and the river, where head chef Pete Durkan finesses terrific ingredients into elegant culinary productions. Many guests choose also to eat in the Fisherman's Pub, an authentic and atmospheric bar with lovely food.

751
4/G13
16 ROOMS
NO PETS
MED-INX
FF

Coach House Hotel & Basilico Restaurant Main St, Oranmore
+353 91 483693 · www.coachhousehotel.ie In the centre of Oranmore just S of Galway, this comfortable hotel is rock-steady, overseen by the team behind the delightful Basilico Restaurant, and just adjacent.
EAT Paolo Sabatini knows both the Italian art of cooking, and the Italian art of eating. His menus in Basilico celebrate west coast artisans, and with these peerless ingredients he weaves that Italian magic that ushers in the 'gift of making art out of life'. The confidence shows right through the menu, and goes all the way to the service, overseen by Fabio Mulas, who also organises a super wine list. Lunch & dinner 7 days.

752
4/G13
8 ROOMS
NO PETS
NO KIDS
NO TV
LL
EXP

Screebe House Rosmuc, Connemara +353 91 574110 · www.screebe.com
Large, Victorian-era lodge which was extensively refurbished back in 2010, and the luxury levels are pretty stratospheric, so settle in with a glass of their own whiskey, before enjoying the house and the grounds – all 42,000 acres. Screebe is owned by a wealthy family from Germany who occasionally arrive with groups of friends but, for most of the year, it operates as a conventional luxury hotel and fishing lodge. Rooms are in both the house and the newer Spa Lodge, which houses the indoor pool.
EAT Thanks to an extensive estate surrounding the beautiful Screebe, filled with lakes and wild game, chef Damian Ring has an abundance of fresh fish such as brown trout from the lakes, and game such as venison, woodcock and wild duck to bring to the table at dinner. Mr Ring is a real talent, and he makes the majestic Screebe even more special.

753
4/G13
141 ROOMS
EXP

Connemara Coast Hotel Furbo · www.connemaracoasthotel.ie ·
+353 91 592108 There is a sharpness, a cutting edge, in every element of the Connemara Coast Hotel, from the attire and attitude of the team, right through to the wonderful cooking at breakfast and dinner. It means that from the first minute when you are greeted at the reception, to the final goodbye as you leave the hotel, there are people looking after you. For us, this is the greatest luxury of all, and the secret to the hotelness of an hotel. Currently for sale as a going concern, we hope the exceptional team here continue to work together. If you are having your nuptials here, incidentally, do note that the bridal suite is one of the very best.

754
4/G13
LOTS

✓✓✓**Aniar** 53 Lower Dominick St +353 91 535947 ·
www.aniarrestaurant.ie A simple, tiny room in Galway's West End, but the simplicity only serves to magnify the Michelin-starred shine of this brilliant enterprise. JP McMahon and his young team are driven and ambitious, and their cooking offers the true tastes of the West of Ireland. The menus, with their simple iteration of ingredients – leek; crab; kohlrabi – give no hint of how creative this kitchen is but, right from the first dish of chicken heart with a burnt hay hollandaise, you are launched on the wildest culinary rollercoaster in the West. Do opt for the wine pairings, as they offer inspired choices. Dinner Tue-Sat, lunch Sat.

755
4/G13
EXP

✓✓✓**Loam** Geata Na Cathrach, Fairgreen +353 91 569727 ·
www.loamgalway.com In Galway's Loam restaurant, chefs Enda McEvoy and Conor Cockram love to cook with things that are barely there: Smoke. Crumb. Foam. Mousse. Meringue. Gel. Pollen. Loam is the culinary equivalent of the Elements. So, a taster of beef tenderloin looks like a prawn cracker. Coolea cheese is turned into a custard. Pickled kohlrabi is like watermelon. Squid becomes translucent noodles. No one else in Ireland cooks like this, and the result is astonishingly sensual. Dinner in Loam is one of the most exciting experiences you can have with food anywhere in Europe, and value for money, in a Michelin-starred restaurant, is exceptional. Dinner Tue-Sat.

756
4/G13
MED.EX
ATMOS

✓✓**Kai Cafe + Restaurant** Sea Rd +353 91 526003 ·
www.kaicaferestaurant.com Jess Murphy is that rare chef who unites ordinary decent food lovers, and food critics. Both are in awe of her ability to max the flavours out of any ingredient she chooses. Her food is simple, funky, unpretentious and different – much like the room, in fact – so you might have a Sea Road fish finger for your lunch, served with wild garlic ranch, and then have monkfish with sea spaghetti and cockles in a broth, before finishing with a Game of Cones sundae. In Kai, eating = fun. David Murphy presides with calm confidence. Mon-Sat breakfast & lunch, Sun brunch, dinner Tue-Sat.

757
4/G13
MED.EX
ATMOS

✓**Ard Bia at Nimmo's** Spanish Arch, Long Walk +353 91 561114 ·
www.ardbia.com Aoibheann MacNamara brought to the restaurant world the hipness and avant-garde perspective of the art world. Fuse the two, and you get Ard Bia, the funkiest, artsiest collation of people and cooking you can find in Ireland. But it's not just hipsterness you get here, for the cooking is soulful and respectful, right from breakfast through to dinner, and the baking is particularly special. Ard Bia is part and pivot of the Galway food revolution. Breakfast & lunch Mon-Fri, brunch Sat-Sun, Dinner 7 days.

758
4/G13
MED.EX

✓**Upstairs @ West** Barna Village +353 91 597000 ·
www.thetwelvehotel.ie Manager Fergus O'Halloran and head chef Martin O'Donnell are the pair of steady heads who have powered The Twelve Hotel in Barna to west coast prominence. There is fine cooking, both in the hotel bar and in their Pizza Dozzina, but Mr O'Donnell's subtle ways with west coast ingredients is a thrill. Start with Castlemine pig ear terrine, or house sloe gin cured salmon, and you are well on the way through Mr O'Donnell's wild creativity. The cheese trolley is one of the best, the wine list exceptional. Lunch Sun, dinner Wed-Sun.

759
4/G13
MED.INX
ATMOS
FF

✓✓ **Cava Bodega** 1 Middle St +353 91 539884 · www.cavarestaurant.ie JP McMahon's Cava Bodega is probably the most popular restaurant in Galway. McMahon and his team love the queer gear of Iberian food – pig's head fritters; chicken hearts with chorizo – and the surprise is that these dishes are just as popular as patatas bravas, or salt cod with romesco, or lomo ham. The atmosphere in the basement dining room is always up to 90 as everyone tears into tasty Spanish tapas and the excellent wines and sherries from Spain, and the dizzying mood is driven on by truly excellent service. Major fun. Lunch Sat-Sun, dinner 7 days.

760
4/G13
MED.INX

✓ **The Kitchen @ Galway City Museum** Spanish Parade +353 91 534883 · www.galwaycitymuseum.ie Michelle Kavanagh and her team make it look as if it's easy to do what they do in The Kitchen, at the City Museum. But it's not easy to be as precise about flavours and textures as the team here are, and their secret ingredient is simply that Ms Kavanagh is a real student of the culinary arts, always finding new ideas, new inspirations. Everything they do has a little riff, like brioche bread and butter pudding with Hazel Mountain chocolate sauce, or their frankfurter with pickled onion. Trying to make your mind up and decide what you want to eat is some sort of agony. Superb cooking. Daytime Tue-Sun.

761
4/G13
CHP

✓ **Builin Blasta** Spiddal Craft & Design Studios, Spiddal +353 91 558 559. www.builinblasta.com Heather Flaherty runs Builin Blasta at the Spiddal Craft Centre, just outside the pretty village of Spiddal. Ms Flaherty is one of the best talents on the West Coast, and everyone heads here for beautiful baking – sourdough rye; brioche; treacle brown bread; carrot cake; sausage rolls – great coffees, and a hearty lunch after a hair-tousling stroll on the beach is just sublime: broccoli and cheddar soup; vegan wrap with beetroot salad; Russian sausages; fish cakes; the classic veggie spag bol; bakewell tart. Kids are properly looked after, too. Daytime 7 days.

762
4/G13
CHP

Anton's 12a Father Griffin Rd + 353 91 582067 · www.antonscafe.com Across the bridge over the River Corrib heading towards Salthill, Anton O'Malley's little corner room does the good thing. We like the calmness of the space, so settle in with a coffee and some buttermilk pancakes, check out the artworks, and mainline that unique, funky Galway culture. Breakfast & lunch 7 days. There is a second Anton's in Salthill, Antons@Ozone, under the Galway Business and Language School at the Galway Cultural Institute.

763
4/G13
CHP

Goya's 2/3 Kirwans Lane + 353 91 567010 · www.goyas.ie Emer Murray's status as the best baker in Galway has never been challenged in over 25 years. In her stylish Kirwan's Lane café and shop, Ms Murray remains the best, a patissier of precision, exactitude and accomplishment. Nothing comes out of the kitchen at Goya's – from the simplest sandwich to the most mellifluously ethereal cake – unless it is the best it can possibly be. Daytime Mon-Sat.

764 **Griffin's Bakery** 21 Shop St + 353 91 563683 · www.griffinsbakery.com
4/G13 Jimmy Griffin's bakery is no mere bread shop. Instead, it is a temple of good things,
CHP and we all come here to pledge fealty to Mr Griffin's devotion to making beautiful
things to eat. Mr Griffin hasn't just continued the family bakery business: he has
super-charged it, steadily broadening the list of breads and cakes, whilst running
a superb tea rooms, and yet never losing their focus on the fact that 'Bread is
not bread unless it is made by an artisan bakery'. Griffin's is that artisan bakery.
Daytime 7 days. From 7.30 am Mon-Sat.

765 **Armorica** Main St, Oranmore +353 91 388343 · www.armorica.ie East of
4/G13 the city in amidst the twisting main street of Oranmore, Armorica had seen several
MED.INX identities come and go until Natasha Hughes and chef Nicolas Denis – both
Galway restaurant veterans – gave the room a makeover and started to serve some
arrestingly creative cooking. It's notable that the menu particularly showcases
seafood – smoked and cured fish with blinis; crab meat with tomato jelly; clams
with velvet crab bisque; mussels with Longueville cider; cod with smoked chicken
sauce. With a smart wine list, and nine fine rooms upstairs at decent prices,
Armorica is a classy destination. Dinner 7 days.

766 **Upstairs @ McCambridge's** 38/39 Shop St +353 91 562259 ·
4/G13 www.mccambridges.com For 90 years, McCambridge's has been the pivot of
CHP Galway's food culture, a shop whose doctrine of excellence and service has only
ATMOS improved with the passing of the years. Eoin McCambridge has spoken of the family's
philosophy that you 'have to reinvest and reimagine the business every few years',
and Eoin and his sister, Natalie, do just that. Their café, Upstairs@McCambridge's
proved to be a pathbreaking success and the shop is also part of the Galway Whiskey
Trail. The shop and café are a cultural catalyst for the city. Daytime Mon-Sat, brunch
Sun, till 8 pm Thur-Sat.

767 **Petit Delice** 7 Mainguard St +353 91 500751 · @LePetitDelice Whilst it is
4/G13 starry chefs who garner the most attention, every food lover knows that Galway's
CHP culinary reputation rests with destinations like Alexandra Saivre's La Petit Delice.
You come to this pretty room for sweet and savoury treats, for teas and coffee, for
the chance to enjoy a moment of respite from the fever that is Galway. Even if you
aren't taking a table in the café, the bread and sweet counter, with its colourful
bricolage of baking, is a treat, and the Petit Delice baguette is regarded as the best
in town. Daytime 7 days, till 7 pm Fri & Sat.

768 **Le Petit Pois** Victoria Pl +353 91 330880 · www.lepetitpois.ie Philippe and
4/G13 Michele Renaut's pretty little upstairs dining room, through the archway and down
MED.EXP a laneway at Victoria Place, just off Eyre Square, offers an intriguing Gallic riff on
excellent Irish ingredients. Michele cooks, whilst Philippe – an oenologist – takes
care of the wines and the room. The menu descriptions are in French, with English
below, and there are usually four starters and main courses on offer, with a quintet
of excellent puddings. Nice cooking – parsnip soup with Roquefort and walnuts;
hake with cardamom butter; sirloin with tomato, courgette and aubergine sauce;
chocolate fondant with Teeling whiskey. Value is very keen, especially for the set
menus, and take Philippe's advice and you will discover excellent wines. Dinner
Tue-Sun.

769   **37 West**   37 Lower Newcastle Rd +353 91 524122 · www.37westcafe.com
4/G13   Gill Carroll's 37 West reveals the strength of Galway's culinary culture. It could
MED.INX   coast by just as a student place – it's across the street from NUI Galway – but
whilst the students are there for the takeaways, the rest of the crowd are here
because 37 West food totally rocks, and to have food of this quality in a modest,
hip room shows just how much depth there is to the city's food. The staff are, of
course, simply brilliant. Daytime 7 days. Gill also runs 56 Central, on Shop Street, in
the centre of town.

770   **Gourmet Tart Company**   171 Salthill Upr +353 91 861667 ·
4/G13   www.gourmettartco.com   The cooking in the GTC is every bit as stylish as
CHP   this gorgeous room. Start the day with a bowl of power porridge with maple
syrup, or Colleran's bacon with a free-range egg, and you'll be back at lunchtime
to try the pasta alla Norma, or the Thai duck salad, with sweet potato fries.
Great for brunch on Sunday – blueberry buttermilk pancakes; eggs Royale. A
real Salthill classic. Daytime, till 6 pm Sun-Thur, 7.30 pm Fri & Sat. There are
several Galway Tart Company locations in Galway city, including Galway
Shopping Centre, Newcastle Rd, Abbeygate St, Raven Ter. and they have a
market stall at the Galway Market.

771   **Hazel Mountain Chocolate**   9 Middle St +353 65 7078847 ·
4/G13   www.hazelmountainchocolate.com   Kasha and John Connolly's bean to bar
CHP   enterprise in the Burren quickly birthed this Galway offshoot, where you can
buy their superb chocolate bars and spreads as well as a delightful menu of hot
chocolate drinks: urban woodsman; gingerbread; 65% Ecuador. Good coffee as
well. Daytime Mon-Sat, till 7 pm. The original Hazel Mountain Chocolate Organic
Cafe is in Belharbour, Co Clare.

772   **The Secret Garden Tea Room**   4 William S W +353 85 7583927 ·
4/G13   www.secretgardengalway.com   Mara Gedrovica's secret place is, happily,
CHP   becoming less of a secret as people discover and warm to this enigmatic and
different room, with its incredible array of teas – rooibos pretty woman, anyone? –
and the lovely areas to relax in and, maybe, smoke a shisha. It's a cult place, left-field,
unorthodox and, thereby, perfectly at home in Galway. Lunch & dinner 7 days.

773   **Delight Health Café**   Renmore Av, Renmore +343 91 761466 · www.delight.ie
4/G13   A little way outside the city in Renmore, Delight is based at the Kingfisher Club
CHP   where Paula Lawrence and her team specialise in healthful cooking: raw power
salad; humous bagel with roasted vegetables; avocado and spinach smoothie.
Clever, holistic cooking. Breakfast & lunch Mon-Sat.

774   **Maxwell's Restaurant**   Williamsgate St + 353 91 568974 ·
4/G13   www.maxwellsrestaurant.ie   Paul O'Meara's bistro is friendly and fun and the
MED.INX   cooking is spot on: good, tasty food with something to suit all ages and also very
FF   affordable. Lunch & dinner 7 days.

The Best Vegetarian & Vegan Restaurants

775   **The Light House**   8 Upper Abbeygate St +353 87 3520198 ·
4/G13   @The.Light.House.Tea.Room   Alison Haslam's vegan cooking in this pretty
CHP   space is vivacious and smart: come on, what's not to love about a vegan Black
Forest gateau! The savoury cooking is just as adventurous – smoked tofu with black
beans and quinoa; vegetarian tart with cashew nut cream. Daytime 7 days.

776   **TGO Falafel Bar**   11 Mary St +353 86 1890655 · @GalwayFalafel   This is the
4/G13   bricks'n'mortar home of The Gourmet Offensive, best known for their busy stall in
CHP   the Galway Market. They have been doing the good vegetarian and vegan thing in
this cosy and colourful space since 2015, so go for The Worx, and get falafels with
humous, salads and pickles in a wholemeal pitta at a giveaway price. Their chips,
in particular, are regarded by many as being the best in the city. Daytime 7 days, till
8/9 pm. Sat & Sun in the Galway Market, where they have traded since 2005.

Where to Eat Brunch

777   **Dela**   51 Lower Dominick S + 353 91 449252 · www.dela.ie   Joe and Margaret
4/G13   Bohan are re-writing the restaurant book in Dela. With their own smallholding
MED.INX   in Moycullen providing the produce for the kitchen, and their own nano-brewing
venture, the couple are sowing, growing, and brewing their way to a unique
distinctiveness. The success of their brunch means that it is now offered 6 days a
week, and the Dela brunch extends beyond the standard eggs-and-things: braised
beef cheeks with Bellingham Blue cheese on sourdough; scrambled egg burrito;
minted feta and felafel wrap. Dinner offers the same smart, well thought-through
food. Daytime & dinner 7 days.

✓✓ **Kai Cafe + Restaurant** Many food lovers say that the best time to enjoy
Kai is brunch time at the weekends. They're right, but you need to get
there early, or be prepared to wait. Report: 756/TOP END RESTAURANTS.

✓ **The Kitchen @ Galway City Museum** Brunch all day from the brilliant
Michelle Kavanagh and her team: don't miss the brioche bread and butter
pudding with Hazel Mountain chocolate sauce. Report: 760/CASUAL
RESTAURANTS.

✓ **Ard Bia at Nimmo's** The riverside destination for the Hippy Fry, or Turkish
baked beans. Report: 757/TOP END RESTAURANTS.

Gourmet Tart Company Nothing better than a big walk along the seafront at
Strandhill, followed by Sunday brunch at GTC: shakshuka with feta; muffins with
poached eggs. Report: 770/CASUAL RESTAURANTS.

Upstairs @ McCambridge's All day brunch is served upstairs in one of the city's
nicest rooms on Sunday. Report: 766/CASUAL RESTAURANTS.

The Best Burgers & Steaks

778 **Burgatory** 1 Quay Lane · www.burgatorybar.com Owners Enda Hoolihaa
4/G13 and Tara Haugh are rewriting the burger book in Burgatory. They source their raw
CHP ingredients from the very best west coast artisans, so this is Slow Food Fast Food:
chicken fingers made with Friendly Farmer birds; bacon cheese burger made with
Castlemine Farm beef and Colleran's bacon. Enda and Tara did things the Galway
way – a food cart at the festivals, then pop-ups, then the room on Quay Lane
– and Burgatory is actually Revolutionary Burger. Great Americana rock 'n' roll
soundtrack sets the raucous mood. Lunch & dinner 7 days.

779 **Handsome Burger** Moycullen Country Market, Moycullen, Co Galway ·
4/G13 @handsomeburger A roving feast, appearing at the Moycullen Country Market
CHP each Friday, and festivals and markets throughout the city and county, and
now with a home in the busy Caribou pub on Wood Quay, a trendy pub with
an emphasis on craft beers. Handsome specialises in burgers and 28-day aged
sirloin steak sandwiches.

✓✓ **Kai Cafe + Restaurant** Jess Murphy serves a dry-aged striploin, from
Brady's butchers in Athenry, with blue cheese butter and sprouting
broccoli, and it's carnivore heaven. Report: 756/TOP END RESTAURANTS.

Brasserie on the Corner McGeough's butchers provide fine sirloin, rib-eye
and fillet, and the Brasserie kitchen will cook them any way you like, from blue
to well-done. Report: 816/BARS WITH GOOD FOOD.

The Best Seafood Restaurants

780 **Oscar's Seafood Bistro** 22 Upper Dominick St + 353 91 582180 ·
4/G13   www.oscarsbistro.ie Michael O'Meara and Sinead Hughes were the first
MED.EX   restaurateurs to colonise Galway's West End in the name of good cooking and,
ATMOS   almost two decades later, O'Meara's seafood cookery, and Ms Hughes' superb
service, keep Oscar's at the top of Galway eating. Mr O'Meara is a curious,
intelligent cook, and his knowledge of the riches of west coast seafood is second-
to-none: his book, *Seafood Gastronomy*, is regarded as a modern classic. Dinner
Mon-Sat.

781 **O'Grady's on the Pier** Seapoint, Barna + 353 91 592223 ·
4/G13   www.ogradysonthepier.com Mike O'Grady's end-of-pier restaurant, is
MED.EX   atmospheric and charming, and has been consistent and reliable for many years.
FF   Seafood is their signature, and the team like to riff on the classics. There are dishes
apart from fish and shellfish, of course, but those are the ones to go for. The restaurant
has a sister establishment, Kirwan's Lane, in Galway city. Lunch & dinner 7 days.

782 **McDonagh's Seafood House** 22 Quay St +353 91 565001 ·
4/G13   www.mcdonaghs.net McDonagh's enjoys nationwide fame for its fish and chip
MED.INX   bar, but their seafood bar on Quay Street offers a comprehensive array of seafood
dishes – monkfish with smoked bacon; ray wing with mussel sauce; lemon sole
with champ. Boisterous, unpretentious, and great fun. Lunch & dinner 7 days.

Hooked Whilst owner Nosheen Jalilvand describes Hooked as 'a fish and chip
restaurant' it's a lot more than that, so bring on the brill with Mediterranean
vegetables, the fish burger with tartare; the john dory with sautéed potatoes; the
chocolate fudge cake. Report: 1462/FISH & CHIPS.

The Best Italian Restaurants

783
4/G13
MED.EXP
ATMOS

Il Vicolo O'Brien's Bridge + 353 91 530515 · www.ilvicolo.ie Gerry McMahon and his Il Vicolo team have a beautiful space in the Bridge Mills building, a trio of stone-clad rooms where the River Corrib – literally – rushes underneath you. Their signature style of Italian small plates, cicchetti, and larger plates is rock-steady and invigorating. The wines are fabulous, the service is smart and hip. Lunch & dinner Tue-Sun.

784
4/G13
MED.EXP

Da Roberta's Ristorante & Pizzeria 161 Upper Salthill + 353 91 585808 · www.darobertas.ie The cooking in Da Roberta is Italy's Greatest Hits: pastas; pizzas; calzones. It's theatrical, and fun. Lunch & dinner 7 days.

785
4/G13
MED.INX

La Collina 169 Upper Salthill + 353 91 450716 · @lacollinagalway You have got to love an Italian restaurant that makes green pasta for St Patrick's Day. But whatever day of the year it is, La Collina's fresh pastas will always be aptly delicious. The pizzas are no slouch either; here is a team, in both the kitchen and at front-of-house, who really do put their Italian heart into it. Dinner from 4pm, 7 days, Sun lunch.

Basilico Report: 751/HOTELS OUTSIDE TOWN.

The Best Pizza

786
4/G13
MED.INX
ATMOS
FF

✓**The Dough Bros** 24 Upper Abbeygate St +353 87 1761662 · www.thedoughbros.ie In 2013 Eugene Greaney lost his job. Three short years later, by way of food carts and pop ups, Mr Greaney and his team at Dough Bros were rockin' it in a super-funky, 70-seater restaurant in one of Galway's historic buildings. The Dough Bros turned adversity into triumph, and they did it by making the coolest pizzas on the west coast. Everything they do is pure Dough Bros, which means it's not like how anyone else would do it. Their pizzas are original, they have their own craft beer, and Dough Bros is the most fun a pizza restaurant can be. So, order up the Buffalo Soldier, or the Hail Caesar, or the Prawn Po'boy, and go with the Dough. No visitor to Galway should miss these pizzas. Lunch & dinner 7 days.

787
4/G13
MED.EXP
FF

Pizza Dozzina Barna + 353 91 597012 · www.thetwelvehotel.ie 'The dough is exactly what you would expect from an Italian wood-fired oven: it's deliciously blistered and blackened around its puffed-up edges while the thin base acts as the perfect vessel for its assorted toppings.' That's *The Irish Times*, singing the praises of the Pizza Dozzina pizzas. Not only are the pizza bases ace, but the groovy toppings are sublime, especially their own signature creations such as The Connemara, with spiced lamb, sage and sesame seeds, and The Barna Crossroads, with Connemara smoked ham, Gubbeen cheese and Irish buffalo mozzarella. Lunch & dinner & takeaway 7 days.

La Collina Report: 785/BEST ITALIAN.
Basilico Report: 751/HOTELS OUTSIDE TOWN.

The Best Ethnic Restaurants

CHINESE

788 **The Royal Villa** 1st Floor, Galway Atlantaquaria, Quincentennial
4/G13 **Drive, Salthill + 353 91 580131 www.royalvilla.ie** The Chang family's
MED.INX Chinese restaurants are amongst the longest-established in Galway – it is
more than 25 years since Charlie Chang opened the original premises in Shop
Street, in the centre of town. Today their stylish Salthill restaurant is housed
in the National Aquarium, where the menus are modern, accessible and pan-
Asian in style, so choosing is easy, and service is polite and helpful. Dinner
7 days (closed Mon off season). A second branch of Royal Villa is at Oranmore.

PAN ASIAN

789 **Xi'An Street Food** 9 Quay St +353 91 534931 · www.xianstreetfood.ie
4/G13 The specialities of Xi'an – biang biang hand-ripped noodles, and the roujiamo
CHP shredded halal meat burgers served in a flat bread bun – have brought the first
taste of Shaanxi province cooking to the centre of Galway. After they have been
slapped and stretched, the noodles are cooked and flavoured with hot pepper and
chilli, and can be ordered as a soup or served with meat or fish. It's not all far out
fare; there are Singapore noodles and massaman curries, but it's great fun to watch
the noodles being made. Noon-midnight 7 days.

790 **Lime Asian Infusion** Flood St, Spanish Arch +353 91 534935 ·
4/G13 **www.limegalway.com** There is a rather nice terrace facing the river at Lime, for
MED.INX fine evenings when the wind is calm. The fusion cooking is broadly based – you
TERRACE can get a 10oz steak with sweet potato fries, or Granny's curry laksa, or Singapore
noodles, and they offer small plates which they call Asian tapas – and it's popular
both for eating and for take-away. Lunch & dinner 7 days.

791 **Asian Tea House** 15 Mary St +353 91 563749 · www.asianteahouse.ie
4/G13 Every detail is very carefully considered in Terry Common's stylish, moody pan-
MED.EXP Asian tea house and eating room. Dark furnishings imported from the Orient set
the mood, and the food follows suit. Start with a good cocktail in the Buddha Bar.
Open Dinner Mon-Sun.

792 **Papa Rich** 3 Daly's Place, Woodquay +353 91 450147 ·
4/G13 **www.paparichkitchen.com** Upstairs above Bar an Chaladh on Woodquay,
MED.INX owners Kevin and Rebecca have summoned their experience working in Galway
restaurants to open up their own place, and Papa Rich quickly caught the attention
of Galway food lovers. The menu is extensive but this is good Asian cooking, even
if it wanders all over the zone and reads like Asia's Greatest Hits. Fantastic value.
There is also a take-away – Papa Rich Express – out on the Headford Rd and a
Papa Rich Bistro upstairs at the Born department store, overlooking the river.
Lunch & dinner 7 days.

793 **JalanJalan** 4 Grianan Gael, Newcastle Rd · www.jalanjalan.ie Out of town,
4/G13 close to the hospital, Jalan Jalan is a colourful home for Asian street food – Japanese
MED.INX gyoza; hot and sour soup; wok-fried duck; beef rendang. Lunch Mon-Fri, dinner, from
3.30 pm 7 days. There is a sister restaurant on Castle St in Sligo.

794 **Chi** 2 Middle St + 353 91 861687 www.chiasiantakeaway.com
4/G13   Andy Bandara and Catherine O'Brien operate two Chi outlets, the city branch
MED.INX in Middle St and the take-away branch in Westside. Their menus and dishes
span the Orient, with specialities from Malaysia, Singapore, Thailand, Vietnam
and China, so you can run the gamut from egg fried rice to roast duck to king
prawn soup. Dinner from 4pm 7 days. Chi Asian Takeaway at Westside Enterprise
Park, Westside.

INDIAN

795 **Tulsi Restaurant** 3 Buttermilk Walk, Middle St @TulsiIndianGalway Tulsi is
4/G13   one of the longest established Indian restaurants in the city, and it's a comfortable,
MED.INX unpretentious room with very engaged staff who look after everyone very well. If
you are in the mood for chicken jalfrezi, and excellent value, then it's the place.
Dinner 7 days.

The Best Sushi & Japanese Restaurants

796 ✓**Wa Café** 13 New Dock St + 353 91 895850 · www.wacafe.net Wa is
4/G13   small, simple and intimate, and immediately captivating. You step in the door
MED.INX out of Galway's Docklands and you are immediately in Kyoto. The clean, precise
food further enhances the fact that any meal here is a cultural as well as culinary
experience. Yoshimi Hayakawa's sushi sets should not be missed, and there are
also bento boxes, noodles, sashimi and osozai – small tapas-like dishes such as
kimpira or pork katsu – and miso. Serene service just makes everything more
enchanting. Evening menu 7 days, lunch Fri-Sun.

797 ✓**Kappa-Ya** 4 Middle St Mews + 353 91 865930 · @kappaya.galway
4/G13   Junichi Yoshiyagawa rewrote the book on fusion cooking when he first paired
MED.INX Irish lamb with miso and blue cheese, then put it on a plate in his tiny, single-room
restaurant. Since then, a wild ride of dishes spills forth from the kitchen.
Lunchtimes are a little more straightforward, with sushi rolls, bento boxes, and
tempura and rice bowls that offer some of the best value in the city. But for that
real walk on the culinary wild side, there is no other experience quite like dinner at
Kappa-Ya. Lunch & dinner Mon-Sat.

798 **Tomodachi Sushi Bar** Colonial Building, 2 Eglinton St + 353 91 564939
4/G13   @tomodachigalway Across from the Brown Thomas department store, and
MED.INX upstairs above Maxwell's restaurant, Tomodachi is home to the only sushi conveyor
in town. There is an open kitchen, and the room is divided into three sections:
tatami seating; table seating, and the conveyor belt zone. It's a pretty room with
lanterns and kimonos and Japanese artworks. Lunch & dinner 7 days.

Raw – Sushi in the Sky Radisson Hotel Report: 743/MAJOR HOTELS.

The Best Original Pubs

799
4/G13
ATMOS

✓✓✓ **Tigh Neachtain** 17 Cross St +353 91 568820 www.tighneachtain.com You pronounce it 'Nokton' and having a drink in what may be the most famous pub in the city is a rite of passage: if you haven't had a glass of Redbreast or Galway Hooker in here, then you haven't actually been to Galway. A sepia-tinged warren of cosy snugs, amiable crowds, and don't miss the excellent daytime dishes, created by Sarah Coffrey and her team in the Kasbah wine bar next door to the pub: Flaggy Shore oysters with Cuinneog buttermilk; stout-braised beef stew; cauliflower and goat's cheesecake. Neachtain's is as classic as an Irish pub can be.

800
4/G13

Garavan's 46 William St +353 91 562537 · www.garavans.ie A Galway institution since they opened the doors in 1937, Garavan's is a classic Irish pub, and one that is also much celebrated for their specialisation in Irish whiskeys. Paul Garavan and his team offer a tasting platter of three Irish whiskeys in special tasting glasses, with tasting notes.

801
4/G13

Freeney's 19 High St +353 91 562609 Opened since 1938, Freeney's used to combine the business of a general merchant – packing their own sugar and tea, bottling their own whiskeys – with the business of running a pub. Today, the general merchant side is confined to the fact that they sell fishing tackle, thereby providing you with the perfect excuse: 'I just nipped out to get a fishing rod, but I walked in the wrong door by mistake!' We believe you.

802
4/G13

E. Brún 55 Lwr Dominick St +353 91 565821 · @ebrun.bar It was a post office before Tom McDonagh opened E Brun a decade ago, and began to play a role in the reinvigoration of the West End. It's a tiny pub, which we like, and we also like the fact that it feels like a real local pub.

803
4/G13
ATMOS

Tig Coili Mainguard St +353 91 561294 · www.tigcoiligalway.com They call themselves 'a country pub in the middle of the city', and that's just right: a real Galway classic, with fantastic musician sessions.

804
4/G13
ATMOS

O'Connor's Famous Pub Salthill +353 91 523468 · www.oconnorsbar.com The Salthill legend that is O'Connor's may look like a stage-Irish pub from a Martin McDonagh play, but it's the real deal. Jam-packed with geegaws, bric-a-brac, memorabilia, paraphernalia and any and every piece of bricolage that you could find in an Irish bar, you only have to step in the door to step back in time, all the way back to 1875 when it opened.

805
4/G13

Dail Bar 42-44 Middle St + 353 91 563777 · www.thedailbar.com The Dail is one of the classic Galway pubs, perennially busy with a young crowd. The name doesn't refer to Ireland's parliament, however: it means a place where people meet to discuss and debate.

806
4/G13
TERRACE

An Púcán 11 Forster St +353 91 376561 · www.anpucan.ie This famous Galway pub, on the corner of Eyre Square is now run by the same people who own the Connacht and Residence hotels in the city. The pub is one of the founding members of the Galway Whiskey Trail, and the selection is breathtaking, including their own cask bottling from Teeling's whiskey, so make sure that is on your tasting platter. Music sessions, DJs, beer garden, and food, and a slew of HD televisions for watching the match. Food served until 8pm.

 The King's Head Atmospheric pub that has stood here since the 13th century. Report: 815/BARS WITH GOOD FOOD.

The Best Craft Beer & Brew Pubs

807
4/G13
ATMOS

✔ **The Salt House** Ravens Terrace +353 91 441550 · www.galwaybaybrewery.com There are scores of bottled artisan beers for sale in this beautiful bar, part of a chain of eleven pubs owned by the Galway Brewing Company. There are also some two dozen craft beers, ales and stouts rotating on tap, so you step in the door of the Salt House and, basically, you step into Beer Heaven. The crew are purist – there are no beers at all from corporate brewers – but they aren't didactic about it, so if you are bewildered by the choice, simply ask what they recommend.

808
4/G13
ATMOS

Oslo Salthill +353 91 448390 · www.galwaybaybrewery.com Oslo is a bustling big bar and brewery, at the seaside end of Salthill. Of most interest to visitors is their range of six craft beers, from their own Galway Bay Brewery: Buried at Sea; Bay Ale; Of Foam & Fury; Stormy Port; Full Sail; Althea. The beers also match up with the modern tasty food served in the bar. Most of the Irish craft beers are also sold, as well as a great range of international brews.

809
4/G13
ATMOS

Bierhaus 2 Henry St +353 91 587766 · www.bierhausgalway.com Bierhaus is a haven for beer heads, and offers the most amazing selection of craft beers in one of Galway's great pubs. Snacks and sandwich menu.

The Best Music Pubs

810
4/G13

Tigh Giblin Spiddal + 353 91 504787 www.tighgiblin.com Brenda and Ned ran various bars in the States before coming home and taking over the famous Tigh Giblin. Great spot for music – musicians play every evening in the summer season. Just bring your bodhran.

811
4/G13

Taaffe's Bar 19 Shop St +353 91 564006 · @TaaffesBarGalway Right in the middle of Shop St, and relatively easy to miss, Taaffe's is respected for the quality of the pint, and for their traditional music sessions. Bar food.

812
4/G13

The Crane Bar 2 Sea Rd +353 91 587419 · www.thecranebar.com Much-loved destination, both as a traditional Galway pub, and as a venue for great music. Music sessions upstairs each evening; less formal, impromptu sessions in the bar.

813
4/G13
ATMOS

Roisin Dubh Dominic St +353 91 586540 · www.roisindubh.net This Galway institution is where you go to listen to headlining bands and great comedy shows — Roisin Dubh is at the heart of the Galway Comedy Festival. For many years the Roisin Dubh has provided a stage for alternative music and upcoming residencies. Silent Disco on Tue nights which is popular with city's students.

814
4/G13

Monroe's Tavern Dominick St +353 91 583397 · www.monroes.ie This great big pub on the edge of Galway's West End has music every night. Bar food.

Tig Cóilí Mainguard St The crowds literally spill out onto Mainguard St from Tig Cóilí, so it's the place for a boisterous music session, but not for a quiet pint. Report: 803/ORIGINAL PUBS.

Bars with Good Food

815
4/G13
MED.INX
ATMOS

✓ **The King's Head** Olde Malt Mall, High St + 353 91 567866 ·
www.thekingshead.ie Paul and Mary Grealish have created a beautiful room in the bistro of the legendary, 800-year-old King's Head pub, with a cosy snug and a neat bar adjacent to the main dining room of the bistro. There is a real tactility in both the room and in the food on the plate. Start the evening with a gin cocktail, have their signature lobster and chips or a great T-bone for the main course, and then head into the King's Head itself for a whiskey or two at their Irish whiskey bar. Lunch & dinner 7 days.

816
4/G13
MED.EXP
ATMOS

Brasserie on the Corner 25 Eglington St +353 91 530333 ·
www.brasseriegalway.com Part of the very busy Blakes Bar, this brick-and-wood brasserie delivers excellent food, further distinguished by a great service team. The selection of brasserie boards are a neat way to sample local artisan foods, superb fresh fish is particularly noteworthy. Great atmosphere late on. Lunch & dinner 7 days.

817
4/G13
MED.INX

Blakes Corner Bar 25 Eglington St +353 91 530053
· www.brasseriegalway.com The sister bar to Brasserie on the Corner has its own menus – carrot and coriander soup; Madras-style chicken and sweet potato curry; lamb stew with barley – and it's a characterful, vivacious pub. Lunch & dinner 7 days.

818
4/G13
MED.INX
ATMOS

The Universal 9 William St W +353 91 728271 · @Theuniversalbar
Super funky – hot and sour dumpling soup; maki roll; Russian salad. Great gins; an excellent selection of craft beers; fantastic jumble-sale chicness, and we really applaud this cool attempt to reimagine the very concept of pub food. Dinner 7 days.

819
4/G13
MED.INX

Front Door High St +353 91 563757 · www.frontdoorpub.com A hugely popular Galway pub, particularly with sports fans, the Front Door boasts four bars spread over two floors, and there is some good cooking. Lunch & dinner 7 days.

820
4/G13

John Keogh's – The Lock Keeper 22 Upr Dominick St +353 91 449431 ·
www.johnkeoghs.ie This handsome, club-like West End bar is serious about its food, and careful sourcing of top-class ingredients makes for some fine gastropub eating.

Oslo Report: 808/CRAFT BEER.

The Best Places to Drink Cocktails

821
4/G13
Bite Club 36 Upper Abbeygate St + 353 91 569824. www.biteclub.ie
The question to ask about Biteclub is not what is it, so much as what isn't it? It's a streetfood discotheque, where you will find fine things to eat for brunch, lunch and dinner – beef slider with beet humous; Louisiana chicken burger – and excellent things to drink – gin and watermelon slushie; bloody Maire; black pepper margarita. It's also a place to hear cool sounds, to do some dancing, to party, to grab a coffee, to do brunch, sip a craft beer, and listen to a DJ. Bites, lunch & dinner Wed-Sun. Food served till late and drinks till 2 am.

822
4/G13
Tribeton 1-3 Merchant's Rd +353 91 421600 · www.tribeton.ie This vast warehouse of a bar and restaurant, down near to the Docks, has created its own list of New Way cocktails, in addition to the classic sours, martinis and negronis. All day beverage menu, brunch, lunch & dinner 7 days.

823
4/G13
Buddha Bar 14 Mary St +353 91 563749 · www.buddhabar.com The next door bar of the highly regarded Asian Tea House serves almost two dozen cocktails, at very fair prices.

✓**The House Hotel** Report 744/BOUTIQUE HOTELS

Nova 1 William St There is an excellent, and comprehensive list of cocktails on offer in Nova, the best known gay bar in the city. Drag acts and DJs at the weekends. Report: 1261/GAY.
The Universal Report: 818/BARS WITH GOOD FOOD
The G Hotel Report: 740/MAJOR HOTELS

The Best Wine Bars

824
4/G13
MED.INX
ATMOS
✓✓**Sheridan's Cheesemongers & Winebar** Yard St +353 91 564829 (shop) + 353 91 564832 (wine bar) · www.sheridanscheesemongers.com
Sheridan's is unique. On the ground floor is the best cheese shop in Ireland. Upstairs is the best wine bar in Ireland, with amazing wines and delicious cheese and charcuterie plates. But it's not just the wines and the cheeses that make Sheridan's special: it's the atmosphere, the ambience, the staff, the buzz that happens when you put a bunch of the most interesting people in a city into one room. It's not a wine bar: it's a salon, and there is nowhere else like it. Instead of Lunch & Dinner, it's Wine and Cheese - that's what they serve all day. 7 days.

825
4/G13
MED.INX
ATMOS
Martine's Quay St Wine Bar 21 Quay St +353 91 565662 · www.winebar.ie Martine put a smart facade on her smart wine bar a few years back but, behind the new surface, this Galway institution continued doing what it does the way it has always done it: cooking nice food, making people happy, ensuring they come back time and again, and doing everything with a smile. Martine and her team could coast on the tourist trade, but they don't: every day they make it new. Superb wine list. Lunch Mon-Sat, brunch Sun, dinner 7 days.

826 **Tartare Cafe and Wine Bar** 56 Dominick St Lwr +353 91 567803 ·
4/G13   @tartaregalway Directly facing his ground-breaking Aniar restaurant, on
MED.EXP Dominick St, JP McMahon's third Galway city venture personifies his ability
to marry high-concept food and wines with simple, modest design. From the
benchmark cheese scones with fermented butter and a cup of coffee, to dazzling
small plates such as oysters with sea lettuce, and beef tartare with pickled onions,
McMahon has once again rewritten the book. Drigin Gaffey's design of the room is
a beaut. Lunch & dinner 7 days.

827 **Kasbah Wine Bar at Tigh Neactain,** 3 Quay St +353 85 7340164 · www.
kasbahwinebar.ie Sarah Coffrey and her team have brought an enriching
culinary tapestry to the wealth of Galway's food scene. Citing the great Diana Henry
as a particular influence, Ms Coffrey cooks smart, soulful food. Elena Dove offers
superb wines in her role as Oste, the person who brings you the good wine, and the
list reads like a juicy novel. Evenings till 11pm/12.30am.

Il Vicolo Report: 783/BEST ITALIAN RESTAURANTS.

The Best Coffee

828 ✓**Coffeewerk + Press** Quay St +353 91 448667 ·
4/G13   www.coffeewerkandpress.com Daniel Ulrichs brings us beautiful
CHP coffee and sweet snacks downstairs, with beans from Berlin's The Barn and
Copenhagen's Coffee Collective, whilst upstairs there are design objects whose
beauty will melt your heart. Mr Ulrichs and his crew are coffee obsessives,
agonising over every detail of the process; the result is spellbinding coffee and hot
chocolate. Mr Ulrichs also seeks out design and art objects 'that appeal to the
physical and aesthetic'; his design objects hit those desired targets with ease.
Daytime 7 days.

829 **Badger and Dodo** Fairgreen Rd +353 87 0532660 · www.badgeranddodo.ie
4/G13   The Fairgreen area of Galway is finally awakening from a lengthy slumber; the first
CHP Badger & Dodo café to open its doors is a bright new player in the zone. Comfy
and cool, the coffees are killer good, and it's great to see eager culinary creativity
returning to this part of the city. Daytime 7 days.

830 **Urban Grind** 8 William St W +353 91 375000 · www.urbangrind.ie
4/G13   Here's how good Urban Grind is: the stellar chefs in Galway will often tell
CHP you that Pádraig and Lisa Lynagh's coffee shop is their fave place. Their house
blend, Momentum, is crafted by coffee wizards 3fe, there are good teas, and the
food is smart. Another brick in the mighty wall of Galway's West End. Daytime
Mon-Sat.

831 **Jungle Beach Break** Seafront, Salthill Beach · @JungleBeachBreak
4/G13   Coffee from Badger & Dodo, pastries, fruits and ice cream on this windy waterfront
CHP beach shack at Salthill. The seats are re-purposed pallets. If the flag is flying beside
TERRACE Jungle Beach, it means they are open. Daytime.

Galway's Main Attractions

832
4/G13
AYR

✓ **Galway Saturday Market** Church Lane · www.galwaymarket.com
Mixing vital local foods with crafts and bric-a-brac, the market winds around Saint Nicholas' church like a crazed panjandrum, a melée of colour and craic that is unmatched by any other Irish market. New arrivals have brought fresh faces and fresh foods in recent years, joining the veteran cohort who established it as one of the most important destinations in the city. Daytime Sat & Sun, Bank hols, and Fri in July/Aug. Christmas market 14th-24th Dec.

833
4/G13

Collegiate Church of St Nicholas Church Lane · www.stnicholas.ie
The phrase City of Tribes was disparagingly coined by Oliver Cromwell to refer to the fourteen merchant families, who traded and governed between the 13th and 19thC. The Collegiate Church of St Nicholas was built when this was a young city on the edge of Europe, and extended by members of the tribal families. Galway was always a city that had pride and ambition, and the church was built bigger than many city cathedrals; it is still the largest parish church in Ireland. The Church is open daily and the Parish Choir is a joy to listen to during their services.

834
4/G13

The Corrib Princess Furbo Hill +353 81 563846 · www.corribprincess.ie
The Corrib Princess tour is a family-run attraction that begins in Galway city, and travels through river to lough in a 90-minute cruise, spotting otters and hawks, and seeing the riverside modern buildings and historical sites from the water. Cruises bookable for private parties, and guests can enjoy their special Irish Coffee, or food provided by Galway's Cava restaurant, including barbecues on board. 7 days with 3 daily sailings in summer.

835
4/G13

Galway Atlantaquaria Salthill Promenade · www.nationalaquarium.ie
An imposing building overlooking Galway Bay is home to a fascinating collection of marine biology information and live species of every type, from tiny wrasse, to awesome ray and sharks. Learn about bloodless starfish, problem-solving invertebrates, hear the story of the rescued turtle, and don't miss the penguins. Daytime 7 days.

836
4/G13
FREE
ADMISSION

Galway City Museum Spanish Parade House, Merchants Rd Lwr
+353 91 532460 · www.galwaycitymuseum.ie Galway's famous Spanish Arch was built as part of the city walls, a defensive structure erected in the 16thC, built on the site of a 12thC Norman battlement. The Spanish misnomer was probably in reference to the European traders, trawlers and galleons which docked here. Christopher Columbus was one of those who moored up to the arches in 1477. In the tsunami that followed the Lisbon earthquake of 1755, the arch was damaged, and later in the 18thC, a route through the quays was created, called The Long Walk. The Galway Museum explores Galway through prehistoric and Medieval times, as well as looking at the city's marine history, including its famous wooden boats. There is an interactive 3D map, where visitors can toggle between the Galway of today and how it looked in the 17th century. Eat in The Kitchen, Report: 760/CASUAL RESTAURANTS. Daytime Tue-Sun.

837
4/G13

Galway Arts Centre 47 Lower Dominick St +353 91 565886 ·
www.galwayartscentre.ie A key element of the West End, the Galway Arts Centre hosts exhibitions of contemporary art in the 3,000 sq ft gallery as well as conducting classes and workshops. Daytime Mon-Sat.

838   **The Claddagh Ring Museum**   Thomas Dillon Jewellers, 1 William St ·
4/G13   www.claddaghring.ie   The Claddagh brings together a heart, for love; a crown, for loyalty; and hands, for friendship. It is traditionally worn on the right hand ring finger, with the heart facing out, when you're unattached, and facing in if, as they say, you are in a relationship. The ring is said to have originated in Galway. Thomas Dillon Jewellers were established in 1750 and during that time, have supplied Claddagh rings to a host of superstars and monarchs.

839   **Salthill Promenade**   Galway to Salthill   The Irish name *Bóthar na Trá* translates
4/G13   as 'the road by the sea' and today the promenade stretches from the town centre,
3KM   at the mouth of the River Corrib, around through playing fields and along the
1-A-1   northern inner shore of Galway harbour to the town of Salthill. Attractions on the route include the tiny Mutton Island, reached by a 1km causeway – popular, allegedly, for wedding proposals; the Aquarium (see previous page) and the Blackrock Diving Tower (1719/SWIMMING).

840   **Charlie Byrne's Bookshop**   Cornstore Mall, Middle St +353 91 561766 ·
4/G13   www.charliebyrne.com   Smashing bookshop, packed to the ceiling with yards of fascinating books. Allow several hours for a visit. Daytime 7 days, till 8 pm Thurs.

the
Best
Regional Hotels
& Restaurants

The Places to Eat & Stay in Ireland's East Co Wicklow

WHERE TO STAY

841
1/R15
86 ROOMS
LOTS
ATMOS
L

The Brook Lodge & Wells Spa Macreddin Village +353 402 36444 · www.brooklodge.com The only organically certified hotel in Ireland. Achieving that is work enough, but owner Evan Doyle is a restless guy, who loves to do the impossible, like creating a feast for 100 people which has zero food miles. In Wicklow! Of course, he pulled it off, and the concept is tribute to his diligence and determination. The Brook Lodge is simply unique.

EAT The principal restaurant of the hotel is The Strawberry Tree, supplemented by their La Taverna Armento Italian restaurant. Thanks to foraging, pickling, preserving, smoking and a visionary attitude towards food, The Strawberry Tree delivers flavours, tastes and textures you simply will not find elsewhere. Armento is a distinctive Italian restaurant, characterised by the use of superlative Italian artisan foods.

842
1/S15
7 ROOMS
LOTSL

Ballyknocken House Glenealy, Ashford +353 404 44627 · www.ballyknocken.ie Catherine Fulvio is one of the small handful of Irish food people who have crossed over into celebrity status. But before she became a star of the small screen, she was celebrated for running a benchmark country house, an excellent cookery school in the family home where her mum first ran a B&B. The house is charming; in addition to the rooms there is self-catering in their converted Blackberry Barn. The cooking is a defining example of Irish country cuisine: gutsy, unfussy and packed with flavour, and is available on Fri and Sat evenings.

843
1/S15
16 ROOMS
TERRACE
ATMOS
L

Hunter's Hotel Rathnew +353 404 40106 · www.hunters.ie Little if anything has changed in Hunter's, an atmospheric country inn with rooms run by the Gelletlie family for five generations, tucked away down a narrow road off the main strip of Ashford. There is melon with fruit coulis to start, leek and potato soup to follow, duck with orange for main course and fruit meringue for pudding. Goodness knows, many people seem to enjoy the comfort of a hotel that still calls Sunday lunch 'luncheon'. Charming gardens make a very chic setting for drinks in the summertime.

WHERE TO EAT

844
1/Q14
CHP

Grangecon Cafe Kilbride Rd, Blessington +353 45 857892 · @GrangeconCafe Richard and Jenny Street's café is situated just off the long main strip of Blessington, on Kilbride Road. The couple are formidable, painstaking and inventive cooks, and their quest for deliciousness is helped by the fact that they work with the produce of talented local artisans and organic farmers. The savoury and sweet baking, in particular, are worth the trip but, in truth, it's all good. Daytime Tue-Sat.

845
1/S14
MED.INX
ATMOS

Firehouse Bakery Old Delgany Inn, Delgany +353 1 85 1561984 · www.thefirehouse.ie Patrick Ryan is one of the foremost bakers in Ireland, and his baking at The Firehouse in Delgany, south of Dublin, sees queues snaking out the door waiting to buy breads, sandwiches and, above all, their flatbreads and pizzas. The pizzas are thin and crispy, with gooey mozzarella and lots of Gubbeen charcuterie, and they are worth anyone's time to get to little Delgany. Open daytime 7 days. Food served 11am-4.30pm. Pizzas available from 12.30pm.

846 Glendalough Green Laragh Village +353 404 45151 ·
1/R15   www.glendaloughgreen.com This fine shop and café is a magnet for the bikers,
TERRACE   hikers, walkers, cyclists and motorcyclists who tour the zone. There is a dish of the
L   day, fresh soups, flapjacks and sweet things to pair with that revitalising cup of
coffee. Clodagh Duff's café is in the back of the shop, but there are tables out front
for those warm Wicklow afternoons. Daytime 7 days.

847 Mount Usher Garden Cafe Ashford +353 404 40116 · www.avoca.com
1/S15   Head gardener Sean Heffernan has created one of the best loved Irish gardens at
CHP   Mount Usher, so once you've done the primula walk and explored this Robinsonian
TERRACE   masterpiece, you will need some sustenance in the café, run by the Avoca group
L   for more than ten years. The cooking is cheering and reviving: duck leg salad with
pomegranate; lamb casserole with giant couscous; croque monsieur with garden
salad. Daytime 7 days.

848 Boxburger 7 Strand Rd, Bray +353 1 5381000 · www.boxburger.ie Housed
1/S14   in a 160-year-old railway building, and right next door to its sister establishment,
CHP   Platform Pizza, Conor and Nicola Duggan offer 14 burgers, including two vegetarian
choices and one vegan creation, made with seitan. These are good burgers, and
their quality explains why there is now a second branch in Eatyard, on Richmond St
in Dublin. Get here on Wed and there is a free beer from the superb Wicklow Wolf
Brewery, along with that burger. Dinner Wed-Fri, Lunch & dinner Sat & Sun.

849 Holland's of Bray 78-80 Main St, Bray +353 1 2867995 ·
1/S14   www.hollandsofbray.com It might be the astonishing selection of craft beers
MED.INX   they offer – more than 350! – that brings you to Holland's the first time, but
some tasty bar food will also make you linger. They have been here for more than
40 years, and comfort and meticulous housekeeping mean the pub is always
pristine. Their wine shop is also superb, and you can bring a bottle to the pub for
minimum corkage. Good 3fe coffee. Lunch & dinner 7 days.

850 Mickey Finn's Pub Main St, River Valley, Redcross +353 404 41661 ·
1/S15   www.wicklowbrewery.ie Leigh and Ashley William's bar is the bar that ran out
MED.INX   of beer. Back in 2015, demand was so high for their five craft beers, that the pub ran
ATMOS   dry. It's a great story, but the real reason to head to Redcross is the fact that these
beers don't make it out of Co Wicklow. So, make the trip – it's just a detour off the
M11 – tour the brewery, buy the T-shirt, enjoy the cooking in the bistro, and do note
that they have rather splendid tree houses for glamping. Lunch & dinner 7 days.

851 The Pigeon House Old Delgany Inn, Delgany +353 1 2877103 ·
1/S14   www.pigeonhouse.ie Brian Walsh and Paul Foley's restaurant is one of the four
MED.EXP   dynamic food businesses that have transformed the Old Delgany Inn, 40 minutes
S of Dublin and a short detour off the N11.They have the upstairs space, and share
the rest of the premises with Roasted Brown Coffee, Firehouse Bakery and the
Delgany Grocer. You can have breakfast, lunch and dinner, and weekend brunch,
and the cooking is savoury and enjoyable. 7 days.

852   **Fern House Café** Avoca, Kilmacanogue +353 1 2746990 · www.avoca.com

1/S14

MED.INX

TERRACE

The Avoca cafés and shops are now owned by the multinational Aramark group, with original boss Simon Pratt still running the show. The group are busy expanding internationally, and the original driver of their success, the Kilmacanogue branch just off the N11 motorway, remains as busy and successful as ever. There are two cafés, in addition to the retail space: the self-service Sugar Tree Café, and the table service Fern House Café. Cooking and baking are reliable and tasty, and the location means it's an ideal pull-over whether heading N or S. Daytime 7 days, dinner Thur-Sat.

If you're in Greystones . . .

WHERE TO EAT

853   ✓**The Happy Pear** Church Rd, Greystones · www.thehappypear.ie

1/S14

CHP

Dave and Steve Flynn have become famous food personalities in Ireland over the last few years; there are few to match them when it comes to social media. But their journey began when they quietly opened a wholefood shop and vegan café on Church Rd, back in 2004, and started converting people to a plant-based, healthful way of eating. Today, HP is permanently packed, so expect to queue. They also have cafes in the nearby Shoreline Leisure Centre and in Walkinstown. Their well-made foods are widely available, from sauces, to coffee, to granolas. A mighty duo, and probably the best food yogis you can meet. Daytime & dinner 7 days - 6/7/9 pm.

854   **La Creperie Pierre Grise** The Harbour, Greystones +353 1 2878352 ·

1/S14

CHP

www.lacreperie.ie Alison and Julien offer buckwheat galettes made with the famous black flour – farine de sarrasin – from Brittany, in a pretty room down at the harbour. The savoury galettes make for good eating, whilst the youngsters will likely want a sweet crepe with lemon, butter and sugar. Nice wines, drinks and syrups, interesting foods in the shop. Daytime 6 days (closed Tue), till 9 pm Fri & Sat.

855   **The Hungry Monk** Church Rd, Greystones +353 1 2875759 ·

1/S14

MED.INX

www.thehungrymonk.ie Julian and Samantha Keown serve the great classics in Greystones' legendary Hungry Monk, a destination which has been feeding the town since 1988. You come for steak au poivre; seafood platter; steak and kidney pie with puff pastry; lobster linguini, and the cooking shows simply that if it ain't broke, there is no need to fix it. Wine lovers also come to enjoy one of the best lists you will find, a bibulous masterpiece, which offers excellent value. Dinner 7 days, lunch Sun.

856   **Chakra by Jaipur** Meridian Point Centre, Greystones +353 1 2017222 ·

1/S14

MED.EXP

www.jaipur.ie Asheesh Dewan's Chakra trio of Jaipur restaurants offers some of the most authentic and well-delivered ethnic food on the E coast. Their riffs on Irish ingredients are particularly noteworthy. Chakra is a big room on the top floor of the Meridian Point Centre, colourful and comfortably plush. Dinner 7 days & Sun lunch.

857   **The Three Qs** Church Rd, Greystones +353 1 2875477 · www.thethreeqs.com

1/S14

MED.INX

The 3 Q's are the brothers Quinn – Brian, Paul and Colin – and this trio do a good, friendly job in their little space, and have done so for a dozen years. Brian and Colin knock out the breakfasts, lunches and dinners, whilst Paul looks after everyone as if they are his BFF, and that's why everyone loves this charming neighbourhood spot. Daytime 7 days, dinner Tue-Sun.

Co Louth

WHERE TO STAY

Ghan House Co Louth Report: 1281/COUNTRY HOUSES.

WHERE TO EAT

858

1/R9
CHP
TERRACE
ATMOS

✓ **Strandfield** Ballymascanlon, Dundalk +353 42 9371856 ·
www.strandfield.com Strandfield is one of the most popular destinations on the east coast, thanks to a great location only 2 mins off the M1 motorway, just N of Dundalk town and S of Newry town, and thanks to excellent cooking. The shop and flower shop are a treasure, but it's the bustling café and the elegant, flavourful, rustic cooking that makes this worth anyone's detour. Time your journey to accommodate coffee or lunch at this gem, but expect to queue. Daytime 7 days.

859

1/R9
7 ROOMS
MED.EXP

Bay Tree Restaurant Newry St, Carlingford +353 42 9383848 ·
www.belvederehouse.ie Conor and Kristine Woods have been the star culinary act of Carlingford for a decade now, hauling in awards for rock-steady cooking. Mr Woods grows a lot of his own gear, and sources well, so his classic style is well served by fresh ingredients. Rooms available for overnight stays in their flower-festooned Belvedere House B&B, above the restaurant. This is a good spot for staying in a charming, medieval village, though street noise can be an issue at busy weekends. Dinner 7 days & Sun lunch.

860

1/R9
MED.EXP

Eno Bar, Grill & Wood Fired Pizza 5 Roden Place, Dundalk +353 42 9355467 ·
www.eno.ie Directly across from St Patrick's Cathedral in the centre of town, Eno's offer revolves around the pizzas from their wood-burning pizza oven, abetted with a menu of antipasti, pasta dishes and grilled meats. Rachel and Victor Graham have a cocktail bar and dining space upstairs from the main dining room, and Eno is a busy, energised space. Dinner Tue-Sun, Lunch Sat & Sun.

If you're in Drogheda . . .

WHERE TO STAY

861
1/R11
16 ROOMS
MED.EXP

Scholars Townhouse Hotel King St, Drogheda +353 41 9835410 ·
www.scholarshotel.com The ornate Victorian style of the dining room and the
rooms of the family-owned Scholars may belong to an earlier age, but chef Matthias
Ecker has brought some modern culinary bangs to the restaurant. Fine bar, with
first-rate gastrolounge menu; all the newest craft beers and gins. Good location for
anyone wanting to spend a few days exploring the riches of the Boyne Valley.

862
1/R11
104 ROOMS
MED.EXP
TERRACE

The d Hotel Scotch Hall, Drogheda +353 41 9877700 · www.thedhotel.com
Taken over by new owners in early 2017, the d Hotel has been undergoing an
extensive refurb. Stunning location beside the River Boyne and a beautiful terrace.
Food is served in The Hops bar, and the Il Ponte restaurant offers a pasta, pizza and grill
menu.

WHERE TO EAT

863
1/R11
MED.INX

✓ **Eastern Seaboard Bar & Grill** Bryanstown Centre, Drogheda
+353 41 9802570 · www.glasgow-diaz.com The fact that the Eastern
Seaboard is in a commercial strip in the middle of a suburban housing estate in the
middle of nowhere makes it even hipper than you could believe. Step in the door of
both the ES – and its sister bakery, Brown Hound – and you step into Coolsville.
Cooking is outstanding, and we have never had a bad dish here in the last decade.
Lunch & dinner 7 days. Brown Hound Bakery, open all day and serves coffee, light
lunches and their own lovely baking.

864
1/R11
MED.EXP

The Kitchen Restaurant 2 South Quay, Drogheda +353 41 9834630 ·
@thekitchenrestaurantdrogheda In a glass-fronted building on Drogheda's
South Quay, Glyn Schneider and Anne Brennan have been knockin' 'em dead with
estimable cooking for several years. Mr Schneider has brought the fruits of his travels
home to Co Louth and he borrows liberally and confidently from the cuisines of the
Middle East and further afield, best shown in his themed dinners. Nice wines, good
value, and excellent service complete a class act. Lunch & dinner Wed-Sun.

865
1/R11
MED.INX

D'Vine Bistro & Tapas Bar Dyer St, Drogheda +353 41 9800440 ·
www.dvine.ie Having created one of the most characterful destinations in
Drogheda, Sonia and Damien have opened a second D'Vine, at Jacks, a handsome
thatched building in Rush, Co Dublin. This pair know how to put the fun into eating
and drinking, and enjoying music, and their tapas plates are slick and enjoyable.
Lunch & dinner Wed-Sun.

866
1/R11

Ariosa Coffee Cafe 1 St Laurence St, Drogheda +353 41 9802505 ·
www.ariosacoffee.com Michael Kelly's Ariosa company is amongst the leading
boutique coffee roasters in Ireland, and Ariosa was one of the first to kick start the
coffee revolution. They run two grinders, one for a blend, one for single estate. It's
a classy, uncluttered room, and the drinks are simply ace. Daytime Mon-Sat.

867
1/R11
CHP

Stockwell Artisan Foods 1 Mayoralty St, Drogheda +353 41 9810892 ·
www.stockwellartisanfoods.ie Two first-rate destinations, a deli-café on Stockwell
St and a café-restaurant on Mayoralty St, means Gwen and Orlaith's shops are places
to eat well, shop well and source carefully crafted meals. Daytime Mon-Sat.

Co Monaghan

WHERE TO STAY

Hilton Park Co Monaghan Report: 1278/COUNTRY HOUSES.

WHERE TO EAT

868
1/Q9
MED.EXP

Courthouse Restaurant 1 Monaghan St, Carrickmacross +353 42 9692848 ·
www.courthouserestaurant.ie The main room of Conor Mee and Charlotte Carr's
Courthouse Restaurant is upstairs. It's an atmospheric arched room with stone walls
and a wooden floor, and the place where you find the best cooking in town. Mr Mee's
menus read straight-head but his food has an energy and finesse that delivers the
flavours. Good local gin and beers, a confident crew, and it's no surprise they haul in
the restaurant awards each year. Dinner Wed-Sun & Sun lunch.

Co Cavan

WHERE TO EAT & STAY

869
1/L8
17 ROOMS

✓ **MacNean House & Restaurant** Blacklion +353 71 9853200 ·
www.nevenmaguire.com Neven Maguire is a culinary superstar in Ireland, a
public figure who is amongst the 3 or 4 best-known chefs in the country. Maguire's
fame means that it is necessary to book dinner months in advance to get a table:
it's worth it. The cooking is expert, finessed, and hugely enjoyable, served by a
charming crew who back their boss to the hilt. Many people choose to stay in one
of the 17 rooms, and Neven has upgraded them steadily, preserving a Restaurant
with Rooms feel. Dinner Mon-Sat & Sun Lunch.

870
1/N9
MED.EXP

The Oak Room 24 Bridge St, Cavan +353 49 4371414 · www.theoakroom.ie
Norbert Neylon is a fine cook, and his town-centre restaurant is the destination
in Cavan town. The menus are diverse but everything is handled deftly and
confidently. Great children's menu, and great value for money. Dinner Tue-Sun.

✓ **The Olde Post Inn** Co Cavan Report: 1317/RESTAURANTS WITH ROOMS

Virginia Park Lodge Co Cavan Report: 1397/HOUSE PARTIES.

Co Meath

WHERE TO EAT & STAY

Headfort Arms Co Meath. Report: 1845/GOLF.
Conyngham Arms Hotel Co Meath Report: 1292/FAMILY FRIENDLY.

Co Westmeath

✓ **Lough Bishop B&B** Collinstown, Co Westmeath Report: 1343/B&B.

If you're in Athlone...

WHERE TO STAY
The Bastion B&B Co Westmeath Report: 1348/B&B.

WHERE TO EAT

871
1/L12
MED.EXP

✓ **The Fatted Calf** Church St, Athlone +353 90 6433371 · www.thefattedcalf.ie
Feargal and Fiona O'Donnell run the benchmark restaurant of the region, here in the centre of town. Mr O'Donnell gathers the best local artisan foods and showcases them with elegance, and big flavours. Slicky run, and great fun, so look for the glass-encased room on Church St. Lunch Thur-Sat, dinner Tue-Sat.

872
1/L12
MED.EXP
ATMOS

Left Bank Bistro Fry Place, Athlone +353 90 6494446 · www.leftbankbistro.com As they head towards 25 years of exemplary service, the Left Bank remains a standard bearer for good food in Athlone, thanks to Annie and Mary's inspired cooking, and innate good taste. The fusion elements of the dishes are smartly executed and the sheer professionalism of the operation gladdens the heart. Daytime and dinner Tue-Sat.

873
1/L12
MED.EXP

Thyme Restaurant Custume Pl, Athlone +353 90 6478850 · www.thymerestaurant.ie Meticulous sourcing and confident plating are the hallmarks of John Coffey's modern, comfortable, understated restaurant. For ten years, Mr Coffey has built his menus on the produce of the best producers; it makes for great eating. Ambitious team, exceptional value. Dinner 7 days and Sun Lunch.

874
1/L12
MED.INX

Kin Khao Thai 1 Abbey Lane, Athlone +353 90 6498805 · www.kinkhaothai.ie Adam and Janya Lyon's Kin Khao has been one of the best ethnic restaurants in the Midlands for a long time. It's an atmospheric, colourful series of rooms, in the old part of town. The dishes range beyond the familiar Thai staples into creations from Laos and Burma. Lunch Wed-Fri & Sun, dinner 7 days.

875
1/L12
CHP

Bastion Kitchen 1 Bastion St, Athlone +353 90 6498369 · www.bastionkitchen.com This cosy little café is directly across from the Bastion B&B and offers one of the best breakfasts in the Midlands: we would walk to Athlone just to have that Castlemine Farm sausage bap, which is pretty much the tastiest breakfast bite in town. Daytime 7 days.

✓ **Sean's Bar** Report: 1419/COUNTRY PUBS

Co Offaly
If you're in Birr...

WHERE TO EAT IN BIRR...

876
1/L14
CHP
EASTER-SEPT
TERRACE

The Courtyard Cafe Birr Castle, Birr +353 57 9169735 · www.birrcastle.com Open between St Patrick's Day and late Sept, the Courtyard Café does simple things supremely well. Mary Walsh-Kinsella and her team cook and bake and put tasty things in the cup and on the plate. Nice food for the kids, picnic service if you want to explore the castle, and they even have Bonios for your doggie. Key address in Birr, even if you aren't visiting the castle. Daytime 7 days. Tearooms open weekends only off season.

877
1/L14

Emma's Café 31 Main St, Birr +353 57 9125678 · @Emma'sCafeBirr Debby and Adrian run a good show here in Emma's, a long-time fixture of the town, and ever-reliable for a coffee break and a lunchtime sandwich. Daytime 7 days.

878 **Nutmeg Bakery** Main St, Birr +353 87 0550473 · @Meganscakebakes
1/L14   It's the sweet baking from baker and owner Megan Curran that is the real draw in
CHP   this cutesy bakery and coffee shop. Whilst Ms Curran is a wizard at wedding and
party cakes, she's also a dab hand with eclairs, tray bakes and fruit pavlovas, so
satisfy that sugar craving here. Daytime 7 days.

Co Kildare

WHERE TO EAT

879 ✓✓ **Canteen Celbridge** Main St, Celbridge +353 1 627 4967 ·
1/Q13   www.canteencelbridge.com Canteen Celbridge is one of the most
EXP   significant restaurants in Ireland, because what you get here is star-status cooking,
but in a provincial town, in a slender, glass-walled room. James Sheridan's cooking
is dazzling, technically flawless, and brimful of flavour. Soizic Humbert matches her
husband's skills at front of house, there are choice vegetarian dishes, good wines,
and value for money for such ambitious cooking. Dinner Tue-Sat, lunch Sat.

880 ✓✓ **Ballymore Inn** Main St, Ballymore Eustace +353 45 864585 ·
1/Q14   www.ballymoreinn.com Georgina O'Sullivan is one of Ireland's greatest
MED.EXP   female chef-proprietors. Her cooking is rustic, yet refined, alert to new influences, and
authoritatively able to deliver the classic dishes. You can order anything she offers and
chances are you will declare it to be amongst the best things you have ever eaten.
They also make the best mashed potato you can find anywhere. Barry O'Sullivan
marshals great drinks, and Ballymore Inn is a star address. Lunch & dinner 7 days.

881 ✓ **Two Cooks** 5 Canal View, Sallins +353 45 853768 · www.twocooks.ie
1/Q13   Husband and wife cookery duo Josef and Nicola have combined their
MED.EXP   considerable culinary chops to create something pretty special. The couple use
technical prowess to fashion short and seasonal menus. Rapid success meant they
quickly had to convert the downstairs wine bar to create more seats, so make sure
you have a booking before heading canalside, and try to get a window seat to enjoy
the views of the water. Dinner Wed-Sat, Lunch Sun.

882 ✓ **Hartes of Kildare** Market Sq, Kildare Town +353 45 533557 ·
1/P14   www.harteskildare.ie On the square in Kildare town, Barry Liscombe's
MED.EXP   cooking has propelled Harte's to the pinnacle of the gastropub league. Mr Liscombe
is a driven talent, and he has a great team behind him who show respect to every
detail of their work, so even the potato skins are special. Excellent modern Irish
cookery is matched by top-class drinks and service. Lunch & dinner Tue-Sun. Note,
they run cookery classes in their cookery school.

883 **The Brown Bear** Two Mile House, Naas +353 45 883561 ·
1/Q14   www.thebrownbear.ie Thanks to paying microscopic attention to the details that
MED.EXP   makes a room welcoming, Jean Grace and her partner, Eugene Brennan, survived
the slump – they opened in 2008 – and have developed an excellent reputation for
fine cooking that people like to eat. Dinner Wed-Sat, lunch Sun.

884 **L'Officina by Dunne & Crescenzi** Kildare Retail Village, Kildare
1/P14   +353 1 2166764 · www.dunneandcrescenzi.com Eileen Dunne and Stefano
MED.INX   Crescenzi are famous for their Dunne & Crescenzi chain of Italian eateries in Dublin
city. L'Officina is their site for offering cooking based on D.O.P. Italian foods and the
food is confidently delivered in a stylish room, complete with delightful Italian staff.
A good detour off the M7 – there is lots of parking – and there is a sister branch at
the Dundrum Shopping Centre in S Co Dublin. Daytime until 7 pm/8 pm.

885 **Zest Cafe** Clane Unit 6, Clane Shopping Centre, Clane +353 45 893222 ·
1/Q13
MED.INX
www.zestcafeandrestaurant.ie Mark Condron runs both Zest Café in the centre of Clane village, and the Jolly Café in nearby Naas. Both are super-professional operations, consistent, reliable and creative, characterised by tasty modern food that perfectly suits any time of day. Lunch & dinner 7 days.

886 **Mad Hatter Café** 1 Keenan's Lane, Castledermot +353 85 7148085 ·
1/P15
CHP
www.madhattercafe.ie This perpetually thronged cafe has been the place to visit for the last ten years. It's a popular spot for breakfasts and lunches, when the blackboard features the daily soup, salad, a fish dish, a curry and a pasta dish. For us it's the savoury and sweet baking that is the star. Tapas nights on the last Sat of each month feature Spain's greatest hits. Daytime Tue-Sun.

Co Laois

WHERE TO STAY

887 **Castle Durrow** Durrow +353 57 8736555 · www.castledurrow.com Sara and
1/N16
46 ROOMS
LOTS
TERRACE
L
Shane Stokes' grand country house is a popular wedding destination, but proximity to Dublin and the M8 motorway also makes it a favoured getaway for Dubliners who want a night away in a grand big house with elegant, manicured gardens, luxe rooms and a smashing terrace for early evening cocktails. Cooking can be good, but service can be flustered when busy.

Roundwood House Co Laois Report: 1282/COUNTRY HOUSES.
Ballyfin Demesne Co Laois Report: 1327/ESCAPES.

WHERE TO EAT

888 ✓**The Gallic Kitchen @ Bramley** Abbeyleix +353 86 6058208 ·
1/N15
CHP
www.gallickitchen.com Across the street from the legendary Morrissey's pub, Sarah Webb shows that even after decades at the stove, she remains one of the finest bakers in Ireland, and her pastry alone is worth the detour into pretty Abbeyleix. No one makes a sausage roll like this great chef. The room is spacious, bright and informal. Daytime 7 days. Gallic Kitchen Cafe is open at The Moat Theatre in Naas.

889 ✓**Tynan's At The Storeyard** Kea Lew Business Park, Portlaoise
1/N15
CHP
+353 57 8688343 · www.tynans.ie Tucked away in the middle of a phantasmagorical furniture warehouse, The Storehouse, Tynan's is an informal place where Imelda Tynan and her team exemplify the great traditions of Irish baking, and Irish hospitality. Whilst the sweet baking is simply outstanding – the rhubarb tart is reason alone to detour into town – the team here are determined, and they never put a foot wrong: everything is good. Daytime Tue-Sat.

890 **The Pantry** 13 Market Sq, Portlaoise +353 57 8681695 ·
1/N15
CHP
@ThePantryPortlaoise Good coffee from superstar Dublin roasters 3fe is just one of the draws in Ladonna McCartan and Mark Healy's town-centre café. Whilst the brews are serious, there are no beards, barnets or top-knots: this is a relaxed and unpretentious country café with good cakes, pies, salads and sandwiches, so look out for their window displays of cute china tea sets. Daytime Mon-Sat.

891 **Bowe's Foodhall & Cafe** The Square, Durrow +353 57 8740669 ·
1/N16
CHP
www.bowescafe.ie Just off the central square in Durrow, Sarah and Shane Bowe's menus offer cooking with considerable ambition and as a result they attract an audience from many miles around, and this is a favourite spot for people to meet up, adjacent to the M8 motorway. Occasional tapas evenings, switched-on service. Daytime Mon-Sat.

The Best Places to Eat & Stay in Ireland's South East

Co Tipperary

WHERE TO STAY

892
2/L17
19 ROOMS

Baileys Hotel Main St, Cashel +353 62 61937 · www.baileyshotelcashel.com
Baileys is a very comfortable hotel, but its most singular merit is the staff who animate the place. If you stay, they give you a ticket for access to the Rock of Cashel, and if you book the penthouse, you can see the Rock from your window.

✓ **The Old Convent** Co Tipperary Report: 1269/COUNTRY HOUSES.

WHERE TO EAT

893
2/K18
MED.EXP

Prime 74 Restaurant 74 Main St, Tipperary Town +353 62 31388 · www.prime74.ie Good, tasty bistro food is what you will find in Prime 74. Chef Martin Lovell's cooking is straight-ahead, and especially valuable in a town with few choices. The downstairs room is the best place to be. Daytime Tue-Sun, dinner Thur-Sat.

894
2/J16
CHP

Ponaire Cafe Main St, Newport +353 61 373713 · www.ponaire.ie An artisan roastery with a hip coffee shop on the main street, Jennifer and Tommy's brilliant Ponaire bespoke coffee company is the destination to get that perfect flat white, or that smoky Americano, and something nice to eat that will put a pep in your step. Daytime Mon-Sat.

895
2/K14
MED.INX
TERRACE
ATMOS

The Derg Inn Terryglass +353 67 22037 · www.thederginn.ie The Derg is a pretty country inn in a pretty country village, and Mick and Joyce's menu hits all the points. This eclectic mix echoes the style of the Inn, a place where a warm fire greets you in the winter, an alfresco table greets you on a sunny day, music greets you at the weekends, and where the whacky bricolage interior is always charming. Bar food daytime & dinner 7 days.

896
2/M18
CHP

Dooks Fine Foods Kerry St, Fethard +353 52 6130828 · www.dooksfinefoods.ie Richard Gleeson worked with Skye Gyngell and Yotam Ottolenghi before coming home to Fethard to open Dooks. His cooking is vivid and creative, and Dooks is a city surprise – in culinary and in design terms – in this agricultural vale. Fethard has seen nothing like Dooks, and it looks as if Mr Gleeson is only starting. Daytime until 3/4pm Tue-Sun.

897
2/K18
CHP

The French Quarter Cafe Excel Centre, Tipperary Annemarie and Loic have brought lovely baking and good drinks to Tipperary for more than ten years now in their cafe in the Excel Arts Centre. Lunch & dinner Wed-Sat.

898
2/L18
CHP

The Cottage Loughmore Templemore, Co Tipperary +353 504 35846 · @TheCottageLoughmore An award-winning community owned shop and tearooms, The Cottage is, somewhat famously, in the middle of nowhere, and way, way off the beaten track. That didn't stop deter Mary Fogarty and Maeve O'Hair from rallying everyone in the village to support their co-operative venture, and they have fashioned a darling, old-style tea rooms, with excellent home cooking. It's worth going all the way to Loughmore just to have a slice of Mary Martin's tea brack and a nice cup of tea. A wee treasure. All day 7 days.

If you're in Thurles . . .

899
2/L17
MED.EXP
Mitchel House Restaurant Mitchel St, Thurles +353 504 90776 ·
www.mitchelhouse.ie Michael O'Dwyer and his team have provided an
invaluable service to Thurles over the last decade. A handsome room, smart
modern cooking from chef Shane Boyle, great drinks, professional service, all
brought together in one successful venture. Value for money is keen. Dinner
Wed-Sat & Sun lunch.

900
2/L17
CHP
Stef Hans The Source Arts Centre, Thurles Ruth Mulhern got Stef Hans up
and running in 2015 in an in-between-the-entrance-and-under-the-stairs space,
in The Source Arts Centre. But what matters is that the cooking, from Stef Hans,
is simply knockout. Great drinks, and service by local ladies is fantastic.
Daytime Tue-Sat.

If you're in Cashel . . .

901
2/L17
EXP
L
ATMOS
✓**Chez Hans** Moor Lane, Cashel +353 62 61177 · www.chezhans.net
Chez Hans is a deconsecrated church sitting under the shadow of the Rock of
Cashel, founded in 1968 – and after 50 years it remains a beloved destination for
food lovers. Jason Matthiae's lush cooking never swerves from its classical path,
and never misses a beat, and the room is one of the best big night out destinations
in Ireland. Dinner Tue-Sat.

902
2/L17
MED.INX
L
✓**Cafe Hans** Moor Lane, Cashel +353 62 63660 · @CafeHans Forewarned is
forearmed: at lunchtime, walk into this narrow room, several hundred yards
from the Rock of Cashel, and you haven't a chance of getting a seat. A seat in Hans
is the most sought after seat in the county, and all the people who know that arrive
early. The alternative, of course, is to arrive late. But their success is the surest
proof that you will eat well here, and it's worth travelling to Café Hans for the spag
bol and garlic bread alone. Daytime Tue-Sat.

903
2/L17
MED.INX
Mikey Ryan's Bar & Kitchen 76 Main St, Cashel +353 52 62007 ·
www.mikeyryans.ie This super-stylish bar has arrived with a bang, thanks to
a hip room, enormous attention to detail – check out those butter paddles from
Hewn spoons – and cooking that has real attitude: plaice with heritage tomatoes;
summer vegetable salad with cashew ricotta; rump steak with buttered greens.
Still early days, but Ryan's has gotten off to a very impressive start. All day and
dinner 7 days.

904
2/L17
CHP
The Spearman 97 Main St, Cashel · @spearmansbakery Elaine Spearman's
simple, country town tea rooms has been a fixture of Cashel for many years,
because it's always been a reliable, relaxing place to eat something good and tasty,
all of it based around their splendid domestic baking. Daytime Mon-Sat.

905 **Country Choice** 25 Kenyon St, Nenagh +353 67 32596 · @CountryChoice
2/K16 Humble things animate Peter Ward's culinary compass. A scone warm from the
CHP oven. A slice of brawn with brown bread. A pickled calf's tongue. The Nenagh
ATMOS butter that creates the canvas for a mince pie. A piece of Parmesan aged for
50 months by his friends in Italy. This is the reality of what this world-class shop
and café does: it makes the choicest of choices, and brings them to us. A warm
scone, Nenagh butter, damson jam, Earl Grey tea... there is no more that you need.
Daytime Mon-Sat. Also Country Choice at Limerick Milk Market.

906 **The Peppermill Restaurant** Kenyon St, Nenagh +353 67 34598 ·
2/K16 **www.thepeppermill.ie** Robert and Mairead Gill's restaurant is professional,
MED.INX unpretentious, and a key destination. The rooms are comfortable and welcoming,
the service is affable, the cooking is assured, and when you put these elements
together you can understand why the Gills' restaurant is a mainstay of Nenagh.
Dinner Tue-Sun.

907 **Larkin's Bar** Portroe, Nenagh+353 67 23232 · www.larkins.ie Whitewashed
2/J15 and topped with a fine thatched roof, Larkin's is the archetype of the country
MED.EXP pub. It's celebrated for traditional and modern music sessions but there is also
bar food served – steaks; burgers; chicken Caesar. Bar food served daytime &
dinner 7 days.

908 **The Pantry Cafe** Unit 12, Quintin's Way, Pease St, Nenagh +353 67 31237 ·
2/K16 **www.thepantrycafe.ie** Grainne Moylan and her team have been feeding the
CHP folks of Nenagh for more than 25 years, and they have the assurance blessed of
experience in their cooking: chicken Marsala with mushrooms; beef & Guinness
casserole; poached haddock with new potatoes. Daytime Mon-Sat.

909 **Cinnamon Alley** Hanly's Place, Nenagh +353 67 33923 · @cinnamonalley
2/K16 Marie Nagle's popular café is particularly celebrated for their bounteous puddings -
CHP Rocky Road; strawberry and mint cheesecake; the psychedelic KitKat and
Smartie cake. But the savoury food is just as precise: chicken satay skewers;
seafood pie. Coffee and a fresh eclair is always the way to make the day better.
Daytime Tue-Sat.

910 **Lily Mai's Cafe** Dove Hill Design Centre, Carrick-on-Suir +353 51 645603 ·
2/M18 **www.lilymais.com** In addition to very professional and accomplished cooking
CHP in the café, the Lily Mai's team also run the nearby Greenheart Cafe in a beautiful
thatched cottage on the campus. Daytime 7 days.

Co Kilkenny
If you're in Kilkenny City . . .

WHERE TO STAY

911
2/N17
46 ROOMS
MED.EXP

Kilkenny Hibernian Hotel 1 Ormonde St, Kilkenny +353 56 7771888 · www.
kilkennyhibernianhotel.com With one of Kilkenny's best chefs, Paul Cullen,
cooking for Harper's Restaurant in the hotel, and manager Joanna Hannick running
the show, the Hibernian Hotel has signalled a dramatic upscaling of ambition. The
hotel's central location is unbeatable and, whilst the rooms are compact, they are
comfortable and stylish. Make sure to get a room at the rear to avoid nightclub noise.

912
2/N17
118 ROOMS
EXP

Kilkenny Ormonde Hotel Ormonde St, Kilkenny +353 56 7723977 ·
www.kilkennyormonde.com Kilkenny is a major weekend destination in
Ireland, especially for groups, so booking a room means trying to get one where
your peaceful sleep will be guaranteed. Despite being right in the centre, we have
always found the Ormonde to be quiet and well run. Secure car park nearby.
EAT in the Ormonde Lounge and Savour restaurant. The head chef, Mark Gaffney,
is one of the best cooks in Kilkenny. Breakfast, if you leave it late, involves a queue.

Langton's House Hotel Co Kilkenny Report: 1313/ROADSIDE INNS.

WHERE TO EAT

913
2/N17
EXP

✓✓**Campagne** 5 The Arches, Gas House Ln, Kilkenny +353 56 7772858 ·
www.campagne.ie Garret and Brid's Campagne is the big destination
restaurant in the SE. Every significant celebration brings revellers to this handsome
room, tucked away on Gas House Lane. Garret Byrne's cooking is devoted to classic
French cuisine, and he has the chops to execute his dishes with exactitude – pork
jowl with choucroute and turnip purée; pheasant en croute with tarragon jus; fig
tart with blackberry ice cream. This is intricate cooking, devotional in its quest for
perfection, and eating here is inspiring, so don't wait for your birthday. Lunch
Fri-Sat, dinner Tue-Sat.

914
2/N17
EXP
ATMOS

✓**Ristorante Rinuccini** 1 The Parade, Kilkenny +353 56 7761575 ·
www.rinuccini.com After almost 30 years, Riccardo Cavaliere's restaurant is
enjoying greater success than ever before. They offer the staples of Italian dining
– the clubby room; the super-Tuscan wines; the smart service; the white
tablecloths; the tiramisu – but they bring a pin-point attention to detail to
everything. So the cooking is sharp, the service is sympathetic, the wines are
superb. Rinuccini is a SE landmark, and it's a pleasure to walk down the steps just
across from Kilkenny Castle. Lunch & dinner 7 days.

915
2/N17
CHP

✓**Cakeface** Irishtown, Kilkenny +353 56 7739971 ·
www.cakefacepastry.com Laura and Rory Gannon have stints at the
Ballymaloe school, The Savoy and The Connacht in their CVs, and that polish shows
in their fine baking and the precision of the food offer in this up-and-coming part
of the city. If they don't make it, they source it from the best, allowing them to
focus on what they do best: patisserie with a rare professional polish. It's well
worth the trip to enjoy these sweet jewels, and the coffee is top-notch, so set aside
plenty of time to enjoy this distinguished baking. Daytime 7 days.

916 **Kernel Bar & Kitchen** 15 Vicar St, Kilkenny +353 56 7786326 Maria Raftery,
2/N17 head chef at the Kernel Kitchen, is one of Kilkenny's finest chefs, and she has
MED.EXP brought her elegant, modern style of food to this bright room in the Kilkenny Inn, a
TERRACE 3-star hotel on Vicar Street. She loves a jolt of freshness in her dishes and her touch
is sure, her cooking always enjoyable. Good craft beers, short wine list, excellent
afternoon tea offer, and a significant addition to the city. Lunch & dinner 7 days.

917 **Anocht** Kilkenny Design Centre, Castle Yard, Kilkenny +353 56 7722118 ·
2/N17 www.kilkennydesign.com Everything in Anocht – the lovely upstairs room, the
MED.EXP service, the setting, the cooking – aims to seduce you, not conquer you. Chef Rory
L Nolan lets great ingredients like Kilkenny black leg chicken dominate the plate,
confident that its taste and texture will get the dish home. Great wines, polite
service, and Anocht is one of those modest restaurants that is all grown up.
Dinner Thur-Sun.

918 **The Gourmet Store** 56 High St, Kilkenny +353 56 7771727 ·
2/N17 @TheGourmetStore Padraig and Irene Lawlor have been giving the people
CHP of Kilkenny great coffee, fine sandwiches and sweet treats, for more than two
decades, and their work has been a defining part of a Kilkenny food culture that
just gets better and better. Daytime Mon-Sat.

919 **Mug*Shot Cafe** 25 James St, Kilkenny +353 56 7777798 ·
2/N17 www.mugshotcafe.ie Aoghan Courtney's Mug*Shot Café, just beside the
MED.INX cathedral, offers modern, tasty cooking in a bright and relaxing room. Great staff
seem to always know what you would like to eat. Daytime Tue-Sat

920 **Foodworks** 7 Parliament St, Kilkenny +353 56 7777696 · www.foodworks.ie
2/N17 Peter Greany and Maeve Moore offer simple and beautifully thought-through food
MED.INX in the elegant, high-ceilinged Foodworks. Because a lot of the foods they use come
straight from their own farm and polytunnel, they offer ingredients in a style that
many modern cooks would describe as unadorned. Subtle, modest food in a lovely
room, in Ireland's loveliest city. Lunch 7 days, dinner Thur-Sat.

Mocha's Vintage Tea Rooms Co Kilkenny Report: 1476/TEA ROOMS.

THE BEST BARS IN KILKENNY CITY
921 **The Tap Room at Sullivan's Brewing Company** 15 John St, Kilkenny +353 56
2/N17 7722907 www.sullivansbrewingcompany.com Sullivan's Brewery preceded
TERRACE the famous Smithwick's Brewery of Kilkenny, being established in 1706, and was
later taken over by Smithwick's. Today, Sullivan's is a collaboration by the families
– Smithwick's ale today is brewed by Diageo – and there is something special
about drinking a Kilkenny red ale in Kilkenny city made by the people who created
brewing in the city. The Tap Room and bar are very modern and stylish, there are
super pizzas from a wood-fired oven housed in a shipping container, and it's all
behind the Wine Centre shop, itself one of the best wine shops in the country.

922 **Left Bank** 1 The Parade, Kilkenny +353 56 7750016 · www.leftbank.ie
2/N17 The Left Bank is indeed an old bank house, and it is a phantasmagoric pub. For a
ATMOS start, it's vast. Secondly, it's home to the most eclectic collection of collectibles
and furnishings you have ever seen in one place, spread over two floors. Their
restaurant, accessed on the Castle side, is Rive Gauche and there is some excellent
cooking here: vegetable risotto Wellington; 14-hour slow cooked lamb shoulder; a
superb prawn cocktail.

923   **Brewery Corner**   29 Parliament St, Kilkenny +353 56 7805081 ·
2/N17   **@brewery.corner**   This bright blue pub is a rare example of a craft brewery pub. It's owned by the Carlow Brewing Company. There are 13 taps for craft, and cask-conditioned beers. Good pizzas, lively music, nice spot run by good staff.

924   **Bridie's Bar & General Store**   72 John St Lwr, Kilkenny +353 56 7765133
2/N17   · **www.langtons.ie**   Bridie's looks like a shop and pub from the Ireland of the
ATMOS   movie *Brooklyn*, but of course it isn't, being a superbly reconstituted facsimile of the same. It's part of the Langton empire, whose bars and hotel stretch all the way along John Street. Great spot.

925   **Tynan's Bridge House**   2 John's Bridge, Kilkenny +353 56 7771291   'This is a
2/N17   pub you'll want to take home with you' said the Bushmills Irish Pub Guide, many
ATMOS   years ago, and we agree: Tynan's is not one of the best-known pubs, but it is one of the most beautiful, and most beautifully preserved. Nothing quite like an early evening drink in here.

926   **Marble City Bar**   66 High St, Kilkenny +353 56 7761143 · **www.langtons.ie**
2/N17   The great Irish designer David Collins worked with the Langton bar and hotel group
ATMOS   on many of their projects, and you can see Mr Collins' stylish classicism at work in the lovely Marble City Bar. It's one of the oldest in town, and downstairs is the Marble City Tea Rooms. Both are extremely busy enterprises.

If you're in Thomastown...

927   **Bassett's Restaurant**   Marsh's St, Thomastown +353 56 7724916 ·
2/N17   **@BassettsThomastown**   John Bassett and Mijke Jansen are maverick talents,
MED.INX   whose unpredictability adds to their brilliance. In Thomastown they have a fine,
TERRACE   minimalist room, and a beautiful stone-walled terrace, and there are pizzas from the wood-fired oven, whilst 60-day beef from their dry-ager is cooked on the big green egg. Lunch & dinner Wed-Sun.

928   **The Blackberry Cafe**   Market St, Thomastown +353 86 7755303 ·
2/N17   **www.theblackberrycafe.ie**   Walking into Jackie Hoyne's café is just like stepping
ATMOS   into a Beatrix Potter book: as the name suggests, this former cobbler's shop is simply sweet. The poem 'Blackberry Picking' by Seamus Heaney has been proudly framed and mounted in the side of the windows, and this is a room where cookery and charm chime happily. One of the stars of Kilkenny. Daytime Mon-Sat.

Co Carlow

WHERE TO STAY

929 **Step House Hotel** Borris +353 59 9773209 · www.stephousehotel.ie
2/P17
20 ROOMS One of the most popular wedding venues in the country, in a pretty town on the
MED.EXP River Barrow. Nice rooms when things quieten down, and this area, between the
River Barrow and Mount Leinster, is special.
MAR-NOV **EAT** The real attraction here is a very fine head chef, Alan Foley, who is one of the
TERRACE most dedicated professionals we know, and whose cooking we have enjoyed for
L many years.

Kilgraney House Co Carlow Report: 1274/COUNTRY HOUSES.
Richmond House Co Carlow Report: 1283/COUNTRY HOUSES.
Coolanowle House Co Carlow Report: 1349/B&B.
Lorum Old Rectory Co Carlow Report: 1350/B&B.

WHERE TO EAT

930 ✓**Sha-Roe Bistro** Main St, Clonegal +353 53 9375636 · www.sha-roe.ie
2/Q16 For more than ten years, Henry and Stephanie have bucked every modern
MED.EXP trend about how to run a restaurant. Their social media presence is subterranean.
Self-promotion? PR strategies? None of that. In eschewing the modern way of
working, they show in little Sha Roe, in little Clonegal, that there is an older, and
more resilient, way of running a restaurant. So, they create a lovely room, welcome
people into it, and cook them imaginative and cheering food. And everyone comes
back. Dinner Thur-Sat & Sun lunch.

931 ✓**Lennon's @ Visual** Visual Arts Centre, Old Dublin Rd, Carlow
2/P16 +353 59 9179245 · www.lennons.ie In a stylish room in the beautiful Visual
CHP Arts Centre, Sinead and Ross Byrne, and chef Gail Johnson, offer artful cooking with
ATMOS ingredients sought with fastidious determination. Intelligence is at work
everywhere. Fantastic staff: the waitress who served us was a Ph.D. candidate.
Daytime 7 days, evenings Thur-Sat.

932 **Mullichain Cafe** The Quay, St Mullins +353 51 424440 ·
2/P18 www.oldgrainstorecottages.ie Right by the banks of the River Barrow, on the
TERRACE quay at St Mullins, the O'Brien family's restored mill and grain store is a magnet for
ATMOS walkers, kayakers, canoeists, and for those exploring the heritage sites. Good food
is served by first-class staff, and everyone is always well looked after. Eating here is
the perfect end to a long walk, and the planned new Barrow Blue Way will see even
more walkers discover these beautiful waterside routes. All day Tue-Sun.

Co Waterford

WHERE TO STAY

✓**Cliff House Hotel** Co Waterford Report: 1270/COUNTRY HOUSES.

Hanora's Cottage Co Waterford Report: 1330/ESCAPES.
Glasha Farmhouse Co Waterford Report: 1352/BEST B&B.

WHERE TO EAT

933 **White Horses** Main St, Ardmore +353 24 94040 On the main street in pretty
2/K20 Ardmore, sisters Christine and Geraldine have been showing for many years that
MED.INX they know their way around a menu. The room is especially vivid, bright and alive in
FEB-DEC the height of summer, except that then, of course, it's well nigh impossible to get a
ATMOS table. Excellent Irish domestic sweet baking means you must leave room for pudding
or go early in the day to try those cakes with coffee. Lunch & dinner Tue-Sun.

934 **Barron's Bakery Coffee Shop** Cappoquin +353 58 54045 ·
2/L20   www.barronsbakery.ie One of Ireland's finest traditional bakeries. Their breads
and Waterford blaas – the traditional local white bread roll – are made in their
classic, traditional Scotch oven, with the bread allowed lots of time to develop and
ferment before it meets the heat, and the final result is sheer goodness. The bakery
also features a neat coffee shop and a bake shop to buy the breads, and it's a vital
destination. Daytime Mon-Sat.

935 **The Copper Hen** Mother McHugh's Pub, Fenor +353 51 330300 ·
2/N19   www.thecopperhen.ie A pretty pub and restaurant, upstairs over Mother
MED.INX   McHugh's pub, in the little village of Fenor on the stunning Copper Coast. Chef
patron Eugene Long is a fastidious cook – the sort of guy who can make roast
potatoes that are both crisp and fluffy. This is some lovely cooking, and the recently
smartened up room is comfortable and welcoming. Dinner Thur-Sat.

936 **Azzurro Italian Restaurant** Dock Rd, Dunmore East +3533 51 383141 ·
2/P19   www.azzurro.ie It's the buzz of Azzurro that is the big attraction, whether you are
MED.INX   in the Ship bar downstairs or enjoying the harbour views from upstairs. Their pizzas
L   and pastas are inexpensive, and there are special deals at lunchtime. It's very busy
during holiday season in pretty Dunmore, so there's always a great crowd of locals
and tourists, and Azzurro is well managed. Dinner 7 days, midweek lunch May-Sep.

937 **The Spinnaker Bar & Restaurant** Dunmore East +353 51 383133 ·
2/P19   www.thespinnaker.ie Niall and Maria look after everyone in The Spinnaker. There
MED.EXP   is fine seafood cooking, but there are also expertly sourced meats for the carnivorous
L   to enjoy. There is an excellent menu for younger eaters, and lots of smart distractions
such as kids' movies, so the parents can catch up with each other and enjoy a drink
in the bar. Lunch & Dinner Mon-Sun. Three rooms also available for staying over.

938 **Lemon Tree Catering & Cafe** Seafield, Coxtown Rd, Dunmore East +353 51
2/P20   383164 · www.lemontreecatering.ie Joan Power was born into the business of
hospitality – her folks ran the landmark Candlelight Inn on Dock Road – so it's no
surprise that the signature of The Lemon Tree is a confident professionalism. There
is good, savoury cooking from breakfast through lunch, but it's at the summertime
weekend dinners that the creative flair comes out to play. Elegant, simple room,
polite service, decking area for sunny days, and good value. Daytime Tue-Sun. Open
dinner Jun-Aug.

939 **The Bay Café** Dock Rd, Dunmore East +353 87 6743572 · @dunmoreeast
2/P20   The Bay is a super-friendly little caff on the harbour. Go for the open crab sandwich
CHP   and the seafood chowder. Breakfasts are good, and the team looks after everyone
TERRACE   extra well. Daytime 7 days.

Jaybees Co Waterford Report: 1489/ICE CREAM.
Baldwin's Farmhouse Ice Cream Co Waterford Report: 1488/ICE CREAM.

If you're in Dungarvan...

940
2/M20
14 ROOMS
EXP

✓✓ **The Tannery** 10 Quay St, Dungarvan +353 58 45420 · www.tannery.ie
The upstairs dining room of The Tannery is the place to enjoy some of the most creative cooking in Ireland. Paul Flynn may not be a youngster anymore, but he has a young chef's curiosity, and the energy in his food is remarkable: we would come here just to eat his crab creme brulée. There are simpler plates in the wine bar, and a stylish private dining room for that big blowout. Maire Flynn runs the room, and is one of the great hostesses. Winebar open evenings Tue-Sun, no reservations. The Tannery Townhouse is just around the corner from the restaurant. The rooms are small but stylish, and breakfast is taken in the restaurant itself. The massive success of the Waterford Greenway means the Tannery rooms have become a favourite with cyclists, so make sure to book in advance. Restaurant Dinner Tue-Sat, Fri & Sun Lunch.

941
2/M20
MED.INX

The Moorings Davitt's Quay, Dungarvan +353 58 41461 · www.mooringsdungarvan.com The Moorings is an archetypal seaside restaurant, down near the quayside. Both the food and the decor have a nautical theme, so expect plenty of Helvick and Ballycotton seafood served in an informal, friendly setting. Small selection of rooms available for B&B.

942
2/M20
MED.INX

Merry's Gastro Pub Lwr Main St, Abbeyside, Dungarvan +353 58 24488 · @merrysgastropub Merry's is a classy pub, and it's one of the key destinations for eating and drinking during the annual West Waterford Food Festival, the sort of dynamic pub that puts the Fun in Fungarvan. Nice cooking, but it's the atmosphere and the excellent drinks that set Merry's apart.

If you're in Waterford City . . .

WHERE TO STAY

943
2/P19
100 ROOMS
MED.INX

The Granville Meagher's Quay, Waterford +353 51 305555 · www.granville-hotel.ie The Granville is a well-run traditional hotel, characterised by very professional staff who really do look after their guests. The gin menu is superb, whilst the food offering is broad, and designed to appeal to a wide demographic.

Faithlegg House Hotel Co Waterford Report: 1841/GOLF.
Waterford Castle Co Waterford Report: 1848/GOLF.

WHERE TO EAT

944
2/P19
CHP

✓ **The Cafe at Grow HQ** Ardkeen, Dunmore Rd, Waterford +353 51 584422 · www.giy.ie Grow HQ is the mothership of the GIY – Grow It Yourself – movement, which has spread like wildfire across Ireland over the last decade. Here, they conduct horticultural classes, run the organisation, and cook what is grown in the gardens outside the beautiful double-height, wood and glass café. It's a dynamic place, and the vibrancy of this largely plant-based cooking – cabbage and smoked tofu risotto; slow-cooked pork neck with red chard; veg cooked 5 ways – is invigorating. Daytime 7 days. Long table Dinner once a month.

945
2/P19
MED.INX
ATMOS

Momo Restaurant Patrick St, Waterford +353 51 581509 · www.momorestaurant.ie Opposite the Omniplex Cinema, in the centre of town, Kamila and Harry have a pretty room where they have enjoyed great success over the last few years. Their sourcing is meticulous – Seagull Bakery bread; GIY beetroot; Crowe's Farm ham – and there is real sense of ambition in Momo, evident in their imaginative vegetarian and children's menus. On a busy night the room fizzes with atmosphere. Lunch & dinner Tue-Sun.

946   Bay Tree Bistro 16 Merchant's Quay, Waterford +353 51 858517 ·
2/P19   www.thebaytreebistro.com Keith Boyle started cooking upstairs above a pub
MED.INX   in Ballybricken, but success was so rapid he had to move to this big barn of a room
down on the Quays. The room isn't hectic, divided as it is into several spaces, but
Mr Boyle's straight-ahead, hard-working food is a winner. Excellent value, and the
cooking is impish and fun. Dinner Tue-Sat.

947   La Boheme 2 George's St, Waterford +353 51 875645 ·
2/P19   www.labohemerestaurant.ie La Boheme is the most handsome dining
EXP   room in the city, a beautiful, arched basement that will put you in mind of a
ATMOS   medieval cathedral. Eric Theze retains the core French culinary repertoire that
has served him so well over the years. Christine Theze runs the room with
superb authority, and choicest drinks get the evening started with a bang.
Dinner Mon-Sat.

948   L'Atmosphere Restaurant 19 Henrietta St, Waterford +353 51 858426 ·
2/P19   www.restaurant-latmosphere.com L'Atmosphere is well-named: part of
MED.EXP   the attraction of Arnaud and Patrice's bistro is the fact that it feels as Gallic as
ATMOS   a 2CV. Exposed stone walls; simple place settings; and cooking that takes you
straight down the River Suir and over to provincial France. Value for set menus
is exceptional, and at the weekends you need a shoehorn to get seated. Lunch &
dinner 7 days.

949   Bodega 54 John St, Waterford +353 51 844177 · www.bodegawaterford.com
2/P19   The question everyone asks about Bodega is this: does any other room enjoy the
MED.EXP   sort of wild energy that seems to be inscribed in the DNA of this restaurant? The
ATMOS   answer is: no. Bodega stands alone. It's the restaurant equivalent of a cocktail:
riotous, colourful, alluring, clamorous. Whilst the menu reads like a standard
modern missal, what animates the food is some superb sourcing, and really
careful, attentive cooking. You can get drunk in here even without hitting the wine.
Lunch & dinner Mon-Sat.

950   Burzza 53 John St, Waterford +353 51 844969 · www.burzza.com Bodega!
2/P19   added a sister restaurant, Burzza, right next door to the mothership, specialising
MED.INX   in burgers and pizza, hence that curious name. A wood-fired oven and some
ATMOS   really fine Italian flour make for lovely thin-based pizzas with a variety of inventive
toppings, and the beef for the burgers comes from Tom Kearney's butchers just
down the street. Burzza has been busy since the day it opened and has needed
almost no fine tuning at all. Lunch & dinner 7 days (closed Tue & Mon Lunch)

951   Berfranks Café 86 The Quay, Waterford +353 51 306032 @Berfranks
2/P19   On The Quay in Waterford city, a vibrant orange frontage announces Berfranks,
CHP   Frank and Bernadette Treyvaud's cafe and restaurant. Frank's impeccable training,
TERRACE   and his many years experience in the restaurant business, ensure that Berfranks is
always a special place. An icon on the Quays. Daytime Mon-Sat.

952   Loko Ardkeen Shopping Centre, Waterford +353 51 841040 ·
2/P19   @LokoWaterford Loko is a funky, colourful space, and the team are crafting
MED.INX   some fine cooking here at the Ardkeen Centre, a couple of miles out of the city. The
ambition of the crew is to offer good food for everyone at any time of the day – they
are open from 11am, until late – and we admire the determination to do everything
with style. All this, and an interactive jukebox: download that sevenpop app now!
Lunch & dinner 7 days. Brunch Sat & Sun.

953
2/P19
CHP
Ginos Waterford The Apple Market, John's St, Waterford +353 51 879513 ·
@GinosW The Dunne family have been making good pizza for the good people of
Waterford for more than 30 years. But it's not just thin-crusted pizza: their home-
made ice cream – especially the hazelnut flavour – is exceptional. Pizza and ice
cream: how bad? Dinner 7 days.

954
2/P19
CHP
ATMOS
Granary Cafe Hanover St, Waterford +353 51 854428 · www.granarycafe.ie
Peter Fowler runs an exceptional café on Hanover Street, a step up from the quay.
His food sourcing gives you a taste of the entire county, indeed of the entire SE,
and he is helped by having one of the best-motivated, most efficient crews working
in the city. Daytime Mon-Sat.

955
2/P19
CHP
ATMOS
Arch Coffee 28a Great George's St, Waterford · www.archcoffee.ie
In this tiny shop, Neill White and George McDonald brought 3fe coffee beans, and
a very clear idea of what they wanted to achieve when they opened up Arch Coffee.
The coffee from Arch is exceptional: depending on what beans are on offer, you
vicariously travel the coffee world here with each cup, so precise is their execution.
George is a dab hand at baking, so there is always a brownie or a coconut slice to
have with your flat white. Daytime 7 days. Opens at 1pm Sun.

956
2/P19
CHP
Larder 111a Henrietta St, Waterford +353 87 4162401 · @Larder It's amazing to
see all the good things that Patrick Murphy manages to squeeze into this tiny space.
Great breads; scones; excellent locally roasted coffee; first-class drinks. And Mr Murphy
is droll and witty, which makes even the quickest visit a pleasure. Daytime Mon-Sat.

THE BEST BARS IN WATERFORD CITY

957
2/P19
TERRACE
ATMOS
Geoff's at The Apple Market Barronstrand St, Waterford +353 51 874787
Geoff's is pretty much a legendary destination in Waterford. Good music, good
drinks, an interior that fuses art gallery with curiosity shop, and a cool back garden
with heaters drive the powerhouse on. The food in Geoff's is particularly worth your
time: modern pub food delivered with confidence.

958
2/P19
ATMOS
Davy Macs 7 John's Ave, Waterford +353 51 843730 · www.davymacs.ie
They offer around about 80 different gins in Davy Mac's and, thankfully, they know
exactly what to do with them. A classic, award-winning Waterford pub with great
staff who make sure everything works.

959
2/P19
ATMOS
Tully's Bar 37 O'Connell St, Waterford +353 51 301639 @tullysbarwaterford
Look out for the bright red livery of Tully's, on O'Connell Street. It's a genuine bar
in the old style, with a classic snug that is a favourite seat in Waterford. Great craft
beer and gin selection.

960
2/P19
ATMOS
J & K Walsh 11 Great George's St, Waterford +353 51 874575 Walsh's has been
the lucky recipient of one of the most sublime restoration projects any Waterford pub
has seen in recent years. It's been made-over, yet left alone, so the wood panelling is
sepia tinged, the apothecary cupboards are all there and – hallelujah! – there are no
televisions. Give these guys a design award for bringing us all back to 1910.

Co Wexford

WHERE TO STAY

961
2/R19
118 ROOMS
EXP
ATMOS
LL

✓ ✓ ✓ **Kelly's Resort Hotel** Rosslare +353 53 9132114 www.kellys.ie
For more than a century, Kelly's has been a benchmark vacation destination, and the standards shown by the staff in this resort hotel, fronting onto the sands of Rosslare beach, are benchmark. This means that Kelly's has, on many occasions, occupancy rates that are north of 99%. Go once to Kelly's Resort Hotel, and you will find – like many other generations – that you will be going back to Kelly's for the rest of your life. Bill Kelly's art collection is one of the finest private collections in the country, and the wine list – Vincent Avril of Chateauneuf-du-Pape is Mr Kelly's father-in-law – is a masterpiece, and offers great value.
EAT Eugene Callaghan, head chef at Beaches Restaurant, won the first ever Roux Brothers' scholarship, and he has been one of the most significant culinary talents in Ireland ever since. Despite coping with very large numbers, the cooking in Beaches is exceptional. There is also simpler food in La Marine Bistro, which has already celebrated 20 years of business: longevity is in the DNA of this extraordinary hotel.

✓ **Monart Destination Spa** Co Wexford Report: 1334/SPAS.

Ferrycarrig Hotel Co Wexford Report: 1295/FAMILY FRIENDLY.

WHERE TO EAT

962
2/R19
MED.EX
L

Wild and Native Strand Rd, Rosslare +353 53 9132668 · www.wildandnative.ie
Fergal and Jodie Dempsey's restaurant and wine bar has been a big hit in Rosslare, thanks to a lovely room, that is cleverly decorated with varnished pallets, fishnets, and twinkling lights, and some spot-on cooking from Fergal. The menu is more or less completely seafood, wild foods are used smartly, and there good dishes for the kids, which means it can be difficult to get a table here during the summer season. Make sure to have a booking, otherwise you will meet the 'We are fully booked, sorry!' blackboard at the gate. Brunch, Lunch & dinner 6 days, closed Tue. TGP opening Wild & Native Gourmet Food store in Wexford.

963
2/P19
3 ROOMS
MED.EXP
ATMOS

Aldridge Lodge Duncannon, New Ross +353 51 389116 · www.aldridgelodge.com Billy Whitty's cooking has many champions, and not just amongst his devoted local audience. Working alongside his partner, Joanne Harding, Mr Whitty runs a class act, and offers some of the best-value cooking in the country. With supplies from his garden and from family members, the sourcing is as good as the cooking. Three comfortable, dormer-style rooms let the traveller really make the most of the experience. Dinner Wed-Sun. Closed 3 weeks in Jan.

964
2/P18
CHP

Cafe Nutshell 8 Sth St, New Ross +353 51 422777 Café Nutshell occupies a special status in New Ross. Patsey and Philip Roger's wholefood shop and café is the food destination in the town, and you time your journey around and across the N25 according to whether you will stop here for breakfast, lunch, or an afternoon break, or just for a sandwich to keep you going as you motor along to Rosslare or to Cork city. It's the proudest, prettiest place in town. Daytime Mon-Sat.

965
2/P19
22 ROOMS
LOTS

Dunbrody House Arthurstown +353 51 389600 · www.dunbrodyhouse.com
Kevin Dundon is one of top Irish celebrity chefs, and with his wife, Catherine, he presides over this elegant 1830's manor house. Dining options include the formal Harvest Room restaurant, with its classic European cooking – sole meuniere; suckling pig plate – and the champagne seafood bar – crab cocktail with lime mayonnaise; Hook Head haddock smokies. There is also simpler food in their bar, The Local.

966 Partridge's 93 Main St, Gorey +353 53 9484040 www.partridges.ie
2/R1 / Christian Pauritsch has a fine speciality food shop at the front of the house, where
CHP the hippest Irish artisan brands feature alongside great wines, and a bistro and tea
rooms at the rere. The cooking is simple, unpretentious and tasty. Paintings by
local artists adorn the walls, which adds to the air of a local hub, and Partridge's is
a special destination. Daytime Mon-Sat.

967 The Wilds 23 Weafer St, Templeshannon, Enniscorthy +353 53 9237799 ·
2/Q18 www.thewilds.ie Housed in an elegant historic building up the hill on Weafer
Street, The Wilds is both café and deli, and a lifestyle store. There are some funky
touches with the cooking and the sweet baking is good, as is the coffee. Good
stopover on the main road S. Daytime Tue-Sun.

968 The Lobster Pot Carne +353 53 9131110 · www.lobsterpotwexford.com
2/R19 The Hearne family's bar and restaurant has been a staple of the SE for more
MED.EXP than three decades. It's a pretty, flower-bedecked building with meticulous
housekeeping, and solid cooking that recalls the cordon-bleu style from when they
first opened. It's always busy. Lunch & dinner Wed-Sun.

969 The Silver Fox Kilmore Quay +353 91 29888 · www.thesilverfox.ie
2/Q19 A stone's throw from the marina, this modest blue bungalow houses a series of
MED.EXP brightly painted dining rooms, festooned with local artworks. Shane and Gopal have
TERRACE been here for more than a decade – though the restaurant has been a feature of
pretty Kilmore village for nearly 30 years. They stick to seafood classics, though there
are meat and chicken choices. Nice verandah is protected from the winds, and there
is a selection of their sauces and dressings to take away. Lunch & dinner 7 days.

WHERE TO EAT IN WEXFORD TOWN...

970 La Cote Church Ln, Ferrybank Sth, Wexford +353 53 9122122 · www.lacote.ie
2/R18 Paul Hynes worked in many great kitchens before heading home to open La Cote,
MED.INX with his partner Edwina. It's a lovely low-key room which looks out over the town's
fleet of mussel trawlers moored along the quayside, and the menu focuses wisely
on seafood. This is good cooking, with fine service and good value.

971 Kelly's Cafe Drinagh Retail Park, Wexford +353 53 9168800 · www.kellys.ie
2/R19 Sister establishment to the legendary Kelly's Resort Hotel of Rosslare, the Kelly's
CHP team offer local Wexford foods handled with care in this huge room in the Meadows
ATMOS & Byrne store at the Drinagh Park roundabout. First-rate pizzas underpin a menu
that reads conventionally, but where ingredients and ambition marry well. It's
exceptionally comfortable, thanks to some great design, and the logo, by Fiona Nash,
is a classic. Daytime 7 days. From noon Sun.

972 Cistín Eile 80 Sth Main St, Wexford +353 53 9121616 ·
2/R18 www.cistineilewexford.com Chef-patron Warren Gillen's restaurant on Main
MED.INX Street is one of the town's culinary destinations, and Mr Gillen's hard working
cooking in this small, simple room has many local admirers. Good value for money.
Lunch Mon-Sat, dinner Wed-Sat.

The Saltee Chipper Co Wexford Report: 1465/FISH & CHIPS.

The Best Places to Eat & Stay in Ireland's South West

East Cork

WHERE TO STAY

973
3/K21
EXP
TERRACE
LL

The Garryvoe Hotel Garryvoe +353 21 4646718 · www.garryvoehotel.com
Facing the 5km blue flag beach at Ballycotton Bay, this family-run hotel under the management of Stephen Belton is one of the best chill-out zones in E Cork. Recent renovations have delivered style and comfort – great pool, buzzing bar – making for one of the great escapes. Popular wedding destination, contained in a separate wing. Sister hotel to The Bayview, across the bay in Ballycotton, is another charmer. **EAT** Samphire Restaurant. We don't know anyone who chines and grills a better lamb chop than Kevin O'Sullivan, so ordering the sharing board of meats should be a first choice. Room strikes an ideal balance between formality and casual; wine list is particularly good.

 Ballymaloe House Co Cork Report: 1267/COUNTRY HOUSES.

WHERE TO EAT

974
3/K21
MED.INX
ATMOS
L

Pier 26 Ballycotton +353 21 20061449 · @pier26restaurant Holly Fitzgerald and Colin Hennessy are doing the good thing at Pier 26, in a simple, bright room in Ballycotton village. They transformed a seasonal restaurant into a year-long project, thanks to scrummy seafood cookery. Up-front flavours are the 26 style and Mr Hennessy shows respect to simple things such as their trademark chowder and the daily offering of fish and chips. Nice wines. Dinner Wed-Sat, 1pm-7pm Sun.

975
3/K21
CHP

The Blackbird Ballycotton +353 21 4647884 · www.blackbirdballycotton.com
If you want to hang out with all the students from the Ballymaloe Cookery School, you will meet them here, in the destination pub in the village. Aside from the drinks and music, everyone comes here to eat the cooking from The Field Kitchen, a food cart that operates out at the beer garden, with good monkfish scampi with aioli; garlic mussels; fish and chips. Nothing better after a long hike along the cliff walk. Afternoon and evening Wed-Sun.

Ballyseedy Garden Centre Report: 1979/GARDEN CENTRES.

976
3/J21
MED.INX
TERRACE
ATMOS
L

Cronin's Pub & Mad Fish Restaurant Crosshaven +353 21 4831829 ·
www.croninspub.com One of the great Irish pubs, and on a fine summer's day the crowds spill outside onto the concourse, happily drinking and eating barbecued seafood. Denis Cronin has steadily taken the food offer in the Mad Fish restaurant upstream in terms of quality, so this is much more than pub grub. Smart cooking, great drinks, and you could spend an eternity just checking out all the memorabilia on the walls. Pub Lunch 7 days, Restaurant Dinner Thur-Sat.

If you're in Midleton...

977
3/K21
EXP

Sage Restaurant The Courtyard, 8 Main St, Midleton +353 21 4639682 ·
www.sagerestaurant.ie Set back in a courtyard, Sage's chef-proprietor Kevin Aherne has pioneered a 12-mile locavore menu, and made it work, thanks to a devoted network of suppliers, and thank to his own formidable technical skills.

The house black pudding – served with salted egg yolk and smoked onions – may be the best in the country. Great staff explain it all. The more informal Greenroom, right next door, serves everyday dishes – breakfasts; burgers; salads; hot sandwiches – and the courtyard is a lovely, casual space that children adore. Dinner Tue-Sat, lunch Sat & Sun.

978
3/K21
MED.INX
ATMOS

✓ **The Café at the Ballymaloe Shop** Ballymaloe House, Shanagarry At the rere of the Ballymaloe Shop is a little room with a small collection of tables and a counter, and some of the best sweet baking that you will find anywhere in Ireland. It's not all sweet stuff – they have fine breakfast and lunch dishes – but the baking here is worth the drive and, if they have made the signature raspberry and chocolate tart, then all is well with the world. Daytime 7 days.

979
3/K21
CHP
TERRACE
ATMOS
FF

✓ **The Cafe at Stephen Pearce Pottery** Shanagarry +353 21 4645065 · www.thecafeatstephenpearce.com Stephen Pearce is one of Ireland's best-known potters, and a visit to his workshop, down a leafy lane off the R632 between the Garryvoe Hotel and the Kilkenny Design Centre has two benefits: you can buy his beautiful craftware; and you can also enjoy the sublime cooking of Christine Crowley, in The Café. Ms Crowley is quite a talent, and she brings an exacting creativity to simple things like her signature bruschetta, a perfect steak sandwich, or excellent carrot and walnut cake. Superb coffees, great staff, and a pretty courtyard for sunny days. Daytime Thur-Mon.

980
3/K21
MED.INX

Ferrit & Lee Midleton +353 21 4635235 · www.ferritandlee.ie On the road into the Midleton Distillery, this popular restaurant changed hands with head chef Stephen Lee taking charge along with Pat Ferriter. These guys are fine cooks and the food delivers on both flavour, and value for money. Great spot for a quick lunch before or after a Distillery tour. Lunch & dinner Tue-Sun.

981
3/K21
MED.INX
ATMOS

Farmgate Coolbawn, Midleton +353 21 4632771 · www.farmgate.ie Marog O'Brien's store and restaurant has been an iconic destination in the town for 35 years, and today Marog works with her daughter, Sally, and they do what Farmgate has always done: cooking E Cork foods with sympathy and imagination, and serving them in one of the county's artsiest and most elegant rooms. Comprehensive selection of local foods to go in the store out front. Daytime Tue-Sat, Dinner Thur-Sat.

982
3/K21
MED.INX

O'Donovan's 58 Main St, Midleton + 353 21 4631255 · www.odonovans.tiz.ie Looks like a standard issue country town pub, but this family-run bar is actually home to some fine restaurant cooking, and is one of the best choices in Midleton. Pat O'Donovan and his team deliver tasty cooking, good service and good value. Dinner Tue-Sat.

983
3/K21
MED.INX
ATMOS
FF

Saturday Pizzas Ballymaloe Cookery School, Shanagarry +353 86 3075749 · www.saturdaypizzas.com Philip Dennhardt makes California-style sourdough pizzas in the wood-fired oven at the Garden Café in the Ballymaloe Cookery School. Classic pizzas, with two funky Saturday Specials – barbecue beef with aioli; beetroot and goat's cheese; Gubbeen cheese with gremolata – feature on a short, smart menu. The pizzas are also available in several stores and supermarkets. With lots of garden space for the kids to explore, this is one of the best Saturday family adventures. Don't miss their excellent pizza book, written with leading food writer Kristen Jensen. Pizzas served Sat 12.30 pm-4 pm.

CF Lennox Co Cork Report: 1458/FISH & CHIPS

West Cork

WHERE TO STAY

984 **Celtic Ross Hotel** Rosscarbery +353 23 8848722 · www.celticrosshotel.com
3/G23 Manager Neil Grant and chef Alex Petit are putting some serious vavavoom! into
66 ROOMS the Celtic Ross, and the recent renovations to this lovely family-owned hotel have
MED.INX given it the style that matches the ambition of the crew. Their Wild Atlantic Way
L menus are particularly fine, and superlatively sourced, and reveal the strengths of
the local food culture. The Celtic Ross is officially a 3-star hotel, but it's got 5-star
ambition. One of the best destinations for afternoon tea.

985 **Eccles Hotel** Glengarriff Harbour +353 27 63003 · www.eccleshotel.com
3/E22 A change of ownership in 2016 has seen a new dynamism arrive in the splendid
64 ROOMS Victoriana of the Eccles Hotel. Situated across the road from the sea at Garinish
EXP Island, as you arrive in Glengarriff heading W, it's a sumptuous big cake of a building,
L and the rooms to go for are those with sea views. On-going refurbishments are
bringing this W Cork icon back to glory.
EAT Head chef Nick Davey has a mighty cv and has worked alongside some of the
leading Irish culinary talents. His menus are alive to W Cork and Kerry ingredients
– Mountain lamb; W Cork charcuterie; Dexter beef; sea vegetables – and here is
a talent to watch. Excellent bar food means this is your N71 stopover: the blue
cheese bruschetta and the chowder are pitch perfect.

986 **Casey's of Baltimore** Baltimore +353 28 20197 · www.caseysofbaltimore.com
3/F23 In addition to their popular hotel, Casey's also offer accommodation in a Townhouse,
14 ROOMS a Lodge and a Cottage. Their own gardens supply a lot of choice ingredients for the
MED.INX kitchen, and be sure to sample the three West Cork Brewing Co. craft beers, made in
their own nano-brewery by Dominic, Kevin and Henry.

✓**Inchydoney Island Lodge & Spa** Co Cork Report: 1333/SPAS

Lis-Ardagh Lodge Co Cork Report: 1365/BEST B&B

WHERE TO EAT

987 ✓✓**Diva Café and Coffeehouse** Ballinspittle, Co Cork +353 21 4778465 ·
3/H22 www.divaboutiquebakery.com Shannen Keane's Diva Café is, indeed,
a diva: a star performer, a headliner. Ms Keane is a culinary Callas, a stylish
individualist with a voice that is uniquely hers. She can go from the high C of
chicken llamas, to the deep bass of a beef and barley soup, and everything is well
within her range: as a cook she has perfect pitch. And she has a mixologist's mind,
so every dish is a deft balance between sweet, sour, bitter, umami, salty. Sister
establishment Diva Boutique Bakery is just down the road.

988 ✓✓**Deasy's Harbour Bar** Ring Village +353 23 8835741 ·
3/H22 @Deasy'sRestaurant Caitlin Ruth is the most generous of cooks. Not
MED.EXP because she delivers generous portions in Deasy's, a water's edge traditional Irish pub
ATMOS in little Ring village, but because she works so hard at every element of every plate. She
LL draws in the produce of her suppliers, farmers and artisans, then brings forth her own
batterie of pickles, ferments, foraged foods, and skills. The result is a meshwork of
flavours on every plate. Darina Allen of Ballymaloe called Ms Ruth 'a beautiful cook',
and that's just right: alive to the beauty of every ingredient, she summons vivid flavours
from her food, and Deasy's is a W Cork icon. Dinner Wed-Sat & Sun lunch.

989 ✓✓ **Pilgrim's** South Sq, Rosscarberry +353 23 8831796 · www.pilgrims.ie
3/G23   Pilgrim's is the most exciting restaurant to have opened in W Cork in
MED.EXP recent years. Mark Jennings puts all the funky stuff on his menus and he has the
ATMOS   skill to deliver this rainbow of influences. The dishes offer wonderful contrasts of
flavour and texture, every bite keeping the taste buds excited, just as the room
offers a tactility that runs between upcycled pine tables, dried and fresh wild
flowers, and gorgeous Patrick Scott paintings. Sarah Jane Pearce and her team are
charming, and for such adept cooking and peerless sourcing, Pilgrim's prices are
remarkably keen. A happening place. Dinner Wed-Sun & Sun lunch.

990 ✓✓ **Good Things at Dillon's Corner** 68 Bridge St, Skibbereen +353 28 51948 ·
3/F23   www.thegoodthingscafe.com Carmel Somer's Good Things is one of the
MED.EXP most beautiful dining rooms on the Wild Atlantic Way, a room where every design
detail chimes to powerful effect, and reveals wit and good taste. The cooking,
then, does exactly the same thing: this is some of the very best W Cork cooking.
Ms Somers' roll-call of classic dishes are amongst the great contemporary Irish dishes,
sure-footed, natural, elegant and soulful. Lunch Thur-Sat, dinner Fri & Sat. Longer
hours high season, shorter hours winter season. Cookery classes run throughout the
year.

991 ✓ **The Mews** Main St, Baltimore +353 28 20572 ·
3/F23   www.mewsrestaurant.ie The Mews opens for six months of the year and this
EXP   pretty room has drawn many admirers over its first three seasons. A change of chef last
APR-OCT season – Ahmet Dede took charge of the kitchen – gave the restaurant new power. It's
a beautiful room, tucked down a laneway as you walk down the hill towards the pier.
Dinner Tue-Sat

992 ✓ **Lettercollum Kitchen Project** 22 Connolly St, Clonakilty
3/G22   +353 23 8836938 · www.lettercollum.ie Lettercollum looks like a
CHP   standard-issue deli, but it's actually home to some of the best savoury cooking
in the county, and what these guys don't know about pastry isn't worth
knowing. Excellent locally-roasted coffee, excellent foods on the shelves.
All Day Tue-Sat.

993 ✓ **Dillon's Restaurant** Mill St, Timoleague +353 23 8869609 ·
3/H22   www.dillonsrestaurant.ie There are two chefs to be discovered in the
MED.EXP cooking of Richard Milnes, of Dillon's Restaurant in little Timoleague. One is
L   Richard Milnes, Modernist, a cook who likes to throw curve balls at everything: he
cooks celeriac, as a steak. Then there is Richard Milnes, Classicist, who cooks pork
belly with lentils as if he had learnt it straight from Fernand Point back in the '50's,
or black Angus sirloin with garlic butter as if we were still in the days of Escoffier.
Happily, these two talents combine to produce some of the best cooking in W Cork,
while Antje Gesche runs the room with unflappable charm. Dinner Fri-Tue (closed
Wed & Thurs), and Sun lunch.

994 ✓ **Monk's Lane** Timoleague +353 23 8846348 · www.monkslane.ie
3/H22   Everyone loves Gavin and Michelle's Monk's Lane, one of the defining
MED.INX gastropubs in the region. So, what's to love? Well, their W Cork tasting platter
ATMOS   is worth the trip itself, but there's also their classic burger, the lamb quesadillas,
the sausages with mash. And there's the music, the craic, the lovely service,
the great drinks. There's a lot to love in Monk's Lane. Lunch Wed-Sat, dinner
Wed-Sun.

995   ✓ **The Coffee Shop**   Union Hall 353 87 1737748 · @Thecoffeeshopunionhall
3/G23   Billy and Jessie's Coffee Shop has taken pretty little Union Hall by storm. At the
CHP   core of their offer is Billy's artful baking. But it's not just the baking that is top-notch:
ATMOS   the chowder is a classic, and the signature pizzas draw in locals from miles around
on weekend evenings. Add in a sweet, modest room that seems to incarnate the
spirit of W Cork, and you can see why The Coffee Shop hits so many hearts. TGP they
are opening a second Coffee Shop in Kinsale. Daytime Tue-Sat.

996   **Hart's Coffee Shop**   8 Ashe St, Clonakilty +353 23 8835583 ·
3/G22   www.hartscafeclonakiilty.com Aileen Hart's little coffee shop and lunch stop is
CHP   a beacon of excellence, and the boss and her team just do everything right. All day
Mon-Sat.

997   **Scannells**   5 Connolly St, Clonakilty +353 23 8834116 · www.scannells.ie
3/G22   Scannells is cool. You might be impressed at first by its pristine interior, but a quick
MED.INX   glance at the menus shows just how hip this Clonakilty landmark really is. Fresh
TERRACE   crab with Clonakilty black pudding, apple and manchego; Ummera smoked chicken
with Crozier Blue cheese; beef cheeks braised in local ale. Lovely imaginative food
from a dynamic kitchen.

998   **Sticky Bun**   21 Rossa Street, Clonakilty + 353 23 8835644 @stickybunclon
3/G22   Kay Burke has the benefit of having a cutting-edge chef, Kevin, for a son, and
CHP   together they have brought lots of imagination to the dishes in this pretty little
room. Kay's sweet baking – homemade custard creams! – is worth the trip on its
own. Daytime Mon-Sat.

999   **The Food Depot – Gourmet Street Kitchen**   Courtmacsherry
3/H22   +353 85 7374437 @FoodDepotGourmetStreetKitchen The Food Depot is a
CHP   food cart that sits on the beach at Courtmacsherry, and is run by Diana Dodog and
LL   her husband, Mike. Ms Dodog is famous because she won Ireland's Masterchef,
but her fame lies with her inspired cooking and eating this food on the beach
is a classic W Cork experience. Thur-Fri 8.30am-2pm, W Cork Technology Park,
Clonakilty, Sun 1pm-4pm Courtmacsherry Beach.

1000   **Puffin Cafe**   Long Strand, Castlefreke +353 86 0816898 Spencer Treacy and
3/G23   Kate Zinkin produce some of the best pizzas in W Cork at their inspired little café at
CHP   the end of Long Strand. The pizzas sound good – the Frankie Knuckles; the Chuck
ATMOS   D – and taste even better. The room is whacky and post-modern, the drinks are
LLL   perfect, and the kids will all want an ice. Spencer and Kate also rent some cool
accommodation: just enquire. And do be warned that walking on Long Strand is
particularly exhausting: that sand is soft! Daytime, seasonal hours.

1001   **O'Callaghan Walshe**   The Square, Rosscarbery +353 23 8848125 ·
3/G23   ocallaghanwalshe.com Martina and Sean cook and serve only wild W Cork fish,
MED.EXP   and their scampi – and their mashed potato – are the stuff of local culinary legend.
Sean is also one of the wittiest hosts in history, so you get a great sense of humour
and plenty of craic along with inspired fish cookery, in a quirky and atmospheric
room. Dinner Tue-Sun.

1002   **O'Neill Coffee**   64 Townshend St, Skibbereen +353 86 3334562 ·
3/F23   @oneillcoffee Colm Crowley sources his beans from two local W Cork roasteries
ATMOS   – W Cork Coffee and Red Strand Coffee – and his sweet and savoury tastes come
from the best local bakeries. Put these in a darling little old grocery shop, and you

have the hippest place in town. A flat white and a lemon and raspberry square and you'll be buzzing. Daytime 7 days.

1003 **Kalbo's** 26 North St, Skibbereen +353 28 21515 · www.kalboscafe.com
3/F23 Siobhan O'Callaghan is one of the best cooks in W Cork, and everything cooked in
CHP the closet-sized space of Kalbo's enjoys her signature of superb sourcing meeting sophisticated kitchen skills. The sausage rolls use their own free-range pork, and the brownies are just the best. All day Mon-Sat.

✓ **Glebe Gardens** Co Cork Report: 1666/GARDENS

▧ If you're in Ballydehob . . .

1004 **Porcelain Room** Staball, Ballydehob +353 87 9263255 · www.ballydehob.ie
3/E23 Joanne switches her culinary character in the Porcelain Room, so whilst the daytime food swerves to the Mediterranean, in the evenings the focus is on Asian-Fusion food. Dinner Thurs-Sat.

1005 **Antonio's Ristorante Pizzeria** Main St, Ballydehob +353 28 37139 ·
3/E23 www.antonioristorante.ie Antonio's charismatic mix of unfussy Italian food and good pizzas is a winning formula. Their signature pasta dishes are really fine, and an evening here is great theatre, and great fun. Dinner Wed-Sun.

1006 **Budds** Main St, Ballydehob +353 28 25842 · www.budds.ie Budds is buzzing,
3/E23 so don't be surprised if you arrive to meet a friend and have to wait for a table. Ballydehob is home to a close-knit community, and Budds has placed itself at the heart of it, with its artisan cheese and meat boards and buffalo burgers, good coffees and relaxed atmosphere. Just about everyone in here is a local, always a great sign for a restaurant. All day Mon-Sun, dinner Thurs-Sat.

▧ If you're on The Mizen Peninsula . . .

WHERE TO STAY
✓ **Fortview House** Co Cork Report: 1344/BEST B&B.

Rolf's Country House Co Cork Report: 1320/RESTAURANTS WITH ROOMS.

WHERE TO EAT
1007 **Hackett's Bar** Main St, Schull +353 28 28625 · www.schull.ie Hackett's is a
3/E23 treasure, as funky, colloquial, and characterful as any traditional pub in W Cork. The
CHP cooking is as punky as the staff, and that's saying something, so this is the place
ATMOS for a bowl of big red, or some bacon and cabbage soup. Unique atmosphere. Food served noon-3pm.

1008 **The Crookhaven Inn** Crookhaven +353 28 35309 ·
3/E23 www.thecrookhaveninn.com Emma and Freddy serve really smashing food in
MED.INX the Crookhaven Inn, and if you find yourself pitching up here with a big appetite
EASTER-OCT after a day on the beach at Barleycove, well you could not be in a better place. Their
LL signature dishes are just delicious. Lunch & dinner 7 days.

If you're on The Sheep's Head . . .

WHERE TO STAY

Blairscove House & Restaurant Co Cork Report: 1273/COUNTRY HOUSES.
Gallan Mor Co Cork Report: 1366/BEST B&B.

WHERE TO EAT

1009 **The Heron Gallery and Cafe** Ahakista +353 27 67278 · www.herongallery.ie
3/E22 Annabel Langrish has opened galleries in both Schull and Kinsale in addition to her
CHP original gallery in Ahakista. Ms Langrish is a one-woman powerhouse, and somehow
APR-AUG also manages to find time to run a lovely wholefood café beside the gallery, in
L addition to maintaining a superb garden, so this is a great stop for lovely food and a
tour of both gallery and garden. All day 7 days.

1010 **Arundels by the Pier** Kitchen Cove, Ahakista +353 27 67033 ·
3/E23 www.arundelsbythepier.com Arundel's bar and restaurant has a drop-dead
LL gorgeous location, and to enjoy something tasty sitting across the road in the
garden at the water's edge on a sunny W Cork day is an experience that is hard to
beat. They serve bar food downstairs, whilst the restaurant is upstairs. Don't miss
the signature dish of Durrus cheese fritters served with poached pears and salad.
Lunch & dinner 7 days.

1011 **Bernie's Cupán Tae** Café Toreen Car Park, Sheep's Head +353 27 67878
3/D23 At the end of the Sheep's Head Way, at the end of Europe, there is a table and on it
CHP there is a cup of tea, and a salmon sandwich, that both have your name on them.
LLL If you have hiked down to Tooreen, with the lighthouse as your destination, then
the tea and the sandwich waiting for you in Bernie Tobin's tea room will taste like
the greatest thing you have ever eaten in your entire life. Daytime 7 days during
summer season. Telephone before travelling.

If you're in Bantry . . .

WHERE TO STAY
Seaview House Hotel Co Cork Report: 1284/COUNTRY HOUSES.
Bantry House Co Cork Report: 1279/COUNTRY HOUSES.

WHERE TO EAT

1012
3/E22
CHP

✓ **Organico Cafe** 3 Glengarriff Rd, Bantry +353 27 55905 · www.organico.ie
Even after 20 years of service, Organico still exudes a just-born energy, thanks to its owners, Hannah and Rachel Dare, and their team of wise, witty women – and the occasional man – who run the shop and the café with calm exactitude. The cooking in the café is as smart as smart gets, whilst the shop and bakery has everything you could possibly need. Organico is the best double act in W Cork, and should not to be missed. Takeaways available. Daytime Mon-Sat.

1013
3/E22
CHP
ATMOS

✓ **The Stuffed Olive** Bridge St, Bantry +353 27 55883 · @TheStuffedOlive
The elegance and dynamism of Trish Messom's cooking and baking, and the efficiency and energy of the front of house team led by Sarah and Bernie, means the Stuffed Olive is a café that punches way above its diminutive weight. One of their signature dishes is 'beetroot, fennel and caraway spelt soda bread' which gives some idea of how funky the food can be: you are a long way from your Mammy's soda bread when you get a slice of this. Great food to go if you are renting nearby; nice wines. Daytime Mon-Sat.

1014
3/F22
MED.INX
ATMOS

✓ **Manning's Emporium** Ballylickey, Bantry +353 27 50456 ·
www.manningsemporium.ie For a lot of visitors to W Cork, eating in Manning's Emporium is one of the defining experiences of the region. Val, Laura and Andrew mainline the zeitgeist of what 'W Cork' is, and then put the foods and flavours of the area in front of you, along with a chilled glass of fino sherry, or a local craft beer. Whether it's a flat white and a slice of coffee cake at 11am, or a plate of tapas and W Cork cheeses with good wines at 7pm, Manning's delivers what is for many people a dream-like food experience. It's all so simple, logical, and unique. And when it's time to head home, you can raid the shop to bring the taste of W Cork back home. Daytime 7 days, till 7/9pm.

1015
3/E22
MED.INX

The Fish Kitchen New St, Bantry +353 27 56651 · www.thefishkitchen.ie
Ann Marie's Fish Kitchen is upstairs above the fish shop, right in the centre of town, and it's a welcoming and simple room in which to enjoy some straight-ahead fish and shellfish cookery. Great service, and great value for money, means the Fish Kitchen really ticks all the boxes, which is why it is always so busy. Lunch & dinner Tue-Sat.

1016
3/E22
MED.INX-
MED.EXP

The Snug and O'D's Pub The Quay, Bantry +353 27 50057 · www.thesnug.ie
No bar in Ireland is as well named as The Snug. Maurice O'Sullivan's bar is an always-welcoming destination, a place for good food and good pints. Whether you are having a quiet lunch of bacon and cabbage with a bottle of mineral water, or a dinner of fresh fish with a few pints of beer, The Snug always feels just right. Their restaurant room – O'D's – has gifted them with much need extra seating, and it's an excellent space. Lunch & dinner 7 days.

Wharton's Co Cork Report: 1459/FISH & CHIPS.

1017
3/D22
MED.INX
LL
Rhonwen's Eyeries Bistro Eyeries, Beara Peninsula +353 27 74884 · www.eyeriesbistro.ie Eating lunch sitting in the backyard of Rhonwen's is so special that it's worth the drive all the way to Eyeries, the prettiest village on the peninsula. Their Beara buffalo burger is really good, but then all the food shows care and attention to detail. Lunch & dinner Tue-Sun

1018
3/D22
MED.EXP
Ocean Wild West End, Castletown Berehaven, Beara Peninsula +353 27 71544 · www.oceanwild.ie Sisters Mairead O'Driscoll and Eileen Quinn opened both Ocean Wild and their wine and tapas bar, Into The Wild, in 2017, and quickly made a splash in this pretty harbour town. They have two pretty rooms, with stone walls and floors and, with a family background in the fishing industry, their sourcing is impeccable. Highly promising. Dinner Thur-Mon.

1019
3/D21
CHP
LLL
Teddy O'Sullivan's Bar Kilmackillogue, Lauragh, Co Kerry +353 64 6683104 The locals call it Helen's – the name of the original licensee – and this is the place for the freshest mussels, or crab, and a pint in this classic pub hard by the pier. Unforgettable, especially when the sun is shining.

North Cork

WHERE TO STAY

1020
3/F21
26 ROOMS
MED.EXP
LLL

✓ **Gougane Barra Hotel** Ballingeary +353 26 47226 · www.gouganebarrahotel.com The Lucey family and their team offer hospitality in its most elemental form in their lakeside hotel up in the woods of Gougane Barra. You could pitch up here, frazzled from the cares of the world, and imagine that you had arrived in a fairy tale. A little lakeside hotel, a small church, a forest, a place set apart, and the purest hospitality you could ever imagine. Mr & Mrs Lucey are modest, charming, and hard-working, and they create nothing less than an archetype of Irish hospitality. **EAT** Katy Lucey's cooking is simple and delicious, the ideal domestic cooking in the right place: Aga-roast chicken with savoury mash; cod with champ and lime butter; Gougane Mess. Good wine list has an excellent selection.

1021
3/G21
60 ROOMS
MED.INX

Castle Hotel Main St, Macroom +353 26 41074 · www.castlehotel.ie Brothers Don and Gerard Buckley are the latest family members to have charge of the Castle Hotel, a welcoming, professional and highly-regarded destination in Macroom. Food is served in the bar, in the Next Door Café, and in B's restaurant, and it's here that the kitchen's solid professionalism comes into its own: chicken stuffed with Clonakilty black pudding; hake with a herb crust; Cork artisan producers board. Do note that the coffee is excellent, and well worth the stop-over. Good pool in the leisure centre.

Longueville House Co Cork Report: 1285/COUNTRY HOUSES.

WHERE TO EAT

1022
3/H21
MED.EXP
TERRACE
ATMOS

✓ **Blairs Inn** Cloghroe +353 21 4381470 · www.blairsinn.ie On the R579, a mile or so past the entrance to the Muskerry Golf Club, Blairs Inn is the rural gastropub every village in Ireland would like to have. Brothers Richard and Duncan have taken the lessons of their parents, Anne and John, and created some of the most impressive pub cooking in Ireland. The dishes are a roll-call of classics – corned beef and cabbage; Cashel Blue and roasted pears; gratin of seafood; roast duck with Grand Marnier; Cork fillet steak; bread and butter pudding – but the cooking sings with flavour, and the bar is quaint and mightily charming: the fire is always lit, the hospitality is always mighty. Lunch & dinner 7 days.

1023
3/G21
MED.INX
MAR–OCT
ATMOS

Toons Bridge Dairy Macroom +353 87 3457790 · www.toonsbridgedairy.com Toby Simmonds and his team make rare caciocavallo cheese at this little dairy, but they also offer some of the best pizzas you can find in the country, in a charming space which is also blessed with a cute food shop, where you can buy all their cheese products. No one else makes cheeses like these in Ireland, so it's well worth the detour. Lunch & dinner Fri-Sun.

1024
3/J21
MED.EXP

The Square Table Blarney +353 21 4382825 · www.thesquaretable.ie Martina Cronin worked in some of Dublin's leading restaurants before she and her twin, red-headed sister, Tricia, opened their little room in the centre of busy Blarney. The cooking, therefore, has more polish and technical finesse than one might expect in a provincial town and together they are a mighty pair, in a mighty charming destination that is the star attraction for many miles around. Dinner Wed-Sat, lunch Sun.

1025
3/G21

The Mills Inn Main St, Ballyvourney +353 26 45237 · www.millsinn.ie This big roadside bar and shop offers some very competent cooking – crab and leek gratin; lamb cutlets with rosemary gravy. Lovely ladies who know all things look after you like you were a native. Comfortable rooms, good music sessions, and owner Don O'Leary is also a brewer, and fashions the superb 9 White Deer craft beers with Gordon Lucey, so this is where you want to be sipping a Stag Rua. Lunch & dinner 7 days.

WHERE TO STAY

1026 **The Brook Lane Hotel** Kenmare +353 64 6642077 · www.brooklanehotel.com
3/E21 Kenmare has lots of distinguished places to stay, and whilst The Brook Lane isn't
19 ROOMS amongst the best-known addresses in town, Una and Dermot Brennan's small boutique
MED.EXP hotel on the Sneem Road has been doing the good thing quietly and efficiently for
some years now. In particular, the quality of the cooking here is superb, as good as the
hospitality from an excellent team. One essential tip when you are staying: don't miss Mr
Brennan's own rare-breed pork, served at breakfast as sausages and on the dinner menu.

The Park Hotel Co Kerry Report: 1337/SPAS.

WHERE TO EAT

1027 ✓**Mulcahy's** Main St, Kenmare +353 64 6642383 ·
3/E21 www.mulcahyskenmare.ie When he first opened in Kenmare, more than
MED.EXP 20 years ago, Bruce Mulcahy was a punky, culinary enfant terrible. He has mellowed
over time, and he now serves his food in a clubby, wood-panelled series of rooms.
But that punky spirit is still there in Mulcahy's food which explains why the tastes
and textures are so vivid and precise, and why he has been the leading restaurant in
the town for two decades. Laura Mulcahy looks after everyone. Dinner Tue-Sat.

1028 ✓**Packie's** Henry St, Kenmare +353 64 6641508 Martin Hallisey's cooking in
3/E21 Packie's, one of the legendary Kenmare addresses, is neither modern nor
MED.EXP traditional, though it has elements of both. Truthfully, it's food that is outside of
ATMOS fashion, and outside of time, so you might have roast duck, or Irish stew, or cod
Provencale, or seafood sausage with beurre blanc, and it will all be delicious.
Service is as genial as the chef and his food, and Packie's is one of the Kenmare
standard bearers. Dinner Mon-Sat.

1029 **Purple Heather** Henry St, Kenmare +353 64 6641016 ·
3/E21 www.thepurpleheatherkenmare.com Grainne O'Connell is one of the select
MED.INX band of Kenmare Food Heroes, the people who carved out the town's reputation
ATMOS for good food, and who also maintain it, day after day, through sheer hard work.
Something about the room always makes us yearn for classic food when we are
here – chicken liver pâté with Cumberland sauce, the mushroom omelette, the
cheese platter, the seafood pie. Class. Lunch Mon-Sat

1030 **The Mews** 3-4 Henry Court, Kenmare +353 64 6642829
3/E21 www.themewskenmare.com Maria O'Sullivan's warm welcome and assured
MED.EXP service, and Gary Fitzgerald's classic cookery have seen The Mews make its mark
quickly in Kenmare. Tucked into a little laneway just off Henry Street, it's a pretty
room where the food and service chime perfectly, so enjoy Dingle Bay crab; Kenmare
chowder; beef with caramelised onion mash; chocolate terrine with berry ice cream.
Dinner Tue-Sun.

1031 **The Strawberry Field** Moll's Gap, Kenmare +353 64 6682977 ·
3/E21 www.strawberryfield-ireland.com You will find Margaret and Peter's
CHP Strawberry Field by turning off down the Sneem Road, at the Avoca store at Moll's
ATMOS Gap. It's an unusual, cute little cottage that also offers a gift shop selling a range of
LL oil paintings, crafts, metal-ware and strawberry-related accoutrements. Margaret
and Peter make exceptionally good crepes and, when you pull up to the cottage

and order up a flour crepe with some ice cream and a cup of tea, you realise just what a fine snack this is for the hungry traveller, not to mention the hungry traveller's children. Daytime 7 days during the summer. Weekends only off season.

▬▬ If you're on The Ring of Kerry . . .

WHERE TO STAY

1032
3/C21
36 ROOMS
EXP
L

Butler Arms Hotel Waterville +353 66 9474144 · www.butlerarms.com
The Huggard family's hotel has a reputation for fine cooking, which they serve in the Charlie's Restaurant – the Charlie is none other than Charlie Chaplin, a frequent guest – in the Fisherman's Bar, and in the bright, colourful Chaplin Conservatory. Great sea views from the front room – the hotel is just across from the ocean – give you the spirit of the real Wild Atlantic Way and the Ring of Kerry. Do note that they offer a two-night stay, with one dinner in the conservatory and a boat trip around the Skelligs, as one of their special offers.
EAT Good fresh seafood in the Fisherman's Bar, and Charlie's Restaurant.

QC's Co Kerry Report: 1318/RESTAURANTS WITH ROOMS.
Sneem Hotel Co Kerry Report: 1291/FAMILY FRIENDLY.
McMunn's Co Kerry Report: 1309/ROADSIDE INNS.
Ard na Sidhe Co Kerry Report: 1328/ESCAPES.
Parknasilla Resort and Spa Co Kerry Report: 1331/ESCAPES.
The Moorings Co Kerry Report: 1308/ROADSIDE INNS.

WHERE TO EAT

1033
3/D20
EXP
ATMOS

Nick's Seafood Restaurant & Gastro Bar Lwr Bridge St, Killorglin +353 66 9761219 · www.nicks.ie Nick's is a legend in Kerry, and has been since they opened in 1976. Today, John Foley runs the restaurant and gastro bar and whilst he pays tribute to some of the restaurant's classic dishes – seafood platter; monkfish and prawn thermidor; surf & turf – the development of the gastro bar has allowed him to introduce lots of modish new dishes. Do note that the bar has a fantastic selection of craft beers from the county, and further afield. Dinner Tue-Sun.

1034
3/D20
MED.INX
ATMOS

Sol y Sombra The Old Church of Ireland, Killorglin +353 66 9762357 · www.solysombra.ie For more than ten years, Cliodhna Foley's inspired venture, serving Spanish-accented food and wine in a former Church of Ireland, has been making people happy. Whilst the accent of the cooking is Spanish, Cliodhna uses a lot of local foods, so Killorglin beef comes in a southern Spanish sauce, and instead of morcilla you will be enjoying Sasta black pudding, whilst the mature cheese on the fries is the brilliant local Wilma's Killorglin farmhouse cheese. There are lots of wonderful wines, and a great cocktail selection. The whole venture is surreal and quite inspired. Dinner Wed-Sun.

1035
3/D20
CHP
ATMOS

Zest Café School Rd, Killorglin +353 66 9790303 · www.zestcafe.ie
Nicola Foley's Zest Café is a pivotal part of the Foley family's trio of establishments in town, a stylish and happening room where every dish they offer, from breakfast to brunch to lunch and on into the afternoon, somehow manages to be healthful and yet comforting. Value and service chime sweetly with every other detail of a café that gives us the zest for living. Daytime Mon-Sat.

1036　**Jacks' Coastguard Restaurant** Cromane, Killorglin +353 66 9769102 ·
3/D20　www.jackscromane.com Jacks' is an icon in and around Cromane, a sure-fire
EXP　success story for professionally cooked seafood, served in a svelte room with
LL　superlative sea views. The Keary family really do their best to look after everyone,
and their caring approach is a delight. Just make sure to get there early if you are
heading to Cromane for Sunday lunch, because they get super-busy super-early.
Dinner Wed-Sun & Sun lunch.

1037　**The Lobster** Main St, Waterville +353 66 9474629 · @thelobsterwaterville
3/C21　James Doyle and his family moved from the stresses of Dublin city to the tranquility
MED.INX　of Waterville and took over the venerable Lobster, one of the best-known pubs
in the town. They quickly carved a reputation for both good cooking and good
hospitality, which makes this a perfect stop-over if you are touring the Ring, or
a good destination for tasty food in a lively bar if you are staying locally. Good
music sessions.

If you're in Killarney . . .

WHERE TO STAY

1038
3/E20
68 ROOMS
LOTS

✓✓ **The Killarney Park Hotel** Town Centre, Killarney +353 64 6635555 ·
www.killarneyparkhotel.ie The Treacy family's hotel, right in the centre of Killarney, defines what a 5-star hotel should be. In every aspect of the hotel, the team show that they are on top of the detail: greeting, information, bar service, spa service, cooking and table service. With Marcus Treacy now returned to the family hotel, after a decade spent working in hotels abroad, the team is better than ever. What sets the KP apart from the legion of Killarney hotels is its endless striving to improve. One of the best destinations.
EAT in the Park Restaurant or the Garden Bar. The restaurant cooking in the Park is very strong – and it's a particularly striking room – but it's a mark of how serious the entire operation is that many regulars still choose to eat in the Garden Bar: you might be eating in a bar but this is not bar food. Don't miss the local Killarney Brewery beers.

1039
3/E20
29 ROOMS
MED.INX
ATMOS

✓ **The Ross** Town Centre, Killarney +353 64 6627633 · www.theross.ie Ciara Treacy runs the show in the uber-stylish The Ross, the Killarney town-centre hotel where her grandmother first established the Treacy reputation as Kerry hoteliers par excellence. It's a tradition continued by her dad, Padraig, who runs the stellar Killarney Park, alongside her brother, Marcus. The Ross has the most stylish rooms in the town.
EAT in the Cellar One restaurant or the Lane Café Bar. The cooking downstairs in the wildly over-the-top glam of the Cellar One restaurant is modern and hip: small plates offer chickpea cakes, or air-dried beef, or Kerry lamb lollipops, whilst large plates have cod fillet with Ted Browne's crab or Skeaghanore duck with duck spring roll. Top-notch cocktails from a good bar team get the night off to the best start.

1040
3/E20
23 ROOMS
EXP
APR-OCT
L

✓ **Killeen House Hotel** Aghadoe +353 64 6631711 ·
www.killeenhousehotel.com In this picture-postcard country hotel, just a few miles outside town, Michael and Geraldine Rosney define what an Irish welcome is. The Rosneys live up to their promise, made more than 25 years ago when they opened, that all guests be called by their christian names. The effect is palpable: never mind that this is a 23-room hotel, because for everyone who stays here, Killeen House feels like home. Except that it's the ideal home, with fine cooking, and the best staff who delight in doing everything for you. Killeen House may be classified as a 3-star hotel, but it offers a 5-star welcome.
EAT in Rozzers Restaurant. Guests in nearby hotels come to Rozzers to enjoy dinner, and chef Paul O'Gorman has the experience to produce consistent and interesting cooking.

1041
3/E20
23 ROOMS
EXP

Muckross Park Hotel & Spa Muckross +353 64 6623400 ·
www.muckrosspark.com In just a few years, manager Sean O'Driscoll has taken the potential of the Muckross Park Hotel and made it a top-class destination. Corralling an operation of this size, with its many disparate elements – from spa to weddings to serious dining – into a cohesive entity is no small feat. Underlying all the elements at self-improvement is Mr O'Driscoll's profound culture of hospitality, which means the focus of the MPH is always on the guest's well-being.
EAT Food is a core element of the hotel, thanks to head chef John O'Leary's cooking, which showcases the foods of Kerry and of the Wild Atlantic Way. His sympathy for his ingredients is palpable, and he creates an alluring portfolio of flavours on every plate.

1042
3/E20
131 ROOMS
EXP

Lake Hotel Muckross Rd, Killarney +353 64 6631035 · www.lakehotel.com
Many admirers of the Huggard family's hotel argue that the Lake Hotel enjoys the most enviable location of any Irish hotel. What's certain is that the vistas, across the lakes and mountains, will take your breath away. The team work hard to ensure that it's not just scenery that makes the Lake a special place, and it's one of those hotels that people return to year after year to get a fix. Good cooking – house smoked sea trout; Ballinskelligs chicken with white onions, monkfish tail with monk liver – and excellent service bring it all home.

The Europe Co Kerry Report: 1335/SPAS.
The Brehon Co Kerry Report: 1336/SPAS.

WHERE TO EAT

1043
3/E20
MED.INX
ATMOS

Celtic Whiskey Bar & Larder 93 New St, Killarney +353 64 6635700 · www.celticwhiskeybar.com The fact that they have some 45 permutations of craft gin and tonic drinks alone, and so many varieties of whiskey from all around the world that you can hardly count them, gives some idea of the scope and scale of the stylish Irish Whiskey Bar & Larder. It's the big sister to the excellent Dublin store, and the menu sticks with good punchy savoury cooking. The Whiskey Experience offers beginners and advanced classes in tasting as well as interesting whiskey and food pairings and cocktail making. A really significant destination in Killarney. Daytime till 9.30pm. Bar open till 11.30pm/12.30am.

1044
3/E20
CHP

Petit Delice 41 High St, Killarney +353 64 6626723 · @Petitdelicekerry
Petit Delice, at the far end of High Street as you head westwards, is the best place to get a decent cup of coffee in Killarney that is not poured from a press button coffee machine. They also have great patisserie, including a very fine croque monsieur. Daytime.

1045
3/E21
MAR-NOV
LL

Avoca Moll's Gap +353 64 6634720 · www.avocahandweavers.com
Never mind that every tour bus heading from W Cork to Killarney stops here: Avoca is worth the detour into the car park for good savoury cooking, and the shop is excellent. Daytime 7 days. Cafe closes at 5pm.

1046
3/E20
CHP
LLL

Altitude Cafe Ladies View, Killarney +353 64 6633430 · www.ladiesview.com
The addition of an open air, first-floor dining area has gifted the Ladies View café and shop with the most extraordinary views out across Black Valley and the lakes of Killarney: this is the place, and these are the vistas, that will show you why the early voyagers compared Killarney to Lake Como. Daytime 7 days.

✓✓ **Murphy's Ice Cream** Co Kerry Report: 1481/ICE CREAM.

If you're on The Dingle Peninsula . . .

WHERE TO STAY

1047
3/C19
25 ROOMS
MED.EXP

Dingle Bay Hotel Strand St, Dingle +353 66 9151231 www.dinglebayhotel.com
Right down on the harbour in the magical town of Dingle (Daingean Uí Chúis), this modest hotel with its friendly bar and music sessions is a heart-warming, friendly base, ideal if visiting for any of the town's Festivals.

✓**Castlewood** Co Kerry Report: 1268/COUNTRY HOUSES.

Greenmount Co Kerry Report: 1347/BEST B&B.
Heatons Guesthouse Co Kerry Report: 1272/COUNTRY HOUSES.
Pax House Co Kerry Report: 1332/ESCAPES.
Dingle Skellig Hotel Co Kerry Report: 1289/FAMILY FRIENDLY.
Ashe's Bar Co Kerry Report: 1315/ROADSIDE INNS.

WHERE TO EAT

1048
3/C19
MED.EXP
APR-SEPT
ATMOS

✓**Global Village** Upper Main St, Dingle +353 66 915 2325
www.globalvillage.com That old line from Bob Dylan – 'I was so much older then, I'm younger than that now' – defines Martin Bealin's cooking as he moves into his confident middle age. He used to be quite controlled and conventional as a chef. Now he's as unruly as an adolescent. It's not only brilliant, it's charming, as the chef has discovered a hidden youthfulness. Great atmospheric room is one of the best in town. Dinner 7 days. Closed Tue off season.

1049
3/C19
CHP
ATMOS

✓**The Little Cheese Shop** Grey's Lane, Dingle +353 87 6255788 ·
www.thelittlecheeseshop.net Maya Binder is an artisan cheesemaker who also runs one of the best cheese shops in Ireland, and TLCS is also a destination for cleverly concocted sandwiches, salads and other savoury treats. The queues for her oozing, melted raclette, during the Dingle Food Festival, are the longest in the town, and this is also a place to find local cheeses in mint condition, not least Ms Binder's own lactic creations, which brilliantly feature seaweeds. Daytime Mon-Sat.

1050
3/C19
EXP
MAR-SEPT
LL
ATMOS

✓**Out of the Blue** Waterside, Dingle +353 66 9150811 ·
www.outoftheblue.ie Tim Mason and his team understand how to cook in the moment. OOTB depends on the day's catch and, depending on what is pulled from the waters of the bay, the team then sets into action, steaming crab claws, fashioning their classic chowder, curing salmon, splashing Pastis onto langoustines as they are flipped in a red-hot pan, stirring the polenta to go with char-grilled john dory. It's this sense of urgent improv that makes the seafood cookery in OOTB so special – from sea to boat to kitchen to table in double-quick time. The wines are superb, the staff are chatty and, even with high prices, for very many people OOTB is first call in Dingle (Daingean Uí Chúis). Dinner 7 days & Sun Lunch.

1051
3/B19
ATMOS
LL

✓**Caifé na Caolóige** Louis Mulcahy Pottery, Clogher Strand, Slea Head
+353 66 9156229 · www.louismulcahy.com The light-filled rooms in the shop and the caife offer the gorgeous pottery that has made Louis Mulcahy's work world-famous, so first you admire the plates, cups and vases and amphorae, and then you pick something delicious in the caife and eat and drink using the pottery. But what makes the Caife special is the beauty of every plate that Emer and her team create. This is a don't-miss! destination on Slea Head. All day Mon-Sat. Open all year.

1052 **Chart House** The Mall, Dingle +353 66 915 2255 ·
3/C19 www.thecharthousedingle.com Jim McCarthy's Chart House is pure charm.
MED.INX This is thanks to the wonderful service by the boss and his team, partly to the
ATMOS domestic and unpretentious nature of the room, partly to the fact that the cooking
is graciously modest, whilst being never other than professionally precise. And, the
vegetables they serve are out of this world: you won't taste a better spud in Kerry. Do
make sure to book, however: this is one busy restaurant. Dinner 7 days. Seasonal.

1053 **Goat Street Social** Goat St, Dingle Goat Street is the town's most hipsterish
3/C19 eatery, with playful blue decor and a light-hearted ambience. Nice fun cooking – tuna
MED.INX burger with black olive chutney; salt 'n' chilli squid – and big generous portions hit
ATMOS the target. Goat Street will put a smile on your face. Daytime till 8pm Tue-Sun.

1054 **Grey's Lane Bistro** Grey's Lane, Dingle +353 66 915 2770
3/C19 www.greyslanebistro.com Ed and Laurence have moved downtown to a bigger
MED.INX room, having outgrown their original Main St premises after more than a decade
ATMOS of success. The new space means they are open from breakfast through to dinner,
but Ed's sure-fire, international style of cooking is in top gear, from the signature
chowder to the excellent duck confit. Daytime 7 days, dinner till 9pm, Fri-Sun.
Limited hours off season.

1055 **Bean in Dingle** Green St, Dingle +353 87 299 2831 www.beanindingle.com
3/C19 Justin Burgess began with an idea for a coffee cart, but that quickly turned into
ATMOS Bean, a bricks-and-mortar setting on Green St where Justin and the team – brother
Luke and sister Georgia – serve a Badger & Dodo blend made just for them. They
caught the zeitgeist right from the off, and have been jammers ever since they got
the doors open. They source breads and pastries from two local bakeries, Bácús
and Blúiríní Blasta, and you can also enjoy Dingle sushi. Daytime.

1056 **My Boy Blue** Holyground, Dingle · @myboybluedingle Stephen Brennan's
3/C19 dramatically minimalist café is top notch. The coffee is superlative – 3fe Momentum
blend – and the breakfast offer is genuinely creative. These guys can make a fish taco
that is worth the trip to Holyground all on its own. Daytime 7 days.

1057 **The Boatyard** Strand St, Dingle +353 66 9150920
3/C19 www.theboatyardrestaurant.ie Charming seafood cookery in the bright, glass-
MED.INX-EXP fronted room of The Boatyard, so head straight across from the marina to enjoy a
MAR-NOV wild Atlantic seafood platter. The crew cap it all with no nonsense service, which
L won praise from *The New York Times*, no less. Lunch & dinner 7 days.

1058 **Gregory's Garden** Main St, Castlegregory +353 86 3621984 ·
3/D19 www.gregorysgarden.ie Greg O'Mahoney has made quite a splash opening Ember
MED.EXP Restaurant, in Milltown in Dublin 6, but it was in Gregory's Garden in little Castlegregory
TERRACE on the northside of the peninsula that he made his name for imaginative cooking,
MAY-SEPT DF inspired by the produce he grows in the raised beds in his garden. All day & dinner 7 days.

1059 **Spillane's Bar & Restaurant** Fahamore, Castlegregory +353 66 7139125
3/D19 www.spillanesbar.com Michael Spillane's bar is a landmark in the Maharees
MED.INX area, home to spontaneous and organised music sessions and some good bar
L food. Lunch & dinner 7 days during the season. Booking advisable if you are going
to travel. Two self-catering rental apartments are available next door, and Michael
knows all about this region.

✓✓ **Reel Dingle Fish Co** Co Kerry Report: 1446/FISH & CHIPS.

WHERE TO STAY

1060
3/E18
42 ROOMS
MED.EXP

Listowel Arms Hotel The Square, Listowel +353 68 21500 ·
www.listowelarms.com This pretty, ivy-clad family hotel on the square in Listowel does a rather nice job, and has been doing so since about 1801. Patrice O'Callaghan and her team run a real community hotel, a place for christening parties and weddings, and for the punters to stay during the Listowel races. Rather lovely.

1061
3/E19
28 ROOMS
EXP

Ballyseede Castle Ballyseede, Tralee +353 66 7125799 ·
www.ballyseedecastle.com In a forested area just outside the town, Ballyseede is a modest castle, and it's home to smashing, friendly staff who bring it to life, not to mention the owner's four dogs, who like to come looking for some love from the guests. Four poster beds, red and burgundy colour schemes and ornate wallpapers give an age-old feel to the experience. A little more focus on the food would elevate eating to the high standard of the hospitality.

McMunn's Co Kerry Report: 1 309/ROADSIDE INNS.

WHERE TO EAT

1062
3/E17
MED.INX

✓**Daroka** Cliff Rd, Ballybunion + 353 68 27911 www.daroka.ie
Dan and Emily O'Brien don't have the greatest room to work with in Daroka, their little two-storey space facing the sea, but no one cares, because in Daroka they have some of the best food you can eat in Kerry. Lots of the ingredients are straight from their own vegetable patch, so the flavours are pristine, and they serve a salad of heritage tomatoes that would lure you to Ballybunion. Mr O'Brien wrings unctuous richness out of ingredients such as pork cheeks, or rib-eye with foie gras jus, but he is just as assured with delicacies such as cured salmon with samphire, or Dover sole with beetroot. Daroka is a quiet gem. Lunch & dinner Wed-Sun. Reduced opening hours Oct-Mar.

1063
3/D19
MED.INX

Spa Seafoods The Spa, Tralee +353 66 7136901· www.spaseafoods.com
Worth the short detour out of Tralee and down the road towards Fenit to eat the best seafood cookery in this part of north Kerry. Actually, Spa Seafoods is worth two detours. One will bring you to a fish shop and delicatessen with gleaming wet fish and shellfish and prepared fish dishes. The second detour will take you upstairs, to a handsome room with some of the best views out over the Dingle peninsula, and delicious seafood cookery: don't miss the oysters with trout caviar. Dinner Tue-Sun, Lunch Fri-Sun.

1064
3/E19
CHP

The Roast House 3 Denny St, Tralee + 353 66 7181011·
www.theroasthouse.ie They have their own on-site coffee roastery in the Roast House, set in the lovely terrace of Denny St in the centre of town, so it's the place for that good cup of Java. But whilst the coffee may bring you in, the cooking will make you linger. Daytime 7 days, till 2pm Sun.

1065   **Roundy's Bar**   5 Brogue Makers Ln, Tralee · @roundysbar   Nothing quite like
3/E19   enjoying a fine carne asada taco, or a grilled cheese, cooked by Nils Kemper in his
rainbow-coloured horse box, and having a good cocktail from the bar in Roundy's
while you are at it. Add in some good tunes, and it's all sorted.

1066   **Lizzy's Little Kitchen**   Main St, Ballybunion +353 87 1497220
3/E17   @lizzyslittlekitchen   Lizzy Lyon's has opened a second little kitchen in Listowel,
CHP   proof that the good people of Kerry can't get enough of the cooking of this fine
MAR-SEP   chef. So join the queue for Rigney's farm pork sausage roll; lentil and bean chilli;
lamb, feta and lemon meatballs with homemade harissa; chocolate buttermilk
cake. Daytime Tue-Sat. Also open all year in the square in Listowel.

Co Limerick
If you're in Limerick City . . .

WHERE TO STAY

1067
3/H17
184 ROOMS
EXP
L

Limerick Strand Hotel Ennis Rd, Limerick + 353 61 421800
www.strandhotellimerick.ie That honeycomb of local artisan honey, sitting proudly on the breakfast counter, tells you all that you need to know about the ambition of chef Tom Flavin at Limerick's Strand Hotel. Mr Flavin goes the extra mile to deliver for his guests the pure flavours of the Wild Atlantic Way, and he works super hard to get there, whether he is cooking breakfast, lunch or dinner. Aside from the finesse of the food, the hotel runs like clockwork. The views across the city, from the upper floor rooms, are spellbinding, and The Strand has the heartbeat of the city.

1068
3/H17
20 ROOMS
MED.INX

No. 1 Pery Square Georgian Quarter, Limerick +353 61 402302 ·
www.oneperysquare.com This stylish Georgian boutique hotel is someplace where – if you are sampling your way through their extensive gin menu – you can order a Traditional Tayto Crisp Sandwich: house bread; Kerrygold butter; Tayto potato crisps. It's this sort of impish humour that sets Patricia Robert's small hotel apart from the crowd. Yes, they have a spa, they have lovely cooking in the Sash restaurant, they have a mighty wine shop, and there is cool luxury everywhere you look. Thankfully, they also have a mighty sense of humour.
EAT You've got to warm to a dinner menu at Sash, in a town with a pork-related history like Limerick's, that offers 'No.1 Pigtown Choucroute'. But No.1 Pigtown is exactly what you will get in Sash, the first-floor restaurant of 1 Pery Square. The choucroute is typical of the unstuffy, funky spirit of the hotel.

The Mustard Seed Co Limerick Report: 1275/COUNTRY HOUSES.

WHERE TO EAT

1069
3/H17
CHP

✓**Canteen** 26 Catherine St, Limerick +353 85 2153212 ·
www.wearecanteen.com It was always apparent that Paul Williams is a singular talent, not just an excellent cook who worked alongside Heston Blumenthal, but a guy who is also a vivid thinker on the subject of food. The Canteen grub defines smart-casual eating, for every time of day. Great coffee. Daytime Mon-Sat.

1070
3/H17
MED.INX

✓**La Cucina Centro** Henry St, Limerick +353 61 517405 · www.lacucina.ie
La Cucina Centro, the city centre restaurant from experienced restaurateurs Bruno and Lorraine Coppola, is the most significant restaurant to open in the city's culinary history. The room is glam-as-all-get-out, a collaboration by designer Tullio Orlandi and sign writer Tom Collins. The staff epitomise the sharp service the Coppolas have always created, and the cooking, from Bruno Coppola and head chef Diarmuid O'Callaghan, drives the feel-good factor down deep into your boots. Just one problem: getting a weekend table is the biggest ask in the city. All day & dinner 7 days. The original La Cucina is in Castletroy.

1071
3/H17
CHP
ATMOS

✓**The Limerick Milk Market** Mungret St, Limerick +353 61 214782 ·
www.milkmarketlimerick.ie The Milk Market is where you head to for some of the best eating and shopping in Limerick. The Market got itself a serious makeover a few years back, and in the process a great space for foods and crafts and culture was created. Whether you fancy sushi or some wet fish, a flat white or a bacon sandwich, a slice of lemon meringue pie or a glass of apple juice, it's all here. Whilst some shopkeepers trade all week, the best days for the Market are Sat

and Sun, when everything is at full tilt, and the space becomes a jamboree of colour and choice. Just make sure you have plenty of time to see everything, including the many stalls that sell arts and crafts and clothes, in addition to all the lovely artisan foods. Daytime Fri-Sun until 3pm.

1072 **Mortell's** 49 Roches St, Limerick +353 61 415457 · www.mortellcatering.com
3/H17   Just down from the Georgian Quarter, off St Patrick St, the modest space that is Mortell's
CHP   is the place to go if you want a genuine Limerick experience. Brian Mortell inherited the
ATMOS   shop from his parents, who sold fish and game here. Everything, absolutely everything, from the puff pastry to the white bread to the fine Limerick ham, is cooked from scratch. This is some of the best fish cooking in the W. Daytime Mon-Sat.

1073 **Freddy's Bistro** Theatre Ln, Lwr Glentworth St, Limerick +353 61 418749
3/H17   · www.freddysbistro.com Liz Phelan and Caroline Kerley run a great show in
MED.INX   Freddy's. Like the best sister 'n' sister teams, they are effortlessly professional. They source and cook lovely food, and don't mess about with it, so flavours are true and the dishes are classics. Dinner Tue-Sat.

1074 **The Grove Veggie Kitchen** 11 Cecil St, Limerick +353 61 410084 ·
3/H17   @TheGroveVeggieCafe The Grove has been looking after Limerick's vegetarian
CHP   foodies since 1981, offering chickpea and hazelnut casserole; baked falafel and radish salad; beetroot and feta tart; buckwheat and raw cacao cake. Lunch Mon-Sat

1075 **Café Noir** Park Point, Dublin Rd, Limerick +353 61 423901 · www.cafenoir.ie
3/J17   Pat O'Sullivan runs one of the best food operations in Limerick, and the Café Noirs
CHP   in Raheen, U.L. and Castletroy are distinguished by a level of consistency and excellence most other places never even get close to achieving. These guys are professionals, so Café Noir is a sure bet for delicious food, and staff who are on top of their game. Raheen; Castletroy; University of Limerick. Daytime Mon-Sat.

1076 **Cornstore Restaurant** Thomas St, Limerick +353 61 609000 ·
3/H17   www.cornstore.ie Cornstore is a rock-steady professional operation, and this
MED.EXP   Limerick champion simply goes from strength to strength, with a great team who relish their work. Look out especially for their unusual cuts of beef – onglet; drunken rump; mighty tomahawk – which are hard to find in other restaurants, and which are worthy of splashing out to enjoy with a special bottle of wine to make for a big night out. Lunch & dinner 7 days.

1077 **House** Howley's Qy, Limerick +353 61 513282 · www.houselimerick.ie
3/H17   Deirdre Daly, who made her reputation cooking at Lir Restaurant, up in Kilkee,
MED.INX   oversees the food in the glamorous House, on Howley's Qy down by the river. Ms
TERRACE   Daly is a marvellous, individualistic cook, and the food here is very moreish. Good spot for breakfast, and there is a delightful terrace. Daytime & dinner 7 days. There is a second branch of House in Dublin.

The Hunt Cafe Co Limerick Report: 1540/HISTORY.

1078 **Copper and Spice** Above Mill Bar, Annacotty Village +353 61 338791 ·
3/J17   www.copperandspice.com Upstairs over the Mill Bar in the village, overlooking
MED.INX   the salmon weir, Brian and Seema Conroy offer authentic and well-delivered Thai and Indian dishes – prawns in tamarind; chicken dopiaza; aloo gosht. The Conroys

have maintained enviably high standards for many years, as well as offering excellent value. Dinner 7 days, Lunch Sun. Takeaway menu available.

THE BEST PUB IN LIMERICK CITY

1079 **Curragower Pub** Clancy's Strand, Limerick +353 61 321788 ·
3/H17 www.curragower.com The cooking in the Curragower, one of Limerick's most
MED.INX famous pubs, is a treat: unfussy, hearty, homely and delicious. It's affordable and
ATMOS satisfying, and a textbook example of a menu that only does a few things, and does them well: scampi and chips; fish chowder; apple and toffee crumble. Cian Bourke and his team do a good job.

▰▰▰ If you're in Adare . . .

WHERE TO STAY

Adare Manor Co Limerick Report: 1847/GOLF.

WHERE TO EAT

1080 √ **1826 Adare** Main St, Adare +353 61 396004 · www.1826adare.ie 1826 is
3/H17 the Wade and Elaine show: he cooks, she serves, and Mr & Mrs Murphy are
EXP as good a double act as you will find in modern Irish food. They have a darling
L room in one of Adare's prettiest thatched cottages, and this understated style serves to amplify the rich goodness of Wade Murphy's cooking. The food has real impact because he always makes apposite pairing. 1826 is a real player. Dinner Wed-Sun.

1081 √ **The Wild Geese** The Rose Cottage, Adare +353 61 396451 ·
3/H17 www.thewild-geese.com If Adare is the prettiest village, then The Wild
MED.EXP Geese is surely the prettiest restaurant in the prettiest village. David Foley's
L cooking is intricate, detailed and beautifully realised, and he's a chef who really cooks from the heart. What ensures that you always have a special night in this special place is the service from Julie Randles, which is as good as service gets. Daytime & dinner Tue-Sat, Sun lunch.

The Best Places to Eat & Stay in the West of Ireland and the Wild Atlantic Way

Co Clare

WHERE TO STAY

1082
4/G16
105 ROOMS
MED.EXP

The Old Ground O'Connell St, Ennis +353 65 6828127 · www.flynnhotels.com
Charming staff who look after all their customers with patience and charm is the defining characteristic of the Flynn family's venerable hotel. A truly lovely country town hotel.
EAT The hotel also owns the Town Hall Bistro in the centre of town. Polished. Popular modern food, and excellent atmosphere.

Morrissey's Bar & Restaurant Co Clare Report: 1311/ROADSIDE INNS.

WHERE TO EAT

1083
4/F15
CHP
MAY-NOV

Copper Pot Artisan Bakery Holland Place, Liscannor +353 85 7743137 ·
@copperpotbakery Iconic local artisans Fabiola and Adam offer the most droolsome selection of sweet and savoury baking, along with the superb local Anam coffee, at their delectable shop and bakery. Grab a stool or a bench and get stuck into those croissants for breakfast, and chances are you will be back for quiche or pizza or that amazing spelt bread made with kombucha starter at lunchtime. Not to be missed. Daytime.

1084
4/F17
CHP

The Potter's Hand 3 Vandeleur St, Kilrush +353 65 9052968 ·
@thepottershandcafe Aisling Hamilton's book-festooned café is the first choice in town for some good baking and proper coffee. The room has a lovely vibe, with lots of gigs, wine tastings and community events. Nice courtyard for when the sun shines. All Day Mon-Sat.

If you're in Loop Head . . .

WHERE TO STAY

1085
2/J16
19 ROOMS
AYR MED.EXP
TERRACE
ATMOS

✓**Stella Maris** O'Connell St, Kilkee +353 65 9056455 ·
www.stellamarishotel.com Stella Maris is a treasurable old resort hotel, and Ann Haugh and her family do a brilliant job of looking after guests. The rooms are cosy, the cooking is very, very good, and the sense that this is an hotel for the community is precious. We once stayed here for several days in January and, even in the depths of winter, we had a terrific time.

1086
4/E16
6 ROOMS
MED.INX
LL

The Strand Bistro & Guesthouse Kilkee +353 65 9056177 ·
www.thestrandkilkee.com The dining room here looks out on the bay – for us it's San Sebastian in microcosm – whilst the views from the bedrooms upstairs are amazing. Che Guevara stayed here back in 1961, and he signed himself 'Rafael Trujillo' in the visitor's book. Johnny and Caroline Redmond's cooking and hospitality in The Strand is true, spirited, and blessed with that lovely Clare generosity.
EAT In The Strand Bistro, Johnny's cooking is popular and big on flavour, and the coffee bar is a great addition, whether you seek an Americano or a craft beer.

1087 **Thalassotherapy Centre Guest House** Grattan St, Kilkee +353 65 9056742 ·
4/E16 www.kilkeethalasso.com Eileen Mulcahy harvests the serrated wrack seaweeds
5 ROOMS she uses for her seaweed baths with her own hands, and then uses them to brew
CHP up the most sublime bath you have ever had. Book one of the five comfortable
rooms upstairs, enjoy a delicious breakfast in the dining room, then plunge into
that old porcelain bathtub for an hour, and you never felt so good in all your life.

Glencarrig B&B Co Clare Report: 1357/BEST B&B.

WHERE TO EAT

1088 ✓**Murphy Blacks** The Square, Kilkee +353 65 9056854 ·
4/E16 www.murphyblacks.ie The crab cakes are so good we would walk a country
MED.INX mile for them. Sweet, yielding, slightly spicy, bound with bechamel, they are one of
ATMOS the culinary stars of Loop Head, the area where Mary Black and Cillian Murphy run
one of the cutest restaurants on the W coast. Murphy Black's is a simple, single
room, comfortable and cosy, with the day's specials chalked on the board. Good
wines and craft beers. Dinner Mon-Sun in high season. Closed Sun & Mon mid
season. Weekends only Oct-Mar.

1089 **Diamond Rocks** West End, Kilkee +353 86 3721063 ·
4/E16 www.diamondrockscafe.com The views from the Diamond Rocks Café out over
CHP Kilkee Bay are simply stunning. Whilst it's a lovely stop-off as you walk the coastal
LL path, it's also a fine destination in its own right. And do check out that groovy
Richard Harris statue! All day Mon-Sun. Reduced hours off season.

1090 **Lir at Kilkee Golf Club** Kilkee +353 65 9056048 · @liratkilkeegolfclub
4/E16 Deirdre Daly is one of the best cooks working on the Wild Atlantic Way. Ms Daly
CHP could serve her food from a Nissen hut in an industrial estate, and we would flock
LL to eat it. Fortunately, at her base in Kilkee, she gives us sublime food, along with
some of the finest sea views on the WAW. It's no surprise that Ms Daly's reputation
has led her to extend her reach to Limerick city, where she oversees food in the
House bar, Howley's Quay. All Day Mon-Sat (closed Wed).

1091 **Naughton's Bar & Restaurant** 45 O'Curry St, Kilkee +353 65 9056597 ·
4/E17 www.naughtonsbar.com There is some fine cooking in the interweaving series
MED.INX of rooms that is Naughton's, with a leaning towards fish and shellfish, and a
FEB-NOV selection of Irish meat dishes. Elaine and Robert carefully source ingredients and
show them proper respect. The result is so successful that it's often impossible to
get a table, either in the bars downstairs or in the beautiful rooms upstairs. Dinner
Mon-Sun. Weekends only Sept & Oct.

1092 **The Pantry Shop & Bakery** O'Curry St, Kilkee +353 65 9056576 ·
4/E17 www.thepantrykilkee.com The Pantry can seem to be the very epicentre
CHP of Kilkee on a busy summer day, with everyone calling in to eat breakfast, buy
EASTER-SEPT Imelda's breads and cakes, sit around over a lazy lunch or read the paper over a
cup of coffee. We suspect many Kilkee holidaymakers are in and out of The Pantry
several times a day. Essential. All day Mon-Sun.

1093 **The Long Dock** Carrigaholt +353 65 9058106 · www.thelongdock.com
4/E17 Start with the pitch-perfect brown bread and seafood chowder, and the seafood pie
MED.INX topped with mashed potato, and you know straight away that you are in the
ATMOS W coast pub of your dreams, except that the cooking is way better: you can even
get takeaway from their Courtyard Kitchen. Lunch & Dinner Mon-Sun. Reduced
hours off season.

WHERE TO STAY

1094
4/F15
9 ROOMS
EXP
LLL

Moy House Lahinch +353 65 708 2800 · www.moyhouse.com Moy is a beautiful house, baronial, welcoming, and blessed with the most amazing sea views. But once chef Matt Strefford's food begins to arrive on the table, then the outside world stops, for the power of this cooking is total.

EAT Mr Strefford has taken to rearing his own livestock for the kitchen, so this is peerless farm-to-fork and top-to-tail cooking and eating. Garden produce completes the picture of a cook with total knowledge and control of every part of the food chain.

1095
4/F15
17 ROOMS
EXP
ATMOS

Hotel Doolin Ballyvoe, Doolin +353 65 7074111 · www.hoteldoolin.ie
Hotel Doolin is distinct, dynamic and different. There is a true sense of creativity about how the team here carry out their work, and it means that they avoid the clichés that make so many hotels humdrum. All the while they are hosting craft beer festivals, writing festivals, music festivals, so stay here and catch that energy. The cooking uses many elements from their garden, and is very fine.
EAT in the Chervil Restaurant, the Stone Wall Cafe & Pizzeria and drink in Fitz's Pub where there is live traditional music.

1096
4/F16
6 ROOMS
MED.EXP
TERRACE
LL

Red Cliff Lodge Spanish Point +353 65 7085756 · www.redclifflodge.ie
John and Brid O'Meara have created a series of six comfortable, one-bedroom Seaview suites for rental, built around the courtyard that houses their pretty Red Cliff Lodge restaurant, where you will find seriously enjoyable cooking: house-smoked salmon with brown bread crumb; Liscannor Bay crab meat with cucumber gel; tomato, lentil and chickpea casserole with gnocchi; espresso creme brulée. The O'Mearas are an impressive and hospitable couple, and they are key players in the wonderful Spanish Point.

1097
4/F16
86 ROOMS
MED.EXP
LL

Armada Hotel Spanish Point +353 65 905 6576 · www.armadahotel.com
The Burke family's Armada Hotel has long been known as a banqueting and wedding destination, but there is much more to this fine hotel than simply catering for big groups. Sea views from the rooms are entrancing and this is one of the best Wild Atlantic Way destinations.
EAT Chef Peter Jackson is one of the county's most talented cooks, and Mr Jackson is fortunate to not only have a troupe of local suppliers, he also has the produce of their own Armada Farm. Johnny Burke's bar, meantime, is special, and not to be missed.

1098
4/F15
20 ROOMS
EXP
APR-NOV
ATMOS

Vaughan Lodge Ennistymon Rd, Lahinch +353 65 7081111 ·
www.vaughanlodge.ie Just up the road from the golf links, Michael Vaughan's smart, modern hotel is the ideal stage for the boss to show how he is one of the great Irish hoteliers. Unpretentious, hospitable, and one of the best in the W.
EAT The VL Restaurant has always produced exceptional cooking. The room itself is informal, but the cooking is creative and striving: halibut with squid ink purée; foie gras and honeycomb. Good value, good wines.

Cullinan's Restaurant & Guesthouse Co Clare Report: 1325/RESTAURANTS WITH ROOMS.
Spanish Point House Co Clare Report: 1359/BEST B&B.
Vaughan's Anchor Inn Co Clare Report: 1310ROADSIDE INNS.
Roadford House Co Clare Report: 1321/RESTAURANTS WITH ROOMS.

WHERE TO EAT

1099 **Stonecutters Kitchen** Doolin +353 65 7075962 ·
4/F15   www.stonecutterskitchen.com Up on the hill above Doolin village,
CHP   Stonecutters excels in offering dishes that are familiar, but which they serve with
EASTER-OCT   their own twist. Simple things like fishcakes, lentil burgers, and fish and chips, are
L   beautifully delivered, and owners Karen and Myles anchor the cooking with careful
ATMOS   sourcing. Great staff, and very, very busy. Daytime 7 days, till 7pm/8pm/9pm
during summer. Hours vary off season.

1100 **Vasco** Coast Rd, Fanore +353 65 7076020 www.vasco.ie. Ross and Karen have
4/F14   done a lot of travelling in their time, and they bring all those influences, memories
MED.INX   and dishes back home. If you seek saganaki – fried cheese, from Greece – or Burren
OCT-FEB   goat meat, or you want to play it straight with some bay prawns with lemon and
TERRACE   garlic mayo, it's all here. The room is colourful and simple, filled with sea light.
LL   Daytime Tue-Sun, open till 7.30 pm Fri-Sun.

1101 **Randaddy's** The Prom, Lahinch +353 65 708 2740 · www.randaddys.ie
4/F15   A big room that is part of the big Beach Front in Lahinch is home to Randy Lewis'
MED.INX   eclectic and well-handled cookery. If you have been out on the waves, Mr Lewis has
L   some punchy, creative cooking that will put the fire back into your battered body.
ATMOS   All day until 7pm Mon-Wed, 8pm Thur & Sun, 9pm Fri & Sat.

1102 **Pot Duggan's** New Rd, Ennistymon +353 65 7071480 ·
4/F15   www.potduggans.com At one time, Ennistymon had a pub for every week of the
MED.INX   year: 52 in total. There are fewer now, and this venture from the Dublin Bodytonic
L   pub team is a great newcomer. They've taken it back to the old days, so step in
ATMOS   the door and it's 1953, apart from the food and drinks, which are hip as all get out.
From noon 7 days.

If you're in The Burren . . .

WHERE TO STAY

1103
4/F15
11 ROOMS
MED.EXP
EASTER-OCT

Sheedy's Hotel Lisdoonvarna +353 65 7074026 · www.sheedys.com The Sheedy family's hotel is a modest delight, a place where everything is made from scratch, and where the hospitality matches the excellence of the cooking. When you stay here you understand what a true 'family-run' hotel is. One of the great Co Clare destinations.

1104
4/G14
32 ROOMS
MED.EXP

Hylands Burren Hotel Main St, Ballyvaughan +353 65 7077037 · www.hylandsburrenhotel.com The Quinn family run both this traditional hotel and bar and their L'Arco restaurant, just down the street. The bar in the hotel has always been famous as a cosy spot to eat and enjoy great music sessions. Open all year.

✓✓✓**Gregans Castle Hotel** Co Clare Report: 1265/COUNTRY HOUSES.

✓✓**Wild Honey Inn** Co Clare Report: 1307/ROADSIDE INNS.

Fergus View Co Clare Report: 1358/BEST B&B.
Ballinsheen House & Gardens Co Clare Report: 1356/BEST B&B.

WHERE TO EAT

1105
4/F15
MED.INX
ATMOS

✓**The Roadside Tavern** Kincora Rd, Lisdoonvarna +353 65 7074432 · www.burrensmokehouse.ie Peter and Birgitta Curtin's traditional pub is a landmark in the county, and it's been made even better with the addition of their own craft beers, and with some genuinely impressive cooking from the kitchen. Chefs Kieran and Viv fire out some very tasty food – don't miss the chowder and the lamb stew. The Curtin family also run the Storehouse – great pizzas – and the Burren Smokehouse, just up the road, which is a don't-miss shop. Great music sessions. Lunch & dinner Mon-Sun.

1106
4/G14
MED.INX
L

✓**Granny's Coffee House** Oughtmara, Belharbour +353 87 9903000 · www.hazelmountainchocolates.com Kasha and John Connolly have created one of the hottest destinations in the Burren, a mile or so up the hill from Belharbour. It's a coffee house, a bean-to-bar chocolate factory and a series of smart tasting rooms, in an idyllic location. Top class. All day Tue-Sun. Lunch served noon-3pm. Booking recommended.

1107
4/G14
CHP

Aillwee Cave Tea Room Ballyvaughan +353 65 707 7036 · www.aillweecave.ie Everything about Aillwee Cave is superbly managed. The design, the structure of the tours, the charm of the staff, the food in the café, the hawk walk and birds of prey area and, of course, their rather special shop. You shop here for their own Burren Gold cheese, but over the years their range has increased exponentially, so there's lots of good things. All day Mon-Sun.

1108
4/G14
MED.INX

An Fear Gorta Pier Rd, Ballyvaughan +353 65 7077023 · www.tearoomsballyvaughan.com Jane O'Donoghue's lovely tea rooms and garden are a Ballyvaughan classic, and have been since opening in 1981. Aside from the famous table, which is always laden with cakes and desserts, there are many savoury choices, and proper sandwiches. A good hike along the coast road followed by afternoon tea is bliss. Day time Mon-Sun. Closed Tue & Wed and limited hours off season.

1109 · **Burren Fine Food & Wine** Corkscrew Hill Rd, Ballyvaughan +353 65 7077046 ·
4/G14 · www.burrenwine.ie Don't miss Cathleen's roadside operation as you climb or
MED.INX · descend the twisty Corkscrew Hill. Not only is the cooking really fine, but service
MAY-SEPT · is gracious and sincere. So, a pizza for you, some lemon drizzle cake for me and
are we happy? More than. Lunch Mon-Sun. BFF&W also have a cycling offer
(1859/CYCLING).

1110 · **Kilshanny House** Kilshanny +353 65 7071660 · www.kilshannyhouse.ie
4/F15 · Kilshanny House may be the most meticulous bar in the country, and everything
ATMOS · gleams so brightly you almost have to wear sunglasses inside. Aidan and Mary
make sure the cooking matches the housekeeping, making for an idyllic stop on
the main road. Bar food 7 days during the summer.

1111 · **The Sanctuary Cafe** Cloonasee, Kinvara, Co Galway +353 91 637444 ·
4/G14 · www.bns.ie The Burren Nature Sanctuary is a great place to explore the many
CHP · natural facets of the Burren – it's a great spot to bring kids – but there is also some
nice cooking in the café, with ingredients coming from their polytunnel: Buddha
bowl; veggie burger; pizza for the youngsters. All day Mon-Sun.

✓**Burren Perfumery Tea Rooms** Co Clare Report: 1954/CONSUMING PASSIONS

Co Galway

1112 · **Gallery Cafe** The Square, Gort +353 91 630630 · www.thegallerycafegort.com
4/H14 · Sarah Harty's Gallery Café on the square is the place to be in Gort, a pair of stylish
CHP · rooms and some interesting cooking. Ms Harty is a painter by training, so the café
ATMOS · is always flower-bedecked and welcoming, with lots of exhibitions and music gigs
at the weekends. All day till 7/9/10pm Wed-Sun.

1113 · **Raftery's Bar** Craughwell +353 91 846708 · www.rafterysbar.ie The pristine
4/H13 · country pub, with a great welcome, good drinks, and delicious food: that's what
MED.INX · you will find in Rachel Raftery's bar, in the centre of Craughwell. The bar has been
in the hands of the Raftery family for four generations, and it's a place where
everything gleams. But what shines brightest is the cooking. Lovely. All day &
dinner Mon-Sun.

1114 · **White Gables** Moycullen Village +353 91 555744 · www.whitegables.com
4/G13 · Kevin and Anne Dunne straddle the decades in White Gables and its sister
MED.EXP · café, Enjoy. In WG, both Mr Dunne's cooking and the style is classical – lobster
thermidor, for heaven's sake – whilst in Enjoy the cooking and the style is casual,
smart and modern. Both are good, both are key destinations on the main street of
the village. Dinner Wed-Sun & Sun lunch.

1115 · **The Old Barracks** Cross St, Athenry +353 91 877406 · www.oldbarracks.ie
4/H13 · Housed in a handsome, window-shuttered townhouse, Fiona and Cathal and the
MED.INX · team take things from scratch in the Barracks, right down to sourcing foods from
their own W coast farms. The bakery and the bistro operate in tandem during the
day, with a good breakfast selection followed from noon by the main dishes of the
day. All day Mon-Sun. Open till 9pm Fri & Sat.

Glenlo Abbey Co Galway Report: 1288/FAMILY FRIENDLY.

Connemara
If you're in Roundstone . . .

WHERE TO STAY

1116
4/D12
5 ROOMS
CHP
L

Bogbean Roundstone +353 95 31006 www.bogbeanconnemara.com
A lively café and a series of five B&B rooms upstairs, in the centre of Roundstone, run by Orla Conneely and Shane McElligott. Orla and Shane are uber-serious sailors and kayak instructors, and can show you how to paddle and stand up on a SUP, courtesy of their company, Roundstone Outdoors. Upstairs, the rooms are comfy and just right, with lovely, locally-made hardwood furniture.
EAT in the Bog Bean Cafe. This where you get the best coffee, fine breakfasts and lunches. Open all day.

1117
4/D12
11 ROOMS
MED.EXP
L

Roundstone House Hotel Roundstone +353 95 35944 ·
www.roundstonehousehotel.com A folky, family-owned and run hotel, and we like its modesty and lack of pretension, and the welcoming hospitality of the Vaughan family. The cooking in Vaughan's bar, and in their restaurant is a favourite with locals, who come here for fresh seafood: hake with a cider sauce; monkfish with bacon and mushrooms; cod with a smoked mussel sauce.

WHERE TO EAT

1118
4/D12
MED.INX
L
ATMOS

O'Dowd's Seafood Bar & Restaurant Roundstone +353 95 35923 ·
www.odowdsbar.com Four generations of the O'Dowd family have run this Connemara institution in statuesque Roundstone, acquiring an international audience along the way. They won their status by cooking good, tasty food – seafood gratin; poached salmon; beef and Guinness stew – both in the classic bar and in the restaurant. They stay open all year, so even when the winter is in full flight, getting a seat by the fire is just the thing. Bar and restaurant serving food from noon-9pm Mon-Sun. Booking advised.

1119
4/E13
L

Coynes Bar & Bistro Kilkerrin, Connemara +353 95 33409 Michael Coyne's family pub and bistro does the simple things well: classic chowder with perfect, sweet brown bread; mussels in white wine sauce; pan-fried sea trout. There are music sessions at the weekends, along with dancing, which is what you will feel like doing after a few glasses of the fine Independent Brewery craft beers, from nearby Carraroe.

If you're in Clifden . . .

WHERE TO STAY

1120
4/D12
14 ROOMS
MEX.EXP
MAR-NOV
LL

✓ Quay House Beach Rd, Clifden +353 95 21369 · www.thequayhouse.com
Paddy Foyle is probably the greatest interior designer in Ireland, and staying in the unique Quay House, down at the water's edge in Clifden, brings you up close to the work of a guy who sees design in a different way from everyone else. 'I remain in awe of the sheer exuberance and lightheartedness of these extraordinary interiors', the blogger Pamela Peterson wrote. What will also leave you in awe is the hospitality, the welcome and the cooking from Julia, Paddy and the family. One of the best W coast houses.

1121
4/D12
20 ROOMS
MAR-NOV
DF
LLL

Rosleague Manor Letterfrack +353 95 41101 · www.rosleague.com
Mark Foyle's house is one of the stateliest of all the Irish country houses. Pretty in pink, with the most to-die-for location and setting overlooking Ballinakill Harbour and hard by the winding N59, it is a quintessential part of Connemara, both elegant and elemental. The Foyle family are legendary hoteliers in this region, and Mr Foyle shares the family's calm professionalism. He's also taken to rearing his own pigs, so look out for interesting porky bits on the menu. Pristine comfort, good cooking – scallop carpaccio; Connemara lamb; turbot with beurre blanc.

1122
4/D12
6 ROOMS
CHP
EASTER-OCT
CASH ONLY
LL

Mallmore Country House Ardbear, Clifden +353 95 21460 · www.mallmore.com
The Hardmore family's house, overlooking the harbour and just off the R341 is one of those perfectly proportioned Georgian houses that seduces the eye from the first glimpse of its finesse. The front door is offset by eight Corinthian columns and, like the best Georgian design, Mallmore impresses because of its restraint. The contrast between the wildness and the charm and fire-lit comfort of the house makes it seem even more welcoming, and the family's hospitality – and the excellent breakfasts – copper-fasten the feeling of having found a Connemara gem.

Clifden Station House Hotel Co Galway Report: 1290/FAMILY FRIENDLY.
Hillside Lodge Co Galway Report: 1360/BEST B&B.
Sea Mist House Co Galway Report: 1361/BEST B&B.

WHERE TO EAT

1123
4/D12
MED.INX

Guy's Bar & Snug Main St, Clifden +353 95 21130 · www.guysbarclifden.com
This is a popular pub, and a good spot to grab a tasty bite of seafood. Make sure to enjoy a pint of the excellent local Bridewell Brewery. Lunch & dinner Mon-Sun.

1124
4/D12
MEX.EXP

Mitchell's Restaurant Market St, Clifden +353 95 21867
www.mitchellsrestaurantclifden.com The service and the food in JJ Mitchell's restaurant enjoy a consistency you don't expect in a tourist town like Clifden. A friend once described Mitchell's as 'the most consistent restaurant I know from visits over the last five years'. That is some accolade, but the team here earn it. Their people-pleasing dishes – fish and chips, a good chowder, crab with brown bread, fish cakes, good lunchtime sandwiches – bring people back time and again at lunchtime and, whilst the evening menu is more extensive, the team are in full control. Lunch & dinner Mon-Sun.

1125
4/D12
CHP

Steam Cafe Station Yd, Clifden +353 95 30600 · @SteamCafeClifden
Steam is housed in the Station Yard in Clifden, a short walk from the town centre, and it's the sort of simple space that survives and thrives because owners Claire and Alan have great taste. Just look at that Cleggan crab on a thick slice of brown bread, with sweet chilli mayo and a crisp salad. It's as good a thing as you could eat on the W coast: sweet, unctuous, saline and subtle. Everything is served with punctilious modesty by a charming team who care deeply about the quality of everything they make. All day Mon-Sat.

If you're in N Connemara...

1126 **The Misunderstood Heron** Leenane +353 87 9915179 · @MisunderstoodHeron
4/E11 Reinaldo and Kim's food cart and picnic benches are set just off the N59 on the edge
LLL of Killary Harbour, 5 miles from Leenane, so as you meander on one of the most
beautiful driving routes in Ireland, pull off the road and get ready to get that appetite
sated with some fine cooking and a cup of Cloud Picker coffee. Don't forget to ask
Kim the true story of that unfortunate heron, as you take in the jaw-dropping views.

✓ **Renvyle House Hotel** Co Galway Report: 1326/ESCAPES.

Letterfrack Lodge Co Galway Report: 1299/HOSTELS.
Paddy Coyne's Public House Co Galway Report: 1425/COUNTRY PUBS.

Co Longford

WHERE TO EAT & STAY IN LONGFORD . . .

1127 ✓ **Viewmount House** Dublin Rd, Longford +353 43 3341919 ·
4/L11 www.viewmounthouse.com We love the fact that James and Beryl Keaney
12 ROOMS work so hard to seek out the correct historical furnishings for this regal house, a
EXP mile or so outside the town. Every aspect of the public and private rooms is
ATMOS apposite, appropriate, and understated, and their Boxty Benedict for breakfast is
one of the most original things you can eat for breakfast anywhere in Ireland.
EAT TGP Young Chef of the Year finalist Bronagh Rogers is the new head chef of
VM restaurant, replacing celebrity chef Gary O'Hanlon.

1128 ✓ **Nine Arches Restaurant** Main St, Ballymahon +353 90 6452895 Partners
4/L12 Daniel Skukalek and Lorna Halligan's Nine Arches has quickly become a
MED.EXP destination restaurant in the zone. Daniel worked with Gary O'Hanlon at
Viewmount and has brought that level of service and detail to this new and
enterprising venture. Dinner Wed-Sat & Sun lunch.

1129 **Aubergine Gallery** 17 Ballymahon St, Longford +353 43 3348633 ·
4/L11 @AubergineGalleryCafe Upstairs on the town's main street, in a building called
MED.INX The White House, Stephen Devlin's bistro is the first choice in the town for tasty,
Mediterranean-style cooking – spinach and ricotta lasagne; pork and apple tart.
Lunch Tue-Sun, dinner Fri-Sun.

Co Roscommon

1130 **Gleesons Restaurant & Rooms** Market Sq, Roscommon +353 90 6626954 ·
4/K11 www.gleesonstownhouse.com Mary and Eamonn Gleeson's restaurant,
20 ROOMS townhouse and food shop are three vital aspects of the town's culinary culture, and
MED.INX since 1991 they have provided a pivotal service for hungry visitors and travellers.
This is lamb country, so don't miss that slow-braised lamb steak.

1131 **Lough Key House** Boyle +353 71 9662161 · www.loughkeyhouse.com
4/K9 Frances McDonagh operates a simple mantra in her pristine, 200-year-old house,
20 ROOMS at the edge of Lough Key forest park: warm hospitality, and real food. She delivers
MED.INX both, in spades. Communal breakfast table means you can expect to make lots of
good new friends.

The Best Places to Eat & Stay in the North West

Co Mayo

If you're In Westport . . .

WHERE TO STAY

1132
5/F10
97 ROOMS
MED.EXP

✓**Knockranny House Hotel** Castlebar St, Westport +353 98 28600 · www.knockrannyhousehotel.ie Up on the hill just outside bustling Westport, Knockranny is an ocean liner hotel: you can walk in the door and vanish from the world, if you wish. It's a big place, but retains the feel of a family hotel, thanks to the careful stewardship of owners Ger and Adrian Noonan.
EAT Chef Seamus Commons brings home the award for best chef in Mayo on an almost annual basis. His cooking in the La Fougere Restaurant is complex, with lots of ingredients in a single dish, but here is a chef who makes every plate work, and does so with ease and style. The restaurant also offers an incredible wine list; sommelier and service skills second-to-none.

1133
5/E10
87 ROOMS
EXP
TERRACE

Westport Plaza Castlebar St, Westport +353 98 51166 · www.westportplazahotel.ie Joe and Anne Corcoran's hotel has a very clear vision of creating a happy workforce as the means by which you create happy guests, and they have made this sympathetic philosophy work, both in the Plaza itself and in its larger, sister hotel, the Castlecourt Hotel. The same company also owns the the Westport Coast Hotel on the Quay, which has sea-facing rooms.

1134
5/E10
52 ROOMS
MED.INX

Clew Bay Hotel James St, Westport +353 98 28088 · www.clewbayhotel.com Maria and Darren's family has a long history of offering hospitality in the town, and they offer good cooking in Madden's Bar – Clew Bay chowder; loaded potato skins; traditional fish and chips – and in the Riverside Restaurant where the cooking is more formal.

WHERE TO EAT

1135
5/E10
MED.EXP
ATMOS

✓**An Port Mor** 1 Bridge St, Westport +353 98 26730 · www.anportmor.com 'We are an Irish restaurant and we serve Irish food, but we also offer a Mayo experience, and we just let the ingredients speak'. That's how chef-proprietor Frankie Mallon describes what he does in An Port Mor, and in his intimate series of rooms he puts that philosophy on the plate, every time. Seafood and Mayo lamb are highlights. Great staff. Dinner 7 days.

1136
5/E10
MED.EXP

Sage 10 High St, Westport +353 98 56700· www.sagewestport.ie Shteryo Yurukov is a very fine cook, and the flavours of his food are clean and bright, whether you have duck tartlet or Belmont venison with oxtail ravioli. Sourcing is meticulous and service under the guidance of Eva Ivanova is pitch-perfect. Informal room, good value, and very popular, so make sure to book. Dinner 7 days.

1137
5/E10
MED.EXP
LL

The Idle Wall The Quay, Westport +353 98 50692 · www.theidlewall.ie Aine Maguire's elegant cottage-style room, a mile or so outside the town, is one of the prettiest dining rooms, and you should come here for shellfish especially: mussels from Kilmeena; N Mayo crab; her classic dish of lamb and clams. Great service from local ladies, who look after everyone like they were your Mammy. Dinner Wed-Sat.

1138 **Pantry & Corkscrew** The Octagon, Westport +353 98 26977 ·
5/E10 www.thepantryandcorkscrew.com The Pantry & Corkscrew epitomises what
MED.INX a west coast restaurant can offer its customers. Dermott and Janice haul in all
the tasty marvels of their hinterland – Mescan beer; Killary Clams; Andarl Farm
pork; Velvet Cloud yogurt; Kelly's putog – and then confect these ingredients into
beautiful dishes. The room at the Octagon is bright and lovely, and do ask to see
their Italian wines. Dinner Wed-Sun.

1139 **Sol Rio** Bridge St, Westport +353 98 28944 · www.solrio.ie Jose and Sinead
5/E10 are professionals to their fingertips, and they make it all seem easy in Sol Rio.
CHP 'Customer is king', Sinead once told us, and they put that philosophy into practice
every day, in the ground-floor café and the upstairs restaurant. Oh, and don't miss
the Portuguese custard tarts, the stuff of legend. Open daily until 10pm 7 days.

1140 **Cian's on Bridge Street** 1 Bridge St, Westport +353 98 25914 ·
5/E10 www.ciansonbridgestreet.com Cian's has been making waves ever since local
MED.INX lad Cian Hayes made over the ground-floor room and started cooking some fine,
bistro-savoury food. They have renovated the first-floor room, the awards have
already started flowing in, and here is a talent to watch closely.

1141 **The Gallery Wine & Tapas Bar** Brewery Pl, Westport +353 83 1091138 ·
5/E10 www.thegallerywestport.com Owner Tom has assembled a list of natural,
organic and biodynamic wines, and put them alongside the Scrabble board, the chess
set, the local foods – look out for Wooded Pig charcuterie – the books and the vinyl
records, in a surreal room set just back from the street. Wonderfully strange, and the
place for good coffee and acoustic music sessions. 2pm-midnight/2am Wed-Sat.

1142 **The Tavern Bar & Restaurant** Murrisk, Westport +353 98 64060 ·
5/E10 www.tavernmurrisk.com Ruth and Myles O'Brien run a veritable paradigm of
MED.INX the modern Irish rural gastropub and restaurant, close to Croagh Patrick in little
ATMOS Murrisk. Pristine housekeeping, great cookery, and the team here have such pride
L in their work that it gladdens the heart. Delightful. Lunch & dinner 7 days.

1143 **Devour Bakery** 3 Church Ln, Ballinrobe + 353 94 9521626 ·
5/F11 www.devourbakery.net Yvonne Murphy's bakery and café is where you will find
CHP some of the best sweet baking in the country. Everything about Devour is modest,
save for Ms Murphy's skill set; this woman is one of the small handful of great Irish
patissiers, so head to Ballinrobe for that magical strawberry eclair. All day Mon-Sat.

1144 **Flanagan's** Brickens, Claremorris +353 94 9380101 · www.flanaganspub.ie
5/H11 Luke and Caroline's gastropub, Flanagan's, transformed a traditional country
MED.INX pub into a modern gastropub by sourcing ingredients from Mayo's finest food
producers, and then cooking those ingredients with sympathy and creativity. Great
local staff look after you. Lunch & dinner Wed-Sun.

If you're in Cong . . .

WHERE TO STAY

1145
5/F12
64 ROOMS &
SUITES
LOTS
DF

✓**The Lodge at Ashford Castle** Cong +353 94 9545400 ·
www.thelodgeac.com The Lodge offers a series of suites arranged around a courtyard at the rere of the house, and they are colourful, tactile and relaxing places to stay, with bedrooms set upstairs from the sitting rooms.
EAT Jonathan Keane's cooking in Wilde's Restaurant is really at a peak these days, and he has harnessed modern technique to deliver great tastes. Service is as good as the cooking; cocktails are some of the very best and should not be missed.

WHERE TO EAT

1146
1/S14
CHP

✓**Hungry Monk** Abbey St +353 94 9545842 · www.hungrymonkcong.com
Aisling Butler speaks fluent food, and cooks with the verve and control of a polymath. In the cottage-style room of the Hungry Monk she demonstrates a mastery of the simple and the elaborate that is convincing, and utterly delicious: we would walk to Cong for her breakfast blaa. Some of the best cooking in the West, and Jonathan Butler minds the room with quiet authority. Daytime Mon-Sat.

1147
4/F12
83 ROOMS
LOTS
DF
LLL

Ashford Castle Cong +353 94 9546003 · www.ashfordcastle.com Ashford Castle has captured the high-roller, de luxe market for the west coast – you can blow €6.5k on their two-day Ashford Castle Fairytale Experience alone if you have that kind of moolah. More importantly, a dynamic service team and an excellent head chef, Philippe Farineau, have brought the castle deserved acclaim and success, and standards here are sky high.

Newport to Mulranny...

WHERE TO STAY

1148
5/E10
41 ROOMS
LOTS
LL
DF

Mulranny Park Hotel Mulranny + 353 98 36000 · www.mulrannyparkhotel.ie
Led by manager Dermot Madigan, the Mulranny Park Hotel is distinguished by having a marvellous team of staff members. Everything they do is thought through, from the superb brown bread, to the design of the rooms – try and get the John Lennon suite! – to the signature dishes which chef Chamila Mananwatta prepares for the Nephin Restaurant. One of the treasures of the Wild Atlantic Way. 20 apartments available for self-catering. Pets allowed in lower floor apartment suite, subject to availability and not in July & Aug due to hotel capacity.
EAT The Nephin Restaurant is a supremely stylish room, and the cooking matches the svelte comfort, showcasing the best Co Mayo ingredients: Curraun blue trout with carrot and lemongrass purée; chicken stuffed with white pudding and chorizo with crispy egg.

Newport House Co Mayo Report: 1286/COUNTRY HOUSES.
Mulranny House Co Mayo Report: 1363/BEST B&B.

WHERE TO EAT

1149
5/E10
CHP

Kelly's Kitchen Main St, Newport +353 98 41647 · @KellysKitchenNewport
Shauna Kelly is one of the legendary Kelly family of Newport, and she shows the same dedication to good food that has characterised her family for decades. Ms Kelly leads the front-of house team in The Kitchen, and happily serves up the iconic Kelly's pork products for breakfast, along with a host of lovely things throughout the day. All day Mon-Sat.

✓**Blue Bicycle Tea Rooms** Co Mayo Report: 1471/TEA ROOMS.

WHERE TO STAY

1150
5/D8
21 ROOMS
EXP

✓**Talbot Hotel** Barrack St, Belmullet +353 97 20484 ·
www.thetalbothotel.ie The Talbot Hotel has a design style every bit as vivid as The G Hotel in Galway. Aside from the décor however, it's the ambitious and well-executed cooking in the dining room that will have you heading back to N Mayo.

Leim Siar B&B Co Mayo Report: 1362/BEST B&B.

WHERE TO EAT

1151
5/F10
CHP

✓**Cafe Rua** New Antrim St, Castlebar +353 94 9023376 · www.caferua.com
Castlebar is twice-blessed for the McMahon siblings, Aran and Coleen, offer both the original Café Rua, and the newer kid on the block, Rua, an ace delicatessen with a fine restaurant upstairs. Ever since their mother, Ann McMahon, first opened Café Rua, in 1995, the family has been devoted to the produce of Co Mayo, and today their menus and shelves spill over with good things from local artisans – Andarl farm bacon croquettes; Killary mussels with coconut and lime; Mayo beef with roast garlic mash; the great Mayo mezze board; West coast crab with avocado and pickles. All day Mon-Sat. Open Fri evenings for dinner. Sister establishment Rua Deli & Cafe on Spencer St, open daily.

1152
5/F10
MED.INX
ATMOS
·

Bar One Rush St, Castlebar +353 94 9034800 · www.barone.ie
Mark Cadden's Bar One is an aleph of the foods of the Wild Atlantic Way. An aleph is a point from which you can see the entire concept, and Mr Cadden's sourcing means that when you eat in this glamorous gastropub, you eat the foods of the western seaboard, and drink the craft beers of the WAW. Fish from Achill and Donegal; ice cream from Cork; beers from the hills of Mayo. Beef, lamb and pork from local farms and local butchers, and farmhouse cheeses come from western islands and Mayo pastures. Great staff bring it all home. Lunch & dinner Mon-Sat.

1153
5/F10
MED.INX

House of Plates Upr Chapel St, Castlebar +353 94 9250742 ·
www.houseofplates.ie Barry Ralph serves a small plates menu, although these are Irish scale tapas plates, rather than Spanish ones. HofP has enjoyed great success in the first year and the cooking is colourful and makes great use of ingredients from their own urban farm. Good brunch choices at the weekend. Dinner Wed-Sun, open from noon Sat & Sun.

If you're in Ballina . . .

WHERE TO STAY

1154
5/G8
10 ROOMS
LOTS
MID FEB-DEC
L

Belleek Castle Hotel Belleek +353 96 22400 · www.belleekcastle.com
Chef Stephen Lenahan is making waves in the neo-Gothic Belleek Castle, and whilst his techniques are contemporary, he also reaches back into history to create dishes such as Gore-Knox pie, made with rare-breed pork and pork fat pastry, and Drunken Bullock, where Mayo beef is flambéed in Jameson whiskey. There is ambition here, in a most characterful castle: make sure to take the tour to learn all about this extraordinary concoction of a castle.

1155
5/G8
32 ROOMS
EXP
LL

Ice House The Quay, Ballina +353 96 23500 · www.icehousehotel.ie
A super-stylish boutique hotel, right beside the River Moy on the Quay just outside Ballina itself. It's popular for spa breaks, and there are seaweed baths, saunas and hot tubs. Great views across the river from the rooms and the restaurant, as well as an amazing terrace.

WHERE TO EAT

1156
5/G9
MED.INX-
MED.EXP

Heifer & Hen Restaurant Market Sq, Ballina +353 96 73528 ·
www.heffernansfinefoods.ie Newish café addition to Anthony Heffernan's family butcher's business. A good aged tagliata and a glass of excellent Italian red will do just nicely. Dinner Wed-Sat & Sun lunch.

Co Sligo

WHERE TO STAY

Coopershill House Co Sligo Report: 1277/COUNTRY HOUSES.

WHERE TO EAT

1157
5/G8
MED.INX

✓**Pudding Row** Main St, Easkey +353 96 49794 · www.puddingrow.ie
Dervla James is making a monumental impact in Pudding Row, in little Easkey, with cooking that is vivid, smart and seasonal. The food is centred around the superb baking of Dervla and her husband, Johny Conlon – don't miss their evening baking courses – and concoctions like courgette, cinnamon and walnut cake, or wild blackberry and pear are to-die-for delicious. The only difficulty in Pudding Row is getting a table so you can enjoy the food and the views. All day Thur-Sun & Bank Hols.

1158
5/J8
MED.INX
ATMOS
L

✓**Shells Cafe and Little Shop** Strandhill +353 71 9122938 ·
www.shellscafe.com Shells Café in Strandhill is a smashing, light-filled room, run by hip young people who are up for it, packed with surfer dudes and holidaymakers, and it is one blast of a destination, the star of Strandhill. Myles and Jane – surfer dudes themselves – cook just the right food for the right room – chicken burger; lamb stew; house baked beans –and everyone is mad for it. Be sure not to miss their delightful shop, beside the café, which is packed with great crafts and lovely foods. All day 7 days.

1159
5/J8
CHP

Nook Cafe and Bakery Main St, Collooney +353 87 3522135 ·
@NookCafeRestaurant Ethna Reynolds is a real powerhouse cook. In a tiny space in little Collooney, she puts out big, big flavours – slow-cooked White Hag beef brisket hash; big local burger with Dozio's cheese, bacon, beetroot and a Ballysadare egg; double chocolate ganache toffee popcorn cake. But the whumpf! of the combinations is balanced by her finesse and delicacy as a cook, so the combinations are smart and successful, and there is nothing on the plate that doesn't need to be there. Worth the detour into the village. All day, till 3/3.30pm Tue-Sat.

1160 Hooked 3 Rockwood Parade, Sligo +353 71 9138591 ·
5/J8 www.hookedsligo.ie Sligo restaurateur Anthony Gray has stepped into his family's
MED.INX back pages with Hooked, which is a tribute to his father's butcher's shop, and even
includes the traditional butcher's block. Chef Joe McGlynn offers and all day menu –
don't miss the pork sausages. Lunch & dinner 7 days.

1161 The Draft House Strandhill +353 71 9122222 · www.thedrafthouse.ie
5/J8 Daniel McGarrigle and his team have boundless ambition, and thoughtfulness, so
MED.EXP here is a gastropub that also offers showers for surfers, and kennels for your puppy,
and features the work of local artists. Strong, professional cooking matches the
manic design style, and it's all great fun, especially after a day on the waves. Lunch
& dinner Mon-Sat, all day Sun.

1162 Eithna's by the Sea Mullaghmore +353 71 9166407 ·
5/J7 www.eithnasrestaurant.com Eithna O'Sullivan is the great food heroine of
MED.INX- Sligo, and her seafood restaurant at the harbour in Mullaghmore has served as a
MED.EXP beacon of creative cooking for 20 years. Ms O'Sullivan's cookery pushes the right
LL buttons, often thanks to the inspired use of foraged ingredients, and the menus
are strong on the classics: lobster thermidor; shellfish platter; Lissadell mussels
in wine and cream. Just lovely. Lunch & dinner Wed-Sun. Eithna also runs the
comfortable Seacrest Guest House, 50m from the beach.

1163 Lang's of Grange Grange +353 71 9163105 · www.langs.ie Lang's is as
5/J7 authentic a bar as any traveller could hope to find, and the Burke family offer good
MED.INX pub grub – steak sandwich; fish and chips; bangers and mash – perfect for enjoying
with a pint of Donegal Blonde. Lunch & dinner Wed-Mon.

1164 Vintage Lane Cafe Rathcormac +353 87 6622600 · @VintageLaneCafe
5/J7 All the design elements are artfully mismatched in Ciaran Walsh's café, and the
CHP cooking and baking are straight-ahead delicious, whether it's the savoury goat's
cheese tart or the sweet lemon drizzle cake. There is an eclectic craft and food
market held here on Saturday mornings, but anytime the wind is whistling over
Benbulben you will find a warm fire blazing in Vintage Lane and an excellent cup of
coffee. All day Mon-Sat.

1165 Drumcliffe Tea House Drumcliffe +353 71 9144956 ·
5/J7 www.drumcliffeteahouse.ie The Tea House is where you go for tea and buns
and some choice retail therapy when you pay your respects to the great W.B. Yeats
in Drumcliffe graveyard. Daytime 7 days.

1166 Feed Cafe Restaurant Millview House, Riverstown +353 71 9165675 ·
5/J8 @feedrestaurant Paul Monaghan's Feed Café, in the Sligo Folk Park, fits perfectly
CHP into that admirable category of unusual Sligo food destinations. It's a great spot
L for freshly baked breads and scones and a good cup of coffee, or an energy-packed
bowl of porridge with fresh fruit, and Paul's lunchtime dishes deliver true, assured
flavours. Mr Monaghan has begun to garner quite a reputation for his cooking and
– especially – for his baking, and this little Sligo secret isn't going to stay a secret
for long. All day Tue-Sat.

If you're in Sligo Town . . .

WHERE TO STAY

1167
5/J8
116 ROOMS
EXP

The Glasshouse Swan Point, Sligo +353 71 9194300 · www.theglasshouse.ie
The central location of The Glasshouse, and the good views over The Garavogue river makes it a fine choice for staying in Sligo. The staff are enthusiastic, the decor has a funky, retro vibe with lots of boldly coloured and stylised artworks and lots of lime and orange on the colour palette.

Down Yonder B&B Co Sligo Report: 1364/BEST B&B.

WHERE TO EAT

1168
5/J8
MED.EXP
ATMOS

✓**Knox** 32 O'Connell St, Sligo +353 71 9141575 · www.knoxsligo.ie
David Dunne and Patrick Sweeney's Knox restaurant met with success right from the day they opened the doors, and the pair have steadily and organically expanded their offer, so you can now go to Knox for breakfast and weekend brunch, for lunch, and go at the weekend evenings to enjoy tapas. Everything is well-chosen and thought-through in Knox, from the furnishings to the concise wine list, from the accomplished baking by Stacey McGowan to the vintage lighting. Knox is the Sligo powerhouse. All day 7 days, dinner Thur-Sat.

1169
5/J8
CHP

✓**Sweet Beat Cafe** Bridge St, Sligo +353 71 9138795 · www.sweetbeat.ie
Carolanne Rushe has opened one of the sharpest new addresses on the west coast, in the lean, smart Sweet Beat. The menu is plant-based: Italian bean stew; sweet potato falafel burger; Sri Lankan vegetable curry; chilli and coriander humous; dark chocolate, spelt and pecan brownie. Simon Hunt is the barista, working with superb, single-origin beans from 3fe roasters, and there is a superb selection of fermented drinks. All day Mon-Sat.

1170
5/J8
MED.EXP
ATMOS

Eala Bhan Rockwood Pde, Sligo +353 71 9145823 · www.ealabhan.ie
Anthony Gray takes the flavours of Sligo and puts them on a plate for you in Eala Bhan, his riverside Sligo restaurant. There is lamb from Sherlocks of Tubbercurry, there is John Flynn's fresh fish, there is Feeney's Sligo pork fillet, and he doesn't mind stepping over the county border to source the superb black and white puddings of Kelly's of Newport. Mr Gray brings great energy and welcome to the room, and it's a good choice. Lunch & dinner Mon-Sun

1171
5/J8
CHP

Kate's Kitchen 3 Castle St, Sligo +353 71 9143022 · www.kateskitchen.ie
Kate, Beth and Jane's magnificent emporium has all the classic artisan brands that your heart could desire. But, first off, grab a stool by the window as it's time for a sausage roll and a cup of Fixx coffee to get the day off to a good start, then hit the shelves, and then head off with one of their delicious takeaway lunches: spiced chicken with Asian chickpea and peanut salad; felafel with cucumber pickle; pork and bean chilli hotpot; pork burrito with pickled onion. All day Mon-Sat.

1172
5/J8
MED.EXP
ATMOS

Hargadon Bros 4 O'Connell St, Sligo +353 71 9153709 · www.hargadons.com
Hargadon Bros opened its doors in 1868, and they haven't needed to do much to this classic pub in all the years since. You step in the door, and you step back 150 years. Lunch & dinner Mon-Sat. Kitchen closed, bar only on Sunday.

1173
5/J8
CHP

Lyon's Cafe & Bakeshop Quay St, Abbeyquarter Nth, Sligo +353 71 9142969 · www.lyonscafe.com Gary Stafford knows his food as well as he knows his customers, and the result for those devoted customers of Lyons Café, on the first floor above the Lyons' department store, is delicious, authentic food, food that zings with health and energy. The downstairs bakery offers some of the best bakes and treats in the NW. All day Mon-Sat.

1174
5/J8
MED.INX

Osta Cafe and Wine Bar Garavogue Weir, off Stephen St, Sligo +353 71 9144639 · www.osta.ie Brid Torrades sources from the artisan suppliers who live and work near to Sligo, and her zeal for the local extends even to breakfast, where her foods come from within a 30-mile radius. She has always been the most perspicacious, committed restaurateur, and her tenure stretches over decades. Ever since the early days, her love for fresh local foods has only gotten deeper, and that zeal is evident in every bite of Osta's dishes. All day until 7pm/8pm 7 days.

Co Leitrim

WHERE TO STAY

1175
5/K10
60 ROOMS
MED.INX

The Landmark Hotel Carrick-on-Shannon +353 71 9622222 · www.thelandmarkhotel.com There has always been an excellent team running things in The Landmark, and they really put the effort into creating good food and offering genuine hospitality. Very friendly, very relaxing.

The Courthouse Co Leitrim Report: 1322/RESTAURANTS WITH ROOMS.

WHERE TO EAT

1176
5/K10
MED.EXP

✓ **The Cottage** Jamestown +353 71 9625933 · www.cottagerestaurant.ie Sham Hanifa's restaurant isn't as famous as London's NOPI, but Mr Hanifa has done for Ireland what chefs Yotam Ottolenghi and Ramael Scully have done for London. He cooks on the culinary tightrope of Irish ingredients and Eastern grace notes – beef carpaccio Thai-style with dry roast peanuts; monkfish with turmeric coconut cream; Pernod panna cotta with star anise poached pear. He makes these matches seem made-in-heaven, the Asian grace notes adding colour, heat and contrast to the Leitrim ingredients. It makes for lovely, unique eating. Dinner Wed-Sun & Sun lunch.

1177
5/K10
MED.EXP
ATMOS

✓ **The Oarsman** Bridge St, Carrick-on-Shannon +353 71 9621733 · www.theoarsman.com Ronan and Conor Maher have helmed the beautiful Oarsman for more than 15 years, giving Carrick-on-Shannon the town's don't-miss gastropub for eating and drinking. Their cooking is original and delicious – sea trout with chive gnocchi; Cloonconra cheese and olive croquettes; Brogan's beef and garlic meatballs; Andarl farm pork loin with swede – and they marshal one of the best teams in the NE. One of the best bars. Lunch & dinner Mon-Sat.

1178
5/K10
EXP

St George's Terrace Carrick-on-Shannon +353 81 9616546 · www.stgeorgesterrace.com Siobhan Smyth and chef Dave Fitzgibbon have brought an unprecedented level of culinary finesse and design consciousness to Carrick-on-Shannon in the shape of St George's, and it's that stylish cooking which has been drawing attention: tea-smoked salmon with blood orange; pork neck fillet with Savoy cabbage; caramel mousse with brioche. Good value for such complex cooking, great views from the dining rooms, and Dave also conducts cookery classes. Dinner Wed-Sun, Sun lunch and afternoon tea Thur-Sat.

1179
5/K0
CHP

Luna Main St, Dromahair +353 9134332
Joe Grogan has worked in some of Sligo's best destinations over the years, and has now taken up the stoves at little Luna, a cottage-style restaurant in tiny Dromahair. Mr Grogan is a real professional, so expect confident cooking, and some ace pizzas. Dinner from 4pm, Tue-Sat. Open Sun from 3pm during high season.

Co Donegal

WHERE TO STAY

1180
6/N2
17 ROOMS
MED.INX
ATMOS

McGrory's Culdaff +353 74 9379104 · www.mcgrorys.ie John Reynolds and his team at the iconic McGrory's Hotel love to surprise us. You might arrive just to enjoy a few days' relaxation, and to enjoy chef Gary McPeake's elegant Donegal food, but then you hear that those Saharan sonic superstars, Bombino, are playing in The Back Room, and you say: for real? For real is right, so the gigs in McGrory's are just as delightful as everything else.

1181
6/L3
MAR-OCT
3 ROOMS
EXP

Breac House Horn Head, Dunfanaghy +353 74 9136940 · www.breac.house Cathrine and Niall's dramatic house on far-flung Horn Head is as idyllic an escape as you can imagine. Best of all is the fact that the house and its contents are tribute to the skills of Donegal craftsmen and women, who have fashioned every aspect of a modern design jewel: the house is an aleph of the county, revealing the talents and the elements of the place.

✓ **Rathmullan House** Co Donegal Report: 1271/COUNTRY HOUSES.

The Mill Co Donegal Report: 1323/RESTAURANTS WITH ROOMS.
Danny Minnie's Co Donegal Report: 1324/RESTAURANTS WITH ROOMS.
The Glen House Co Donegal Report: 1369/BEST B&B.

WHERE TO EAT

1182
6/L4
CHP

✓ **The Counter Deli & Wine** Canal Rd, Letterkenny +353 74 9120075 · www.thecounterdeli.com The Counter is a wine and food shop that is also a café; it's a day-time place that can be rebirthed into an evening destination. It's informal, but stylish. And the food you find in The Counter has one characteristic: it is bespoke. They cook the food they like to cook, so you might have a lentil curry with a fig raita, while your kid tucks into a ham and cheese toastie. And you might eat breakfast here, and then find yourself back at 2.30pm for a late lunch. The Counter is multi-purpose: it gives you what you want, and it's a bit genius. All day Mon-Sat.

1183
6/L4

Burrito Loco Port Rd, Letterkenny, Co Donegal +353 74 9126380 · @burritolocolk Casual Mexican takeaway with a big heart, great cooking and a huge hit in the Letterkenny community. They pride themselves as being a takeaway that doesn't own a deep fat fryer, and their delicious burritos are served with real juices.

1184
5/K6
MED.EXP

The Village Tavern Mountcharles +353 74 9735622 · www.villagetavern.ie the Tavern offers the taste of West Donegal, right down to having their own craft beer, Salty Dog, made in Ballyshannon. They put the bounty of the county on the plate – summer lobster salad with marinated watermelon; pan-seared scallops with slow-braised tomato broth; Drimarone lamb with pea risotto. The cooking is modest and wise, service is excellent. Lunch & dinner 7 days.

1185 **Aroma Coffee Shop** The Craft Village, Donegal +353 74 9723222
5/K6 Tom and Arturo's Aroma, at the Donegal Craft Village, is but a tiny single room and
CHP it is perennially packed. Arturo cooks European staples – risotto; polenta; pasta –
just as well as he cooks his native chimichangas and quesadillas – and Tom's
baking is superlative: if you haven't had the Tunisian orange cake, you haven't
lived. All day Mon-Sat.

1186 **Quay West** Quay St, Donegal +353 74 9721590 · www.quaywestdonegal.ie
5/K6 Debbie and Jo are amongst the most experienced restaurateurs in Donegal town,
MED.INX and their move to the sleek, glass-fronted Quay West, with its fantastic views of the
LL bay, has given them a new lease of life. They offer steaks from the char-grill, lots of
local seafood, and classics like braised Donegal lamb, and Jo's service is super-
friendly. Dinner 7 days, from 3pm Sun.

1187 **Olde Castle Bar and Red Hugh Restaurant** Tirconnell St, Donegal
5/K6 +353 74 9721262 · www.oldecastlebar.com A minute's walk away from the
MED.EXP Diamond, and the Olde Castle bar and restaurant is home to unpretentious,
gimmick-free local seafood, with the sort of menu that every Donegal destination
should offer: Killybegs seafood pies; Lily Boyle's fishcakes; seafood chowder; cod
in breadcrumbs; grilled lobster; seafood platter. Red Hugh's restaurant upstairs
is more formal, service is svelte, and the food for children is thoughtful. Lunch &
dinner 7 days.

1188 **The Blueberry Tearooms** Castle St, Donegal +353 74 9722933 ·
5/K6 @TheBlueberryTearooms The Blueberry is a small, flower-bedecked room
CHP where Brian and Ruperta Gallagher take care of everyone as if they were family
and where tasty, clever food makes sure that everyone who visits comes back. The
honesty and hard work of this couple is inspiring, and don't miss Ruperta's great
puddings and desserts. All day till 7pm Mon-Sat.

1189 **Kitty Kelly's Restaurant** Killybegs +353 74 9731925 · @KittyKellys
5/J6 Remy Dupuy and his wife Donna took over this landmark destination, on a
MED.EXP sharp bend on the R263 a few miles west of Killybegs, after decades cooking in
Dunkineely. M. Dupuy brought his classic signature dish of prawns and monkfish
with him – eating this is a rite of passage in Donegal – and a smart makeover has
transformed a traditional farmhouse into a welcoming spot. Dinner Wed-Sun

1190 **Nancy's of Ardara** Front St, Ardara +353 74 9541187 · www.nancysardara.com
5/J5 'Nancy's is one of those pubs that just captures the imagination', wrote *The Irish*
MED.INX *Times*. Too right. No fewer than seven generations of the McHugh family have
ATMOS manned the bar in this Donegal icon, one of the county's most legendary pubs,
serving tasty food and pulling great pints. It's a must-visit on the WAW, simple as
that. Lunch & dinner 7 days.

1191 **The Cove** Port Na Blagh, Dunfanaghy +353 74 9136300 ·
6/L3 @CoveRestaurantDonegal Siobhan Sweeney's vivid, Asian-accented cooking
MED.EXP is soulful – hake with yellow split peas and chorizo; fresh cannelloni with spinach
LL and ricotta; organic salmon with pearl barley risotto – food that is precise and
punky, every bit as good to eat as it is to look at. Peter Byrne runs the room with
good humour, and there are good beers and wines to kick off the evening in the bar
upstairs as you wait. Dinner Mon-Sun.

1192 **The Shack** Marble Hill, Port Na Blagh, Dunfanaghy +353 86 7238318 ·
6/L3   www.shackcoffee.ie Overlooking Marble Hill beach and Sheephaven Bay, Tom
CHP TERRACE   and Min offer artisan coffee and good ice cream in a wooden beachside shack:
ATMOS LL   what's not to love? All day, seasonal.

1193 **The Rusty Oven** Behind Patsy Dan's Bar, Main St, Dunfanaghy ·
6/L3   @therustyoven Underneath the fairy lights in the cool back garden of Patsy
CHP   Dan's famous pub is where you will find the crew of The Rusty Oven, wearing the
TERRACE   cool T-shirts and making everyone happy with some really fine pizzas. Very busy, so
get there early. Dinner Fri-Sun, and open 7 days during the summer holidays.

1194 **Olde Glen Bar & Restaurant** Carrigart +353 83 1585777 · @oldeglenbar
6/L3   The Olde Glen is a true original that dates back a couple of hundred years, and
CHP   it has worn those years well. Make sure to get there early to get a table to enjoy
some good cooking in the restaurant: crab linguini; roast duck; hake with spinach
velouté; buttered lobster. Great music sessions, great craft beers. Meals Mon-Fri,
from 3pm, from noon Sat & Sun.

1195 **House Winebar & Taproom** 21 Lwr Main St, Letterkenny +353 74 9109815 ·
6/L4   @housewinebarandtaproom House is a super-stylish, walk-up-the-stairs-
MED.INX   and-ring-the-doorbell club, with table service, good wines and craft beers, and
ace cocktails. The vibe is meant to feel like being at home, except that, unlike your
own modest pad, you are now in a groovy place with wood-fired pizzas, cheese and
meat boards, and Kinnegar Brewery beers on tap. Dinner Tue-Sun.

1196 **Berry Layne** Houston House, 32 Upr Main St, Letterkenny +353 74 9111002 ·
6/L4   www.berrylayne.com This wine bar and coffee shop has a neat small plates
MED.INX   and pizza offering, along with a coffee, cakes and lunchtime offer, and it's a great
addition to the fast-improving food scene in Letterkenny. For the evenings, there
are cheese and charcuterie boards, baked camemberts, and nice pizzas: Margarita;
Hawaiian; Vegetarian, and the Berry Layne special. All day until 10pm 7 days.

1197 **The Lemon Tree** 32 Courtyard Shopping Centre, Letterkenny
6/L4   +353 74 9125788 · www.thelemontreerestaurant.com The Molloy family
MED.EXP   siblings – Chris, Gary and Thomas in the kitchen; Linda and Trudy at front of house
– power this ambitious Letterkenny destination. Nice, friendly cooking and good
service, and value for money, as with many Donegal restaurants, is excellent.
Dinner 7 days.

1198 **Wholegreen** Church Lane, Letterkenny +353 74 9112296 · www.wholegreen.ie
6/L4   Wholegreen is a vegetarian and vegan restaurant, so if you are seeking plant-based,
CHP   healthy dishes you will find them here in Anna Good's café: sweet potato and lentil
curry; root vegetable chowder with samphire, the signature fresh juices such as
Green Monster juice made with cucumber, kale, spinach, lemon, green pepper and
basil. All day Mon-Sat.

1199 **The Red Door** Carrowmullin, Fahan +353 74 9360289 · www.thereddoor.ie
6/M3   Sean Clifford has charge of the kitchens in The Red Door in Fahan, an elegant
MED.EXP   country house with a sublime location on the water's edge in Fahan. It's a great
spot for afternoon tea, and Mr Clifford's cooking in the restaurant is imaginative
and creative: salmon en croute; fillet steak with smoked celeriac purée; Killybegs
monkfish with spinach, chorizo and chickpeas. On weekday evenings they have a
Grill Night, where Mr Clifford gets all funky with his Big Green Egg. Dinner Wed-
Sun, lunch Sat & Sun. Four double rooms are available for B&B on Saturdays only.

1200 **The Beach House** The Pier, Swilly Rd, Buncrana +353 74 9361050 ·
6/M3 www.thebeachhouse.ie Claire McGowan is a great restaurateur, and The Beach
MED.EXP House is an archetype of the dependable, trustworthy country town restaurant,
welcoming you with delicious cooking and wonderful wines. Dinner, from 5pm,
Thur & Fri, lunch & dinner Sat & Sun.

1201 **Nancy's Barn** Ballyliffin Village +353 86 8432897 · @nancysbarn Chef Kieran
6/M2 Duey of Nancy's has won the all-Ireland chowder championship on two separate
MED.INX occasions, and followed that with victory in the Chowder Cook Off in Rhode Island.
So a bowl of chowder and buttermilk soda bread is reason enough to get to pretty
Ballyliffin, even if you aren't a golfer. But there is much more to enjoy here, from a
chef who is at the top of his game. All day 7 days.

1202 **Kealy's Seafood Bar** The Harbour, Greencastle +353 74 9381010 ·
6/P2 www.kealysseafoodbar.ie Kealy's of Greencastle has always been one of
MED.EXP the great Donegal destinations, a pioneering seafood restaurant where fish
and shellfish are showcased to produce the most delicious dishes:
Greencastle chowder; hake with smoked salmon and lemon bon-bon and
Noilly Prat beurre blanc; monkfish and cod bake with crab sauce. Kealy's is
an ageless, charming restaurant. Lunch & dinner Thur-Sun. Self-catering
accommodation available.

1203 **Hardy Baker** Unit 3 Bundoran Retail Park, Bundoran +353 71 9833865 ·
5/K7 @HardyBaker Situated in the Bundoran retail park, Laura Hardaker's café is
worth the detour for top class scratch baking, good coffee, and for a blast of that
casual, surfer vibe that is transforming this once-sleepy coastal town. Good
home-made treats to take away, but it's Laura's wizardry with sweet things that
will have you coming back for another taste of that Great Bundoran Bake Off.
Daytime Tue-Sun.

The Best Hotels & Restaurants in Northern Ireland
Co Londonderry

WHERE TO STAY

1204   **Ardtara Country House & Restaurant**   8 Gorteade Rd, Upperlands
6/Q4   +4428 79644490 · www.ardtara.com   Recently taken over by the team who
9 ROOMS   run Browns (1210/WHERE TO EAT), this glorious country house has a great history
EXP   of entertaining stylishly in the N, and the union between this grand house and
Browns restaurant was an exciting match. Ian Orr is the leading chef in the region,
and Ardtara is one of the most beautiful houses; together they make a very special
destination.

WHERE TO EAT

1205   ✓**Harry's Shack**   Portstewart Beach +4428 70831783 · @HarrysShack
6/Q3   Sited at the eastern end of the magnificent Portstewart Strand – familiar to
MED.INX   *Game of Thrones* fans – Harry's Shack has been a phenomenon since the day it
TERRACE   opened in August 2014. It's a wooden shack on the beach, inside you sit on school
LLL   chairs and eat off tables hewn from untreated wood, and everyone wants to be in
this room. Top-class cooking, of course, but it's the fact that Harry's represents
everyone's dream beach food shack that makes it so important. Lunch & dinner
7 days till 7/8.30/9pm

1206   ✓**Lost & Found**   2 Queen St, Coleraine · www.wearelostandfound.com
6/Q3   Lost & Found is the coolest room in NI, and it's always filled with the coolest
CHP   people. The team working this glass-fronted room on Queen St are so on top of
their game that everyone wants a piece of their action, and L&F is one of the most
significant players in the country. Simple and delicious cooking hits all the points
and, if you fused Chez Panisse with The Spotted Pig, the result would be something
inspiring like L&F. All day Tue-Sat.

1207   **The Lime Tree**   60 Catherine St, Limavady +4428 77764300 ·
6/P3   www.limetreerest.com   Stanley and Maria Matthews have run the destination
MED.INX   restaurant in Limavady for more than two decades. We like the fact that it isn't
concerned to offer the latest food fashions, and ploughs its path with dishes like
sirloin with forestiere sauce, or cod thermidor, or duck confit with potato bread.
Ageless, and blessed with excellent service and great value. Lunch Thur-Fri,
dinner Tue-Sat.

WHERE TO STAY

1208 · **Bishop's Gate Hotel** 24 Bishop St +4428 71140300 ·
6/N4 · www.bishopsgatehotelderry.com The restoration of the old Northern Counties
30 ROOMS · listed building has been sensitively handled – save for the branded awnings, which
EXP · should be removed – and the BG team, under manager Ciaran O'Neill, show a
real pride in their work in this architectural jewel. The main focus for eating is The
Gown restaurant, which offers classic dishes but there is also daytime food in
The Wig, their champagne bar, and afternoon tea in The Hervey library.

1209 · **Beech Hill House Hotel** 32 Ardmore Rd +4428 71349279 · www.beech-hill.com
6/N4 · A couple of kilometres outside the city, and set amidst mature grounds, The
30 ROOMS · Beech Hill has for decades been the first choice for events and celebrations in
EXP · Londonderry (Derry). Conor Donnelly and his team are real strivers, always seeking
to improve, and a lot of the cooking is now plot-to-plate.

WHERE TO EAT

1210 · ✓ **Browns Restaurant** 1 Bonds Hill, Waterside +4428 71345180 ·
6/N4 · www.brownsrestaurant.com Browns delivers some of the most interesting,
EXP · nuanced contemporary cooking you will find anywhere, and the crew deliver the
ATMOS · goods in both the original Waterside restaurant, and in Browns in Town in the city
centre. Head chef Ian Orr is one of the great Northern chefs. He also oversees the
grand Ardtara House, near Maghera (1204/WHERE TO STAY) where Eddie Atwell
heads up the kitchen. Lunch & dinner Tue-Sat & Sun lunch.

1211 · ✓ **Pyke'n'Pommes** Foyleview, Strand Rd +44 75 94307561 ·
6/N4 · www.pykenpommes.ie Kevin Pyke cooks some of the best food in the NW,
CHP · and the fact that he serves it from a pod – a converted container from an articulated
L · lorry – at the edge of the River Foyle, only makes his food taste better. P'n'P has
gotten posher over the years – there are seats and tables out front now, and plants
and flowers – but the quality and consistency of the cooking has never faltered.
Mr Pyke's latest riff is some fine cooking with tacos, so put some mescal in the hip
flask. Noon-4pm 7 days. Pyke'n'Pommes also operates as a Food Truck from a
converted van named Moe, and serves the food at Blackbird (1218/BEST BARS).

1212 · **Harry's Derry** 20 Craft Village +4428 71371635 · @HarrysDerry
6/N4 · Part of the quixotic complex of the Derry Craft Village, and sibling restaurant to
MED.INX · Harry's Shack (1205/WHERE TO EAT). The restaurant is blessed with an enviable
ATMOS · supply chain, including their own walled garden that brings the best produce
straight in the door. The food is simple, and pretty perfect. All day till 8.30/9pm
Wed-Sat.

1213 · **The Sooty Olive** 160 Spencer Rd +4428 71346040 · www.thesootyolive.com
6/N4 · Sean Harrigan and the team are going from strength to strength in the Sooty Olive.
MED.INX · With a second polytunnel supplying the kitchen, and gigs with the likes of Tom
Kerridge, this crew are pushing hard. The cooking hits the spot: Kilkeel crab with
avocado, grapefruit and Asian dressing; salt-baked celeriac with cod; sea trout with
braised baby gem and crayfish. Nice cocktails, chatty staff, and a 'sooty olive' by the
way, is a fisherman's lough fly used to catch wild trout. Lunch & dinner 7 days.

1214 · **Primrose Restaurant Delicatessen Cocktail Bar** 53 Strand Road
6/N4 · +44 28 71264622 · www.primrose-ni.com Melanie and Ciaran Breslin are
CHP · dynamic food figures in the city, with ventures ranging from butcher's shops to
excellent cafes, all united by fastidious attention to detail. The Primrose Restaurant

on Strand Road teams them with one of the finest modern chefs, Derek Creagh, in a radical new culinary venture that is proof of the emergence of Londonderry (Derry) as a pivotal food lovers' destination. Lunch & dinner 7 days.

1215 **Saffron** 2 Clarendon St +4428 71260531 · **www.saffronderry.co.uk**
6/N4 Saffron is the place where good restaurateurs in Londonderry (Derry) take their staff
MED.INX for their annual Christmas party. The food is a curious mix of Indo-European, but the cooking is so poised that a dish like risotto of chickpea - essentially a chickpea dhal, with Asian mushrooms, Indian spicing, Fivemiletown Creamery soft cheese and pesto - actually works. Their chips are ace. Dinner, from 4.30pm, 7 days.

1216 **Guild** Ground floor, The Guildhall, Guildhall Sq +4428 71360505 ·
6/N4 www.guildcafe.co.uk The Londonderry (Derry) Guildhall is gorgeous, and so is
CHP Guild, the glamour of the room matched by Claire McGowan's expert food. All of the virtues Ms McGowan exhibits in her Buncrana restaurant, The Beach House, are here in spades: colourful, delicious cooking, beautiful baking, simple good taste. All day 7 days.

THE BEST BARS

1217 **The Walled City Brewery** 70 Ebrington Sq +4428 71343336 ·
6/N4 www.walledcitybrewery.com Brewer James Huey worked at St James Gate in Dublin before returning to NI with his wife, Louise, to set up his dynamic craft brewery and restaurant. The beers are wickedly good, and impishly named: Boom, a DPA (Derry Pale Ale); Stitch, an IPA; Kicks, a pilsner; and Cherry/Londoncherry, a fruit beer. The cooking in the restaurant is just as smart as the beers, with a selection of pintxos, and classic mains like pulled pork, walled city burger and porchetta. If you want to feel the creative energy that has transformed Londonderry (Derry) in recent years, you can mainline it right here. Food served 5pm-9pm Tue-Thur, lunch & dinner Fri-Sun

1218 **Blackbird** 24 Foyle St +4428 7136211 Kevin Pyke's street food, from his inspired
6/N4 Pyke 'n' Pommes food cart, is a big attraction at this stylish, and hugely busy Londonderry (Derry) bar. Excellent craft beers and cocktails, and lots of music. Food served 11.30pm-late.

■■■ Co Antrim

WHERE TO STAY

1219 **Bushmills Inn Hotel** 9 Dunluce Rd, Bushmills +4428 20733000 ·
6/Q2 www.bushmillsinn.com The Bushmills Hotel is one of the original north coast
41 ROOMS destinations, and it's always been a beacon of confident professionalism. Good,
MED.EXP savoury cooking in the restaurant, in the old converted stable block, and in the Gas
TERRACE · ATMOS Bar, though prices are relatively high for NI. Good cocktails.

1220 **Galgorm Resort & Spa** 136 Fenaghy Rd, Ballymena +4428 25881001 ·
6/R4 www.galgorm.com Galgorm is ultra luxe, and spacious: 12 rooms in total,
12 ROOMS divided between those in the house itself and a series of cabins and cottages
EXP distributed throughout the 160-acre estate. Their spa is a major attraction, and it's one of the busiest wedding venues in the NE.
EAT in River Room Restaurant This is the flagship eating venue, a super-glam room with views of the River Maine. The cooking is modern in style and description – brill, scallop, pea, romanesco – is a typical tasting menu dish. Food also in their Italian Ristorante Fratelli, and in the Gillies Bar.

1221 **Marlagh Lodge** 71 Moorfields Rd, Ballymena +44 28 25631505 ·
6/R4 www.marlaghlodge.com Marlagh Lodge was a Victorian wreck when Robert and
3 ROOMS Rachel Thompson took it over and, today, it stands as one of the most perfectly
MED.INX executed labours of love: a most beautiful place to stay. The same heroic attention
to detail is true of Mrs Thompson's cooking, which is amongst the best country
cooking you can eat. Great base for exploring.

WHERE TO EAT

1222 ✓**Babushka Kitchen Cafe** S Pier, Portrush +44 77 87502012 ·
6/Q2 ✓@babushkaportrush George Nelson's Babushka Café, on the S pier at
CHP Portrush, is one of that handful of dynamic new destinations which have had a
LL major impact on the food culture in NI. It's little more than a tiny room on the pier,
but it's the star of Portrush simply because they do everything so well, from the
coffee to the bacon bap to the very best salted caramel slice. All day 7 days.

1223 **The Ramore Restaurants** The Harbour, Portrush +44 28 70824313 ·
6/Q2 www.ramorerestaurant.com George and Jane McAlpin's suite of five
LL restaurants and pub serve more customers every week than any other destination
in Ireland. They have re-birthed the old seaside town of Portrush, and have done it
by having something for everyone: pizzas in Coast; wine bar classics in the Ramore;
Asian-accented dishes in Neptune & Prawn; wood-fired meats in the Harbour
Bistro; small plates and sharing plates in The Mermaid; small bites and good gins
in the Harbour Bar. It's generous, gregarious, and mighty fun, and the McAlpins'
achievement in this once-neglected town is monumental. 7 days.

1224 **Bothy** 164 Whitepark Rd, Bushmills +4428 20732311 ·
6/R2 www.bothycoffee.com The simple sign for Bothy: Coffee gives little indication
of the stylishness of the room, and the hipness of the team, who know how to
brew up a London Fog, or fashion a fine chicken Caesar salad as the daily special.
Bothy is an essential element of the experience of crossing the Carrick-a-Rede rope
bridge, and exploring the coastline. Daytime Mon-Sat. Another branch in Mallusk.

If you're in Ballycastle . . .

1225 **Marine Hotel** 1-3 North St, Ballycastle +4428 20762222 ·
6/R2 www.marinehotelballycastle.com The hotel faces the sea and a big, expensive
34 ROOMS revamp is currently underway, so hopefully the full potential of the hotel can
MED.INX be realised.

1226 ✓**Ursa Minor Bakehouse** 45 Ann St, Ballycastle ·
6/R2 ✓www.ursaminorbakehouse.com
CHP Dara and Ciara's Ursa Minor is a craft bakery and café, but thanks to being an
Economusee that showcases their artisanal skills it is much more than that. This is
one of the food businesses that is transforming the food culture of the north coast,
committed to excellence and enjoyment. A true jewel. All day Tue-Sat.

1227 **Central Wine Bar** 12 Ann St, Ballycastle +4428 2076 3877 ·
6/R2 www.centralwinebar.com
MED.INX There is some tasty cooking here, and four of us all ate well on a recent visit. The
McHenry family run an efficient, charming place. Make sure to try a pint of the very
local Glens of Antrim craft beers in O'Connor's Bar, just across the street, before
having dinner. Lunch & dinner 7 days.

If you're in Lisburn & Hillsborough . . .

1228 **Hilden Brewing Company and Tap Room** Hilden House, Grand St, Hilden,
6/S6 Lisburn +4428 92660800 · www.hildenbrewing.com Ireland's original craft brewery
MED.INX survives to this day, creating and serving excellent beers and ales, and fashioning some
very tasty cooking to go with them. There aren't many destinations in this area, so
Hilden is especially valuable. Tap Room lunch & dinner Tue-Sat & Sun lunch.

1229 **The Square Bistro** 18 Lisburn Sq, Lisburn +4428 92666677 ·
6/S6 www.squarebistro.co.uk Stephen Higginson's ever-busy room is the star of
MED.INX Lisburn city. There is some seriously well executed cooking produced here by a
ATMOS bunch of professionals who know exactly what they want to do. Great value and
the staff are just brilliant. All day & dinner Mon-Sat.

1230 **The Parson's Nose** 48 Lisburn St, Hillsborough +4428 92683009 ·
6/S7 www.ballooinns.com Sister restaurant to the acclaimed Balloo House, in
MED.INX Killinchy, and a sure-fire sender of good, modern Irish food, served in excellent
rooms in NI's quaintest town. Lunch & dinner 7 days.

1231 **The Plough Inn** 3 The Square, Hillsborough +4428 92682985 ·
6/S7 www.ploughgroup.com The Patterson family's popular destination is right on
MED.INX the square in Hillsborough. Food is served in both the bar and their bistro, where
good steaks and gourmet burgers are a sure bet. Lunch 7 days.

1232 **Pizza Boutique** 6D Lisburn St, Hillsborough +44 28 92683881
6/S7 It's a bit of a drive, but worth it to see what James Neilly - who teaches at the
Belfast Cookery School - gets up to with pizza: smoked lamb sausage with
halloumi; beef brisket with pickles; chicken and bacon Caesar with ricotta. This is
funky stuff, and worth a detour. There are also pork and ginger dumplings; hickory
chicken wings; polenta fries. Dinner from 4pm Wed-Sun.

Co Tyrone

1233 **Oysters Restaurant** 37 Patrick St, Strabane +4428 71382690 ·
6/M5 www.oystersrestaurant.co.uk Oysters is one of the few restaurants that offers the
MED.EXP old NI idea of 'high tea', which they serve between 4pm and 7pm. A la carte menus are
pretty extensive, and strive to offer something for everyone. Lunch & dinner 7 days

1234 **The Brewer's House** 73 Castlecaulfield Rd, Donaghmore, Dungannon
6/P6 +4428 87761932 · www.thebrewershouse.com Kieran McCausland's stone-
MED.INX built pub, in pretty Donaghmore, has won a mighty reputation over the last several
years. It's one of the oldest pubs in Ulster, and it's worth the detour into the
village for some particularly ambitious gastropub food – beef sausages with mash;
bookmaker sandwich; crispy oysters; brill with Madeira – and it's good to see a
proper kids' menu in a pub. Nice cocktails. Dinner Mon-Sun, lunch Fri-Sun.

Co Down

WHERE TO STAY

1235
6/T7
14 ROOMS
MED.EXP
ATMOS LL

✓**Portaferry Hotel** The Strand, Portaferry +4428 42728231 ·
www.portaferryhotel.com A landmark S Down destination, the Portaferry
has been raised to new heights since being taken over by the local Arthurs family.
Everything chimes here: the comfort of the rooms; the excellent cooking; the
amiability of the staff; the great waterside location. A wee treasure.

1236
6/R7
3 ROOMS
LOTS

✓**Blackwell House** 33 Mullabrack Rd, Scarva +4428 2838832752 ·
www.blackwellhouse.co.uk Joyce Brownless is a formidable hostess, and a
formidable cook. Her skills make Blackwell one of the outstanding country houses,
and staying and eating here is a sublime experience. If you want a masterclass in
NI baking, this is the place to be. Benchmark in every way.

1237
6/T8
3 ROOMS
MED.INX

The Carriage House 71 Main St, Dundrum +4428 43751635 ·
www.carriagehousedundrum.com Maureen Griffith's house is an artsy
and delightful place to stay, and the best accommodation for exploring the
region.

WHERE TO EAT

1238
6/T6
MED.INX-EXP
ATMOS

✓**Balloo House** 1 Comber Rd, Killinchy +4428 97541210 ·
www.ballooinns.com Head chef Danny Millar's cooking is amongst the best
in the N. He cooks mostly in the upstairs restaurant, where his extemporisations
with artisan ingredients can be exhilarating. Downstairs, there is simpler but no
less precise cooking in the very busy bar. Pub food noon-9/9.30pm 7 days. Upstairs
dining dinner Fri & Sat.

1239
6/T7
MED.INX

The Lobster Pot 9 The Square, Strangford, Downpatrick +44 28 44881288 ·
www.thelobsterpotstrangford.com Sarah Kilgore runs a most handsome bar
and restaurant, just metres from the ferry at Strangford. The water's edge location
means it's the perfect place to enjoy Strangford Lough mussels – one of their
signature dishes – or Kilkeel lobster, though there is a fine Shorthorn burger. They
cater for *Game of Thrones* dinners, right down to the wooden tankards, and the
menu is also notable for a fine selection of vegetarian and vegan choices. Lunch &
Dinner 7 days.

1240
6/R7
CHP

Blend & Batch 104 Newry St, Banbridge +4428 40238050
www.blendxbatch.com Good sourcing of ingredients and good coffee lifts
Marion and Peter Fairbairn's smart coffee shop far above the ordinary. It's a
welcoming room, and the salads and savoury food are all delivered with attentive
care. All day till 8pm 7 days.

1241
6/R7
MED.INX

The Vault 50 Bridge St, Banbridge +4428 40620662 ·
www.thevaultpizza.com The vault is an associate of Quail Fine Foods, just up
the town, and is home to excellent pizza cookery. It's a great, atmospheric room.
Dinner Tue-Sun.

1242
6/R7
CHP

Quails Fine Foods 13 Newry St, Banbridge +4428 40662604 ·
www.quailsfinefoods.co.uk Quails is one of the best food shops, and at the rere
of the shop there is a small cafe with good savoury cooking. Nice food to go also.
All day Mon-Sat.

1243 **The Buck's Head** 77 Main St, Dundrum +4428 43751868 · @TheBucksHeadInn
6/T8 Chef Alison Crothers and her husband, Michael, have offered excellent cooking
MED.INX in little Dundrum for many years, and are the local food heroes in the region.
TERRACE Strangford oysters; Dromara beef; Kilkeel hake are just some of the superb
ATMOS ingredients that animate Alison's creativity. Lunch & dinner 7 days.

1244 **Rostrevor Inn** 33-35 Bridge St, Rostrevor +4428 41739911 ·
6/R9 www.therostrevorinn.com Seth Linder revamped the old Crawford's bar
MED.INX to create the stylish Rostrevor Inn, adding seven simple, compact bedrooms
upstairs to create a modern coaching inn in this pretty village.The daily specials
are the dishes to go for, and do try the local Farmageddon beers, which are sheer
explosions of hops. Lots of folk music sessions. Lunch & dinner 7 days.

▉ If you're in Holywood . . .

WHERE TO STAY
1245 **Culloden Estate & Spa** Bangor Rd, Holywood +4428 90421066 ·
6/T5 www.hastingshotels.com The grand Culloden Hotel, a couple of kilometres E
105 ROOMS of Holywood, is the flagship of the Hastings Group. It's an extremely comfortable
LOTS place to stay, and the grounds are majestic, overlooking Belfast Lough.

1246 **Rayanne House** 60 Demesne Rd, Holywood +4428 90425859 ·
6/S6 www.rayannehouse.com Conor McClelland's cooking in Rayanne House has
10 ROOMS won many admirers over the years, so staying here, just up the hill from Holywood,
MED.EXP a few kilometres E of Belfast is a good bet if you don't want to go out for dinner.
A 9-course Titanic menu is Mr McClelland's signature offering.

WHERE TO EAT
1247 ✓**Noble** 27a Church Rd, Holywood +4428 90425655
6/S6 www.nobleholywood.com Saul McConnell and chef Pearson Morriss's
MED.INX restaurant offers terrific cooking in Noble, the best food that Holywood has seen in
years. They have an upstairs room, staff attired in the required Enrich & Endure
aprons, minimalist design, and ace cooking: crubeens with pickled vegetables;
salt-aged lamb with lovage gremolata; plum frangipane. Super-slick, super-
professional, and the only caveat is that getting a table can be difficult. Lunch
Thur-Sun, dinner Wed-Sun.

1248 ✓**The Bay Tree** 118 High St, Holywood +4428 90421419 ·
6/S6 www.baytreeholywood.co.uk Holywood's busiest and best-loved dining
MED.INX room is always jam-packed. A lot of eaters come for their legendary cinnamon
ATMOS buns, many more come to pack out the Friday evening dinners. The cooking is right
on target: pork casserole with apple; mushroom and sweet potato frittata. Their
motto is 'Serving the food we love to eat', but it could be 'Serving the food you love
to eat'. All day Mon-Sun, dinner Fri from 5.30pm-9pm

1249 **Dirty Duck Ale House** 3 Kinnegar Rd, Holywood +4428 90596666
6/S6 www.thedirtyduckalehouse.co.uk Mark McCrory's loughside gastropub is one
MED.INX of the busiest in the county, and they offer superb beers alongside tasty, smart
ATMOS food. Great views over Belfast Lough from the upstairs, nice cosy fire downstairs.
L Lunch & dinner 7 days.

1250 **The Coffee Yard** 102 High St, Holywood +4428 90427210 ·
6/S6 www.coffeeyard.com Queue to order at the counter from their crafted casual
CHP menu of sandwiches and home-made soup, and then sit in one of a series of
rooms, choosing a sofa, or a table, depending on how you feel. All day Mon-Sat.

1251 **Homebird Cafe** 69 High St, Holywood +4428 90427061 · @HomebirdCafe
6/S6 Good cafe cooking, strong on breakfasts and filled Belfast Baps, including their
CHP famous fish finger sandwich. Queues on Sun morning. Daytime 7 days.

Co Armagh

WHERE TO STAY

1252 ✓**Newforge House** Magheralin +4428 92611255 · www.newforgehouse.com
6/R7 John and Louise Mathers run an exemplary country house, in the little hamlet
6 ROOMS of Magheralin, close to Moira. The setting is picture-postcard-pretty, the
MEX.EXP cooking, by John, is beautifully executed, and for many people this is their
favourite country house. The gin and tonics, incidentally, are superlative, so don't
miss them.

WHERE TO EAT

1253 **4 Vicars** 4 Vicar's Hill, Armagh +4428 37527772 · www.4vicars.com
6/Q7 A handsome Georgian house on Vicar's Hill, close to the pair of cathedrals, is where
MED.EXP Gareth and Kasia Reid offer the best food in the city. Mr Reid makes the most of his
ATMOS local foods, from Kilkeel fish to Armagh Bramley apples, and with a bright, modern
room, excellent wines and keen prices, 4 Vicars is blessed. All day till 3pm Wed-Sat,
Fri dinner 6pm-8.30pm & Sun lunch.

1254 **The Moody Boar** Palace Stables, Palace Demesne Public Park, Armagh
6/Q7 +4428 37529678 · www.themoodyboar.com Sean Farnan is a most interesting
MEX.INX cook, and he does things quite differently to most chefs in The Moody Boar,
which is situated in the beautiful grounds of the Armagh Palace Demesne.
Expect the unusual, and expect to enjoy it. Breakfast Fri-Sun, lunch & dinner
Tue-Sun.

1255 **The Yellow Door** 74 Woodhouse St, Portadown +4428 38353528 ·
6/R7 www.yellowdoordeli.co.uk Simon Dougan's Yellow Door delis are rock-solid
CHP reliable destinations for tasty, modern Irish food. All day Mon-Sat. There are Yellow
Door Cafes in Market Square in Lisburn, The MAC in Belfast and the Ulster Museum.

1256 **Wine & Brine** 59 Main St, Moira +4428 92610500 · www.wineandbrine.co.uk
6/R6 The exterior of Wine & Brine gives no hint of the scale and style of Chris and Davina
MEX.EXP McGowan's slick restaurant, on the main street of pretty Moira. Mr McGowan spent
years working beside Richard Corrigan in London, so his food is as professional and
perfectly executed as you would expect. Excellent value, terrific service and great
wines. Lunch & dinner Tue-Sat & Sun lunch.

Gay Ireland the Best

On, Friday, May 22nd, 2015, Ireland became the first country in the world to legalise same-sex marriage by popular vote. All but one of the country's 43 parliamentary constituencies voted Yes in the referendum to amend the Constitution. Here are some gay friendly venues that celebrate gay culture, or regularly host LGBT events.

1257 **The George 89 Sth Gt Georges St,** Great Georges St, Dublin 2 +353 1
1/R13 6776943 · www.thegeorge.ie The George is Ireland's original gay pub, spread over two floors and in the middle of Dublin's gay nightzone between Capel St, Parliament St and Sth Gt George's St. There's a dance-tastic atmosphere here 7 days with everything from bingo to glitterbomb to sickening drag antics. The George also provides links to all kinds of LGBT support through their Facebook page. 7 days.

1258 **Mother Club** The Hub, Eustace St, Temple Bar, Dublin 2 ·
1/R13 www.motherclub.ie Describing itself as an old school club night for disco-loving gays and their friends, this underground space in Temple Bar is your Saturday night destination in Dublin to hear electronic, synth and disco. Visiting guests have included the Scissor Sisters, LCD Soundsystem and Daithi. Two thumbs up! DJs from 11pm every Saturday.

1259 **PantiBar 7-8** Capel St, Dublin 1 +353 1 8740710 · www.pantibar.com
1/R13 Owned by the Queen of Ireland, Panti Bliss, the bar is a homo activity centre with 7 days of fun. Panti herself is the stage name of Rory O'Neill, activist and Irish legend. Panti's most famous speech about homophobia was described by *Irish Times* columnist Fintan O'Toole as 'the most eloquent Irish speech in 200 years' so whilst there's wickedly fun entertainment this is also a beacon for gay rights, and Panti is a national treasure. 7 days.

1260 **The Roundy** 1 Castle St, Cork +353 21 4222022 · www.theroundy.com
3/J21 Gay-friendly pub, music venue and exhibition space, and home to vinyl institution Plugd Records. Upstairs at The Roundy is now a record and print store, a gallery, event space and cafe open four days a week. The Roundy bar also serves as a comedy club, and there are craft beers and live gigs.

1261 **Nova** 1 William St, Galway +353 91 725693 · www.novagalway.ie
4/G13 The West End in Galway is Galway's happening zone, and this LGBT friendly pub is one of its key locations. Great cocktails, DJ and drag shows at weekends.

1262 **Kremlin** 92 Donegall St, Belfast, NI +44 28 90316060 · www.kremlin-
6/S6 belfast.com Belfast has a vibrant LGBT scene, and one of the top Gay Pride parades. The leading LGBT club is Kremlin, gay owned and managed with a Soviet-inspired decor and an electric atmosphere that includes a cocktail lounge, disco bar and club arena. DJs, live acts and theme nights. 7 days.

1263 **Union Street** 8 Union St, Belfast, NI +44 28 90316060 · www.
6/S6 unionstreetbar.com Converted shoe factory, now home to glitzy bar,
TERRACE restaurant, cocktail bar and entertainment centre, featuring drag queens and
karaoke, as well as Sunday bingo.

1264 **Rainbow** 67 Botanic Ave, Belfast, NI +44 28 90237077 · www.
6/S6 rainbowbelfast.weebly.com Supperclub, venue, restaurant and cocktail bar,
this is an over-25 spot for gay and lesbian people and their friends in the heart of
Belfast's university quarter.

Bow Lane www.bowlane.ie Dublin Don't miss their famous Drag Brunch.
Report: 361/BEST COCKTAILS.
The Bodega Cork Report: 657/CRACKING CORK PUBS.
Roisin Dubh Galway Report: 813/BEST MUSIC PUBS.
Ma Murphy's Bantry Report: 1443/COUNTRY BARS.

the
Best
Particular Places
to Stay

Superlative Country House Hotels

1265
4/G14
21 ROOMS
LOTS
MAR-OCT
LLL

✓ ✓ ✓ **Gregans Castle Hotel** Corkscrew Hill Rd, Ballyvaughan, Co Clare +353 65 7077005 · www.gregans.ie For many food lovers, Gregans Castle, on the winding Corkscrew Hill in the heart of the Burren, offers the finest country house experience in Ireland. Simon and Freddie Haden's house is a tone poem of elegant design, and a statement of feng shui: everything is exactly where it needs to be in order to construct a feeling of idyllic repose.
EAT in Gregans Castle Restaurant and The Corkscrew Bar where David Hurley's cooking is amongst the best in Ireland. Complex, transformatory and yet ultimately soulful food is rendered with patient diligence. If you can't get into the restaurant, the bar food is smashing.

1266
3/K20
6 ROOMS AND
GLAMPING
EXP
ATMOS

✓ ✓ **Ballyvolane House** Castlelyons, Co Cork +353 25 36349 · www.ballyvolanehouse.ie Justin and Jenny Green have shown in Ballyvolane House how the second generation of a family can utterly transform the country house experience. Before taking over from Justin's parents, the pair worked in top-notch international hotels, and they have brought that experience and polish back to Ballyvolane, in the process creating one of the best country houses, one of the best wedding venues, and one of the best glamping venues. World class, and don't miss their own Bertha's Revenge gin, made using milk whey.

1267
3/K21
LOTS
ATMOS

✓ ✓ **Ballymaloe House** Shanagarry, Co Cork +353 21 4652531 · www.ballymaloe.ie Myrtle Allen created both the modern Irish food revolution, and the country house hotel concept, when she opened the doors of Ballymaloe House in 1964. The house sits at the centre of a working farm, surrounded by landscaped lawns and vegetable beds and a number of related businesses, including the Ballymaloe shop and café, the Golden Bean coffee roastery and The Grainstore, which hosts conferences, concerts and weddings. Accommodation is in the house itself and a number of adjacent buildings in the courtyards. Despite its international reputation, Ballymaloe remains a simple, elegant and understated destination: no bells and whistles, no lifts, no pomposity.
EAT at the Yeats Room Restaurant. If you want to be blown away by the flavour of a potato, or the taste of braised cabbage, or the sweetness of a fillet of fish, then you are in the right place: Ballymaloe offers flavours that are elemental and ancient. Breakfast, incidentally, can be even better, especially in autumn when the fruits are harvested. In the Ballymaloe Cafe at the End of the Shop, there is scrumptious baking: we have never forgotten a slice of chocolate and raspberry tart that we enjoyed here years ago, a rare taste of utter perfection.

1268
3/C19
12 ROOMS
MED.EXP
L

✓ **Castlewood** The Wood, Dingle, Co Kerry +353 66 9152788 www.castlewooddingle.com Castlewood House is one of the handful of Irish addresses that feature amongst the best international destinations in the world. To understand why, just look at their breakfast table, for example: there isn't a better breakfast cooked and served anywhere in the world. The housekeeping never dips below a standard of daunting meticulousness. And, most importantly, the welcome from Helen and Brian Heaton is always the same: spontaneous, generous, modest, sincere, welcoming. Being out of town, down near the distillery, also means you get a great night's sleep when Dingle (Daingean Uí Chúis) is in party mode.

1269
2/L19
7 ROOMS
EXP-LOTS

✓ **The Old Convent** Mount Anglesby, Clogheen, Co Tipperary +353 52 7465565 · www.theoldconvent.ie An old convent sounds like an austere, self-denying place to stay, yet Dermot Gannon's 8-course Tipperary tasting menus are amongst the most bacchanalian feasts cooked in Ireland. What's more, the

NO KIDS
L
sleek interior of the house is colourful and sybaritic. It's one hell of a double act, and explains why this is one of the most treasured destinations in the country. No one cooks the foods of the county better than Mr Gannon.

1270
2/L21
39 ROOMS
LOTS
TERRACE
LLL
✓ **Cliff House Hotel** Middle Rd, Ardmore, Co Waterford +353 24 87800 · www.cliffhousehotel.ie Adriaan Bartels is one of the finest hotel managers in the country and under his direction the striking, modernist Cliff House – it is perched on a cliff face, looking over Ardmore Bay – maintains sky-high standards. **EAT** Head chef Martin Kajuiter has headed the kitchen since the hotel opened, and his modern European cuisine perfectly echoes the style of the hotel. Less challenging, but just as enjoyable, is the cooking in the hotel bar, which attracts both guests and locals.

1271
6/M3
32 ROOMS
LOTS
LL
ATMOS
✓ **Rathmullan House** Rathmullan, Co Donegal +353 74 9158188 · www.rathmullanhouse.com For more than 50 years, the Wheeler family have welcomed guests to their gorgeous country house, on the shores of Lough Swilly. Their achievement is immense, yet they never rest on their laurels, and are always occupied with new developments. **EAT** There is fine cooking in the hotel's Cook & Gardener Restaurant, but their great success in recent years has been The Tap Room, where world-class pizzas pair with the craft beers of the local Kinnegar Brewery to dazzling effect.

1272
3/C19
16 ROOMS
MED.INX
L
Heatons Guesthouse The Wood, Dingle, Co Kerry +353 66 9152288 www.heatonsdingle.com Cameron, Nuala and David Heaton seem able to read their guests' minds, so you will have scarcely made a request for something or other before they have it sorted. Their hospitality is only mighty, and the water's edge location, in The Wood, down near the Dingle Distillery, is perfect.

1273
3/E22
4 SUITES
EXP
MAR-OCT
TERRACE
Blairscove House & Restaurant Durrus, Co Cork +353 27 61127 · www.blairscove.ie Arriving at Blairscove House, just outside the little village of Durrus, you drive down the winding track to the house, then look out over beautiful Dunmanus Bay from the side of the house, to complete one of the most magical moments in Irish journeying. Stepping into the elegant, vaulted dining room with its centrepiece buffet table, its wood fire and its piano, is yet another magical moment. All this before the gutsy, tasty cooking raises the crescendo of voices to a pitch. Here is a house which is on a roll, powered by youthful energy. Dinner Tue-Sat.

1274
2/N17
4 ROOMS
EXP
MAR-NOV
TERRACE
Kilgraney Country House Bagenalstown, Co Carlow +353 59 9775283 · www.kilgraneyhouse.com There is nowhere else quite like Kilgraney House. It has an air of glamour and an aesthetic which are unique. It has a style which, over the course of 25 years – Bryan Leech and Martin Marley first opened their doors to guests way back in 1994 – has not aged, but which has simply matured, the sign of truly great design. In addition to the food and the aesthetic, Bryan and Martin are hosts who try to 'be true to what we set out to deliver back in 1994'. They are true to that vision, and their dedication explains why people return to Kilgraney House time, after time.

1275
3/H18
17 ROOMS
EXP
ATMOS
The Mustard Seed Echo Lodge, Ballingarry, Co Limerick +353 69 68508 · www.mustardseed.ie John Edward Joyce has taken over the day-to-day running of this fine manor house, on the edge of Ballingarry village, following three decades when Daniel Mullane powered Echo Lodge to a preeminent place in Irish hospitality. The house is quirky, colourful, elegant and Mr Joyce is sincerely hospitable. It's a special place.

EAT at the Mustard Seed Restaurant. The cooking, both at dinner and breakfast, is better than it has ever been, powered by a welter of ingredients grown in the gardens at the rere of the house. Don't miss their own black pudding at breakfast.

1276 **Tankardstown** Rathkenny, Slane, Co Meath +353 41 9824621 ·
1/Q11
14 ROOMS
EXP

www.tankardstown.ie The Conroy family's posh, meticulously maintained and very grand country house offers a tea rooms, a cellar restaurant, and their luxurious Brabazon restaurant, where chef Adrian Cassidy brings modernist kitchen techniques to really ace ingredients.The glamour of the house and gardens makes Tankardstown a very popular wedding venue. A simpler destination is their sister hotel, the nearby Conyngham Arms Hotel - Report: 1292/FAMILY FRIENDLY.

1277 **Coopershill House** Riverstown, Co Sligo +353 71 9165108 ·
5/J8
8 ROOMS
LOTS
APR–OCT
ATMOS

www.coopershill.com It's thrilling to see a grand country house re-animated by a new generation, and Simon O'Hara and Christina McCauley are propelling the pristine Coopershill, in east Co Sligo, to a new level of achievement, and acclaim, the seventh generation of the family to work here. Every aspect of this couple's endeavour – cooking, design, development – articulates a straining for the just-right note of comfort and welcome.

1278 **Hilton Park** Clones, Co Monaghan +353 47 56007 · www.hiltonpark.ie
1/N8
6 ROOMS
LOTS

Tha Madden family's enormous mansion dates back as far as 1734, and the house is jam-packed with memorabilia stretching back through the centuries. Fred and Joanna Madden are the ninth generation to welcome guests and, thanks to Fred's training as a chef – he worked at Kensington Place with Rowley Leigh – the standard of cooking is far above normal country house fare, and makes the most of the produce from their elegant gardens.

1279 **Bantry House** Bantry, Co Cork +353 27 50047 · www.bantryhouse.com
3/E22
APR–OCT
LL

The views from the upper lawns of Bantry House, out over Bantry Bay and across to Whiddy Island, are spellbinding. The house is one of the grandest Irish houses, and particularly noted for its gardens – and the 100 steps up to the summit! Today, it's managed by Sophie Shellswell-White, who oversees the weddings and the B&B guests who occupy the six rooms of the east wing. Guests have the use of the house library, and the billiards room.

1280 **Castle Leslie** Glaslough, Co Monaghan +353 47 88100 · www.castleleslie.com
1/P7
49 ROOMS
PLUS MEWS &
COTTAGES
LOTS

Sammy Leslie's huge house is surrounded by 1,000 acres and a magnificent lake. The architecture is baronial, the scale is epic, and includes several ghosts. It's nice and unpretentious, with accommodation provided in the house itself, in the restored Lodge, which has 29 rooms and is sited at the entrance to the estate, and in the Mews and the Village Cottages. Their equestrian centre is particularly popular, and offers a water complex and more than 300 cross country jumps, along with an indoor arena.

1281 **Ghan House** Carlingford, Co Louth +353 42 9373682 · www.ghanhouse.com
1/R9
12 ROOMS
MED.EXP

Paul Carroll's small country house, on the outskirts of the medieval village of Carlingford, is one of those destinations that gets better with each year. Mr Carroll is a true professional, and his optimism and drive powers an excellent team, the sort of folk who simply can't do enough for you. A charming getaway, and very popular with Northerners who nip across the border.
EAT Fine, gutsy country cooking is centred on pristine local ingredients – Mourne lamb; Carnbrooke beef; Carlingford crab – and value for money is exceptional. Dinner and Sun Lunch.

1282 **Roundwood House** Mountrath, Co Laois +353 57 8732120 ·
1/M15   www.roundwoodhouse.com Hannah and Paddy Flynn have taken charge of
10 ROOMS   Hannah's family home, an elegant, nicely scuffed Arcadian treasure, and Paddy's
EXP   good country cooking has been attracting lots of attention – trout eclairs, Laois
DF   lamb with leeks. If you have a big group, then this is one of the best places to
ATMOS   convene a house party. Two self-contained cottages in the grounds mean you can
bring the pets if you wish, and you can also book dinner.

1283 **Richmond House** Cappoquin, Co Waterford +353 58 54278 ·
2/L20   www.richmondhouse.net Paul and Claire Deevy are masters at creating an
10 ROOMS   elemental sense of welcome and friendship in their lovely country house, just
MED.INX   outside Cappoquin. There is the blazing fire, the tea and scones and cakes when
you arrive, and the promise of a beautiful dinner cooked by Mr Deevy and served by
gracious ladies in the ageless dining room. Mrs Deevy is one of the most gracious
hosts, and runs the house with calmness and grace.

1284 **Seaview House Hotel** Ballylickey, Co Cork +353 27 50073 ·
3/F22   www.seaviewhousehotel.com A new chapter has begun in Seaview House,
25 ROOMS   one of W Cork's defining destinations. Ronan O'Sullivan has taken up the reins,
EXP   succeeding his aunt, Kathleen, who brought the hotel to prominence as a singular
place to stay and eat. Part of the secret of Seaview is that it feels more like a
country house than an hotel, yet it has hotel standards of service, cooking and
attention to detail.
EAT W Cork locals eat here, always a good sign for a hotel restaurant. We love the
quaint, almost domestic style of the rooms, and the generous country cooking.

1285 **Longueville House** Mallow, Co Cork +353 22 47156 ·
3/H20   www.longuevillehouse.ie William and Aisling O'Callaghan's huge family home
26 ROOMS   is like a big, pink birthday cake that sits high on the hill, overlooking the original
LOTS   O'Callaghan castle. It's a delight to stay here, thanks to Aisling's hospitality, and it's
a house that makes you feel special everytime.
EAT The Presidents' Restaurant: Austere portraits of Ireland's various Presidents
glare down at you from the walls of the Presidents' Restaurant, setting a sombre
tone which is at odds with the panache and joie de vivre of William O'Callaghan's
cooking. He is one of the most masterly country cooks, with capacious technique,
and superb garden ingredients deliver a tumult of flavours.

1286 **Newport House** 7 Main St, Newport, Co Mayo +353 98 41222 ·
5/E10   www.newporthouse.ie The tiny back bar in Newport House is one of our
14 ROOMS   favourite places to enjoy a drink, but its charm is just one element of Kieran
LOTS   Thompson's resplendent Georgian mansion. The house is right on the edge of
MAR-OCT   the single street of Newport village and, whilst its original reputation was focused
on catering for fishing parties in search of a salmon or a sea trout, the house has
always been home to excellent cooking, whilst the wine list is a treasure trove of
great bottles.

✓ **Newforge House** Magheralin Report: 1252/NI

Marlagh Lodge Ballymena Report: 1221/NI

Family Friendly Hotels

1287   **Westin Hotel** College Green, Westmoreland St, Dublin 2 +353 1 6451000
1/R13   · www.thewestindublin.com Even though it's a slick, international hotel with
172 ROOMS   a heart-of-the-city location, the Westin wisely has lots of offers for the younger
LOTS   traveller, including an in-room glamping gig, where they set up a tent in the
parents' room, with an airbed, a torch and a book butler string bag. Ultra cool, and
the kids' menus are excellent.

1288   **Glenlo Abbey** Kentfield Bushy Park, Galway +353 91 519600 ·
4/G13   www.glenloabbeyhotel.ie Two miles outside Galway on the N59, the Glenlo
172 ROOMS   is best known for offering dining in two former Orient Express train carriages, an
LOTS   experience that is pretty awesome for the kids. Like their sister property in Dublin,
the Westin, they can also organise glamping for the kids in your room.

1289   **Dingle Skellig Hotel** Dingle, Co Kerry +353 66 9150200 ·
3/C19   www.dingleskellig.com We have friends with large families who take their kids
113 ROOMS   down to the Dingle Skellig Hotel year after year. The kids get to enjoy the creche,
EXP   the children's dinners, and the Kids Club, whilst the parents can grab a moment to
LL   themselves. Excellent staff are the bedrock of a Kerry institution, and the seaside
location offers some of the finest views of Dingle Bay.

1290   **Clifden Station House Hotel** Clifden, Co Galway +353 95 21699 ·
5/E10   www.clifdenstationhouse.com The bar and restaurant of the Station House
78 ROOMS   Hotel, on the outskirts of pretty Clifden, is actually the old station master's house,
MED.INX   and the original railway platform of the Galway-Clifden railway line is a prominent
feature. The hotel offers a Railways Children's Club during the summer holidays
and school breaks, with a supervised swim club, and there is also a special kids' tea.

1291   **Sneem Hotel** Goldens Cove, Sneem, Co Kerry +353 64 6675100 ·
3/D21   www.sneemhotel.com The hotel's Fun4Kids Club operates during school
28 ROOMS   holidays and will keep the kids busy during the evenings with movie nights and lots
MED.EXP   of play activities. For older kids, the sea and kayaking trips on Kenmare Bay are just
TERRACE   the ticket, whilst they also offer motorised kayak trips down the Sneem River to
DF LL   Sneem harbour.

1292   **Conyngham Arms Hotel** Slane, Co Meath +353 41 9884444 ·
1/Q11   www.conynghamarms.ie This handsome coaching inn in pretty Slane village
15 ROOMS   offers a Tayto Park Adventure Package for 2 nights, for 2 adults and 2 kids. The
MED.INX   youngsters can wear themselves out on the swings and slides, and then the
parents can get to enjoy a quiet dinner. Sister hotel to Tankardstown, also in Slane.
Report: 1276/COUNTRY HOUSES.

1293   **The Gleneagle Hotel** Muckross Rd, Killarney, Co Kerry
3/E20   +353 64 663600 · www.gleneaglehotel.com This relaxed and friendly family-
244 ROOMS   run hotel, sister to the Brehon Hotel (1336/SPAS) is loved by all the generations for
MED.INX   its laid back style and unpretentious atmosphere. Part of the complex that houses
Killarney's INEC Convention Centre, kids entertainment includes kids' club, soft
play area, entertainment spaces and pool-side birthday parties at the Aquila Club

in their Leisure Centre. The field opposite will often give grazing to large numbers of wild deer. Family rooms and apartments complete the package.

1294   **Radisson Blu Hotel & Spa**   Ditchley House, Cork +353 21 429700 ·
3/J21   www.radissonblu.com/Cork The larger family rooms in the Radisson Blu can
126 ROOMS   sleep 2 adults and up to 4 kids, and there is a kids' club during school holidays. There
MED.INX   is a playground, and special swimming hours for the youngsters lets them splash to
their heart's content. Even better is the fact that the Fota Wildlife Park, a 75-acre site
with birds and mammals from all across the globe, is just 10 minutes away.

1295   **Ferrycarrig Hotel**   Ferrycarrig, Co Wexford +353 53 9120999 ·
2/R18   www.ferrycarrighotel.ie Five kms outside the town, overlooking the Slaney
102 ROOMS   Estuary, the Ferrycarrig is a very popular hotel with the local community, thanks
MED.EXP   in part to a fine pool and leisure centre. Lots of kids during the summer season,
AYR   but they do keep a section of Reed's Restaurant adult only. Lots of good local
ingredients on tasty menus and staff are professional and unpretentious.

✓ ✓ ✓ **Kelly's Resort**   Co Wexford Many years ago we were staying in
Kelly's Hotel and got chatting to a 16-year-old dude from NI. The
young man had stayed in Kelly's Hotel 16 times: every year of his life! For many
families, an annual visit to this seaside getaway is simply taken for granted, and
they book for the next year when they are departing. Top-class facilities for kids
who are well looked after; luxury for the parents. Don't miss the sandcastle
competition. Report: 961/THE SOUTH EAST.

Cork International Airport Hotel   Co Cork Thanks to their Cloud 9 cinema –
it's exactly like an aeroplane interior – and a kids' club, this superbly run hotel is
a good choice for kids, who also enjoy the friendly cooking. Family rooms are
large and colourful. Report: 592/CORK HOTELS.

The Best Hostels

1296
4/G13
MED.INX

✓ **The Nest Boutique Hostel** 108 Upr Salthill, Galway +353 91 450944 ·
www.thenestaccommodation.com The Nest is a hostel, but it's known by
locals as a "Poshtel", which gives you a clue as to the stylish decor and witty and
artistic style that owner Keith Kissane has gifted to this fine old house, out in Salthill,
close to the sea. The aesthetic value of the Nest is exceptionally chic, being modern,
classic, simplistic and clean. The lobby is the epicentre of the house, where guests
enjoy a very sophisticated breakfast, with local fresh breads, scones and little pots of
muesli to be enjoyed with yogurt.

1297
1/R13
MED.INX

Generator Hostel Smithfield Square, Dublin 7 + 353 1 9010222 ·
www.generatorhostels.com This stylish, international chain of hostels is
extremely well managed by enthusiastic staff, and the fact that it was formerly a
hotel means that it looks and feels pretty luxurious for a hostel. They offer every
sort of accommodation: up to ten-bed dorms, female-only dorms, there is a big,
capacious cinema room downstairs, laundry facilities, and luggage storage means
you can park the backpack whilst you explore the city. Terrific location, of course,
but don't imagine that it's cheap.

1298
1/R13
CHP-MED.INX

Isaacs Hostel 2-5 Frenchmans Lane, Dublin 1 +353 1 8556215 · www.isaacs.ie
Close to both Connolly train station – you can hear the trains! – and the Busaras
bus depot, Isaacs has been a backpackers' magnet for decades. It's a handsome
old 19thC wine store, with accommodation ranging from 8-bed dorms to private
rooms, with prices descending depending on how private you want to be. Free
sauna, good laundry facilities, friendly staff.

1299
4/D12
CHP-MED.INX
ATMOS

Letterfrack Lodge Letterfrack, Co Galway +353 95 41222 ·
www.letterfracklodge.com Whilst the creative and elegant cooking from Mike
and his team is the big draw at The Lodge, they also offer hostel accommodation:
the house has three kitchens and the rooms are divided into double, triple, dorm
and family, and there are also sitting rooms and a laundry room. But be sure not
to miss the excellent cooking in their funky restaurant, which showcases fantastic
local ingredients. Great service in what is the most cosmopolitan room in the W.

1300
4/C11
EASTER-OCT
NO PETS
MED.INX
LL

Inishbofin Island Hostel Inishbofin, Co Galway +353 95 45855 ·
www.inishbofin-hostel.ie The hostel is a converted farmhouse, and still has the
traditional stove from way back when. There are dorms, family rooms and private
rooms, as well as camping, and there's a neat conservatory with great views. The
hostel is about 700 metres from the pier after you disembark following the 30
minute ferry trip from Cleggan Pier.

1301
4/G13
CHP-MED.INX

Kinlay Hostel Eyre Sq, Galway +353 91 565244 · www.kinlaygalway.ie
Located just around the corner from Eyre Square and the bus station, on Merchant
Rd, Kinlay had a big refurb in early 2017, so the dining and public areas here are
pretty glam. Good ensuite rooms and all manner of dorms, free wi-fi and iMacs,
and check out that old telephone booth.

1302   **Kinlay House**   Bob & Joan's Walk, Shandon, Cork +353 21 4508966 · www.
3/J21   **kinlayhousecork** How could you not love a hostel situated on 'Bob and Joan's
190 BEDS   walk', which is where you will find the Kinlay, in the pretty and atmospheric
MED.INX   Shandon district, north of the River Lee. They have everything from multi-bed
dorms to family rooms, and even promise that 'local rock stars work at the
reception.' Cork has rock stars? Who knew!

1303   **Glendalough International Hostel**   The Lodge, Glendalough, Co Wicklow
1/R15   +353 404 45342 · www.anoige.ie/hostels A chalet-style house, once known as
MED.INX   Swiss Cottage, the GIH offers all en suite rooms, and the setting, in a wooded valley
in one of the most beautiful parts of the county, is just peachy.

1304   **Kilfenora Hostel**   Main St, Kilfenora, Co Clare +353 65 7088908 · www.
4/F15   **kilfenorahostel.com** The hostel is right next door to Vaughan's Pub, which has a
9 ROOMS   fine reputation for good Irish cooking – and traditional music sessions – so you are
MED.INX   sorted for dining, drinking and dancing if staying in Kilfenora. Breakfast and linen
included, en suite rooms, good kitchen facilities.

1305   **Ballyhoura Hostel**   West End, Kilfinane, Co Limerick · www.
3/J18   **ballyhourahostel.ie** There is a lot of care taken by owners Seamus and Theresa
7 ROOMS   to make sure you are comfortable in this supremely welcoming lodgings. From
MED.INX   the hand-made wooden furniture to the sauna, to the hotel-standard mattresses,
the hostel is a good base for those enjoying mountain biking, horse riding or
geocaching; all pursuits available in the zone.

1306   **Belfast International Youth Hostel**   22 Donegall Rd, Belfast, NI +44 28
6/S6   90315435 · www.hini.org.uk With a city centre location – on the grimy Donegall
54 ROOMS   Rd – the BIYH offers good value in simple rooms and dorms. They have strict
CHP-MED.INX   rules on group bookings and alcohol, and the Causeway Café is handy for cheap
breakfasts and lunch. Some street noise, as you would expect.

Pure Magic At The Lodge Achill Island, Co Mayo Report: 2022/THE ISLANDS
Island Accommodation & Discovery Sherkin Island, Co Cork
Report: 1991/THE ISLANDS
Go Explore Hostel Clare Island, Co Mayo Report: 2016/THE ISLANDS

The Best Roadside, Seaside & Countryside Inns

1307
4/F15
14 ROOMS
MED.INX
MAR-OCT

✓✓ **Wild Honey Inn** Kincora Road, Lisdoonvarna, Co Clare +353 65 7074300 · www.wildhoneyinn.com Aidan and Kate's Wild Honey is the idyllic archetype of the country inn. The bar is charming, the cooking is serious but fun, the rooms are simple and inexpensive. Put it all together in an old Victorian house a mile outside Lisdoonvarna, and you have a true classic: one of the best loved places on the W coast. Mr McGrath's cooking works with ruddy cuts, like lamb neck fillet, or pork cheek, and he brings a lightness of touch that is revelatory – he seems to conduct his ingredients every bit as much as he cooks them. Dinner Tue-Sat.

1308
3/B21
17 ROOMS
MED.EXP
LL

The Moorings Portamagee, Co Kerry +353 66 9477108 · www.moorings.ie You will have to wade your way through the phalanxes of *Star Wars* fans, now that the world knows all about the fact that the crew of the movie ate and drank in Gerard and Patricia Kennedy's family bar and B&B. 'Rich with characters, music, set dancing and great food' was how *The Irish Times* summed up this charming destination in the centre of Portmagee. Noel Dennehy's cooking is excellent, the sort of simple, tasty cooking you want in a coastal bar.

1309
3/E17
10 ROOMS
MED.INX
MAR-OCT

McMunn's Strandhill Rd, Ballybunion, Co Kerry +353 68 28845 · www.mcmunns.com Greg and Una McMunn have been doing the good thing in their bar and restaurant with rooms in little Ballybunion for more than a decade. The cooking is straight-ahead tasty – oysters from the tank; seared scallops with Athea black pudding; Hereford beef sirloin; lobster thermidor. Open for weekends only pre-Christmas and off season.

1310
4/F15
7 ROOMS
MED.EXP
NO KIDS

Vaughan's Anchor Inn Main St, Liscannor, Co Clare +353 65 7081548 · www.vaughans.ie Most people travel to Vaughan's to enjoy Denis Vaughan's ambitious, cheffy food, but do note that they also offer three ensuite rooms, including a family room, above the restaurant and bar for guests. The cooking is pretty mighty: there aren't too many Irish pubs where you can enjoy lobster with foie gras, or 21-day chateaubriand. Lunch & dinner Mon-Sun.

1311
4/E16
6 ROOMS
MED.INX

Morrissey's Bar & Restaurant Doonbeg, Co Clare +353 65 905 5304 · www.morrisseysdoonbeg.com There are half a dozen clean and comfortable rooms in this classic Irish village pub, on the main street in Doonbeg. You can't book a table in Hugh Morrissey's very popular bar and restaurant, so if you are planning a trip in high season, then go early at 6 o'clock, or late. The cooking is very good – direct, tasty and suitable for all ages – and when the kids have finished they can scamper around the gardens at the river's edge. Open for dinner Wed-Sun & Sun lunch.

1312
2/L17
67 ROOMS
EXP

The Horse & Jockey Horse & Jockey, Co Tipperary +353 504 44192 · www.horseandjockeyhotel.com Always jammers, despite the fact that it was bypassed a decade ago by the main Dublin-Cork road. No matter: everyone still meets up here, eats here, and stays here. Quite what the attraction is, we're not sure, but H&J has to be one of the busiest places in the Midlands.

1313   **Langton's House Hotel**   69 John St, Kilkenny, Co Kilkenny +353 56 7765133 ·
2/N17   www.langtons.ie The Langton family's hotel is a legendary Kilkenny destination
34 ROOMS   The rooms are set up above a labyrinth of bars and dining rooms, and they are
MED.EXP   spacious and comfortable, although street noise can be an issue if you are staying at
the John St side of the hotel. Good safe car parking at the rere. Make sure to check
out the retro Bridie's Bar: it's our favourite of their portfolio of drinking places.

1314   **Weir's Bar and Restaurant**   Multyfarnham, Co Westmeath +353 44 9371111
1/N11   · weirsmultyfarnham.ie Pat and Una prepare fine food and they have been
MED.EXP   serving choice, hearty cooking for more than a decade now, making their bar and
ATMOS   restaurant the star of little Multyfarnham. It's a short detour off the N4, between
Loughs Owel and Derravaragh, and it's worth the detour because the bar is a real
country classic, with a wild energy at weekends. Bar open 7 days, Restaurant open
Wed-Sun, lunch & dinner.

1315   **Ashe's Bar**   Main St, Dingle, Co Kerry +353 66 9150989 · www.ashesbar.ie
3/C19   Ashe's is one of the classic Dingle (Daingean Uí Chúis) pubs, and offers excellent
3 ROOMS   seafood cooking in their restaurant. There are three rooms upstairs – two doubles
MED.EXP   and a twin – and the location on Main St couldn't be better. Lunch & dinner Mon-
ATMOS   Sun during the season. Closed for annual holiday mid Nov-mid-Dec and 3 weeks
in Jan.

1316   **The Cuan**   6 The Square, Strangford Village, Co Down, NI +44 28 44881222
6/T7   · www.thecuan.com Peter McErlean's fine seasonal and seafood cookery has
9 ROOMS   always been the big attraction in Strangford's pretty Cuan Inn. But with nine
MED.INX   comfortable but simple rooms upstairs in the Inn, it's worthwhile making a booking
and making a big night of it, and The Cuan also offers a great base for touring this
beautiful region. *Game of Thrones* fans will, of course, be on the hunt for one of the
10 GoT carved doors. Just off the A25 and overlooking Strangford Lough.

The Best Restaurants with Rooms

1317
1/N9
6 ROOMS
MED.EXP

✓ **The Olde Post Inn** Cloverhill, Co Cavan +353 47 55555 ·
www.theoldepostinn.com The old, red-bricked post office building in little
Cloverhill has been steadily added to by Gearoid and Tara Lynch, so in addition to
the rooms there is a comfortable conservatory for pre-dinner drinks. It's a cosy
house, and the hospitality is real and sincere.
EAT Discovering that he was coeliac gifted Gearoid Lynch with a new blast of energy,
and this dynamism is reflected in his food, which is amongst the most elegantly
crafted cooking in Ireland. His ability to coax various textures from his ingredients is
superlative, and this is one of the best restaurants along the Borderlands.

1318
3/C21
5 ROOMS
EXP
L

QC's Caherciveen, Co Kerry +353 66 9472244 · www.qcbar.com With five
stylish new suites added in 2016, Kate and Andrew Cooke's QC's is a Ring of Kerry
dynamo, a place for enjoying creative fish cooking, and blissful comfort in the
most stylish rooms on the Ring. One of them even has its own Pac-Man arcade
machine! Breakfast is taken in the room – fruits and yogurts and smoked salmon
in the fridge, fresh bakes delivered and hung on the door, Nespresso machine. The
cooking in the restaurant is rock steady and has a Spanish swerve which perfectly
utilises the freshest seafood. It's a great, tavern-like room, always filled with
energy, and happy people enjoying happy food.

1319
2/N17
13 ROOMS
MED.EXP
ATMOS

Zuni Restaurant & Boutique Hotel 26 Patrick St, Kilkenny +353 56
7723999 · www.zuni.ie Zuni is a definition of class; the monochrome modernist
bedrooms are intimate spaces. Breakfast is simple and succeeds because of using
quality ingredients. The restaurant is a chic and stylish room that likes to be
funky and to get as much fun on the plate as possible. Excellent value, and one
of the city's best rooms. Good cocktails also in the smart bar at the front of the
townhouse.

1320
3/F23
10 ROOMS
MED.INX
DF

Rolf's Country House Baltimore, Co Cork +353 28 20289 ·
www.rolfscountryhouse.com Johannes and Frederike have a characterful
restaurant and splendid rooms in this lively and unpretentious hostelry, which
has been a staple of Baltimore for decades, ever since the Haffner family opened
in 1979. The place has changed much over the years, but it has always been
characterful and fun, and the good cooking by Johannes brings in the W Cork locals
as well as summertime visitors to Baltimore. Dogs allowed in their self-catering
holiday cottages, which sleep 4-5 people.

1321
4/F15
6 ROOMS &
SUITES
MED.INX
APR-NOV
DF

Roadford House Doolin, Co Clare +353 65 7075050 ·
www.roadfordrestaurant.com In the centre of always-bustling Doolin village,
Frank and Marian Sheedy bring professional polish to the business of running a
restaurant with rooms. Accommodation includes a two-bedroom suite and a two-
bedroom apartment, and both are pet friendly. Mr Sheedy is an excellent cook, and
particularly renowned for his desserts, which are artful masterworks, so don't even
think of skipping pudding. Delicious breakfasts the next morning will set you on
your way in style.

1322 **The Courthouse Restaurant** Main St, Kinlough, Co Leitrim
5/K7 +353 71 9842391 · www.thecourthouserest.com Piero Melis has been making
MED.INX pretty little Kinlough into a slice of Sardinia for more than 20 years, cooking curious
and surprising dishes that showcase the style of a truly individual chef. Wonderful
Sardinian wines help you believe you are somewhere out in the middle of the
Mediterranean Sea. Dinner Wed-Sun. Weekends only during winter. There are three
small rooms available for rent over the restaurant.

1323 **The Mill** Dunfanaghy, Co Donegal +353 74 9136985 ·
6/L3 www.themillrestaurant.com Beautiful rooms upstairs in The Mill have epic
7 ROOMS views of New Lake, which is immediately adjacent to the house. In the restaurant,
EXP Derek Alcorn keeps it local: his brother, Thomas, brings in the lamb and beef; his
LL nephew, Richard, is responsible for the kid meat; Ivan McElhinny catches the fish
and shellfish; and Stephen Kerr does the butchering. This rock-steady supply team
allows Mr Alcorn to weave his confident culinary signature right through the dinner
menus, and the effect is simple deliciousness. Great value.

1324 **Danny Minnie's** Annagry, The Rosses, Co Donegal +353 74 9548201 ·
6/J4 www.dannyminnies.ie The well-appointed rooms, with fine old brass, and
5 ROOMS four-poster beds, make for luxurious lodging. The O'Donnell family's restaurant
MED.EXP with rooms is one of the longest established restaurants and bars in Co Donegal,
with a history stretching back over many generations. The dining room is grand
and ceremonial, a place to enjoy Brian O'Donnell's cooking in classic dishes like
Silverhill duck with cassis sauce, or monkfish with crab bisque sauce. Dinner Mon-
Sun & Sun Lunch.

1325 **Cullinan's Restaurant & Guesthouse** Doolin, Co Clare +353 65 7074183 ·
4/F15 www.cullinansdoolin.com James and Carol Cullinan's restaurant with rooms in
MED.INX the centre of Doolin offers good cooking, comfortable rooms, and good breakfasts
MAR-NOV will set you up for that promising day ahead. Dinner Mon-Sat. Restaurant closes
Wed & Sun evenings.

✓✓**The Tannery** Co Waterford Report: 940/THE SOUTH EAST.

Aldridge Lodge Co Wexford Report: 963/THE SOUTH EAST.

Great Escapes

1326
4/D11
70 ROOMS
MED.EXP
MAR-NOV
DF
LL

✓ **Renvyle House Hotel** Renvyle, Co Galway +353 95 43511 ·
www.renvyle.com You might call them a pair of veterans, but when you
watch Tim O'Sullivan and Ronnie Counihan go about their work in the confines of
Renvyle House, you see two guys who skip about with the energy of eternal youth.
They bring a virtuosity to the cooking, and to the art of hospitality, and it is gilded
with a sprezzatura confidence that means they make it all look easy. You turn up
here, at the edge of the world, and you tune out and lose yourself in great food,
good times, and serene comfort, thanks to a pair of master practitioners.

1327
1/M14
20 ROOMS
LOTS

Ballyfin Demesne Ballyfin, Co Laois +353 5787 55866 · www.ballyfin.com
Owned by American billionaires Fred and Kay Krehbiel, who have lavished a small
fortune on the house, Ballyfin is characterised by a superb team of staff, and by
extraordinary prices: you could blow the cost of an entire holiday here in just 24
hours. If you have the money, then it won't matter that an all-inclusive stay here is
probably the most expensive in the country. But, everything is extremely well done,
and the service is simply world class.

1328
3/D20
18 ROOMS
EXP
LL

Ard na Sidhe Caragh Lake, Killorglin, Co Kerry +353 66 9769105 ·
www.ardnasidhe.com Sister hotel to the well-known Europe and Dunloe
hotels, Ard na Sidhe is a most gorgeous Arts & Crafts building which has been
meticulously restored by the Liebherr family. It operates a fairly short season,
opening from May until October, and this is a dream-like destination, on the edge
of Caragh Lake. There are 18 rooms, with ten in the main house and eight in the
garden house, and the attention to detail lavished on the house is supreme: every
little thing is magic.

1329
1/L12
29 ROOMS
EXP
L

Wineport Lodge Glasson, Co Westmeath +353 90 6439010 ·
www.wineport.ie Nestling on the shore of Lough Ree, on the edge of Glasson
village, just a short journey from Athlone town, this was one of the first destinations
to create a culinary identity for the Irish Midlands. An elemental, eco setting and
elegant, luxe rooms provide a great getaway for frazzled city dwellers – you can get
here from Dublin and Galway in about an hour. Good cooking completes the picture
of one of the best escapes. Good wines and craft beers on a keenly-priced list.

1330
2/M19
10 ROOMS
MED.EXP
NO KIDS
L

Hanora's Cottage Nire Valley, Ballymacarbry, Co Waterford +353 52 6136134
· www.hanorascottage.com Get chatting to your fellow guests in the Wall
family's remote lodge and restaurant and you will quickly find that most of them
have stayed at Hanora's on multiple occasions. For many folk, it's one of the
perfect escapes to get up into the hills, switch off, walk for miles, and enjoy, at the
start of the day and the end of the day, some fantastic cooking. Their breakfasts, in
particular, are a superlative, Wagnerian-scale drama, of what the meal can be.

1331
3/D21
85 ROOMS
LOTS
LLL

Parknasilla Resort and Spa Sneem, Co Kerry +353 64 6675600 ·
www.parknasillaresort.com Parknasilla enjoys a jaw-dropping location,
and enjoys the skills of John Foley, restaurant manager, and Peter Farndon, the
executive chef, at the helm of their Pygmalion restaurant, two guys on top of their
game. The cooking is classical and assured, and it's pretty difficult to leave after a
couple of days here in the heart of the Ring of Kerry.

1332   **Pax House**   Upr John St, Dingle, Co Kerry +353 66 9151518 · www.pax-house.com

3/C19

7 ROOMS

MED.INX-EXP

L

John O'Farrell could just as easily have called his house Sea View, because the views from the sea-facing side of the house, and from the patio, are stupendous. Sipping a glass of wine on the terrace as the sun sets, or enjoying breakfast as the sun rises, is one of the great Dingle (Daingean Uí Chúis) experiences, and the rooms are subtle and sumptuous.

✓✓✓ **Gregans Castle** Co Clare   Report: 1265/COUNTRY HOUSES.

✓✓ **Ballyvolane House** Co Cork   Report: 1266/COUNTRY HOUSES.

✓ **The Old Convent** Co Tipperary   Report: 1269/COUNTRY HOUSES.

✓ **Blairscove House & Restaurant** Co Cork   Report: 1273/COUNTRY HOUSES.

✓ **The Mustard Seed** Co Limerick   Report: 1275/COUNTRY HOUSES.

✓ **Coopershill House** Co Sligo   Report: 1277/COUNTRY HOUSES.

The Best Spas

1333 ✓ **Inchydoney Island Lodge & Spa** Inchydoney, Co Cork +353 23 8833143 ·
3/G23 www.inchydoneyisland.com Surfers will argue that the best spa experience
57 ROOMS in Inchydoney are the waves that beat up on the beaches at the front of the hotel, a
EXP couple of miles outside little Clonakilty. But, if you don't want to don a wetsuit, but
LLL do want the living benefits of seawater, then their Island Spa has several seawater
spa treatments, in additional to more conventional treatments. The hotel itself is
one of the highlights of W Cork.

1334 ✓ **Monart Destination Spa** Enniscorthy, Co Wexford +353 53 9238999
2/Q17 www.monart.ie This adults-only spa and hotel has been an enormous
70 ROOMS success from the day they opened, back in the mid-noughties. The complex is a
MED.EXP series of rooms built in two wings in the woodlands and skirting the lake, arrayed
NO KIDS around the original Georgian house, with two suites in the house itself. Their secret
is simple: the staff are an exceptional team, both in the house and in the spa itself,
which has on a number of occasions claimed the title as the best spa in the
country. Excellent cooking completes a pretty idyllic picture.

1335 **The Europe** Fossa, Co Kerry +353 64 6671300 · www.theeurope.com
3/E20 The spa at the luxurious and enormous The Europe Hotel – on the outskirts of
181 ROOMS Killarney town – regularly wins awards as the best in Ireland. What we enjoy the
LOTS most, as you swim in the pool, is the view of the lakes and the mountains that first
LLL made travellers compare Killarney to Lake Como: it's a singularly stunning vista.
Excellent staff.

1336 **The Brehon** Muckross Rd, Killarney, Co Kerry +353 64 6630700 ·
3/E20 www.thebrehon.com Sister hotel to the next-door Gleaneagle Hotel, this grand
125 ROOMS 4-star is home to the only Angsana Spa in the country, and all their therapists have
EXP trained at the Banyan Tree spa academy in Thailand. The Vitality pool is adult-only
– if you are travelling with kids they can use the 15-metre pool in the Gleaneagle
Hotel.

1337 **The Park Hotel** Kenmare, Co Kerry +353 64 6641200
3/E21 · www.parkkenmare.com When they first opened their Samas Spa, the Park
46 ROOMS Hotel even went as far as to commission a set of musical suites from Roxy
LOTS LL Music saxophonist Andy McKay, so there would be no threat of Andean pipe
FEB-NOV & music twittering in the background as you undergo their three-hour sequence of
CHRISTMAS treatments. Hyper luxe, amazing setting.

✓ **The Shelbourne** Co Dublin Report: 119/MAJOR HOTELS.

The Best Retreats

1338 ✓✓ **Dzogchen Beara Buddhist Meditation Centre** Allihies, Co Cork
3/D22   +353 27 73032 · www.dzogchenbeara.org Situated on 150 acres of
LLL   dramatic clifftop with a mind-boggling view of the Atlantic, Dzogchen Beara is a
spiritual centre that has always offered support to those with long-term or
life-threatening illnesses, helping guests to achieve a sense of personal peace and
acceptance. The centre now offers a limited space to those seeking time to unwind
and recharge in secluded retreat rooms, suited to all budgets, including hostel
accommodation. They offer guided meditation, deep listening, relationship healing
and help with those facing loss and bereavement. Their rest and renewal breaks are
for those who simply want to escape from the stresses of everyday life, either alone
or with family and friends.

1339 **Cliffs of Moher Retreat** Liscannor, Co Clare +353 86 8517710 ·
4/F15   www.cliffsofmoherretreat.com Yoga retreat centre, purpose built around a
L   glass-walled studio, with amazing views of the sea. Vinyasa yoga is at the heart of
the offer, but they also run walking and wellness weekends. Accommodation is in
the form of twin, single and quad rooms with shared bathroom. Anti-gravity yoga
sessions are a real treat.

1340 **Burren Yoga & Meditation Centre** Lig do Scith, Cappaghmore, Kinvarra, Co
4/G14   Galway · www.burrenyoga.com In the heart of the incredible Burren limestone
L   Geopark, this yoga retreat specialises in mindfulness and meditation, or you could
opt for bootcamp and recharge. Vegetarian cooking. Activities include guided
walks, and access to outdoor pursuits like kayaking and surfing. Recommended for
single holiday makers. Rooms are dorms, quads, single and double.

1341 **Ard Nahoo** Mullagh, Dromahair, Co Leitrim +353 71 913439 ·
5/K8   www.ardnahoo.com Family-run retreat centre made up of eco cabins that can
be rented for holidays and allow access to massage treatment rooms, yoga studio,
lovely grounds and vegetarian meals. The materials used to build the cabins were
carefully considered: sustainable cedar, hemp, natural paints – no petrochemicals.
The cabins are self catering, but most people order up their meals which are
delivered each evening. Popular for alternative Hen Parties.

1342 **Cloona Health Retreat** Westport, Co Mayo +353 98 25251 · www.cloona.ie
5/E10   Visitors who travel to Cloona, situated between mountain and sea, in the woodland
foothills of Croagh Patrick, come for weight loss, detox, juice-fasting, to quit
smoking or simply for mind and body balancing. Programmes include walking,
meditation, massage, while your accommodation is probably a single room, with –
needless to say – digital detox as well: it's a wifi-free zone.

1343
1/N11
3 ROOMS
MED.EXP

✓ **Lough Bishop House B&B** **Derrynagarra, Collinstown, Co Westmeath** +353 44 9661313 · www.loughbishophouse.com Chris and Helen Kelly's work at Lough Bishop House is one of the most significant acts of cultural conservation in modern Ireland. As agricultural and architectural curators, the Kellys have created the Derrynagarra herd of Moiled cattle, and their draught horses also carry the Derrynagarra prefix. They have restored their fine farmhouse, recreating its elegant beauty. Best of all, they have fashioned a modern concept of country conservatism, where 'everyone is a conservative about the things they love'. Very special.

1344
3/E23
3 ROOMS
MED.INX
NO TV

✓ **Fortview House** **Gurtyowen, Toormore, Goleen, Co Cork** +353 28 35324 · www.fortviewhouse.ie It's a commonplace to hear people describe Fortview as 'the best B&B', as they head off, having enjoyed meticulous breakfast cookery, superb hospitality, and the warm mature style of this fine, working farmhouse, hard by the road as you head down to little Goleen, in deepest W Cork, on the Mizen peninsula. Violet Connell is a great hostess. Self-catering cottage on the farm also available.

1345
4/G13
11 ROOMS
MED.INX
ATMOS

✓ **The Stop** **38 Father Griffin Rd, Galway** + 353 91 586736 · www.thestopbandb.com From the outside, The Stop looks like every other suburban house. But The Stop is like an Asian bowl, because when you lift the lid – or open the door – then this tone poem of superb design will stop you in your tracks. Russ and Emer's house betrays their gallerist backgrounds, thanks to the precise and perfect placing of every object, and the result is feng shui heaven. The rooms are small in comparison to hotel rooms, but the style is so perfect that this becomes irrelevant. Excellent breakfast, and Russ and Emer are superb hosts.

1346
1/S11
3 ROOMS
MED.INX
LL

The White Cottages **Balbriggan Rd, Skerries, Co Dublin** +353 1 849 2231 · Jackie and Joe O'Connor's meticulous house has the most extraordinary views out over Dublin Bay, a portmanteau of sea, horizon and sky that is mesmerising. The views are so extraordinary that they distract you initially from the bright, handsome interiors, but once breakfast arrives you will only have eyes for Jackie's confident, stylish cookery. Their USP is afternoon tea and, if the sun is shining and you can enjoy it out on the terrace, hard by the sea, then it is an unforgettable treat.

1347
3/C19
14 ROOMS
MED.EXP

Greenmount **Upr John St, Dingle, Co Kerry** +353 66 9151414 www.greenmounthouse.ie The Curran family have been beacons of hospitality since they opened Greenmount to guests back in 1977 and, if you ask anyone who has stayed here to explain the appeal of this Dingle (Daingean Uí Chúis) icon, you will be told that it is the handmade nature of so much of what they do. Breakfast, with fresh handmade breads, handmade preserves, poached fruits, and freshly cooked hot dishes, is a masterclass. John Curran is a formidable authority on the peninsula and if you can persuade him to escort you on a tour, you will discover all the secrets of Dingle.

1348
1/L12
7 ROOMS
CHP

The Bastion B&B **2 Bastion St, Athlone, Co Westmeath** +353 90 6494954 · www.thebastion.net This is a really characterful and comfortable bed and breakfast, with just the right sort of rive gauche vibe and style that you hope to find when travelling. The best bet for breakfast is to walk across the street to the very fine Bastion Kitchen, who make excellent scrambled eggs and an ace sausage bap.

1349 **Coolanowle House** Ballickmoyler, Co Carlow +353 59 8625544 ·
1/P15 www.coolanowle.com Jimmy and Bernadine Mulhall's farmhouse is set in the
9 ROOMS midst of a working organic farm, so you can enjoy the organic beef, lamb, pork and
MED.INX chicken reared on the farm at dinnertime. The Mulhalls are visionary, and tireless,
DF and great craic, so staying here is both relaxing and invigorating. Accommodation
ATMOS in a Log House and a self-catering cottage as well as the house itself. Excellent
cooking. Small pets welcome by prior arrangement only, if guests are staying in
their self-catering cottage.

1350 **Lorum Old Rectory** Kilgraney, Bagenalstown, Co Carlow +353 59 9775282 ·
2/P17 www.lorum.com Bobbie and Rebecca Smith both exude a natural, caring
4 ROOMS hospitality, which means that whilst the Rectory is rather grand, it quickly feels like
EXP your favourite place, especially when enjoying a superb breakfast in the drawing
FEB-NOV room, with a blazing fire warming your soul. Every tiny detail of design, cooking
ATMOS and comfort in the house is attended to with painstaking deliberation by these
formidable women, and it makes for one of the great Irish houses.

1351 **Ivyleigh House** Bank Place, Church St, Portlaoise, Co Laois +353 57 8622081
1/N15 · www.ivyleigh.com It is worth staying in Dinah Campion's svelte Georgian house
6 ROOMS just to enjoy one of the most perfect breakfasts offered in the Midlands: poached
APRIL-NOV plums; melon balls with fresh orange; cinnamon poached prunes and apricots;
MED.INX homemade granola; homemade muesli; just-squeezed orange juice; tea in a silver
teapot. Sheer indulgence, and culinary perfection, in a charming house just at the
edge of town.

1352 **Glasha Farmhouse** Ballymacarbry, Co Waterford +353 52 6136108 ·
2/L19 www.glashafarmhouse.com Olive O'Gorman's country house is up in the hills
9 ROOMS amidst splendid walking territory amongst the Comeragh and Knockmealdown
MED.INX Mountains, in Ballymacarbry, and there is no better place to set off from after a
NO KIDS heroic breakfast, or to return to when the feet are aching, and then to be able
L to enjoy a rack of Comeragh lamb and a glass of red wine. Mrs O'Gorman is a
formidable host, and her meticulous small country house is a great place to escape
to and enjoy the real peace of the countryside.

1353 **Garnish House** Western Rd, Cork +353 21 4275111 · www.garnish.ie
3/J21 There are scores of B&B's on Cork's Western Road, stretching alongside the
30 ROOMS campus of the University, but there is only one Garnish House. No other B&B
MED.INX owner spoils you the way Hansi Lucey spoils you – chocolate eclairs for breakfast,
anyone? – and the hospitality means the house is always filled with returning
guests. Pure Cork.

1354 **Ballinterry House** Rathcormac, Co Cork +353 25 87835 · @BallinterryHouse
3/K20 A listed building, dating from the 1690's, Ballinterry is a Queen Anne house, and
3 ROOMS Ann O'Sullivan and Michael Garvey have gifted it with one of the most magnificent
MED.EXP restoration jobs ever undertaken in Ireland: it's a jewel. It's been renovated and
renewed, and the result is a house that is supremely relaxing. Guests can order
dinner, and walk amidst field of bluebells as if you were a character in a Jane
Austen novel. A special destination for restoration fanatics.

1355 **Old School House B&B** Cross, Carrigaholt, Co Clare +353 86 1549402 ·
4/D17
3 ROOMS
CHP
DF
@theoldschoolBandBcross Ian and Theresa brought a near-derelict National School back to vibrant life when they restored the Old School House. Ian bakes delicious treats for breakfast, and it's quite a feeling to enjoy them in the old, light-filled classroom. Theresa is a guide at the Loop Head lighthouse, and between them they know everything about the region.

1356 **Ballinsheen House & Gardens** Lisdoonvarna, Co Clare +353 65 7074806 ·
4/F15
MED.INX
www.ballinsheen.com Terrific housekeeping and hearty breakfasts mean that the handsome Ballinsheen House, just on the edge of Lisdoon', is a perfect stop for anyone pausing on the WAW to spend a few days hiking and exploring.

1357 **Glencarrig B&B** Ramona, Carrigaholt, Co Clare +353 65 9058209 ·
4/E17
4 ROOMS
MED.INX
www.fishandstay.com Mary Aston is one of the best Irish bakers we know. Mrs Aston bakes in the Irish vernacular style, that sweetly-savoury style that blesses scones, cakes and pastries with a maternal signature – simple, precise, designed to please, not to astonish. The house is very comfortable, set in a beautiful part of beautiful Loop Head, and Luke Aston takes you fishing in his boat so, yes, there will be fresh mackerel for breakfast – Glencarrig is actually the accommodation side of Carrigaholt Sea Angling Centre.

1358 **Fergus View** Kilnaboy, Corofin, Co Clare +353 65 6837606 ·
4/G15
6 ROOMS
CHP
EASTER–OCT
www.fergusview.com Fergus View, a couple of miles outside Corofin village, has been a star destination in Co Clare for more than 55 years. Margaret Kelleher opened the doors here in 1962, with her son and daughter-in-law, Declan and Mary, taking over the running of the house in 1978, so Declan and Mary are celebrating their own four decades of offering great hospitality and great cooking to guests. Charming.

1359 **Spanish Point House** Spanish Point, Co Clare +353 86 1701814 ·
4/F16
10 ROOMS
EXP
L
www.spanishpointhouse.ie Pat and Aoife O'Malley's grand, 10-bedroom house was once upon a time a convent for the nuns who taught the children of Spanish Point. Today, it's a stylish B&B, beautifully restored to its past glory, with amazing sea views – 8 of the 10 rooms have sea views, so these are the ones to chase. Excellent breakfasts feature some of the best Co Clare foods.

1360 **Hillside Lodge** Sky Rd, Clifden, Co Galway +353 95 21463 ·
4/D12
6 ROOMS
MED.INX
MAR–OCT
NO KIDS
www.hillside-lodge.com Is that Sting's bass guitar I see before me, in Ruth and Stuart Morgan's B&B, Hillside House, just on the outskirts of Clifden, heading N on the WAW? Indeed it is, and Sting had the decency to autograph the guitar, a tribute to the regard in which Stuart Morgan is held as a guitar technician to the stars. You come here to enjoy the U2 room, or the Beatles' room, and to revel in rock 'n' roll memorabilia. But you also come to enjoy Ruth's brilliant design and decorative flourishes, for Hillside is also a tribute to a hostess with great design skills.

1361 **Sea Mist House** Clifden, Co Galway +353 95 21441 · www.seamisthouse.com
4/D12
4 ROOMS
CHP-MED.INX
MAR–NOV
ATMOS
When you are sitting in the conservatory of Sheila Griffin's Sea Mist House, just look out the window and study the gorgeous array of flowers that Sheila grows: the tulips and bluebells, the clematis and the roses, the peonies and campanula, the angel's fishing rods and the aquilegia. Wave after wave of colour, and all of them overlooked by the bust of Mark Anthony. Ms Griffin's zest for the garden is matched by her zest for hospitality, and her hospitality shares an organic sense of origin, colour, and naturalness that matches her horticulture. Sea Mist is simply peachy.

1362   **Leim Siar Bed & Breakfast** Blacksod Bay, Belmullet, Co Mayo +353 97 85004
5/D9 · www.leimsiar.com Hannah Quigley's B&B. Léim Siar, enjoys an amazing
4 ROOMS setting, way, way down Erris Head at Blacksod Bay, at the extremity of the Wild
CHP Atlantic Way, the place that readers of *The Irish Times* acclaimed as the best place
L to go wild in Ireland. You might turn up initially for the wildness, but Hannah's
cooking will be what lures you back. The Irish breakfast is beautifully sourced and
perfectly cooked, the soft fruits from the garden will put real wildness into your
day. The house is modern and comfortable, the perfect shelter from the storms of
W Mayo. Self-catering apartment also available.

1363   **Mulranny House** Mulranny, Co Mayo +353 98 36953 ·
5/E10 www.mulrannyhouse.ie Sarah and Nick's house is high up the hill on the N59,
MID.INX with audaciously beautiful views out over Clew Bay: you could sit and simply watch
L the waves and sky change all day long. Nick and Sarah are hospitality professionals,
and offer light-filled, stylish rooms, good breakfasts, and they will make up a picnic
for anyone hiking or cycling the Greenway.

1364   **Down Yonder B&B** Rosses Point, Sligo, Co Sligo +353 89 2103639 ·
5/J7 www.downyonder.ie Eavan O'Hara's Down Yonder is a super-luxurious B&B in
4 ROOMS Rosses Point, with capacious furnishings creating superlative comfort, fabulous
MED.EXP views from the bedroom windows, great hospitality and a fine breakfast. There are
22 acres in which to roam, and the house is a gift for golfers, being adjacent to Co
Sligo Golf Course - it actually overlooks the 9th hole.

1365   **Lis-Ardagh Lodge** Union Hall, Co Cork +353 28 34951 ·
3/G23 www.lis-ardaghlodge.com A brisk walk up the steep hill from pretty Union Hall,
3 ROOMS Ian and Carol's Lis Ardagh offers B&B and two cottages for self-catering. It's a
CHP friendly, lively house, with big, generous breakfasts.

1366   **Gallan Mor** Kealties, Durrus, Co Cork +353 28 62732 · www.gallanmore.com
3/E22 Lorna and Noel's purpose-built B&B is on the eastern ridge of the Sheep's Head
4 ROOMS Peninsula, so it's the perfect base for anyone who wishes to walk the entire Sheep's
MED.INX Head Way. The house sits on a small hill overlooking Dunmanus Bay, offering the
NO KIDS visitor jaw-dropping views over the water across to the Mizen Peninsula. There is
MAR-OCT also a sweet self-catering cottage for rent which is very comfortable, and ideal for a
L longer break. Two-night minimum stay throughout the year.

1367   **Carbery Cottage Guest Lodge** Durrus, Co Cork +353 27 61368 ·
3/E22 www.carbery-cottage-guest-lodge.net Mike and Julia are both hospitable and
3 ROOMS professional, and their confidence means that Carbery Lodge is a spiffing W Cork
MED.INX destination. Mike will cook dinner by arrangement, and he is a good cook – wild
DF Atlantic fish pie; fillet steak with balsamic onions; mushroom risotto. Excellent
breakfasts use top notch local ingredients, as well as produce from the garden. The
three rooms include one two bedroom suite. Self-catering cottage also available.

1368   **Sea View House** Fisher St, Doolin, Co Clare +353 87 2679617 ·
4/F15 www.seaview-doolin.ie Niall and Darra's pretty house overlooks the Aille river
4 ROOMS and Doolin village. Special breakfasts are the USP here, using their own eggs in
MED.EXP signature dishes such as frittata with St Tola goat's cheese, and they count the
MAR-NOV food miles for every dish, so this is a super-eco destination, and the comfort and
location couldn't be bettered.

1369 **The Glen House** Straid, Clonmany, Co Donegal +353 74 9376745 ·
6/M2 www.glenhouse.ie Sonia McGonagle's The Glen House, in little Clonmany, is
9 ROOMS a beautiful house in a beautiful setting, distinguished further by the creativity of
MED.INX a dedicated hostess. The house has comfortable rooms, and a fine tea room to
L relax in after a visit to the Glenevin Waterfall. The Glen is a house that pushes all
the buttons, and we can't think of anything nicer than a few days walking on the
beaches and through the Urris Hills and the Mamore Gap, then the return to The
Glen to end a perfect day.

1370 **Dufferin Coaching Inn** 33 High St, Killyleagh, Co Down, NI +44 28 44821134 ·
6/T7 www.dufferincoachinghouse.com Leontine Haines is doing a super job in this
7 ROOMS lovely, early 19thC coaching house in pretty Killyleagh. Part of the Dufferin was
MED.EXP formerly a bank but, unlike most Irish banks, Ms Haines actually knows how to run
a business properly and professionally. The rooms and bathrooms are beautifully
appointed, the towels are fluffy, the Bircher muesli at breakfast is as scrumptious
as all the other home-made ingredients that comprise the feast that starts the day.
Many guests choose to eat next door at the friendly Dufferin Arms, or at Balloo
House (1238/NI) where the brilliant Danny Millar cooks up a storm.

1371 **Strandeen** 63 Strand Rd, Portstewart, Co Antrim, NI +44 28 70833872 ·
6/Q3 www.strandeen.com Sitting high on the hill above the beautiful Portstewart
5 ROOMS Strand, with views out across the water, Strandeen offers five exquisitely styled
rooms, boasting Plum & Ashby toiletries and White Company towels and robes.
Patient development and renovation has seen a conventional coastal house reborn
beautifully as a high luxe destination. Debbie Caskey also offers very healthful and
invigorating treats at breakfastime, so you will have plenty of gas in the tank for
running along the strand, or conquering that golf course.

1372 **The Saddler's House** 36 Gt James St, Derry, Co Londonderry, NI
6/N4 +44 28 71269691 · www.thesaddlershouse.com Joan Pyne's restoration work
7 ROOMS on two major Londonderry (Derry) destinations – The Saddler's House and The
Merchant's House – is both valuable and important, so it's a treat to stay in these
lovely houses, each of which enjoys a very precise, and precisely maintained,
aesthetic. And, even better, the location of both is smack in the centre of town,
and Joan's breakfasts are ace: don't miss their legendary marmalade! The Merchant
House is at 16 Queen Street.

Laurel Villa Magherafelt Report: 1648/LITERARY PLACES.
Rayanne House Holywood Report: 1246/NI.
Maddybenny Farmhouse Portrush Report: 1396/GLAMPING.

Camping, Glamping, Yurts, Pods, Treehouses & Gypsy Wagons

1373   **Portsalon Luxury Camping** Cashelpreaghan, Portsalon, Co, Donegal
6/M2   +353 87 6016654 · www.donegalglamping.com Five luxurious Mongolian yurts,
NO PETS   with king-size beds, carpets and a wood-burning stove, are the luxe USPs of Sean
L   and Helen's fantastically remote and romantic site. It's close to Ballymastocker
Bay, which *The Observer* once called the second most beautiful beach in the world.
The Observer was wrong: this is the most beautiful beach in the world. There is also
a bell tent for hire, but it's the yurts that you want.

1374   **The Phoenix** Shanahill East, Castlemaine, Co Kerry +353 66 9766284 ·
3/D19   www.thephoenixrestaurant.ie Lorna Tyther's much-loved vegetarian restaurant
is one of the signature destinations of the Dingle peninsula, and their grounds also
offer two Romany wagons, which sleep two (with or without kids) and there is a
field in which to pitch a tent. Bathrooms in the house, where there are also some
rooms for B&B. Lorna wrote an excellent cookery book, *A Culinary Adventure*, a few
years back, so make sure to get a copy to bring her fine vegetarian recipes home
with you.

1375   **Eagle Point Camping** Bantry, Co Cork +353 27 50630 ·
3/E22   www.eaglepointcamping.com Siobhan and Elizabeth's caravan and camping
APR–SEPT   park enjoys the most spectacular location, on a small, 20-acre peninsula in the
NO PETS   inner waters of Bantry Bay, where the Ouvane and Coomhola Rivers meet the sea.
LL   There is a slipway if you are trailering a boat, tennis and basketball courts, and all
the necessary facilities. For many people, it's a site to return to year after year.

1376   **The Apple Farm** Moorstown, Cahir, Co Tipperary +353 52 7441459 ·
2/L18   www.theapplefarm.com Con Traas, who runs The Apple Farm, is the smartest
MAY–SEPT   farmer in Ireland. From a smallholding he produces exquisite fruits and juices of
NO PETS   the highest order, and we all drive to the barn to buy boxes of apples, plums, juices
and cider vinegars. When he isn't grafting new stock, Mr Traas takes care of the
small caravan and camping site on the farm. So, stay here, and you can tell people
you stayed on the smartest farm in Ireland.

1377   **River Valley Holiday Park** Redcross Village, Co Wicklow +353 404 41647 ·
1/S15   www.rivervalleypark.ie Not too many caravan and camping parks have a craft
MAR–OCT   brewery attached, but River Valley is also home to the Wicklow Brewery, so you
NO PETS   can pitch your tent, then go and have a brewery tour and a pint of St Kevin's Red
in Mickey Finn's pub. The Park features really funky glamping microlodges – which
look like something from a sci-fi movie – and tree house camping, where the cabin
sits 8ft up in the sky. If you need to escape the youngsters, then there is camping
for adults in the secret garden.

1378   **Battlebridge Caravan & Camping Park** Leitrim Village, Carrick-on-Shannon,
4/K9   Co Leitrim +353 71 9650824 · www.battlebridgecaravanandcamping.ie
On the banks of the River Shannon, Battlebridge offers glamping in eco pods and
tree houses, in addition to pitches for tents and caravans, and is unusual in having
a traditional pub and restaurant – Beirnes – on the site. There is a private marina
for those cruising the Shannon to tie up, and if you are navigating the Shannon
Blueway by bike or boat or on foot, it's a perfect destination.

1379 **Nore Valley Park** Annamult, Bennettsbridge, Co Kilkenny +353 56 7727229
2/N17 · www.norevalleypark.com Thanks to featuring a petting farm with ostriches,
MAR–OCT goats, sheep and many more animals, Nore Valley is kiddie heaven. You can hire a
mobile home or one of the simple wooden lodges, or bring the tent or camper van.
In addition to the farm, there are lots of kiddie activities – go karts; crazy golf; trailer
rides.

1380 **Wolohan's Caravan and Camping Park** Silver Strand, Dunbur Upr, Co
1/S15 Wicklow +353 404 69404 · www.silverstrand.ie The famous Silver Strand, one
EASTER–SEPT of the most beautiful east coast beaches, is the big attraction here. The Wolohan
DF family have 22 acres for camping and caravans, and there is a shop in an old
L shipping container which sells all the stuff you forgot to bring with you. Dogs on
lead welcome, but not on the beach.

1381 **Pod Umna Glamping Village** Dominick St, Portumna, Co Galway
4/K14 +353 90 9759499 · www.podumnavillage.ie Pod Umna is unique inasmuch
as it is right in the heart of Portumna. There are bell tents, a shepherd's hut and
heated pods, and it can accommodate up to 40 people.

1382 **Mannix Point Camping Park** Cahirciveen, Ring of Kerry +353 66 9472806 ·
3/C21 www.campinginkerry.com With pitches for tents, caravans and motorhomes,
EASTER–SEPT Mannix Point has been welcoming guests for over 30 years. It's well-known for
DF lively music sessions in the campers' sitting room, and there is a well-stocked
L kitchen, a barbecue area and a picnic zone. This area is the Kerry International Dark
Sky Reserve, and is the only Gold Tier Reserve in the northern hemisphere: on a
fine, clear night, the night sky and the orchestra of stars will blow your mind.

1383 **Renvyle Beach Caravan and Camping Park** Tullybeg, Renvyle, Co Galway
4/D11 +353 95 43462 · www.renvylebeachcaravanpark.com There is direct access
EASTER–OCT to a sandy beach on this 4.5 acre site, which caters for campers and caravanners.
NO DOGS It's on the N side of the road running between Tullycross and Renvyle House Hotel,
and they have three mobile homes for hire. If you're in the area, don't miss the
Harry Clarke stained glass windows in the church in Tullycross, and
Paddy Coyne's pub.

1384 **Dromquinna Manor** Sneem Rd, Kenmare, Co Kerry +353 64 6643888 ·
3/E21 www.dromquinnamanor.com Seven huge South African safari tents are the
MAY–SEPT luxurious attraction at Dromquinna, on the shores of Kenmare Bay. As you would
L expect from the people who also run Kenmare's luxe Park Hotel, it's seriously
stylish: good cotton sheets, goose feather duvets, fresh coffee in the morning, and
the adjacent Boat House Bistro will take care of dinner just perfectly.

1385 **Rock Farm** Slane Castle Demesne, Slane, Co Meath +353 41 9884861 ·
1/Q11 www.rockfarmslane.ie Famous for massive rock concerts, and for whiskey, the
APR–NOV Slane Castle estate also offers glamping in yurts and shepherd's huts, on a hillside
overlooking the castle. There is also the Lime House, which can sleep up to 22
people, and they offer various packages for hen and stag groups, and even for
wedding parties. Outdoor hot tub and pizza oven, and a variety of food packages
are available to order.

1386 **Crann Og Eco Holidays** Derrymore, Drummin Gort, Co Galway +353 85
4/H15 1453535 · www.ecostayireland.com They call it Re-naturing at Crann Og, where you can do everything from foraging to sound baths to yoga to nature therapy walks, all on an organic farm. They offer cabins, yurts and bell tents for those staying on the farm, but virtually everything is off-grid: no wifi, no internet, no television.

1387 **Pure Camping** Querrin, Kilkee, Co Clare +353 65 9057953 ·
4/E17 www.purecamping.ie Trea and Kevin were amongst the first people to offer
APR-SEPT stylish bell tents and timber-clad eco huts for guests, set amidst a 10-acre native
L woodland. There is an on-site pizza oven, an eco-sauna, and Satyananda yoga classes are taught by Trea.

1388 **Clifden Eco Beach Camping & Caravanning Park** Claddaghduff Rd, Clifden,
4/C12 Co Galway +353 95 44039 · www.actonsbeachsidecamping.com
MAR-OCT Ten minutes outside Clifden, and known locally as Acton's, this is a climate-neutral
DF site to bring your caravan or tent, and to start a beach fire to cook the dinner.

1389 **Lough Key Caravan & Campsite Park** Lough Key Forest Park, Boyle, Co
4/K9 Roscommon +353 71 9673122 · www.loughkey.ie This family-focused site
APR-SEPT sits on the edge of a 750-acre forest park, where you can cycle, walk, zip wire and
DF Segway. A lot of the features are wheelchair friendly, and there is good swimming
L at the marina.

1390 **Morriscastle Strand Holiday Park** Kilmuckridge, Co Wexford
2/R17 +353 53 9130124 · www.morriscastlestrand.com A 20km strand of soft, white
MAR-SEPT sand and a Blue Flag beach is a big part of the charm of this Wexford institution, where the Darcy family have been welcoming guests since 1969. There is a shop and a takeaway, and the site offers all necessary facilities. Mobile homes on the site are privately owned and are not for rent. Lots of activities for the kids, and music nights for the adults.

1391 **Top of the Rock Pod Páirc** Drimoleague, Co Cork +353 86 1735134 ·
3/F22 www.topoftherock.ie David and Elizabeth Ross have been garnering award after
L award for their pioneering Pod Pairc since opening in the Ilen River Valley in 2014. The pods were designed by Ian Bone and their corbel roofs borrow design elements from the Gallarus Oratory in Dingle (Daingean Uí Chúis). They are super cosy, both in summer and winter, and you can rent super pods that are equipped with everything you might need, whilst the other family pods can use all the facilities of the site. This is a magnificent area for walking, contemplating, and getting away from it all. As Elizabeth Ross says, the area has 'a beauty that feeds the soul'.

1392 **Finn Lough Resort** 33 Letter Rd, Enniskillen, Co Fermanagh, NI
6/L6 +4428 68380360 · www.finnlough.com Finn Lough is an eco-luxury estate on
NO DOGS the shore of Lough Erne, and has already begun to feature in the various Cool Lists
L of the lifestyle magazines. There are various choices of accommodation – lodges, cottages and catered suites – but of particular interest are the bubble domes – transparent spherical living spaces with four-poster beds that are designed to maximise star gazing as night draws on. The latest part of the development has been the opening of the spa, and thanks to a kitchen you have many good food choices. Lots of activities on the Lough.

1393 **Pink Apple Orchard** Corry, Drumkeeran, Co Leitrim +353 83 4886645 ·
5/K8 www.irelandglamping.com There is nothing quite like apple blossom time, if
L you are staying in a yurt, a Hobbit house, or a teepee at Pink Orchard, in amongst
the cider apple orchard, at the top of Lough Allen, between Drumkeeran and
Dowra. There is a communal kitchen and showers and a big pizza oven, and Martin
and Jess have really fashioned something funky and punky here, a classic example
of Co Leitrim's punky counter-culture, and that's before you get a taste of that
organic cider.

1394 **Burren Glamping** Kilfenora, Co Clare +353 65 7088931 ·
4/F15 www.burrenglamping.com As well as rearing the cutest pigs on the planet, Eva
and Stephen also offer a converted horse truck, just the sort of accommodation
that kids dream about, and which they will find to be an unforgettable experience:
talk about the archetypal happiness anchor. The truck has two double beds and a
settle bed converts into a couch during the day. Get the kids to bring back the eggs
for breakfast, and get the day off to the perfect start.

1395 **Ballinacourty House & Caravan Camping Park** Glens of Aherlow, Co
2/K18 Tipperary +353 62 56000 · www.camping.ie Ballinacourty House is a converted
EXP courtyard with a restaurant, some rooms for B&B and two self-catering cottages.
In addition there is a touring park for campers, caravans and motorhomes, and it's
an ideal base for exploring the Glen of Aherlow. It's just off the R663, close to the
village of Lisvernane.

1396 **Maddybenny Farmhouse** Loguestown Rd, Portrush, Co Antrim, NI +4428
6/Q3 70823394 · www.maddybenny.com Maddybenny has long been one of the most
famous B&Bs in NI, and if you are touring the Causeway Coast in a camper, they
have a site with grass pitches and electric hook-up. There are also attractive self-
catering cottages, and two excellent houses for rent.

✓✓ **Ballyvolane House** Co Cork Report: 1266/COUNTRY HOUSES.

The Best for House Parties

1397 **Virginia Park Lodge** Virginia, Co Cavan +353 49 8546100 ·
1/N10 www.virginiaparklodge.com Celebrity chef Richard Corrigan took over this big,
L 100-acre estate just outside the village of Virginia, and has been busy transforming every element of it, from garden to table to the plush interiors. The lakeside site is quite magical, and partly explains why the Park Lodge has quickly become a very popular wedding destination, but they also specialise in renting the house to groups and for private parties.

1398 **Inishbeg Estate** Baltimore, Co Cork +353 28 21745 · www.inishbeg.com
3/F23 Paul and Georgie Keane's expansive water's edge estate, just off the narrow road
L outside Baltimore, offers a wide range of stylish accommodation, including The Boathouse, perhaps the most covetously desired getaway in the country. Being so desirable makes it elusive, but there are many other excellent choices here for family and friends to escape to, including Roma caravans, cottages, the Forester's House, and more. When staying, make sure to visit the Saturday Skibbereen market to get all the best local foods and to mainline those W Cork tastes.

1399 **Dunowen House** Clonakilty, Co Cork +353 23 8869099 ·
3/G23 www.dunowenhouse.ie Several miles westwards out along the coast from
L Clonakilty, heading towards Red Strand, Dunowen offers a unique potion of history with rock 'n' roll credentials: the house dates from the 1700's and, for 30 years, was home to Noel Redding, bass player in the Jimi Hendrix Experience. Kela and Stephen Hodgins have created one of the most sought-after escapes here, in a house that is as comfortable as it is beautiful. A gem.

1400 **Enniscoe House** Castlehill, Ballina, Co Mayo +353 96 31112 ·
5/F9 www.enniscoe.com Susan and DJ Kellett's fine house has a dining room that seats 30 people, a scale that was normal for people building fine mansions way back in the 1790's. With extra accommodation available in the Courtyard rooms, you have all you need for that big anniversary bash or alumni get-together

1401 **Liss Ard Estate** Castletownshend Rd, Skibbereen, Co Cork +353 28 40000
3/F23 · www.lissardestate.com The modernist interior of Liss Ard is one of the
L best-realised pieces of interior design of any Irish country house. Add in the mesmerising James Turrell Sky Garden in the expansive and idyllic grounds, and you have two major features that will charm everyone. The 25 bedrooms in the house can accommodate up to 50 people for house parties, and there is further space for groups in the Lake Lodge. The house is just a couple of miles outside Skibbereen, heading to Castletownshend.

1402 **Temple House** Ballinacarrow, Ballymote, Co Sligo +353 71 9183329 ·
5/J9 www.templehouse.ie You can rent the Perceval family's entire mansion per night, and they also specialise in weddings, as well as leisure and pleasure guests.

1403 **Montalto** Ballynahinch, Co Down, NI +4428 90566100 ·
6/S7 www.montaltoestate.com Montalto is an almost impossibly perfect house. Every aspect of every aspect – house; grounds; woodlands; stable yard; lake; interiors – seems to exist in a state of airbrushed preparation for an *Architectural Digest* photo shoot. Weddings are specifically catered for in the Carriage Rooms, which can accommodate 180 people. It's close to Ballynahinch town but, in truth, it's a world unto itself, providing you have the wherewithal to rent it, of course.

1404 **Delphi Lodge** Leenane, Co Galway +353 95 42222· www.delphilodge.ie
5/E11 Peter Mantle's country house and estate is world-renowned, especially by
L fishermen; a beautiful house in one of the most beautiful places in Ireland. It is
quaint, characterful, a fine 1830's house that is perfectly suited for house parties
and small weddings, for groups ranging from four to forty, for a 2-night minimum.
There are also five holiday cottages on the estate.

1405 **Crosshaven House** Crosshaven, Co Cork +353 21 4832005 ·
3/J21 www.crosshavenhouse.ie Noel Corcoran's majestic four-storey Georgian
house is the house on the hill in little Crosshaven. The house has a most unusual
arrangement: there are five grand rooms in the house for B&B, whilst the
basement – known by the coordinates of the house, 51 Degrees North – is a super-
slick hostel-style arrangement of three rooms with bunk beds: one sleeps 6 people,
the other two rooms sleep 4 each. 51 has a sauna, cinema, and a kitchen with an
Aga, and you have to book all of the bunks, so it's perfect for groups and getaways.
Cronin's pub in the village is the place where you will be enjoying dinner, and good
wines and craft beers.

1406 **Bellingham Castle** Castlebellingham, Co Louth +353 42 9372176 ·
1/R10 www.bellinghamcastle.ie The Corscadden family, who own Markree Castle
in Co Sligo, Cabra Castle in Co Cavan and Ballyseede Castle in Co Kerry, took
over Bellingham in 2002, and have developed the castle to cater to their niche
marketing in castle weddings and as an event venue. There are 19 bedrooms in the
hotel itself, and they aso cater for B&B guests at certain times of the year.

1407 **Tyrella House** Downpatrick, Co Down, NI +4428 44851422 David Corbett's
6/T8 skills as a host set the tone of the elegant Tyrella, whether he is welcoming
you with a cup of tea, or cooking an excellent dinner which the guests take
communally, or telling a raft of interesting stories after dinner. The house is a
fascinating synthesis of architectural styles, and has its own private beach: no
surprise it's popular with film crews looking for quixotic locations for filming. Cross-
country horse riding and polo are big elements of the house.

1408 **Martinstown House** The Curragh, Co Kildare +353 45441269 ·
1/P14 www.martinstownhouse.com Built by the renowned Victorian architect,
Decimus Burton, Martinstown is a rare gothic cottage. Edward and Roisin Booth
offer six rooms for guests, who take dinner communally at the dining table. It is
a very popular wedding venue, and is also available for private hire and for house
parties. Proximity to the Curragh racecourse, and the fact that it's only an hour
from Dublin, explain the popularity.

Stay in a Lighthouse or a Martello Tower

1409 **Clare Island Lighthouse** Clew Bay, Co Mayo +353 87 6689758 ·
5/D10 www.clareislandlighthouse.com Leave the mainland behind when you stay
DF here, arriving at Clare Island after a ferry journey from Roonagh Pier on Co Mayo.
LLL The cottages at the lighthouse sleep 12 people, and Clare Island is unique in
offering B&B and evening meals to visitors. The owners also operate Killadangan
House, on the outskirts of Westport town on the mainland, a sanctuary-style house
where they host retreats, private events and self-catering accommodation.

1410 **Galley Head Lighthouse** Clonakilty, Co Cork +353 1 6704733 ·
3/G23 www.irishlandmark.com The Irish Landmark Trust restored two lightkeepers'
LLL houses adjacent to the lighthouse itself, which was the most powerful lighthouse
in the world when built in 1875. Two houses, each sleeps 4, with a minimum
3-night stay. It's a truly W Cork adventure to stay here.

1411 **Loop Head Lighthouse** Kilbaha, Co Clare +353 1 670 4733 ·
4/D17 www.irishlandmark.com The symbol of the dynamic group of artisans and
DF hospitality operators who have made Loop Head a significant destination.
LLL Even if you can't stay, this is an essential visit and tour when navigating the area
around Kilbaha. Operated by Irish Landmark Trust, cottage sleeps 5, minimum
5-night stay.

1412 **St John's Point Lighthouse** Killough, Co Down, NI
6/T8 +353 1 6704733 · www.irishlandmark.com Not to be confused with the St
LLL John's Point in W Donegal, this bumblebee-coloured lighthouse has two cottages
operated by the Irish Landmark Trust. Each cottage sleeps 4 people, with a
minimum 3-night stay. At a towering 40m, this is the tallest onshore lighthouse on
the coastline.

1413 **Blackhead Lighthouse** Whitehead, Co Antrim, NI +353 1 6704733 ·
4/F14 www.irishlandmark.com At the North East approach to Belfast Lough, the
LLL three cottages, right beside the lighthouse itself, can sleep 16 people, so this is a
good group getaway location, just north of the town of Whitehead. Operated by
Irish Landmark Trust, there is a minimum 3-night stay. Lovely coastal walk into
Whitehead.

1414 **Fanad Head Lighthouse** Araheera, Portsalon, Co Donegal +353 83 8091199
6/M2 · www.fanadlighthouse.com The lighthouse cottages are just about as far north
LLL as you can possible stay in Ireland, perched on the cliff at the entrance to Lough
Swilly, one of only three glacial fjords in the country. If you stay here, you need to
know that the winds are of an almost unearthly power: be careful opening the
door of your car. Ten guests can be accommodated in the three cottages.
There is a Visitors' Centre, and tours of the lighthouse every half hour. Minimum
7-night stay. If you need to be at the end of the earth, here it is.

1415 **St John's Point Lighthouse** Dunkineely, Co Donegal +353 1 6704733 ·
5/J6   www.irishlandmark.com The lighthouse keepers' cottages were restored and
LLL   are operated by Irish Landmark Trust. Eight visitors can be accommodated in two
        houses, with a minimum 3-night stay. Dunkineely is a wild and wonderful location,
        and check out the famous pink sands of Coral Beach.

1416 **Wicklow Head Lighthouse** Dunbur Head, Co Wicklow +353 1 6704733 ·
1/S15   www.irishlandmark.com Want to get fit, lose some weight, and stay in a
DF   lighthouse? At Wicklow Head, you can do all three. This is a rare chance to actually
LLL   stay in the Lighthouse itself, which sleeps 4 people, all of whom will need to ascend
        no fewer than 109 steps up to the kitchen. Fit? You'll be doing an Ironman next. It's
        operated by Irish Landmark Trust, and a minimum 3-night stay.

1417 **Martello Tower** Red Rock, Sutton, Co Dublin +353 86 1642671 ·
1/S13   www.martellotowersutton.com This is the only Martello Tower in Ireland that
LLL   you can rent. The towers were built at the beginning of the 19thC as lookouts
        and defences in the event of an invasion by Napoleon, and they appear all along
        the east coast. The two bedrooms are in the base of the tower, with a living room
        and kitchen above and, above that, another room with lighthouse-like windows
        running all around. With 10ft thick walls, and a winding staircase, this makes for an
        extraordinarily atmospheric place to stay, with extraordinary views.

the
Best
Good Food & Drink

The Best Country Bars

1418 ✓✓✓ **Dick Mack's** Green St, Dingle, Co Kerry +353 66 9151787 ·
3/C19 @DickMack'sPub Dick Mack's is the most polyglot pub in Ireland,
ATMOS maybe in the world. It attracts visitors of every nationality, and on an evening when
the place is packed – which is most evenings – the roar of voices seems to fashion
a brand new international Esperanto: you could get tipsy in Dick Mack's and never
touch a drop of drink. But, if you are having a sip, then there are few better pubs in
which to drink whiskey, and Finn McDonnell and his team work hard at offering an
extraordinary array, more than enough to win them national titles as the best
whiskey bar in Ireland.

1419 ✓ **Sean's Bar** 13 Main St, Athlone, Co Westmeath +353 90 6492358 ·
1/L12 www.seansbar.ie Sean's is one of the truly legendary pubs, and claims to be
ATMOS the oldest pub in Ireland, but don't mistake it for a tourist dive: this is the real deal,
long and narrow, and strangely regal. It may also be the busiest bar in the
Midlands, so jammers with punters that just raising that pint of Galway Hooker to
your lips can involve yogic contortions. You will find it in the old part of Athlone.
Great music sessions.

1420 ✓ **Matt Molloy's** Bridge St, Westport, Co Mayo +353 98 26655 ·
5/E10 www.mattmolloy.com Matt Molloy is one of Ireland's most famous
ATMOS musicians – a founder member of the extraordinary The Bothy Band, flute player
with The Chieftains, don't you know – but in Westport he is famous as a man who
runs one of the nicest traditional pubs in Ireland. Molloy's is a classic of the genre
– crowded, sociable, affable, with fabulous music every evening, and it's a great
place to hunt down the craft beers of Mayo.

1421 ✓ **De Barra's** 55 Pearse St, Clonakilty, Co Cork +353 23 8833381 ·
3/G22 www.debarra.ie More than any other Irish pub, De Barra's of Clonakilty is
ATMOS synonymous with music. For almost 40 years, De Barra's Folk Club has been a
home for the best musicians and the best gigs, to such an extent that the great
Christy Moore argues De Barra's has equal status to the Royal Albert Hall, the
Sydney Opera House and Carnegie Hall. Aside from the music, it's a darling W Cork
pub with lots of Lusitania memorabilia, lots of Jimi Hendrix memorabilia – Noel
Redding gigged here regularly – and a handsome, flower-bedecked exterior.

1422 ✓ **Connolly's of Leap** Main St, Leap, Co Cork +353 28 33215 ·
3/G23 www.connollysofleap.com Mid-way between Clonakilty and Skibbereen on
ATMOS the N71, Connolly's was a celebrated W Cork venue for gigs for many years. Now
re-born with Sam McNicholl in charge, it's a punky, surrealist space, and home to
great gigs once again, even to famous names like James Vincent McMorrow and
others, who like to road-test new material here.

1423 ✓ **Levis Corner House** Main St, Ballydehob, Co Cork +353 28 37118 ·
3/E23 www.leviscornerhouse.com Joe and Caroline O'Leary rebirthed the
ATMOS legendary Levis' bar in the most sympathetic way possible, retaining the unique
ambience that Joe's grand-aunts, Nell and Julia, blessed the pub with, whilst the
addition of truly excellent music sessions, craft beers and Irish gins has made the
space contemporary and funky. Levis' is a template for the Irish country pub in the
modern age.

1424 ✓ **McCarthy's Bar** The Square, Castletownbere, Co Cork +353 27 70014 ·
3/D22 www.maccarthysbar.com McCarthy's was a famous pub long before the late
ATMOS Pete McCarthy's delightful book, *McCarthy's Bar* declared that it 'might just be the

best pub in the world'. Charming, comforting, convivial, it's the epicentre of Castletownbere, and an iconic part of W Cork and the Beara Peninsula. If you get the chance, do ask Adrienne to tell you about the wartime service of her dad, Aidan: it's an unbelievable story, and one that was made into the documentary film, *A Doctor's Sword*.

1425
4/D11
ATMOS

✓ **Paddy Coyne's Public House** Tullycross, Co Galway +353 95 43499 ·
@PaddyCoynesPub Paddy Coyne's is the pub with a gravestone in the centre of the pub. Every year, it's the epicentre of the Connemara Mussel Festival, and there is some good cooking to be enjoyed, though the coffee needs a rethink. If you get lucky, you can hear some really darling singing in here. Fantastic pub.

1426
5/J8

Thomas Connolly Markievicz Rd, Sligo +353 71 9194920 ·
www.thomasconnollysligo.com The river of history runs through Thomas Connolly's, and its magical interior, with its flagstone floor and cosy snugs. It's dreamlike but, thankfully, it's real, set hard by the river in the centre of town. The premises first had a licence in 1861, and by 1890 it was in the care of Thomas Connolly, who returned to Ireland having made his money on the railroads in America. Ironically, one of the things that made Connolly's famous was its selection of teas and, if you look behind the bar, you can see the six tea bins. That sort of attention to detail, and the dedicated hospitality of the staff, makes Connolly's special.

1427
1/N15

Morrissey's Main St, Abbeyleix, Co Laois +353 57 8731281 Televisions have intruded into the otherwise undisturbed and gloriously ramshackle interior of the legendary Morrissey's, on the middle of Abbeyleix village. If you fused an Irish grocer's emporium from 1948 with a provincial pub from the same era, you might create Morrissey's. What you could not create would be the pantechnicon effect, and the atmosphere, that comes with having old biscuit tins, bicycles, ham slicers, stoves, cash registers and counters disassembled throughout this big room, with its cluster of snugs, partitions and soft ceiling lights.

1428
1/R9

PJ O'Hares Tholsel St, Carlingford, Co Louth +353 42 9373106 ·
www.pjoharescarlingford.com PJ's is a pristine traditional pub, and you will know it from the old Shell petrol pump – labelled 'oyster fuel' just on the corner. Charming interior, good music sessions, and just the place for some oysters, brown bread and stout.

1429
5/H8
L

The Beach Bar Aughris, Co Sligo +353 71 9176465 ·
www.thebeachbarsligo.com When we used to visit the beach bar at Aughris, 30 years ago, any stranger would be met with suspicious silence from the locals drinking at the bar. Today, with surf schools having colonised the beach at Aughris, the bar is buzzy, friendly, and always busy. You turn off at Skreen, heading W on the Sligo-Ballina Road, just past the church, and head down to the sea along some lovely, winding boreens and then suddenly: there it is.

1430
1/Q11

O'Connell's Hill of Skryne, Co Meath O'Connell's is such a quintessential archetype of the classic Irish bar that it even featured in a Guinness Xmas advert. 'A cinnamon-hued step back in time to a 1950's country bar' is how the writer Turtle Bunbury has described a bar that hasn't changed in decades. Locals know it as Mrs O's, after the late Mrs O'Connell who ran it until her death aged 95, and who never touched a drop of drink. It's also known as The Yankee, or Yankee Connell's. Founded in the 1870's, it sits opposite the church – you can see the church tower when driving the M3, a few miles past Dunshaughlin – on a site where St Columba founded a monastery, and where his followers kept his relics.

1431 Peadar O'Donnells Bar 63 Waterloo St, Derry, Co Londonderry, NI
6/N4 +4428 71267295 · www.peadars.com This is Londonderry (Derry)'s most famous
ATMOS music pub, in the centre of the city on Waterloo St, with a global reputation
and, hence, lots of tourists. There are actually three bars on the premises –
O'Donnell's, The Gweedore, and Gweedore Upstairs. Lots of organised gigs, but the
spontaneous sessions are the best.

1432 O'Connor's Bar Ann St, Ballycastle, Co Antrim, NI +4428 20762123 ·
6/R2 www.oconnorsbar.ie An excellent gin menu and the chance to find the fine
ATMOS local craft beers – Lizzie's Ale; Fairhead Gold and Rathlin Red, made by Pat and
Isabella of the Glens of Antrim Brewery, and only distributed locally – will cause
you to linger in this famous, green and gold-painted pub on the Main Street of little
Ballycastle. It's a popular spot for eating, and there are good music sessions on
Thursday evenings. Rugby regalia all around means there are TVs switched to the
sports channels.

1433 The Sky & The Ground 112 Sth Main St, Wexford +353 53 9121273 The Barron
2/R18 family have made the Sky & The Ground into a Wexford institution over the last
20 years or so. They took a burned-out old pub, and made it into a classic country
town pub, and one that looks as if it has been here forever. But their secret has
been to keep developing all the time, with excellent music gigs, a smashing beer
garden, a separate space for watching the matches away from the bar, and a
fantastic array of craft beers and gins. A glass of White Gypsy Blond and a white
gypsy sausage in a bun: that's the stuff, now.

1434 O'Shea's Borris, Co Carlow +353 59 9773106 Pretty as a picture on the outside,
2/P17 with its potted plants at the door, Michael O'Shea's grocery-bar has the most
gorgeous candy-striped bar imaginable. You might come in off the Main Street
of Borris for a pint, and leave with some WD-40, or a sweeping brush, or some
other essential piece of hardware. There aren't an awful lot of shop-style pubs still
surviving, so don't miss this slice of old Ireland.

1435 Jim O' the Mill Upperchurch, Co Tipperary +353 0504 54400 Jim Ryan and his
2/L17 family open their bar for one night – one night – each week – Thursday, remember
– and yet the reputation and fame of the pub is extraordinary. The house managed
to secure a licence back in the 1900's, and the Ryan family kept it extant by
opening one evening each week. Today, Jim's is a magnet for musicians, not least
Jim's five daughters, talented singers and musicians all.

1436 Geoff's 9 John St, Waterford +353 51 874787 ·
2/P19 @geoffscafebarwaterford Geoff's is not just the busiest pub in Waterford, it's
also the coolest, the hippest, and attracts the biggest queue to get in the doors at
the weekend for the music gigs and the DJs. By day it's a cafe-bar, serving good
food. By night, it is heaving with good sounds, good drinks and people having a
good time.

1437 Harry's Bar Rosses Upr, Sligo +353 71 9177173 · www.harrysrossespoint.com
5/J8 Five generations of the Ewing family have welcomed visitors to Rosses Point, to
this quixotic pub, with its famous well in the bar, down into which you can peer
to see the goldfish. The bar, with its amazing nautical memorabilia, is welcoming
and characterful, their musical evenings are legendary, and the cooking is much
respected.

1438   O'Sullivan's Inn Crookhaven, Co Cork +353 28 35319 ·
3/E23   www.osullivanscrookhaven.ie Plates of toasted sandwiches, bowls of chowder, pints of stout, and chats with the nautical types who colonise the idyllic port of Crookhaven during the summer, is the order of the day in Dermot O'Sullivan's classic bar, which announces itself as serving 'the most southerly pint in Ireland'. The bar is festooned with ancient currency notes left by visitors from all over the globe, and the next door Nottages bar and restaurant is run by the same family.

1439   South Pole Inn Lwr Main St, Annascaul, Co Kerry +353 66 9157388 ·
3/C19   @SouthPoleInn As the extraordinary adventures of the Antarctic explorer Tom Crean have become better known, so more and more people make their way to little Annascaul – it's only a short detour from the main road to Dingle (Daingean Uí Chúis) – to pay their respects at the pub Tom ran when he returned to Kerry. Great atmosphere, but we can't recommend the food.

1440   Brick's Brew Pub Ballyferriter, Co Kerry +353 87 6822834 ·
3/B19   www.brickspub.westkerrybrewery.ie Adrienne Heslin is a great brewer, and there is nothing nicer than a trip to the beach at Wine Strand, followed by a few bottles of Beal Ban dark ale in the atmospheric bar, the most south-westerly craft brewery in the country. Four rooms, which share a kitchen and living room, make for cosy accommodation.

1441   Egan's Liscannor, Co Clare + 353 65 7081430 You could lock us into Egan's
4/F15   anytime you like, and leave us alone to explore the fantastic, oh-so-classy clarets and other great global wines that the Egan family has collected, and which adorn the shelves of this most beautiful bar. If your taste leans more towards the grain than the grape, it's a great place for a quiet drink, or a noisy session. A unique destination.

1442   O'Loclainn's Bar Ballyvaughan, Co Clare + 353 65 7077006 ·
4/G14   www.irishwhiskeybar.com O'Loclainn's is one of the most beautiful bars
ATMOS   in Ireland. Intimate, zen-like, handsome, and with a jaw-dropping selection of whiskeys, it is probably the Irish pub we would most like to be locked into. Time stands still from the second you walk through the narrow green doors.

1443   Ma Murphy's Bar New St, Bantry, Co Cork +353 27 50242 @MaMurphysBar
3/E22   Sean and Mary make everyone welcome in Bantry's classic bar, a lovely warren of
ATMOS   rooms and nooks and snugs, and a bar that is as authentic as it gets. A fantastic range of local craft beers just puts the cherry on the cake.

1444   Nora Murphy's Bar Brandon Pier, Brandon, Co Kerry + 353 86 343 0267 ·
3/C19   www.murphysbarbrandon.com Pádraig Murphy is the fifth generation of the
TERRACE family to run this classic bar, hard by the water's edge at Brandon Pier, and in the shadow of the mountain. One of Padraig's crab sandwiches, and a Kerry craft beer, whilst sitting in front of a warm fire and, oh my goodness, you won't want to leave this Kerry classic. Nora's is a little bit of a detour from the WAW, and about 40 minutes from the town of Dingle (Daingean Uí Chúis), and well worth the drive.

1445   Powers Thatch, Bar & Restaurant Main St, Oughterard, Co Galway
4/F12   +353 91 557597 · @powersthatch With a beautifully restored reed thatched roof, Powers is one of the most handsome bars in the W, a picture postcard perfect pub. But you can also bring an appetite to Rory and Louise Clancy's bar, for the cooking is mighty: lamb burger with spiced yogurt; quinoa salad; spiced beef wrap; honey roast duck. A glorious pub.

The Best Vegetarian Restaurants

The cities Dublin, Galway and Cork all have sections recommending Vegetarian restaurants. The following are places that make a special effort for vegetarians in the regions and Northern Ireland.

✓ ✓ ✓ **OX** 1 Oxford St, Belfast, NI Report: 475/ULSTER COOKING.

✓ ✓ **The Brook Lodge & Wells Spa** Co Wicklow Report: 841/THE EAST.

✓ ✓ **Canteen Celbridge** Celbridge, Co Kildare Report: 879/THE EAST.

✓ ✓ **Deasy's Harbour Bar** Co Cork Report: 988/THE SOUTH WEST.

✓ ✓ **Pilgrim's** Rosscarbery, Co Cork Report: 989/THE SOUTH WEST.

✓ **Grangecon Cafe** Blessington, Co Wicklow Report: 844/THE EAST.

✓ **Firehouse Bakery** Delgany, Co Wicklow Report: 845/THE EAST.

✓ **The Happy Pear** Greystones, Co Wicklow Report: 853/THE EAST.

✓ **MacNean House & Restaurant** Blacklion, Co Cavan Report: 869/THE EAST.

✓ **The Cafe at Grow HQ** Waterford Report: 944/THE SOUTH EAST.

✓ **Momo Restaurant** Waterford Report: 945/THE SOUTH EAST.

✓ **Lettercollum Kitchen Project** Clonakilty Report: 992/THE SOUTH WEST.

✓ **Pudding Row** Easkey, Co Sligo Report: 1157/THE NORTH WEST.

✓ **Sweet Beat Cafe** Sligo Report: 1169/THE NORTH WEST.

✓ **Organico Cafe** Bantry, Co Cork Report: 1012/THE SOUTH WEST.

Chakra by Jaipur Greystones, Co Wicklow Report: 856/THE EAST.
The Heron Gallery and Cafe Ahakista, Co Cork Report: 1009/THE SOUTH WEST.
The Strawberry Field Kenmare, Co Kerry Report: 1031/THE SOUTH WEST.
The Grove Veggie Kitchen Limerick Report: 1074/THE SOUTH WEST.
Vasco Coast Rd, Fanore, Co Clare Report: 1100/THE SOUTH WEST.
Dooks Fine Foods Fethard, Co Tipperary Report: 896/THE SOUTH EAST.
Mikey Ryan's Bar & Kitchen Cashel, Co Tipperary Report: 903/THE SOUTH EAST.
Osta Cafe and Wine Bar Sligo Report: 1174/THE NORTH WEST.
Wholegreen Letterkenny, Co Donegal Report: 1198/THE WEST.
Home Belfast, NI Report: 912/BELFAST CAFES.
Coppi Belfast, NI Report: 497/BELFAST ITALIAN.
Graze Belfast, NI Report: 513/BELFAST CAFES.
Kaffe O Belfast, NI Report: 492/BELFAST BRUNCH.

The Best Fish & Chips

1446 **✓✓ Reel Dingle Fish Co** Bridge St, Dingle, Co Kerry +353 66 9151713
3/C19 If you want to see fish and chips practised as an art form, there is only one destination, and here it is. Mark Grealy is the Rick Stein of fish and chips, a maestro of the art, and you can't eat better fish and better chips than you will find in this tiny, narrow room. Every part of the operation here is considered, sustainable, local and hand-made. Unmissable. 1pm-10pm 7 days.

1447 **Fish Shop** 76 Benburb St, Dublin 6 · www.fish-shop.ie + 353 15571473
1/R13 Fish and chips, for the 21stC, served with natural wines, in a tiny wee place with high stools. As cool a destination as you can find in Dublin. Lunch Tue-Fri, dinner Tue-Sun.

1448 **Leo Burdock** 2 Werburgh St, Christchurch, Dublin 8 +353 1 4540306 ·
1/R13 www.leoburdock.com Dublin's most famous chip shop is the place where Bruce Springsteen buys his fish and chips when he's in Dublin. Leo Burdock also operate chippers in Temple Bar; Dundrum; Phibsborough; Rathmines, and Cookstown Tallaght. They switched over from beef tallow many years ago, but the chips are still excellent, the staff burly and witty. Lunch & dinner Mon-Sun.

1449 **Beshoff Bros** 12 Harbour Rd, Howth, Co Dublin +353 1 8321754 ·
1/R13 www.beshoffbros.com Beshoffs were the first Irish takeaway to be awarded the Marine Stewardship Council (MSC) certification, certifying that they use only sustainably caught wild fish. They also pay a great deal of attention to the quality of their spuds for the chips, which they fry in vegetable oil. The Beshoff family has a long history of fishmongering in Dublin. Lunch & dinner Mon-Sun. Also branches at **Clontarf** (5 Vernon Avenue, D3 +353 1 8339725); **Mespil Rd** (75 Mespil Road, D4 +353 1 6607463); **Dame St** (71 Dame Street, D2 +353 1 6337956); **Malahide** (New Street Mall, Co Dublin +353 1 5620050).

1450 **Cervi** Super Miss Sue, 2-3 Drury St, Dublin 2 + 353 1 6799009 ·
1/R13 www.supermisssue.com Serial restaurateur John Reynolds knows what elements it's important to foreground in his various places, so the chips in Cervi are cooked in beef lard, just as you hoped. Lunch & dinner Mon-Sun.

1451 **Henry & Rose** 6 Florence Rd, Bray, Co Dublin +353 1 282 9342 ·
1/R13 www.henryandrose.ie With branches in Bray, Kilcoole and Newtown, Henry & Rose are particularly recommended for their chips, made with real potatoes, and cooked in beef dripping.

1452 **KC & Son & Sons** East Douglas St, Douglas, Cork +353 21 4361418 ·
3/J21 www.kcandco.ie KC's has the longest queue of any chipper in the country, but it's also the happiest queue, because everyone knows that at the end there is some ace food. Pure Cork, as they say. Open evening 7 days, till 1am Fri & Sat. Open lunchtime Thur & Fri.

1453 **Jackie Lennox Chipper** 137 Brandon Rd, The Lough, Cork +353 21 4316118 ·
3/J21 @JackieLennoxChipShop The most famous chipper in Cork, and a rite of passage for anyone who comes to live in the city. Great staff, superb beef fat chips and, whilst they would never permit themselves any bias, Cork people reckon Lennox's has no equal anywhere in the world. Noon-1am 7 days.

1454 **The Fish Wife** 45 MacCurtain St, Cork +353 87 2644266 · @thefishwifecork
3/J21 Lard for frying the chips, and vegetable oil for frying the fish is the one-two secret of the Fish Wife, a very highly regarded Cork institution. Noon-11.30pm 7 days, till 1am Fri & Sat. There is a second branch of The Fish Wife on Grand Parade.

1455 **Golden Fry** Ballinlough Rd, Ballinlough, Cork +353 21 4292909 ·
3/J21 @GoldenFryBallinlough The O'Connell family's pristine business is heading towards half-a-century of serving great food to the good people of Cork. The cooking shows real verve – steamed mussels; spicy calamari; tempura of hake; Ballycotton scampi; Bresnan's burger with garlic and chive mayonnaise; cheese and onion potato pie; herb-crusted Toonsbridge mozzarella. From 4/5pm-11pm 7 days.

1456 **The Chunky Chip** 1 Western Rd, Clonakilty, Co Cork · @thechunkychip
3/G22 Superbly fried chips cooked in beef fat: crisp, dry, luscious, and a stylish room in which to enjoy them. They only offer one fish – hake – but they cook it beautifully. Sister premises to Wharton's in Bantry, and just as good.

1457 **Quinlan's** 77 High St, Killarney, Co Kerry +353 64 6620666 ·
3/E20 www.seafoodbar.ie Quinlan's use rapeseed oil for frying their fish and chips, and the Cork premises has had a smart makeover. Smart rooms, excellent fish from their own boats. Noon-9pm 7 days. There are Quinlan's Seafood Bars in Cork, Tralee, Kenmare and Killorglin.

1458 **CF Lennox** 81 Main St, Midleton, Co Cork +353 21 4639678 · @cflennoxs
3/K21 A separate company to the famous Jackie Lennox in Cork city, CF Lennox also use beef dripping for their excellent chips. High standards and really satisfying food. Noon-midnight 7 days, from 1.30pm Sun, till 3am Fri & Sat.

1459 **Wharton's** New Street, Bantry, Co Cork One of the most pristine chippers in
3/E22 the country, and a room where everything gleams. Even the vinegar is organic. Chips are cut to order and cooked in lard. Pretty perfect.

1460 **Sailor's Catch** Patcheen's Bar, Annascaul, Co Kerry + 353 66 9767869
3/C19 This is where the locals come for good fish, chips cooked in lard, and a pint of porter. There's also a takeaway.

1461 **McDonagh's Seafood House** 22 Quay St, Galway +353 91 565001 ·
4/G13 www.mcdonaghs.net No one was surprised when the fish and chip-loving
MED.INX readers of *The Irish Times* voted their approval of Galway's legendary McDonagh's, when the newspaper polled its readers as to which fish and chip shop was the best in Ireland. McDonagh's was right up there with the best of the fish and chip specialists from everywhere else in Ireland. The chip shop is to the side of their hugely popular fish restaurant. Lunch & dinner Mon-Sun.

1462 **Hooked** 65 Henry St, Galway +353 91 581751 · www.hookedonhenryst.com
4/G13 The fish comes straight from their sister operation, Ali's Fish Market, which is just
MED.INX around the corner, so the piscine quality is top notch at this fish and chips and seafood restaurant. The space is a nice, modest mix of chipper, cafe and restaurant and it has a great ambience. Dinner Tue-Sun, lunch & dinner Wed-Sun.

1463 **Donkey Ford's** 22 John St, Limerick +353 61 411757 Donkey Ford's is the
3/H17 favourite place of best-selling thriller writer Darren Shan. Like the rest of us, Darren loves the chips cooked in beef fat. No, we don't know why they have protective grilles on the windows either. A Limerick institution, and often voted the best in the country.

1464 **Luigi's** 6 Main St, Longford +353 43 3341228 A favourite chipper for all those
4/L11 who traversed the country and made a stop-over in Longford town to break the
journey to Galway. Today, you have to detour off the motorway to get to Luigi's, but
it's worth it. Vegetable oil is used for frying. 7 days.

1465 **The Saltee Chipper** Kilmore Quay, Co Wexford +353 53 9129911 Just across
2/Q19 from the harbour at Kilmore Quay, this modest room has some nice verandah
seating outside, and celebrated chips. There are pizzas and burgers also, but that's
not why you are here in Kilmore Quay: so chips and beer-battered haddock it is.
12.30pm-9.30pm 7 days.

1466 **The Galley** Kilkeel Rd, Annalong, Co Down, NI +4428 43767253 ·
6/S9 www.thegalleyannalong.co.uk Joey and Aileen have both a takeaway and a
super-smart cafe, and use vegetable oil for frying their sustainably sourced fish.
Meticulous care is evident in every aspect of this pristine and professional outfit,
and the fryer's skills create sublime meals. A heart warming place.

1467 **Long's** 3 Athol St, Belfast, NI +4428 90321848 · www.johnlongs.com It
6/S6 doesn't look like much from the outside, with its barricaded windows and mesh
shutters, but Long's is a Belfast institution, and has been serving superb fish and
dripping-fried chips for more than 100 years. The fish and chips are the equal of
any of the great chippers in Ireland and whilst owner John Copeland keeps things
the way they have always been – the formica booths are still in place – there are
small but steady innovations, and you can order simply grilled fish with lemon or
chilli. All day Mon-Sat.

1468 **Fish City** 33 Ann St, Belfast, NI +4428 90 231000 · www.fish-city.com In
6/S6 a city where chippers tend to stick to fish, chips, pasties and burgers, the smart
Fish City is a surprise. It's the first MSC (Marine Stewardship Council) chipper
in NI, serves wine and beer, offers a 'healthy menu', and chips that are cut to a
scientifically optimum size and cooked in either beef dripping or vegetable oil
(which takes longer to cook). Fish City's innovative approach, and the stylish and
comfortable room, is radical. The Taste of Belfast tours include a visit to enjoy fish
and chips here. All day till 8/9pm 7 days, from 1pm Sun.

1469 **The Dolphin** 19 Georges St, Dungannon, Co Tyrone, NI +44 28 87752400 ·
6/P6 www.dolphindungannon.co.uk Malachy Mallon's shop was voted best chipper
in NI in 2017, and regularly features in the top ten UK chipper list. Beef dripping for
the chips, of course.

1470 **McNulty's** 84 Main St, Limavady, Co Londonderry, NI +4428 77762148
6/P3 www.mcnultysfishandchips.com Brian McNulty is a perfectionist, which
explains why McNulty's legendary chips are first blanched in beef dripping, and
then cooked in vegetable oil. No one takes such care of their food as this Limavady
institution.

The Priory Cork Report: 678/COFFEE.

The Best Tea Rooms

1471
5/E10
MAY-OCT

✓**The Blue Bicycle Tea Rooms** 8 Main St, Newport, Co Mayo
+353 98 41145 · www.bluebicycletearooms.com Philly Chamber's Blue Bicycle is a charmer. The room is girly, the cooking and baking is soulful, and there is a beautiful courtyard out back for when the sun shines. The BB is just the sort of place you dream of finding as you cycle the Mayo Greenway, with delicious food that will get you back on the saddle. Daytime 7 days

1472
5/K8

Village Tea Rooms Dromahair Main St, Dromahair, Co Leitrim
+353 86 2542505 @TheVillageTeaRoomsDromahair Quaint little establishment in the village of Dromahair, set beside the River Bonet serving a selection of teas and cakes; also casual lunches and morning coffees. All day 7 days.

1473
1/R13

Vintage Tea Tours Pick up @ CHQ, 1 Custom House Quay, Dublin 1
+353 1 5266961 · www.vintageteatours.ie Afternoon tea - on a bus! The Tea Tours bus is decked out for a vintage repast, complete with tiered cake stands, and crustless sandwiches. The bus travels through the Phoenix Park, and passes sites such as Trinity College and St Stephen's Green. There is no running commentary, just a chance to sit back, enjoy the tea and see the sites. Book online. Three tours per day.

1474
2/P16

The Tea Rooms at Duckett's Grove Rainestown, Bennekerry, Co Carlow
+353 85 1136075 · @TheTeaRoomsAtDuckettsGrove Everyone loves what Madeleine and Mary-Kate do here in the tea room at Duckett's Grove. They make proper sandwiches – just-roasted chicken; just-boiled ham – and bake rustic cakes and scones, and you ask yourself why everyone everywhere can't do it like this. Charming ruins, excellent acoustic sessions, but it's that ham sandwich that will bring you back to this little gem.

1475
3/H17

Miss Marples Tea Rooms 15 Racefield Centre, Father Russell Rd, Limerick
+353 89 4219889 · @missmarpleslimerick Colette O'Farrell and Jane Harris take great care with the cakes and preserves served with their afternoon teas and morning coffees, making hedgerow jams, freshly baked breads, cakes and meringues. Both breakfasts and lunches are good too, with satisfying sandwiches and home-made soups. All day Mon-Sat.

1476
2/N17

Mocha's Vintage Tea Room 4 The Arches, Gas House Ln, Kilkenny
+353 56 7770565 · @thevintagetearoomsbymocha Every surface of this pretty room is bounteously spilling over with the accoutrements of a classic tea, served on china plates – mismatched of course. The cakes and tarts and traybakes are all luscious, portions are generous. Also a tremendous spot for brunch. All day Mon-Sat.

1477
4/G13
CHP

Cupán Tae 8 Quay Ln, Galway +353 91 895000 · www.cupantae.eu
The frills and the chintz are a big part of the appeal of Cupan Tae, and they add to the daintiness and character of this little room, close to the traffic lights at Spanish Arch. Multi-lingual staff members means that it's no problem to order a cup of Formosa Dong Ding Oolong and a slice of tart in Hungarian. Daytime 7 days.

1478
5/K6

The Olde Village Tea Rooms Main St, Mountcharles, Co Donegal
+353 87 3382763 · @TheOldeVillageTeaRoom As well as being a bakeshop, the Village Tea Rooms serves as a community meeting spot with book clubs, walking groups and art groups. The location, in the picturesque village of Mountcharles, is also a favoured stopping point for cyclists. Cakes, breads and bakes are all homemade, and there are also savoury sausage rolls and pork pies. All day Wed-Sat till 4.30pm.

1479 **SD Bell's Coffee House and Tea Rooms** 516 Upr Newtownards Rd, Belfast, NI
6/S6 +44 28 904/1/74 www.sdbellsteacoffee.com Four generations of the Bell family
have run this distinguished tea blending and coffee roasting business. For fully forty
years, the Leaf & Berry Bar has been an important East Belfast destination for eating
and drinking, and for listening to some good local bands on Thursdays and Saturdays.
Till 5pm, 7 days (closed Sun afternoon).

1480 **The Old Post Office** 191 Killinchy Rd, Lisbane, Co Down, NI +44 28 97543335 ·
6/S6 www.oldpostofficelisbane.co.uk The Post Office is one of the prettiest traditional
buildings in Northern Ireland, set hard by the side of the road. It's a charming warren
of rooms, and changed hands in late 2017 when Stuart and Julia took over. A pretty
garden and a pantry of local foods adds to the charm of an idyllic destination. Daytime
Mon-Sat.

The Best Places for Afternoon Tea

✓**The Merrion Hotel** Dublin 2 The original afternoon tea, expect to be dazzled
with artful gateaux, curds, and exquisite sandwiches. Report: 120/MAJOR HOTELS.

✓**The Westbury Hotel** Dublin 2 Served in extravagant luxury the menu
features brioche rolls, clotted cream, smoked salmon and Champagne. One of
their tea menus crafts pastries into homages of Ireland's milliners, and this work is
quite honestly inspired. Blueberry cheesecake made to resemble a Wendy Louise
Knight Jasper hat. We love it! Report: 121/MAJOR HOTELS.

The Morrison Hotel Dublin 1 They offer both an afternoon tea and a
Gentlemen's Tea, which features a steak sandwich and a pint of craft beer. Report:
126/MAJOR HOTELS.

Ariel House Dublin 4 The team here at Ariel pay enormous respect and attention
to detail to the afternoon tea that they serve to residents and non residents in
their little dining room at the back of the guesthouse in D4. Report: 133/SUPERIOR
LODGINGS.

White Cottages Co Dublin Waterside accommodation in Skerries, that also
makes a feature of serving summer afternoon teas on the terrace.
Report: 1346/B&B.

Kernel Bar & Kitchen Kilkenny The afternoon tea here subverts the convention
of finger sandwiches and cupcakes, and instead offers maki rolls with Goatsbridge
trout caviar, arancini and mini brioche burger buns. Inventive, feminine and totally
delicious. Report: 916/THE SOUTH EAST.

The G Hotel & Spa Galway Like everything about The G - the afternoon tea here
is colourful, witty and full of style. Expect sugarcraft, pinwheel sandwiches, cornets
and lots of pink. Report: 740/MAJOR HOTELS.

The Celtic Ross Hotel Co Cork The Celtic Ross team puts a huge amount of
effort into everything they do; their afternoon tea is no exception. 'Little Guests' tea
for younger visitors, featuring sandwiches, cakes and hot chocolate.
Report: 984/THE SOUTH WEST.

The Best Ice Cream & Ice Cream Parlours

1481
3/C19

✓✓ **Murphy's Ice Cream** Strand St, Dingle, Co Kerry +353 66 9152644 ·
www.murphysicecream.ie Kieran and Sean Murphy are the Emperors of
Ice Cream, and they have achieved the impossible: they have gotten Irish people to
eat ice cream, all year round. How did they do it? The answer is simple: they are
master artisans, and restless perfectionists. Ally these qualities to a Midas touch,
and you begin to understand how they have been able to develop out from their
stronghold of Dingle (Daingean Uí Chúis) to Killarney, Galway and Dublin. Their
terrific team backs up the brothers' flights of fancy with service that is gracious and
humorous: the Emperors of Ice Cream in the Kingdom of Kerry.

1482
1/R13

Teddy's Ice Cream Store 1a Windsor Terrace, Dun Laoghaire, Co Dublin
+353 86 4529394 · www.teddys.ie Teddy's is something of a legend in S Dublin,
an ice cream store and van that is part of the fabric of society, part of the culture
and a must on a hot day in Dun Laoghaire. The store has been opened since the
'50s, and is still making memories for children, 65 years and three generations
after it first opened. All day till 8pm 7 days, depending on weather. There is
another **Teddy's** store in Bray, as well as vintage ice cream vans available for
events.

1483
1/R13

Aussie Ice Dundrum Shopping Centre, Sandford Rd, Dublin 16
+353 1 2968044 An ultra posh set-up in the Dundrum Centre, offering flavours
as diverse as Tahitian vanilla or fresh mango sorbet. Owner Kevin Cahill is a
trained chocolatier, so anything flavoured with chocolate is a good bet. All day
7 days.

1484
1/R13

Scoop 22 Sandford Rd, Dublin 6 · www.scoopgelato.ie Scoop is a dessert
parlour, so there are crepes, waffles and milkshakes as well as the gelato which
comes in flavours such as Irish Coffee, Piña Colada or Ferrero Rocher. Gluten-
free cones available, they think of everything. All day 7 days. Open from noon
Sat & Sun.

1485
1/R13

Scrumdiddly's Crofton Rd, Dun Laoghaire, Co Dublin ·
www.scrumdiddlysworld.com The striped candy colours of the ice cream cups
almost seem muted compared to the colourful range of toppings for their soft
scoop ices. There are jelly beans, fizzy cola, candy mini eggs, wine gums, melted
Maltesers, marshmallows, and many other options, all topped with lashings of
chocolate or strawberry sauce. This is a no-holds barred establishment when it
comes to sweetness. They also do filled crepes and waffles piled high. Noon-9pm
7 days. There is a second branch of Scrumdiddly's in Donabate.

1486
1/R13

Storm in a Teacup The Harbour, Skerries, Co Dublin ·
@storminateacupskerries The ice cream shop of dreamland, this tiny
whitewashed stone store on the harbour is perennially busy. Much loved in
Skerries, so expect to queue, whatever the weather. Noon-9pm 7 days, from
11am Sat.

1487
6/U6

Glastry Farm Ice Cream 43 Manse Rd, Kircubbin, Co Down, NI
+4428 42738671 · www.glastryfarm.com The dairy ice cream from the Glastry
herd on the Ards Peninsula, is the real deal. Look out for it in farm shops and

stores and restaurants throughout NI. Their Vanilla Bean is a particular favourite, and Yellowman is an NI speciality, so even more precious for that.

1488 **Baldwin's Farmhouse Ice Cream** Killeenagh, Knockanore, Co Waterford
2/L20 +353 86 3220932 · www.baldwinsicecream.com Baldwin's comes from the SE of Ireland, and you can often spot them in markets and events. The ice cream is made from milk from their 70 dairy cows. A genuine farmhouse product available in a good range of flavours.

1489 **Jaybees** Dunmore East, Co Waterford +353 51 382305 · @jaybeeslocalshop
2/P19 Jaybees is an Amish Mennonite community who have made themselves indispensable in Waterford for their famous chocolate brownies, their carrot cake and their soft scoop 99s. All available from their cute shop and petrol station in Dunmore East. 8am-7pm Mon-Sat.

1490 **Idaho Gelato** 19 Caroline St, Cork +353 21 4276376 Everybody loves Idaho
3/J21 (606/CASUAL RESTAURANTS) and so everyone is ecstatic when they open their home-made pop-up ice cream shop next door. So much so that their Twitter will trend nationally when they reopen each summer.

1491 **Sundays Ice-Cream & Coffee Bar** 1 Pearse St, Kinsale, Co Cork ·
3/J22 www.sundays.ie If Kinsale is an archetypal seaside destination, then Sundays is the archetypal ice-cream parlour to match. Their '50s-style parlour sells sundaes, shakes, brownies and their own ice cream in many flavours. For the savoury minded they also have hot dogs. All day, weather dependent.

1492 **Casanova Gelato** 13 George's Quay, Cork · www.casanovagelato.ie
3/J21 Barbara and Andrea Bonato use only organic milk to make their ice creams, and they also offer dairy-free and vegan. Kids love their blue ice cream, which is actually flavoured with spirulina algae; it delivers a punch of health boosters as well as tasting delicious.

1493 **Sundaes Ice Cream Parlour** Ballybunion, Co Kerry +353 86 0523089
3/E17 Banana splits, knickerbocker glories, sundaes, doughnuts are all available in this
APR-OCT splendid institution in the seaside town of Ballybunion. Legend. All day from noon-9pm Mon-Sat, till 6pm Sun.

1494 **Valentia Island Farmhouse Dairy** Kilbeg, Valentia Island, Co Kerry
3/C21 +353 66 9476864 · www.valentiadairy.com Joe and Caroline Daly operate a small dairy farm on Valentia Island, from which they make and sell their completely natural – no artificial flavourings, colouring or preservatives – ice cream from the full-fat milk of their herd. Any visit to the island is incomplete without a visit to the dairy. If you can't get to the island, you'll find the ice cream in local Kerry supermarkets. Open May to Oct 7 days.

1495 **Café Linnalla** New Quay, Co Clare +353 65 7078167 · www.linnallaicecream.ie
4/G14 Roger and Brid Fahy make gorgeous artisan ice creams using the milk of their own herd on their own farm, and a visit to their café to enjoy the ices – and lots of other nice things – is one of the great treats of the WAW. All day 7 days. Weekends only during winter.

1496 **Indigo Coffee & Gelato** 86 Stranmillis Rd, Belfast, NI +4428 90687296 ·
6/S6 @indigocoffeegelato Coffee shop, cafe and brunch restaurant is half of the story – the other half is their gelateria, with home-made ice cream in flavours like peanut butter, strawberry and basil - and even sweet potato. Splendid vegan menu of ice creams come in flavours such as avocado, or lychee, made with coconut milk. All day 7 days.

1497 **Cafe Mauds** 551 Lisburn Rd, Belfast, NI +4428 93329988 · www.mauds.com
6/S6 Mauds ice creams are found in many locations throughout Ulster, and it's hard not to love their Poor Bear Honeycomb. All day till 10pm 7 days.

1498 **Tickety Moo Ice Cream** 38 Tully Rd, Oghill, Irvinestown, Enniskillen, Co
6/M7 Fermanagh, NI +4428 68628779 The Tickety Moo farm of jersey cows opens seasonally as an ice-cream farm shop, where you can see every stage of the process from cows eating grass in field to the full-flavoured (balsamic strawberry? Bubblegum Mallow?) ice cream. Farm shop opens Easter to Sept.

1499 **Fabio's Ice Cream** Wine St, Sligo +353 87 1772732 · @fabiosicecream
5/J8 Italian-style ice cream in the W of Ireland - with flavours like mascarpone and caramelised fig; ricotta, cinnamon and pistachio; liquorice; banoffee – and Nutella on top! All day 11am-6pm 7 days, from 1pm Sun.

1500 **Fiorentini's** 67 Strand Rd, Derry, Co Londonderry, NI +4428 71260653
6/N4 Fiorentini's is the oldest cafe still trading in Londonderry (Derry), specialising in fish and chips, and ice cream – especially their knickerbocker glory. A legend in the city.

The Best Delis

1501
1/R13

✓✓ **Sheridans Cheesemongers** 11 Sth Anne St, Dublin 2 +353 1 6793143 · www.sheridanscheesemongers.com The Sheridan brothers shops in Galway and Dublin are cheese temples, but in addition to perfectly matured cheese – the affinage is carried out at their headquarters in Co Meath – they have lots of the best Irish artisan goods. They also have stalls in several Dunnes stores. All day Mon-Sat. Sheridans have counters and supply cheese to delis and supermarkets throughout Ireland, and also have shops in Kells, Co Meath, Galway city.

1502
1/R13

✓✓ **Fallon & Byrne** 11 Exchequer St, Dublin 2 +353 1 4721010 · www.fallonandbyrne.com Fallon & Byrne transformed Dublin food shopping right from the day it opened in 2006. No one had ever done anything on this scale before. The shop is a glorious emporium with all the key Irish artisan brands, and the deli, meat and cheese counters are exceptional. In addition to the store, and the snack and coffee counter on the ground floor, there is also a cool brasserie room on the first floor, and a wine cellar in the basement. Head chef Joe Rumberger has a nice way of working around his ingredients. It's a beautiful, light-filled room with luxe red banquettes and a welcoming bar, and the cocktails are excellent. All day till 9pm Mon-Sat, Sun from 11am-7pm.

1503
2/P19
CHP

✓✓ **Ardkeen Quality Food Store** Dunmore Rd, Waterford +353 51 874620 · www.ardkeen.com The Jephson family's supermarket is just that: a market of superlative food products, with most of the artisan products coming from the counties of the SE. Shopping here is a genuinely pleasing experience, thanks to brilliant staff, and a truly special ambience. The deli cooks restaurant-quality food to go and you can get juices and great coffee. All day until 9pm 7 days.

1504
1/R13

Liston's 25 Lwr Camden St, Dublin 2 +353 1 4054779 · www.listonsfoodstore.ie Karen Liston's shop was the act of transformation for Camden St, the event that transformed this formerly run-down area into Dublin's Food Central. Ms Liston remains ahead of the curve today, and her store is exceptional in every detail. All day Mon-Sat.

1505
1/R13

Lotts & Co 12 Bath Ave, Dublin 2 +353 1 6697800 · www.lottsandco.ie Terrific sourcing means you will want to fill the basket with pretty much everything they have in Lotts & Co. Having a resident butcher is a huge attraction, and this is the very definition of a boutique food store: everything is good, from breads to cheeses to coffee to seafood. All day 7 days.

1506
1/R13

Lilliput Stores 5 Rosemount Tce, Arbour Hill, Dublin 7 +353 1 6729516 · www.lilliputstores.com One of the city's best food shops is out in hipster Stoneybatter, where Brendan O'Mahoney has been feeding the people of Dublin 7 with great Irish foods for a decade. Excellent coffee from Ariosa brings the punters back day after day, and everything is well chosen, and choice. All day 7 days.

1507
1/R13
MED.EX

Picado Mexican Pantry 44A Richmond St Sth, Dublin 2 +353 1 4792004 · www.picadomexican.com Picado is a shop and website selling Mexican ingredients, and they run legendary Mexican evening events, where they teach and cook Mexican food alongside you, and then you all enjoy the feast you have created. Tue-Sun.

1508 **Morton's** 15 Dunville Ave, Ranelagh, Dublin 6 +353 1 4971254 ·
1/R13 www.mortons.ie Out in leafy Ranelagh, the Morton family's store is the original Dublin classic, and maintained standards through all the years when supermarkets destroyed quality retail stores. No other shop has a vibe quite like this. All day 7 days. There is a second branch of **Morton's** on Hatch St. in the city centre.

1509 **The Good Food Store** Serpentine Court, Serpentine Ave, Ballsbridge,
1/R13 Dublin 4 +353 1 6674541 · www.thegoodfoodstore.ie Melissa Clark's pair of super delis show the boss's assured culinary chops: there isn't an idly considered thing on the shelves, and the cooking for takeaway is restaurant standard. All day 7 days. There is a second **Good Food Store** on Sth Gt George's St.

1510 **Dollard & Co** 2 Wellington Quay, Dublin 2 +353 1 6169606 ·
1/R13 www.dollardandco.ie Dollard & Co has stepped up the definition of a deli, with its pizza oven, 40-seater food area and open kitchen, dry-aging chamber for meat, a fish counter and a bakery, as well as all the expected Irish and international cheeses, charcuterie, breads and artisan goods. It's ambitious, and further sign of the culinary life that is rebirthing this part of Dublin's quayside.

1511 **Caviston's Food Emporium** 58 Glasthule Rd, Sandycove, Co Dublin
1/R13 +353 1 2809120 · www.cavistons.com We walked into Caviston's 30 years ago, and came out not just with some smoked haddock, but also with a recipe for onion sauce to serve with it, delivered verbally by Peter Caviston. It's the original southside classic, always bustling, always brilliant. All day Mon-Sat, till 7pm Tue-Fri.

1512 **Select Stores** 1 Railway Rd, Dalkey, Co Dublin +353 1 2859611 ·
1/R13 www.selectstores.ie Oliver and Mairead McCabe's store and juice bar is one of the pivotal destinations in pretty Dalkey village. Mr McCabe is an expert nutritionist, and a great cook, so there is lots of advice along with all the good things. All day Mon-Sat.

1513 **Glasraí and Goodies** Main St, Gowran, Co Kilkenny +353 56 7733799 ·
2/P17 www.glasraiandgoodies.com In a tabernacle tiny shop, Siobhan Lawless packs in all the good things she can find, filling this tiny space to the rafters – literally. Pound for pound, Glasrai outpunches everyone else. All day Mon-Sat.

1514 **Bradley's** 81 Nth Main St, Cork +353 21 4270845 · www.bradleysofflicence.ie
3/J21 Bradley's is unmatched as a place to buy craft beers, as well as superb wines and interesting spirits. But the deli section of the shop is just as good, making this one of the most vital elements of Cork's food culture. All day Mon-Sat.

1515 **O'Keeffe's Shop** 2 Wellington Rd, St Lukes Cross, Cork +353 21 4502010 ·
3/J21 www.okeeffes-shop.ie Up the hill in Montenotte, Donal O'Keeffe's store is a Cork classic, and a culinary Tardis: how do they manage to cram so much good stuff into such a tiny space? All day till 10pm 7 days.

1516 **Urru Culinary Store** McSwiney Quay, Bandon, Co Cork +353 23 8854731 ·
3/H22 www.urru.ie The curious name stands for URban/RUral, and owner Ruth Healy
CHP synthesises a city professionalism with a country woman's appreciation of great food in this stylish shop, which is simply one of the best places to eat and buy artisan foods in the country. There is a fine selection of wines, a distinguished library of cookbooks, and the lunchtime sandwiches are peerless. Daytime Mon-Sat.

1517   **Morton's of Galway** Lower Salthill, Galway +353 91 522237 ·
4/G13   www.mortonsofgalway.ie Eric Morton's store is one of the most masterly examples of culinary editing that you will find in Ireland. Mr Morton sells everything you need, and no more. He has the best of the best, and that's all he offers. Morton's is a model enterprise. All day 7 days.

1518   **The Connemara Hamper** Market St, Clifden, Co Galway +353 95 21054 ·
4/D12   www.connemarahamper.com The hamper is just that: a little space, packed chock-a-block with lovely things. Like a good hamper, it unveils itself slowly, as you come to realise just how many things Sally and Brendan have managed to pack onto the shelves. All day Mon-Sat, noon-6pm Sun during Jul & Aug.

1519   **Indie Fude** 5a High Street, Comber, Co Down, NI +44 7510728109 · www.
6/T6   indiefude.com Johnnie McDowell and Laura Bradley turned their pop-up into the excellent Indie Fude, nestled in a courtyard just off High Street. All the best NI foods are here, chosen by a pair with a keen eye for the best. Do note their fine specialist food and drink evenings, and don't miss the superb cheese ageing room. Over the Goose Café.

1520   **Arcadia Deli** 378 Lisburn Rd, Belfast, NI + 44 28 90381779 ·
6/S6   www.arcadiadeli.co.uk Laura and Mark Brown have taken the venerable Arcadia to new heights over recent years, proven by their ability to create hampers that feature only NI artisan cheeses. Everything else in the store is something you just need to try.

1521   **Sawers** 5 Fountain Centre, College St, Belfast, NI +44 28 90322021 ·
6/S6   www.sawersbelfast.com A Belfast legend for decades – John McKenna shopped here when he was a wee lad, many years ago – Sawers has more stuff on the shelves than you could ever believe, so it's the shop that feels like a souk.

1522   **SuperValu Mount Merrion** 27 The Rise, Merrion, Dublin +353 1 2881014
1/R13   Think of any great Irish artisan food, and if you want to be certain of getting your hands on it, then you only need to head to SuperValu Mount Merrion, where Damien Kiernan will have them waiting for you. The finest artisans want their products here because they know their care and dedication are respected and appreciated in this superlative shopping destination. 7 days.

1523   **The Cheese Press** 10 Main St, Ennistymon, Co Clare +353 85 7607037 ·
4/F15   @CheesePressEnnistymon Cheese runs in Sinead ni Ghairbhith's family – Sinead used to make cheese alongside her sister, Siobhan, who makes the lush St Tola goat's cheese, in nearby Inagh. A lovely store with superb cheeses, locally roasted coffee, and great breads. All day Mon-Sat.

Country Choice Co Tipperary Report: 905/THE EAST.
The Little Cheese Shop Dingle, Co Kerry Report: 1049/THE SOUTH WEST.
Kate's Kitchen Castle St, Sligo Report: 1171/THE NORTH WEST.
The Happy Pear Greystones, Co Wicklow Report: 853/THE EAST.

The Best Distillery & Brewery Tours

1524 **Listoke Distillery and Gin School** Listoke, Ballymakenny Rd, Drogheda, Co
1/R11 Louth +353 87 2405283 · www.listokedistillery.ie Ireland's first gin school,
where visitors learn about botanicals and then design their own 700ml bottle. A
fun and educational day and a great concept.

1525 **Teeling Whiskey Visitor Centre** 13 Newmarket, Merchants Quay, Dublin 8
1/R13 +353 1 5310888 · www.teelingwhiskey.com Dublin's only operational distillery
opens its doors to those who want to understand how the Water of Life is created.
Shop, cafe and bar onsite in this characterful Dublin zone that once was teeming
with brewers and distillers. Open all day 7 days.

1526 **Tullamore D.E.W. Visitor Centre** Bury Quay, Tullamore, Co Offaly
1/M13 +353 57 9325015 · www.tullamoredew.com Visitors' centre in an old bonded
warehouse where you can learn about this triple-distilled, triple blend whiskey and
experience a tutored tasting. Restaurant and gift shop. All day 7 days.

1527 **Killarney Brewery Tour** Muckross Rd, Killarney, Co Kerry +353 64 6636505
3/E20 · www.killarneybrewing.com The tour takes place in the old Killarney mineral
water drinks facility, converted into a brewery and tap room. Water for the beer
comes from a spring from the Devil's Punch Bowl mountain and a tour guides you
through their flavour profile, and allows you to meet the brewer. Pizza served from
their wood-fired oven Tue-Sun from 3pm-9.30 pm. No reservations.

1528 **The Dingle Distillery** Dingle, Co Kerry +353 66 4029011 ·
3/C19 www.dingledistillery.ie The famous Dingle Gin is now one of three spirits made
here at the atmospheric waterfront Distillery. 2017 saw the release of their new
whiskey, and they also make Dingle vodka.This is one of the very best distillery
tours you can do in Ireland.

1529 **Kilkenny Whiskey Guild** Kilkenny · www.kilkennywhiskeyguild.com
2/N17 The Kilkenny Whiskey Guild is a grouping of ten pubs throughout the city, that
each stocks at least 60 whiskeys and are ready and willing to talk through the
options with customers. They also hold regular events and tastings. Find the trail
members on their website.

✓**The Jameson Experience** Co Dublin Report: 6/MAIN ATTRACTIONS.

Guinness Storehouse Dublin Report: 403/DUBLIN ATTRACTIONS.

the
Best
Historical Places

Best History & Heritage

1530
5/F7
APR-NOV

✓ **Céide Fields** Ballycastle, Co Mayo +353 96 43325 ·
www.heritageireland.ie The stone age people who cleared the forests and divided this land into fields for cattle rearing were a peaceful community of farmers, builders and craftspeople. The fields on which they lived remained covered by blanket bog for 6,000 years until the system was uncovered by father and son Patrick and Dr Seamus Caulfield, who noted that the buried stone walls predated the bog, which was being cut for turf. The visitors' centre that is now built over the bog features a stunning, award-winning building, and the museum uncovers not only stone age life, but also the life of the bog that covers it. All day, 7 days.

1531
4/D12

✓ **Derrigimlagh Bog & the Alcock & Brown Monument** Clifden, Co Galway +353 91 563081 By extraordinary coincidence, the wireless station where Guglielmo Marconi transmitted the first wireless messages to America is the same blanket bog where Alcock and Brown crash landed after the first non-stop Atlantic flight. Their journey was a harrowing one, with both men having to leave the cockpit and manually clear the ice from parts of the aircraft after the controls began to freeze. The Derrigimlagh bog, where they landed, was also the site of Marconi's wireless station, and they mistook the bog for a landing strip. The nose of the plane sunk into the bog, but neither pilot suffered injury. They received a reward of £10,000 from the *Daily Mail* and a triumphant journey from Clifden to London, where they were knighted by King George. To have two phenomenal transatlantic historical achievements in the same Connemara field has got to be a reason to visit. In 2016 the Derrigimlagh looped walk opened – a 5km boardwalk cutting through the bog. The Monument - an aircraft tail, is on the hillside that overlooks the bog.

1532
2/N17
AYR

✓ **Medieval Mile Museum** 2 St Mary's Lane, High St, Kilkenny +353 56 7817022 · www.medievalmilemuseum.ie St Mary's Church was built in the 13thC, and in its 800 years of life it has seen many architectural changes. The church was designed by William Marshal (1533/HOOK LIGHTHOUSE), son-in-law of Strongbow and Aoife (1534/REGINALD'S TOWER); also the man credited with re-designing Kilkenny Castle after it had been destroyed by the O'Briens in 1173. A clever 21stC redesign of St Mary's, undertaken by McCullough Mulvin Architects, has transformed it into the MMM, the trailhead of Kilkenny's Medieval Mile. All day, 7 days, till 6pm summer, till 4.30pm winter.

1533
2/P20
AYR

✓ **Hook Lighthouse** Hook Head, Co Wexford · www.hookheritage.ie This is still fully operational 800 years after its construction. The 13thC medieval lighthouse tower stands four storeys high and has walls up to 4m thick. The tower was built by William Marshal, a renowned jousting champion, whom the Archbishop of Canterbury declared to be 'the greatest knight that ever lived'. He was also the designer of Kilkenny Castle and St Mary's Church, now the Medieval Mile Museum (see above). Tours of the lighthouse all year (weather permitting); the compound has an on-site bakery. See also Ring of Hook drive, Report: 1748/ DRIVING ROUTES.

1534
2/P19
AYR

✓ **Reginald's Tower** The Quay, Waterford +353 51 304220 · www.heritageireland.ie Reginald was a Viking ruler, but in 1170 the Tower was occupied by Richard de Clare (aka Strongbow). Strongbow had been invited to Ireland by deposed Leinster King, Diarmait Mac Murchada, and was given the hand in marriage of Eva of Leinster, aka *Aoife Rua*. The tower was where they met and married. This marked the beginning of the Anglo-Norman involvement in Ireland. Aoife became the ancestress of many kings of England, including the current

British royal family. The Tower is the oldest complete building in Ireland, the first to use mortar in its construction. Its walls are 3-4m deep. The museum, part of three museums known as Waterford Treasures in the Viking Triangle, is home to a number of Viking relics. All day, 7 days. Closed Mon-Tue off season.

1535
3/D23
MAR-OCT

✓ **Mizen Head Signal Station** Goleen, Co Cork +353 28 35115 · www.mizenhead.ie Beginning in the visitors' centre shop and cafe, visitors proceed to the signal station over an unforgettable arched bridge, which crosses over a gorge, beside cliff faces and the swelling sea. Once at the signal station, learn the life of the lightkeepers, and also see the Marconi Radio Room, for it was in nearby Crookhaven that Marconi attempted to get his first radio message across the Atlantic. All day, 7 days.

1536
2/P19
AYR

Medieval Museum Waterford The Mall, Viking Triangle, Waterford www.waterfordtreasures.com The museum employs costumed actors to bring to life the stories of medieval Ireland. Artefacts on display include the Cloth-of-Gold Vestments and the Great Charter Roll of Waterford dating from 1373. The museum is sited in the atmospheric Choristers' Hall with its Wine Vault underneath, which dates from the 15thC. All day, 7 days.

1537
2/P18
AYR

The Dunbrody Irish Emigrant Experience New Ross, Co Wexford +353 51 425239 · www.dunbrody.com Reproduction of the type of emigrant vessel that undertook the 6-week Atlantic crossing during the 19thC, when people fled Ireland due to the Great Hunger. Known as coffin ships, an average of 20% and sometimes 50% of those travelling died on board and were buried at sea. The ship tells the story of the brave emigrants from the Irish diaspora in a moving and very different working museum. All day, 7 days.

1538
1/Q14
AYR

Newbridge Silverware Museum of Style Icons Newbridge, Co Kildare +353 45 431301 · www.newbridgesilverware.com The Museum features garments worn by iconic figures of the 20thC – clothing and artefacts pre-owned by Audrey Hepburn, Greta Garbo, Princess Grace and Princess Diana, Michael Jackson, an umbrella by Marilyn Monroe. Even Kim Kardashian. Downstairs room devoted to the silverware and jewellery. The Silver Restaurant serves huge numbers of customers. All day, 7 days.

1539
3/F23
MAR-OCT

Skibbereen Heritage Centre Old Gas Works, Upr Bridge St, Skibbereen, Co Cork +353 28 40900 · www.skibbheritage.com Skibbereen was one of the worst affected areas of the famine in the 1840s and this atmospheric heritage centre looks at the town's experience through personal accounts of people involved at every level. It also tells the history of local sea lough, Lough Hyne, a fascinating place, both through its natural life and its folklore. All day Mon-Sat.

1540
3/H17
AYR

The Hunt Museum The Custom House, Rutland St, Limerick +353 61 312833 · www.huntmuseum.com A former 18thC Custom House houses the private collection of art and antiquities owned originally by the Hunt family. Highlights include paintings by Jack B. Yeats, a menu card by Pablo Picasso, a bronze age cauldron and a gold cross owned by Mary, Queen of Scots. The Hunt Cafe is self-service with carefully-made food overseen by Helen O'Donnell. All day Mon-Sat, & Sun afternoon.

1541
4/F15

The Rock Shop Derreen, Liscannor, Co Clare +353 65 7081830 · www.therockshop.ie Liscannor Stone is characterized by the fossil tracks of a marine worm dating from when the rock was formed 350m years ago. The stone has a bluey-black colour and a textured surface, the non-slip property which makes it ideal for paving. The Rock Shop has developed into more of a retail space than a museum. All day, 7 days.

1542 **Foynes Flying Boat & Maritime Museum** Foynes, Tarbert, Co Limerick
3/G17 +353 69 65416 · www.flyingboatmuseum.com The museum, in the original
MAR-NOV Airport Terminal, harks back to the 30s and 40s, and the days when JFK, Bob
♿ Hope, Eleanor Roosevelt and various movie stars landed at Foynes as transatlantic
passenger flights criss crossed the Atlantic via commercial carriers including Pan
Am, and BOAC. Foynes is also the place where, in 1942, chef Joe Sheridan served
the first Irish Coffee to passengers from a flying boat that had been forced to return
to the airport due to bad weather. All day, 7 days.

1543 **Kylemore Abbey** Kylemore, Co Galway +353 95 41146 ·
4/D12 www.kylemoreabbeytourism.ie The silver grey of the granite facade of Kylemore,
reflected in the lake on a calm day, framed by its steep mountain backdrop is one
of those views that stops your breath when you first see it. This is an iconic building
in an incredible location. For many years a boarding school and home to an order
of Benedictine nuns, the Abbey itself was built in 1867 by a local surgeon, Mitchell
Henry, for his wife Margaret. Nowadays, it's a big tourist operation, with 350,000
people visiting the shop, self-service café and walled gardens to enjoy garden tours,
lakeshore walks and visits to the Gothic church and the ground floor rooms of the
Abbey. 9am-6pm, 7 days. Entrance fee, family tickets available.

1544 **Connemara Marble Visitor Centre** Moycullen, Co Galway +353 91 555102 ·
4/G13 www.connemaramarble.ie Connemara marble has been quarried in the W of
AYR Ireland since the early 19thC, though use of the marble goes back to the stone age.
The colours of the marble are distinctive - so called 'forty shades of green' with
a white vein. At the Joyce's Visitor Centre, you can look through their museum
collection of vintage jewellery, as well as early Irish furniture, pottery and carvings.
During the summer, they offer tours of the jewellery factory. All day, 7 days during
summer, Mon-Fri during winter.

1545 **Doagh Famine Village** Doagh Island, Inishowen, Co Donegal
6/N2 +353 74 9378078 · www.doaghfaminevillage.com The village is, in fact, the
APR-SEPT home of the owner's family, Pat Doherty, who had a vision of telling the story of
the people of Doagh Island, and how they survived from famine times until modern
day. It's the story of a community living on the edge of Europe, the hardships and
the humour: today the village is visited by thousands from all over the globe. All
day, 7 days.

1546 **Armagh Planetarium** College Hill, Armagh, NI +4428 37523689 ·
6/Q7 www.armaghplanet.com The Planetarium in Armagh was the first in Ireland,
and is one of the most respected and technologically-advanced planetaria in the
world. The first planetarium to show moving images by projecting video, Armagh
has especially comfortable seats donated by Belfast aircraft company Shorts. All
day Mon-Sat.

1547 **Ulster Folk & Transport Museum** Cultra, Holywood, Co Down, NI
6/T5 +4428 90428428 · www.nmni.com A way-of-life museum, where you can visit
MAR-SEPT real buildings that have been re-erected, and learn about how country life was
DF lived, through costumed visitor guides. There are demonstrations of basket-
making, printing, weaving, and open-hearth baking. The Transport Museum
displays original horse-drawn carts, trams, fire-engines, and vintage bikes and cars.
Daytime Tue-Sun.

The Best Castles to Visit

1548 **Dublin Castle** Dame St, Dublin 2 +353 1 6458813 · www.dublincastle.ie
1/R13 This impressive 13thC castle has been rebuilt every century from the 17thC
AYR to almost the present day. The castle was selected by the Normans as their
🖵 stronghold, and it became the seat of the UK government's administration in
Ireland until the formation of the Republic. During its life it has been used as a
prison, a treasury and a court. Tours of the castle are available daily. The castle
complex includes the Garda Museum, the Revenue Museum and the Chester
Beatty Library.

1549 **Kilkenny Castle** The Parade, Kilkenny +353 56 7704100 ·
2/N17 www.kilkennycastle.ie The castle has a stunning location that befits its
FEB-OCT impressive structure, overlooking the River Nore, in the centre of medieval
Kilkenny, and set in its own extensive parklands. The castle, which has been altered
many times during its eight centuries of life, was originally designed by jousting
champion William Marshal, son-in-law of Norman lord Strongbow. Three of the
original castle walls built by William Marshal, who reputedly became the richest
man in the British Isles, and also built St Mary's Church (now the Medieval Mile
Museum), Hook Head Lighthouse and Black Abbey, still stand. The castle later
became the property of the Butler family for five centuries and is now home to
the Butler Gallery, displaying solo exhibitions for emerging and mid-career artists.
Open for tours daily.

1550 **Cahir Castle** Cahir, Co Tipperary +353 52 7441011 · www.heritageireland.ie
2/L18 The impressive keep within Cahir Castle is exceptionally well preserved, as are the
AYR walls, the still-working portcullis and the crenellations at the top of each part of
the building. The castle was said to be the most impregnable castle in Ireland.
Built on a rocky island in the River Suir, much of the structure still remains, even
though two cannonballs are embedded in the walls from a battle in 1599. Home
to the Butler family, the most powerful aristocratic family in Tipperary, who arrived
in Ireland in the 12thC, the gate still shows the Butler coat of arms. In 1650 Oliver
Cromwell took over the castle without a fight, which probably saved the building
from destruction. All day, 7 days.

1551 **Birr Castle** Rosse Row, Birr, Co Offaly +353 57 9120446 · www.birrcastle.com
1/L14 For a period of 70 years the Birr telescope was the largest in the world, and this
AYR great piece of technology is viewable in the castle grounds. The castle was always
🖵 a centre of scientific discovery and innovation, and today is home to a Science
Centre explaining discoveries in photography, engineering, astronomy and botany
through a series of interactive galleries. In the gardens there is a treehouse with
an adventure playground, and, with its river garden, terraces, and arboretum, the
garden is also record breaking - it has the world's tallest box hedges. Tours of the
castle and its grounds, summer months. Cafe open Mar-Nov.

1552 **Lismore Castle Gardens** Lismore, Co Waterford +353 58 54061 ·
2/L20 www.lismorecastlegardens.com Present home of the Duke of Devonshire,
MAR-OCT and while the house itself is not open to the public, you can rent part of it (at a
🖵 price!), and tours of the garden and exhibition gallery are well worth seeing. The
castle was originally built in 1185 on the ecclesiastical site of a 7thC monastery
and abbey. In 1589 the house was leased and later owned by Sir Walter Raleigh,
leader of the army who were responsible for the massacre of the Siege of Smerwick
(1634/BATTLEGROUNDS). It is a majestic building, well placed overlooking the River

Blackwater, but do go for the outstanding, gorgeous gardens. There is a nature trail and a sculpture trail, cafe and sales of preserves and plants from the garden. All day, 7 days, last entry 4.30pm.

1553   **Trim Castle**   Trim, Co Meath +353 46 9438619 The largest Anglo-Norman castle
1/Q12   in Ireland, built in the 12thC by Hugh de Lacy, who had been given the Kingdom of
AYR   Midhe (Meath and lands west of it) by Henry II. It took about 30 years to build, but
NO DOGS   thereafter it was not added to or remodelled during any later period. The fortress
was built over a large area of land, next to the River Boyne, so no modern buildings
have intruded on its landscape. The castle keep is three storeys high, with 20
sides, including four towers which flank it. Because the castle has kept its original
shape and style, and still dominates the landscape surrounding it, we can really
appreciate one of the great examples of Norman architecture as it was originally
intended. Access to the keep by guided tour only.

1554   **Ross Castle**   Killarney, Co Kerry +353 64 6635852 · @rosscastlekillarney
3/E20   The siting of this 15thC medieval stronghold will take your breath away. Tours to
MAR-OCT   the castle book up, so you might enjoy the day more by taking a boat trip from here
around the Lakes of Killarney and observing the castle from the water. The castle
is sited on the banks of Lough Leane, and overlooks Innisfallen Island. Cromwell's
Roundheads attacked it in the Confederate Wars of 1652. It was one of the last
fortifications to surrender to the New Model Army, where it was defeated not from
its land side but from the lough. Tours of the castle by pre-booking only. Boat trips
by Ross Castle Boat Tours +353 85 1742997.

1555   **King John's Castle**   King's Island, Limerick +353 61 360788 Much of this fine
3/H17   medieval castle still stands, well preserved, and a battlement walk gives panoramic
AYR   views over the River Shannon and Limerick. The battlements and castellated
corner towers are still standing, though damage was done during the Great Siege
of Limerick. Recently a visitor centre was constructed on the site, and, during
construction, the remains of a Viking settlement were uncovered. King John was
the youngest of five sons of Henry II and Eleanor of Aquitaine. He was appointed
Lord of Ireland, but became King of England after the death of his brother, Richard
the Lionheart, who died childless. King John is probably best known as the
signatory of the Magna Carta. The castle was built on his orders. Visitor centre open
all day, 7 days.

1556   **Bunratty Castle**   Bunratty Village, Co Clare +353 61 711200 During its violent
4/H16   history Bunratty Castle has been built, routed, rebuilt, laid waste, ruined, restored,
AYR   surrendered and finally rebuilt and returned to its former splendour in 1954. After
this restoration the castle opened to the public as a National Monument and the
building, now fully complete, enjoys 15th and 16thC furnishings and tapestries, and
is part of Bunratty Folk Park. Famous for hosting medieval banquets twice nightly
for pre-booked visitors. The castle is also visited each year by Santa. Last tour at
4pm. Banquets served at 5.30pm & 8.45pm daily during summer months.

1557   **Dromoland Castle**   Newmarket-on-Fergus, Co Clare +353 61 368144 ·
4/G16   www.dromoland.ie This beautiful dark blue limestone castle is now a 5-star
AYR   hotel. Once the ancestral home of the O'Briens, direct descendants of the
Gaelic High King of Ireland, Brian Boru, the castle underwent many rebuilds and
renovations over the centuries and narrowly escaped destruction during the Irish
revolutionary period in the early 20thC when many ancestral houses were burned
down by the IRA: philanthropic relief work by the Inchiquin Lords during the famine
years saved the house. In 1962 the house was bought by an American Industrialist

and opened as a luxury hotel. In 2017 the castle underwent further renovation. Bill Clinton, George W Bush, Nelson Mandela, Muhammad Ali, Jack Nicholson and Johnny Cash have all stayed here.

1558 **Parke's Castle** Kilmore, Fivemilebourne, Co Leitrim +353 71 9164149 ·
5/J8　www.heritageireland.ie Named after Robert Parke, but it is for the original
APR-OCT　owner, Sir Brian O'Rourke, that the castle is remembered. O'Rourke was the first man to be extradited within Britain over 'crimes' committed in Ireland. He was sentenced to death, and hung and quartered in the Tower of London. Under the 16thC Plantation system, his lands were given to Captain Parke, who demolished O'Rourke's tower house, and used the stone to build the three-storey castle. The ruins of the castle are now the property of the Irish State, and was completely restored during the 1980s. All day, 7 days.

1559 **Donegal Castle** Castle St, Donegal +353 74 9722405 ·
5/K6　www.heritageireland.ie Built in 1474, Donegal Castle was constructed and
EASTER-SEPT　inhabited by the O'Donnell clan and, later, Red Hugh O'Donnell in the 1580s. Red Hugh O'Donnell was one of the architects of the ill-fated Battle of Kinsale in 1601, Report: 1632/BATTLEGROUNDS. The defeat marked the end of the old Gaelic order, and soon after O'Donnell fled to Spain, followed by other Irish chieftains – the 'Flight of the Earls'. The castle was taken over by the British a decade after the Battle of Kinsale, and was given to army captain, Sir Basil Brooke, who was also given the title Lord of Donegal. Many of the Brooke family descendants entered politics, including the 1st Viscount Brookeborough, another Basil Brooke, who was famously opposed to the granting of civil rights to Catholics and was involved in the formation of the infamous 'B Specials' a militarised Protestant constabulary in Ulster. All day, 7 days.

1560 **Ashford Castle** Cong, Co Mayo +353 94 9546003 · www.ashfordcastle.com
4/F12　The name is sometimes spelt de Burgo, sometimes Bourke, sometimes de Burgh, and sometimes a straight Burke, but this ancient family is reputed to have built no less than 121 castles in Co Galway, chief amongst them Ashford Castle, built in 1228. In the 19thC, ownership of the house passed to the Guinness family, and more recently – in 2013 – the castle was purchased by Red Carnation hotels, who invested significant millions to restore it, adding a 30-seat cinema, a billiards room and a cigar terrace, as well as an ultra-modern, lavishly decorated spa. Now a celebrated wedding venue for celebs, though its reputation for romance goes back to John Ford's *The Quiet Man*, which made many fall in love with the idea of Ireland.

✓ ✓ **The Rock of Cashel** Report: 1561/RUINS.

✓ **Dunluce Castle** Report: 1564/RUINS.

Blarney Castle Report: 1590/MONUMENTS.

1561 ✓✓ **Rock of Cashel** Cashel, Co Tipperary +353 62 61427 · www.cashel.ie
2/L17 *Caiseal* means 'stone fort' and, hovering dramatically on its hilly outcrop,
AYR the Rock of Cashel overlooking Ireland's Golden Vale, in Co Tipperary, is a towering landmark. There are many folk tales as to how the Rock came to be where it is, but there is no argument that it was built around the 12thC. Cormac's Chapel, which dates from the early 12thC, features beautiful details in its arches and corbels, and contains some of the oldest Romanesque wall paintings in Ireland. The surrounding grounds are home to an extensive graveyard packed with impressive high crosses. Brian Boru, most famous of the High Kings of Ireland, was crowned High King in Cashel in 990. He was the only High King to rule the whole island in unity. All day till 4.30/5.30pm & 7pm Jun-Sept.

1562 ✓✓ **Gallarus Oratory** Dingle, Co Kerry +353 66 9155333 ·
3/B19 www.heritageireland.ie Taking the shape of an upside down boat bow, the Gallarus Oratory is 12thC, a beautiful dry-stone chapel that still remains waterproof. There are divisions about exactly when it was built and what it was for: some call it a chapel, others a shelter for pilgrims, or even a funeral chapel. The oratory stands at the foot of Mount Brandon, and overlooks the harbour at Ard na Caithne, scene of a massacre in 1580 (1634/BATTLEGROUNDS). Visitors' centre only open during the summer, but access to the Oratory is available all year.

1563 ✓ **Muckross Abbey** Killarney, Co Kerry Founded in 1448 by Daniel McCarthy
3/E20 Mor, the most dramatic sight is the yew tree which twirls up loftily in the very centre of the building. Yew trees are often seen in churchyards, it is believed on account of their extreme longevity – a yew tree can live up to 1,000 years, and the yew tree in Muckross is said to date from the year the Abbey was founded, making it more than 600 years old. The church itself, and the graveyard around it, is said to have inspired Bram Stoker, when he was writing *Dracula*. Open to the public all year. Park on the N71 and walk in.

1564 ✓ **Dunluce Castle** Bushmills, Co Antrim, NI +353 28 20731938 Dunluce is
6/Q2 perched on the extreme edge of a basalt rock face, dropping down to the sea.
AYR To get to the castle, you need to cross over a bridge. It was built in the 13thC and
NO DOGS the spectacular ruin is loved by photographers and drone operators, who take pictures at sunset, with backdrops of red moons and, more recently, showered in the green flashes of an aurora borealis. There is an internet myth that part of the castle fell into the sea, taking seven cooks from the kitchen as it plunged. This is not true, but it makes a good story. A true story, however, is that the castle had its own gallows. An image of the castle was used on the Led Zeppelin LP, *Houses Of The Holy*. All day, 7 days.

1565 **Mellifont Cistercian Abbey** Tullyallen, Drogheda, Co Louth +353 41 9826459
1/R11 One of the wealthiest and most influential monastic houses in medieval Ireland,
JUN-AUG Mellifont, the first Cistercian Abbey in Ireland, was founded by St Malachy and a community of French and Irish monks in 1142. William of Orange used Mellifont Abbey House as his headquarters during the Battle of the Boyne in 1690. Most of the abbey is now destroyed.

1566 **King John's Castle** Carlingford, Co Louth At the southern shores of Carlingford
1/R9 Lough, King John's castle was originally built in and around 1200 on a rocky outcrop
AYR overlooking the lough. The castle has been added to over the centuries, and is
FREE an atmospheric presence on the shore, just outside the town. You can't miss it,
ADMISSION driving the R173 on the S side of the lough.

1567   **Jerpoint Abbey**   Thomastown, Co Kilkenny +353 56 7724623 ·
2/N17   www.heritageireland.ie Visit to marvel at the magnificent tomb sculptures,
AYR   dating from the 13th to 16thC, particularly the 'Tomb Weepers' carved into the
stone chests. The remains of the 15thC cloister arcade are also decorated with
atmospheric and detailed carvings of knights in armour, and the carvings are said
to have been taken from medieval manuscripts. The Abbey declined after the
Dissolution of the Monasteries in Reformation times, during the reign of Henry VIII.
Guided tours daily in summer. Pre-booked tours only during winter.

1568   **Kells Priory**   Kells, Kilkenny, Co Kilkenny This Augustinian Priory is essentially
2/N17   a walled field, with seven medieval tower houses evenly built into the structure.
JUN-AUG   The tower houses give the priory its local name: Seven Castles. Built in 1193, and
founded by Geoffrey FitzRobert, a brother-in-law to Strongbow, and a knight of
William Marshal (1549/KILKENNY CASTLE). As a structure, it is fortress-like rather
than ecclesiastical. In 1540, Henry VIII dissolved the priory and divided the lands.
It is currently being restored by OPW. Take the sign for Kells off the R697, and the
Priory is 300m on the left. All day Wed-Sun. Tours by prior arrangement.

1569   **Holycross Abbey**   Holycross, Co Tipperary +353 86 1665869 ·
2/L17   www.visitholycross.com The abbey was, for ten centuries, a destination for
AYR   pilgrims who came to see the fragment relic of the True Cross, which was brought
FREE ADMISSION   here around 1233 and is still held in the abbey. The abbey was a ruin from the
15thC until the 1970s, when it was restored completely. There is a meditation
garden which overlooks the River Suir.

1570   **The Samson Crane**   Cliff Walk, Ardmore, Co Waterford The wreck of a floating
2/L21   crane-ship is a dramatic site when completing the Cliff Walk from Ardmore (Report:
1786/CLIFFS & COASTAL WALKS). The ship was being towed when the towline snapped
in a gale and the huge metal structure ended up on the Rocks at Ardmore. The two
crew members were rescued.

1571   **Affane Church**   Lismore, Co Waterford Built in 1819, this ruined, three-bay
2/L20   Church of Ireland sits within a graveyard. Most of the original form of the church
is still intact. Affane was the place where, in 1565, a battle took place between the
Fitzgeralds of Desmond, and the Butlers of Ormond, and there is an Irish dance set,
the Battle of Affane, named after the battle.

1572   **The Port Lairge**   Bannow Bay, Co Wexford Known locally as the Mud Boat, the
2/Q19   Port Lairge was the last remaining steam-driven dredger to operate in Ireland. It
now lies rusting gracefully in Bannow Bay. It is the subject of many photographs.

1573   **MV Plassey**   Inis Oirr, Aran Islands, Co Galway The *Plassey* was a steam trawler
4/E14   that sank in a storm on 8th March 1960. All the crew members were saved thanks
to the bravery of the islanders of Inis Oirr. The boat was swept up on a wave and
has stayed there ever since, and the rusty site became the image of Craggy Island
in *Father Ted*, and is now world famous.

1574   **Menlo Castle**   Menlo, Co Galway On the banks of the River Corrib, and
4/G13   accessible by a riverside walk, is the 16thC castle which has ruined gracefully as an
ivy-clad landmark in the centre of Galway, opposite the NUIG on the other side of
the river. Tragedy came to the house, when it was burned down in 1910. The house
was owned by the Blake family, and the fire claimed the life of Eleanor, their invalid
daughter and two other women. Only the walls of the house remained.

1575 **Kilmacduagh Monastery** Gort, Co Galway The monastery is noted for its
4/H14 leaning tower: it leans over half a metre. This is the tallest of Ireland's distinctive
round towers, built as places of refuge, a place where monks could retreat using
the high front door – in this tower, the door is over 7m above ground. Once in
the tower, they could withdraw the ladder. Kilmacduagh was built in the 10thC,
300 years after the establishment of the monastery. You can see the Crozier of St
Colmáin, who established the monastery, on display in the National Museum of
Ireland.

1576 **Leamaneh Castle** Kilnaboy, Co Clare The shell of Leamaneh Castle, standing five
4/G15 storeys high and with its distinctive stone windows, is a memorable landmark as you
enter the Burren in Co Clare. It's a splendid ruin and was even more splendid when it
was inhabited by Máire Rua MacMahon, aka Red Mary. Red Mary is remembered in
the Burren for her fierce temper. Legend has it, she kept a stallion and visitors who
fell foul of her temper would be challenged to ride the horse, who would then throw
its rider over the Cliffs of Moher. The word Leamaneh means 'horse's leap', and the
house is now said to be the most haunted house in Ireland.

1577 **Chetwynd Viaduct** Bandon Rd (N71), Cork This imposing construction was
3/J21 built by the company that built the Crystal Palace in London. The viaduct was
damaged in the Irish Civil War, but repaired and used regularly until the railway line
was closed in 1961.

1578 **Lispole Viaduct** Lispole, Co Kerry Splendid piece of railway engineering, a
3/C19 seven-span stone and iron viaduct, dating from the era of the Tralee to Dingle
(Daingean Uí Chúis) railway line, which ran from 1891 to 1953. The scene of a
derailment in 1907, the railway closed for passengers in 1939, and shut finally in
1946.

1579 **MV Ranga** Coumeenoole Beach, Dingle, Co Kerry The *Ranga* was a 1,586
3/B20 tonne Spanish container ship washed up on her maiden voyage in 1982. She lost
power during a storm and was wrecked at Dunmore Head. She landed, and is still
visible in Coumeenoole, just off the Slea Head Drive, the R559.

1580 **Fahan Beehive Huts** Slea Head, Dingle, Co Kerry Visible from the Slea Head
3/B20 drive, these huts, or *Clochán*, are situated on the southside of Mount Eagle. You
will see handmade signposts alerting you to them, and you can catch a glimpse
as you drive by. The dry-stone huts, in classic beehive shape, are said to date
back to the 12thC, when farmers were resettled to the marginal land at the end
of the peninsula, chased out by Norman invaders. As many as 460 huts have
been registered in Fahan, believed to have been built over a number of centuries.
Signposted about 14km W of Dingle (Daingean Uí Chúis). Landowners usually
charge a token entrance fee to visit the sites on private land.

1581 **The Deserted Village** Slievemore, Achill Island, Co Mayo There are up to
5/D9 around 100 stone cottages, spread along a stretch of hillside, about a mile in
length, S of Slievemore mountain, and these houses have become known as the
'Deserted Village'. The houses are from what was known as a *booley* settlement
– this was the transhumance practice of grazing cattle in different pastures,
depending on the season. The cottages of the deserted village were used as
summer dwellings before the practice was abandoned and the village lay empty.
3km from Keel on the Slievemore Road.

The Best Prehistoric Sites

1582
1/R11

✓ ✓ ✓ **Newgrange Stone Age Passage Tomb** Brú na Bóinne Visitor
Centre, Donore, Co Meath +353 41 9880300 ·
www.worldheritageireland.ie/bru-na-boinne 1,000 years older than the
Pyramids, Newgrange is a UNESCO heritage site, which puts it alongside the Great
Wall of China, the Pyramids of Egypt, and Stonehenge. It is a Neolithic Ritual
Centre and Passage Tomb, the oldest astronomical observatory in Europe, and
completely intact since the Stone Age. It is estimated that a workforce of 300
laboured over 30 years to fashion the mound using 200,000 tonnes of stone. The
entrance to the tomb was re-discovered in 1699, and on the winter solstice the
inner chamber is illuminated by the rising sun for 17 minutes. No direct access to
the tombs, all access is through the Visitor Centre, then bus to tomb. 9am-7pm
Jun-Sept, with slightly shorter hours during winter season.

 ✓ ✓ **Dun Aonghasa** Report: 2002/THE ISLANDS.

1583
4/G14

✓ **Poulnabrone Dolmen** Ballyvaughan, Co Clare Portal tomb from the
Neolithic period, the burial place of a race of people who lived a life of toil,
infection, violence and early death but who were, despite these hardships,
considered worthy of this impressive burial tomb. The simple but awe-inspiring
collection of stones makes a vivid outline on the landscape, an iconic structure that
is one of the most photographed monuments in all of Ireland. The name has been
translated as 'Hole of Sorrows'. You can see the Dolmen halfway between the
Kilnaboy to Ballyvaughan Road, about 8km S of Ballyvaughan.

1584
6/M4

✓ **Grianán of Aileach** Burt, Inishowen, Co Donegal It's hard to decide which
is more impressive: the stone fort, or the views from it, from where, on a good
day, you can see five counties. The simple circular shape, built on summit of
Greenan Mountain just outside the town of Burt, is incredibly pleasing, with an
encircling wall that measures around 23m in diameter. The entrance passage
reveals the depth of the structure and why it has lasted so well. The hill fort was
constructed around the 8th or 9thC, but there are remains on the site that link this
hillside to a structure dating from 1000BC. Well signposted in the area.

1585
1/Q12
MAY-SEPT

Hill of Tara Navan, Co Meath +353 46 9025903 · www.hilloftara.org
A primeval site with an impressive number of ancient monuments, said to have
been used for the coronation of the Irish High Kings, and some say a site where
142 kings were crowned. From the hill, you can see more than half of Ireland's 32
counties. Also the site of a stone age passage tomb. The whole hillside is steeped
in history, and has an extraordinary aura that is powerful and atmospheric. Wear
protective clothing against the rain, and walking shoes suitable for uneven terrain.
12km S of Navan. All day, 7 days.

1586
3/G23

Drombeg Stone Circle Rosscarbery, Co Cork Seventeen standing stones form
a circle on this S facing hillside, and the placing of these rocks, standing between
1-2m high, are believed to have been built to catch the sun rays of the winter
solstice, which fall on the altar stone at the entrance to the circle. The rocks have
stood in this spot since the Bronze Age. Nearby there is a *fulacht fiadh*, a stone-age
cooking pit. At Rosscarbery, turn onto the R597 and after about 4 km there is a left
turn, signposted Drombeg Circle. There is a car park, and the circle is a short walk
from here.

1587   **Medb's Cairn** Knocknarea, Sligo Sligo is dominated by the distinctive,
5/J8   mountainous forms of Ben Bulben to the N and Knocknarea to the S. Knocknarea
is topped with a cairn, known as Medb's Cairn. You can walk to the top of the
hill and see the cairn, which is massive – about 55m wide and 10m high. Medb
herself was said to be a stone age queen who, for a gift, was given the province of
Connacht. The grave was thought to have been constructed around 3000 BC.There
is a carpark at the base of the mountain, about 3km from Strandhill, and the walk
to the top takes about an hour.

1588   **Garfinny Bridge** Dingle, Co Kerry Said to be the oldest surviving drystone
3/C19   bridge in Ireland, and the only bridge in Ireland to have been declared a National
Monument. This bridge was possibly the route taken by the troops on their way
to Smerwick Harbour, where 600 men were massacred. The bridge is beautifully
constructed in a radial arch, a piece of engineering that has lasted the centuries.

Great Monuments, Memorials & Follies

1589   **The Spire**   O'Connell St, Dublin 1 Dubliners have a penchant for nicknaming the
1/R13   city's monuments and statues, so when the Spire was unveiled in 2002, everybody
waited to see what it would be known as – the 'Stiletto in the Ghetto', the 'Nail in
the Pale', the 'Stiffy by the Liffey', or the 'Erection at the Intersection' all quickly
entered Dublin patois, and the Spire was immediately part of the city. Standing
120m high, and only 3m in diameter at its base, the elegant structure is lit from the
top by LEDs, and bathes in the ambient lighting of the street as soon as darkness
falls. It is built to withstand the storms that can have it sway 1.5m and was
designed by London-based architect Ian Ritchie.

1590   **The Blarney Stone**   Blarney Castle, Blarney, Co Cork +353 21 4385252 ·
3/J21   **www.blarneycastle.ie** The Blarney Stone is a lump of limestone rock built into
the battlements of the medieval stronghold, Blarney Castle. To say someone
has 'kissed the stone' usually refers to a person's ability to speak with loquacity,
expressiveness and persuasion. In order to actually touch the stone with one's lips
you have to lean backwards over the edge of the parapet, holding on to iron cross
rails. The rock's linguistic blessings don't come that easy, but many thousands
have tried. 9am-6/7pm 7 days. Shorter hours during winter.

1591   **The Beacon**   Baltimore, Co Cork Known locally as 'Lot's Wife' the navigation
3/F23   beacon that overlooks Baltimore Harbour is an atmospheric circular, freestanding
edifice, on the cliff's edge. The beacon is made from rubble stone that has been
painted lime-wash white. It is topped with a slender iron finial cap, which is what
gives the structure drama and an almost Celtic, sculptural aura. Practically, it is a
distinctive landmark which has guided mariners for more than a century.

1592   **Father Ted's House**   Carron, Co Clare · **www.fathertedshouse.com**
4/G15   Glanquin Farmhouse was the location for filming the global hit comedy series,
Fr Ted, and, due to the flocks of visitors who regularly visit to pay their respects,
the McCormack family decided to open the house for pre-booked afternoon tea –
strictly by appointment. Contact via the website.

1593   **Tacumshane Windmill**   Broadway, Co Wexford ·
2/R19   **www.meylersmillhouse.com** With its revolving straw thatched top, the windmill
is an arresting site. The last commercially worked windmill in Ireland, it was built
in 1846 and was in continuous use until 1936. Almost all the timber used in its
construction was either driftwood, or timber from local shipwrecks. The windmill
stands three storeys high. If you want to visit, then you can get the keys from the
local Millhouse Bar and Restaurant, who also offer tours to groups.

1594   **The Metal Man**   Tramore, Co Waterford The Metal Man came into existence
2/N20   because, from the sea, it is easy to confuse Waterford Harbour with Tramore Bay.
The insurers Lloyds of London, following the loss of life of 360 men, women and
children in 1816 in the sinking of the HMS *Sea Horse*, commissioned and paid for a
group of five large beacons to be erected and, in 1815, the figure of 'Jack Tar' was
cast, designed by Thomas Kirk (who also designed Dublin's ill-fated Nelson's Pillar).
The slightly dandyish gentleman at the top of one of the beacons is said to be
pointing to the safe harbour, and is dressed in the uniform of British sailors at the
time. There is a second Metal Man, in Sligo, once again pointing to the deep water
channel.

1595 **Scrabo Tower** Newtownards, Co Down, NI The haunting site of Scrabo,
6/T6 towering over the whole of N Down and across Strangford Lough, is the subject of
many an amateur landscape watercolour. Check out any art gallery in Ulster, and
you'll recognise its Rapunzel-style windows and turrets. The tower is 160m high,
higher than the Spire, higher than any cathedral steeple and, until the age of wind
farms and radio transmitters, one of the tallest structures in Ireland. Grounds open
Mon-Thurs, grounds and Tower Mon-Sun. Last admission 3.40pm.

1596 **The National Famine Monument** Murrisk, Co Mayo The Monument at Murrisk
5/E10 was erected to commemorate the more-than-a-million Irish people who died in
the Great Famine in the mid 19thC in Ireland. The monument depicts a three-
masted ship, with skeleton bodies forming the rigging. Irish famine victims, like
many migrants, fled the country in overcrowded ships, which became known as
Coffin Ships. The monument was unveiled in 1997, and is the work of sculptor John
Behan. There is a second famine memorial in Dublin, which features painfully thin
sculptural figures, situated as if walking to the coffin ships on the Dublin Quayside.
The sculpture, entitled Famine, was created by Edward Delaney.

1597 **Kindred Spirits** Bailic Park, Midleton, Co Cork During the time of the Great
3/K21 Famine an extraordinary contribution was made by the Native American Choctaws,
who donated the then substantial sum of £111 to famine-relief. This gorgeously
evocative sculpture is there to commemorate this act of generosity, and to
remember the story of two separate nations, tied together in suffering. The statue
represents Choctaw feathers – eagle feathers – made from stainless steel, arranged
in a circle, symbolising an empty bowl. Visible from the N25.

1598 **The Sky Garden** Liss Ard Estate, Skibbereen, Co Cork +353 28 40000 ·
3/F23 www.lissardestate.com To get to the Sky Garden, you walk through a dark
passageway, as if you are entering a tomb. Halfway through the passage there is
a shaft of light, and at the end there are stairs, the tread of which are a little too
high for comfort, so you experience an *Alice in Wonderland* moment as you pull
yourself upwards. Then, magic. You are in a scooped out bowl of grassy earth,
where the 'garden' is the sky. The viewing platform is a stone grave-like bed, where
you lie and contemplate the clouds. Renowned American artist, James Turrell,
knows how to play with all your emotions. This astonishing Turrell sculpture was
commissioned by a previous owner of Liss Ard, and was intended to be one of
three, but only the Sky Garden was completed. Not recommended for anyone
with physical disability. From Skibbereen follow signs for Castletownshend, A596,
entrance to hotel 1km on right.

1599 **Phil Lynott Statue** Harry St, Dublin 2 Phil Lynott of Thin Lizzy was a true
1/R13 Dublin hero, and his statue is outside Bruxelles pub, near Grafton St, supposedly a
hostelry that he knew well. In 2013 Phil's bass guitar was snapped in half in a traffic
accident, but the Paul Daly bronze was restored and today is visited by fans who
snap selfies beside his life-size image. Phil Lynott died in 1986, and his grave is in
Sutton.

1600 **Molly Malone Statue** Suffolk St, Dublin 2 The 'Dolly with the Trolley', the
1/R13 'Trollop with the Scallop', the 'Flirt in the Skirt', the 'Tart with the Cart' are all Dublin
names for this bronze sculpture, subject of the ballad anthem, '*Cockles and mussels,
alive, alive, oh*'. The sculpture, designed by Jean Rynhart, was presented to Dublin
by the Jury's Doyle Group to mark the Millennium. It's hilarious to watch tourists
taking selfies of themselves pretending to grope the bosomy barrow trader.

1601 **An Tarbh, The Wire Bull of Cooley** J15, M1, Co Louth This gorgeous statue of a
1/R10 bull, by artist Michael McKeown, represents the great Irish folk epic, where Queen
Maeve of Connacht fought with her husband Ailill over ownership of the bull.

1602 **Dromana Gate** Cappoquin, Co Waterford Ireland's only Hindu Gothic gate –
2/L20 said to have been inspired by the Royal Pavilion in Brighton. It still stands proudly
at the bridge, at the entrance to the Dromana Estate in Cappoquin.

1603 **Holy Well & Rag Tree** Tully, Co Kildare St Brigid, according to Irish mythology,
1/P14 was a Celtic goddess, and there are many holy wells dedicated to her memory. Holy
wells are often accompanied by rag trees, where people tie a piece of clothing. The
offering, which is first dipped in the well with accompanying prayer for its owner, is
called a 'clootie'. St Brigid's Day is 1st Feb, officially the first day of Spring in Ireland,
and a day when many people still make a cross formed out of rushes. OS Map 55, a
few kilometres from the National Stud, and signposted.

1604 **Rise** Belfast, Co Antrim, NI The massive globe, rising nearly 40m high and 30m
6/S6 wide is at the Broadway roundabout at the junction of the Westlink and the M1
Motorway in Belfast. The roadside gateway to the city, where nearly 100,000 cars
flow by each day. The structure is two geodesic domes, and it's an awe-inspiring
landmark as you arrive in Belfast. There was considerable discussion about the cost
– £400,000 – for a piece of public art. It is Belfast's largest piece of public artwork
and represents a new rising sun to celebrate peace in the city.

1605 **Joey and Robert Dunlop Memorial Gardens** Castle St corner of Seymour St,
6/Q3 Ballymoney, Co Antrim, NI +44 28 27660230 George Best is NI's best-known
sporting legend, but the motorcyclist Joey Dunlop was actually a figure more
beloved than Best: his funeral in 2000, following his death at a race in Estonia,
attracted more than 60,000 people from all over the world. Joey's brother, Robert,
died in 2008 at a qualifying race for the North West 200, and his garden adjoins the
memorial garden dedicated to his brother, Joey. Open all year; admission free.

1606 **The Peace Bridge** Derry, Co Londonderry, NI A cycle and pedestrian bridge
6/N4 which symbolically, and practically, joins the two communities on either side of
the River Foyle in the centre of Londonderry (Derry). On one side, the Unionist
Waterside, on the other, the Nationalist Cityside. It's an elegant bridge, 235m long,
designed by the architects who also designed the Sutong Yangtze River Bridge and
Gateshead Millennium Bridge. Londonderry (Derry) has never been the same after
the bridge was built: its creation unleashed a dynamic creative and community
spirit, and the city has been flourishing ever since.

The Most Interesting Abbeys, Cathedrals & Churches

1607 **St Andrew's Parish Church** Westland Row, Dublin 2 ·
1/R13 www.standrews.ie/parish The Doric portico at the front of the church makes St Andrew's a distinctive landmark on Westland Row. The church was consecrated in 1834 and designed by John Bolger, based on plans for another church by James Leeson.

1608 **St Paul's Church** Arran Quay, Dublin 7 · @stpaulschurcharranquay
1/R13 A striking site when driving down the Liffey quays, built soon after Catholic emancipation in Ireland. The copper dome, Italianate bell tower and elegant ionic columned portico give the building great stature. The three figures on the roof are Saints Peter, Patrick and Paul. Nowadays the church has reinvented itself as a church for young people.

1609 **St Stephen's 'Pepper Canister' Church** 2 Mount St Cres, Dublin ·
1/R13 www.peppercanister.ie A popular album cover location and, today, a popular music venue, the Pepper Canister church was named not for its distinct shape, but due to its being built on the site of a medieval leper hospital. Parishioners of this Church of Ireland included Oscar Wilde and William Butler Yeats, and it sits elegantly in the centre of this handsome Georgian streetscape.

1610 **St Finbarr's Oratory** Gougane Barra, Ballingeary, Co Cork +353 87 7842534
3/F21 A thrillingly cute church, on an island, on a lake, in a valley, between mountains
ATMOS and a forest, the Oratory at Gougane Barra is today a favoured wedding venue.

1611 **St Barrahane's Church** Main St, Castletownshend, Co Cork One of a good
3/F23 number of country churches that boasts a Harry Clarke window. This church actually has three, as well as windows made by James Powell & Sons, 17thC glass-maker and stained glass manufacturers. The church porch also displays an oar from a SS *Lusitania* rescue boat.

1612 **All Saints Church** Drimoleague, Co Cork Built 1954, and a powerful example of
3/F22 mid-20thC church architecture, it was constructed from limestone and concrete: the square bell tower has louvred windows, the windows on the side of the church are classic '50s design. Inside the church there are no pillars, just a huge cavernous space – a splendid feat of modern engineering. The stained glass wall is a concertina of colour. Services Sat, 7.30pm, Sun noon

1613 **St Mary's Cathedral** Killarney, Co Kerry The work of trailblazing architect
3/E20 A.N.W. Pugin, who was born in London in 1812 and has been called 'God's architect'. Pugin was said to have been largely responsible for the interior of the Palace of Westminster in London, and the design of Big Ben, though he never received credit in his lifetime. Before his early death, he suffered a breakdown and spent some time in Bedlam Hospital. St Mary's is recognised as a masterpiece in Gothic Revival architecture.

1614 **Lurganboy Church** Lurganboy, Manorhamilton, Co Leitrim Known as the 'Tin
5/K7 Church', Lurganboy is made from corrugated-iron. The arched windows have cast-iron lattice work, painted glass and a decorative wrought-iron gate. This is a rare example of corrugated-iron architecture, built in 1862.

1615   **St Aengus Church** Burt, Co Donegal Taking inspiration from the nearby
6/M3   Grianan of Aileach (1584/PREHISTORIC SITES), the Burt Chapel is a Liam McCormick
masterpiece dating from the '6os. The circular shape comes directly from the late
Bronze Age hilltop fort, but clever touches include the off-centre roof, the Cubist
stained glass windows, and the ingenious engineering which means the church is
circular both outside and inside, but still has room for extra space due to the placing
of the internal structure. Awarded 'Building of the Century' in a millennium poll.

1616   **Down Cathedral** Downpatrick, Co Down, NI · www.downcathedral.org
6/17   The burial ground of St Patrick, the building stands on the site of a 12thC
monastery, and there are several high crosses on the site from the 9th, 10th, and
12th centuries. A granite slab marks St Patrick's grave.There is a 132-km Pilgrim
walk, which begins at Navan and ends at the cathedral. Cathedral shop and
facilities. All day Mon-Sat.

Kylemore Abbey Report: 1543/HISTORY.
St Patrick's Cathedral Report: 415/DUBLIN ATTRACTIONS
Christ Church Cathedral Report: 410/DUBLIN ATTRACTIONS.

The Most Interesting Graveyards

1617 **Glasnevin Cemetery** Finglas, Dublin 11 · www.glasnevinmuseum.ie
1/R13 Glasnevin is the largest burial place in Ireland, and a cemetery for all denominations. It was established by political leader 'The Liberator' Daniel O'Connell as a place where Catholics could be buried according to their own religious rules, something that had not previously existed in Ireland. The round tower, built in the mid 19thC commemorates him – though it was blown up in 1971, a Loyalist reprisal to the destruction of Nelson's Pillar on O'Connell St. (It is now restored.) The first person buried in Glasnevin was 11-yr-old Michael, and his grave took eight hours to dig. Since then more than 1.5m have followed, including many famous Irish people including Charles Stewart Parnell, Maud Gonne, Brendan Behan, Constance Markievicz and Christy Brown. The graveyard now has its own museum, tours daily. 7 days.

1618 **Huguenot Cemetery Merrion Row,** St Stephen's Green, Dublin 2 Normally
1/R13 locked, but you can look through the railings and see the gravestones in this tiny city centre graveyard for the descendants of Huguenots – French Calvinists, who chose exile in Ireland, rather than having to give up their religion in 17thC Catholic France.

1619 **Grangegorman Military Cemetery** Blackhorse Ave, Cabra, Dublin 7 Opened
1/R13 in 1876, and the place where British servicemen were buried, along with their relatives. There are graves from both world wars. Some of the war dead were relocated from other graveyards. The site is near the Irish National War Memorial Gardens in Islandbridge, dedicated to the 49,400 Irish soldiers who gave their lives in the Great War of 1914-1918.

1620 **Ballybough Jewish Cemetery** 65 Fairview Strand, Dublin 3 The oldest Jewish
1/R13 site in Ireland, dating from 1718. A number of the graves are unmarked, others are inscribed in Hebrew, with the Jewish calendar month of death. The oldest dated tombstone is from 1777. The gate lodge, just down from Fairview Park, bears the inscription *'Built in the year 5618'* from the Hebrew Calendar. Ballybough translates as 'town of the poor' in Irish. Fairview was the place where Bram Stoker grew up – legend has it the cemetery influenced his account of Count Dracula.

1621 **Dunlewey Church** Poisoned Glen, Co Donegal The Poisoned Glen, at the foot
6/K4 of Mount Errigal, is the stunning location of a ruined 19thC Protestant church, the Church of Dunlewey. The graveyard contains the grave of a man whose wife – who died later – is buried in the Catholic Church of the Sacred Heart across the valley. Her grave faces across the valley to her husband's, and is the only grave to do so: all the other grave stones in the Catholic Church face the other way.

1622 **Famine Graveyard** Abbeystrewry, Skibbereen, Co Cork This peaceful plot,
3/F23 overlooking the River Ilen, just W of Skibbereen town centre, is the location of a famine burial pit, where it is thought 8-10,000 coffinless people were buried. Skibbereen was one of the worst affected towns by the 1840's famine, which is now recognised as a humanitarian catastrophe.

1623 **Carrowmore Megalithic Cemetery** Carrowmore, Co Sligo +353 71 9161534
5/J8 · www.heritageireland.ie The largest prehistoric cemetery, and one of the
APR-NOV oldest cemeteries in Ireland, with over 60 tombs, about 30 of which are above ground. The oldest tomb predates Newgrange by 700 years, and is older than the

Pyramids. Sadly the ravages of time, farming and general site removal has reduced the number of stones significantly, but this is still one of the most important prehistoric sites in Ireland. Visitor centre, Apr-Nov 7 days, on the R292 heading S out of Strandhill.

1624 **Yeats Grave** Drumcliff Parish Church, Co Sligo 'Cast a cold Eye On Life, on
5/J7 Death Horseman pass by' W.B. YEATS June 13th 1865, January 28th 1939. This is the inscription on this famous grave in Drumcliff, under Ben Bulben. The words were Yeats' own epitaph, and he also gave instruction that the grave should consist of 'no marble, no conventional phrase'. The words come from one of his last poems, *Under Ben Bulben*.

1625 **Arthur Guinness' Grave** Oughterard, Co Kildare Just off the N7 at Kill (no
1/Q13 significance in the name, Kill means 'Village' in Ireland) you find Oughterard cemetery, the final resting place of Arthur. The inscription on his grave reads 'In the adjoining vaults are deposited the mortal remains of Arthur Guinness late of James's Gate in the city'. The grave has become a visitors' attraction bringing people from all over the globe.

1626 **Flann O'Brien's Grave** Deansgrange Cemetery, 2 Dean's Grange Rd,
1/R13 Co Dublin The first person to be buried in Deansgrange was Anastasia Carey in 1865, in the N (Catholic) section, near the Catholic chapel. Protestants had their own chapel and were on the S side. Deansgrange is the burial site of satirist Flann O'Brien (Brian Ó Nualláin), author of *At Swim-Two-Birds*, *The Third Policeman* and others. Visiting hours 10am-4.30pm 7 days.

1627 **Rory Gallagher's Grave** St Oliver's Cemetery, Ballincollig, Co Cork
3/J21 You can't miss the grave of iconic guitarist Rory Gallagher in St Oliver's Cemetery. The headstone depicts the sun's rays, a replica of an award he received in 1972 when he was named International Guitarist of the Year. There is also a bronze statue of Rory Gallagher in his hometown of Ballyshannon in Co Donegal and a lending, reference and archival library – the Rory Gallagher Music Library – in the Cork City Library, the city where he grew up.

Great Irish Battlegrounds

1628   **The Battle of the Boyne**   Drogheda, Co Louth   The Battle of the Boyne took
1/R11   place at Oldbridge, in 1690, a fordable bend in the Boyne River, four miles W of
Drogheda. The fight was between the Dutch-speaking Protestant, William of
Orange and his Catholic father-in-law, James II. William's forces outnumbered the
opposing army (Jacobites) by three to one and, after managing to lure a bulk of the
Jacobites towards Slane, the actual battle pitched 26,000 Williamites against 6,000
Jacobites. All the fighting took place on the S side of the river, and about 1,500 men
were killed. William then travelled to Dublin, and his victory assured Protestant
supremacy in Ireland, the symbolic importance of which is still celebrated in NI
every 12th July.

1629   **The Battle of Clontarf**   Clontarf, Co Dublin   Clontarf, N Dublin, was the location
1/R13   for the famous battle between Brian Boru, High King of Ireland, and King Sitric
Silkenbeard, his Viking adversary. The battle supposedly took place on Good Friday
in 1014, when at least 10,000 men died. It was a victory for Brian, and his brother
Wolf the Quarrelsome, but it resulted in the death of Brian, who was killed in his
tent just hours after victory by Viking Brodir, who himself was brutally dealt with by
Wolf the Quarrelsome.

1630   **Siege of Drogheda**   Drogheda, Co Louth   Cromwell arrived in Ireland in
1/R11   1649 with his New Model Army of 12,000 men, and between 1649 and 1653
approximately 20% of the population of Ireland died, be it from violence, famine
and disease. Nearly 400 years later, the Irish have not forgiven him. Cromwell
was both politically and religiously hostile to Ireland and he was revengeful of
the deaths of English and Scottish Protestants in the Irish Rebellion of 1641.
After arriving in Ireland, he first attacked Rathmines, and then the port town of
Drogheda where, in 1649, his troops killed around 3,500 people *after* the town had
been captured, including civilians, prisoners and priests.

1631   **The Easter Rising**   GPO, O'Connell St, Dublin 1   The Easter Rising was a
1/R13   rebellion against British rule that took place in Dublin between Easter Monday
(24th) and 29th April 1916. Technically it was a failure, and the British military
response was swift. Ultimately, however, its legacy lay in turning the majority
of Irish people away from the idea of British Home Rule, and towards a fully
independent Irish Republic. The GPO on O'Connell St in Dublin was the rebellion
headquarters, where Patrick Pearse, James Connolly and their group were able to
hoist the flag on an Irish Republic and read the Proclamation of Independence.

1632   **Battle of Kinsale**   Kinsale, Co Cork   In 1601, Kinsale was the location for a bloody
3/J22   battle between the English and the combined Irish and Spanish forces, but history
tells that the Irish were defeated even before the Spanish entered battle. The
battle brought to an end Gaelic rule and the Ulster leaders, Hugh O'Neill and Red
Hugh O'Donnell, left for exile in Spain in what was known as the Flight of the Earls.
England made peace with Spain, and began its rule over Ireland.

1633 **Irish Civil War** Béal na mBláth, Co Cork The Irish Civil War happened in
3/H21 response to the Treaty of 1921 between the English and the Irish, in which Ireland
was to become a Free State, but Ulster would remain under British rule. Michael
Collins, signatory of the Treaty, was ambushed in Béal na mBláth near Coppeen
in W Cork, and assassinated. There is still considerable sadness in Ireland over
the violence that occurred between former comrades. Béal na mBláth is S of
Crookstown on the R585, and there is a monument to Collins in the location
of the ambush.

1634 **The Siege of Smerwick** Ard na Caithne, Dingle, Co Kerry In this peaceful
4/F16 headland, just off the Slea Head drive on the N Dingle peninsula, the Papal forces
of Spanish, Italian and Irish who had surrendered to the British forces led by Sir
Walter Raleigh were beheaded in an execution of 600 men that took two days,
and supposedly took place in a field, known locally as *Gort a Ghearradh* – the Field
of the Cutting. Their bodies were thrown into the sea. Archaeologists found many
16thC skulls in another field known as *Gort na gCeann* (the Field of the Heads),
which verified the accounts of this terrible massacre. Follow signs to Fort del Oro,
until you get to the car park. There are some self-catering cottages and a golf
course on the little spit of land.

1635 **Spanish Armada** Spanish Point, Co Clare In 1588, the Spanish Armada began
4/F16 its fateful journey as a massive flotilla of 130 ships. Their purpose was to overthrow
the Protestant Queen, Elizabeth I. As the ships travelled Northward they were
attacked by the English, led by Sir Francis Drake and, having been cut off from
returning via the English Channel, took the perilous strategy of sailing N, around
Scotland, NI, with the plan of returning to Spain via the W Coast of Ireland. The
storms raged, and the Spanish were ill equipped to make the journey. Many of the
ships were wrecked on their journey S. Some landed, but their half starved, half
drowned crew were massacred.

1636 **The Murals** Belfast, NI The history and culture of Belfast is often told by
6/S6 the murals painted on the gable ends of the houses in the different religious
communities. While the history behind these stories is often war-torn and tragic,
they are often extremely descriptive, and tell a story of a city that was effectively a
battleground for many years. Some of the murals are political, depicting nationalist
and loyalist heroes. Others depict NI's sporting heroes, particularly George Best.
The so-called International Peace Wall depicts other international conflicts and
global campaigns. Finally, there are cultural walls depicting, for example, the work
of CS Lewis and The Undertones. Many of the city bus tours take in the murals, as
do the Black Taxi tours.

The Important Literary Places

1637 **Samuel Beckett Theatre** Trinity College Dublin, College Green, Dublin 2
1/R13 Beckett was a star student at Trinity College, and the theatre is nowadays home
to the School of Drama, Film and Music. It was opened in 1992, celebrating the
quadricentenary of TCD, and in addition to its college role, it also houses visiting
dance and theatre productions, in addition to events at the Dublin Theatre Festival.

1638 **Kavanagh's Seat** Grand Canal, Dublin 4 There are actually two seats
1/R13 commemorating the great Monaghan poet, on the Grand Canal. The best known is
on the N bank, on Mespil Road, and has a statue of the poet, by John Coll. Less well
known is the simple wood and granite seat, at the lock gates near Baggot St Bridge,
unveiled in 1968, shortly after Kavanagh's death.

1639 **James Joyce Tower & Museum** Sandycove, Co Dublin ·
1/R13 www.jamesjoycetower.com This Martello tower, close to the sea at Sandycove,
memorably features in the opening pages of *Ulysses*, and houses a splendid
collection of Joycean memorabilia. It is maintained voluntarily by the members of
the Friends of Joyce Tower Society, and is open all year. Free admission.

1640 **Frank McCourt Museum** Leamy House, Hartstonge St, Limerick
3/H17 +353 61 319710 · www.frankmccourtmuseum.com *Angela's Ashes* was an
enormously successful memoir written by Irish American author, Frank McCourt,
who grew up in abject poverty in Limerick. The museum is in the Georgian Quarter
of Limerick City, on the site that was Frank's former school. All day Mon-Fri till
4.30pm. By appointments only on Sat & Sun.

1641 **Synge's Cottage** Inis Meain, Aran Islands, Co Galway The house where JM
4/E14 Synge stayed when he visited the Aran Islands, between 1898 and 1902, has been
restored, and is a splendidly authentic tribute to the great playwright. The family
who looked after Synge still own the cottage, and maintain it beautifully. The small
admission charge goes towards the upkeep of the cottage. Make sure to also visit
Synge's Chair, where the dramatist would go to write.

1642 **Pearse's Cottage** Ros Muc, Co Galway +353 91 574292 ·
4/E13 www.heritageireland.ie Patrick Pearse, leader of the 1916 uprising, built his
cottage in Ros Muc in 1909, and thatched it in the style of the local country
dwellings. Today, an adjacent visitor centre provides an introduction to the Irish
language and Gaeltacht culture, in addition to Pearse's connection to Ros Muc. All
day, 7 days, till 4pm winter, 6pm summer.

1643 **Coole Park Nature Reserve** Coole, Gort, Co Galway +353 91 651804 ·
4/H14 www.coolepark.ie The home of Lady Gregory, who founded the Abbey Theatre
with W. B. Yeats and Edward Martyn, the house was the centre of the Irish Literary
Revival in the early 20thC. Today it is a 1,000-acre nature reserve, with a complex
wetland and turlough system which is of global importance. There are two
waymarked trails, and a visitors' centre.

1644 **John B Keane's Pub** 37 William St, Listowel, Co Kerry +353 68 21127 ·
3/E18 @JohnBKeane When he wasn't penning hugely popular plays, John B. Keane
was a publican in Listowel, having bought the premises on William St after he was
outbid on a grocer's shop. The pub has been in the family for more than 60 years
and is today run by John B's son, Billy.

1645 **Oscar Wilde Memorial Statue** Merrion Square Park, Dublin 2 The raffish
1/R13 statue of Oscar Wilde in the beautiful Merrion Sq was created by the sculptor
Danny Osborne, and erected in 1997. It's right across the street from Wilde's
birthplace at No 1, Merrion Square. The work uses a variety of precious stones, and
there are two accompanying pieces.

1646 **Yeats Tower** Gort, Co Galway · www.yeatsthoorballylea.org W. B. Yeats
4/H14 wrote some of this finest poetry whilst living with his wife and family in Thoor
Ballylee, the 15thC tower house built by the De Burgo family. But the tower was
more than a home, becoming a hugely important symbol and monument to
the poet, not least the tower's winding stair. In 2017 the tower celebrated the
centenary of the first work carried out on Thoor Ballylee. Open 7 days during the
summer months.

1647 **Seamus Heaney Home Place** 45 Main St, Bellaghy, Co Londonderry, NI
6/Q5 +4428 79387444 · www.seamusheaneyhome.com The Nobel Laureate's deep
connection to the area around Bellaghy is explored over the two floors of the
Home Place, and artefacts include his school satchel and school desk, and many
manuscripts.

1648 **Laurel Villa Guest House** 60 Church St, Magherafelt, Co Londonderry, NI
6/Q5 · www.laurel-villa.com Geraldine and Eugene Keit's guest house has hosted
4 ROOMS poetry festivals and poetry evenings, and is closely associated with Seamus Heaney,
who both read here and was patron of the festival. Visitors to the Heaney Home
Place in Bellaghy, a 10-minute drive away, often stay in the comfortable rooms.

1649 **Tyrone House** Kilcolgan, Co Galway Dramatic shell of a late 19thC house, ready
4/G14 to collapse but still beautiful and in dire need of conservation. The house inspired
the Somerville and Ross novel *The Big House of Inver*. Follow the road past Moran's
of the Weir, off the N18 at Kilcolgan heading for Stradbally, head in the direction of
the sea. You'll see the house on the right.

1650 **Bronte Homeland Drive** Church Hill Rd, Drumballyroney, Rathfriland,
6/R7 Co Down, NI +4428 40620232 The plain, simple church and the school where
Patrick Brunty, father of Emily and Charlotte, preached and taught have been
restored into a small museum and interpretive centre that is the beginning of a 10-
mile driving tour around various Bronte points in S Co Down. Well signposted.

1651 **The Searcher Sculpture & the CS Lewis Trail** Holywood Arches Library,
6/S6 Holywood Rd, Belfast, NI Clive Staples (CS) Lewis was born in Belfast. There is a
CS Lewis Trail which begins at the statue of Lewis, by Ross Wilson, at the Holywood
Road Library, and which tours the city exploring key addresses in Lewis's young life
in the city. The tour takes approximately two hours.

✓ ✓ ✓ **Gregans Castle** Visited by Tolkien, who is said to have based Middle
Earth on the Burren landscape. Report: 1265/COUNTRY HOUSES.
✓ **Hungry Hill** Fictionalised by Daphne du Maurier. Report: 1727/WATERFALLS.

St Patrick's Cathedral Report: 415/DUBLIN ATTRACTIONS. Dean Swift/Gulliver's
Travels. Also Cave Hill - where the silhouette of a gigantic profile is thought to be
the inspiration for *Gulliver's Travels*. Swift lived in Carrickfergus, nearby.
Deansgrange Cemetery Burial place of Brian Ó Nualláin, aka Flann O'Brien.
Report: 1626/GRAVEYARDS.
Glasnevin Cemetery Burial place of Brendan Behan. Report: 1617/GRAVEYARDS.

the
Best
Outdoor Places

Ireland's Remarkable Landscape

1652
6/Q2
✓ ✓ ✓ **Giant's Causeway** Causeway Rd, Bushmills, Co Antrim, NI
+4428 20731855 · www.giantscausewaytickets.com A UNESCO World Heritage site, it is a rocky shoreline made from over 40,000 interlocking hexagonal basalt columns; nobody *really* knows how they got there.
Of course, we know that it is something to do with the cooling of lava flow, but the ambiguity has left open the opportunity to believe that there might be a mystical reason why the rocks stand as they do. Enter the giant, Finn McCool, and all the folklore that comes with his story. Visiting the shoreline starts at the National Trust visitors centre, with exhibitions and explanations and, if you like, you can pick up an audio guide. Walk, or shuttle bus. 9am-9pm July-Aug, with earlier closing for the rest of the year. See *Scotland the Best*, Staffa report 2209 for the other end of the ancient lava flow.

1653
4/G15
✓ ✓ **The Burren** From the Flaggy Shore, S towards Corofin, Co Clare The Burren region in Co Clare is the great Irish paradox. When you see it first, one word comes to mind: barren. And yet, it is uniquely fertile. 'Plants normally found in regions as far apart as the Arctic and the Mediterranean occur together in the Burren', the naturalist Gordon D'Arcy has written. Come here between April and June, when the Spring gentian is in flower, and marvel at how it grows on the limestone, all the way down to sea level, fragile, yet intense. The word Burren is derived from the Irish term boireann: a rocky place. But, here's the other paradox: the secret of the Burren is not rock, but water. Under the limestone karst there are countless caves and, in time, it is water that will destroy the Burren, just as it was water that created it. Reports: 1103–1111/THE WEST.

1654
4/F15
✓ **Cliffs of Moher** Cliffs of Moher Visitor Experience, Liscannor, Co Clare
+353 65 7086141 · www.cliffsofmoher.ie The popularity of the Cliffs of Moher as a visitor destination means that the traveller has to have a strategy. Visit them early in the day, or late in the afternoon, after the tour coaches have left. But note that there are more tactile and enjoyable cliff walks at Kilkee, in Loop Head, further south in the county, and at Slieve League, in Donegal. Or consider a water vista of the cliffs, by taking a boat trip from Doolin or from Liscannor, which gives a better sense of the scale and majesty of the cliffs. 'One of Ireland's most visited attractions, which is why you should consider skipping them', *The New York Times* sagely noted. The cliffs centre often closes due to overcrowding. Visit after 4pm recommended. 7 days, 9am-8/9pm during summer, with earlier closing Jan-Jun and Sept-Dec. Reports: 1074–1102/THE WEST.

1655
4/E17
✓ **Loop Head & The Cliffs of Nowhere** Kilkee, Co Clare ·
www.loophead.ie The horseshoe bay of Kilkee has always attracted bathers and walkers, and the accessible sea cliff walk, known locally as The Cliffs of Nowhere, in deference to the more famous cliffs up the road. The cliff walk is accessible from behind the Diamond Rocks café, and loops around with incredible views of cliffs and sea stacks. Loop Head tourism group has protected this environment with slow and careful development. There are several restaurants, great walks and don't miss the lighthouse at the end of the headland. Reports: 1085–1093/THE WEST.

1656 ✓ **Gap of Dunloe and the Lakes of Killarney** Killarney, Co Kerry The Gap of
3/E20 Dunloe is a narrow mountain pass, 11km long, forged by glacial flows between
the mountain ranges MacGillycuddy Reeks and Purple Mountain. The Lakes of
Killarney are three lakes that can best be seen from Ladies View on the N71 road
between Kenmare and Killarney. (So called after a visit from Queen Victoria's
ladies-in-waiting.) You can drive both, or take a tour, and a popular way of seeing
the Gap is by jaunting car (the horse-drawn wagons available to hire — at a price!
In Killarney town).

1657 ✓ **Killary Fjord** Leenane, Co Mayo www.killaryfjord.com Killary is Ireland's
4/D11 only fjord, and stretches 16km inland, to the village of Leenane. The
philosopher Ludwig Wittgenstein stayed in a cottage, in the building that is now
the youth hostel, in Rosroe, for six months in 1948, and described this region as
'the last pool of darkness'. Local legend has it that tea chests, filled with his notes,
were found in the attic when the youth hostel was being developed. The locals,
believing Wittgenstein to have been insane, suggested the notes be burnt, which
they were. Modern aquaculture developments on the fjord have created
unfortunate visual disturbance, but the surrounding areas and the major route of
the N95 are amongst the most beautiful vistas in the country. Ferry trips of the
fjord leave from close to Leenane.

1658 **Killarney** Co Kerry The Victorians made Killarney famous – Queen Victoria
3/E20 visited in 1861 and sailed on the royal barge across the lakes, from Ross Castle to
Glena Cottage, and then through Muckross Lake and into the Upper Lake. Shelley
compared Lake Como to the Arbutus Islands of Killarney, and Sir Walter Scott
visited in 1825, at the height of his extraordinary fame. Friedrich Engels visited
twice in 1856 and 1869, and when William Wordsworth came, he climbed both
Carrauntoohil and Mangerton Mountain. Wordsworth probably had to be careful
not to trip over a painter's easel, for the hills and lakes have attracted landscape
painters since the 18thC. Today, many visitors pay too much attention to the town
of Killarney, and too little to the lakes and mountains. But it's only when you get
down to the shoreline, around the lakes, that you can understand the sublime
beauty that captivated the Victorians. Reports: 1038–1046/IF YOU'RE IN KILLARNEY.

1659 **The Dark Hedges** Bregagh Rd, Stranocum, Ballymoney, Co Antrim, NI The
6/R3 Dark Hedges fascinated people even before this short stretch of road became the
King's Road in HBO's *Game of Thrones*. The hedges are a simple row of beech trees
that were planted in the 18thC to form a driveway as they approached Gracehill
House. The trees somehow grew into one another, a tangle of boughs that seem to
catch the light from all sides and now the roadside has become a global image that
very many people recognise. If you want to get that classic photo with the empty
road and the trees, then it's only dawn or dusk when this is possible.

The Best Gardens

1660 **Ashtown Walled Garden Phoenix Park,** Dublin 8 +353 1 6726454 ·
1/R13 www.heritageireland.ie In the centre of the Phoenix Park, this walled garden,
AYR maintained by Ireland's Office of Public Works, is adjacent to the location for
FREE Ireland's Bloom gardening festival. The focus of the garden is the growing of fruit
ADMISSION and vegetables as well as a colourful planting of herbaceous cottage garden plants
that are planted between the formal walkway that allows one to see every part of
the garden. Organic growing techniques are followed and the plants team with life
and vibrancy.

1661 **Hunting Brook Gardens** Lamb Hill, Blessington, Co Wicklow
1/R14 +353 87 2856601 · www.huntingbrook.com Just N of Blessington, under
APR-SEPT Lamb's Hill in Co Wicklow, Hunting Brook is a garden of world renown. Jimi Blake
is a plant collector who has been on many expeditions, always collecting. Jimi
NO DOGS was the head gardener of Airfield Gardens in Dundrum, but now his work in both
gardening and teaching and running workshops happens here. Hunting Brook is
full of excitement, a cult garden. 11am-5.30pm Wed-Sun. Jimi also runs tours of
gardens in the UK.

1662 **Powerscourt Gardens** Powerscourt Estate, Enniskerry, Co Wicklow
1/S14 +353 1 2046000 · www.powerscourt.com 20km and about 30 minutes S of
AYR Dublin, the Palladian mansion of Powerscourt overlooks an ornate garden spread
over 47 acres. The house overlooks Triton Lake, and between it, a series of terraces,
complete with statuary, and formal planting. Beyond it is the distinctive Sugar Loaf
mountain in the Wicklow hills. Gardens include a walled garden with Ireland's
largest herbaceous border. A Japanese garden was planted in 1908 with a grotto.
There is a tower, constructed of old church stones that is supposedly shaped like
the family pepper pot. 6km away from the house is Powerscourt Waterfall – one of
the highest in Ireland. The garden in the Garden of Ireland. All day 7 days. Mornings
only May-Sept.

1663 **Burtown House** Athy, Co Kildare +353 59 8623865 · www.burtownhouse.ie
1/P15 A mile from the M9, leave the motorway at exit 3, heading towards Athy until you
FEB-DEC see the sign. Burtown House still feels like a family home, and there is a sense of
the generations of family each putting their stamp on the house and gardens. Most
recently, the Green Barn has opened up as a shop and restaurant. The restaurant
uses produce from the gardens, and is ambitious in its scope. Sometimes it gets
too busy, and its non-professional nature works against it, rather than for it. If you
visit the restaurant, don't miss the walled vegetable garden or a walk through the
woods. 11am-5.30pm Wed-Sun.

1664 **The Bay Garden** Camolin, Co Wexford +353 53 9383349 ·
2/R17 www.thebaygarden.com On the N11 Dublin to Rosslare road, just S of Camolin,
MAY-SEPT heading towards Ferns. Two-acre garden of an 18thC farmhouse, which includes
a bog garden, a pond garden, woodland and vegetable garden. A mass of colour,
between neatly cropped pathways. Frances and Iain MacDonald have put 20 years
of love and planning to create garden 'rooms' each with its own theme. Afternoons
Sun May-Sept, Fri Jun-Aug, or by appointment.

1665 **Bellefield House & Gardens** Birr, Co Offaly www.angelajupe.ie Just N of
1/L15 Roscrea on the R492, near Lough Boora Bog nature park, Angela Jupe's garden in
JUN-SEPT this Georgian farmhouse setting has a large walled garden walled with Tipperary
sandstone, with its own folly; a salvaged Victorian-style glasshouse, and some

unusual and ebullient planting - a fernery, notable iris displays, old roses and snowdrops. 11am-5pm Wed-Sat or by appointment.

1666 **Glebe Gardens** Baltimore, Co Cork +353 28 20579 · www.glebegardens.com
3/F23 Established by Jean and Peter Perry, Glebe Gardens is just at the entrance to
AYR Baltimore, sloping down to the sea. The garden now features a brilliant cafe,
⌨ a seasonal shop, and opens up to become an open-air venue in summer. The gardens are natural and calmly idyllic, with lots of emphasis on edible planting for the cafe. There is a little pen of baby goats for children to admire, and thereafter goat is on the menu. All day Wed-Sun.

1667 **Ballymaloe Cookery School** Shanagarry, Co Cork www.cookingisfun.ie
3/K21 As with every part of the Cookery School, just off Shanagarry village, everything in
AYR the garden is considered, well planned and carried out with impeccable care and environmental responsibility. Don't miss the glasshouses, which were established by Ivan Allen, husband of Myrtle Allen of Ballymaloe House, for this was always the Allen's home. There are pigs and chickens, a shell house, formal gardens and an orchard. An inspirational space. All day Mon-Sat. Gardens tours may be booked.

1668 **Cluain na dTór** Ballyconnell, Falcarragh, Co Donegal +353 74 9135640 ·
6/K3 www.seasideplants.eu Location is everything and this N Donegal wilderness
AYR garden credits its maritime situation, its gulfstream-influenced climate and its sheltered surroundings. The garden is sometimes playful, almost whimsical, sometimes restful, pleasing, and best seen in the late summer, early autumn, when borders reach their exotic peak. 10am-6pm Mon-Sat.

1669 **Altamont Gardens** Ballon, Tullow, Co Carlow +353 59 9159444 ·
2/Q16 www.heritageireland.ie Altamont is of interest all year round, starting with their
AYR magical snowdrop collection and finishing the year with the autumn colours of
FREE the mature trees that gift the garden with its settled character. The garden design
ADMISSION dates from Victorian times, and features rare plants such as the Tulip Tree. The
⌨ lawns slope down to a lake. One of the glories of Ireland. All day 7 days. You can buy plants from the Walled Garden.

1670 **Kells Bay** Kells, Cappamore, Co Kerry +353 66 9477975 · www.kellsbay.ie
3/C20 On the N side of the Ring of Kerry - 13km beyond Glenbeigh, look for their sign.
AYR Kells Bay is full of incomparable surprises. The longest rope bridge in Ireland, 35m
⌨ long and 12m over the river. A Thai restaurant in a Kerry country house; owner Billy Alexander has travelled extensively in SE Asia, so why not. Outside there are dinosaur tree sculptures in a Tasmanian-style forest – Pieter Koning was here, and designed these massive creatures to fit their jungle-type setting. It's all here, in this beautiful Gold Medal-winning garden. The tree ferns are astonishing – 12ft tall, and all descended from one 120-yr-old tree fern – the largest fern forest in the northern hemisphere. You can stay in the house, as well as enjoy their terrace and conservatory cafes. 9am-7pm 7 days. Open until 9pm during some, till 4.30pm Nov & Dec.

1671 **Derreen Garden** Lauragh, Kenmare, Co Kerry · www.derreengarden.com
3/D22 Smack in the middle of the spectacular scenery on the N side of the Beara, with
AYR views of both the Caha mountains and sea, Derreen is one of those gulf stream gardens where subtropical plants thrive and amaze. They encourage you to bring a picnic and spend the day. 10am-6pm 7 days.

1672 **Brigit's Garden** Pollagh, Rosscahill, Co Galway +353 91 550905 ·
4/F13 www.brigitsgarden.ie Call it Celtic Zen, but there is something about the quiet
AYR contemplativeness of Brigit's Garden, in Rosscahill, that is both stimulating, yet
☕ mellow. Happily, the excellent tea rooms share this deep aesthetic, so the whole
experience syncs beautifully, and it makes for an excellent family day out.
All day 7 days.

1673 **Glenveagh Castle Gardens** Glenveagh National Park, Church Hill,
6/L3 Letterkenny, Co Donegal +353 76 1002537 · www.glenveaghnationalpark.ie
AYR The dreamy 19thC castle, set in the context of granite mountains and overlooking
☕ a lake, is one reason why Glenveagh is so much loved and visited, but the garden
is reason again. Formal planting in a series of gardens, developed by the various
private owners of the castle, and taken over by the state include a collection of
southern hemisphere species especially rhododendrons, maples and pines. Tea
room, open AYR, and the Glenveagh Restaurant Easter-Sept are particularly good.
Midges can be a problem.

1674 **Mount Stewart** Portaferry Rd, Newtownards , Co Down, NI +4428
6/T6 42788387 · www.nationaltrust.org.uk Mount Stewart is a 19thC neo-classical
AYR mansion, owned and managed by the National Trust on the E shore of Strangford
☕ Lough. Both the interior of the house and the extensive gardens are open to the
DF public. Close to the house, the gardens have a formal, Mediterranean feel, and
include a walled garden and Italian garden. As you walk further into the mature
woodland, the gardens evolve into a softer, more natural landscape, culminating in
a lake walk. 9am-5.30pm 7 days, till 4pm Sat & Sun.

Ilnacullin Garinish Island, Glengarriff, Co Cork Report: 1995/THE ISLANDS.
Lismore Castle Garden Co Waterford Report: 1552/CASTLES.
Mount Usher Gardens Co Wicklow Report: 847/THE EAST.

The Best Beaches & Bays

1675
2/R18
✓ **Curracloe** Co Wexford 10km NE of Wexford town, this beach is famous for being the location for the extraordinary D-Day beach scenes in *Saving Private Ryan*. Curracloe is a seven-mile expanse of soft sand that stretches from Raven Point to Ballyconnigar. The area surrounding the beach is designated an area of scientific interest because of the elaborate dune system held together with marram grass. Leave the village of Curracloe on the R743 until you reach the beach.

1676
2/N19
✓ **Tramore** Co Waterford This beach is very much associated with the seaside town of Tramore. A spit of land, 5km long, it is popular as a surfing destination. The sand dunes are some of the highest in Ireland. Behind the spit lies the tidal wetland lagoon known as Backstrand which is a popular place for bird spotting. Report: 1755/BIRDS. At the town of Tramore, follow the N25 and take the first exit left on the second roundabout through Riverstown, until you reach the beach.

1677
3/G23
✓ **Long Strand** Castlefreke, Co Cork Long Strand lives up to its name: if you set out to walk its deep sandy stretch, you will be very tired by the time you finish. Many people instead prefer to walk up in the dunes, where the grass gives better grip. Puffin Cafe. Report: 1000/THE SOUTH WEST.

1678
3/D23
✓ **Barleycove** Mizen, W Cork Barleycove beach was created by the tidal wave that followed the 1755 Lisbon earthquake. It is a special area of conservation, with dunes and sea lakes. Visitors approach the beach on a causeway. There are lifeguards on duty during the season, and be aware that the nearby Chimney Cove beach is dangerous, due to strong currents. This is a popular beach for sandcastles and dams for the river channels, but hesitate to swim without lifeguards present.

1679
3/C22
✓ **Derrynane** Caherdaniel, Co Kerry The natural harbour of Derrynane Bay, with its long sandy beach, is one of the glories of Kerry. Despite its idyllic setting, parts of the beach aren't safe – to such an extent that the main stretch of sand is known as 'Danger Beach'. But the section with the dangerous currents is marked out during the summer, and there are lifeguards on duty. To the W end of the beach, on a small spit of land, you can find one of the most beautiful monastic sites in Ireland, and the atmospheric ruins of St Finian's Abbey, dating back to the 6th century. The salt marshes behind the beach are a great spot for foraging for samphire.

1680
3/D19
✓ **Inch Beach** Dingle Peninsula, Co Kerry This three-mile long sand spit at the start of the S side of the Dingle Peninsula is everyone's vision of the perfect beach and, of course, played a starring role in the movie *Ryan's Daughter*. It is a major destination for surfers and wind-surfers, and produces some of the longest waves in Europe. Accessible from the R561 road towards Dingle (Daingean Uí Chúis), and there are cafes both on the beach and just up the hill heading towards Dingle town.

1681
4/C12
✓ **Omey Island** Claddaghduff, Co Galway Omey Island is designated a Special Area of Conservation and is home to a number of rare flora and fauna. To find the strand and the island, follow the small road beside the large church in the centre of Claddaghduff. You can park at the car park and walk across to the island, or you can drive across the sand at half-to-low tide. Make sure to check the tides coming back. Look out for shell middens, and visit the remains of St Feichin 7thC church, which was part of an early monastic settlement on the island. Today, one of the best ways to explore the beaches of Aughrus, is on horseback. See Cleggan Beach Riding Centre www.clegganridingcentre.com.

1682
6/M3 ✓ **Ballymastocker Beach** Portsalon, Co Donegal Ballymastocker is a beautiful beach of pristine white sand, and is recognised as one of the most serenely beautiful beaches in the world, not just in Ireland. But, be warned: in wintertime the winds here are so severe that they are known locally as a 'lazy wind': too lazy to go around you, they simply go straight through you. You've never felt a chill like it. The prize, however, is that this is one of the most idyllic beaches in Ireland.

1683
6/Q3 ✓ **Portstewart Strand** Co Antrim, NI Portstewart is one of the N W's most popular beaches, with miles of hard sands that are perfect for that invigorating walk with the dogs. Lots of sportsmen train here also, and *Game of Thrones* fans take selfies up in the dunes. Harry's Shack, a National Trust wooden pavilion at the Portstewart entrance, is the most charming beach restaurant in which to enjoy great cooking, but make sure to book before taking that walk.

1684
6/S8 ✓ **Murlough National Nature Reserve** Keel Point, Dundrum, Co Down, NI Murlough is one of the best blue flag beaches in S Co Down. Home to a 6,000-yr-old dune system, it became Ireland's first nature reserve in 1967, and is the best example of a dune heath in Ireland. Over 600 species of moth and butterfly – including the important Marsh Fritillary – have been identified. Lifeguard on the beach during the summer season. Signposted from the A2, and there is a series of linear and circular walking and cycling routes, and *Game of Thrones* pilgrims.

1685
2/P19 **Baginbun** Fethard, Co Wexford This sandy cove is at the tip of the Hook Peninsula, near to the famous Hook Lighthouse. You reach the beach via a track, and the sand is surrounded by cliffs. Swimmers use the beach thankful of its sheltered location. While the beach is a tranquil spot for families, it has a violent history and was the scene of an Anglo-Norman invasion around 1170AD.

1686
2/M20 **Stradbally Cove** Copper Coast, Co Waterford This sheltered cove, protected on all sides by mature trees and cliffs, is a popular spot for families and swimmers, though very young children are warned to swim only on the right-hand side of the bay, away from tidal pull of the River Tay, which is concealed on the incoming tide. At high tide, the beach almost disappears. Take the R675 from Dungarvan in the direction of Tramore. Turn right at the signpost for Stradbally, and then turn again at the signpost for Stradbally Cove.

1687
2/N20 **Ballydowane Bay** Copper Coast, Co Waterford This is a stony beach with a number of rock pools for exploring. Impressive red-tinged cliffs and sea stacks. This is a classic Copper Coast experience, showing the volcanic, quartz-veined rocks in all their glory – but be careful of falling rocks and rip tides.

1688
3/H23 **Inchydoney Island** Clonakilty, Co Cork Inchydoney is a small island, just outside the town of Clonakilty, connected to the mainland by two causeways. There are two halves to the beach, either side of the headland, and in between the two is the notable Inchydoney Island Lodge & Spa (1333/SPAS). The Inchydoney Surf School www.inchydoneysurfschool.com gives surf lessons, rents surf equipment, and operates summer surf camps (1876/OUTDOOR ACTIVITIES). Inchydoney is 4km from Clonakilty, and signposted from the N71.

1689
3/G23 **Owenahincha** Rosscarbery, Co Cork Owenahincha is one of a string of beautiful beaches on the route between Clonakilty and W Cork. This is a blue flag beach, with lifeguards, but be warned — the sea here can be rough at times and there have been a number of fatalities on this beach. Do not attempt to swim if the lifeguard

is not present. There is a notice board on the beach detailing lifeguard attendance. There is a lovely cliff walk from Owenahincha to Warren Strand. Report. 1789/WALKS.

1690 **Ballyrisode Beach** Toormore, Co Cork Three beaches actually running into one
3/E23 another within the Toormore bay area just W of Schull. Very sheltered spot as well as being a Special Area of Conservation and a National Heritage area. Popular with families — the only problem being the single track road fills up and traffic jams are frequent in summer weather. If you arrive early, make sure your car is pointing towards the way out before parking!

1691 **Ladies and Men's Beaches** Ballybunion, Co Kerry Ballybunion is a quaint
3/E17 seaside town with no less than two beaches. 'Ladies Beach' and 'Men's Beach' named for their modest history. The beaches are divided by a cliff, on which stands a ruined castle.

1692 **Rossbeigh** Co Kerry Rossbeigh is a great local amenity for families in N Ring
3/D20 of Kerry. There is a children's playground and a shop at the beach and lots of opportunity for water sports.

1693 **Coral Beach** Sneem, Co Kerry Made from dried and sun-bleached algae rather
3/D21 than sand, this beach is a geological rarity. The only other beach made from this material in Ireland is Trá an Dóilín, in Carraroe (1700/BEACHES). The beach, near a little pier at Gleesk, is part of the Kerry Geopark. Follow signs for the pier from Sneem.

1694 **Banna Strand** Tralee, Co Kerry Known as the landing point for nationalist Roger
3/D18 Casement. The views here are legendary, miles of beach overlooked by the Dingle Peninsula and Kerry Head. This is also a great spot for shore fishing. 15km from Tralee, follow the R551 through Ardfert and then on to the beach.

1695 **Ballinskelligs** Co Kerry Overlooked by the McCarthy Mór Tower House, this
3/C21 sheltered bay is within the Kerry Dark-Sky Reserve. The Skellig Monks called it 'the nearest thing to heaven' and it has always been a spiritual centre.

1696 **Kilkee** Co Clare Kilkee's horseshoe bay is protected by Duggerna Reef, and this
4/E17 is a classic town beach with an impressive sea wall and even a bandstand. The beach leads to the Cliffs of Nowhere (1785/WALKS) and is home also to the famous Pollock Holes (1718/SWIMMING).

1697 **Fanore Beach** Ballyvaughan, Co Clare Fanore Beach is part of the Burren and
4/F14 Cliffs of Moher Global Geopark. It has an expanse of sand dunes, on which you can find the wild Burren flora that makes this area so special. Good small waves for surfing beginners.

1698 **The Flaggy Shore** New Quay, Co Clare It's the rocks, rather than the sand that
4/G14 make this beach special. The large rocks along the shore are called 'biokarst'. The Flaggy Shore, whose limestone rocks feature fossils embedded within them, is made famous by the Seamus Heaney poem.

1699 **Salthill** Galway, Co Galway Popular as much for the promenade that follows the
4/G13 line of the beach, and its flatness is a major attraction for joggers. Parking all along the promenade. Follow signs for Salthill.

1700 **Trá an Dóilin, Coral Strand** Carraroe, Co Galway Like a similar beach in
4/E14 Sneem, Co Kerry, the beach here in Carraroe is made from biogenic gravel, which is
in fact, dried, sun-bleached algae. From Spiddal, head towards Casla, and turn left
onto the R343 towards Carraroe. Go through the village of Carraroe, following signs
for the beach.

1701 **Silverstrand** Galway, Co Galway Just on the outskirts of Galway city, and
4/G13 signposted from the R336, what begins as a sandy beach, becomes a rocky
strand, overlooked by cliffs and rocks, which is an area that is brilliant for seaweed
foraging. The Irish name is Trá na gCeann. Swimming is good at low tide, as the
beach almost disappears during full tide.

1702 **Sellerna Beach** Aughris Peninsula, Co Galway One of a number of beaches on
4/C12 the Aughris Peninsula, Sellerna is a classic white strand, close to Cleggan. Follow
the small road to the right as you leave Cleggan driving towards the end of the
Peninsula. Look out for the sign – 'Tra' just at the edge of the village. It's a safe
beach, lovely and sandy and is prized by locals who use it for a sunset stroll.

1703 **Mulranny** Co Mayo The town of Mulranny is on an isthmus between Clew Bay to
5/E10 the S and Blacksod Bay to the N, and the point of entry to the Curraun Peninsula.
The strand is accessible via the Mulranny Causeway, which links the beach to the
village and the popular Mulranny Park Hotel (1148/THE WEST). The sunsets here
are wonderful. Mulranny is one of the European Destinations of Excellence (EDEN).

1704 **Mullaghmore Beach** Co Sligo Mullaghmore is sadly best known as the location
5/J7 for the bomb that killed Lord Mountbatten. In happier days, it is a long expanse of
sand, overlooked by dunes and views of Tievebaun and Truskmore mountains. The
beach is enjoyed by swimmers and windsurfers and the nearby harbour provides
a sheltered anchorage. There is a designated area for wheelchair access, which
is also good for buggies. Turn left just beyond Cliffony onto the R27, signposted
Mullaghmore.

1705 **Aughris Beach** Co Sligo Aughris Beach is signposted from the main road, the
5/H8 N59, and is also the home of the Beach Bar which overlooks the bay. This is a
beach where people learn to surf, overlooked by the Ox mountains, Knocknarea
and Benbulben.

1706 **Maghera Strand and Caves** Ardara, Co Donegal This beach is well known as
5/J5 being the point of access for the Maghera Caves. When the tide is out, the beach
stretches back 5km. Access to the cave only at low tide. Look out for the Aladdin's
Cave signpost as you come to Ardara.

1707 **Marble Hill Beach** Dunfanaghy, Co Donegal Dunfanaghy is becoming a bit
6/L3 of an alternative holiday destination, and if Marble Hill Beach is at the heart of it,
then **The Shack** is its soul. The beach is one of two blue flag beaches in the area,
the other being Killahoey Beach. This is a white strand surrounded by dunes and
the beach is used for all types of watersports. Take the N58 NE direction from
Cloughaneely towards Portnablagh. After Portnablagh turn left down towards
the beach.

1708 **Benone Bay** Coleraine, Co Antrim, NI Benone is one of the longest Irish
6/P3 beaches, with seven miles of sand, which makes it popular with windsurfers and
blokarters. There is a popular caravan park resort – Benone Tourist Complex – with
caravans, glamping and spaces to pitch tents, and many NI families take their
annual holidays there. Access off the A2 Sea Coast Road.

1709 **White Park Bay** Ballycastle, Co Antrim, NI Three magnificent miles of white
6/R2 sand between two headlands, ammonite fossils, and the sand actually sings when
the wind blows through it. Turn down to the beach off the A2 Whitepark Road,
halfway between the Carrick-a-Rede bridge and the Giant's Causeway, and be
prepared for the walk down to the beach. If the cows have come down to lie on the
sands, give them plenty of room.

1710 **Whiterocks Beach** Portrush, Co Antrim, NI Now famous as a stop on the
6/Q2 great tourism opportunity afforded by *Game Of Thrones*, Whiterocks is a simply
magnificent beach stretching to Dunluce Castle. Consistent waves throughout the
year also attract surfers, and do explore the caves and arches. Report: 1564/RUINS.

1711 **Tyrella Beach** Downpatrick, Co Down, NI 2km of sand backed by dunes, with
6/T8 lifeguards in attendance during July and August. A blue flag beach for over 20 years;
entrance fee during the summer season. Popular with windsurfers.

1712 **Laytown & Bettystown** Co Wicklow Laytown is the only beach in Europe where
1/R11 a horse race is run under Turf Club rules, and it's been happening here on the sand
since 1868. The races attract between 5,000 and 10,000 spectators, so it's a big
day out to watch the horses race each September, on a course ranging from 6 to
7 furlongs. Bookmakers, burgers, 99s, and all the fun of the fair, then the beach
returns to normal for the rest of the year. Can get very busy with Dublin daytrippers
on sunny days.

1713 **Skerries** Co Dublin Do ask the locals all about the story of St Patrick's Footprint,
1/S11 one of the signature stories of the bright town of Skerries. N beach is more
sheltered than S beach, and there are play areas, walks and views out to the
Rockabill lighthouse. Lots of excellent places in the town for eating and drinking
when you've gotten off the sand.

1714 **Velvet Strand** Portmarnock, Co Dublin 5km in length, and nice smooth sand
1/S12 makes Velvet Strand an ideal day out, with views across to Lambay Island and
Ireland's Eye. Conservation measures taking place include the planting of more
marram grass to help the dunes. Gets very busy, especially the N beach, but there
is ample parking, and a short walk through the dunes to the sand.

1715 **Ladies' Cove** Greystones, Co Wicklow Ladies' Cove sits between Greystones'
1/S14 N and S beaches, and it's got excellent rocks for the youngsters to jump off into
the waves, followed by a trip up town to join the eternal queue at The Happy Pear
restaurant.

The Best Wild & Outdoor Swimming Places

1716 ✓ **Guillamene** Tramore, Co Waterford The cove here is no longer for Men
2/N20 Only, but the sign remains as a relic of the past. Nowadays families use this deep water pool, accessed via steep steps against the cliff face that take you into the cove, which has a concrete diving platform. For many wild swimmers, Guillamene is the archetypal experience. 2km from Tramore, take the coast road until you reach the car park.

1717 ✓ **Lough Hyne** Skibbereen, Co Cork Lough Hyne is a deep, deep seawater
3/F23 lough that has been a marine nature reserve for many years. Swimmers get into the water via the slipway, and then the more experienced of them swim over to the island in the middle of the lough.

1718 ✓ **The Pollock Holes** Kilkee, Co Clare Three sea pools on the Duggerna Reef,
4/E16 which are uncovered at low tide. The pools are calm and protected from the Atlantic just beyond. Take the coast road out of Kilkee until you come to a car park. Take the steps onto the flagstones — there are always swimmers to follow, and ask a local for directions if you get lost. There are several good swimming spots on Loop Head, including Byrnes Cove, Edmund's Point, and Newfoundout, where diving boards have recently been reinstated.

1719 ✓ **Blackrock Diving Tower** Salthill, Galway The high boards of the diving
4/G13 platform stretching out into the sea from Salthill's promenade, just W of the city, are a magnet for youngsters who want to show off their diving and depth-charge moves. Diving into the water on the last day of the school term is how you truly enter summertime.

1720 **The Forty Foot** Sandycove, Co Dublin James Joyce's *Ulysses* mentions the Forty
1/S13 Foot. So does Flann O'Brien in *At Swim-Two-Birds*. It has depth, so even at low tide you can jump in. Swimmers use it all year round, and it's great at Christmas. There is a good changing area, and it's very well maintained. The Forty Foot is behind the James Joyce Tower and Museum, just off the R119 in Sandycove.

1721 **Seapoint** Dun Laoghaire, Co Dublin Seapoint beach is well maintained by the
1/S13 county council, there are good facilities, including an outdoor shower. Parking is tricky, and the beach fills up on a sunny day. Choose the tide time carefully – on a low, you have to walk quite far before there is any depth. At high tide the water comes right up to the stone steps.

1722 **The Springers Bathing Area** Skerries, Co Dublin This is a sociable bathing
1/S11 area with deep water and steps to the sea. Good for competent swimmers who can handle the strong currents, and who meet and swim here throughout the year. Take the harbour road out of Skerries, and follow it until you reach the parking area. Look for the signs and the steps into the water.

1723   **Vico Road** Dalkey, Co Dublin There are steps down to the sea and a ladder.
1/S13   This swimming destination, though not as well known as the Forty Foot, has its
devotees, who come to this very well-heeled area to swim.

1724   **Ballina Riverside Pool** Ballina, Co Tipperary +353 87 2293793 Unusual in
5/G9   Ireland – this is a well-kept, heated outdoor swimming pool, which is maintained
by N Tipperary County Council. Check opening times on their Facebook @
ballinariversidepool, before travelling, but the pool is usually open in the afternoons
from 2pm. There is a small entry charge, and the pool is 1m deep at its shallow
end, and 25m long. There are dressing rooms, with showers, and lifeguards are on
duty when the pool is open.

1725   **The Blue Pool** Glengarriff, Co Cork The Blue Pool is also the place where the
3/E22   ferries leave for Garinish Island. This sheltered pool is actually within Bantry Bay,
and there are stone steps to help you get into the water. The Blue Pool is within
walking distance of the centre of town.

1726   **West End Bathing Pool** Bundoran, Co Donegal The West End is a sea water
5/K7   pool on the shoreline, located between large, flat rocks, onto which steps have
been fixed. A man-made sea wall keeps the water in the pool. The West End
Bathing Pool is signposted in Bundoran.

Spectacular Waterfalls

1727
3/D22
✓ **The Mare's Tail** Hungry Hill, Co Cork It's also been named after the mane of the mare, and this waterfall is one of the highest waterfalls in Ireland and the UK. It cascades water from Coomadavallig Lake over impermeable sandstone. *Hungry Hill* is the title of the novel by Daphne du Maurier. The story is alleged to be based on the ancestors of a friend of du Maurier, and the descriptions of the mountain are recognisable to anyone who has walked here.

1728
3/E20
✓ **Torc Waterfall** Owengarriff River, Muckross, Killarney, Co Kerry At the base of the Torc mountains, about 7km from Killarney and near the entrance to Muckross House is the Torc waterfall. There are viewing stations at the car park off the N71, and at 100 steps higher, where you can see the lake as well. The waterfall is about 20m high and fed by the Owengarriff river. The waterfall gets busy with tour buses during the summer months.

1729
1/R14
✓ **Powerscourt House & Gardens** Enniskerry, Co Wicklow Located 6km from the main Powerscourt Estate, this Wicklow Mountains waterfall drops a massive 121m, making it one of the highest waterfalls in Ireland. To reach the falls, you walk through a woodland with giant redwoods, oaks, beach and larch. Bring a picnic. Admission charge applies. Open daily AYR. Pass Powerscourt entrance and follow the signs. Report: 1662/GARDENS.

1730
1/M14
✓ **Glenbarrow Waterfall** Glenbarrow Trailhead Car Park, Co Laois Situated in the Slieve Bloom mountain region. The source is the River Barrow — the second longest river in Ireland. It's a three-tiered waterfall in a woodland setting. Best seen in Spring when it is surrounded by bluebells. There is a looped walk taking in the waterfall. Start at the Glenbarrow Trailhead car park, which gets very full. Be prepared to queue for parking on sunny days.

1731
6/M2
✓ **Glenevin Waterfall** Straid, Co Donegal Looking like a waterfall from a shampoo ad, Glenevin plunges 30 feet into a quiet stream. There is a gentle, well sign-posted ramble up to the waterfall, and the Glen House B&B and tea room and craft shop is at the start of the walk, and makes a lovely spot to return to. Report: 1369/B&B. 2km NW of Clonmany village in the far N reaches of the Inishowen Peninsula.

1732
5/J5
Assaranca Waterfall Ardara, Co Donegal Near the town of Ardara and on the road to the Maghera Caves, the waterfall tumbles into a black pool. Much photographed with slow shutter speeds and long exposures. The nearby wood sculpture is by Mike Henderson. 8.5km SW of Ardara.

1733
2/M19
Mahon Falls Comeragh Mountains, Co Waterford An essential stop on the Comeragh Mountain drive. Park the car and you will see the waterfall in the distance. It's a stroll along a gravel track to get there, and thereafter you can climb alongside the waterfall and up the scree to the top. Follow the signs for Comeragh Drive, exiting off the Dungarvan/Waterford N25 towards Mahon bridge.

1734
5/J7
Glencar Waterfall Glencar Lake, Manorhamilton, Co Leitrim 'Where wandering water gushes' wrote W.B. Yeats in *The Stolen Child*, describing the 50ft high waterfall, gushing from steep, steep hills and wandering down to Glencar Lough. There is another, lesser-known waterfall nearby called 'The Devil's Chimney'. With the right wind conditions and after heavy rain, the water sprays back over the cliff and you understand how the waterfall got its name. OS No 16.11km W of Manorhamilton.

1735   **Glenmacnass Waterfall**   Laragh, Co Wicklow   The Old Military Rd follows the
1/R14   River Glenmacnass from Sally Gap down to Laragh, and from the road you can
see the water as it plunges and flows over the hillside, like a giant treacherous
waterslide. The waterfall marks the beginning of the glaciated Glenmacnass valley.
There is a car park just beside.

◼◼◼◼ The Best Wildlife Reserves

1736   **Lough Hyne Nature Reserve**   Skibbereen, Co Cork   An important sea lough
3/F23   that has been carefully studied and recorded for many years. 8,000 years ago, it
was a freshwater lake and the sea level outside the lough was about 15m lower.
Nowadays, it's a saltwater lake, which meets the sea at a narrow passage – the
Lough Hyne rapids, which can be flat calm at the turn of the tide, or can run in
either direction, depending on the ebb and flow. The lough is like a living textbook
of every type of seaweed that grows on the Irish coastline, there are also urchins
and a wealth of sea fish just under the clear water level – this is a great spot for
snorkling. Every now and then a dolphin makes its way into the lake, and there
are plenty of otters. There is evidence of prehistoric life around the lake including
ruins of four ring forts, suggesting medieval dwellers. The Vikings raided, and
the Normans settled. The original rapids wall, built in 1847 was what is known
as a 'famine wall'. But it is for marine research that Lough Hyne is probably most
famous. 7.5km S of Skibbereen.

1737   **The Raven Nature Reserve**   Wexford   The Raven is a spit of land at the N
2/R18   entrance to Wexford harbour, a wildlife reserve with dune flora and marine birds.
Butterfly conservation and monitoring is observed, and visitors are invited to note
the butterflies they see. Looped walk that goes through the wood to the tip of the
headland and then back via the beach. Close to Curracloe beach, where *Saving
Private Ryan* was filmed.

1738   **Connemara National Park**   Letterfrack, Co Galway   The National Park was
4/D12   opened in 1980 to try to encapsulate the unique Connemara landscape – including
man-made: standing stones, old wall systems, megalithic tombs and nature:
blanket bogs, salmon running streams, heaths and Dalradian rock formations. The
best way to navigate the park is by following the Sruffaunboy Nature Trail, a 1.5km
way-marked route starting at the Visitor Centre. Views of Ballinakill Harbour and
Tully Mountain. The trail is named after the muddy water coming from the stream
running from Diamond Hill: *sruthán* (stream) *buí* (yellow).

Glengarriff Woods Nature Reserve   Co Cork   Report: 1809/WALKS.
Knockomagh Wood Nature Reserve   Co Cork   Report: 1810/WALKS.
Union Wood Nature Reserve   Co Sligo   Report: 1811/WALKS.
Ballyarr Wood Nature Reserve   Co Donegal   Report: 1812/WALKS.
Dromore Wood   Co Clare   Report: 1808/WALKS.

Scenic Driving Routes

1739
3/J22

✓ ✓ ✓ **The Wild Atlantic Way** The Foyle Bridge, Londonderry (Derry), Co Londonderry, NI to Kinsale, Co Cork We anticipate a flood of future tourism studies which will attempt to examine why the Wild Atlantic Way concept caught fire right from the off, and succeeded in pulling visitors and Irish travellers to the west coast in their droves. The route stretches from Kinsale in Cork to the Foyle Bridge in Londonderry (Derry), so there are 2,400km of breath-taking scenery to navigate. Our advice is to do it as slowly as possible.

1740
2/N20

✓ **The Copper Coast** Co Waterford The 17km-long Copper Coast, between Fenor in the east and Stradbally in the W, is a UNESCO Global Geopark, with a visitor centre in Bunmahon, housed in a converted church. The name derives from the copper mining that was carried out here in the 19thC, particularly in Bunmahon, and you can see the ruins of several of the mines today. The coastline is rugged, dramatic and peaceful, and boasts several blue flag beaches, and extraordinary sea stacks.

1741
2/L19

✓ **The Vee** Co Waterford This short but steep drive between Lismore and Coppeen is notable for the spectacular views across Tipperary from The Vee Gap, the hairpin bend on the Sugarloaf Hill in the Knockmealdown Mountains, at a height of about 2,000ft (609m). The route is popular with serious cyclists because of the steep climb. Legend has it that the nearby Bay Lough is haunted, by a lady of loose morals who was banished there with the task of emptying the lake with a thimble.

1742
3/D21

✓ **The Ring of Kerry** Co Kerry People drive the Ring of Kerry, because it's there and because it's world famous. But, it is also very busy with large coaches who hog the road, so if you want to do the drive, do it early in the morning or towards sunset, and drive clockwise. At 180km, it's a big drive, with a lot of potential stops, so allow a full day to explore the towns and villages, and to have time to cross over to Valentia Island. A charming route is the Skellig Ring: turn down the R567 to Ballinskelligs, then cross over to Valentia Island, and reconnect with the mainland via the ferry at Knightstown.

1743
3/D22

✓ **The Ring of Beara** Co Cork You could drive around the Beara Peninsula, from Glengarriff to Kenmare, and each excursion will seem to be completely different from the last time you toured this other-worldly escarpment of mountain, sea and stone. Everything is always changing, as you head SW down to Castletownbere – the major fishing port of the region – then continue up the N coast. Two detours are worth the effort: go as far S as you can and take the cable car over across the water to Dursey Island. And make time to cut across the peninsula via The Healy Gap (R574), an inspiring drive, where the sheep own the road.

1744
3/B19

✓ **Slea Head Drive** Dingle Peninsula, Co Kerry There are two loop drives here, at the westernmost extent of the Dingle Peninsula. The R559 is the shorter loop, but it is worth adding on the R549 loop, and heading through Ballydavid, before turning S to drive back to Dingle (Daingean Uí Chúis). The roads are good, but narrow, the number of historical and monastic sites – including the 1,300 year-old Gallarus Oratory – is almost astonishing for such a remote region. Make sure to stop at Tig Bhric, a few miles past Ballyferriter village, a brew pub where Adrienne Heslin fashions mighty craft beers using her own well water.

1745 ✔ **The Causeway Coastal Route** Co Antrim, NI It's best to think of the
6/S3 Causeway Coast as two separate drives. Firstly, the dramatic stretch between
Larne and Cushendun on the A2, north of Belfast, has been described as 'the
perfect coastal drive' and boasts two fine arches through which you drive,
especially Red Arch, which was carved from red sandstone. The second drive turns
up to the coast at Cushendun, travelling on narrow roads through Torr Head – with
its views across to the Mull of Kintyre – and Fair Head and onto Ballycastle,
finishing in Portstewart. This is one of the most spectacular coastal drives in
Europe, and the fact that it includes the Carrick-a-Rede rope bridge, the Giant's
Causeway, Dunluce Castle and the Bushmills Distillery means it is difficult to resist
the superlatives. Good coffee and cakes in the Bothy Cafe, close to the Carrick-a
Rede bridge.

1746 **Boyne Valley Drive** Co Meath The Boyne Valley drive stretches fully 225km, and
1/Q11 includes major historical sites such as the Hill of Tara, Trim Castle, the passage
forts at Knowth and Newgrange, the High Crosses near Kells, Mellifont Abbey
and Monasterboice, and the site of the 1690 Battle of the Boyne. The driving is
unremarkable, but this rich procession of ancient sites is extraordinary, though
exhausting to accomplish on one outing. Signposting of the sites is very good.

1747 **Comeragh Mountains Drive** Co Waterford Walking to the waterfall at Mahon
2/M19 Falls is the culmination of the drive after you turn off the N25 at the signpost and
head uphill to the Comeragh Drive – you have a 15-minute walk from the car park.
But the drive is worthwhile for the spectacular views from the hills, across the Tay
valley and the Mahon River valley and down to the Copper Coast, and for the Magic
Road, where your car will appear to travel uphill. Wonderfully quiet.

1748 **Ring of Hook Peninsula** Co Wexford The short journey around the Hook Head
2/P19 will take you to the oldest working lighthouse in the world. The black-and-white
striped beacon of the Hook Lighthouse was begun way back in the 13th century.
There are 115 steps up to the top of the lighthouse, so you will need to catch your
breath, before the beautiful sea views take it away again. Make time to detour into
Tintern Abbey and its Colclough walled garden, take a guided tour of Duncannon
Fort, and visit Loftus Hall, reputedly the most haunted house in Ireland.

1749 **The Sky Road** Co Galway With blind crests, blind brows, single-car sections
4/D12 and other vertigo-inducing frights, you need to be a confident driver to undertake
the Sky Road, as it twists out of Clifden along the coast by Clifden Bay. The views
are spectacular, so take your time and enjoy the vistas out towards Inishturk
and Turbot Island. You can simply do the loop and come back on the road along
Streamstown Bay, to rejoin the main N59, N of Clifden.

The Best Places for Spotting Birds

1750 **East Coast Nature Reserve** Newcastle, Co Wicklow A BirdWatch Ireland
1/S14 Reserve, covering 92ha of the Murrough Wetlands where you will see whooper swans, little egret, an all-white heron, wintering geese and perhaps the blue flash of a kingfisher. There are three observation hides and boardwalks. The central fen feels like another world. Open 7 days in daylight hours.

1751 **Lough Boora Discovery Park** Tullamore, Co Offaly · www.loughboora.com
1/L14 Former peat-harvesting site which has been developed into a nature reserve by Bord na Móna and the Irish tourist board. Situated on the edge of Loch an Dochais, visitors can explore a series of natural and man-made lakes and wetlands. There are bird hides at Tumduff and over 110 bird species have been identified in this expansive wetland. All day 7 days.

1752 **Clara Bog Visitor Centre and Boardwalk** Ballycumber Rd, Clara, Co Offaly
1/M13 +353 57 9368878 464 hectares of raised bog provides a haven for some unusual bird life in this wetland centre. Resident curlews, with their beautiful and distinctive call, are now red-listed in Ireland, but they find a breeding habitat in Clara Bog. You can also see woodcock, meadow pipit, stonechat, kestrel and Ireland's smallest bird of prey (yet able to catch birds four times its own weight), the merlin. All day Mon-Fri.

1753 **Slieve Bloom Mountains Nature Reserve** Mountrath, Co Laois ·
1/M15 www.npws.ie Slieve Bloom (1773/WAYS), enjoys its Special Protection Area status due to the nest sites of the hen harrier and the red grouse, rare and secretive birds that nest on the ground on the blanket bog and heath. Other birds spotted here include meadow pipits, skylarks, snow buntings, merlin, peregrine falcon and golden plover. There are three marked boardwalk walking routes on the site with fine viewing points.

1754 **Wexford Wildfowl Reserve** North Slob, Ardcavan, Wexford
2/R18 +353 76 1002660 · www.wexfordwildfowlreserve.ie Over 250 species of birds have been recorded on the reserve, where you will find an 8m-high observation tower and three hides. The centre is run by the National Parks and Wildlife Service and Birdwatch Ireland. Expect to see Greenland white-fronted geese in their number, as well as mute swans, ducks, waders, grebes and even some birds of prey. All day 7 days. Car park and entrance gates locked at 5pm.

1755 **Backstrand** Tramore Bay, Co Waterford Behind the spit of sand dunes at
2/N19 Tramore Bay, the estuary, saltmarsh habitat of the Backstrand sees divers, egrets, curlews, gulls, redstarts, and more rarely you might see buzzards, brent goose, pied flycatcher and brambling. Access from a range of points along the coast road, and there is a car park at Saleen, on the opposite side of of the bay.

1756 **Harper's Island** Cork, Co Cork Harper's Island is a small but significant Nature
3/J21 Reserve between Little Island and Fota. The N25 drives over it, and the water that surrounds it is Lough Mahon, and beyond it, Cobh and Cork harbour. TGP Birdwatch Ireland are building a bird reserve on this spot, which is planned to open late 2017. The island was once a quayside where inland canal boats, or 'lighters' would land their cargoes of sand or lime. It is also a haven for wintering black-tailed godwits and redshank, who hide in the fields waiting for the tide to drop.

1757 **Rosscarbery Estuary** Co Cork Just opposite the Celtic Ross Hotel, on the N71,
3/G23 outside the village of Rosscarbery, the inlet just over the bridge is good for foraging
for samphire, and also for spotting a huge variety of seabirds, most particularly the
flocks of lapwing and golden plover which over-winter in this spot.

1758 **Mulranny Beach** Mulranny, Co Mayo The word machair is a Gaelic word
5/E10 meaning 'fertile plain' and it is also a scientific term to describe the grassland that
is associated with the dune landscape in Western Scotland and Ireland. A number
of beaches in the NW coast support Machair Grass, one of these is Mulranny,
where the machair/beach landscape sees cormorants, shags, terns, gulls,
kittywake, snipe and lapwing. The nearby mudflats support curlew, oystercatcher,
sanderling, godwits and plover. The beach is accessible from opposite the Mulranny
Park Hotel.

1759 **Inch Island Wildfowl Reserve** Lough Swilly, Co Donegal Inch is a lough island
6/M3 in Lough Swilly, just at the narrow point between Rathmullan to the W and Fahan
to the E, on the Inishowen peninsula. Entrance to the island is via two old railway
embankments, a stunning environment for both birdwatchers and birds. Look out
for whooper swans, greylag geese, black-headed gulls, kingfishers and cormorants.
You might well also spot an otter. Take the road opposite the church in Burt. There
is a car park, with directions to two hides. There is an 8km-looped pathway around
the island for walkers and cyclists.

1760 **Rathmullan Wood Nature Reserve** Glenveagh National Park, Church Hill,
6/S6 **Letterkenny, Co Donegal** +353 76 1002537 · www.glenveaghnationalpark.ie
Birdlife here, in this ancient oak woodland, includes jays, treecreepers, buzzard
and sparrowhawk. The woodland, which also has species of holly, downy birch and
beech, is part of Glenveagh National Park which has an impressive visitor centre, a
castle and a good seasonal restaurant. There is a 1km-woodland loop trail to follow.

1761 **Window On Wildlife, Belfast Lough** Belfast, NI +4428 90461458 · www.
6/S6 rspb.org.uk This is an extremely comfortable site, ironically placed just adjacent to
the shipyard in Belfast. The site is manned by knowledgeable staff, who are happy
to talk to novices, even lending books to help identify what you're looking at. If
you're lucky, in Spring, you might see a black-tailed godwit just before they head N
to breed. The reserve is situated on the Airport Rd W which runs parallel to the A2.
It's best to visit at high tide.

✓ **Cliffs of Moher** Liscannor, Co Clare It's the puffins that bring birdwatchers
to the Cliffs of Moher – this is the only place on the mainland where they
breed. You can spot them nesting in the cliffs during April and May. Other cliff and
sea birds to spot are razorbills, choughs, and gulls all visible from the cliff walk.
Report: 1654/LANDSCAPE.

The Best Sea Tours

1762   **Cork Whale Watch**   Castlehaven, Co Cork +353 86 3850568 ·
3/F23   www.corkwhalewatch.com Colin Barnes is a retired fisherman, and his boat the *Holly Jo* now hosts trips that leave Reen Pier in Castlehaven in search of minke, fin and humpback whales. As long as the weather is fair, Colin works year round to share his passion for sea mammals. The trips take a minimum of four hours, and often longer, as Colin criss crosses the sea to find the whales. In the summer there are usually two trips per day, morning and afternoon, and in the winter, just one.

1763   **Baltimore Sea Safari**   Baltimore, Co Cork +353 28 20753 ·
3/F23   www.baltimoreseasafari.ie The beautiful marine landscape of W Cork is the backdrop of this sea adventure. See the Baltimore Beacon from the sea, tour Sherkin Island, and visit the seal colonies at the mouth of the Ilen River. W Cork is a wonderful natural habitat for whales, dolphins and porpoise and the two ribs used by Baltimore Sea Safari are manoeuvrable with a shallow draft so they can get close up to the action and have unobstructed panoramic views of the coastline and its wildlife.

1764   **Whale Watch West Cork**   Carrigillihy, Union Hall, Co Cork
3/F23   +353 86 1200027 · www.whalewatchwestcork.com Nic Slocum is a zoologist, and a knowledgeable and companionable navigator of the seas, and his onboard commentaries are part of what makes Whale Watch W Cork a popular trip for those who want to see sunfish, whales, dolphins, porpoises and, if lucky, even killer whales, turtles and blue sharks. Tours take place on *Voyager*, a twin-engine catamaran that is built specifically for whale and dolphin watching tours, and is licensed to carry 12 passengers. There is also a larger boat available that can take up to 50 passengers. Boats leave Baltimore Harbour daily at 9.30am and 2.15pm. Arrive 20 minutes before scheduled departure. Booking essential.

1765   **Dolphinwatch Carrigaholt**   Carrigaholt, Co Clare +353 65 9058156 ·
3/F23   www.dolphinwatch.ie The Shannon estuary is teeming with life, and Geoff and Susanne Magee run an informative tour of the river mouth running a Dolphin and Nature Boat Trip, on which you might see the bottlenose dolphins as well as grey seals and pelagic sea birds. Times of tours are all dependent on weather but they travel most days. Call for sailing times.

1766   **Dingle Dolphin Tours**   Dingle, Co Kerry +353 66 9152626 ·
3/C19   www.dingledolphin.com Fungie is the famous dolphin who has inhabited the natural harbour of Dingle (Daingean Uí Chúis) for the last 32 years. Meet Fungie with this tour and follow in the footsteps of passengers like Pierce Brosnan and Jean Kennedy Smith, who have taken this boat trip to meet one of Ireland's most enduring characters, a bottlenose dolphin who always makes an appearance, or your money back.

the Best

Strolls, Walks & Hikes

The Irish Ways

Ireland has an extensive network of National Waymarked Trails, spanning the whole country and divided into long and medium distance walks with a duration spanning anything from 2 to 6 days. Here are some of the best-known trails, and some looped walks that feature within them, from different geographical locations.

Many of the maps and route plans of the walks mentioned here are available online. Where a walk is associated with a website, we have added it here, and we also recommend various books. Otherwise www.irishtrails.ie is a very good resource for details of walking in Ireland.

1767
6/S6
1000KM
XCIRK
3-C-3

✓✓ **The Ulster Way** NI · www.walkni.com The Ulster Way is made up of nine sections, linked by six link sections, which are on public roads – walkers are advised to take public transport on the link sections and walk the rest. The route circumnavigates the entire Province in a route of over 1,000km. The way marker disc is blue with a yellow leaf. You can download route maps of each section from the WalkNI website.

1768
3/E22
175KM
CIRC
2-C-3

✓✓ **The Sheep's Head Way** Durrus, Co Cork · www.thesheepsheadway.ie An extraordinarily beautiful walkway taking you over and around W Cork's smallest peninsula, with views of Bantry Bay to the N and Dunmanus Bay to the S. You can do the whole walk as a circular ramble, or do selected parts of it. Highlights are the ever present Atlantic, the lighthouse, blowholes, seeing dolphins in the distance, the friendly villages and the feeling of freedom as you walk those wild heathery hills breathing in the sea air. OS No 85 and 88. Follow a yellow arrow on black background. The paths are well maintained, and there are excellent books and maps describing the walks.

1769
4/F15
114KM
XCIRC
2-C-3

✓✓ **The Burren Way** Lahinch, Co Clare Tolkien is said to have been inspired by The Burren to write the story of Middle Earth, and this extraordinary landscape of limestone pavement interspersed with wild flowers is one of Ireland's greatest treasures. Expect to see many ancient relics and ruins, fascinating terrain, stone fields, and plenty of wild flowers. Pure magic. OS 51, 52, 57 & 58. Yellow arrow on a black background.

1770
1/R9
40KM
CIRC
2-B-3

✓ **The Tain Way** Carlingford, Co Louth The Cooley peninsula is a place of beauty and myth. This is where, in legend, Queen Maeve of Connacht and Cú Chulainn fought over a Brown Bull in the saga known to all Irish school children as *The Cattle Raid of Cooley*. The Tain Way walk is a loop walk around the peninsula. Start at Carlingford and follow the yellow arrow on a black background. OS No 36. The full walk should take about 2 days.

1771
1/R13
144KM
XCIRC
1-A-2

✓ **Royal Canal Way** Dublin, Co Dublin This route follows the Royal Canal that connected Dublin with the River Shannon in 1790. The walk takes place on towpaths, with some interesting historical industrial architecture to spot as you walk, including the Ryewater Aqueduct which carries the canal over the River Rye. OS Nos 40, 41, 48, 49 & 50.

1772 ✓ **The Wicklow Way** Marlay Park, Rathfarnham, Co Dublin ·
1/R13   www.wicklowway.com This was Ireland's first waymarked trail and it
129KM wanders between moorland and mountain. The most dramatic part of the route is
XCIRC the journey through Glendalough. The entire route lies between Marlay Park in
1-C-2 Rathfarnham and Clonegal in Co Wicklow, OS No 50, 56, 61 and 62. The walk takes
just over a week. Follow a yellow arrow on black background. The website suggests
accommodation en route.

1773 ✓ **The Slieve Bloom Way** Glenbarrow, Co Laois · www.slievebloom.ie
1/M14   Along with the Massif Central in France, these are the oldest mountains in
70KM   Europe. Supporting a mountain blanket bog ecosystem, the Slieve Bloom is the
CIRC   largest state-owned Nature Reserve in Ireland. The route here is a circular one,
1-C-2 starting and ending in Glenbarrow. OS No 54. Follow a yellow arrow on a black
background.

1774 ✓ **The Kerry Way** Killarney, Co Kerry · www.kerryway.com This route
3/F20   circumnavigates Kerry's Iveragh peninsula - the driving route in the same
214KM peninsula is called the Ring of Kerry, and is world famous. The names of the
CIRC   locations themselves sum up the wonderful landscape that the walk traverses –
3-C-3 Black Valley, Windy Gap, Macgillycuddy's Reeks. The walk takes you across
mountain passes, into valleys and through delightful local towns. Yellow arrow on
black background, OS No 78, 83, 84, 70 & 85.

1775 ✓ **The Dingle Way** Tralee, Co Kerry · www.dingleway.com The peninsula is
3/D19   around 50km long and feels like the end of the world. This circular route takes
162KM you the whole length of the peninsula, passing Inch beach and over Mount
CIRC   Brandon. Expect to see ancient beehive huts, castles and ring forts. There are some
2-C-3 ascents, but no significant climbs. Overnight in any of the B&Bs, hear music in the
pubs, and sample the great food, and you'll never want to leave. OS No 70 & 71.
Beginning and ending in Tralee. Yellow arrow on black background marks the trail.

1776 ✓ **The Western Way - Galway** Oughterard, Co Galway ·
4/E11   www.thewesternway.ie A linear route that takes you from Leenane to
55KM   Ballycastle, through mountain and moorland, bog and around lakes. Mayo is
XCIRC considered to be one of the most remote parts of Ireland, and this route is an
2-C-3 unforgettable pilgrimage that takes in the holy mountain of Croagh Patrick, with its
views over Clew Bay. OS No 23, 31, 37 & 38. Yellow arrow on a black background.

Wild Atlantic Way Report: 1739/SCENIC DRIVING ROUTES.

Hill & Mountain Walks

1777 ✓ **Croagh Patrick Hiking Trail** Westport, Co Mayo Moderate to strenuous
5/E10   4-hour hike up Mayo's third highest mountain. Probably the most famous
7KM   Pilgrim Path in Ireland. The summit has a little church at 762m above sea level.
XCIRC   Stunning views of Clew Bay. The last section of the walk is very rocky, and we
2-A-2   always end up scrambling up to the peak on all fours.

1778 ✓ **Devil's Ladder** Carrauntoohil, Co Kerry Carrauntoohil is the highest
3/D20   mountain in Ireland. There are eight different routes to the summit, which
11KM   offer challenging but achievable climbing on rough tracks, and you must allow at
XCIRC   least six hours for the climb. Devil's Ladder is the best known 'tourist route' up the
3-C-3   mountain, but even that path is unstable. Start your climb at Cronin's Yard, where
there are showers and tea facilities. Find more info on www.kerrymountainrescue.ie.

1779 ✓ **Knocknarea** Strandhill, Co Sligo A walk up to the massive cairn on the top
5/J8 2.5KM   of Knocknarea, the Queen Maeve trail takes about 2 hours. The route is
XCIRC 2-A-1   marked with red arrows. OS no 25.

1780 ✓ **Mourne Wall Challenge** Hilltown, Co Down, NI · www.walkni.com
6/S8 36KM   This is a challenging route up Slieve Binnian, following the extraordinary
CIRC 3-C-3   Mourne Wall. The dry stone wall, 35km in length, is made of granite – around 1.5m
high, 60cm thick, and passes over no less than 15 mountains. Mind blowing!

1781 **Blackstairs Mountain Loop Walk** Enniscorthy, Co Wexford A gentle eco-zone
2/Q17 13.5KM   with much to see and appreciate in nature. The walk takes around half a day –
CIRC 3-C-2   allow 5 hours – through green fields and quiet lanes. OS No 68.

1782 **The Nire Valley Gap Walk** Comeragh Mountains, Ballymacarbry, Co
2/L19   Waterford A linear walk through the Comeragh Mountains, which has long been a
6KM XCIRC   place of pilgrimage. Takes about an hour and a half. Start in Ballymacarbry and walk
2-A-2   to Nire Valley car park. OS No 75.

1783 **Cuilcagh Legnabrocky Trail** Florence Court, Co Fermanagh, NI ·
6/L8   www.marblearchcavesgeopark.com Start at the Legnabrocky car park, which
7KM   is 1km from the entrance to the Marble Arch Caves. The walk takes you up to the
XCIRC   summit with the help of a newly laid boardwalk that protects the blanket bog from
3-A-3   erosion. Six-hour walk, with a significant ascent, but worth it for the incredible
views. Ancient cairn at the summit.

Cliff & Coastal Walks

1784
5/H6
10KM
CIRC
3-A-2
☞

✓ ✓ **One Man's Pass** Sliabh Liag Cliffs, Co Donegal To reach the start, drive 6km beyond Teelin to Bunglass Point Car Park (through a gate). The lower car park is recommended. Note, you will find the road disappears from your field of vision due to steep gradients. Once parked, follow the marked path for the summit. The path goes inland, but rejoins the cliff edge later. At one point, you reach a very narrow passage with steep slopes on either side. If this is too scary, you can choose an alternative route via the Pilgrim's inland path and rejoin the route after a few hundred metres. Follow the pass to the summit. You can then descend via the Pilgrim's Path, known as 'Old Man's Pass' which takes you past the ruins of a small chapel. The Sliabh Liag Cultural Centre in Ti Linn has a very good cafe.

1785
4/E16
8KM
CIRC
2-A-1

✓ **The Kilkee Cliff Walk** Loop Head, Co Clare The Cliffs of Nowhere, as it's known, in deference to its more famous cliffside neighbour. But don't be put off by its lack of hype and fame, because this is a stunning, natural pathway that leads you right along the edge of the cliffs, overlooking crashing water and giant sea stacks. Join the walk at the Diamond Rocks Café, and follow the line of the cliff. At the top, the walk curls inland and back down to the town via a country lane.

1786
2/L21
5KM
CIRC
1-A-1

✓ **Ardmore Cliff Walk** Ardmore, Co Waterford · www.visitwaterford.com Starting and ending at the Cliff House Hotel, this walk – OS No 82 – follows the edge of the cliff, passing a holy well, a coastguard station, Ardmore Head, spectacular views of the Samson Crane (1570/RUINS) before you get to the lookout post at Ram Head. After another holy well, the road sweeps back inland and back past the round tower and oratory, to the Cliff House. Cliff House Hotel, Report: 1270/COUNTRY HOUSES.

1787
1/S14
7KM
XCIRC
2-A-1

✓ **Bray Head Cliff Walk,** Bray Seafront, Co Dublin The walk follows the coastal path between Bray and Greystones, and there is a simple way back to your starting point via the DART. The walk leads to the top of Bray Head from where you can see the Wicklow Mountains and the Irish Sea. It's a solid footpath, well marked with red arrows.

1788
3/E17
2.7KM
CIRC
1-A-1

Ballybunion Cliff Top Loop Walk Ballybunion, Co Kerry There is a short walk around the Ballybunion beaches that includes the Nine Daughters Blow Hole, where a local chief supposedly threw his own daughters to avoid the possibility of them eloping with Vikings. There is also the secluded Nun's beach, named after the convent that overlooked the bay. Access to the beach is down a steep track, but there is a rope for assistance. Start and end in Ballybunion.

1789
3/G23 2KM
XCIRC 1-A-1

Owenahincha to Warren Strand Owenahincha, Co Cork Short cliff walk that takes you over the rocky headland that joins two of W Cork's most popular sandy beaches.

1790 **Rathbarry, Castlefreke and Long Strand** Castlefreke, Co Cork This walk
3/G23 starts and finishes at the Long Strand car park. It is not well signposted, but there
7KM are few ways to get lost. Take the walk uphill through the dead forest, leafless
XCIRC Maritime Pines that have not survived the maritime climate. At the top of the steep
1-A-2 hill there stands a tall Celtic cross, erected in 1902, in memory of her husband,
by Mary, Lady Carbery of Castlefreke. The track swings by the atmospheric ruin of
Rathbarry Church – lovely place for a picnic! – and down again to Kilkerran Lake,
after which you can cross through the sand dunes and back onto Long Strand.

1791 **Keem Bay Walk** Achill Island, Co Mayo There are several astoundingly beautiful
5/C9 walks crossing the island: this one is a moderate walk that begins steeply, but
7KM becomes less strenuous after the initial climb. The walk takes you to the tip of
CIRC Achill Head. Begin at Keem beach car park and walk to the top of Carraig Fhada.
2-A-2 That's the hard bit done. The path travels parallel to the cliff top before turning
inland and down hill back to Keem. It should take you about two and a half hours.
Report: 2021/THE ISLANDS.

1792 3/D23 **Mizen Head Visitor Centre** Mizen, Co Cork · www.mizenhead.net The centre
2KM XCIRC features a series of paths, wood and rock, with hand rails, that take you to the cliff
1-A-1 ☕ face, and over the famous Mizen bridge.

1793 **Malin Head Coastal Walk** Inishowen, Co Donegal Ireland's most northerly
6/M2 point. There is a short walk from the car park, at the Caffe Banba coffee cart, to
5KM the tip at Banba's Crown, but because of the wind, the walk seems longer, and the
CIRC wind is unrelenting. The word Eire, placed in stones, was to signify neutral Ireland
1-A-1 to passing planes during the war. Banba's Crown is marked by an early 20thC
☕ tower, later used as a signal station.

1794 **The Gobbins Cliff Path** Islandmagee, Co Antrim, NI ·
6/T5 www.thegobbinscliffpath.com A 2½ hour guided walk through the Gobbins
2KM Experience, a narrow path set into the cliff face. A good level of fitness is required
CIRC to traverse the walk, which takes you over bridges and through tunnels and up
2-A-1 at least 50 flights of steps. But it's worth it, this is an awesome experience, on a
path that has existed since the early 20thC, but has only recently been rebuilt as a
tourist attraction.

1795 **Inchydoney Island Loop** Inchydoney, Co Cork This is a flat seaside walk over
3/H23 sand and hillside. Knowledge of the local tide time is absolutely essential, as the
6.5KM walk is inaccessible at high tide. Consult a tide timetable, and do not start the walk
CIRC past mid-way on an incoming tide. Start at the hotel and walk in either direction,
2-A-1 on either beach. Thereafter follow the headland and loop back behind the hotel
DF and back to the beach.

River Walks

1796 ✓ **The Barrow Way** Athy, Co Kildare to Carlow The River Barrow was a
1/P15 commercial waterway until the 1960s. Originally it was serviced by shallow-
20KM draft boats called 'cots', but in order to make it navigable for larger boats, lengths of
XCIRC canals were built, with a towpath for horses. The river walk is now popular with
2-A-1 leisure walkers. The section from Athy to Carlow can be completed in about 5
hours, and the walk takes place on road, track and canal towpath. OSi map No 55 &
61. The full Barrow Way runs from Robertstown to Graiguenamanagh, and a
significant upgrade of the Way is planned.

1797 ✓ **Hurt Hill (Hurtle)** Faithlegg, Co Waterford The Hurtle, or Whortle runs
2/P19 along the River Barrow, and there is a walk that takes you from Faithlegg in a
12KM circle through Minaun, adjacent to the river confluence where the Rivers Nore, Suir
XCIRC and Barrow empty into Waterford Harbour, on the newly re-opened Hurtle (Hurt
1-A-1 Hill) and back to Faithlegg. Andrew Doherty's blog about Waterford harbour is a
good source of knowledge about the area @whtidesntales. Look out for the Barrow
Bridge viaduct which, for a short time after it was erected, held the record for the
longest span of a viaduct across water. TGP there are plans to make this part of the
Waterford Greenway.

1798 **The Nore Valley Walk** Kilkenny to Bennettsbridge The walk begins by
2/N17 following the River Nore as it meanders past mills that produced wool, stored grain,
12KM made paper and sawed wood. This is where the black marble, from which Kilkenny
XCIRC gets its name The Marble City, was honed ready for use. If you're lucky you might
NO DOGS see a kingfisher or an otter. Once the trail leaves the river, it heads along the Sion
2-A-1 Rd for 600m then crosses through a field, and back to the riverbank. The trailhead
in Kilkenny is from Ossory Bridge; from Bennettsbridge it starts or ends under the
six arch bridge beside Tynan's butchers shop.

1799 **Glengarriff Woods River Walk** Glengarriff, Co Cork Just outside the village
3/E22 on the Kenmare Road – the entrance is actually on a nasty bend in the road – the
1KM Nature Reserve offers walks to suit all abilities, in one of the finest sessile oak
XCIRC woods in the country. There is a short river walk, a waterfall walk, a trail through
1-A-1 the woodland, whilst the longest hike amongst the routes is the easy 3.5km walk
to the Big Meadow. The short river walk is magical for children, and there are picnic
seats at the end of it. Also magic for children is the nearby Ewe Experience. Report:
1889/ACTIVITIES FOR FAMILIES.

1800 **The Lagan Towpath** Belfast, NI This path takes from you Stranmillis in Belfast,
6/S6 along the towpath to Lisburn through the picturesque Lagan Valley. Access is from
20KM Lockview Road, and you can park near Stranmillis College. The walk highlights a
XCIRC mixture of quiet rural river paths, and industrial architecture, including the old
DF gasworks and various locks. There are several opportunities to exit the route, if you
1-A-1 don't want to go the whole distance.

1801 **Lough Foyle Walk** Derry, Co Londonderry, NI Where Londonderry (Derry)'s
6/N3 River Foyle empties into the Lough, there is a lough-side walk that starts at
8KM Ballykelly and travels along the bank of the Foyle until you get to the River Roe
XCIRC DF Estuary National Nature Reserve. Look out for the wreck of a WWII aircraft at low
1-A-1 water just after you cross the footbridge.

Woodland Walks

1802
3/E20
2KM
CIRC
1-A-1

✔ ✔ **Killarney National Park Muckross Abbey Loop** Killarney, Co Kerry
You can take a guided walk with a local guide (www.killarneyguidedwalks.
com), or follow the trails. Expect to see red and sika deer, mountain goats, and
hope to see sea eagles. Look out for the Arbutus Strawberry Tree. The Muckross
Abbey Loop takes in the mesmeric Muckross Abbey, the lake and the woods.

1803
3/F21
2.4KM
XCIRC
1-A-1

✔ **Gougane Barra Woodland Walk** Co Cork The Forest Park covers 400ha,
and there are six marked trails. The longest is Sli Sleitbhe, at 2.4km, which
takes around 2 hours and offers great views. Also spectacular is the waterfalls walk,
which has two viewing platforms along the 65m climb. To make it special, arrange
to stay and have dinner in the terrific Gougane Barra Hotel (1020/CORK), just
across from the chapel on the island, and let Neil and Katy look after you.

1804
3/G17
1KM
CIRC
1-A-1

✔ **Coillte Forest Park** Curragh Chase, Kilcornan, Co Limerick ·
www.coillteoutdoors.ie At the centre of Curragh Chase is the shell of an
18thC mansion house, Curraghchase House. The house was the home of poet and
author Aubrey de Vere. The house is magnificent, but the grounds are special too.
The house overlooks a lake, and is surrounded by Curragh Chase forest. The looped
trails, in the 313ha of mixed woodland, are especially fun for cycling as well as
walking. There is even a barbecue spot, where families can grill their own sausages
after trailing through the woods.

1805
2/P15
4KM
CIRC
1-A-1

Oak Park Forest Park Carlow +353 59 9130411 · www.carlowgardentrail.com
120 acres of mixed woodland species, mainly beech, oak, scots pine, silver fir, larch
and sycamore. The wood is crossed by a series of walkways, with boardwalks over
muddy or slippy areas. There is a picnic area, a playground and adult fitness area
which overlooks the lake. The forest is a recognised bat habitat, and there are hides
for bird watching. Access off Dr Cullen Park Rd, on the outskirts of the town, and
from the N9 at Knocknagee Cross.

1806
2/P19
3KM
CIRC
1-A-1

Dunmore East Woods Walk Dunmore East, Co Waterford Dunmore East is
a centre for walkers, with an open policy from local landowners and a welcoming
village. For the woodland walk, park at the Azzurro restaurant (936/THE SOUTH
EAST) down by the harbour, and follow the forest trail which opens out to lovely
views of Waterford harbour. There is a gravel footpath the whole route.

1807
2/L20
2KM
CIRC
2-A-1

The Towers Walk Lismore, Co Waterford This woodland walk takes you to a
strange collection of gothic-style ruins, known locally as The Towers. They were
built in 1850 as the gates to a much bigger property, but the money ran out, and
only the gates were built. Access the loop at the entrance car park, 3.5km NE of
Lismore, travelling on the R666 towards Ballyduff. Walk through the woods until
you get to the towers, and then loop back.

1808
4/G15
6KM
CIRC
1-A-1

Dromore Wood Loop Ruan, Ennis, Co Clare Dromore Woods is a continuation
of the Burren landscape with limestone pavement, and flooding turloughs and
callows. The diverse nature of the wood also supports fen peat and reed beds. The
woodland is a mixture of native ash and hazel. There are also beech, blackthorn,
hawthorn and guelder rose. There are conifers including Scots pine and Japanese

larch, also Norway spruce. O'Brien castle is an 18thC ruin by the lough, and fauna living happily here includes pine marten, red squirrel, stoat, fox and hare, as well as shrews, wood mice and plenty of bats. There are many dragonflies. The Trailhead loop is at Killian, Ruan, and the loop is well marked. There are shorter trails marked out in the wood.

1809 **Glengarriff Wood Esknamucky Walk** Glengarriff, Co Cork The forest park
3/E22 is one of the most important native woodlands, and comprises 300ha of old oak
3KM woodland, which includes the Arbutus – or Strawberry – tree, a native evergreen
CIRC that is found here, over the border in Kerry and around Lough Gill in Sligo. It is
1-A-1 notable for having the same species of plants and invertebrates that can be found in Spain, Portugal and the Pyrenees – these are known as the Hiberno-Lusitanian species – and include the Kerry slug, which is regarded by naturalists as an attractive slug, as slugs go. The River Glengarriff is also home to the freshwater pearl mussel, which can live for up to 130 years. You can see bats at dusk. The Esknamucky Walk is known as the high walk, the trail starts just off the N71 N of Glengarriff.

1810 **Knockomagh Wood Nature Reserve** Lough Hyne, Co Cork The name
3/F23 Knockomagh means bent or crooked hill, and the uphill ramble criss crossing the
3KM hillside reminds you that it was well named. Mixed broadleaf woodland grows over
CIRC about 31 acres. As the trail rises – steeply! – native plants begin to thrive. At the
1-A-2 top of the hill, your climb is rewarded by a magnificent view over the coastline and its islands that stretches from the Stags to Cape Clear, from land at Galley Head to Mount Gabriel. After the summit the trail can be hard to follow, but all roads lead back to the carpark.

1811 **Union Wood Loop** Sligo, Co Sligo A large portion of the wood is set aside for
5/J8 growing mature sessile oak mixed with downy birch, holly and rowan in this
5.5KM ancient woodland site. The mixture of commercial coniferous forestry and old oak
CIRC woodland supports a diverse fauna population, including pine marten, badger, fox
2-A-1 and red squirrel, and deer. The forest has a car park, a picnic site and about 8km of pathways and forest trails. To reach the trailhead follow the road to Keadue, and look for the signs. OS No 25.

1812 **Ballyarr Wood Nature Reserve** Co Donegal Ballyarr is being managed as a
6/L3 semi-natural native woodland. Wild oak flourishes in what was always a wild forest.
4KM There are frogs, and butterflies, as well as badgers, stoats, foxes and deer. Bird
CIRC life to look out for include buzzards, ravens and jays. Pathways and boardwalks
2-A-1 have been built to make the wood more accessible to walkers. OS No 6. From Letterkenny take the N56 N. Head right at Ellistrin junction, and the forest is 4km N, on the left. The circular path takes you through the oldest part of the woodland.

Pilgrim Paths, Famine Walks & Butter Roads

1813
1/Q14
30KM
XCIRC
3-C-3

✓ **St Kevin's Pilgrim Path** Hollywood, Co Wicklow · www.pilgrimpath.ie
Following the footsteps of St Kevin on his journey through Wicklow to the monastic village of Glendalough. At the highest point the path takes you through the Wicklow Gap and then descends into the Glendalough valley. The next valley beyond Glendalough is home to the now inaccessible 'St Kevin's Bed' from which the Saint 'reputedly hurled a seductive maiden into the lake below, in a determined effort to preserve his chastity'. The Pilgrim way is part of a new 'Irish Camino' which offers walkers a 120km series of walks. Complete the lot and you can receive a Irish Pilgrim Walks Certificate from Ballintubber Abbey.

1814
3/F22
37KM
XCIRC
2-B-2

✓ **St Finbarr's Pilgrim Path** Drimoleague, Co Cork · www.pilgrimpath.ie
The route takes you over three mountain systems and into four valleys, traversing the Ilen, Mealagh, Ouvane and Lee Valley basins, and usually takes 2 days. Recreating the journey of St Finbarr, the route travels from Drimoleague through the mountains and valleys via Gougane Barra and down to the Sheep's Head Way. It then travels the Beara Breifne Way, ending N of Kealkil. A number of pilgrims and walkers choose to stay in the Top of the Rock Pod Páirc & Walking Centre when embarking on the walk www.topoftherock.ie. One of the five Pilgrim Walks, and *The Irish Times* has described it as 'simply the most beautiful country walk on the island of Ireland'.

1815
5/F11
35KM
XCIRC
2-B-2

✓ **Tóchar Phadraig** Ballintubber, Co Mayo · www.pilgrimpath.ie The 35km route begins at Ballintubber Abbey and then follows the path to Croagh Patrick. It's believed, however, that the route dates back to pagan times, and there are Bronze Age relics along the way, along with a round tower, a holy well, St Patrick's bed and his 'bath', and a sacred tree. One of the five Pilgrim Paths that allows you to qualify for a Pilgrim Path Passport when you have walked them all.

1816
3/B19
18KM
XCIRC
2-B-2

✓ **Cosa na Naomh (Saints Road)** Ventry, Co Kerry · www.pilgrimpath.ie A pilgrim path of 17.7km, across the Dingle peninsula from S to N, from Ventry to An Baile Breac. This is a straightforward walk with no major challenges, and with spectacular sea and mountain views on one of the old pilgrimage roads.

1817
3/C21
9KM
XCIRC
2-A-2

✓ **Cnoc na dTobar Sacred Mountain Walk** Cahersiveen, Co Kerry · www.pilgrimpath.ie Cnoc na dTobar is associated with the pre-Christian Festival of Lúghnasa – harvest, which was celebrated on its summit. There is a 9km pilgrim path, which starts from Coonanna Harbour, and is marked by 14 stations of the cross, leading eventually to the Celtic Cross that has been erected on the summit plateau. The trail is clearly marked and is suitable for all ages. From the mountain top you can see the Skelligs, Dingle Bay and W Cork. One of the five Pilgrim Paths.

1818
4/E11
12KM CIRC
2-A-2

✓ **The Famine Walk** Killary Fjord, Connemara, Co Galway
A 12km looped walk along the only fjord in the Republic, which was once a hiding place for U-boats. This is a moderate walk along a famine relief path with stunning views of the fjord and Mweelrea Mountain.

1819 ✔ **Ballyhoura Way** Mallow, Co Cork to Limerick Junction, Co Tipperary
3/G19 The 89km route from Newmarket to Tipperary follows part of the path of the
89KM heroic and doomed march of Donal Cam O Suilleabhain, chief of the O'Sullivan
XCIRC clan, following defeat at the Battle of Kinsale in 1602. Donal planned to walk
3-C-3 500km to Leitrim with 1,000 clan members, setting out in the depths of winter.
Only 15 finally made it to Leitrim. There are no significant climbs apart from a few
steep sections, and the highest point is at Seefin in the Ballyhoura Mountains at
500m. Most of the terrain is forest tracks and tarmac roads, though some of the
roads can be busy, and some of the upland sections can be wet. OS nos 66, 73, 74.

1820 **Butter Road Walk** Ballydehob, Co Cork Butter Roads are so named to describe
3/E23 the routes that people took with their horse and cart, taking butter to the Cork
10KM Butter Market. There are butter roads throughout Cork and Kerry. This walk takes
XCIRC in the 12-arch railway bridge in Ballydehob, the old graveyard at Stouke, the Mill
1-A-1 House at Coosheen and Cadogan's Strand in Schull. Basically it is the old road
between Ballydehob and Schull in W Cork, travelling just S of the R592 main road.

1821 **St Declan's Way Walk** Ardmore, Co Waterford to Cashel, Co Tipperary
2/L21 A 96km walking route between Ardmore and Cashel, the St Declan's route crosses
96KM the Knockmealdown Mountains, with a highest elevation of 537m, but most of the
XCIRC route is through farmland. It's a mix of old pilgrim paths and trading routes with
3-C-3 many sites of historic and archaeological significance. St Declan was a 5thC saint
who brought Christianity to the southern part of the country, and who established
his monastery in Ardmore.

Croagh Patrick The Holy Mountain. Report: 8/ATTRACTIONS.

the
Best
Outdoor Activities

Ireland has 50 of the 200 golf links in the world (a seaside course typically over an area of coastal sand dunes).

1822
6/S8

Royal County Down 36 Golf Links Rd, Newcastle, Co Down, NI +44 28 43723314 · www.royalcountydown.org Ireland has 50 of the 200 golf links in the world and, in Royal Co Down, it has the finest links, and perhaps the finest golf course on the planet. The Old Tom Morris course presents a unique challenge, even before the winds whip in off Dundrum Bay.

1823
6/Q2

Royal Portrush Golf Club Dunluce Rd, Portrush, Co Antrim, NI +44 28 70822311 · www.royalportrushgolfclub.com The Dunluce Course, designed by Harry Colt, is the star attraction – and will stage the 2019 Open Championship. The par-3 14th, popularly known as 'Calamity Corner', will feature endlessly in your golfing nightmares.

1824
3/E18

Ballybunion Golf Club Sandhill Rd, Ballybunion, Co Kerry +353 68 27146 · www.ballybuniongolfclub.com Be careful driving in and around Ballybunion: the roads have curious fall offs into the ditch, and locals tend to drive in the middle of the road. Once you have made it to the course, you are faced with two of the finest links courses: The Old Course was created in 1893, whilst the Cashen Course was opened in 1984, and designed by Robert Trent Senior.

1825
4/F15

Lahinch Golf Club Lahinch, Co Clare +353 65 7081003 · www.lahinchgolf.com Popularly known as 'The St Andrews of Ireland', the Alister MacKenzie course was modernised in 2000 by Martin Hawtree, though the two most famous holes, Klondyke and The Dell, have remained untouched since Old Tom Morris first laid out the course in 1894.

1826
5/J8

The County Sligo Golf Club Rosses Point, Co Sligo +353 71 9177134 · www.countysligogolfclub.ie Popularly known as 'The West', and a Harry Colt-designed course that hosts the W of Ireland championship, the course enjoys the most magnificent setting between the sea and towering Ben Bulben.

1827
3/C21

Waterville Golf Links Waterville, Co Kerry +353 66 9474102 · www.watervillegolflinks.ie Established in 1889, the Waterville links features high in golfer's dream links courses. Tom Fazio updated the old Eddie Hackett course in recent years, and from the back tees the course extends to more than 7,300yds (6675m).

1828
5/G8

Enniscrone Golf Club Enniscrone, Co Sligo +353 96 36297 · www.enniscronegolf.com It's not just surfers who come to Enniscrone, though the beach is celebrated for its big waves. The town also boasts a par 73 championship course, and there are a further 9 holes as well. Regularly features in the lists of the Top 100 courses in Ireland and the UK.

1829
6/Q3

Portstewart Golf Club 117 Strand Rd, Portstewart, Co Londonderry, NI +44 28 70835791 The first and second holes of the Strand course are regarded as two of the finest in the country, up here on the most north-westerly links course. There are 52 more holes spread over the three courses, but the 7,000yds (6400m) of the Strand links are the big challenge.

1830 **Tralee Golf Club** West Barrow, Ardfert, Tralee, Co Kerry
3/D18 +353 66 7136379 · www.traleegolfclub.com An Arnold Palmer course, opened in 1984, the club originally dates back to 1896. The beach, adjacent to the first and second holes, was the location for the beach scenes filmed for the movie *Ryan's Daughter*. Bill Murray is a fan of the course.

1831 **County Louth Golf Club** Baltray, Drogheda, Co Louth +353 41 9881530 ·
1/R11 www.countylouthgolfclub.com 125 years old, and little has changed at the Baltray links since Tom Simpson and Molly Gourlay redesigned the course in 1938. The greens are regarded as some of the best on the east coast.

1832 **Ballyliffin Golf Club** Inishowen, Co Donegal +353 74 9376119 ·
6/M2 www.ballyliffingolfclub.com Ballyliffin offers two links courses. The Old Course has been refashioned by Nick Faldo, whilst the newer Glashedy Links, constructed around 7,210yds (6592m) of dunes, is set to host the Irish Open. Many visitors stay in the hotel in Ballyliffin village, and make sure to get a bowl of chowder in Nancy's Barn, where the chef is world champion chowder king Kieran 'Duey' Doherty.

1833 **Donegal Golf Club** Murvagh, Co Donegal _353 74 9734054 ·
5/K6 www.donegalgolfclub.ie The locals call it Murvagh, and this Eddie Hackett course is often nicknamed the 'Muirfield of Ireland'. At 7,300yds (6675m) from the back tees, the two loops of 9 holes offer quite a challenge.

1834 **Dooks Golf Links** Glenbeigh, Co Kerry +353 66 9768205 ·
3/D20 www.dooks.com Dooks is one of the oldest courses in the country – founded in 1889 – and for almost 100 years it was a 9-hole course. Eddie Hackett, and then Martin Hawtree, extended the course to a full 18 holes. The scenery is spectacular, the club and bar are friendly places.

1835 **Narin & Portnoo Golf Club** Portnoo, Co Donegal +353 74 9545107 · www.
5/J5 narinportnoogolfclub.ie Founded in 1930, and originally a 9-hole course, Narin & Portnoo today is a par 73, and will demand all your special links shots to navigate the course, especially the pair of par fives on the way home. Greenkeeper Jim McCole tended the course between 1934 and 1977.

1836 **Killarney Golf & Fishing Club** Killarney, Co Kerry +353 64 6631034 · www.
3/E20 killarneygolfclub.ie Just 5 minutes from the centre of town, on the shores of Lough Leane, there are two 18-hole courses, and the 9-hole Lackabane Course. The 7,250yds (6629m) Killeen is the jewel of the complex.

1837 **Old Head Golf LInks** Kinsale, Co Cork +353 21 4778444 ·
3/J23 www.oldhead.com The spit of land that houses the course extends a full 3km into the Atlantic Ocean, so the Old Head enjoys as spectacular a location as any course. The area is also a bird haven, and boasts more than 100 native botanicals. There are 15 suites, and a spa, in the complex, with food in the Lusitania bar and the De Courcey restaurant, whilst the terrace has extraordinary views.

Good Golf Courses in Great Places

1838
2/N17
LOTS

✓ **Mount Juliet Estate** Thomastown, Co Kilkenny +353 56 7773000 ·
www.mountjuliet.ie Sumptuous grounds, heavily populated with grey
squirrels, gives the Mount Juliet estate an enviable calm, and there are few things
nicer than to borrow one of the hotel bicycles and careen around the place early in
the morning. At the Lady Helen Restaurant, chef Ken Harker has held onto his star
from the Guide Michelin for several years now, and he offers lush cooking: veal
sweetbread with truffle; crubeens with sauce gribiche; foie gras with oxtail vinegar.
Jack Nicklaus designed the course; Trackman technology available as part of golf
tuition.

1839
6/L3

✓ **Rosapenna Hotel & Golf Resort** Sheephaven Bar, Downings,
Letterkenny, Co Donegal +353 74 9155301 · www.rosapenna.ie There are
two courses: the Sandy Hills Links, designed by Pat Ruddy, and the Old Tom Morris
Links. The Casey family has always demonstrated very high standards throughout
their 65-room hotel, pool and spa, and there are stunning views from the Vardon
Restaurant.

1840
6/L7
LOTS

✓ **Lough Erne Resort** Belleek Rd, Enniskillen +4428 66323230 ·
www.loughrneresort.com The rooms in this great big confection of an hotel
are amongst the biggest we have ever stayed in. In the Catalina Restaurant, leading
chef Noel McMeel offers subtle, delicately crafted cooking and offers the best food
in the county. The Nick Faldo designed course is highly regarded as one of the best
modern courses.

1841
2/P19
EXP
L

Faithlegg House Hotel & Golf Resort Faithlegg, Co Waterford
+353 51 382000 · www.faithlegg.com The centre of the hotel is an 18thC
mansion house, and this sylvan setting near to the Waterford Estuary, just E of the
city, is home to all types of events: golf, weddings, ladies' charity lunches, corporate
family days out, and they do it all very well. The staff always find time for a chat,
and the cooking, overseen by chef Tom Spruce, is considered and imaginative.
Patrick Merrigan-designed parkland course has no fewer than five lakes waiting to
claim your golf ball.

1842
4/E16
LOTS
LL

Trump International Golf Links Doonbeg, Co Clare +353 65 9055600 ·
www.trumpgolfireland.com Designed by Greg Norman, and later enhanced by
Martin Hawtree, the course extends to just over 7,000yds (6400m) from the back
tees. Eating in the bar and the Ocean View restaurant, lavish rooms.

1843
3/K21
LOTS

Castlemartyr Resort Castlemartyr, Co Cork +353 21 4219000 ·
www.castlemartyrresort.ie The huge Castlemartyr resort extends over 220 acres
with a Norman castle and a spa complex, and is now owned by the UK hotelier
Martin Shaw, best known for his Old Thorns Manor Hotel, in Hampshire. It's hyper-
luxurious – €70m euro was spent developing the resort – but it's still early days for
the new team. Par 72, 6,728yd (6152m) course designed by Ron Kirby, which they
describe as an inland links style course.

1844
1/S14
LOTS
LL

Powerscourt Hotel Powerscourt, Co Wicklow +353 1 2748888 ·
www.powerscourthotel.com Part of the Marriott Group's Autograph Collection
of hotels, the Powerscourt is a de luxe destination surrounded by 1,000 acres, with
almost 200 rooms, a pair of golf courses, a massive spa, and views out across the
Sugar Loaf Mountain from the windows of their Sika Restaurant. East and West
courses are 6.412yds (5863m) and 6,345yds (5801m) respectively.
Report: 1662/GARDENS.

1845 **Headfort Arms** Headfort Place, Kells, Co Meath +353 46 9240063 ·
1/P11   www.headfortarms.ie Olivia Duff's family-run hotel is a real charmer, rich with
MED.EXP   the natural warmth that you can only experience from well-trained, experienced
local staff who enjoy their work. Good eating in their Vanilla Pod restaurant.
Headfort Golf Club, with two courses, is 2 minutes from the hotel and the 6,515yds
(5957m) New Course is regarded as one of the best parkland courses.

1846 **The K Club** Straffan, Co Kildare +353 1 6017200 · www.kclub.ie Two Arnold
1/Q13   Palmer courses, one of which was famously home to the Ryder Cup victory by the
LOTS   European team in 2006. 5-star hotel which opened in 1991 is high luxe, with the
Byerley Turk their best-known dining destination. If you can afford to drink old
vintages of Petrus and DRC, here they are.

1847 **Adare Manor** Adare, Co Limerick +353 61 605200 · www.adaremanor.com
3/H17   The businessman and philanthropist JP McManus has spent several fortunes on
LOTS   refurbishing the great big pile that is Adare Manor, a luxury hotel, spa and parkland
LL   golf resort at the northern end of Ireland's prettiest village. The golf course,
originally designed by Trent Jones Sr, has been rebuilt by Tom Fazio, with new tees
and greens and Subair technology under the greens. Long way from the mashie
niblick, then.

1848 **Waterford Castle** The Island, Waterford +353 51 878203 ·
2/P19   www.waterfordcastleresort.com Having changed ownership in 2015, the grand
LOTS   castle is steadily getting back on track, and they have lots of ambitious plans to
LLL   maximise the appeal of one of the jewels of the SE. Michael Thomas is heading up
the kitchen, whilst their notable mixologist Ilario Alberto Capraro makes gorgeous
cocktails. The castle is on an island, which requires a short, delightful ferry journey
over to the castle and golf course.

1849 **Druids Glen Hotel & Golf Resort** Newtownmountkennedy, Co Wicklow
1/S14   +353 1 2870800 · www.druidsglenresort.com Druids Glen was the first 5-star
LOTS   hotel to open in Co Wicklow, and it got through the recession thanks to a good
LL   crew in the hotel and the kitchen, and a very well-regarded golf course which has
been host to several major championships.

1850 **Portmarnock Hotel and Golf Links** Strand Road, Portmarnock, Co Dublin
1/S12   +353 1 846 0611 · www.portmarnock.com The links course at the hotel was
LL   designed by Bernhard Langer and opened in 1995. Of course, it is the nearby
Portmarnock Golf Club that is the celebrated links, a course about which Arnold
Palmer once enthused that the 15th hole was 'the best par 3 in the world'. The
course has hosted a dozen Irish Opens.

The Best Cycling Routes & Greenways

EASY AND MODERATE TRAILS

1851
2/N19
XCIRC
46KM

✔✔ **The Waterford Greenway** Waterford ·
www.visitwaterfordgreenway.com An off-road Greenway, taking the route of the old railway line between Waterford and Dungarvan, the Waterford Greenway has been a massive success with locals who have got on their bikes in their numbers. The route takes in eleven bridges, three viaducts, an atmospheric tunnel, and travels from river to sea. Start at WIT West Campus. Sensible people choose to stay the night in The Tannery (940/THE SOUTH WEST) and return the following day.

1852
5/E10
XCIRC
42KM

✔✔ **The Great Western Greenway** Westport to Achill Island ·
www.greenway.ie This is the longest off-road trail in Ireland, extending from Westport to Achill Island, and cyclists take the whole route, or just parts of it. The route travels between the Nephin Beg Mountains and the sea, going through the picturesque towns of Newport and Westport where the trail begins. There are several access points but if you want to start from the beginning take the route down one of the Westport Quays. The people of Mayo are very proud of this award-winning route, and there are lots of facilities, places to stay and things to see and do in the zone.

1853
1/R13
XCIRC
3.3KM

The Metals Dun Laoghaire, Co Dublin The Metals is a cycle and pedestrian way from Dun Laoghaire over the traditional route that carried stone from Dalkey Quarry to the harbour in Dun Laoghaire. Over 600,000 tons of stone was dragged by horse along a railway, which is now known as The Metals. The route follows the DART line, and if you want to take the train back, it's good to know bikes are allowed onto the DART during off peak travel periods, including all weekend.

1854
1/R9
XCIRC
7KM

The Great Eastern Greenway Carlingford to Omeath, Co Louth ·
www.louthcoco.ie The trail follows the southern shore of Carlingford Lough, and is built mostly along the old railway line. This is a great place for family cyclists, and affords views across the Lough, and over to the Mountains of Mourne, and Slieve Foy. There are old level crossings, and bridges, and most of the track is off road. Only 300m is on public road. Access the trailhead at Carlingford Marina, just off the R173. From Omeath, the access point is in the centre of town, next to the pier. The trail is well marked. OS Discovery Map: No 36.

1855
2/P17
CIRC
64KM

East Kilkenny Cycle Route Co Kilkenny · www.trailkilkenny.ie Suitable for moderate to experienced cyclists, the East Kilkenny Cycle route takes in some of the most significant cultural spots around Kilkenny, passing through Thomastown, Bennettsbridge and the beautiful village of Gowran (where you should buy your picnic from Glasrai & Goodies (1513/THE EAST). The route is designed to travel on the quieter roads and laneways, and the views are of Brandon Hill and the two rivers, Barrow and Nore. There is a N and S Kilkenny route as well, which are slightly more challenging, also a cycle loop around N & S Kilkenny, which are slightly shorter.

1856
2/R19
XCIRC
110KM

The Norman Trail & the EuroVelo Route Rosslare Harbour, Co Wexford ·
www.thenormanway.com The EuroVelo cycle trail follows the route of Europe's western border, from Portugal to Norway. The first leg of the route in Ireland to be fully developed with EuroVelo route signs is The Norman Trail in Co Wexford. The route begins in Rosslare Harbour, and travels to New Ross and takes in Norman towers & castles, the Tacumshane Windmill, and Hook Head Lighthouse.

1857   **The Kelly Legacy** Dungarvan, Co Waterford · www.irishtrails.ie Waterford-born
2/M20   Sean Kelly is recognised as being Ireland's greatest cyclist, and this route is where
CIRC   he trained. The route is a circuit of the Comeragh Mountains, beginning and ending
105KM   in Dungarvan, and travelling via Carrick-on-Suir and through the picturesque village
of Ballymacarbry. Though it is a mountain route, it never enters mountain terrain,
for that tougher route, opt for The Kelly Comeragh Challenge.

1858   **Skibbereen Atlantic Route** Skibbereen, Co Cork · www.explorewestcork.ie
3/F23   Start at Skibbereen post office, travel down to the roundabout on the Baltimore
CIRC   Rd, and follow signs to Tragumna beach. You will pass Liss Ard, and Lough
24KM   Abisdealy (where you can pop in for a wild swim if you're feeling inclined) and
after Tragumna, you face a climb to the headland at Toe Head, but the views will
ease the pain. Thereafter the road descends and you travel the arresting coastal
landscape towards the charming village of Castletownshend. Then back inland to
Skibbereen.

1859   **The Burren Fine Wine Early Morning Guided Cycling Tour** Burren Fine Wine,
4/G14   **Ballyvaughan, Co Clare** · www.burren.ie/do/burren-fine-wine-cycling
CIRC   There is so much to see on the various Burren Fine Wine guided cycling tours: ring
20KM   forts, caves, cairns, fulacht fiadh, deserted village, holy wells, and portal tombs
MAY-SEPT   – plus wild flowers and lovely countryside. They run a popular Early Bird Cycle
that ends with a cycle down the magnificent Corkscrew Hill, before heading for
breakfast in Burren Fine Wine. Usually Thurs morning. Bikes provided. Starts at
7.30am when the roads are quiet.

1860   **The Head Road Route** Mournes & Slieve Croob, Co Down, NI ·
6/S9   www.cycleni.com Moderate cycle with some ascent. Start Lwr Square, Kilkeel
26KM   town centre. The route proceeds through the beautiful Silent Valley, then climbs
CIRC   steeply. The Head Rd offers panoramic views. From a clear day you can see Howth
Head and the Isle of Man and Scotland.

MOUNTAIN BIKE TRAILS

1861   **Ballyhoura Mountain Biking** Ardpatrick, Kilmallock, Co Limerick
3/J19   +353 63 81300 · www.visitballyhoura.org 92km of trails running through the
Ballyhoura mountains makes this the largest trail network in Ireland. The trails
are a combination of singletrack and boardwalk, forest road climbs laid out in five
loops, each loop connecting to the next. Suitable for beginners and advanced. Bike
rental from www.trailriders.ie.

1862   **Rostrevor Mountain Bike Trails** Kilbroney Park, Rostrevor, Co Down, NI ·
6/R9   @RostrevorMountainBikeTrails On the shores of Carlingford Lough, and
⌨   through the Rostrevor Mountains, 27km of red route beginning with an ascent
of Slieve Martin, and – for experienced cyclers only – 19km black route and two
purpose-built downhill tracks for adrenaline junkies. The centre also offers training
for beginners and kids over 14.

1863   **Castlewellan Mountain Bike Trails** Castlewellan Forest Park, Co Down,
6/S8   NI +44 28 43779664 · @CastlewellanMountainBikeTrails Suitable for all
levels of bikers, the location of the centre, with its panoramic views of the Mourne
Mountains, and the Victorian castle grounds and Castlewellan Forest Park offers
green, blue, red and black trails, including the adventure-lovers 'Dolly's Chute'.

The Best Watersports Centres

1864 ✓✓✓ **Atlantic Sea Kayaking** Skibbereen, Co Cork +353 28 21058 ·
3/F23 www.atlanticseakayaking.com Over the last several years, Jim and Maria Kennedy's kayak company has made nighttime paddling a must-do! part of any visit to W Cork, and Mr Kennedy has become the public face of Irish sea kayaking. The nighttime paddling regularly features amongst the lists of best things to do when in Ireland. Just as good as the paddling is Mr Kennedy's masterful raconteuring: he sure knows how to tell a story.

1865 ✓ **Inish Adventures** Moville, Co Donegal +353 87 2202577 ·
6/P3 www.inishadventures.com An impressive centre, based in a commanding building at the water's edge in Moville in N Donegal. Adrian Harkin is from Moville, and the company is very rooted in the zone, both through extra curricular cultural activities and a deep knowledge of just about every rock on the Inishowen shoreline. The crew here are all high-level coaches. Join them, and you'll have one of the best adventures.

1866 **Bray Adventures** 'Aisling' Royal Marine Terr, Strand Rd, Bray, Co Wicklow
1/S14 +353 1 2760973 · www.brayadventures.ie Activities include SUP, kayaking, raft building, and the new-to-Ireland sport of coasteering. This is where gangs climb rocks, only to jump off again and swim round and do it all over again. While a certain level of fitness and water ability is needed for coasteering, other activities are great for beginners and young people. Land-based courses also - abseiling, rock climbing and hill walking.

1867 **Long Line Surf School** 53 Benone Ave, Limavady, Co Londonderry, NI
6/P3 +44 7738 128507 · www.longlinesurfschool.co.uk Long Line is a holistic surf and SUP provider who join all the dots when it comes to learning on the water – education, environment, motivation and adventure. It is their aim to equip their clients with a life skill as well as simply having fantastic fun. One of the courses they run is for people with disabilities. They are also serious coffee heads and the cafe is fab.

1868 **Oceanics Surf School** The Red Cottage, Tramore, Co Waterford
2/N19 +353 51 390944 · www.oceanics.ie Paul and Linda Tuohy both have a background in lifeboat, lifeguard, and cliff rescue. Courses are focused on marine education as well as having fun. Coastinghacking is a course they have developed, and it involves what they call 'extreme rockpooling'. Sustainability is one of their guiding principles.

1869 **Unique Ascent** Tullaghobegley Irish, Falcarragh, Co Donegal ·
6/K3 www.uniqueascent.ie Iain Miller is an adventurer, author and mountain leader, so you're in good hands if you take on the somewhat dare-devil activity of climbing sea stacks with him in the NW. Unique Ascent is not for the faint hearted. Children's rock climbing is one of the experiences they offer.

1870 **The Irish Experience** Fethard-on-Sea, Co Wexford ·
2/P19 www.theirishexperience.com Get out of your comfort zone and join them in an adventure, be it sea kayaking against the backdrop of the Copper Coast, or hiking the Comeragh Mountains. Their USP is to work in small groups, and they put a special emphasis on the environmental nature of what they offer – they are affiliated to the Irish Wildlife Trust.

1871 **Sligo Kayak Tours** Auburn Lodge, Strandhill Rd, Sligo +353 86 1999015 ·
5/J8 www.sligokayaktours.com Barry Mottershead runs small groups of kayakers
in relatively sheltered areas – Lough Gill, and Glencar, and the estuaries around
Dernish island and within Ballisodare Bay. The emphasis of this tour is on the
natural environment and wildlife of the lakes and inner shore. Suited to people of
all levels of fitness.

1872 **Jamie Knox Watersports** The Maharees, Castlegregory, Dingle Peninsula,
3/D19 Co Kerry +353 66 7139411 This is a great spot in which to learn windsurfing, and
indeed there is a shop selling all sorts of windsurfing equipment, so that you can
take your new learned skill to another level. Jamie Knox is one of the longest-
serving and best kitted-out adventure providers in Ireland.

1873 **Emerald Outdoors** Kenmare, Co Kerry +353 83 0317011 ·
3/E21 www.emeraldoutdoors.ie Colin Wong and Jamie Stevenson-Hamilton have
serious kayaking cred – James has worked as a whitewater guide on the River Nile
in Uganda: Colin has kayaked 2000km of the Arabian Gulf. They have the skills and
the knowledge and the experience. But what is just as important in developing a
tourism facility, they are as good teaching children and complete beginners as they
are taking experts on Level Four pursuits.

1874 **Roundstone Outdoors** The Bogbean, Roundstone, Co Galway
4/D12 +353 87 2265403 · www.bogbeanconnemara.com In 2015 outdoor
educationalist Shane teamed up with Orla from Connemara and they opened the
Bogbean, a delightful little cafe with B&B. Shane keeps his kayaking skills alive with
Roundstone Outdoors, a mobile provider of SUP, kayaking tuition and guided tours.

1875 **Clare Surf Safari** Co Clare +353 87 6345469 · www.claresurfsafari.com
4/F15 Do you want to learn to surf? The Clare Surf Safari is a mobile operator who will
come to any zone throughout Clare and give you the basics or improve on your
skills. All ages are catered for and they will work on a one-to-one basis.

1876 **Inchydoney Surf School** Inchydoney Island, Clonakilty, Co Cork
3/H23 +353 86 8695396 · www.inchydoneysurfschool.ie Inchydoney beach is
a treasure among beaches, and a brilliant location to learn to surf. The surf
school here has been in business for going on for two decades. Just about every
schoolchild in W Cork has been through the school, where they provide everything
from toasty winter wetsuits, to surfboards, boots, hoods and gloves.

1877 **Killary Adventure Company** Derrynacleigh, Leenane, Co Galway
4/E11 +353 95 43411 · www.killaryadventure.com Killary Fjord is a 16km glacial
☐ harbour that cuts through the mountains on the edge of Connemara, and if you
want a Wild Atlantic Way adventure, then this outfit is well placed to provide it. The
large centre, which operates as a hostel as well as an adventure centre, has been in
business for 35 years and offers an enormous number of activities.

1878 **Carrigaholt Sea Angling Centre** Rahona, Carrigaholt, Kilrush, Co Clare
4/E17 +353 65 9058209 · www.fishandstay.com Luke Aston is a fisherman's friend,
and many a seasoned rodman will return again and again to experience his fishing
charter. The estuary here is teaming with turbot, skate, cod and even bluefin tuna
and shark. But you don't have to be an expert to hop on this little blue boat: Luke
takes out novices as well, and there's nothing better than catching a few mackerel
and taking them back to the B&B, where Mary will serve them for breakfast.

1879 **Skelligs Watersports** Ballinskelligs, Co Kerry +353 87 9178808 ·
3/C21 www.skelligsurf.com Ballinskelligs is one of Ireland's most exceptional beaches, (1695/BEACHES), and this company operate here, and around Reen Rua beach, where storms recently revealed an ancient prehistoric forest. The zone is well protected, and the waters are clean, and it's a great place to learn water skills.

1880 **Leitrim Surf Company** Leitrim Village, Co Leitrim +353 86 3494013 ·
4/K9 www.leitrimsurf.ie The Shannon Blue way runs all the way from Drumshanbo to Carrick-on-Shannon and this company specialises in SUP safaris up and down the river, through the scenery that they accurately describe as 'Amazonian' during the verdant summer. They also do SUP yoga, which sells out very quickly.

Clare Island Adventures Clare Island, Co Mayo Report: 2016/THE ISLANDS.

Famous Surfing Beaches

1881 **Spanish Point** Miltown Malbay, Co Clare The name of this wide sandy bay
4/F16 comes from the battles with the Spanish Armada. It's a great place to begin to learn to surf. Take the R482 to the beach, which is 3km W of Miltown Malbay.

1882 **Carrowniskey Strand** Louisburgh, Co Mayo This beach is as famous for beach
5/D11 horse racing, as it is for surfing. There are changing facilities on the beach and a lifeguard operates here during the summer. 5km outside the village of Louisburgh and well signposted.

1883 **Rossnowlagh** Co Donegal Rossnowlagh is a good beach for all levels of ability,
5/K6 especially beginners and improvers. There are no rips or shore breaks, and the waves are consistent. Take the R231 from Ballyshannon, and after the village of Coolmore take a left to the beach.

1884 **Bundoran** Co Donegal Bundoran is the surf capital of Ireland, with some of the
5/K7 best waves. Winter or summer you'll find surfers here.

1885 **Lahinch Beach** Co Clare At the head of Liscannor Bay, the strand at Lahinch
4/F15 stretches for 2km and is home to surfers who come for both the surf and the social life. The flooding tide is also popular for kite surfing.

1886 **Mullaghmore Back Strands** Co Sligo This exposed reef has consistent surf and
5/J7 relative shelter, which makes it great for surfing throughout the year. When the surf is up, this is a very busy surfing destination.

1887 **Strandhill** Co Sligo Great waves mean Strandhill can be jammers for most of
5/J8 the summertime. If you have time, make sure to book a visit to the Voya seaweed baths (1955/CONSUMING PASSIONS).

1888 **Enniscrone** Co Sligo The 5km sandy beach is a destination beach for surfers, but
5/G8 because it's so extensive it never feels crowded. The village is also home to the Victorian Kilcullen's seaweed bath house. Pints afterwards in The Pilot Bar.

Inch Beach Dingle, Co Kerry Report: 1680/BEACHES.

1889 ✓✓ **The Ewe Experience** Glengarriff, Co Cork +353 27 63840 · www.
3/E22 theewe.com The Ewe sculpture garden is just extraordinary, powerful, wonderful! It's right out of the way and hard to get to, but the journey is worth every second of your time. Humorous and bitingly political. Look out for the vintage car and oversize driver and stick men at the entrance 5km N of Glengarriff.

1890 **Tayto Park** Kilbrew, Ashbourne, Co Meath +353 1 8351999 ·
1/R12 www.taytopark.ie Tayto potato crisps occupy that pantheon in Irish affections which is reserved in other countries for similar iconic treats and drinks – Hershey bars; Irn Bru; Kit-Kat; Haribo; Dr Pepper. Their adventure park is extremely popular, with a series of rides involving splashes, slides, carousels, ferris wheels, zip lines and climbing walls. Open 9.30am-7pm, shorter hours off season.

1891 **Corkagh Park** Naas Road, Clondalkin, Co Dublin Dublin parkland, maintained
1/R13 by the S Dublin County Council, but not your usual municipal park. This one has a
AYR fairy path, a pet farm, and sports and playing pitches. All day until 5pm/6pm/7pm
FREE ADMISSION winter, 8pm/9pm in summer.

1892 **Castlecomer Discovery Park** The Estate Yard, Castlecomer, Co Kilkenny
2/N16 +353 56 4440707 · www.discoverypark.ie Orienteering trails, pedal boating
APR-SEPT around the lake and some high wire fun with their twin ziplines – the longest
🖸 over-water in Ireland at 300m. Tree-top adventure in the sycamore trees allow a 7m high Leap of Faith, tree-top walk and climbing wall. The Jarrow Café serves tasty cooking. Open 7 days from 8.30am until dusk.

1893 **Greenan Maze** Ballinanty, Greenan, Rathdrum, Co Wicklow
1/R15 +353 86 8845624 · www.greenanmaze.com You can enter the half acre maze
🖸 or watch the confused walkers from the viewing tower. There's a second maze as
AYR well, more contemplative than the first, also a farm museum, a nature walk, and farm animals, some of them very cute and pettable. 10am-6pm 7 Days, weekends only off season.

1894 **Russborough House** Blessington, Co Wicklow +353 45 865239 ·
1/Q14 www.russborough.ie A hive of activity including the National Bird of Prey
MAR-NOV Centre, owl handling sessions - popular with Harry Potter fans. There are sheepdog
🖸 demonstrations and horse and carriage rides.The gardens have an enormous 2,000m maze of beech hedging. All day 7 days.

1895 **Lullymore Heritage Park** Rathangan, Co Kildare +353 45 870238 ·
1/P13 www.lullymoreheritagepark.com Lullymore is a peatland reserve, a 'mineral island' in the Bog of Allen which, on the fun side, features a little train, a pet farm, and 18-hole crazy golf course with a difference, a treasure hunt and a smashing adventure playground. Hidden underneath all this fun, of course, is a grand element of learning and discovery.

1896 **Irish National Stud & Gardens** Tully, Co Kildare +353 45 521617 ·
1/D14
AYR
☞
www.irishnationalstud.ie There's a fairy village in the Irish National Stud for the younger visitors, and a horse museum for those many young people who are obsessed with all things equine. Visitors can call in to see the stud itself and visit the famously soulful Japanese Gardens.

1897 **Durrow Scarecrow Festival** Durrow, Co Laois ·
1/N16
1ST WEEK IN
AUG
www.durrowscarecrowfestival.com Book early to be a part of the Round Bale Decorating Competition that is one unusual event in this family festival that takes place at the end of July, beginning of August. There is also a summer camp and a craft workshop that includes Fairy Door Making for children.

1898 **Irish Steam Rally** Stradbally Hall, Stradbally, Co Laois +353 86 3890184 ·
1/N15
AUG BK HOL.
WEEKEND
www.irishsteam.ie Organised by the Irish Steam Preservation Society, the narrow gauge railway at Stradbally with its vintage trains is straight out of the imagination of a child. This really shows off these working steam engines at their best.

1899 **Rathbeggan Lakes** Dunshaughlin, Co Meath +353 1 8240197 ·
1/Q12
www.rathbegganlakes.com Drive a mini Land Rover, take aim and get soaked in the water pistol zone, create in the art barn, pet the animals, have a picnic. Welcome to Fun Valley! Also part of the price – the Stone Age Family Adventure park is particularly impressive.

1900 **Wells House & Gardens** Ballyedmond, Gorey, Co Wexford +353 53 9186737
2/R17
AYR
DF
· www.wellshouse.ie 'We all love to play' say the good people of Wells House, and activities here include clay target shooting, an animal farm and falconry centre, and archery. There are swings and slides, and a picnic area, and honestly, you'd be doing well to get it all done in a day.

1901 **Waterford and Suir Valley Heritage Railway** Kilmeaden Station,
2/N19
APR-SEPT
Kilmeaden, Co Waterford +353 51 384058 · www.wsvrailway.ie Pop on the narrow gauge railway, and follow 6km of track, along the route of the old Waterford to Dungarvan line. The train runs through the valleys and banks of the River Suir. The stock is a restored Simplex 60sp locomotive and two of the carriages are partly open.

1902 **Ballyhass Lakes Centre** Cecilstown, Mallow, Co Cork +353 22 27773 ·
3/H19
www.ballyhassaquapark.ie It is compulsory to get wet in the Ballyhass Lakes. Under 12s must be accompanied by an adult in the water, and need to be able to swim 50m. Families hire a session that lasts 60 minutes. Also wakeboarding in their wake park.

1903 **Fota Wildlife Park** Co Cork +353 21 4812678 · www.fotawildlife.ie Fota is a
3/J21 zoological experience on 70 acres. The first animals arrived in the park in 1982, and
since then the park has grown to become one of Ireland's leading attractions. Don't
forget to check the feeding times before you visit.

1904 **Leap Scarecrow Festival** Leap, Co Cork Halloween festival that has got bigger
3/G23 and bigger, and the drive through Leap – beginning a mile either side of the village –
OCT is a scream at the end of Oct. TGP there were 150 scarecrows featured, which isn't
FREE ADMISSION bad for a village with a population of 240.

1905 **Stonehall Visitor Farm** Curragh Chase Forest Park, Kilcornan, Co Limerick ·
3/H17 www.stonehallvisitorfarm.com What started as a family pet farm, has, 12 years
MAR-DEC on earned zoo status — the Stonehall Wildlife Park is a centre for conservation and
play. Nature trails are set out to help children recognise different flowers and see
animals in their natural habitats.

the
Best
Consuming
Passions

Irish Design

DONEGAL TWEED

1906 **The Tweed Project** Galway · www.thetweedproject.com The Tweed
4/G13 Project creates one-off garments from Irish tweed and linen, covetable
creations that both look back at tradition, but also innovate, bringing Japanese
cutting techniques to Irish fabrics. Their collection has quickly established itself in
the forefront of Irish fashion, seriously trend-setting and desirable. Visit their
Atelier by appointment, or buy online.

1907 **Eddie Doherty** Front St, Ardara, Co Donegal +353 74 9541304 ·
5/J5 www.handwoventweed.com Eddie Doherty has been weaving Donegal
Tweed by hand since the age of 16 using Donegal spun yarns. A legendary local
character in Ardagh, he now makes tweed for Armani, Burberry and Ralph Lauren.

1908 **Molloy & Sons** Ardara, Co Donegal · www.molloyandsons.com After the
5/J5 18thC, tweed overtook linen as the fabric of choice in Ireland. Molloy & Sons have
been making tweed for five generations.

WOOL & WEAVING

1909 **Muckross Weavers** Killarney, Co Kerry +353 64 6670144 ·
3/E20 www.muckross-house.ie The weavers supply shops worldwide, and are also part
of the Muckross House working museum, where visitors can call into the workshop
and see traditional spinning and weaving in progress. All day 7 days. 'Til 7pm
summer, 5.30pm winter.

1910 **Cushendale Woollen Mills** Mill Rd, Graiguenamanagh, Co Kilkenny
2/P17 +353 59 9724118 · www.cushendale.ie The mill has been in operation through
many generations of the Cushen family, using natural fibres to create beautiful
textiles. The materials used are brushed mohair, bouclé mohair, Irish wool,
lambswool and cotton chenille. Most special is the Zwartbles Collection. The mill
shop is open daily Mon-Sat.

1911 **Fiadh Handwoven Design** Main St, Dingle, Co Kerry +353 87 7542141 ·
3/C19 www.fiadh.ie Fiadh Durham hand-weaves gorgeous scarves and shawls that
echo the colours of the landscape in which she works – the yellow of lichen on
a rock; mackerel purples and blacks, seaweed greens. Her triangular scarves are
hugely collectible and it's a challenge to leave her shop/workshop without one
around your neck.

NORTHERN IRISH LINEN

1912 **Irish Linen Centre & Lisburn Museum** Market Square, Lisburn,
6/S6 Co Antrim, NI +4428 92663377 · www.lisburnmuseum.com In the old Market
House, in the centre of Lisburn city, is a country museum dedicated not only to
the local history of the area, but also to the story of Irish linen, from flax to fabric.
You can see live spinning and weaving demonstrations here and buy genuine linen
from the museum shop. All day, AYR, Mon-Sat.

1913
6/R7

Enrich & Endure Banbridge, Co Down, NI +4428 40669522 ·
www.enrichandendure.com E&E make beautiful aprons from Irish linen for the restaurant industry, and you can buy their colourful creations online. They also sell napkins from the linen offcuts.

MODERN IRISH JEWELLERY DESIGNERS

1914
3/E21

✓ **PFK** Henry St, Kenmare, Co Kerry +353 64 6642590 · www.pfk.ie PFK's 'Ring of Kerry' has caught the public imagination and the ring has been presented to style icons Michelle Obama and the late Maureen O'Hara. Paul works with precious stones, but his work with semi-precious stones, like the pool-coloured tourmaline, is equally alluring. Paul is also a part-time fisherman. Shop open all day Tue-Sat (closed lunch 1pm-2pm).

1915
1/R13

✓ **Seamus Gill** Studio 21, The Design Tower, Pearse St, Dublin 2 +353 1 6775701 · www.seamusgill.com Seamus Gill's jewellery is born looking ancient and expressive. It has the simplicity of a seed pod, the drama of a medieval relic. Seamus uses a hammer and anvil to make his jewellery, and it produces work that enjoys pure form, beauty in the way that a leaf shape appeals, or a wedge shape, or a knot. The inspiration for his Flow collection comes from beach glass.

1916
1/R13

✓ **Alan Ardiff** Studio 36, The Design Tower, Trinity Enterprise Centre, Pearse St, Dublin 2 +353 1 6713098 · www.alanardiff.com The whimsical, storybook images within the silver and gold windows of Alan Ardiff's jewellery shop have a cartoon-like appeal. Pixar could make a great movie using the cars in his silver 'Going Nowhere' M50/M25 cufflinks, or his busy bee set in a circular pendant, or any of his birds. Every piece tells a story, or captures a moment.

1917
1/R13

✓ **Chupi** Top Floor, Powerscourt Townhouse, Sth William St, Dublin 2 +353 1 5554644 · www.chupi.com Like some super-confident modern-day celebrity chef @Chupi is a jewellery designer for Generation Z. Social media savvy – get with the #lovechupi hashtag – her packaging is as carefully considered as an Apple iPhone. And the jewellery? It stands up to all the hype. All day Mon-Sat and Sun afternoon.

1918
1/N9

✓ **Elena Brennan** Lisreagh, Cavan +353 86 988 2427 · www.elenabrennan.com There is a sculptural element to Elena's jewellery, and her work has movement and drama, whilst always intricate. One of her collections is based on artefacts from the National Museum of Ireland. Her rings are delightful. Visitors to her Cavan studio welcome, but call in advance.

1919
2/N16

✓ **Inga Reed** River House, Johnswell, Co Kilkenny · www.ingareed.com Inga Reed's jewellery has the complexity of elements found in nature. Her chokers can look like winged seed, ash keys, her brooches like pebbles on the beach, her necklaces remind you of washed-up drying seaweed. Stockists listed on her web page.

1920 **Martina Hamilton** 4 Castle St, Sligo +353 71 9143377 ·
5/J8 www.martinahamilton.ie Martina Hamilton's jewellery sits comfortably on woollen shawls, knitted jumpers, tweed scarfs. It reminds you of marram-grass beaches and cliff edges. Her pieces capture the essence of Ireland and the Wild Atlantic Way.

1921 **Enibas** Main St, Schull, Co Cork Spell Enibas backwards and you get Sabine
3/E23 (Lenz), the name of the innovative pioneer of Irish jewellery who founded the Enibas shops and jewellery collections. The Enibas shop has always been an inspiring place to showcase Sabine's work, and other pieces. Blessed with a wonderful eye, Sabine can place precious jewels beside pieces made from rubber and glass, and you want them.

1922 **Stonechat Jewellers** Westbury Mall, Dublin 2 +353 1 6710103 ·
1/R13 www.stonechat.ie In the heart of Dublin's shopping district, Stonechat is a hub for Irish jewellery design, giving an outlet to contemporary designers throughout the country. They offer their own collections, and the work of a number of guests. All day Mon-Sat, late opening Thur 'til 7pm.

1923 **Designworks** Cornmarket St, Cork +353 21 4279420 · www.corkjewellery.ie
3/J21 Designworks is a jewellery store with a difference. Part retail shop, it also functions a bit like a gallery and a bit like a workshop. Watch the goldsmiths at work and discover jewellery from a mix of in-house produced collections and contemporary Irish designers. All day Mon-Sat.

1924 **Steensons** Bedford House, Bedford St, Belfast, NI +4428 90248269 ·
6/S6 www.thesteensons.com Steensons are a dynamic family of goldsmiths who sell from Belfast, but craft their jewellery in Glenarm on the Causeway Coast. Their workshop is an Économusée, a working museum, where visitors are welcome to come along and watch the goldsmiths at work. Open all day Mon-Sat, till 8pm Thurs.

ARAN SWEATERS

1925 ✓ **Inis Meáin Knitting Co** Aran Islands, Co Galway +353 99 73009 Tarlach and
4/E14 Aine at the Inis Meáin Knitting Co long ago realised that the traditional fisherman's clothing worn by the islanders, with their meaningful stitches and fit-for-purpose materials, were iconic. Throughout their career, Turlough and Aine have not only stemmed emigration by providing employment on the island, worked sustainably, and made beautiful clothes, they have also documented a glorious clothing culture and kept it alive. If you can't make it to the island to buy one, you can pick one up at Barney's in New York, one of their select handful of top-notch retailers.

1926 **Aran Sweater Market** Inis Mór, Aran Islands, Co Galway ·
4/E14 www.aransweatermarket.com The wool for genuine Aran sweaters is oiled and unbleached to protect against the elements. Aran stitches are symbolic - cable stitching represents the fishing ropes; plaited cable represents family life; moss stitch represents the soil; Trinity stitches are religious; honeycomb stitches represent rich rewards, and on it goes. A classic Aran sweater is a simple item of clothing, yet one that is richly decorated, and highly regarded: there is an Aran sweater on display at MOMA in New York, selected as a timeless example of 20thC design. The Aran Sweater Market has always had a branch on Inis Mór, which gives it cred in a world where many people copy the design. There are also Aran Sweater Market stores on Grafton St, Dublin and College St, Killarney. All day 7 days.

IRISH CRYSTAL & GLASS

1927 ✓ **Jerpoint Glass** Stoneyford, Co Kilkenny +353 56 7724350 ·
2/N17 www.jerpointglass.com To watch the craftsmen at work at the furnace, fashioning the molten glass into beautiful creations, is good reason enough to visit Jerpoint Glass studios. Glass is blown to create bowls, glasses, vases and jugs with vivid splashes of Murano-like colour, lots of movement, lots of flow. The studio is housed in a 19thC stone building, still owned by the Leadbetter family. Open Mar-Nov. Glass blowing demos daily. All day Mon-Sat, open 7 days in summer.

1928 **House of Waterford** The Mall, Waterford +353 51 31700 ·
2/P19 www.waterfordvisitorcentre.ie In the tour of the Waterford Crystal factory you follow every step of the glass-making process, starting with the mould room, to the blowing platform, to the cutting room. The tour brings together 200 years of craftsmanship as you watch the master blowers working with the molten crystal, followed by the absolute precision required in cutting and engraving. Tours take place Mon-Fri. Shop open 7 days.

MUSICAL INSTRUMENTS

1929 **Roundstone Music, Craft and Fashion** The Monastery, Roundstone, Co
4/D13 Galway +353 95 35808 · www.bodhran.com The Bodhrán (pron. bow-rawn) began life as a tray, made of goatskin, used for drawing turf from the bog. But soon enough it was discovered that if you beat it with your hand, it makes a lyrical haunting sound. The traditionally made and designed instruments sold from this Roundstone Monastery are made by Malachy Kearns, who has supplied Bodhráns to musicians and travellers for a generation. All day 7 days.

1930 **The Bodhrán Maker** Unit 137 Baldoyle Ind Est, Dublin 13 +353 87 2569672
1/S13 · www.thebodhranmaker.com Paraic McNeela makes Bodhrán drums and has worked with musicians like Christy Moore, the Chieftains and the Corrs. Having worked at the forefront of Irish music since 1979, Paraic produces instruments with a 'hand crafted tone' and he keeps the tradition alive.

LEATHERWORKS

1931 ✓✓ **Holden Leathergoods** Burnham East, Dingle, Co Kerry
3/C19 +353 66 9151796 · www.holdenleathergoods.com A visit to the Holden Workshop, just on the water's edge looking across the harbour at Dingle (Daingean Uí Chúis), is one of the very best experiences you can have while touring the peninsula. What first assails you is the wonderful leathery smell. They offer coffee, served in Dingle pottery, and the leather items are all classics, beautifully finished and items to treasure. There is a shop in Dingle town, but don't miss the workshop.

1932 ✓ **De Bruir** Monasterevin Road, Kildare Town +353 87 6182290
1/P14 Garvan de Bruir's collection of leather goods is wide ranging and includes cabin bags, office storage, furniture, even aprons. His very fine work echoes the equestrian culture of the county, using leather that is tanned for saddlery. Workshop open 10am-5pm Mon-Fri, phone in advance for evenings or weekends.

IRISH WOOD DESIGN

1933
4/F13

✓ ✓ **Liam O'Neill** Spiddal, Co Galway +353 91 553633 · www.liamoneill.com Liam O'Neill is a world-class artist, whose wood-turned pieces and sculptures are of museum quality. His bowls and platters make use of petrified wood, and though delicate and perfectly formed, the pieces have a kind of wabi sabi beauty from the natural flaws in the wood. Some of his pieces have a Bronze Age quality, it's as if he's freeing the form from the wood. Liam O'Neill's Wood Gallery and Sculpture garden is in Spiddal, one mile out of town on the Moycullen Road, on the road just opposite the caravan park.

1934
5/F10

✓ **HEWN** Corrig, Sandyhill, Westport, Co Mayo · www.hewn.ie Éamonn O'Sullivan's spoons are a treat and a treasure. To watch him at work, hewing a piece of wood, is to see a guy who operates on pure instinct, and who also works at lightning speed. He works with sycamore, elm, beech, and ash and creates spoons, paddles and boards of the most artful utility.

1935
6/R3

✓ **Scullion Hurls** 16 Lough Rd, Loughguile, Ballymena, Co Antrim, NI +4428 27641308 · www.scullionhurls.com Michael Scullion followed his father into the business of making hurls, the elegant ash sticks used by players of hurling, the finest, most balletic sport on the planet. These are beautiful implements, and surprisingly inexpensive, whether you ever line out for a team or not. They have weekly hurley making demonstrations at the economusée. All day Tue-Sat, till 7pm Thurs.

1936
2/Q16

Bunbury The Lisnavagh Timber Project Ltd, Lisnavagh, Rathvilly, Co Carlow +353 59 9161784 · www.bunbury.ie William Bunbury began producing his wooden chopping boards, from trees felled on the family estate at Lisnavagh, Co Carlow, in 2007. Every chopping board, indeed every piece they produce, has an original number which allows the owner to trace it right back to the tree from whence it came, and the history of the tree and the board. You can order online, and the boards are also sold through specialist retailers.

1937
3/J21

Tony Farrell Woodturner Gables Gallery, Ballinora, Co Cork + 353 87 2380756 tonyfarrell.ie Tony's ashwood plates are beautiful objects, but also ruggedly utilitarian, a difficult balance to strike with a wooden plate. He also makes beautiful bowls and boards and – glory be! – the most lovely wooden buttons. But those wooden plates are the thing.

1938
5/L10

Roy Humphreys Wood Turner Lurga, Mohill, Co Leitrim +353 71 9631031 · www.royhumphreyswoodturner.ie The raw-edged wooden bowls made by Roy Humphreys are a wonder, the beautiful bowls are finished with the natural bark edging. It's a challenging craft, but the result is spectacular. Roy also makes tables, platters, vases and lamp stands using predominantly ash and beech.

HAND MADE KNIVES

1939
3/E23

✓ ✓ **Fingal Ferguson Knives** Schull, Co Cork ·
www.fingalfergusonknives.com Fingal Ferguson is one of the pillars of
the artisan Gubbeen Farmhouse in W Cork, producers of cheeses, smoked foods,
charcuterie, drinks, a splendid book and more, an enterprise that sells predominantly
through farmers' markets. In recent years, Fingal has given himself time and space to
indulge his passion for making knives, and the knives are extraordinarily beautiful,
and wildly covetable. The sad news is the waiting list is long.

1940
3/F22

✓ **Rory Conner Knives** Bantry, Co Cork · www.roryconnerknives.com
Based in a little workshop in Ballylickey, near to Bantry in W Cork, Rory Conner
has been making beautiful knives for over 25 years. He offers knives in both
stainless and carbon steel, as well as Damas steel for a patterned finish. Rory
makes field knives – which come with hand-stitched leather sheaths – as well as
kitchen knives, oyster knives, cleavers, boning knives and cheese knives. Distinctive
and urgently beautiful.

METALWORK

1941
3/F23

✓ **Paddy McCormack** Munig, Skibbereen, Co Cork +353 86 0848029 ·
www.paddymccormack.com Paddy McCormack works in copper, iron and
bronze. His bowls, candleholders, vases and lamps are wondrous things.

PORCELAIN, POTTERY & CERAMICS

1942
3/B19
⌨

✓ ✓ **Louis Mulcahy** Ballyferriter, Dingle, Co Kerry +353 66 9156229 ·
www.louismulcahy.com Louis Mulcahy pottery is pleasing, colourful
and durable, and it has also been an important industry in Ballyferriter, right down
at the end of the Dingle Peninsula. The pottery and its accompanying restaurant
stay open all year and provide a focus for visitors, who can come to the pottery,
learn to throw a pot, buy a lovely momento, complete a collection. Open all year, all
day, 7 days.

1943
2/N16
⌨

✓ ✓ **Rosemarie Durr Pottery** Castlecomer Estate Yard, The Discovery
Park, Castlecomer, Co Kilkenny +353 87 6833639 · www.
rosemariedurr.com Such is the delicacy of Rosemarie's pottery, people often
mistake it for china. Her pots have a soft glaze, coloured powder blue, or blue with
jade, and an oatmeal cream. There is a sophistication and finesse to her work that
is rare. Report: 1892/ACTIVITIES FOR FAMILIES.

1944
2/N16

✓ ✓ **Andrew Ludick Ceramics** Castlecomer Estate Yard, Co Kilkenny
+353 87 9108927 · www.andrewludick.blogspot.ie Each piece of
Andrew Ludick's pottery is a work of art. Everything he makes is unique. The work
is influenced by indigenous arts and the work is vivid, colourful, perplexing and
pleasing, with child-like forms, reminiscent of Picasso. Andrew shares his pottery
studio with his wife Rosemarie Durr, and they both share a striving for perfection.

1945
2/N17
⌨

✓ **Nicholas Mosse** Bennettsbridge, Co Kilkenny +353 56 7727505 ·
www.nicholasmosse.com The lavishly-pattened Nicholas Mosse pottery is
inspired by the botanical richness of Bennettsbridge in Co Kilkenny. Susan Mosse is
the artist who creates the vivid, cheerful patterns, taken from flowers, farm animals
and woodland. Nicholas and his team then develop the theme and apply it, using
traditional spongeware technique, which has a long tradition in Irish pottery. Cafe
is recommended for lunch or tea.

1946 **Stephen Pearce Pottery** The Old Pottery, Shanagarry, Co Cork
3/K21 +353 21 4646807 · www.theshanagarrypottery.com The Stephen Pearce
classic collection of pottery is immensely tactile, you want to brush your hand over
it. The warm-coloured terracotta – distinctively made from clay that they process
themselves, dug in Youghal - is trimmed with a white glaze. The pottery also
continues to make the older Shanagarry range of earthenware developed by his late
father, Philip Pearce. Visitors are welcome to the pottery, where the cafe is more
than good. Visiting children get a lump of clay to play with.

1947 **Belleek** 3 Main St, Belleek, Co Fermanagh, NI +4418 68658501 ·
6/K7 www.belleek.com Belleek have been making china for 160 years, the company
was founded in 1857. The pottery has always been trademarked with a little stamp,
and if you have a piece of Belleek, you can date it, by checking with the date
designs on their website. Pottery Museum and Visitors Centre open all day 7 days.
Weekdays only off season.

1948 **Karen Morgan Porcelain** Market St, Thomastown, Co Kilkenny
2/N17 +353 86 1663691 · @karenmorganporcelain Hand-thrown at the potter's
wheel, Karen Morgan creates contemporary pottery that is both decorative and
functional. Karen also gives pottery courses at Grennan Mill Craft School, and her
studio and gallery is in the heart of Kilkenny craft country, near to Jerpoint Glass
Studio, so a visit is worthwhile.

1949 **Claire Molloy Ceramics** Rossenarra, Kilmoganny, Co Kilkenny
2/N18 +353 87 2146328 · www.clairemolloyceramics.com Claire specialises in horsehair
and smoke-fired ceramics, using hair from horse's manes and tails to decorate her
pots, as well as the materials used to care for her horses, which she breeds herself –
straw, hay and wood shavings. The raku pots are powerful, tactile, appealing.

1950 **Dunbeacon Pottery** Dunbeacon, Durrus, Co Cork +353 27 61036 ·
3/E23 www.dunbeaconpottery.com Woodland green, bog-cotton white and ocean
blue, these are the colours of Helen Ennis's Dunbeacon pottery. All her pieces are
made on the wheel in her workshop overlooking Dunmanus Bay. Visitors welcome.
Call ahead.

1951 **Marianne Klopp Pottery** Coast Road, Ardgroom Inward, Beara Peninsula,
3/D22 Co Cork +353 27 74919 · www.mklopp-pottery.ie Marianne Klopp has carved
a successful career out of making pit-fired ceramics, bowls and sculptures in far
W Cork on the Beara Peninsula, one of a generation of German and Dutch people,
who migrated to Ireland, and enriched W Cork with their skills in cheesemaking
and craft. You can find her pieces in craft shops throughout Ireland.

1952 **Geoffrey Healy** The Rocky Valley, Kilmacanogue, Co Wicklow
1/S14 +353 1 2829270 · www.healy-pottery.com These days, master potter Geoffrey
Healy is as much a teacher as he is a craftsman. He runs regular workshops.
Geoffrey has been making his richly-glazed pots and jars in the Rocky Valley since
1992. He loves visitors and often posts the times he is going to fire up the kiln on
his Facebook page. Visitors welcome, but call ahead.

IRISH BEAUTY

1953 ✓ **Cloon Keen Atelier** 21A High Street, Galway + 353 91 565 736
4/G13   www.cloonkeenatelier.com 'Dramatic simplicity' is a phrase used by Cloon
Keen Atelier to describe their products, and scents of Cloon Keen are a way of
capturing everything that is lovely about this county and bringing it home to enjoy.
Their fragrances, when experienced through the medium of liquid soaps or scented
candles, are generous, powerful and superbly crafted.

1954 ✓ **The Burren Perfumery** Carron, Co Clare +353 65 7089102 ·
4/G15   www.burrenperfumery.com The best thing about the Burren Perfumery is
AYR   that you can visit, you can look at all the bottles and jars, the apothecary centre of
☞   bubbling activity. You can eat in the lovely cafe. Call into the amazing loo – a
beautiful piece of architecture! – and you can pick up bottles and bars of soap from
the shelves, and walk around the garden. All day, 7 days.

1955 ✓ **VOYA** Strandhill, Co Sligo +353 71 9168686 · www.voya.ie VOYA is a
5/J8   family business in Sligo that started from a seaweed bath house, and has now
become a global brand. Seaweed is at the heart of all their products. Voya products
include balms, washes and moisturisers. The seaweed baths are still open in Sligo.
Report: 1887/ACTIVITIES.

IRISH CARPETS

1956 **Connemara Carpets** Moyard, Connemara, Co Galway +353 95 41010 ·
4/D12   www.connemaracarpets.ie The carpets are handmade in the NW of Ireland,
in glorious Connemara. The yarns are spun for the company, who then tuft them
into lustrous designs. This company made the distinctive modern carpets in the G
Hotel, and have many singular clients.

BASKET MAKING

1957 ✓ **Joe Hogan Baskets** Loch na Fooey, Finny, Clonbur, Co Galway
4/E12   +353 94 9548241 · www.joehoganbaskets.com Joe Hogan is so talented a
basket-maker that he frees the form from any idea you might have in your head
about what a basket shape is. He makes hats from twigs, or artistic baskets that
wrap themselves organically around pieces of driftwood. Joe Hogan is an author
and teacher as well as craftsman, and he has written the definitive work on basket
making in Ireland.

1958 **Baurnafea Studios** Baurnafea, Castlewarren, Co Kilkenny +353 59 9726947
2/P16   · www.baurnafeastudio.ie Heike Kahle and Klaus Hartmann are the couple
behind Baurnafea Studios, making classic willow baskets of all shapes and sizes.
They also take commissions for living willow structures, and teach basket-making
courses. Catch them at various markets around the country.

1959 **Kathleen McCormick** Watering Hollow, Ballinakill, Broadford, Co Kildare
1/P12   +353 86 8807208 · www.kathleenmccormickbaskets.com Kathleen
McCormick grows the willow for her baskets in Co Kildare, harvests it herself, and
makes a range of traditional baskets, including trugs, fisherman's creels, bicycle
baskets and some contemporary free-form sculptural works. A talented artisan, she
also makes a range of homespun carpets and woven cushion covers.

The Best Craft Shops

1960
3/E22

✔ **Adrigole Arts** Adrigole, Ring of Beara, Co Cork +353 27 60234 ·
@Adrigole Arts Adrigole Arts is something of a design Mecca in far W Cork.
Very astute curation of Irish crafts: jewellery, pottery, woodwork. You can also get a
good cup of coffee and home-made cakes, so a visit is worth travelling for.

1961
3/G22

✔ **Etain Hickey Collections** 40 Ashe St, Clonakilty, Co Cork
+353 23 8821479 This is a gallery, and a showcase for emerging artists and
classic masters of craft. The collection includes greenwood chairs, metal and
basket work, jewellery, and a wonderful selection of ceramics, some made by Etain
herself, and some by her husband Jim Turner, who makes glorious sculptural pods,
full of texture in a soft, earthy palette.

1962
3/K21

✔ **The Ballymaloe Shop** Ballymaloe House, Shanagarry, Co Cork
+353 21 4652032 · www.ballymaloeshop.ie A much-loved shop of great
character, the Ballymaloe Shop sells the best kitchen necessities, from spatulas to
saucepans. Everything here is the best there is, whether it is a kitchen knife, or the
board on which to chop. There is a super cafe at the end of the shop, and they also
sell books, foodstuffs and some clothing. All day, 7 days.

1963
5/G9

Foxford Woollen Mills Visitor Centre Providence Rd, Foxford, Co Mayo
+353 92 56104 · www.foxfordwoollenmills.com A working mill, with scarves,
throws and blankets sold throughout the world. The mill is open for visitors daily.
Tours of the working mill Mon-Fri. Call in advance to book. All day Mon-Sun, from
noon Sun.

1964
1/R13

Cleo Ltd 18 Kildare St, Dublin 2 +353 1 6761421 · ww.cleo-ltd.com Cleo began
selling sweaters from the Aran Islands, and now sells a range of Irish clothing made
from natural fibres. The family-run store, right in the heart of Dublin city, now sells
socks, felt, knitted toys and shawls as well as storm jackets and aran sweaters. You
can buy their range online.

1965
4/G13

Ó'Máille The Original House of Style 16 High St, Galway +353 91 562696 ·
www.omaille.com A bit of an institution in Galway, Anne O'Máille employes
170 knitters, from remote regions in Connemara, W Clare, and N Mayo who are
part of the team of people making traditional Irish clothing and crafts for sale
here. This shop is a tourist attraction as well as a practical place to buy lovely
clothing.

1966
2/N17

Kilkenny Design Centre Castle Yard, Kilkenny +353 56 7722118 ·
www.kilkennydesign.com Kilkenny is the undisputed craft capital of Ireland, and
the Kilkenny Design Centre, in the Castle Yard of magnificent Kilkenny Castle, is the
place to find all the Kilkenny and other Irish crafts under one roof. The list includes
ceramics, crystal, textiles, jewellery, and other hand-made gifts. As well as that
there is a cafe and food hall, and, at night, the shop transforms into the evening
time Anocht restaurant with a totally different character (917/THE SOUTH EAST). All
day till 7pm 7 days.

1967   **The Leitrim Design House** The Dock Arts Centre, St George's
5/K10   Terrace, Carrick-on-Shannon, Co Leitrim +353 71 9650550 ·
www.leitrimdesignhouse.ie Located in the Dock Arts Centre, this is a showcase
for the best of Irish craft and design, from textiles, to wood, to jewellery and
ceramics, you can find it here, and understand who makes it, and what motivates
the makers to do what they do. Invaluable. All day Mon-Sat.

1968   **The Cat And The Moon** 4 Castle St, Sligo +353 71 9143686 ·
5/J8   www.thecatandthemoon.ie Having your work featured in the Cat And The Moon
is an ambition for many an Irish craftsperson. This is an especially good place to
find contemporary Irish jewellery, but there are also cabinets of pottery and glass,
and they sell textiles, and even soaps and candles. All day Mon-Sat.

1969   **Ardmore Pottery & Gallery** Ardmore, Co Waterford +353 24 94152 ·
2/L21   www.ardmorepottery.com As well as selling their own characterful white
and blue hand-thrown earthenware pots – which you can watch them create on
site – the Ardmore Gallery also sells the work of more than 150 Irish craftworkers,
including glass, candles, paintings and ceramics. From 2pm Sun-Thur, all day
Fri & Sat.

1970   **The Craft Shop** 11 Glengarriff Rd, Bantry, Co Cork +353 27 50003 ·
3/E22   www.craftshopbantry.com The selection of crafts for sale in this shop is
brought together by the careful eye of Christine, whose excellent good taste has
sourced crafts that are beautiful and functional. You will find pottery from Geoffrey
Healy and Rosemarie Durr, metalwork from Paddy McCormack, knives from Rory
Connor, Tedagh Candles, Martin O'Fynn baskets, Marika O'Sullivan's jewellery and
a fantastic selection of local leather bags and shoes from Brendan Jennings. A
pandora's box of Irish craftsmanship. All day Mon-Sat. Closed Wed during winter.

1971   **Old Mill Stores** Connonagh, Rosscarbery, Co Cork +353 86 3919237 ·
3/G23   www.theoldmillstores.ie The Old Mill Stores is a breath of fresh air in terms of
being a funky craft shop, specialising in well-designed and well-priced crafts and
gifts from Ireland and internationally. They began by selling Ovne Antique Stoves
(yes, they supplied Harry Potter), but the shop has developed to selling homewares
that you didn't realise you needed, but you do. Opening times vary. Telephone
before travelling.

1972   **Wooden Heart** 3 Quay St, Galway +353 91 563542 ·
4/G13   www.woodenheart.ie The place to go if you're looking for well-made, ethical
and safe wooden toys, the shop is a haven and a delight, with robust wooden
crafts hanging from every nook and crevice on every shelf and in every corner. The
Ulrich family are also the dynamic team behind Galway's CoffeeWerk + Press just
opposite on Quay St, (828/COFFEE), where not only can you get the best coffee in
town, you can also shop for beautiful cards and posters. And upstairs, beside an old
vinyl system, there are beautiful objects for the home. All day, 7 days.

1973 **The White Room** 22 Henry St, Kenmare, Co Kerry +353 64 6640600 ·
3/E21 www.thewhiteroomkenmare.com The White Room specialises in Irish linen and lace. It's packed to the gills with damask, doilies, bedlinens and hankies. But it sells more than just fabrics – there are gifts and wedding favours, and this is an enjoyable shop to visit at Christmas, when they have everything for the tree and the home. All day, Mon-Sat. The same company also run **The Linen Chest**, in Dingle (Daingean Uí Chúis).

1974 **O'Reilly & Turpin** Bridge St, Westport, Co Mayo +353 98 28151 ·
5/E10 www.oreillyturpin.ie Find Irish ironwork, woodwork, jewellery, ceramics and glass under one roof here as well as what they call their Quirky collection. Corry O'Reilly and Antoinette Turpin are a brilliant shopfront for Irish design. All day, Mon-Sat.

1975 **Donegal Craft Village** Donegal Town +353 74 9723222 ·
5/K6 www.donegalcraftvillage.com A village of craftsmen and women offering weaving, felt, wood, jewellery and painting. And the added bonus of **Aroma Cafe**, which is a destination in itself. The craft village is very well run, with landscaped grounds, a picnic area and a pretty courtyard. Needless to say, the crafts are all deeply desirable. All day Mon-Sat. Closed Mon during winter.

1976 **Kilbaha Gallery** Kilbaha, Loop Head, Co Clare +353 65 9058843 ·
4/D17 www.kilbahagallery.com Kilbaha is pretty much the end of the end of Loop Head, in S Co Clare, so could there be a better place to open a gorgeous craft shop? Home also to the **Henry Blake Heritage Centre** as well, a mini museum dedicated to the life of a native son of Kilbaha: a blind dancer, story-teller and craftsman. All day 7 days in summer. Weekends Oct-Christmas.

1977 **The Irish Design Shop** 41 Drury St, Dublin 2 +353 1 6798871 ·
1/R13 www.irishdesignshop.com As its name suggests, Clare Grennan and Laura Caffrey have pulled together a host of beautiful Irish crafts from contemporary Irish designers and craftspeople. Good-looking NTN watches, made in Dublin, greenwood stools from Wicklow, soap dishes from W Cork, and their own jewellery, amongst many other enticing handicrafts. All day 7 days, from 1pm Sun.

Not just Garden Centres, More a Way of Life

1978 ✓ **Future Forests** Kealkill, Bantry, Co Cork +353 27 66176 ·
3/F22 www.futureforests.net Future Forests became famous for being a force behind Mary Reynold's gold medal winning Chelsea garden, and for a long time it represented the alternative W Cork lifestyle, all dreadlocks and piercings, festival chic, and a casual attitude to life. But this belies the truth of the garden centre as it is today, a well-run, well-stocked venture with a leaning towards wild and native. Staff are helpful and informed.

1979 **Ballyseedy Garden Centre** Fota Retail Park, Carrigtwohill, Co Cork
3/K21 +353 21 4881010 · www.ballyseedy.ie Part garden centre, part department store, part restaurant, sometime country market, sometime gardening college, Ballyseedy in both Cork and Tralee is all about spending the day browsing, shopping and grazing. The cafe here is recommended. Wed farmers' market. All day, 7 days.

1980 **The Garden House** Mabestown, Backroad, Malahide, Co Dublin
1/S12 +353 1 5312020 · www.thegardenhouse.ie The Garden House is all about making the most of an al fresco lifestyle. There are barbecues, garden furniture, and beautiful plants. Everything you need for the room outside. This is a whole shopping experience, so check out the jewellery, handbags and scarves, and the excellent cookery. All day, 7 days.

1981 **Arboretum Home & Garden Heaven** Old Kilkenny Rd, Leighlinbridge,
2/P16 Co Carlow +353 59 9721558 · www.arboretum.ie Arboretum boasts Ireland's largest covered outdoor garden area, with a retractable roof, which can open in sunny weather and close when the rain comes down. There is a kitchen store, gift shop, a whole fashion floor, BBQ and garden furniture. This is designed to be more than just a garden centre, and you could spend a day here quite happily. Rachel's Garden Cafe is their capacious food space. All day 7 days.

1982 **Rathwood** Rath, Tullow, Co Carlow +353 59 9156285 · www.rathwood.com
1/Q16 Before you ever get to talk about the plants in this garden centre, Rathwood is also home to a maze, planted in the shape of Ireland, with each county built to scale. There is a mini railway, with a working express train that runs around their animal park, there is a fashion floor selling designer shoes, jackets and fashion labels, and a playground. There is a deer park, a forest walk, a bird of prey centre, furniture showrooms, and there is a 300-seater restaurant which is popular for breakfast and lunch. You could come here and never leave.

1983 **Creative Garden Centres** 34 Stockbridge Rd, Donaghadee, Co Down, NI
6/T5 +4428 91883603 · www.creativegardens.com This dynamic garden centre group has three branches, the two others are in Bushmills and Galgorm Castle. Each centre offers all-year-round garden goodies, and all of them make a great feature of having a top-rate food offering. The Bushmills centre even offers a BBQ experience in a converted barn. The restaurants are almost as important as their well-sourced pots, plants and giftware. All day, Mon-Sun.

1984 **Hillmount** 56 Upr Braniel Road, Gilnahirk, Belfast, NI +44 2890 448213 ·
6/S6 www.hillmount.co.uk Hillmount is a long-established garden centre with two stores, Belfast and Bangor, and has a reputation for providing everything, absolutely everything a gardener might need. They also run two imaginative cafes.

the
Best
The Islands

The Islands

EAST COAST ISLANDS

1985 **Lambay Island** Skerries, Co Dublin 6 miles off Rush in N Co Dublin, Lambay
1/S12 Island is the private home of Alexander Baring, Lord Revelstoke, of the banking
family, who still lives in the castle. The castle itself is an important Edwardian
country house, and the only Irish country house designed by Sir Edwin Lutyens.
The gardens were designed in collaboration with Gertrude Jekyll, and the house is
the only remaining Lutyens/Jekyll collaboration that still belongs to the family that
commissioned the work. The island is, strangely, also home to a family of wallabies,
first brought to the island by the Lord Lambay of three generations ago. If you want
to visit the island, trips are arranged by **Skerries Sea Tours** who also do tours
around the **Skerries Islands**, and the scenic **Rockabill Lighthouse**, which is a
breeding site for roseate tern: 35% of the European population of tern breed here.
Lambay is home to the only grey seal colony on the E coast.
Skerries Sea Tours +353 86 3043847 · www.skerriesseatours.ie

1986 **Ireland's Eye** Howth, Co Dublin Just off Howth in N Co Dublin, this uninhabited
1/S12 but popular island boasts a Martello tower built in 1803, one of three built in Howth
against the possible invasion by Napoleonic troops. St Nessan's Church dates from
the 8thC. It is an important bird sanctuary, particularly for gannets. **Ireland's Eye
Ferries** operate tours of the island leaving from the end of the W pier in Howth.
Operating 10am-6pm, 7 days AYR weather permitting.
Ireland's Eye Ferries +353 86 07773021 · www.irelandseyeferries.com

1987 **North Bull Island** Dublin Bay The Bull Wall provides access to the island; you
1/S13 can drive as far as the causeway. The island is a wildlife sanctuary, notable for
the Irish hare, and rich birdlife, including whimbrels under observation, bearing
coloured rings – they ask you to report sightings. A man-made island, Bull was
created when they built the N Bull Wall to Dublin Port 200 years ago. It is actually
still growing into the sea, and its habitats are made up of beach, dunes, mud flats,
grassland and marsh.

1988 **Dalkey Island** S. Co Dublin Dalkey is a heritage town, 12km to the S of Dublin,
1/S13 with an offshore island that you can reach by ferry from Coliemore Harbour. It has a
Martello tower, and the medieval St. Begnet's church, as well as goats. A visit to the
Dalkey Castle & Heritage Centre is a good place to start or end the island visit,
where you can learn about the island's 6,500 years of history.
Dalkey Island Tours Ken Cunningham +353 85 2426516
Dalkey Castle & Heritage Centre +353 1 2858366 · www.dalkeycastle.com

1989 **Saltee Islands** Kilmore Quay, Co Wexford The Saltee Islands present an
2/Q20 unforgettable vista of sea birds, land birds and migrant birds, an ornithologist's
dream island, where you will see the mesmeric black-eyed gannets with their
enormous wingspan, the cheerful puffin, whose male parent helps to incubate
their single egg, great black-backed gulls and many other glorious birds who
congregate in large numbers on these islands. Day visits are allowed between
11.30am and 4.30pm only. There are several charter boat companies operating out
of Kilmore Quay marina, offering fishing trips and day trips to the islands.
Saltee Islands · www.salteeislands.info

SOUTH COAST ISLANDS

1990 **Spike Island** Cork Harbour Its proximity to land, combined with its island
3/K21 nature has given Spike Island a fascinating history as a monastery, a fortress and
a gaol. Like the locations of many of the Martello towers along the E coast, the
star-shaped Fort Mitchel, was built initially to withstand the threat of invasion by
Napoleon in 1804, but the fort soon became a place where men were kept in rather
than kept out. Tours to Spike island are immensely popular, especially the After
Dark Tour.
Spike Island Discovery +353 85 8518818 · www.spikeislandcork.ie

1991 **Sherkin Island** Co Cork Sherkin Island is one of the inhabited islands around
3/F23 Ireland's coastline, with a population of about 100. The island is 4.8km long and
is home to an Art School, awarding a BA in Visual Art in a 4-year honours degree
programme. There are two pubs, self-catering cottages and an excellent hostel
and retreat centre. The island landscape is a mixture of heathlands, salt marshes
and glorious beaches. The **Sherkin Island Marine Station** has made a significant
contribution to the marine life of W Cork, producing a series of useful nature
guides. Sherkin is a place where Irish music is played in lively sessions, especially in
the summer months.
Dublin School of Creative Arts Sherkin Island College · www.dit.ie
The Islander's Rest +353 28 20116 · www.islandersrest.ie
The Jolly Roger +353 28 20662 · @TheJollyRogerPub
Murphy's Pub +353 28 20116
Island Accommodation & Discovery +353 87 61853368 ·
www.sherkinnorthshore.com
Sherkin Island Marine Station · www.sherkinmarine.ie

1992 **Heir Island** Skibbereen, Co Cork Heir Island is one of the inner islands in
3/E23 Roaringwater Bay, a swimmable distance from Cunnamore Pier, 14km S of
Skibbereen. The island is 2.5km long — easy also to circumnavigate by kayak.
The island boasts a Bread Cookery School and a well-known restaurant, which
now also functions as an Art Gallery, displaying the work of chef and artist, John
Desmond. **Island Cottage**, the restaurant he runs with partner Ellmary Fenton is
internationally known. Dinner is served Wed-Sun between the months Jun-Sept.
Pre booking essential, fixed menu. The **Firehouse Bread School** operates a
Saturday bread baking course where students learn a range of techniques and
recipes, and pizzas are cooked on their wood-fired oven. Heir Island is also home
to the **Heir Island Sailing School**, an RSA approved Training Centre. One of the
most notable aspects of the island is that all the houses are made in the design of
a traditional cottage, and all recent development has harked back to this 1920's
design.
Island Cottage +353 28 38102 · www.islandcottage.com
The Firehouse Bread School +353 85 1561984 · www.thefirehouse.ie
Heir Island Sailing School +353 87 1488127 · www.heirislandsailingschool.com

1993 **Cape Clear** Baltimore, Co Cork Cape Clear is an Irish-speaking *Gaeltacht* island,
3/E23 where many a school child has completed summer camps in an effort to get to
grips with the language. The island is the most southern of W Cork's group of
islands, it is accessed from Baltimore, landing at the beautiful harbour on its
N side. A magical island of Megalithic standing stones, characterful ruins and a
centre for bird watching and spotting whales, turtles, sunfish, dolphins and sharks.
There are about 120 people living on the island, speaking both English and Irish.
One of the main attractions of the island is the **Goat Farm**, run by blind goat
herder, Ed Harper. The farm is open to visitors and you can buy their delicious
homemade goat's ice cream. **Sean Rua's Restaurant**, operating also as a shop, is

a recommended stop for a pizza or some really fresh fish. And **Cotter's Bar** is the island pub. In winter, the island is battered by sea storms coming in from the S W, and the island is only 4.8km from the famous **Fastnet Rock Lighthouse**.

Cape Clear · www.capeclearisland.ie
Cape Clear Ferries · www.capeclearferries.com
Cape Clear Goat Farm +353 87 7973056 · goat@iol.ie
Sean Rua's Restaurant +353 28 39099 · www.seanruasrestaurant.com
Cotter's Bar · www.capeclearisland.ie/FoodAndDrink
Fastnet Rock Lighthouse · www.mizenhead.net

WEST COAST ISLANDS

1994 **Whiddy Island** Bantry, Co Cork Once a centre for curing pilchards, Whiddy
3/E22 Island, in beautiful Bantry Bay now has an economy driven by fishing and tourism, but the island is also home to a large oil terminal, which stores a strategic reserve of oil for Ireland. Sadly, the island is also known for the Whiddy Island Disaster, when a tanker landing with crude oil exploded on the terminal, killing 50 people. Bantry moved on from the disaster, and the location became the home of Bantry Bay mussel farming. It is an island visited by locals on a summer's day, and there is a restaurant, which is operated by the same family who run the ferry.

Whiddy Ferry and Bank House · www.whiddyferry.com

1995 **Garinish Island** Glengarriff, Co Cork The famous island garden of Ilnacullin is
3/E22 situated on Garinish Island, in Glengarriff harbour in Bantry Bay. The island garden now belongs to the Irish state and is a bucket list adventure for many a garden enthusiast, locally and internationally. The garden is open all days 7 days, Apr-Oct. Be prepared to pay twice, once to the ferry operator, and then again to enter the garden. There is a cafe and toilet facilities on the site. Boats take the trip via Seal Island to see the languishing seals. The Blue Pool where the boats leave to take you to the island is a popular swimming spot.

Ilnacullin +353 27 63149 · www.heritageireland.ie
Garinish Island Ferry & Blue Pool Ferry www.harbourqueenferry.com & www.bluepoolferry.com

1996 **Bere Island** Berehaven, Co Cork Its strategic site at the end of Bantry Bay has
3/D22 made Bere Island an important military base, and it has been used by both the British and the Irish army, indeed to this day it is still used for training exercises. A number of restaurants have come and gone on the island, but none seem to survive. So if you're going to see the wedge graves, the birds, the angling, swimming or cycling, don't forget to bring a picnic.

Bere Island · www.bereisland.net

1997 **Dursey Island** Beara, Co Cork Dursey is a small, inhabited island at the far,
3/C22 far, far W of the Beara Peninsula. The island is only approachable by the cable car which has been running precipitously over Dursey Sound since 1969. It runs continually back and forth between the hours of 9.30am-11am, 2.30pm-5pm and returning only from 7pm to 8pm. Because of the high volume of traffic it is recommended to go early and come back early. The experience of travelling over the sea will make your fingers and toes sweat. The bird population of Dursey – one of the main reasons for visiting – is made up of resident seabirds, shearwaters, guillemots, razorbills and puffins, and also, during the migration season it serves as a resting point for migrant birds. There is a loop walk around the island that you wouldn't want to undertake without a pair of binoculars around your neck.

Dursey Island · www.durseyisland.ie

1998 **Valentia Island** Portmagee, Co Kerry Valentia Island is joined to the mainland
3/B21 via a bridge over the Portmagee channel. It is home to a marine radio station, an ice
cream dairy and a quarry that provided the slate for the British House of Commons.
Geographical landmarks are the Bray Head Cliffs and the beach at Glanleam. Today,
the radio station monitors emergency frequencies in the maritime bands, and
responds to calls for assistance from vessels getting into difficulties, or medical
problems. **Valentia Farmhouse Dairy** is run by Joe and Caroline Daly, who make
beautiful milk, and ice cream from their Valentia dairy herd. You can visit the parlour
during the summer months. Not actually on the island, but just overlooking the
bridge to the island is **The Moorings Restaurant & Bar**, a handy place to stay
and eat if you are visiting the Skelligs along with all the other Star Wars fans. The
Moorings has rooms, and is open all day, and dinner, 7 days. Note, there is a small
island — **Beginish Island** — tucked into Valentia harbour. The island offers a
spectacular loop walk, and many swim around the island.
Valentia Island Dairy Kilbeg +353 87 2843276 · @valentiaicecream

1999 **The Blasket Islands** Co Kerry You can take a day trip to the Blasket Islands via
3/A20 **Blasket Island Ferries**. With luck, you might see dolphins and whales and even
orcas en route, and on the island you might spot wheatears, stonechats, pipits,
black-backed gulls and terns. There are more than 17 different species of sea bird
breeding on the islands, including Manx shearwaters and storm petrels.
The Blasket Centre is also located on the mainland, in Dunquin, telling the story
of life on the island. **Blasket Islands Eco Marine Tours** based in Dingle (Daingean
Uí Chúis), offer boat tours on the MV Blasket Princess with skipper Mick Sheerin. Tra
Ban beach is considered to be one of the best beaches in Ireland. Dunquin Harbour
itself, is a spectacular drive, winding down the mountain face to the harbour.
The Blasket Centre Dunquin · www.blasket.ie
Blasket Islands Eco Marine Tours Ventry, Dingle, Co Kerry +353 86 3353805
· www.marinetours.ie
Blasket Island Ferries Dunquin +353 85 7751045 · www.blasketisland.com

2000 **Scattery Island** Kilrush, Co Clare A day trip to Scattery Island is much
4/E17 recommended to see the monastic settlement, which was founded in the 6thC,
by local saint St Senan. There are actually the ruins of no less than six churches on
the island and one of the highest round towers in the country – a lofty 120ft high.
The island history is full of invasions and reclamations. Brian Boru recaptured the
island from the Vikings. Situated at the mouth of the River Shannon, this is one of
the best places to spot dolphins. Boat trips to the island depart from Kilrush marina
daily during the summer. There is a small visitors' centre for those looking for a
deeper knowledge of the island.
Scattery Island Visitor Centre +353 65 6829100 ·
@scatteryislandvisitorcentre
Dolphin Discovery Kilrush, Co Clare +353 65 9051327 ·
www.discoverdolphins.ie

ARAN ISLANDS
2001 'Stepping stones out of Europe' is how Seamus Heaney described the three Aran
4/E14 Islands. Arriving on these slender outcrops of limestone you do feel that you have
stepped out of familiar climes, and arrived in a place of captivating clarity. Sadly,
90% of the 120,000 visitors to the main island, Inis Mor, are day trippers, and these
visitors get little or no idea of what the island is truly like. They crowd the tour
buses, crowd the significant tourist sites, then hightail it back to the mainland.

But it is only before they arrive, and after they leave, that you can really see the subtle magic of stone and field and sea. Then there is time to have a swim in Kilmurvey Bay or in Poll na bPeist. You can cycle the roads safely without the madcap tour drivers threatening to drive you into the ditch. You can explore the cenotaphs and funerary cairns which lie along the main roads of the island. You get a sense of the extraordinary fort that is Dun Aonghasa, and of Aran as a whole.

INIS MÓR

2002
4/E14
Dun Aonghasa Inis Mór, Aran Islands, Co Galway +353 99 61008 · www.heritageireland.ie The Acropolis of Aran is a mystery. Who built this Stone Age fort, arranged around a cliff face 100 fathoms deep, and why they did so, is a mystery. The writer Tim Robinson expressed it best when he wrote that 'Dún Aonghasa, heavy with centuries, dreams upon a pinnacle of another world'. It is easy to imagine that other world when you wander the walls on a quiet evening, facing off into the Atlantic Ocean at the edge of Europe. The fort is open all year. Free admission if you are staying overnight in an Inis Mór participating accommodation.

2003
4/E14
Aran Camping & Glamping · www.irelandglamping.ie On Frenchman's Beach, which is a short distance from the ferry at Kilronan, ACG has a neat campsite, and ten handsome pods, whose style is based on monastic beehive huts, called *Clochan na Carraige*. They sleep four people, have a shower room, a deck area, and are close to the barbecue and cooking area of the site. Nice way to create a life-long happiness anchor for the kids, in particular.

2004
4/E14
Ted Fest · www.tedfest.org At the end of February each year, Inis Mor becomes Craggy Island, and Fathers Ted, Dougal and Jack are reborn, in their hundreds and in their clerical collars, along with binders of Lovely Girls. It's quite mad, and mighty craic.

2005
4/E14
Cáis Gabhair Árann Goat's Cheese · www.arangoatcheese.com Gabriel Faherty has made a great success of his goat's cheese, made with milk from his handsome Saanen and Nubian goats. In addition to his cheese, Gabriel also conducts tours of the island for groups, which includes a chance to visit the cheese rooms, and this is the tour we would book.

2006
4/E14
Kilmurvey House · www.aranislands.ie/kilmurvey-house Treasa and Bertie run the best B&B on the island, and make the best breakfasts. They are consummate, kindly hosts and, if you stay here for a few days, Aran will creep quietly into your soul.

2007
4/E14
Joe Watty's Bar & Restaurant · www.joewattys.ie A lively pub that is an Aran institution. Decent food, nice music sessions, and a pleasant walk up the hill out of Kilronan will build up that thirst.

2008
4/E13
Aran Island Ferries 37 Forster St, Galway · www.aranislandferries.com Leaves from Rossaveal daily. Bicycles need to be pre-booked, as space can be restricted.

2009
4/F15
Doolin Ferries +353 65 7074455 · www.doolinferries.com Daily sailings from Doolin, Co Clare, to the three islands as well as excursions to see the Cliffs of Moher.

2010   **Aer Arann** · www.aerarannislands.ie

4/F13   You can charter a flight from this company to either visit, or just fly over, the islands.
Synge's Cottage Report: 1641/LITERARY PLACES.
Aran Sweater Market Report: 1926/IRISH DESIGN.

INIS MEÁIN

2011   **Inis Meáin Restaurants and Suites** +353 86 8266026 · www.inismeain.com

4/E14   Ruairi and Marie-Therese de Blacam have created one of the most desirable destinations in Europe, in a stunning architect-designed restaurant and suites on little Inis Meain. Its global reputation means that you have to book well in advance to secure one of the suites, and to get a table in the restaurant where a set menu is cooked for 16 people each evening. The combination of staying and eating here is extraordinary, and worth every cent.

2012   **An Dún** · www.inismeainaccommodation.ie Just up the road from JM Synge's

4/E14   Cottage, in the centre of the island and down a boreen across from the post office, Teresa Faherty's simple B&B and restaurant has been a fixture of Inis Meain since 1989. Mrs Faherty is a charming hostess, and her cooking is true and generous, based on produce from her garden and polytunnel.
Inis Meáin Knitting Co Report: 1925/IRISH DESIGN.

INIS OIRR

2013   **Teach an Tea** · www.cafearan.ie Alissa and Micheál Donoghue's family home is

4/E14   the location for their smashing café and tea rooms. Come and eat fresh mackerel with some of Micheál's Orla potatoes and leaves from the garden, or the signature hen's egg salad on brown bread, followed by a slice of rhubarb and almond tart, and the world will seem a perfect place. Alissa has a real cook's touch.
MV Plassey Report: 1573/SHIPWRECKS.

2014   **Inishbofin Island** Cleggan, Connemara, Co Galway Once upon a time, 1,000

4/C11   people lived on Inishbofin, 11km off the coast of W Connemara, and settlement here goes back to the Bronze Age. Today, the population is down to 165 people, but those people are a dynamic bunch. They organise literary, cultural, music and food festivals, run a hotel – The Dolphin – and an acclaimed bar and restaurant with rooms, Day's Bar. In 2016 Inishbofin became the first island to be awarded an international ecotourism award, and that's why a trip across on the ferry to the Island of the White Cow is merited: for bird watching and nature photography; walking and angling trips and tours; stand-up paddle-boarding; horse riding; eating well and drinking late; and meeting stimulating people at the hog roasts and the Inish conversations.
Inishbofin Information · www.inishbofin.com
Inishbofin Ferry +353 86 1718829 (call or text) ·
www.inishbofinislanddiscovery.com
The Beach, Days Bar & B&B · www.thebeach.ie
Dolphin Hotel · www.dolphinhotel.ie
Inishbofin Island Hostel Report: 1300/HOSTELS.

2015   **Inishturk** Roonagh Pier, Co Mayo Fewer than 60 people now live on Inishturk,

5/C11   and they're a sparky bunch: during the 2016 US presidential election, the island offered 'refuge' to Americans who were terrified at the prospect of a Trump presidency. Excellent loop walks cross the island, nice B&Bs, fabulous cliff formations, and O'Malley Ferries operate daily ferries to the island from Roonagh Pier, which is 6km from Louisburgh.

O'Malley Ferries +353 86 8870814 · www.omalleyferries.com
Tranaun House +353 87 7616582 · www.tranaunhouse.com
Community Club +353 87 1317426 · www.inishturkisland.com

2016
5/D10

Clare Island Clew Bay, Co Mayo 'A quiet place for coastal walks and bird watching' said *The New York Times*, whilst *National Geographic* suggests exploring Pirate Queen Grace O'Malley's tower house and her grave in the Cistercian Abbey. We reckon a Clare Island adventure weekend, followed by a good steak after a day's coasteering and snorkelling, would be just the ticket. Clare Island is the highest of the offshore islands, and from Knockmore, at a height of 462m, you have amazing views of the Co Mayo coast. The Clare Island lighthouse offers luxury accommodation and a communal dinner, whilst Sailor's Bar is where all the walkers and bikers head to at day's end. Ferry from Roonagh Pier takes about 20 minutes.
Island Information · www.clareisland.ie
Go Explore Hostel +353 98 26307 · www.goexplorehostel.ie
Clare Island Adventures +353 87 3467713 · www.clareislandadventures.ie
Clare Island Lighthouse Clew Bay, Co Mayo Report: 1409/PLACES TO STAY.
Clare Island Ferry · www.clareislandferry.com

2017
5/C9

Achill Island Co Mayo Connected to the mainland by a bridge at Achill Sound, but there is no question that you are entering a different world when you cross over. The island is the most populous of Ireland's islands – about 2,500 people live here year round – but sometimes it can feel that is the local blackface mountain lambs who are really in charge, as they saunter down the roads, and cross down to the beach to munch on the seaweeds that make them taste so absurdly delicious – Achill blackface lamb is one of the finest meats that you can eat. Look out also for the particularly fine Achill sea salt, and craft beers from the Achill Island brewery. There is a marvellous sense of community on Achill, and there are lots of festivals, marathons, races and celebrations each year. The island made global headlines in 2017 when the beach at Dooagh, which had disappeared in 1984, reappeared over the space of several weeks.

2018
5/D9
14 ROOMS
MED.INX
LLL

Bervie Keel, Achill Island, Co Mayo +353 98 43114 · www.bervieachill.com
An old coastguard station which has been a well-regarded and very comfortable B&B for many years. John and Elizabeth Barrett have many visitors who return year after year, enjoying the peace, the extraordinary light, the beach at the end of the garden, and some good cooking.

2019
5/D9
CHP
EASTER-NOV
TERRAC

The Beehive Craft Coffee Shop Keel, Achill Island, Co Mayo
+353 86 8542009 · @TheBeehiveCraftCoffeeShop In summertime, it seems that everyone in Achill is in The Beehive, Michael and Patricia Joyce's bustling coffee shop, craft shop and restaurant. Michael and Patricia have steadily and surely expanded every aspect of their essential enterprise, and the laid-back vibe and the tasty cooking means The Beehive is a key destination on Achill. All day Mon-Sun.

2020
5/D9 10 ROOMS
MED.INX LL

Achill Cliff House Hotel Keel, Achill Island, Co Mayo +353 98 43400 ·
www.achillcliff.com The McNamara family's little hotel is an understated, welcoming destination and the team work hard at their job.

2021
5/C9

Keem Bay Achill Island, Co Mayo Keem Bay is at the western end of Achill Island, a blue flag sandy strand bordered by steep cliffs. The drive is not for the faint hearted. For many years it was associated with shark fishing, using currachs. Keem Bay is probably the location for the famous Paul Henry painting *Launching The Currach* (now in the National Museum). Last time we visited there was a handy little food cart selling snacks.

2022 **Pure Magic** Slievemore Rd, Dugort, Achill Island, Co Mayo +353 85 2439782
5/D9 puremagic.ie/achill In addition to the highly-regarded pizzas they serve at this adventure centre and hostel, there is also a restaurant, a bar, a coffee shop and some nice rooms at this activity centre. Their core activities are windsurfing and SUP (Stand-Up Paddle-boarding) but they can also organise bikes, horses, you name it.
The Deserted Village Report: 1581/RUINS.
Keem Bay Walk Report: 1791/WALKS.

NORTH COAST ISLANDS

2023 **Aranmore** Co Donegal The largest inhabited island off the W coast of Donegal,
6/J4 it has a population of just over 500 people, and is generally known simply as 'Aran'. It is a Gaeltacht speaking zone, speaking Donegal Irish. The island is a place where students come to improve their Irish. Access to the island is by car passenger ferry. The crossing takes 15 minutes. There is a fine circular walk of the island.
Aranmore Ferry +353 87 3171810 · www.aranmoreferry.com

2024 **Tory Island** Co Donegal Nine miles off the coast of Donegal in the far NW,
6/K2 with an Irish-speaking population of just over 100 people, Tory Island is the most remote inhabited island, rugged and beautiful. It is named for the high tors at its eastern end, and the cliff faces are dramatic and vertiginous. Balor of the Evil Eye, the legendary giant of the island had his stronghold here, before he met his end at the hands of his grandson, Lewey Long-Arms. Look out for the very unusual Tau Cross, beside the Round Tower in West Town, one of only two in Ireland. Visitors stay at the 12-room Harbour View Hotel, run by the Doherty family. Passenger sea crossings available from Bunbeg and Magheroarty, daily Apr-Oct and five days a week, weather permitting, all year. The island has been home to a significant school of naive painters, started by the artist Derek Hill, and some of the works can be seen at Glebe House, Hill's home near Glenveagh National Park, now run by the Office of Public Works and open to the public.
The Dixon Gallery +353 86 2620154 · www.toryislandpaintings.com
Tory Island Ferry +353 74 9531320 · www.toryislandferry.com

2025 **Rathlin Island** Ballycastle, Co Antrim, NI Rathlin is celebrated in legend as
6/R2 the place where, in the year 1306, Robert the Bruce was inspired by the efforts of a spider in a cave to continue his fight against the English. Today, between April and July, many bird watchers take the six-mile journey across the Sea of Moyle to Rathlin Island in order to see the puffins that congregate on this cliffy island habitat. There is a seabird centre on the island, and visitors come also to see fulmar, shag, kittiwake, razorbill and guillemot on the cliff edges. In addition to these cliff birds, eider live in the harbour, and, to the S of the island, you can occasionally see choughs, lapwings, corncrakes and snow buntings. There is a ferry to the island from Ballycastle and once on the island you can avail of a minibus service or bicycle hire to get around. Note, there 89 steps to viewing platform from the centre. Centre open all day Apr-Sept.

West Light Seabird Centre Rathlin Island, Ballycastle, Co Antrim, NI · www.repb.org.uk
Rathlin Ferry +4428 20769299 · www.rathlinballycastleferry.com

Maps

Key to Map pages

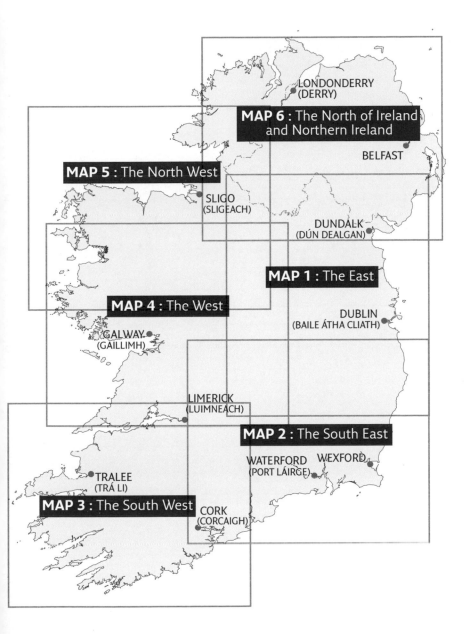

LONDONDERRY
(DERRY)

MAP 6 : The North of Ireland
and Northern Ireland

BELFAST

MAP 5 : The North West

SLIGO
(SLIGEACH)

DUNDALK
(DÚN DEALGAN)

MAP 1 : The East

MAP 4 : The West

DUBLIN
(BAILE ÁTHA CLIATH)

GALWAY
(GAILLIMH)

LIMERICK
(LUIMNEACH)

MAP 2 : The South East

WATERFORD   WEXFORD
(PORT LÁIRGE)

TRALEE
(TRÁ LI)

MAP 3 : The South West   CORK
(CORCAIGH)

379

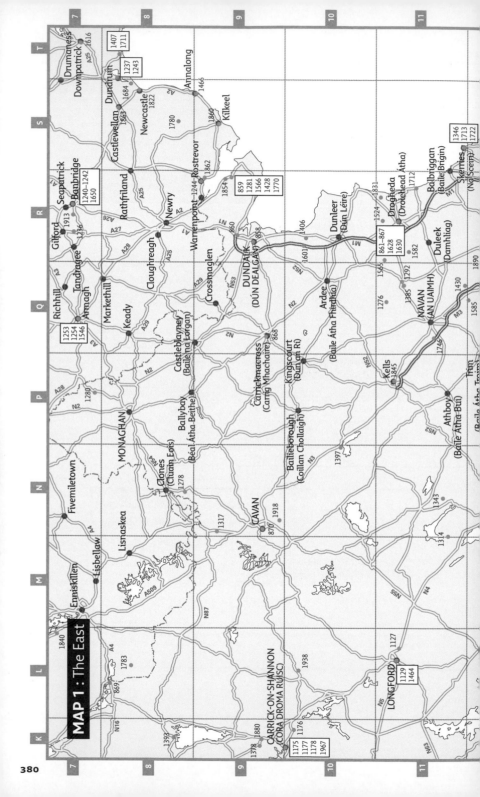

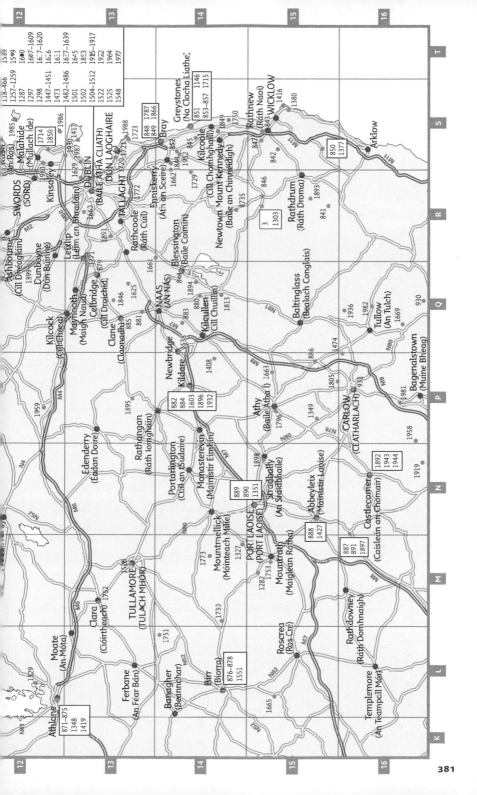

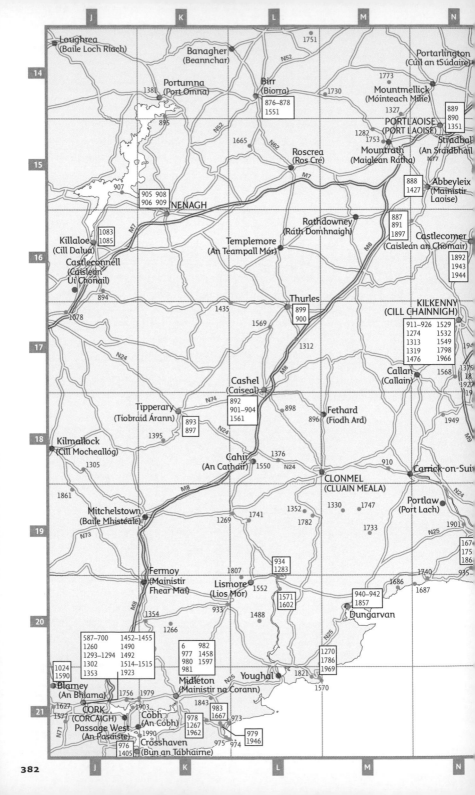

Loughrea
(Baile Loch Riach)

Banagher
(Beannchar)

Portarlington
(Cúil an tSúdaire)

1751

N52

1773

14

Portumna
(Port Omna)
1381

Birr
(Biorra)
876–878
1551

1730

Mountmellick
(Móinteach Míle)
1327

889
890
1351

895

N52

1282
1753

PORTLAOISE
(PORT LAOISE)

Stradbal
(An Stráidbhail)

N77

1665

N62

Roscrea
(Ros Cré)

Mountrath
(Maiglean Rátha)

907

905 908
906 909

888
1427

Abbeyleix
(Mainistir
Laoise)

NENAGH

15

Killaloe
(Cill Dalua)

1083
1085

Rathdowney
(Ráth Domhnaigh)

887
891
1897

Castlecomer
(Caisleán an Chomair)

16

Castleconnell
(Caisleán
Uí Chonaill)

M8

1892
1943
1944

894

1078

Templemore
(An Teampall Mór)

Thurles

899
900

KILKENNY
(CILL CHAINNIGH)

1435

1569

911–926 1529
1274   1532
1313   1549
1319   1798
1476   1966

N24

1312

17

Cashel
(Caiseal)

M8

Callan
(Callain)

1568

194

1379
18
1927
19

Tipperary
(Tiobraid Árann)

N74

892
901–904
1561

898

Fethard
(Fiodh Ard)
896

893
897

1949

1395

N24

Kilmallock
(Cill Mocheallóg)

Cahir
(An Cathair)

1376

1550

N24

CLONMEL
(CLUAIN MEALA)

910

Carrick-on-Suir

18

1305

1861

M8

Portlaw
(Port Lach)

1901

19

Mitchelstown
(Baile Mhistéale)

1269

1741

1352

1330   1747

1782

1733

N25

N73

1686

1740

935

167
175
186

Fermoy
(Mainistir
Fhear Maí)

1807

934
1283

940–942
1857

1687

20

1354

933

Lismore
(Lios Mór)

1552

1571
1602

Dungarvan

1266

1488

587–700   1452–1455
1260   1490
1293–1294 1492
1302   1514–1515
1353   1923

6   982
977 1458
980 1597
981

N25

1270
1786
1969

1024
1590

1756

1979

Midleton
(Mainistir na Corann)

Youghal

1821

1570

Blarney
(An Bhlarna)

1627

1903

1843

N25

1571

CORK
(CORCAIGH)

Cóbh
(An Cóbh)

983
1667

973

979
1946

21

Passage West
(An Pasáiste)

1990

978
1267
1962

975 974

N71

976
1405

Crosshaven
(Bún an Tábhairne)

MAP 2 : The South East

383

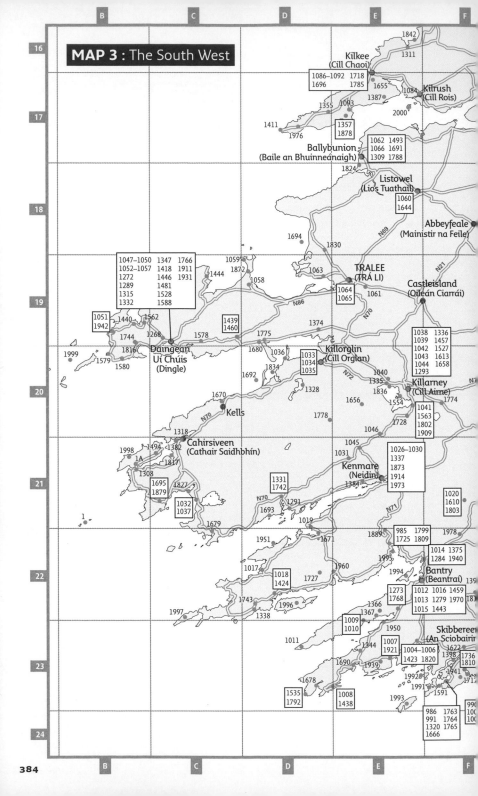

MAP 3 : The South West

Kilkee
(Cill Chaoi)
1086–1092 1718
1696   1785

1655
1387
1084 Kilrush
(Cill Rois)
2000

1355
1093
1411
1976
1357
1878

Ballybunion
(Baile an Bhuinneánaigh)
1062 1493
1066 1691
1309 1788
1824

Listowel
(Lios Tuathail)
1060
1644

Abbeyfeale
(Mainistir na Feile)

1694
1830

1059
1872
1444
1058
1063

TRALEE
(TRÁ LÍ)
1064
1065   1061

Castleisland
(Oileán Ciarraí)

1047–1050 1347 1766
1052–1057 1418 1911
1272   1446 1931
1289   1481
1315   1528
1332   1588

1051
1942

1440 1562
1268

1439
1460

1578

1775

1374

1038 1336
1039 1457
1042 1527
1043 1613
1044 1658
1293

1999

1579
1580

1816
1744

Daingean
Uí Chúis
(Dingle)

1680
1036

1692

1834

1033
1034
1035

Killorglin
(Cill Orglan)

1040
1335
1836

Killarney
(Cill Airne)

1554
1728

1041
1563
1802
1909

1774

1670

Kells

1328

1778

1046

1045

1031

Kenmare
(Neidín)
1384

1026–1030
1337
1873
1914
1973

1318

1318

Cahirsiveen
(Cathair Saidhbhín)

1020
1610
1803

1998
1A
1494 1382
1817
1308
1695 1827
1879

1032
1037

1331
1742

1291
1693
1019

1889

985 1799
1725 1809

1978

1

1679

1951

1671

1960

1995

1014 1375
1284 1940

1994

Bantry
(Beantraí)

139

1017
1018
1424

1727

1273
1768

1012 1016 1459
1013 1279 1970
1015 1443

18

1743

1996
1338

1366
1367

1009
1010

1950

Skibbereen
(An Sciobairín)

1997

1011

1344

1007
1921

1004–1006
1423 1820

1622
1398
1941
1591

1736
1810

990
100
100

1690

1939

1992
1991

1717

1535
1792

1678

1008
1438

1993

986 1763
991 1764
1320 1765
1666

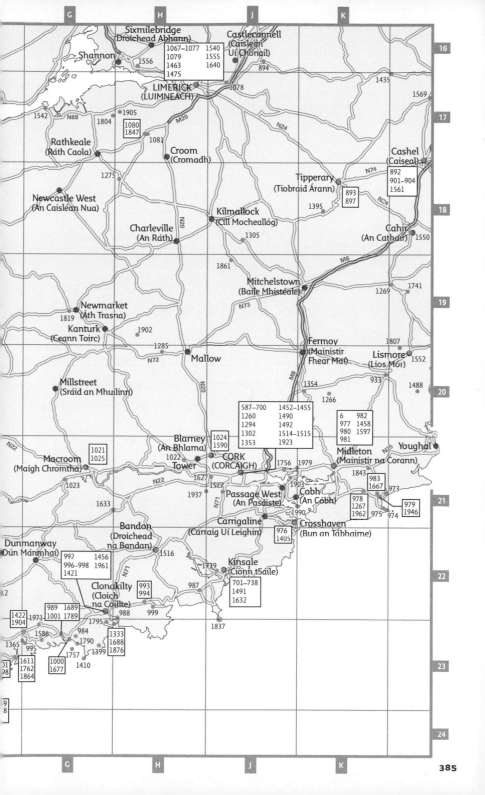

Sixmilebridge
(Droichead Abhann)

Shannon

Castleconnell
(Caisleán Uí Chónail)

1067–1077	1540
1079	1555
1463	1640
1475	

1556

894

1435

1569

LIMERICK
(LUIMNEACH)

1078

1542

N69

1804

1905

M20

1080
1847

1081

Rathkeale
(Ráth Caola)

Croom
(Cromadh)

Cashel
(Caiseal)

| 892 |
| 901–904 |
| 1561 |

N74

1275

Newcastle West
(An Caisleán Nua)

Tipperary
(Tiobraid Árann)

893
897

N24

1819

Charleville
(An Ráth)

Kilmallock
(Cill Mocheallóg)

1305

N20

1395

Cahir
(An Cathair)

1550

1861

Newmarket
(Áth Trasna)

1902

Mitchelstown
(Baile Mhistéale)

1269

1741

Kanturk
(Ceann Toirc)

N73

1285

N72

Mallow

Fermoy
(Mainistir
Fhear Maí)

1807

Lismore
(Lios Mór)

1552

933

Millstreet
(Sráid an Mhuilinn)

N20

1354

1266

1488

587–700   1452–1455
1260   1490
1294   1492
1302   1514–1515
1353   1923

6   982
977   1458
980   1597
981

N22

1021
1025

Macroom
(Maigh Chromtha)

Blarney
(An Bhlarna)

1024
1590

Midleton
(Mainistir na Corann)

Youghal

1022

Tower

CORK
(CORCAIGH)

1756   1979

1843

983
1667

973

1023

1627

1577

1903

978
1267
1962

979
1946

1633

1937

N71

Passage West
(An Pasáiste)

Cobh
(An Cóbh)

975   974

1990

Carrigaline
(Carraig Uí Leighin)

Crosshaven
(Bun an Tábhairne)

976
1405

Bandon
(Droichead
na Bandan)

Dunmanway
(Dún Mánmhaí)

992   1456
996–998   1961
1421

1516

1739

Kinsale
(Cionn tSáile)

701–738
1491
1632

Clonakilty
(Cloich
na Coillte)

993
994

987

989   1689
1001 1789

1422
1904

1971

988

999

1586

984

1795

1333
1688
1876

1837

995

1790

1365

1757

1399

1611
1762
1864

1000
1677

1410

G   H   J   K

385

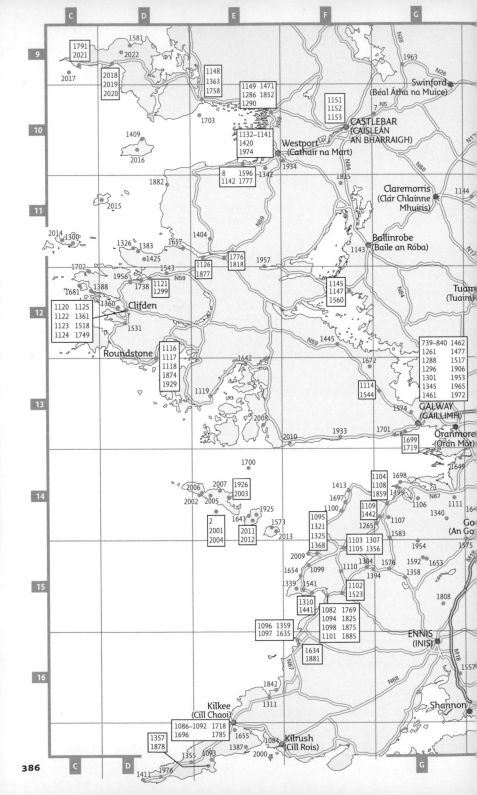

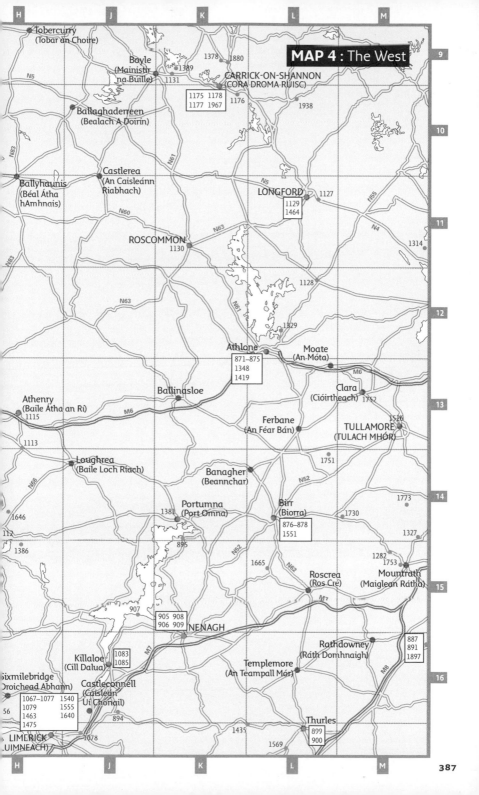

MAP 4 : The West

Tobercurry
(Tobar an Choire)

Boyle
(Mainistir
na Buille) 1131
1378 1880
1389
CARRICK-ON-SHANNON
(CORA DROMA RUISC)
1175 1178
1177 1967 1176
1938

Ballaghaderreen
(Bealach A Doirin)

Castlerea
(An Caisleánn
Riabhach)

Ballyhaunis
(Béal Átha
hAmhnais)

LONGFORD
1129
1464
1127
N5

ROSCOMMON
1130
1314

1128

1829

Athlone
871–875
1348
1419

Moate
(An Móta)

Clara
(Cióirtheach) 1752

Ballinasloe

Athenry
(Baile Átha an Rì)
1115

Ferbane
(An Féar Bán)

TULLAMORE
(TULACH MHÓR)
1526

1113

Loughrea
(Baile Loch Riach)

Banagher
(Beannchar)

1751

1773

1646

Portumna
(Port Omna)
1381

Birr
(Biorra)
876–878
1551
1730

1327

1386

895

1665
1282
1753

Roscrea
(Ros Cré)

Mountrath
(Maiglean Rátha)

907

905 908
906 909
NENAGH

Killaloe
(Cill Dalua)
1083
1085

Rathdowney
(Ráth Domhnaigh)
887
891
1897

Sixmilebridge
(Droichead Abhann)

Castleconnell
(Caisleán
Uí Chonaill)

Templemore
(An Teampall Mór)

1067–1077 1540
1079 1555
1463 1640
1475

894

1078

1435

Thurles
899
900

1569

LIMERICK
(LUIMNEACH)

MAP 5 : The North West

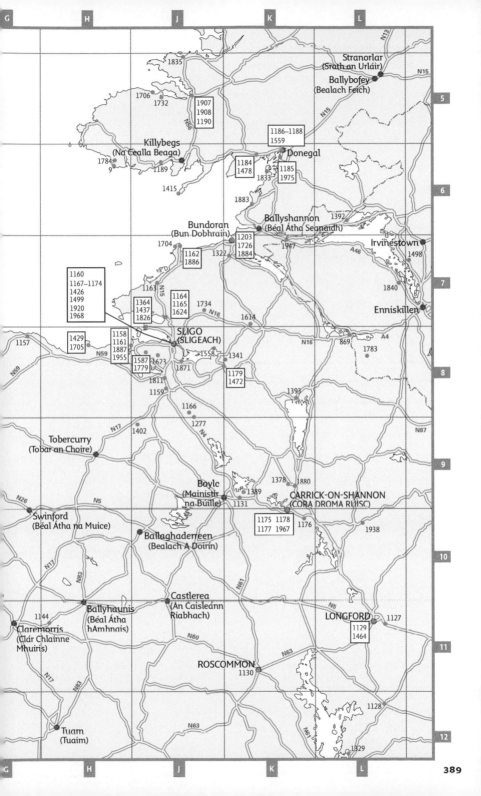

389

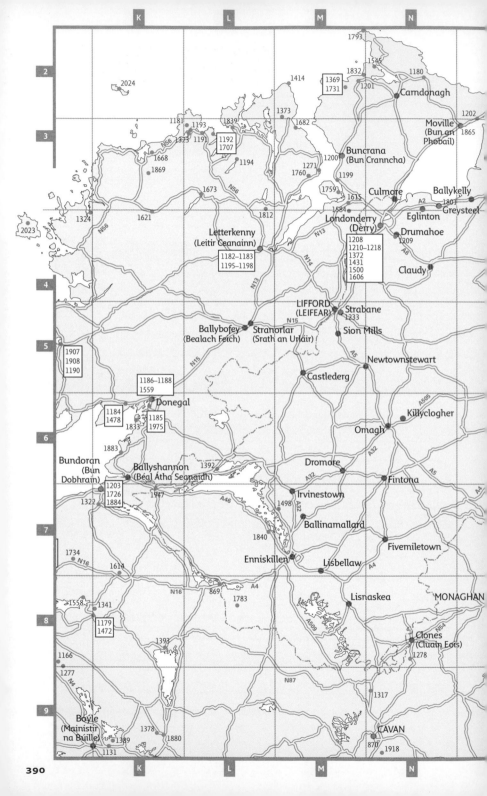

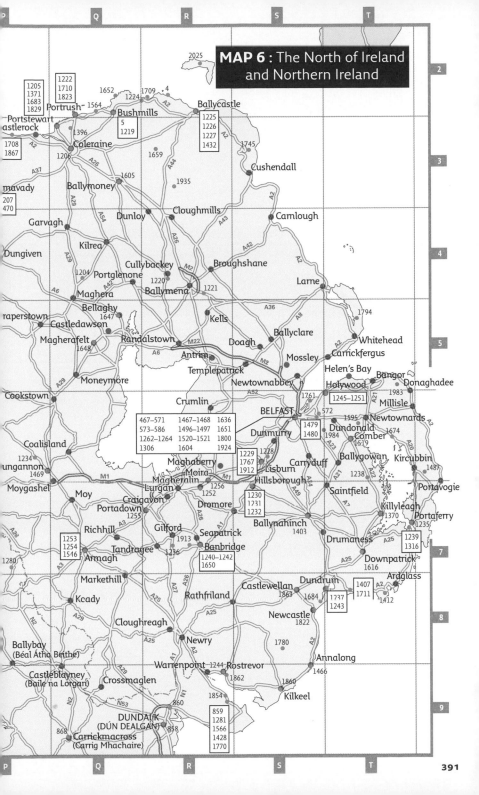

MAP 6 : The North of Ireland and Northern Ireland

Index

The numbers listed against index entries refer to the page on which the entry appears and not the entry's item number.

Acknowledgements

We would like to thank the following people who have been enormously influential and helpful in writing this book:

Constance, Samuel and PJ McKenna. Eamon Barrett, Leslie Williams, Caroline Hennessy and William Barry. Margie Deverell, Lelia McKenna, Belinda, Portia and Phoebe Preston. Frank McKevitt and Edwina Murray. Dr Denis Cotter.

We'd like to thank Pete Irvine for creating this wonderful template, along with Collins' Reference Publisher, Jethro Lennox. Also Judith Casey and Keith Moore who worked closely with us to bring it all together. And finally to all the very creative people we've had the joy to describe in this book.

John and Sally McKenna are happy to receive comments about this edition and recommendations for entries in the next (**the.best@harpercollins.co.uk**). They are, however, unable to reply to submissions personally.

The McKennas are Social! Follow @McKennasGuides on Facebook, Twitter and Instagram. #IrelandTheBest to share your experiences.